**Fodor's** 4th Edition

# New Mexico

The Guide
for All Budgets

Completely
Updated

Where to Stay, Eat,
and Explore

On and Off
the Beaten Path

When to Go,
What to Pack

Maps, Travel Tips,
and Web Sites

Fodor's Travel Publications • New York, Toronto, London, Sydney, Auckland
www.fodors.com

**EDITOR:** Constance Jones

**Editorial Contributors:** Andrew Collins, Tracy Dingmann, Marilyn Haddrill, Holly Hammond, Georgia de Katona
**Maps:** David Lindroth, *cartographer*; Robert Blake, Rebecca Baer, *map editors*
**Design:** Fabrizio La Rocca, *creative director*; Guido Caroti, *art director*; Jolie Novak, *senior picture editor*; Melanie Marin, *photo editor*
**Cover Design:** Pentagram
**Production/Manufacturing:** Yexenia (Jessie) Markland
**Cover Photo** (Museum of Fine Arts, Santa Fe): Thomas Hoepker/Magnum Photos, Inc.

## Copyright

Fourth Edition

ISBN 1–4000–1087–X

ISSN 1526–4734

## Important Tip

Although all prices, opening times, and other details in this book are based on information supplied to us at press time, changes occur all the time in the travel world, and Fodor's cannot accept responsibility for facts that become outdated or for inadvertent errors or omissions. So **always confirm information when it matters,** especially if you're making a detour to visit a specific place.

## Special Sales

Fodor's Travel Publications are available at special discounts for bulk purchases for sales promotions or premiums. Special editions, including personalized covers, excerpts of existing guides, and corporate imprints, can be created in large quantities for special needs. For more information, contact your local bookseller or write to Special Markets, Fodor's Travel Publications, 1745 Park Avenue, New York, NY 10019. Inquiries from Canada should be directed to your local Canadian bookseller or sent to Random House of Canada, Ltd., Marketing Department, 2775 Matheson Boulevard East, Mississauga, Ontario L4W 4P7. Inquiries from the United Kingdom should be sent to Fodor's Travel Publications, 20 Vauxhall Bridge Road, London SW1V 2SA, England.

PRINTED IN THE UNITED STATES OF AMERICA

10 9 8 7 6 5 4 3 2 1

# CONTENTS

**Maps**

# ON THE ROAD WITH FODOR'S

A trip takes you out of yourself. Concerns of life at home completely disappear, driven away by more immediate thoughts—about, say, what marvels will beguile the next day, or where you'll have dinner. That's where Fodor's comes in. We make sure that you know all your options, so that you don't miss something that's around the next bend just because you didn't know it was there. Mindful that the best memories of your trip might have nothing to do with what you came to New Mexico to see, we guide you to sights large and small all over the state. You might set out to visit an Indian Pueblo, but back at home you find yourself unable to forget the flamenco performance at that intimate Spanish restaurant, or the view of the Milky Way from the terrace of your casita. With Fodor's at your side, serendipitous discoveries are never far away.

## About Our Writers

Our success in showing you every corner of New Mexico is a credit to our extraordinary writers. Although there's no substitute for travel advice from a good friend who knows your style, our contributors are the next best thing—the kind of people you would poll for travel advice if you knew them.

Santa Fe resident **Andrew Collins**, a former Fodor's editor, updated Smart Travel Tips A to Z, Destination New Mexico, Santa Fe, and Background for this edition. He has authored more than a dozen guidebooks, including *Fodor's Gay Guide to the USA*. He also writes a syndicated weekly newspaper travel column and has contributed to *Travel & Leisure* and the *Holland Herald*.

As a longtime arts writer for the *Albuquerque Journal,* Albuquerque updater **Tracy Dingmann** knows what's going on in the Duke City. A resident of New Mexico since 1990, she can find the best margaritas, sopaipillas, and out-of-the-way Mexican lunch spots. Dingmann was born in Minneapolis and graduated from the University of Wisconsin-Madison, but no one in New Mexico seems to hold that against her.

A lifelong resident of southern New Mexico, Southeastern New Mexico and Southwestern New Mexico contributor **Marilyn Haddrill** was born in Carlsbad and now lives in Las Cruces. She was a *Roswell Daily Record* reporter-photographer and a full-time New Mexico writer for the *El Paso Times*; as a freelance writer since the early 1990s she regularly scours the region for news and feature ideas.

Taos and Northeastern New Mexico updater **Holly Hammond** moved to Taos after a brief visit there, lured by the landscape and the cultural riches of northern New Mexico. She previously worked on *Fodor's California* and Fodor's *Cityguide Los Angeles.*

**Georgia de Katona,** who updated the Northwestern New Mexico chapter, is a freelance writer who has spent her life exploring the western United States by foot, car, and motorcycle. The beauty of the high desert and the quirky diversity of Western people hold particular interest for her. Despite a passion for travel and new experiences, Georgia always returns home to New Mexico.

You can rest assured that you're in good hands—and that no property mentioned in the book has paid to be included. Each has been selected strictly on its merits, as the best of its type in its price range.

## How to Use This Book

Up front is Smart Travel Tips A to Z, arranged alphabetically by topic and loaded with tips, Web sites, and contact information. Destination: New Mexico helps get you in the mood for your trip. Subsequent chapters in the guide are arranged regionally. All city chapters begin with exploring information, with a section for each neighborhood (each recommending a good tour and listing sights alphabetically). All regional chapters are divided geographically; within each area, towns are covered in logical geographical order, and attractive stretches of road between them, or interesting sights along the way, are indicated by the designation En Route. To help you decide what you'll have time to

# New Mexico

50 miles

75 km

N

TEXAS

MEXICO

Ciudad Juárez

El Paso

Las Cruces

Anthony

San Miguel

Mesilla

Old Mesilla

Organ

San Andreas Nat'l Wildlife Refuge

San Andreas Mts.

Radium Springs

Fort Selden State Mon.

Hatch

Nutt

Cooke's Peak

Deming

Columbus

Pancho Villa S.P.

Hachita

Ascensión

CORONADO NAT'L FOR.

Lordsburg

Redrock

GILA NAT'L FOR.

Silver City

City of Rocks S.P.

Bayard

Pinos Altos

Gila Cliff Dwellings Nat'l Mon.

Inner Loop Scenic Dr.

Kingston

Lake Valley

Mogollon

Glenwood

APACHE NAT'L FOR.

Datil

Magdalena

Socorro

Polvadera

Bosque del Apache Nat'l Wildlife Refuge

Fort Craig Nat'l Historic Site

Elephant Butte Lake S.P.

Elephant Butte Lake

Truth or Consequences

Caballo Lake S.P.

Rio Grande

Winston

Chloride

CIBOLA NAT'L FOR.

Carrizozo

Three Rivers Nat'l Petroglyph Site

Three Rivers

WHITE SANDS MISSILE RANGE

WHITE SANDS NAT'L MON.

Valley of Fires Nat'l Rec. Area

Alamogordo

Tularosa

Mescalero

MESCALERO APACHE INDIAN RES.

Cloudcroft

Ruidoso

6563

LINCOLN NAT'L FOR.

Capitán

San Patricio

Lincoln

Picacho

Bottomless Lakes S.P.

Roswell

Dexter

Hagerman

Lake Arthur

Artesia

Bitter Lake Nat'l Wildlife Refuge

Elkins

Elida

Floyd

Portales

Dora

Loco Hills

Hobbs

Tatum

McDonald

Lovington

Eunice

Jal

Kermit

Oil Center

Carlsbad

Loving

Whites City

Living Desert Zoo and Gardens S.P.

CARLSBAD CAVERNS NAT'L PARK

GUADALUPE MTS. NAT'L PARK

Pine Springs

Cornudas

GUADALUPE MTS.

LINCOLN NAT'L FOR.

Brantley Lake S.P.

Pecos R.

Black R.

Rio Hondo

Rio Peñasco

Pecos R.

Rio Grande

Gila R.

Ramon

Mesa

Mescalero

State Mon.

TAINS

Pancho Villa S.P.

1 US highway and state route shields including 88, 114, 206, 70, 20, 247, 246, 54, 55, 380, 532, 82, 70, 244, 130, 48, 37, 13, 24, 360, 249, 457, 172, 31, 62, 180, 176, 18, 128, 285, 996, 524, 137, 7, 82, 180, 10, 54, 70, 82, 25, 28, 9, 10, 11, 180, 27, 26, 146, 9, 90, 464, 113, 338, 80, 10, 70, 15, 35, 61, 152, 159, 163, 52, 59, 51

visit, all chapters begin with our writers' favorite itineraries. (Mix itineraries from several chapters, and you can put together a really exceptional trip.) The A to Z section that ends every chapter lists additional resources. At the end of the book you'll find Background, including an essay, a glossary, and a list of books and movies suggested as enriching reading and viewing.

## Icons and Symbols

★     Our special recommendations
✕     Restaurant
🏠     Lodging establishment
✕🏠     Lodging establishment whose restaurant warrants a special trip
⚠     Campground
🖑     Good for kids (rubber duck)
☞     Sends you to another section of the guide for more information
✉     Address
☎     Telephone number
🕑     Opening and closing times
💰     Admission prices (those we give apply to adults; substantially reduced fees are almost always available for children, students, and senior citizens)

Numbers in white and black circles ③ ❸ that appear on the maps, in the margins, and within the tours correspond to one another.

For hotels, you can assume that all rooms have private baths, phones, TVs, and air-conditioning unless otherwise noted and that all hotels operate on the European Plan (with no meals) if we don't specify another meal plan. We always list a property's facilities but not whether you'll be charged extra to use them, so when pricing accommodations, do ask what's included. For restaurants, it's always a good idea to book ahead; we mention reservations only when they're essential or are not accepted. All restaurants we list are open daily for lunch and dinner unless stated otherwise; dress is mentioned only when men are required to wear a jacket or a jacket and tie. Look for an overview of local dining-out habits in the Pleasures and Pastimes section that follows each chapter introduction.

## Don't Forget to Write

Your experiences—positive and negative—matter to us. If we have missed or misstated something, we want to hear about it. We follow up on all suggestions. Contact the New Mexico editor at editors@fodors.com or c/o Fodor's at 1745 Broadway, New York, NY 10019. And have a fabulous trip!

*Karen Cure*

Karen Cure
*Editorial Director*

# ESSENTIAL INFORMATION

## AIR TRAVEL

### BOOKING

When you book **look for nonstop flights** and **remember that "direct" flights stop at least once.** Try to avoid connecting flights, which require a change of plane. Two airlines may operate a connecting flight jointly, so ask if your airline operates every segment of the trip; you may find that the carrier you prefer flies you only part of the way. To find more booking tips and to check prices and make on-line flight reservations, log on to www.fodors.com.

### CARRIERS

Most major airlines provide service to the state's main airport in Albuquerque; just over the border in Texas (near Las Cruces and Carlsbad), El Paso International Airport is served by American, Southwest, Delta, Continental, America West, and Frontier. The state is also served by a few regional carriers. Mesa Airlines offers shuttle flights between Albuquerque and Farmington, Colorado Springs, Clovis, Roswell, Hobbs, Carlsbad, Alamogordo, Silver City, and Gallup; fares typically range from about $140 to $165 round-trip. Rio Grande Air operates daily flights between Albuquerque and Taos, Ruidoso, and Durango, Colorado (which is fairly close to Farmington); fares are about $140 to $280 round-trip. Charter flights also are available. Great Lakes Aviation flies daily from Denver to both Farmington and Santa Fe; round-trip fares are usually around $250. Frontier Airlines flies daily from Denver to El Paso, stopping in Albuquerque; fares are usually around $200 or more between Denver and Albuquerque, but only around $100 to $125 between Albuquerque and El Paso.

➤ MAJOR AIRLINES: **America West** (☎ 800/235–9292). **American**
(☎ 800/433–7300). **Continental** (☎ 800/525–0280). **Delta** (☎ 800/221–1212). **Northwest** (☎ 800/692–7000). **Southwest Airlines** (☎ 800/435–9792). **TWA** (☎ 800/221–2000). **United** (☎ 800/241–6522). **US Airways** (☎ 800/428–4322).

➤ SMALLER AIRLINES: **Frontier** (☎ 800/432–1359). **Great Lakes Aviation** (☎ 800/554–5111). **Mesa Airlines** (☎ 800/637–2247). **Rio Grande Air** (☎ 877/435–9742).

➤ FROM THE U.K.: **British Airways** (☎ 0345/222–111). **Delta** (☎ 0800/414–767). **United Airlines** (☎ 0800/888–555).

### CHECK-IN AND BOARDING

Always **ask your carrier about its check-in policy.** Plan to arrive at the airport about two hours before your scheduled departure time for domestic flights and 2½ to 3 hours before international flights. Assuming that not everyone with a ticket will show up, airlines routinely overbook planes. When everyone does, airlines ask for volunteers to give up their seats. In return, these volunteers usually get a certificate for a free flight and are rebooked on the next flight out. If there are not enough volunteers, the airline must choose who will be denied boarding. The first to get bumped are passengers who checked in late and those flying on discounted tickets, so **get to the gate and check in as early as possible,** especially during peak periods.

Always **bring a government-issued photo ID to the airport;** even when it's not required, a passport is best.

### CUTTING COSTS

The least expensive airfares to New Mexico are priced for round-trip travel and must usually be purchased in advance. Albuquerque has relatively few direct flights to other parts of the country, and virtually none to the Northeast. Because the discount airline Southwest serves Albuquerque, fares from here to airports served by Southwest are often 25% to 35% less than to other airport. For instance, it's almost always cheaper to fly from Hartford, Providence, or Baltimore to Albuquerque than from Boston, New York, or Washington. Airlines generally allow you to change your return date for a fee; most low-fare tickets, however, are nonrefundable. It's smart to **call a number of airlines,** and when you are quoted a good price, **book it on the spot**—the same fare may not be available the next day. Always **check different routings** and look into using alternate airports. Also, price off-peak flights, which may be significantly less expensive than others. Travel agents, especially low-fare specialists (☞ Discounts and Deals, *below*), are helpful.

Consolidators are another good source. They buy tickets for scheduled international flights at reduced rates from the airlines, then sell them at prices that beat the best fare available directly from the airlines. Sometimes you can even get your money back if you need to return the ticket. Carefully read the fine print detailing penalties for changes and cancellations, purchase the ticket with a credit card, and **confirm your consolidator reservation with the airline.**

When you **fly as a courier,** you trade your checked-luggage space for a ticket deeply subsidized by a courier service. There are restrictions on when you can book and how long you can stay. Some courier companies list with membership organizations, such as the Air Courier Association and the International Association of Air Travel Couriers; these require you to become a member before you can book a flight.

➤ CONSOLIDATORS: **Cheap Tickets** (☎ 800/377–1000 or 888/922–8849, WEB www.cheaptickets.com). **Discount Airline Ticket Service** (☎ 800/576–1600). **Unitravel** (☎ 800/325–2222, WEB www.unitravel.com). **Up & Away Travel** (☎ 212/889–2345, WEB www.upandaway.com). **World Travel Network** (☎ 800/409–6753).

➤ COURIER RESOURCES: **Air Courier Association** (☎ 800/282–1202, WEB www.aircourier.org). **International Association of Air Travel Couriers** (☎ 352/475–1584, WEB www.courier.org).

## ENJOYING THE FLIGHT

**State your seat preference** when purchasing your ticket, and then repeat it when you confirm and when you check in. For more legroom, you can request one of the few emergency-aisle seats at check-in, if you are capable of lifting at least 50 pounds—a Federal Aviation Administration requirement of passengers in these seats. Seats behind a bulkhead also offer more legroom, but they don't have under-seat storage. Don't sit in the row in front of the emergency aisle or in front of a bulkhead, where seats may not recline.

Ask the airline whether a snack or meal is served on the flight. If you have dietary concerns, **request special meals when booking.** These can be vegetarian, low-cholesterol, or kosher, for example. It's a good idea to pack some healthy snacks and a small (plastic) bottle of water in your carry-on bag. On long flights, try to maintain a normal routine, to help fight jet lag. At night, **get some sleep.** By day, **eat light meals, drink water** (not alcohol), and **move around the cabin** to stretch your legs. For additional jet-lag tips consult *Fodor's FYI: Travel Fit & Healthy* (available at bookstores everywhere).

## FLYING TIMES

Flying time between Albuquerque and Los Angeles is 2 hours; Chicago, 3 hours; New York, 5½ to 6½ hours (there are no direct flights); Dallas, 1 hour and 45 minutes.

## HOW TO COMPLAIN

If your baggage goes astray or your flight goes awry, complain right away. Most carriers require that you **file a claim immediately.** The Aviation Consumer Protection Division of the Department of Transportation publishes *Fly-Rights,* which discusses airlines and consumer issues and is available on-line. At PassengerRights.com, a Web site, you can compose a letter of complaint and distribute it electronically.

➤ AIRLINE COMPLAINTS: **Aviation Consumer Protection Division** (✉ U.S. Department of Transportation, Room 4107, C-75, Washington, DC 20590, ☎ 202/366–2220, WEB www.dot.gov/airconsumer). **Federal Aviation Administration Consumer Hotline** (☎ 800/322–7873).

## RECONFIRMING

Check the status of your flight before you leave for the airport. You can do this on your carrier's Web site, by linking to a flight-status checker (many Web booking services offer these), or by calling your carrier or travel agent.

### AIRPORTS

The major gateway to New Mexico is Albuquerque International Sunport, which is 65 mi southwest of Santa Fe, 130 mi south of Taos, and 180 mi southeast of Farmington. Some travelers to Chama, Raton, and Taos prefer to fly into Denver (four to five hours' drive), which has far more direct flights to the rest of the country than Albuquerque—it's a scenic drive, too.

The gateway to southern New Mexico is El Paso International Airport, 50 mi southeast of Las Cruces, 160 mi southeast of Silver City, 135 mi southwest of Ruidoso, and 160 mi southwest of Carlsbad. The flight between El Paso and Albuquerque takes 50 minutes. The state's easternmost side can also be accessed via major airports in Texas, including Lubbock (170 mi east of Roswell) and Amarillo (105 mi northeast of Clovis).

➤ AIRPORT INFORMATION: **Albuquerque International Sunport** (✉ Sunport Blvd. off I–25, 5 mi south of downtown, ☎ 505/244–7700, WEB www.cabq.gov/airport). **Denver International Airport** (✉ 8500 Peña Blvd., off I–70, Exit 285, ☎ 303/342–2000, WEB www.flydenver.com). **El Paso International Airport** (✉ 6701 Convair Dr., off I–10, Exit 25, ☎ 915/780–4749, WEB www.elpasointernationalairport.com).

➤ MUNICIPAL AIRPORTS: **Cavern City Air Terminal (McCausland Aviation), Carlsbad** (✉ 1505 Terminal Dr., off U.S. 62/180, 8 mi southwest of downtown, ☎ 505/885–5236). **Four Cor-**

ners **Regional Airport, Farmington** (✉ 1260 W. Navajo St., 2 mi northwest of downtown, ☎ 505/325–2867). **Grant County Airport, Silver City area** (✉ 188 Airport Rd., Hurley, 20 mi southeast of Silver City via U.S. 180, ☎ 505/538–2142). **Las Cruces International Airport** (✉ 9000 Zia Rd., off I–10, 10 mi west of Las Cruces, ☎ 505/524–2762). **Roswell Municipal Airport** (✉ 1 Jerry Smith Cir., 8 mi south of Roswell via U.S. 285, ☎ 505/624–6700). **Santa Fe Municipal Airport** (✉ Airport Rd. off NM 284, 10 mi southwest of downtown, ☎ 505/955–2908). **Sierra Blanca Regional Airport, Ruidoso area** (✉ 1 Airport Rd., 16 mi northeast of Ruidoso, ☎ 505/336–8111). **Taos Municipal Airport** (✉ U.S. 64, 12 mi west of Taos, ☎ 505/758–4995).

## AIRPORT TRANSFERS

Shuttle buses between the Albuquerque International Sunport and Santa Fe take about 1 hour and 20 minutes and cost approximately $20–$25 each way. Shuttle service runs from Albuquerque to Taos and nearby ski areas; the ride takes 2¾ to 3 hours and costs $35–$50. In southern New Mexico there are daily trips between El Paso International Airport and Las Cruces (1 hour), Deming (2½ hours), and Silver City (3½ hours); the trip costs $28–$38 each way. There's also Greyhound bus service between Albuquerque International Sunport and many New Mexico towns and cities; fares are considerably less than those charged by the shuttle services listed here.

➤ BETWEEN ALBUQUERQUE AND SANTA FE: **Gray Line/Coach USA** (☎ 800/256–8991). **Sandia Shuttle Express** (☎ 505/474–5696 or 888/775–5696, WEB www.sandiashuttle.com). **Santa Fe Shuttle** (☎ 505/243–2300 or 888/833–2300, WEB www.santafeshuttle.com).

➤ BETWEEN ALBUQUERQUE AND TAOS: **Faust's Transportation** (☎ 505/758–7359 or 888/830–3410, WEB www.newmexiconet.com/faust1.htm). **Pride of Taos** (☎ 505/758–8340 or 800/273–8340).

➤ BETWEEN EL PASO AND SOUTHERN NEW MEXICO DESTINATIONS: **Las Cruces Shuttle Service** (☎ 505/

525–1784 or 800/288–1784, WEB lascrucesshuttle.com).

## BIKE TRAVEL

Bicycling, both on- and off-road, ranks among the most popular recreational activities in New Mexico. It's easy to find bike-rental and -repair shops in the state's major tourist areas, and local tourist boards often distribute bike maps. Because of New Mexico's many hilly and winding roads, often with high automobile speed limits, biking can be dangerous here—always use the proper safety equipment, and inquire locally about the safest areas and times for cycling.

The New Mexico Public Lands Information Center also has a variety of maps and information for outdoor recreation. Cycling events in New Mexico include the Santa Fe Century (50- or 100-mi recreational rides), the Sanbusco Hill Climb (a race to the Santa Fe Ski Area), and the Tour de Los Alamos (road race and criterium).

➤ BIKE MAPS: **New Mexico Public Lands Information Center** (✉ 1474 Rodeo Rd., Santa Fe 87505, ☎ 505/438–7542, WEB www.publiclands.org).

➤ CYCLING EVENTS: **New Mexico Touring Society** (☎ 505/237–9700, WEB www.swcp.com/russells/nmts).

### BIKES IN FLIGHT

Most airlines accommodate bikes as luggage, provided they are dismantled and boxed; check with individual airlines about packing requirements. Airlines sell bike boxes, which are often free at bike shops, for about $15 (bike bags start at $100). International travelers often can substitute a bike for a piece of checked luggage at no charge; otherwise, the cost is about $100. Domestic and Canadian airlines charge $40–$80 each way.

## BUSINESS HOURS

### BANKS AND OFFICES

Banks generally are open 9 to 3 or 4 on weekdays and 9 or 10 to noon on Saturday. Post offices usually are open 8 or 9 until 5 on weekdays and until noon on Saturday.

### GAS STATIONS

Along interstates and major U.S. and state highways, and in larger towns and cities, you'll find at least a handful of stations open 24 hours; in small towns stations often keep very limited hours. Keep in mind, however, that it can be 40 or 50 mi between towns with gas stations in rural parts of the state. When driving long distances, it's a good idea to fill up whenever the opportunity presents itself.

### MUSEUMS AND SIGHTS

Museums in New Mexico are generally open daily from 9 or 10 AM to 5 or 6 PM, although hours may vary seasonally. Even in summer, some facilities close at 4 PM. Many are closed on Monday. Some are open for extended hours on Friday evening. Some pueblos are closed to visitors for short periods throughout the year.

### PHARMACIES

There aren't many all-night pharmacies in New Mexico, so plan ahead. Albuquerque has several; other cities with 24-hour pharmacies include Las Cruces and Santa Fe.

➤ 24-HOUR PHARMACIES: **Walgreens** (✉ 6201 Central Ave. NE, Albuquerque, ☎ 505/255–5511; ✉ 5001 Montgomery Blvd. NE, Albuquerque, ☎ 505/881–5050; ✉ 1096 St. Francis Dr., Santa Fe, ☎ 505/982–4643).

### SHOPS

Most shops and galleries are open between 10 and 5 or 6, sometimes with limited hours on weekends. Store and commercial hours also vary according to the flux of tourist seasons.

## BUS TRAVEL

Bus service on Texas, New Mexico & Oklahoma Coaches, affiliated with Greyhound Lines, is available to Farmington, Gallup, Taos, Santa Fe, Las Cruces, Clovis, Las Vegas, Raton, Roswell, Carlsbad, El Paso (TX), and several other towns and cities. Las Cruces Shuttle Service can get you from Silver City to Deming, Las Cruces, and El Paso.

### FARES AND SCHEDULES

Sample one-way fares are $10 from Albuquerque to Santa Fe, $55 from Raton to Las Cruces, $13 from Roswell to Carlsbad, and $27 from Farmington to Albuquerque. Make reservations several weeks in advance of major holidays or other special events such as the Kodak Albuquerque International Balloon Fiesta in October.

## CUTTING COSTS

Greyhound offers the **North America Discovery Pass,** which allows unlimited travel in the United States within any 7-, 10-, 15-, 21-, 30-, 45-, or 60-day period ($199–$549, depending on length of the pass), and the similar International Ameripass (for non-U.S. residents only), which offers 4- to 60-day passes for $135–$494. Greyhound also has senior citizen, children's, and student discounts.

➤ BUS INFORMATION: **Greyhound/ Texas, New Mexico & Oklahoma Coaches** (☎ 505/243–4435 or 800/ 231–2222). **Las Cruces Shuttle Service** (☎ 505/525–1784 or 800/288– 1784, WEB lascrucesshuttle.com).

## CAMERAS AND PHOTOGRAPHY

New Mexico's wildlife and rugged landscape are extremely photogenic. The striking red sandstone cliffs and soil of northern New Mexico make a terrific backdrop. Photographers also flock to White Sands National Monument, where the stark white sand dunes offer unlimited opportunity for abstract shots such as sand ripples or contrast for brightly dressed models. New Mexico air generally is so clean and pure (except during dust storms) that you can't go wrong. It's best to take photographs in the early morning or late evening to take advantage of more subtle lighting and escape the glare of the bright sun. **Check the rules on Indian reservations** before you take photographs there. In many cases, you must purchase a permit. Restrictions can range from no built-in telephoto lenses to no photography altogether. Be sure you have permission to photograph any Native American you encounter, since beliefs regarding this practice vary. Additionally, your actions might be interpreted as downright rude.

The *Kodak Guide to Shooting Great Travel Pictures* (available at bookstores everywhere) is loaded with tips.

➤ PHOTO HELP: **Kodak Information Center** (☎ 800/242–2424, WEB www. kodak.com).

## EQUIPMENT PRECAUTIONS

**Don't pack film and equipment in checked luggage,** where it is much more susceptible to damage. X-ray machines used to view checked luggage are becoming much more powerful and therefore are much more likely to ruin your film. Try to **ask for hand inspection of film,** which becomes clouded after repeated exposure to airport X-ray machines, and **keep videotapes and computer disks away from metal detectors.** Always **keep film, tape, and computer disks out of the sun.** Carry an extra supply of batteries, and **be prepared to turn on your camera, camcorder, or laptop** to prove to airport security personnel that the device is real.

In New Mexico, dust can be a problem. Keep cameras and video equipment in cases while not in use. Also, keep in mind that extreme heat can ruin film. Don't leave your equipment in a hot car or under direct sunlight.

## CAR RENTAL

A typical rate at the Albuquerque International Sunport is about $28 to $35 daily and $160 to $200 weekly for an economy car with air-conditioning, automatic transmission, and unlimited mileage. Prices are about the same in El Paso. If you want to explore the backcountry, consider renting an SUV, which will cost you about $45 to $60 per day and $260 to $300 per week.

➤ MAJOR AGENCIES: **Alamo** (☎ 800/ 327–9633, WEB www.alamo.com). **Avis** (☎ 800/331–1212; 800/879– 2847 in Canada; 02/9353–9000 in Australia; 09/526–2847 in New Zealand; 0870/606–0100 in the U.K.; WEB www.avis.com). **Budget** (☎ 800/ 527–0700; 0870/156–5656 in the U.K.; WEB www.budget.com). **Dollar** (☎ 800/800–4000; 0124/622–0111 in the U.K., where it's affiliated with Sixt; 02/9223–1444 in Australia; WEB www.dollar.com). **Hertz** (☎ 800/654– 3131; 800/263–0600 in Canada; 020/ 8897–2072 in the U.K.; 02/9669– 2444 in Australia; 09/256–8690 in New Zealand; WEB www.hertz.com).

National Car Rental (☎ 800/227–7368; 020/8680–4800 in the U.K.; WEB www.nationalcar.com).

## CUTTING COSTS

For a good deal, **book through a travel agent, who will shop around.** Also, **price local car-rental companies**—whose prices may be lower still, although their service and maintenance may not be as good as those of major rental agencies—and **research rates on-line.** Remember to ask about required deposits, cancellation penalties, and drop-off charges if you're planning to pick up the car in one city and leave it in another. If you're traveling during a holiday period, also make sure that a confirmed reservation guarantees you a car.

By renting your car elsewhere, you can duck a hefty 10% tax charged extra at the Albuquerque International Sunport and at municipal airports.

➤ LOCAL AGENCIES: **Enterprise** (☎ 800/325–8007). **Sears** (☎ 800/527–0770). **Thrifty** (☎ 800/367–2277).

## INSURANCE

When driving a rented car you are generally responsible for any damage to or loss of the vehicle. You may also be liable for any property damage or personal injury that you may cause while driving. Before you rent, see what coverage you already have under the terms of your personal auto-insurance policy and credit cards.

For about $15 to $20 a day, rental companies sell protection, known as a collision- or loss-damage waiver (CDW or LDW), that eliminates your liability for damage to the car; it's always optional and should never be automatically added to your bill. In most states you don't need a CDW if you have personal auto insurance or other liability insurance. However, **make sure you have enough coverage to pay for the car.** If you do not have auto insurance or an umbrella policy that covers damage to third parties, purchasing liability insurance and a CDW or LDW is highly recommended.

## REQUIREMENTS AND RESTRICTIONS

Most agencies won't rent to you if you're under the age of 21.

## SURCHARGES

Before you pick up a car in one city and leave it in another, **ask about drop-off charges or one-way service fees,** which can be substantial. Note, too, that some rental agencies charge extra if you return the car before the time specified in your contract. To avoid a hefty refueling fee, **fill the tank just before you turn in the car,** but be aware that gas stations near the rental outlet may overcharge. It's almost never a deal to buy the tank of gas in the car when you rent it; the understanding is that you'll return it empty, but some fuel usually remains. Surcharges may apply if you're under 25. You'll pay extra for child seats (about $6 a day), which are compulsory for children under five, and for additional drivers (about $5 per day).

## CAR TRAVEL

A car is a basic necessity in New Mexico, as even the few cities have minimal public transportation. Distances are considerable, but you can make excellent time on long stretches of interstate and other four-lane highways with speed limits of up to 75 mph. If you wander off major thoroughfares, slow down. Speed limits here generally are only 55 mph, and for good reason. Many such roadways have no shoulders; on many twisting and turning mountain roads speed limits dip to 25 mph. For the most part, the scenery you'll take in while driving makes the drive a form of sightseeing in itself.

Interstate 40 runs east–west across the middle of the state. Interstate 10 cuts across the southern part of the state from the Texas border at El Paso to the Arizona line, through Las Cruces, Deming, and Lordsburg. Interstate 25 runs north from the state line at El Paso through Albuquerque and Santa Fe, then angles northeast to the Colorado line through Raton.

U.S. highways connect all major cities and towns with a good network of paved roads—a major highway improvement plan of the past few years has widened several U.S. highways, including large stretches of U.S. 285 and U.S. 550, to four lanes with limited access and high speed limits. You can make nearly as good time on these roads as you can on interstates. State roads are mostly paved two-lane thoroughfares, but some are well-graded gravel. Roads on Native American lands are designated by wooden, arrow-shape signs and you'd best adhere to the speed limit; some roads on reservation or forest land aren't paved. Even in cities, quite a few surface streets are unpaved and often bumpy and narrow—Santa Fe, for instance, has a higher percentage of dirt roads than any other state capital in the nation.

## EMERGENCY SERVICES

Depending on the location, either the New Mexico State Police or the county sheriff's department responds to road emergencies. Call the city or village police department if you encounter trouble within the limits of a municipality. Indian reservations have tribal police headquarters, and rangers assist travelers within U.S. Forest Service boundaries.

## GASOLINE

There's a lot of high, dry, lonesome country in New Mexico—it's possible to go 50 or 60 mi in some of the less-populated areas between gas stations. For a safe trip **keep your gas tank full.** Self-service gas stations are the norm in New Mexico, though in some of the less populated regions you'll find stations with full service. At press time, the cost of unleaded gas at self-service stations was about $1.10 per gallon in most of the state, and $1.25 to $1.40 in Santa Fe, Taos, and certain out-of-the-way spots off the beaten path.

## ROAD CONDITIONS

Arroyos (dry washes or gullies) are bridged on major roads, but lesser roads often dip down through them. These can be a hazard during the rainy season, July–early September. Even if it looks shallow, **don't try to cross an arroyo filled with water**—it may have an axle-breaking hole in the middle. Wait a little while, and it will drain off almost as quickly as it filled. If you stall in a running arroyo, get out of the car and onto high ground if possible. In the backcountry, never drive (or walk) in a dry arroyo bed if the sky is dark anywhere upstream. A sudden thunderstorm 15 mi away could send a raging flash flood down a wash in a matter of minutes.

Unless they are well graded and graveled, **avoid unpaved roads in New Mexico when they are wet.** The soil contains a lot of caliche, or clay, which gets very slick when mixed with water. During winter storms roads may be shut down entirely; call the State Highway Department for road conditions.

At certain times in fall or spring, New Mexico winds can be vicious for large vehicles like RVs. Driving conditions can be particularly treacherous in passages through foothills or mountains where wind gusts are concentrated.

New Mexico has a very high incidence of drunk driving and uninsured motorists. Factor in the state's high speed limits, many winding and steep roads, and eye-popping scenery, and you can see how important it is to drive as alertly and defensively as possible. On the plus side, major traffic jams are a rarity even in cities—and 2001–2002 improvements to the state's busiest intersection, the I-40/I-25 interchange in Albuquerque, has helped to reduce rush-hour backups there.

➤ ROAD CONDITIONS: **State Highway Department** (☎ 800/432–4269).

## ROAD MAPS

Signage is spotty in many rural areas, and relatively few communities are laid out in an easy-to-follow grid pattern; it's important to invest in a good road map if you're planning extensive exploring. You can pick up a free, detailed state map from area tourism offices or from the New Mexico Department of Tourism. GTR Mapping produces topographical maps of the state that depict back-roads and recreational sites—these are available at many bookshops and convenience stores.

Smart Travel Tips A to Z

> MAPS: **New Mexico Department of Tourism** (☎ 505/827–7400 or 800/733–6396 ext. 0643, WEB www.newmexico.org). **GTR Mapping** (☎ 719/275–8948).

## RULES OF THE ROAD

The speed limit along the interstates in much of New Mexico is 70 or 75 mph; it's 65 to 70 on U.S. highways (55 in more populated areas). Right-on-red turns are permitted except where signs indicate otherwise. Speed limits are strictly enforced, especially along interstates and major U.S. and state highways. Radar detectors are legal in New Mexico. U.S. Border Patrol checkpoints are set up on all major roadways from El Paso, Texas, into southern New Mexico. If stopped, you'll be asked what your citizenship is.

The use of seat belts in the front of the car is required by law in New Mexico. Always **strap children under age five into approved child-safety seats.** The state has an unusually high incidence of drunken driving–related accidents, and you might encounter sobriety checkpoints. The legal adult blood-alcohol content (BAC) limit is .08.

## CHILDREN IN NEW MEXICO

If you are renting a car, don't forget to **arrange for a car seat** when you reserve. For general advice about traveling with children, consult *Fodor's FYI: Travel with Your Baby* (available in bookstores everywhere).

### FLYING

If your children are two or older, **ask about children's airfares.** As a general rule, infants under two not occupying a seat fly at greatly reduced fares or even for free.

Experts agree that it's a good idea to use safety seats aloft for children weighing less than 40 pounds. Airlines set their own policies: U.S. carriers usually require that the child be ticketed, even if he or she is young enough to ride free, since the seats must be strapped into regular seats. Do **check your airline's policy about using safety seats during takeoff and landing.** Safety seats are not allowed everywhere in the plane, so get your seat assignments as early as possible.

When reserving, **request children's meals or a freestanding bassinet** (not available at all airlines) if you need them. But note that bulkhead seats, where you must sit to use the bassinet, may lack an overhead bin or storage space on the floor.

## LODGING

Most hotels in New Mexico allow children under a certain age to stay in their parents' room at no extra charge, but others charge for them as extra adults; be sure to **find out the cutoff age for children's discounts.** Another lodging option when traveling with kids is to consider resort accommodations. In many cases, especially for larger families, these work out to be much cheaper than hotels. Adventure holidays for children and families abound in the Southwest. Operators will organize wagon rides, safaris, and other activities for children and adults.

> BEST CHOICES: **Best Western Hotels** (☎ 800/528–1234, WEB www.bestwestern.com). **Bishop's Lodge** in Santa Fe (☎ 505/983–6377 or 800/732–2240, WEB www.bishopslodge.com). **Holiday Inns** (☎ 800/465–4329, WEB www.holiday-inn.com).

> CONDOMINIUMS AND RESORTS: **Fort Marcy Hotel Suites** (☎ 505/982–6636 or 800/745–9910, WEB www.fortmarcy.com).

## SIGHTS AND ATTRACTIONS

Carlsbad Caverns National Park and White Sands National Monument (☞ Chapter 7) are otherworldly settings that will impress even the most jaded 13-year-old. The many rural areas in this sparsely populated state offer many outdoor activities for energetic kids, ranging from hiking to fishing, and ample numbers of family restaurants can be found. However, you'll find relatively few kid-specific attractions in these remote areas. If you're planning to travel into Mexico even for a few hours with children, *see* Southwestern New Mexico A to Z *in* Chapter 8 for document requirements. Places that are especially appealing to children are indicated by a rubber-duckie icon (☺) in the margin.

> ADVENTURE HOLIDAYS: **Santa Fe Detours** (☎ 505/983–6565 or 800/338–6877, WEB www.sfdetours.com).

## CONSUMER PROTECTION

Whether you're shopping for gifts or purchasing travel services, **pay with a major credit card** whenever possible, so you can cancel payment or get reimbursed if there's a problem (and you can provide documentation). If you're doing business with a particular company for the first time, **contact your local Better Business Bureau and the attorney general's offices** in your state and (for U.S. businesses) the company's home state as well. Have any complaints been filed? Finally, if you're buying a package or tour, always **consider travel insurance** that includes default coverage (☞ Insurance, *below*).

➤ BBBs: **Council of Better Business Bureaus** (✉ 4200 Wilson Blvd., Suite 800, Arlington, VA 22203, ☎ 703/276–0100, FAX 703/525–8277, WEB www.bbb.org). **Better Business Bureau** (✉ 2625 Pennsylvania NE, Suite 2050, Albuquerque 87110, ☎ 505/884–0500; 800/873–2224 in New Mexico; FAX 505/346–0696, WEB www.bbbnm.com).

## CUSTOMS AND DUTIES

When shopping abroad, **keep receipts** for all purchases. Upon reentering the country, **be ready to show customs officials what you've bought.** If you feel a duty is incorrect, appeal the assessment. If you object to the way your clearance was handled, note the inspector's badge number. In either case, first ask to see a supervisor. If the problem isn't resolved, write to the appropriate authorities, beginning with the port director at your point of entry.

### IN AUSTRALIA

Australian residents who are 18 or older may bring home A$400 worth of souvenirs and gifts (including jewelry), 250 cigarettes or 250 grams of tobacco, and 1,125 ml of alcohol (including wine, beer, and spirits). Residents under 18 may bring back A$200 worth of goods. Prohibited items include meat products. Seeds, plants, and fruits need to be declared upon arrival.

➤ INFORMATION: **Australian Customs Service** (Regional Director, ✉ Box 8, Sydney, NSW 2001, ☎ 02/9213–

2000 or 1300/363263; 1800/020504 quarantine-inquiry line; FAX 02/9213–4043; WEB www.customs.gov.au).

### IN CANADA

Canadian residents who have been out of Canada for at least seven days may bring in C$750 worth of goods duty-free. If you've been away fewer than seven days but more than 48 hours, the duty-free allowance drops to C$200; if your trip lasts 24 to 48 hours, the allowance is C$50. You may not pool allowances with family members. Goods claimed under the C$750 exemption may follow you by mail; those claimed under the lesser exemptions must accompany you. Alcohol and tobacco products may be included in the seven-day and 48-hour exemptions but not in the 24-hour exemption. If you meet the age requirements of the province or territory through which you reenter Canada, you may bring in, duty-free, 1.5 liters of wine *or* 1.14 liters (40 imperial ounces) of liquor *or* 24 12-ounce cans or bottles of beer or ale. If you are 19 or older you may bring in, duty-free, 200 cigarettes and 50 cigars. Check ahead of time with the Canada Customs and Revenue Agency or the Department of Agriculture for policies regarding meat products, seeds, plants, and fruits.

You may send an unlimited number of gifts (only one gift per recipient, however) worth up to C$60 each duty-free to Canada. Label the package UNSOLICITED GIFT—VALUE UNDER $60. Alcohol and tobacco are excluded.

➤ INFORMATION: **Canada Customs and Revenue Agency** (✉ 2265 St. Laurent Blvd. S, Ottawa, Ontario K1G 4K3, ☎ 204/983–3500, 506/636–5064, or 800/461–9999; WEB www.ccra-adrc.gc.ca).

### IN NEW ZEALAND

All homeward-bound residents may bring back NZ$700 worth of souvenirs and gifts; passengers may not pool their allowances, and children can claim only the concession on goods intended for their own use. For those 17 or older, the duty-free allowance also includes 4.5 liters of wine or beer; one 1,125-ml bottle of spirits; and either 200 cigarettes, 250 grams of tobacco, 50 cigars, *or* a combination of the three up to 250 grams. Meat products, seeds, plants, and fruits must be declared upon arrival to the Agricultural Services Department.

➤ INFORMATION: **New Zealand Customs** (Head office: ✉ The Customhouse, 17–21 Whitmore St. [Box 2218, Wellington], ☎ 09/300–5399 or 0800/428–786, WEB www.customs. govt.nz).

### IN THE U.K.

From countries outside the European Union, including the United States, you may bring home, duty-free, 200 cigarettes or 50 cigars; 1 liter of spirits or 2 liters of fortified or sparkling wine or liqueurs; 2 liters of still table wine; 60 ml of perfume; 250 ml of toilet water; plus £145 worth of other goods, including gifts and souvenirs. Prohibited items include meat products, seeds, plants, and fruits.

➤ INFORMATION: **HM Customs and Excise** (✉ St. Christopher House, Southwark, London SE1 OTE, ☎ 020/7928–3344, WEB www.hmce. gov.uk).

### IN THE U.S.

U.S. residents who have been out of the country for at least 48 hours may bring home, for personal use, $400 worth of foreign goods duty-free, as long as they haven't used the $400 allowance or any part of it in the past 30 days. This exemption may include 1 liter of alcohol (for travelers 21 and older), 200 cigarettes, and 100 non-Cuban cigars. Family members from the same household who are traveling together may pool their $400 personal exemptions. For fewer than 48 hours, the duty-free allowance drops to $200, which may include 50 cigarettes, 10 non-Cuban cigars, and 150 milliliters of alcohol (or perfume containing alcohol). The $200 allowance cannot be combined with other individuals' exemptions, and if you exceed it, the full value of all the goods will be taxed. Antiques, which the U.S. Customs Service defines as objects more than 100 years old, enter duty-free, as do original works of art done entirely by hand, including paintings, drawings, and sculptures.

You may also send packages home duty-free, with a limit of one parcel per addressee per day (except alcohol or tobacco products or perfume worth more than $5). You can mail up to $200 worth of goods for personal use; label the package PERSONAL USE and attach a list of its contents and their retail value. If the package contains your used personal belongings, mark it PERSONAL GOODS RETURNED to avoid paying duties. You may send up to $100 worth of goods as a gift; mark the package UNSOLICITED GIFT. Mailed items do not affect your duty-free allowance on your return.

➤ INFORMATION: **U.S. Customs Service** (for inquiries, ✉ 1300 Pennsylvania Ave. NW, Washington, DC 20229, ☎ 202/354–1000, WEB www.customs.gov; for complaints, ✉ Customer Satisfaction Unit, 1300 Pennsylvania Ave. NW, Room 5.5A, Washington, DC 20229; for registration of equipment, ✉ Office of Passenger Programs, 1300 Pennsylvania Ave. NW, Room 5.4D, Washington, DC 20229, ☎ 202/927–0530).

## DINING

New Mexico has some of the best Mexican food in the Southwest, and ingredients and style vary even within the state. Most longtime residents like their chili (which is seasoned with red or green chile) with some fire—in the Santa Fe, Albuquerque, and Las Cruces areas, chili is sometimes celebrated for its ability to set off smoke alarms. Most restaurants offer a choice of red or green chili with one type typically being milder than the other (either color can be hot or mild). Excellent barbecue and steaks also can be found throughout New Mexico. The restaurants we list are the cream of the crop in each price category. Properties indicated by an ✗🏠 are lodging establishments whose restaurant warrants a special trip.

| CATEGORY | COST* |
| --- | --- |
| $$$$ | over $25 |
| $$$ | $18–$25 |
| $$ | $10–$17 |
| $ | under $10 |

*per person for a main course at dinner*

## RESERVATIONS AND DRESS

Reservations are always a good idea; we mention them only when they're essential or not accepted. Book as far ahead as you can, and reconfirm as soon as you arrive. (Large parties should always call ahead to check the reservations policy.) We mention dress only when men are required to wear a jacket or a jacket and tie. Even at nicer restaurants in New Mexico, dress is usually casual.

Statewide, many kitchens stop serving around 8 PM, so **don't arrive too late** if you're looking forward to a leisurely dinner.

## SPECIALTIES

The glossary in Chapter 9 explains various southwestern ingredients and dishes you'll find on menus.

## WINE, BEER AND SPIRITS

Like many other states, New Mexico has some fine microbreweries, with the largest production facility found in the unlikely and highly remote location of Carrizozo, in south-central New Mexico. New Mexico also has a modest number of wineries. Franciscan monks first planted their vines here before moving more successfully to northern California.

## DISABILITIES AND ACCESSIBILITY

Most of the region's national parks and recreational areas have accessible visitor centers, rest rooms, campsites, and trails.

➤ LOCAL RESOURCES: **National Park Service, Intermountain Support Office** (✉ Box 728, Santa Fe 87504, ☎ 505/988–6091).

## LODGING

In Carlsbad, the Best Western Motel Stevens has two large, accessible guest rooms with parking directly outside the rooms. Accessible kitchenettes also are available. The Hilton of Santa Fe, just a few blocks from the historic Plaza, has several accessible guest rooms. The Hyatt Regency in Albuquerque has eight accessible rooms in both smoking and non-smoking sections. The rooms have flashing alarm lights, with TTY and closed-captioned television available.

Braille guidebooks can also be obtained here. Shadow Mountain Lodge in Ruidoso offers one accessible room on the ground floor, with a rest room equipped with a handheld shower-head and grab bars.

Despite the Americans with Disabilities Act, the definition of accessibility seems to differ from hotel to hotel. Some properties may be accessible by ADA standards for people with mobility problems but not for people with hearing or vision impairments, for example. Furthermore, many accommodations in New Mexico are historic or quite small and do not conform even to ADA mobility standards.

If you have mobility problems, ask for the lowest floor on which accessible services are offered. If you have a hearing impairment, check whether the hotel has devices to alert you visually to the ring of the telephone, knock at the door, and a fire/emergency alarm. Some hotels provide these devices without charge. Discuss your needs with hotel personnel if this equipment isn't available, so that a staff member can personally alert you in the event of an emergency.

If you're bringing a guide dog, get authorization ahead of time and write down the name of the person you spoke with.

➤ ACCESSIBLE ROOMS: **Best Western Motel Stevens** (☎ 505/887–2851, WEB www.bestwestern.com). **Hilton of Santa Fe** (☎ 505/988–2811, WEB www.hiltonofsantafe.com). **Hyatt Regency** (☎ 505/842–1234, WEB albuquerque.hyatt.com). **Shadow Mountain Lodge** (☎ 505/257–4886, WEB www.smlruidoso.com).

## RESERVATIONS

When discussing accessibility with an operator or reservations agent, **ask hard questions.** Are there any stairs, inside *or* out? Are there grab bars next to the toilet *and* in the shower/tub? How wide is the doorway to the room? To the bathroom? For the most extensive facilities meeting the latest legal specifications, **opt for newer accommodations.** If you reserve through a toll-free number, consider also calling the hotel's local number to confirm the information from the central reservations office. Get confirmation in writing when you can.

## SIGHTS AND ATTRACTIONS

Santa Fe has many narrow streets and walkways and ancient buildings that can be less than convenient for wheelchairs. The same is true of Old Mesilla near Las Cruces and much of Taos. Carlsbad Caverns National Park is accessible on the 1¼-mi Red Tour, which goes directly into the Big Room via elevator; wheelchair users are advised never to try this alone. Reserved parking is available at the cavern's lower amphitheater, where the summer bat flights take place. Parking and picnic areas at White Sands National Monument are wheelchair accessible, but only limited access is available to the sand dunes, where there are no developed trails. New Mexico has several free guidebooks for travelers with disabilities.

➤ NEW MEXICO GUIDEBOOKS: **Albuquerque Convention and Visitors Bureau** (☎ 800/284–2282, WEB abqcvb.org/visitors/info). **Developmental Disabilities Planning Council** (☎ 505/827–7590, pputnam@state. nm.us). **Governor's Concerns on the Handicapped** (☎ 505/827–6465; 505/827–6329 TDD; 877/696–1470 in New Mexico; WEB www.state.nm. us/gcch/accessnm.htm). **New Mexico Department of Tourism** (☎ 505/827–7400 or 800/733–6396 ext. 0643, WEB www.newmexico.org/visitor/disabled. html).

## TRANSPORTATION

Specially equipped vehicles can be rented from **Wheelchair Getaways of New Mexico** (✉ Box 93501, Albuquerque 87199, ☎ 505/247–2626 or 800/408–2626, WEB www. wheelchair-getaways.com). Automatic wheelchair lifts or ramps along with hand controls are included in vans, which will be delivered to the Albuquerque International Sunport upon request. Rentals also are available from this El Paso, Texas, franchise.

➤ COMPLAINTS: **Aviation Consumer Protection Division** (☞ Air Travel, *above*) for airline-related problems. **Departmental Office of Civil Rights** (for general inquiries, ✉ U.S. Department of Transportation, S-30, 400 7th St. SW, Room 10215, Washington, DC 20590, ☎ 202/366–4648, FAX 202/366–3571, WEB www.dot.gov/ost/docr/index.htm). **Disability Rights Section** (✉ NYAV, U.S. Department of Justice, Civil Rights Division, 950 Pennsylvania Ave. NW, Washington, DC 20530; ☎ ADA information line 202/514–0301, 800/514–0301; 202/514–0383 TTY; 800/514–0383 TTY; WEB www.usdoj.gov/crt/ada/adahom1. htm).

## TRAVEL AGENCIES

In the United States, the Americans with Disabilities Act requires that travel firms serve the needs of all travelers. Some agencies specialize in working with people with disabilities.

➤ TRAVELERS WITH MOBILITY PROBLEMS: **Access Adventures** (✉ 206 Chestnut Ridge Rd., Scottsville, NY 14624, ☎ 716/889–9096, dltravel@ prodigy.net), run by a former physical-rehabilitation counselor. **Accessible Vans of America** (✉ 9 Spielman Rd., Fairfield, NJ 07004, ☎ 877/282–8267; 888/282–8267 reservations; FAX 973/808–9713; WEB www.accessiblevans.com). **Flying Wheels Travel** (✉ 143 W. Bridge St. [Box 382, Owatonna, MN 55060], ☎ 507/451–5005, FAX 507/451–1685, WEB www.flyingwheelstravel.com).

## DISCOUNTS AND DEALS

Be a smart shopper and **compare all your options** before making decisions. A plane ticket bought with a promotional coupon from travel clubs, coupon books, and direct-mail offers or purchased on the Internet may not be cheaper than the least expensive fare from a discount ticket agency. And always keep in mind that what you get is just as important as what you save.

## DISCOUNT RESERVATIONS

To save money, **look into discount reservations services** with Web sites and toll-free numbers, which use their buying power to get a better price on hotels, airline tickets, even car rentals. When booking a room, always **call the hotel's local toll-free number** (if one is available) rather than the central reservations number—you'll often get a better price. Always ask about special packages or corporate rates.

➤ AIRLINE TICKETS: ☎ 800/AIR–4LESS.

➤ HOTEL ROOMS: **Hotel Reservations Network** (☎ 800/964–6835, WEB www.hoteldiscount.com). **RMC Travel** (☎ 800/245–5738, WEB www.rmcwebtravel.com). **Turbotrip.com** (☎ 800/473–7829, WEB www.turbotrip.com).

## PACKAGE DEALS

Don't confuse packages and guided tours. When you buy a package, you travel on your own, just as though you had planned the trip yourself. Fly-drive packages, which combine airfare and car rental, are often a good deal.

## ECOTOURISM

New Mexico has a wide variety of cactus species, which grow so abundantly that it might seem harmless to dig up a plant or two as a souvenir. Don't do it. Laws prohibit this practice, as certain species are becoming scarce. Avoid picking up lizards or related species, which also are becoming increasingly protected. It's also illegal to carry off Indian artifacts such as arrowheads or pottery from public land. On U.S. Bureau of Land Management land, it's okay to collect many types of rock samples, but clarify rules depending on the district you're visiting. Southern New Mexico has many caves open to visitors mostly by permit. If you visit a cave, don't leave any traces of yourself (pack it in, pack it out) and don't touch the delicate formations.

## ETIQUETTE AND BEHAVIOR

*See* Reservations and Pueblos *in* the Pleasures and Pastimes section of Chapter 1 for information about proper etiquette when visiting Native American lands.

## GAY AND LESBIAN TRAVEL

According to the 2000 U.S. Census, Santa Fe is second only to San Francisco in the percentage of households headed by same-sex couples. Taos and Albuquerque also have very high numbers of lesbian and gay residents and visitors. Elsewhere in the state and in El Paso, somewhat more conservative attitudes prevail, but overall New Mexico is fairly tolerant.

Nevertheless, there's very little in the way of a gay singles scene in New Mexico. You'll find many romantic, gay-friendly inns and also gay-owned shops and eateries in Santa Fe, Taos, and Albuquerque—especially the funky Nob Hill Historic District near the University of New Mexico. But gay nightlife is limited to a handful of bars in Albuquerque (most of them mixed male-female, one of them mostly gay-male, and one mostly lesbian) and one mixed gay-straight club in Santa Fe. The monthly *Out! Magazine* (no relation to the national magazine *Out*) provides coverage of New Mexico.

A chapter in *Fodor's Gay Guide to the USA* (available at bookstores everywhere) covers Santa Fe, Taos, Albuquerque, and El Paso, Texas.

➤ RESOURCES: *Out! Magazine* (☎ 505/243–2540, WEB www.outmagazine.com).

➤ GAY- AND LESBIAN-FRIENDLY TRAVEL AGENCIES: **Different Roads Travel** (✉ 8383 Wilshire Blvd., Suite 902, Beverly Hills, CA 90211, ☎ 323/651–5557 or 800/429–8747, FAX 323/651–3678, lgernert@tzell.com). **Kennedy Travel** (✉ 314 Jericho Turnpike, Floral Park, NY 11001, ☎ 516/352–4888 or 800/237–7433, FAX 516/354–8849, WEB www.kennedytravel.com). **Now, Voyager** (✉ 4406 18th St., San Francisco, CA 94114, ☎ 415/626–1169 or 800/255–6951, FAX 415/626–8626, WEB www.nowvoyager.com). **Skylink Travel and Tour** (✉ 1006 Mendocino Ave., Santa Rosa, CA 95401, ☎ 707/546–9888 or 800/225–5759, FAX 707/546–9891), serving lesbian travelers.

## GUIDEBOOKS

Plan well and you won't be sorry. Guidebooks are excellent tools—and you can take them with you. You may want to check out color-photo-illustrated *Compass American Guide: New Mexico,* and *Compass American Guide: Santa Fe,* thorough on culture and history, or *Fodor's Road Guide USA: Arizona, Colorado, New Mexico,* for comprehensive restaurant, hotel, and attractions listings for driving vacations. Both are available at on-line retailers and bookstores everywhere.

## HOLIDAYS

New Mexico is an exceptional destination at Christmastime, particularly Santa Fe and Taos. There's an excellent chance for snow to put you in the holiday mood, but usually not too much of it and at tolerable temperatures. Farolitos (paper-bag lanterns) line sidewalks and the roofs of adobe buildings. Similar scenes are repeated throughout most of New Mexico, reflecting traditions dating back several centuries. In a nationally recognized Christmas tour at Carlsbad, home owners provide several miles of brightly lit backyard displays for the benefit of evening boat cruises along the Pecos River.

Major national holidays include New Year's Day (Jan. 1); Martin Luther King Jr. Day (3rd Mon. in Jan.); President's Day (3rd Mon. in Feb.); Memorial Day (last Mon. in May); Independence Day (July 4); Labor Day (1st Mon. in Sept.); Thanksgiving Day (4th Thurs. in Nov.); Christmas Eve and Christmas Day (Dec. 24 and 25); and New Year's Eve (Dec. 31).

## INSURANCE

The most useful travel-insurance plan is a comprehensive policy that includes coverage for trip cancellation and interruption, default, trip delay, and medical expenses (with a waiver for pre-existing conditions).

Without insurance you will lose all or most of your money if you cancel your trip, regardless of the reason. Default insurance covers you if your tour operator, airline, or cruise line goes out of business. Trip-delay covers expenses that arise because of bad weather or mechanical delays. Study the fine print when comparing policies.

U.K. residents can buy a travel-insurance policy valid for most vacations taken during the year in which it's purchased (but check pre-existing-condition coverage).

Always **buy travel policies directly from the insurance company**; if you buy them from a cruise line, airline,

or tour operator that goes out of business you probably will not be covered for the agency or operator's default, a major risk. Before making any purchase, **review your existing health and home-owner's policies** to find what they cover away from home.

➤ TRAVEL INSURERS: In the United States: **Access America** (✉ 6600 W. Broad St., Richmond, VA 23230, ☎ 800/284–8300, FAX 804/673–1491 or 800/346–9265, WEB www.accessamerica.com). **Travel Guard International** (✉ 1145 Clark St., Stevens Point, WI 54481, ☎ 715/345–0505 or 800/826–1300, FAX 800/955–8785, WEB www.travelguard.com).

## FOR INTERNATIONAL
## TRAVELERS

For information on customs restrictions, *see* Customs and Duties, *above.*

### CAR RENTAL

When picking up a rental car, non-U.S. residents need a reservation voucher for any prepaid reservations that were made in the traveler's home country, a passport, a driver's license, and a travel policy that covers each driver.

### CAR TRAVEL

Interstate highways—limited-access, multilane highways whose numbers are prefixed by "I–"—are the fastest routes. Interstates with three-digit numbers encircle urban areas, which may have other limited-access expressways, freeways, and parkways as well. Tolls may be levied on limited-access highways. So-called U.S. highways and state highways are not necessarily limited-access but may have several lanes.

Along larger highways, roadside stops with rest rooms, fast-food restaurants, and sundries stores are well spaced. State police and tow trucks patrol major highways and lend assistance. If your car breaks down on an interstate, pull onto the shoulder and wait for help, or have your passengers wait while you walk to an emergency phone. If you carry a cell phone, dial *55, noting your location on the small green roadside mileage markers.

Driving in the United States is on the right. Do **obey speed limits** posted along roads and highways. Watch for lower limits in small towns and on back roads. On weekdays between 6 and 10 AM and again between 4 and 7 PM **expect heavy traffic.**

## CONSULATES AND EMBASSIES

➤ REGIONAL OFFICES: **Australia** (✉ 2049 Century Park E, 19th floor, Los Angeles, CA, ☎ 310/229–4840). **Canada** (✉ 300 S. Grand Ave., Los Angeles, CA, ☎ 213/346–2700). **New Zealand** (✉ 4365 Executive Dr., No. 1600, San Diego, CA, ☎ 619/ 699–2993). **United Kingdom** (✉ 11766 Wilshire Blvd., No. 400, Los Angeles, CA, ☎ 310/477–3322).

## CURRENCY

The dollar is the basic unit of U.S. currency. It has 100 cents. Coins include the copper penny (1¢); the silvery nickel (5¢), dime (10¢), quarter (25¢), and half-dollar (50¢); and the golden $1 coin, replacing a now-rare silver dollar. Bills are denominated $1, $5, $10, $20, $50, and $100, all green and identical in size; designs vary. The exchange rate at press time was US$1.42 per British pound, 63¢ per Canadian dollar, 53¢ per Australian dollar, and 44¢ per New Zealand dollar.

## ELECTRICITY

The U.S. standard is AC, 110 volts/60 cycles. Plugs have two flat pins set parallel to each other.

## EMERGENCIES

For police, fire, or ambulance, **dial 911** (0 in rural areas).

## INSURANCE

Britons and Australians need extra medical coverage when traveling overseas.

➤ INSURANCE INFORMATION: In the United Kingdom: **Association of British Insurers** (✉ 51 Gresham St., London EC2V 7HQ, ☎ 020/7600–3333, FAX 020/7696–8999, WEB www. abi.org.uk). In Australia: **Insurance Council of Australia** (✉ Level 3, 56 Pitt St., Sydney, NSW 2000, ☎ 02/ 9253–5100, FAX 02/9253–5111, WEB www.ica.com.au). In Canada: **RBC Insurance** (✉ 6880 Financial Dr.,

Mississauga, Ontario L5N 7Y5, ☎ 905/816–2400 or 800/668–4342, FAX 905/813–4704, WEB www.rbcinsurance. com). In New Zealand: **Insurance Council of New Zealand** (✉ Level 7, 111–115 Customhouse Quay [Box 474, Wellington], ☎ 04/472–5230, FAX 04/473–3011, WEB www.icnz. org.nz).

## MAIL AND SHIPPING

You can buy stamps and aerograms and send letters and parcels in post offices. Stamp-dispensing machines can occasionally be found in airports, bus and train stations, office buildings, drugstores, and the like. You can also deposit mail in the stout, dark blue steel bins at strategic locations everywhere and in the mail chutes of large buildings; pickup schedules are posted.

For mail sent within the United States, you'll need a 37¢ stamp for first-class letters weighing up to 1 ounce (23¢ for each additional ounce) and 23¢ for postcards. You pay 80¢ for 1-ounce airmail letters and 70¢ for airmail postcards to most other countries; to Canada and Mexico, you need a 60¢ stamp for a 1-ounce letter and 50¢ for a postcard. An aerogram—a single sheet of lightweight blue paper that folds into its own envelope, stamped for overseas airmail—costs 70¢.

To receive mail on the road, have it sent c/o General Delivery at your destination's main post office (use the correct five-digit ZIP code). You must pick up mail in person within 30 days and show a driver's license or passport.

## PASSPORTS AND VISAS

When traveling internationally, **carry your passport** even if you don't need one (it's always the best form of ID) and **make two photocopies of the data page** (one for someone at home and another for you, carried separately from your passport). If you lose your passport, promptly call the nearest embassy or consulate and the local police.

Visitor visas are not necessary for Canadian citizens, or for citizens of Australia and the United Kingdom who are staying fewer than 90 days.

➤ AUSTRALIAN CITIZENS: **Australian State Passport Office** (☎ 131–232, WEB www.passports.gov.au). **United States Consulate General** (✉ MLC Centre, 19–29 Martin Pl., 59th floor, Sydney, NSW 2000, ☎ 02/9373–9200; 1902/941–641 fee-based visa-inquiry line; WEB www.usis-australia.gov/index.html).

➤ CANADIAN CITIZENS: **Passport Office** (to mail in applications: ✉ Department of Foreign Affairs and International Trade, Ottawa, Ontario K1A 0G3, ☎ 819/994–3500 or 800/567–6868, WEB www.dfait-maeci.gc.ca/passport).

➤ NEW ZEALAND CITIZENS: **New Zealand Passport Office** (☎ 04/474–8100 or 0800/22–5050, WEB www.passports.govt.nz). **Embassy of the United States** (✉ 29 Fitzherbert Terr., Thorndon, Wellington, ☎ 04/462–6000, WEB usembassy.org.nz). **U.S. Consulate General** (✉ Citibank Bldg., 3rd floor, 23 Customs St. E, Auckland, ☎ 09/303–2724, WEB usembassy.org.nz).

➤ U.K. CITIZENS: **London Passport Office** (for application procedures and emergency passports, ☎ 0870/521–0410, WEB www.passport.gov.uk). **U.S. Consulate General** (✉ Queen's House, 14 Queen St., Belfast, Northern Ireland BT1 6EQ, ☎ 028/9032–8239, WEB www.usembassy.org.uk). **U.S. Embassy** (for general information, enclose an SASE to: ✉ Consular Information Unit, 24 Grosvenor Sq., London W1 1AE; to submit an application via mail, ✉ Visa Branch, 5 Upper Grosvenor St., London W1A 2JB; ☎ 09068/200–290 recorded visa information; 09055/444–546 operator service, both with per-minute charges; WEB www.usembassy.org.uk).

## TELEPHONES

All U.S. telephone numbers consist of a three-digit area code and a seven-digit local number. Within most local calling areas, you dial only the seven-digit number. Within some area codes, you must dial "1" first for calls outside the local area. To call between area-code regions, dial "1" then all 10 digits; the same goes for calls to numbers prefixed by "800," "888,"

"877", and "866"—all toll-free. For calls to numbers preceded by "900" you must pay—usually dearly.

For international calls, dial "011" followed by the country code and the local number. For help, dial "0" and ask for an overseas operator. The country code is 61 for Australia, 64 for New Zealand, 44 for the United Kingdom. Calling Canada is the same as calling within the United States. Most local phone books list country codes and U.S. area codes. The country code for the United States is 1.

For operator assistance, dial "0." To obtain someone's phone number, call directory assistance, 555–1212 or occasionally 411 (free at public phones). To have the person you're calling foot the bill, phone collect; dial "0" instead of "1" before the 10-digit number.

At pay phones, instructions are usually posted. Usually you insert coins in a slot (10¢–50¢ for local calls) and wait for a steady tone before dialing. When you call long-distance, the operator tells you how much to insert; prepaid phone cards, widely available in various denominations, are easier. Call the number on the back, punch in the card's personal identification number when prompted, then dial your number.

## LODGING

The lodgings we list are the cream of the crop in each price category. We always list the facilities that are available—but we don't specify whether they cost extra: when pricing accommodations, always ask what's included and what costs extra. Accommodations in New Mexico include chain hotels in all price categories, many bed-and-breakfasts, small alpine lodges near ski resorts, and low-budget motels. Rates are highest during the peak tourist months of July and August and during Christmas and winter ski season. Off-season rates, which fluctuate, tend to be 20% lower than peak rates. You can book rooms (and rental cars and outdoor and other activities) by calling New Mexico Central Reservations.

| CATE-GORY | GREATER SANTA FE* | OTHER AREAS* |
|-----------|-------------------|--------------|
| $$$$ | over $220 | over $170 |
| $$$ | $160–$220 | $120–$170 |
| $$ | $100–$160 | $70–$120 |
| $ | under $100 | under $70 |

*All prices are for a standard double room, excluding tax (5.6%–7%), in peak season.*

Assume that hotels operate on the **European Plan** (EP, with no meals), unless we specify that they use the **Continental Plan** (CP, with a Continental breakfast), **Breakfast Plan** (BP, with a full breakfast), **Modified American Plan** (MAP, with breakfast and dinner), or the **Full American Plan** (FAP, with all meals).

➤ RESERVATIONS: **New Mexico Central Reservations** (☎ 800/466–7829, WEB www.nmtravel.com).

## APARTMENT AND HOUSE RENTALS

If you want a home base that's roomy enough for a family and comes with cooking facilities, **consider a furnished rental.** These can save you money, especially if you're traveling with a group. Home-exchange directories sometimes list rentals as well as exchanges.

## LOCAL AGENTS

Vacation home, condo, and cabin rentals are numerous, particularly in mountain resort areas of New Mexico. Management companies include Taos Vacation Rentals in Taos, the Management Group in Santa Fe, and Green Mountain Real Estate in Cloudcroft.

➤ MANAGEMENT COMPANIES: **Green Mountain Real Estate** (☎ 800/748–2537, WEB www.greenmnt.com). **The Management Group** (☎ 505/982–2823, WEB www.santafe-rentals.com). **Taos Vacation Rentals** (☎ 800/788–8267, WEB www.taosvacationrentals.com).

## BED-AND-BREAKFASTS

B&Bs in New Mexico run the gamut from rooms in locals' homes to grandly restored adobe or Victorian homes. Rates in Santa Fe and Taos tend to be high; they're a little lower in Albuquerque and rival those of chain motels in the outlying areas. Good deals can be found in southern New Mexico as well.

➤ RESERVATION SERVICES: **Bed and Breakfast of New Mexico** (☎ 505/982–3332, WEB www.santafebnb.com). **New Mexico Bed and Breakfast Association** (☎ 505/766–5380 or 800/661–6649, WEB www.nmbba.org).

## CAMPING

If you're into camping the way the pioneers did, New Mexico is the place for you. Primitive sites, where you'll likely not see a ranger (or even another camper) for miles, are plentiful. Many of the state and national parks have developed sites. The New Mexico Department of Tourism (☞ Visitor Information, *below*) has information about public and private campgrounds in the state. The state also has a surprising number of lakes, including the expansive Elephant Butte and Navajo Lake. Campers can load up their boats with gear and head for primitive backcountry away from roads and crowds.

## HOME EXCHANGES

If you would like to exchange your home for someone else's, **join a home-exchange organization,** which will send you its updated listings of available exchanges for a year and will include your own listing in at least one of them. It's up to you to make specific arrangements.

➤ EXCHANGE CLUBS: **HomeLink International** (✉ Box 47747, Tampa, FL 33647, ☎ 813/975–9825 or 800/638–3841, FAX 813/910–8144, WEB www.homelink.org; $106 per year). **Intervac U.S.** (✉ 30 Corte San Fernando, Tiburon, CA 94920, ☎ 800/756–4663, FAX 415/435–7440, WEB www.intervacus.com; $90 yearly fee for a listing, on-line access, and a catalog; $50 without catalog).

## HOSTELS

No matter what your age, you can **save on lodging costs by staying at hostels.** New Mexico hostel accommodations range from the elegant surroundings of a bed-and-breakfast in Silver City (The Carter House) to the casual, camping out–style environment of a hot-springs locale in Truth or Consequences (Riverbend Hot Springs) to the no-frills friendliness of the Abominable Snowmansion in Arroyo Seco (just north of Taos).

In some 4,500 locations in more than 70 countries around the world, Hostelling International (HI), the umbrella group for a number of national youth-hostel associations, offers single-sex, dorm-style beds and, at many hostels, rooms for couples and family accommodations. Membership in any HI national hostel association, open to travelers of all ages, allows you to stay in HI-affiliated hostels at member rates; one-year membership is about $25 for adults (C$35 for a two-year minimum membership in Canada, £13 in the United Kingdom, A$52 in Australia, and NZ$40 in New Zealand); hostels run about $10–$30 per night. Members have priority if the hostel is full; they're also eligible for discounts around the world, even on rail and bus travel in some countries.

➤ ORGANIZATIONS: **Hostelling International—American Youth Hostels** (✉ 733 15th St. NW, Suite 840, Washington, DC 20005, ☎ 202/783–6161, FAX 202/783–6171, WEB www. hiayh.org). **Hostelling International—Canada** (✉ 400–205 Catherine St., Ottawa, Ontario K2P 1C3, ☎ 613/237–7884 or 800/663–5777, FAX 613/237–7868, WEB www.hihostels.ca). **Youth Hostel Association of England and Wales** (✉ Trevelyan House, Dimple Rd., Matlock, Derbyshire DE4 3YH, U.K., ☎ 0870/870–8808, FAX 0169/592–702, WEB www.yha.org. uk). **Youth Hostel Association Australia** (✉ 10 Mallett St., Camperdown, NSW 2050, ☎ 02/9565–1699, FAX 02/9565–1325, WEB www.yha.com. au). **Youth Hostels Association of New Zealand** (✉ Level 3, 193 Cashel St. [Box 436, Christchurch], ☎ 03/379–9970, FAX 03/365–4476, WEB www.yha.org.nz).

## HOTELS

If you plan to visit Albuquerque in October, be sure and check dates for the Kodak Albuquerque International Balloon Fiesta or you might be stranded if you haven't booked at least four months in advance. Premium hotel rooms in the state capital of Santa Fe tend to fill up during sessions of the New Mexico Legislature, typically conducted during the first three months of the year. Summer weekends can pack hotel rooms in smaller tourist-oriented communities such as Ruidoso, Taos, and Carlsbad, so make sure you have reservations in advance. All hotels listed have private bath unless otherwise noted.

➤ TOLL-FREE NUMBERS: **Best Western** (☎ 800/528–1234, WEB www. bestwestern.com). **Choice** (☎ 800/424–6423, WEB www.choicehotels. com). **Comfort Inn** (☎ 800/424–6423, WEB www.choicehotels.com). **Days Inn** (☎ 800/325–2525, WEB www.daysinn.com). **Doubletree and Red Lion Hotels** (☎ 800/222–8733, WEB www.hilton.com). **Embassy Suites** (☎ 800/362–2779, WEB www. embassysuites.com). **Fairfield Inn** (☎ 800/228–2800, WEB www.marriott. com). **Hilton** (☎ 800/445–8667, WEB www.hilton.com). **Holiday Inn** (☎ 800/465–4329, WEB www. sixcontinentshotels.com). **Howard Johnson** (☎ 800/654–4656, WEB www.hojo.com). **Hyatt Hotels & Resorts** (☎ 800/233–1234, WEB www. hyatt.com). **La Quinta** (☎ 800/531–5900, WEB www.laquinta.com). **Marriott** (☎ 800/228–9290, WEB www. marriott.com). **Quality Inn** (☎ 800/424–6423, WEB www.choicehotels. com). **Radisson** (☎ 800/333–3333, WEB www.radisson.com). **Ramada** (☎ 800/228–2828; 800/854–7854 international reservations; WEB www. ramada.com or www.ramadahotels. com). **Sheraton** (☎ 800/325–3535, WEB www.starwood.com/sheraton). **Sleep Inn** (☎ 800/424–6423, WEB www.choicehotels.com). **Westin Hotels & Resorts** (☎ 800/228–3000, WEB www.starwood.com/westin).

## MOTELS

➤ TOLL-FREE NUMBERS: **Econo Lodge** (☎ 800/553–2666). **Hampton Inn** (☎ 800/426–7866). **La Quinta** (☎ 800/531–5900). **Motel 6** (☎ 800/466–8356). **Rodeway** (☎ 800/228–2000). **Super 8** (☎ 800/848–8888).

## MEDIA

Because of its sparse and scattered communities, New Mexico has more demand for radio stations and newspapers than ordinarily found (per capita) in more urbanized areas. These islands of population generally have their own media outlets, except for network television stations that are concentrated in Albuquerque and El Paso, Texas. Albuquerque television station affiliates are set up in Roswell, while public television and radio stations operate on university campuses at Albuquerque, Las Cruces, and Portales.

### NEWSPAPERS AND MAGAZINES

New Mexico has about 15 daily and quite a few more weekly newspapers. Only one newspaper, the *Albuquerque Journal,* circulates statewide. The *Santa Fe New Mexican* often takes a political tone, since it's based in the state capital. In more rural areas, agriculture reporting is predominant in newspapers such as the *Courier* in Hatch and *Quay County Sun* in Tucumcari. Two magazines with headquarters in Santa Fe, *New Mexico* (travel and cultural features) and *Outside* (outdoor recreation articles), are nationally recognized publications. Find out what's happening in the arts, culture, and nightlife by picking up the free weeklies that are available in Albuquerque, Santa Fe, and Taos: the *Alibi, Crosswinds Weekly,* and the *Santa Fe Reporter.*

### RADIO AND TELEVISION

National Public Radio affiliates are found on major university campuses in New Mexico, including **KUNM** (89.9 FM) at Albuquerque's University of New Mexico, **KRWG** (90.7 FM) at New Mexico State University in Las Cruces, and **KENW** (89.5 FM) at Eastern New Mexico State University in Portales. The state has about 40 radio stations, ranging from Christian broadcasts to rock to country-and-western. Major network affiliates in New Mexico are all based in Albuquerque, including **KOB** (NBC, Channel 4), **KASA** (Fox, Channel 2), **KRQE** (CBS, Channel 13), and **KOAT** (ABC, Channel 7).

Major network affiliates in El Paso, Texas, serve many southern New Mexico locations. Public television station outlets are found on university campuses, including **KNME** (Channel 5) in Albuquerque, **KRWG** (Channel 22) in Las Cruces, and **KENW** (Channel 3) in Portales.

## MEXICO SIDE TRIPS

Visitors to El Paso, Texas, and other border towns often make an excursion into Mexico. If you're planning to cross the border to Mexico, **note the travel requirements** detailed in Southwestern New Mexico A to Z in Chapter 8, passport information under For International Travelers, *above,* and customs information under Customs and Duties, *above.*

### SAFETY

The U.S. State Department has issued a warning regarding travel in Ciudad Juárez. Crime rates in Juárez are high, and gangland-style hits associated with internal drug wars have taken place in public places.

Since tourists are sometimes targeted for foul play, **don't take the family van with U.S. license plates into Mexico** and never drive in Mexico after dark. Desirable model vehicles from the United States are often stolen when left parked in unsupervised areas.

Be cautious about eating in smaller restaurants, since water and food quality controls are not as stringent as they are in the United States. It's best to order bottled beverages and packaged food, if you're in doubt. **Never carry firearms across the border,** as there are severe penalties, including long-term incarceration.

The odds of encountering trouble are slim, as long as you obey laws and practice common-sense precautions that would apply in any large metropolitan area. You can peruse travel warnings for many international locations including Mexico at the U.S. State Department Web site.

➤ U.S. GOVERNMENT OFFICES: **U.S. Consulate General's Office** (✉ Avenida Lopez Mateos 924-N, Ciudad Juárez Mexico, ☎ 011/52–16–113000). **U.S. State Department**

(✉ U.S. Department of State, 2201 C St. NW, Washington, DC 20520, ☎ 202/647–4000, 🖿 www.travel.state. gov).

## MONEY MATTERS

In New Mexico, Santa Fe is by far the priciest city: meals, gasoline, and motel rates are all significantly higher in the state's capital. Lodging costs in Santa Fe typically run 30% to 50% higher than in any other New Mexico city. Taos, too, can be a little expensive because it's such a popular tourist destination, but you have more choices for economizing there than in Santa Fe. Lodging and dining throughout much of the rest of the state are a genuine bargain. Depending on the establishment, $7 can buy you a savory Mexican dinner in Farmington, Old Mesilla, or Silver City. As the state's largest metropolitan area, Albuquerque has a full range of price choices. Prices throughout this guide are given for adults. Substantially reduced fees are almost always available for children, students, and senior citizens. For information on taxes, see Taxes, below.

### ATMS

Look for ATMs in larger communities, since isolated rural areas are not as widely served. ATMs are available in banks, bank branches, chain grocery stores, and shopping malls.

### CREDIT CARDS

Throughout this guide, the following abbreviations are used: AE, American Express; D, Discover; DC, Diners Club; MC, MasterCard; and V, Visa.

➤ REPORTING LOST CARDS: American Express (☎ 800/441–0519). Discover (☎ 800/347–2683). Diners Club (☎ 800/234–6377). MasterCard (☎ 800/ 622–7747). Visa (☎ 800/847–2911).

## OUTDOORS AND SPORTS

The New Mexico Department of Tourism (☞ Visitor Information, below) distributes a booklet, Outdoors New Mexico, with information about the many recreational activities that take place within the state.

### BIRD-WATCHING

New Mexico is fortunate to be home to tens of thousands of migrating birds, and the refuges offer viewing platforms for observing the flocks of snow geese, sandhill cranes, and other migratory birds using this popular stopover.

➤ REFUGES: Bitter Lake National Wildlife Refuge (✉ 4065 Bitter Lakes [Box 7, Roswell 88202], ☎ 505/622–6755). Bosque del Apache National Wildlife Refuge (✉ Box 1246, Socorro 87801, ☎ 505/835–1828, 🖿 www.friendsofthebosque.org).

## CANOEING, KAYAKING, AND RIVER RAFTING

Most of the hard-core river rafting is done in the Taos area; for statewide information concerning river recreational activities, contact the New Mexico Department of Tourism (☞ Visitor Information, below). For additional operators, see the A to Z listings at the end of individual chapters or contact local tourism offices.

## FISHING

Anyone over 12 who wishes to fish must buy a New Mexico fishing license. Including a trout-validation stamp, the license costs out-of-state visitors $8 per day or $16 for five days. Habitat Improvement stamps also must be purchased for an extra $5 for fishing on U.S. Forest Service or Bureau of Land Management lands. The year-round nonresident fee is $39 ($17.50 for state residents). About 225 sporting-goods and other stores, in addition to the offices of the New Mexico Game and Fish Department, sell fishing licenses.

Fishing on Native American reservations is not subject to state regulations but will require tribal permits; the Indian Pueblo Cultural Center (☞ Visitor Information, below) can provide further information.

➤ INFORMATION: New Mexico Game and Fish Department (✉ 1 Wildlife Way, off Caja Del Rio Rd. [Box 25112, Santa Fe 87504], ☎ 505/476–8000 or 800/862–9310, 🖿 www. gmfsh.state.nm.us).

## GOLF

The Sun Country Amateur Golf Association has a list of courses and telephone numbers for each club regarding greens fees and hours.

► INFORMATION: **Sun Country Amateur Golf Association** (✉ 10035 Country Club La. NW, Suite 5, Albuquerque 87114, ☎ 505/897–0864 or 800/346–5319, WEB www.newmexicogolf.org).

## HIKING

Hiking opportunities abound throughout the state—whether in the Gila National Forest, the Lincoln National Forest, Sandia Mountains, Taos Ski Valley, or Santa Fe area.

► INFORMATION AND MAPS: **New Mexico State Parks Division** (✉ 2040 S. Pacheco St. [Box 1147, Santa Fe 87504], ☎ 505/827–7173 or 888/667–2757, WEB www.emnrd.state.nm.us/nmparks).

## SKIING

Winter in the New Mexico mountains can be particularly pleasant for skiers, because bright sunshine often beams down on mounds of snow. However, compared with other notable ski areas, the state also is more susceptible to extended periods of dry weather that can create massive meltdowns. Major ski resorts have snow machines, but you should **check conditions first** to avoid disappointment.

► INFORMATION: **Ski New Mexico** (☎ 505/982–5300 or 800/755–7669, WEB www.skinewmexico.com).

► RESORTS: **Angel Fire Resort** (✉ Drawer B, Angel Fire 87710, ☎ 800/633–7463, WEB www.angelfireresort.com). **Enchanted Forest Cross-Country Ski Area** (✉ Box 219, Red River 87558, ☎ 505/754–2374 or 800/966–9381, WEB www.enchantedforestxc.com). **Pajarito Mountain Ski Area** (✉ Box 155, Los Alamos 87544, ☎ 505/662–5725 or 800/444–0707, WEB www.skipajarito.com). **Red River Ski Area** (✉ Box 900, Red River 87558, ☎ 505/754–2223, WEB www.redriverskiarea.com). **Sandia Peak Ski Area** (✉ 10 Tramway Loop NE, Albuquerque 87122, ☎ 505/242–9133, WEB www.sandiapeak.com). **Sipapu Lodge and Ski Area** (✉ Box 29, Vadito 87579, ☎ 505/587–2240 or 800/587–2240, WEB www.sipapunm.com). **Ski Apache** (✉ Box 220, Ruidoso 88355, ☎ 505/336–4356, WEB www.skiapache.com). **Ski Santa Fe**

(✉ 2209 Brothers Rd., Suite 220, Santa Fe 87505, ☎ 505/982–4429 or 800/776–7669, WEB www.skisantafe.com). **Taos Ski Valley** (✉ Box 90, Village of Taos Ski Valley 87525, ☎ 505/776–2291 or 800/776–1111, WEB skitaos.org).

## PACKING

Typical of the Southwest, temperatures can vary considerably from sunup to sundown. You should **pack for warm days and chilly nights.**

The areas of higher elevation are considerably cooler than the low-lying southern portions of the state. Any time of year pack at least a few warm outfits and a jacket; in winter pack very warm clothes—coats, parkas, and whatever else your body's thermostat and your ultimate destination dictate. Sweaters and jackets are also needed in summer, because though days are warm, nights at the higher altitudes often dip well below 50°F. And **bring comfortable shoes;** you're likely to be doing a lot of walking.

New Mexico is one of the most informal and laid-back areas of the country, which for many is part of its appeal. Probably no more than three or four restaurants in the entire state enforce a dress code, even for dinner, though men are likely to feel more comfortable wearing a jacket in the major hotel dining rooms, and anyone wearing tennis shoes may feel out of place.

The western look has, of course, never lost its hold on the West, though western-style clothes now get mixed with tweed jackets, for example, for a more conservative, sophisticated image. You can wear your boots and big belt buckles in even the best places in Santa Fe, Taos, or Albuquerque, but if you come strolling through the lobby of the Eldorado Hotel looking like Hopalong Cassidy, you'll get some funny looks.

**Bring skin moisturizer;** even people who rarely need this elsewhere in the country can suffer from dry and itchy skin in New Mexico. And **bring sunglasses** to protect your eyes from the glare of lakes or ski slopes. High altitude can cause headaches and dizziness, so check with your doctor about medication to alleviate symptoms. Sunscreen is a necessity. When planning even a short day trip, especially if there's hiking or exercise involved, always pack a bottle or two of water—it's very easy to become dehydrated in New Mexico.

In your carry-on luggage, **pack an extra pair of eyeglasses or contact lenses and enough of any medication** you take to last a few days longer than the entire trip. You may also ask your doctor to write a spare prescription using the drug's generic name, since brand names may vary from country to country. In luggage to be checked, **never pack prescription drugs or valuables.** And don't forget to carry with you the addresses of offices that handle refunds of lost traveler's checks. Check *Fodor's How to Pack* (available in bookstores everywhere) for more tips.

To avoid customs and security delays, carry medications in their original packaging. Don't pack any sharp objects in your carry-on luggage, including knives of any size or material, scissors, manicure tools, and corkscrews, or anything else that might arouse suspicion.

### CHECKING LUGGAGE

You are allowed one carry-on bag and one personal article, such as a purse or a laptop computer. Make sure that everything you carry aboard will fit under your seat or in the overhead bin. Get to the gate early, so you can board as soon as possible, before the overhead bins fill up.

If you are flying internationally, note that baggage allowances may be determined not by piece but by weight—generally 88 pounds (40 kilograms) in first class, 66 pounds (30 kilograms) in business class, and 44 pounds (20 kilograms) in economy.

Airline liability for baggage is limited to $2,500 per person on flights within the United States. On international flights it amounts to $9.07 per pound or $20 per kilogram for checked baggage (roughly $640 per 70-pound bag) and $400 per passenger for unchecked baggage. You can buy additional coverage at check-in for about $10 per $1,000 of coverage, but it excludes a rather extensive list of items, shown on your airline ticket.

Before departure, **itemize your bags' contents** and their worth, and label the bags with your name, address, and phone number. (If you use your home address, cover it so potential thieves can't see it readily.) Inside each bag, **pack a copy of your itinerary.** At check-in, **make sure that each bag is correctly tagged** with the destination airport's three-letter code. If your bags arrive damaged or fail to arrive at all, file a written report with the airline before leaving the airport.

Attendants at Albuquerque's and El Paso's airports match your luggage's baggage claim ticket to the number placed on your boarding pass envelope, so **have the envelope handy as you exit the baggage claim area.**

## PARKS AND FORESTS

There are 11 national monuments in New Mexico and a few state monuments and parks preserving natural or cultural treasures such as northern Indian cliff dwellings or the white sands in the south. Several monuments yield insight into the 19th-century Territorial period of New Mexico, including exploits of the infamous Billy the Kid.

Carlsbad Caverns National Park, in the southeastern part of the state, has one of the largest and most spectacular cave systems in the world. For information about New Mexico's six national forests and the Kiowa National Grasslands (part of the Cibola National Forest), contact the USDA Forest Service (☞ Visitor Information, *below*).

*See also* Pleasures and Pastimes *in* Chapter 1, and individual park and monument listings *in* Chapters 2 through 8.

➤ GENERAL INFORMATION: **Monument Division, Museum of New Mexico** (✉ Box 2087, Santa Fe 87504, ☎ 505/476–5021 or 800/204–6850, WEB museums.state.nm.us/mnm/mnm.html). **New Mexico State Parks Division** (✉ 2040 S. Pacheco St. [Box 1147, Santa Fe 87504], ☎ 505/827–7173 or 888/667–2757, WEB www.emnrd. state.nm.us/nmparks). **National Park Service** (⊠ Box 728, Santa Fe 87504, ☎ 505/988–6091).

➤ NATIONAL MONUMENTS AND PARKS: **Aztec Ruins National Monument** (⊠ Box 640, Aztec 87410, ☎ 505/334–6174, WEB www.nps.gov/azru). **Bandelier National Monument** (⊠ HCR 1, Box 1, Suite 15, Los Alamos 87544, ☎ 505/672–0343, WEB www.nps.gov/band). **Capulin Volcano National Monument** (⊠ Box 40, Capulin 88414, ☎ 505/278–2201, WEB www. nps.gov/cavo). **Carlsbad Caverns National Park** (⊠ 3225 National Parks Hwy., Carlsbad 88220, ☎ 505/785–2232, WEB www.carlsbad.caverns. national-park.com). **Chaco Culture National Historical Park** (⊠ Box 220, Nageezi 87037, ☎ 505/786–7014, WEB www.nps.gov/chcu). **El Malpais National Monument and Conservation Area** (⊠ 123 E. Roosevelt Ave., Grants 87020, ☎ 505/285–4641, WEB www.nps.gov/elma). **El Morro National Monument** (⊠ Rte. 2 [Box 43, Ramah 87321], ☎ 505/783–4226, WEB www.nps.gov/elmo). **Fort Union National Monument** (⊠ Box 127, Watrous 87753, ☎ 505/425–8025, WEB www.nps.gov/foun). **Gila Cliff Dwellings National Monument** (⊠ HC 68, Box 100,Silver City 88061, ☎ 505/536–9461, WEB www. nps.gov/gicl). **Guadalupe Mountains National Park** (⊠ HC 60, Box 400, Salt Flat, TX 79847, ☎ 915/828–3251, WEB www.nps.gov/gumo). **Kasha-Katuwe Tent Rocks National Monument** (⊠ Bureau of Land Management, 435 Montano Rd. NE, Albuquerque 87107, ☎ 505/761–8700, WEB www.nm.blm.gov/www/aufo/tent_rocks/tent_rocks.html). **Pecos National Historic Park** (⊠ Box 418, Pecos 87552, ☎ 505/757–6032 or 505/757–6414, WEB www.nps.gov/peco). **Petroglyph National Monument** (⊠ 6001 Unser Blvd. NW, Albuquerque 87120, ☎ 505/899–0205, WEB www.nps.gov/petr). **Salinas Pueblo Missions National Monument** (⊠ Box 517, Mountainair 87036, ☎ 505/847–2585, WEB www.nps.gov/sapu). **White Sands National Monument** (⊠ Box 1086, Holloman AFB, NM 88330, ☎ 505/479–6124, WEB www.nps.gov/whsa).

➤ NATIONAL FORESTS: **Apache-Sitgreaves National Forest** (⊠ 309 S. Mountain Ave. [Box 640, Springerville, AZ 85938], ☎ 928/333–4301, WEB www.fs.fed.us/r3/asnf). **Carson National Forest** (⊠ 208 Cruz Alta Rd. [Box 558, Taos 87571], ☎ 505/758–6200, WEB www.fs.fed.us/r3/carson). **Cibola National Forest** (⊠ 2113 Osuna Rd. NE, Suite A, Albuquerque 87113, ☎ 505/346–2650). **Gila National Forest** (⊠ 3005 E. Camino del Bosque, Silver City 88061, ☎ 505/388–8201, WEB www.fs.fed.us/r3/gila/content. htm). **Lincoln National Forest** (⊠ Federal Bldg., 1101 New York Ave., Alamogordo 88310, ☎ 505/434–7200). **Santa Fe National Forest** (⊠ 1474 Rodeo Rd., Santa Fe 87504, ☎ 505/438–7840).

➤ STATE MONUMENTS: **Coronado State Monument** (⊠ NM 44, off I–25 [Box 95, Bernalillo 87004], ☎ 505/867–5351). **El Camino Real State Monument** (⊠ Bureau of Land Management, 198 Neel Ave., Socorro 87801, ☎ 505/838–1255). **Fort Selden** (⊠ Radium Springs exit off I–25, 13 mi north of Las Cruces [Box 58, Radium Springs 88054], ☎ 505/526–8911). **Fort Sumner** (⊠ 2 mi east of the town of Fort Sumner, on Billy the Kid Rd. [Box 356, Fort Sumner 88119], ☎ 505/355–2573). **Jemez State Monument** (⊠ NM 4, 1 mi north of Jemez Springs [Box 143, Jemez Springs 87025], ☎ 505/829–3530). **Lincoln State Monument** (⊠ U.S. 380, 12 mi east of Capitan, Courthouse Museum [Box 36, Lincoln 88338], ☎ 505/653–4372).

## DISCOUNT PASSES

Look into discount passes to save money on park entrance fees. For $50, the National Parks Pass admits you (and any passengers in your private vehicle) to all national parks, monuments, and recreation areas, as well as other sites run by the National Park Service, for a year. (In parks that charge per person, the pass admits you, your spouse and children, and your parents, when you arrive together.) Camping and parking are extra. The $15 Golden Eagle Pass, a hologram you affix to your National Parks Pass, functions as an upgrade, granting entry to all sites run by the

NPS, the U.S. Fish and Wildlife Service, the U.S. Forest Service, and the Bureau of Land Management (BLM). The upgrade, which expires with the parks pass, is sold by most national-park, Fish and Wildlife, and BLM fee stations. A percentage of the proceeds from pass sales funds National Parks projects.

Both the Golden Age Passport ($10), for U.S. citizens or permanent residents who are 62 and older, and the Golden Access Passport (free), for those with disabilities, entitle holders (and any passengers in their private vehicles) to lifetime free entry to all national parks, plus 50% off fees for the use of many park facilities and services. (The discount doesn't always apply to companions.) To obtain them, you must show proof of age and of U.S. citizenship or permanent residency—such as a U.S. passport, driver's license, or birth certificate—and, if requesting Golden Access, proof of disability. The Golden Age and Golden Access passes, as well as the National Parks Pass, are available at any NPS-run site that charges an entrance fee. The National Parks Pass is also available by mail and via the Internet.

➤ INFORMATION: **National Park Foundation** (✉ 1101 17th St. NW, Suite 1102, Washington, DC 20036, ☎ 202/785–4500, WEB www. nationalparks.org). **National Park Service** (✉ National Park Service/Department of Interior, 1849 C St. NW, Washington, DC 20240, ☎ 202/208–4747, WEB www.nps.gov). **National Parks Conservation Association** (✉ 1300 19th St. NW, Suite 300, Washington, DC 20036, ☎ 202/223–6722, WEB www.npca.org.)

➤ PASSES BY MAIL: **National Park Foundation** (WEB www.nationalparks. org). **National Parks Pass** (✉ 27540 Ave. Mentry, Valencia, CA 91355, ☎ 888/GO–PARKS or 888/467–2757, WEB www.nationalparks.org); include a check or money order payable to the National Park Service for the pass, plus $3.95 for shipping and handling.

## PASSPORTS AND VISAS

The best time to apply for a passport or to renew is in fall and winter.

Before any trip, check your passport's expiration date, and, if necessary, renew it as soon as possible. When traveling internationally, **carry your passport** even if you don't need one (it's always the best form of ID) and **make two photocopies of the data page** (one for someone at home and another for you, carried separately from your passport). If you lose your passport, promptly call the nearest embassy or consulate and the local police.

U.S. passport applications for children under age 14 require consent from both parents or legal guardians; both parents must appear together to sign the application. If only one parent appears, he or she must submit a written statement from the other parent authorizing passport issuance for the child. A parent with sole authority must present evidence of it when applying; acceptable documentation includes the child's certified birth certificate listing only the applying parent, a court order specifically permitting this parent's travel with the child, or a death certificate for the non-applying parent. Application forms and instructions are available on the Web site of the U.S. State Department's Bureau of Consular Affairs (www.travel.state.gov).

## SENIOR-CITIZEN TRAVEL

Many stores, restaurants, and tourist attractions in New Mexico offer senior-citizen discounts, and certain RV parks throughout the state specifically to senior citizens.

To qualify for age-related discounts, **mention your senior-citizen status up front** when booking hotel reservations (not when checking out) and before you're seated in restaurants (not when paying the bill). Be sure to have identification on hand. When renting a car, ask about promotional car-rental discounts, which can be cheaper than senior-citizen rates.

➤ EDUCATIONAL PROGRAMS: **Elderhostel** (✉ 11 Ave. de Lafayette, Boston, MA 02111-1746, ☎ 877/426–8056, FAX 877/426–2166, WEB www. elderhostel.org). **Interhostel** (✉ University of New Hampshire, 6 Garrison Ave., Durham, NH 03824, ☎ 603/862–1147 or 800/733–9753,

FAX 603/862–1113, WEB www.learn.
unh.edu).

## SHOPPING

New Mexico is a treasure trove of
antiques originating from old ranch
houses and attics of family homes.
You can find some real bargains in
out-of-the way places. Authentic
Indian jewelry and handcrafted items,
along with goods imported from
nearby Mexico, like leatherwork and
ceramics, are unique to this region.
You can stock up on western-style
clothing and cowboy boots here, too.
The Wingspread Collectors Guide
compiles useful listings of art galleries
throughout the state.

➤ WINGSPREAD GUIDES OF NEW MEX-
ICO, INC.: **Wingspread Guides of New
Mexico, Inc.** (✉ Box 13566, Albuquerque 87192, ☎ 505/292–7537
or 800/873–4278, WEB www.
collectorsguide.com).

### KEY DESTINATIONS

Old Town in Albuquerque is full of
wares reflecting the state's Spanish
and Indian origins. Santa Fe once was
a trading post, and its downtown
area retains an atmosphere of barter
with outdoor vendors, shops, and
galleries scattered among historic
adobe buildings. Old Mesilla near Las
Cruces is an authentic Mexican-style
adobe village where shops and galleries offer high-quality handcrafted
jewelry and clothing at bargain prices.
Taos is an artist's haven, and an array
of styles appears in the galleries. Most
pueblos or reservations sell Native
American arts, crafts, and jewelry.
Shops there are often also artisan's
homes, and you should check for
signage indicating open hours.

### SMART SOUVENIRS

Authentic Navajo blankets are always
a good buy, since they gain value over
time. In Taos and Santa Fe, Overland
Outfitters carries sheepskin footwear,
coats, hats, and mittens. In El Paso,
Texas, you can find Old West items
such as famous handcrafted Tony
Lama boots and far-out souvenirs
such as hand-painted cow skulls.
New Mexicans love their roadrunners
(the state bird); you'll find plenty of
depictions of this feathered denizen.

### WATCH OUT

In New Mexico and other southwestern states, shysters marketing fake
Indian jewelry and blankets are a
continuing problem. Your best guar-
antee of authenticity, particularly
involving Navajo blankets, is to
purchase directly from a reputable
reservation outlet; the goods sold
at the Palace of the Governors in
Santa Fe are also all guaranteed
handmade by Indian artisans and are
high quality. At other shops, **ask for
a certificate of authenticity, written
verification of a piece's origin, or a
receipt** that lists the materials that
make up an item. The Indian Arts and
Crafts Association offers free information on what to look for in Indian-
made goods and sells buyers' guides
as well.

➤ INDIAN ARTS AND CRAFTS ASSOCIA-
TION: IACA (✉ 4010 Carlisle NE,
Suite C, Santa Fe 87592-9780, ☎
505/265–9149, WEB www.iaca.com).

## STUDENTS IN NEW MEXICO

Four-year universities and colleges
can be found in cities such as Albuquerque, Santa Fe, Las Vegas,
Roswell, Grants, Carlsbad, Alamogordo, Silver City, Socorro, Las
Cruces, and Portales. Many branch
colleges are located in other communities. Discounts are commonly
offered to university students.

➤ IDS AND SERVICES: **STA Travel**
(☎ 212/627–3111 or 800/781–4040,
FAX 212/627–3387, WEB www.sta.com).
**Travel Cuts** (✉ 187 College St.,
Toronto, Ontario M5T 1P7, Canada,
☎ 416/979–2406 or 888/838–2887,
FAX 416/979–8167, WEB www.
travelcuts.com).

## TAXES

### SALES TAX

The standard state gross receipts tax
rate is 5%, but municipalities and
counties enact additional charges at
varying rates. Even with additional
charges, you will encounter no sales
tax higher than 7%.

## TIME

New Mexico and a small portion of
west Texas (including El Paso) observe mountain standard time, switch-
ing over with most of the rest of the

country to daylight saving time in the spring through fall. In New Mexico, you'll be two hours behind New York and one hour ahead of Arizona (except during daylight saving time, which Arizona does not observe) and California.

## TIPPING

In New Mexico, as elsewhere in the country, a 15%–20% tip is standard for restaurant service.

## TOURS AND PACKAGES

Because everything is prearranged on a prepackaged tour or independent vacation, you spend less time planning—and often get it all at a good price.

### BOOKING WITH AN AGENT

Travel agents are excellent resources. But it's a good idea to collect brochures from several agencies, as some agents' suggestions may be influenced by relationships with tour and package firms that reward them for volume sales. If you have a special interest, **find an agent with expertise in that area**; the American Society of Travel Agents (ASTA; ☞ Travel Agencies, *below*) has a database of specialists worldwide.

Make sure your travel agent knows the accommodations and other services of the place being recommended. Ask about the hotel's location, room size, beds, and whether it has a pool, room service, or programs for children, if you care about these. Has your agent been there in person or sent others whom you can contact?

Do some homework on your own, too: local tourism boards can provide information about lesser-known and small-niche operators, some of which may sell only direct.

### BUYER BEWARE

Each year consumers are stranded or lose their money when tour operators—even large ones with excellent reputations—go out of business. So **check out the operator.** Ask several travel agents about its reputation, and try to **book with a company that has a consumer-protection program.** (Look for information in the company's brochure.) In the United

States, members of the National Tour Association and the United States Tour Operators Association are required to set aside funds to cover your payments and travel arrangements in the event that the company defaults. It's also a good idea to choose a company that participates in the American Society of Travel Agents' Tour Operator Program (TOP); ASTA will act as mediator in any disputes between you and your tour operator.

Remember that the more your package or tour includes the better you can predict the ultimate cost of your vacation. Make sure you know exactly what is covered, and **beware of hidden costs.** Are taxes, tips, and transfers included? Entertainment and excursions? These can add up.

➤ TOUR-OPERATOR RECOMMENDATIONS: **American Society of Travel Agents** (☞ Travel Agencies, *below*). **National Tour Association** (NTA; ✉ 546 E. Main St., Lexington, KY 40508, ☎ 859/226–4444 or 800/682–8886, WEB www.ntaonline.com). **United States Tour Operators Association** (USTOA; ✉ 275 Madison Ave., Suite 2014, New York, NY 10016, ☎ 212/599–6599 or 800/468–7862, FAX 212/599–6744, WEB www.ustoa.com).

➤ ARCHAEOLOGY: **Archaeological Conservancy** (✉ 5301 Central Ave. NE, Suite 1218, Albuquerque 87108–1517, ☎ 505/266–1540, WEB www.americanarchaeology.com).

➤ GENERAL: **New Mexico Guides Association** (✉ Box 2463, Santa Fe 87504, ☎ 505/466–4877, WEB www.nmguides.com).

## TRAIN TRAVEL

Amtrak's *Sunset Limited,* from Orlando, Florida, to Los Angeles, stops in El Paso, Texas; Deming; and Lordsburg on Tuesday, Thursday, and Saturday eastbound, and Monday, Thursday, and Saturdaywestbound. Amtrak's *Southwest Chief,* from Chicago to Los Angeles via Kansas City, stops in Raton, Las Vegas, Lamy (near Santa Fe), Albuquerque, and Gallup daily.

### FARES AND SCHEDULES

Sample one-way fares on the *Sunset Limited* are $108 from Los Angeles to

El Paso, and $93 from San Antonio, Texas, to Deming. Sample one-way fares on the *Southwest Chief* are $134 from Chicago to Lamy; $97 Raton to Gallup; and $123 Albuquerque to Los Angeles.

➤ TRAIN INFORMATION: **Amtrak** (☎ 800/872–7245, WEB www.amtrak. com).

## TRANSPORTATION
## AROUND NEW MEXICO

A tour bus or car is the best way to take in the entire state. Public transportation options do exist in metropolitan areas, but they are not very convenient. City buses and taxi service are available only in a few larger communities such as Albuquerque, Santa Fe, and Las Cruces. Don't expect to find easy transportation for rural excursions. Bus or van service exists for virtually every community on the map, but be prepared for frequent stops for pickups along rural routes.

For information on specific transportation options in New Mexico, *see* Air Travel, Bike Travel, Bus Travel, Car Travel, and Train Travel, *above*.

## TRAVEL AGENCIES

A good travel agent puts your needs first. Look for an agency that has been in business at least five years, emphasizes customer service, and has someone on staff who specializes in your destination. In addition, **make sure the agency belongs to a professional trade organization.** The American Society of Travel Agents (ASTA)—the largest and most influential in the field with more than 24,000 members in some 140 countries—maintains and enforces a strict code of ethics and will step in to help mediate any agent-client disputes involving ASTA members if necessary. ASTA (whose motto is "Without a travel agent, you're on your own") also maintains a Web site that includes a directory of agents. (If a travel agency is also acting as your tour operator, *see* Buyer Beware *in* Tours and Packages, *above*.)

➤ LOCAL AGENT REFERRALS: **American Society of Travel Agents** (ASTA; ⊠ 1101 King St., Suite 200, Alexandria, VA 22314, ☎ 800/965–2782

24-hr hot line, FAX 703/739–3268, WEB www.astanet.com). **Association of British Travel Agents** (⊠ 68–71 Newman St., London W1T 3AH, ☎ 020/7637–2444, FAX 020/7637–0713, WEB www.abtanet.com). **Association of Canadian Travel Agents** (⊠ 130 Albert St., Suite 1705, Ottawa, Ontario K1P 5G4, ☎ 613/237–3657, FAX 613/237–7052, WEB www.acta.ca). **Australian Federation of Travel Agents** (⊠ Level 3, 309 Pitt St., Sydney, NSW 2000, ☎ 02/9264–3299, FAX 02/9264–1085, WEB www. afta.com.au). **Travel Agents' Association of New Zealand** (⊠ Level 5, Tourism and Travel House, 79 Boulcott St. [Box 1888, Wellington 6001], ☎ 04/499–0104, FAX 04/499–0827, WEB www.taanz.org.nz).

## VISITOR INFORMATION

For general information before you go, contact the city and state tourism bureaus. If you're interested in learning more about the area's national forests, contact the USDA. For information about Native American attractions, call or visit the Indian Pueblo Cultural Center.

➤ CITY INFORMATION: **Albuquerque Convention and Visitors Bureau** (⊠ 20 1st Plaza NW [Box 26866, Albuquerque 87125], ☎ 505/842–9918 or 800/284–2282, WEB www.abqcvb.org). **Santa Fe Convention and Visitors Bureau** (⊠ 201 W. Marcy St., Santa Fe 87501, ☎ 505/955–6200 or 800/ 777–2489, WEB www.santafe.org). **Taos County Chamber of Commerce** (⊠ Drawer I, Taos 87571, ☎ 505/ 758–3873 or 800/732–8267, WEB www.taoschamber.com).

➤ STATEWIDE INFORMATION: **New Mexico Department of Tourism** (⊠ 491 Old Santa Fe Trail, Santa Fe 87503, ☎ 505/827–7400 or 800/ 733–6396 ext. 0643, WEB www. newmexico.org).

➤ NATIONAL FORESTS: **USDA Forest Service, Southwestern Region** (⊠ Public Affairs Office, 333 Broadway SE, Albuquerque 87102, ☎ 505/842–3292, WEB www.fs.fed.us/r3).

➤ NATIVE ATTRACTIONS: **Indian Pueblo Cultural Center** (⊠ 2401 12th St. NW, Albuquerque 87102, ☎ 505/843–7270; 800/766–4405 outside New Mexico; WEB www.indianpueblo.org).

➤ FROM THE U.K.: **New Mexico Tourism** (✉ Garden Studios, Suite 302, 11–15 Betterton St., Covent Garden, London WC2H 9BP, ☎ 020/7470–8803, FAX 020/7470–8810).

## WEB SITES

Do check out the World Wide Web when planning your trip. You'll find everything from weather forecasts to virtual tours of famous cities. Be sure to **visit Fodors.com** (www.fodors. com), a complete travel-planning site. You can research prices and book plane tickets, hotel rooms, rental cars, vacation packages, and more. In addition, you can post your pressing questions in the "Travel Talk" section. Other planning tools include a currency converter and weather reports, and there are loads of links to travel resources.

For more information on events in New Mexico, try visiting the Web sites of major newspapers and alternative newsweeklies in the area (☞ Media). Also take a look at the Web sites listed for regional and local tourism offices in the A to Z sections at the end of each chapter.

## WHEN TO GO

Most ceremonial dances at the Native American pueblos occur in the summer, early fall, and at Christmas and Easter. The majority of other major events—including the Santa Fe Opera, Chamber Music Festival, and Indian and Spanish markets—are geared to the traditionally heavy tourist season of July and August. The Santa Fe Fiesta and New Mexico State Fair in Albuquerque are held in September, and the Kodak Albuquerque International Balloon Fiesta is in October.

The relatively cool climates of Santa Fe and Taos are a lure in summer, as is the skiing in Taos and Santa Fe in winter. Christmas is a wonderful time to be in New Mexico because of Native American ceremonies as well as the Hispanic religious folk plays, special foods, and musical events. During the Christmas season Santa Fe is at its most festive, with incense and piñon smoke sweetening the air and the darkness of winter illuminated by thousands of farolitos. A custom believed to have derived from Chinese lanterns, the glowing paper-bag lanterns are everywhere, lining walkways, doorways, rooftops, walls, and window sills. The songs of Christmas are sung around corner bonfires (luminarias, as the holiday bonfires are called in Santa Fe). With glowing lights reflected on the snow, Santa Fe is never lovelier.

Hotel rates are generally highest during the peak summer season but fluctuate less than those in most major resort areas. If you plan to come in summer, **be sure to make reservations in advance for July and August.** You can avoid most of the tourist crowds by coming during spring or fall.

### CLIMATE

Depending on where you're headed in New Mexico, you may find the sun strong, the air dry, and the wind hot and relentless. Northern New Mexico is significantly cooler on the whole than destinations in the southern part of the state, although colder mountain regions are scattered throughout the South, too. Timing is everything in this land of seasonal temperature extremes. Desert regions can be delightful in late fall and winter months but can surprise you with rare snowfall. Spring weather is unpredictable; it can be mild and cool, or hot and gusty. Certain desert regions in summer months can see temperatures climb above 100°F. During these times, you should head for the cool mountains. Higher elevations are usually within a reasonable drive just about anywhere in New Mexico. October is one of the best months to visit: the air is crisp, colors are brilliant, and whole mountainsides become fluttering cascades of red and gold.

➤ FORECASTS: **Weather Channel Connection** (☎ 900/932–8437), 95¢ per minute from a Touch-Tone phone.

The following are average daily maximum and minimum temperatures for areas of the state.

## ALBUQUERQUE

| Jan. | 46F | 8C | May | 78F | 26C | Sept. | 84F | 29C |
|------|-----|-----|------|-----|-----|-------|-----|-----|
|      | 24  | −4  |      | 51  | 11  |       | 57  | 14  |
| Feb. | 53F | 12C | June | 89F | 32C | Oct.  | 71F | 22C |
|      | 28  | −2  |      | 60  | 16  |       | 44  | 7   |
| Mar. | 60F | 16C | July | 91F | 33C | Nov.  | 57F | 14C |
|      | 33  | 1   |      | 64  | 18  |       | 32  | 0   |
| Apr. | 69F | 21C | Aug. | 89F | 32C | Dec.  | 48F | 9C  |
|      | 42  | 6   |      | 64  | 18  |       | 26  | −3  |

## LAS CRUCES

| Jan. | 56F | 13C | May  | 87F | 31C | Sept. | 87F | 31C |
|------|-----|-----|------|-----|-----|-------|-----|-----|
|      | 29  | −2  |      | 57  | 14  |       | 62  | 17  |
| Feb. | 62F | 17C | June | 97F | 36C | Oct.  | 78F | 26C |
|      | 34  | 1   |      | 64  | 18  |       | 50  | 10  |
| Mar. | 70F | 21C | July | 96F | 36C | Nov.  | 66F | 19C |
|      | 40  | 4   |      | 68  | 20  |       | 38  | 3   |
| Apr. | 79F | 26C | Aug. | 94F | 34C | Dec.  | 57F | 14C |
|      | 48  | 9   |      | 67  | 19  |       | 30  | −1  |

## RUIDOSO AREA

| Jan. | 45F | 7C  | May  | 71F | 22C | Sept. | 73F | 23C |
|------|-----|-----|------|-----|-----|-------|-----|-----|
|      | 19  | −7  |      | 37  | 3   |       | 41  | 5   |
| Feb. | 49F | 9C  | June | 82F | 28C | Oct.  | 66F | 19C |
|      | 19  | −7  |      | 44  | 7   |       | 30  | −1  |
| Mar. | 53F | 12C | July | 82F | 28C | Nov.  | 52F | 11C |
|      | 24  | −4  |      | 47  | 8   |       | 23  | −4  |
| Apr. | 62F | 17C | Aug. | 77F | 25C | Dec.  | 53F | 12C |
|      | 27  | −3  |      | 46  | 8   |       | 19  | −7  |

## SANTA FE

| Jan. | 39F | 4C  | May  | 68F | 20C | Sept. | 73F | 23C |
|------|-----|-----|------|-----|-----|-------|-----|-----|
|      | 19  | −7  |      | 42  | 6   |       | 48  | 9   |
| Feb. | 42F | 6C  | June | 78F | 26C | Oct.  | 62F | 17C |
|      | 23  | −5  |      | 51  | 11  |       | 37  | 3   |
| Mar. | 51F | 11C | July | 80F | 27C | Nov.  | 50F | 10C |
|      | 28  | −2  |      | 57  | 14  |       | 28  | −2  |
| Apr. | 59F | 15C | Aug. | 78F | 26C | Dec.  | 39F | 4C  |
|      | 35  | 2   |      | 55  | 13  |       | 19  | −7  |

## FESTIVALS AND SEASONAL EVENTS

➤ DEC.: **Christmas Native American Dances** (☎ 505/843–7270, WEB www. indianpueblo.org) take place at most pueblos. The Spanish-inspired dance-drama *Los Matachines* is performed at Picurís Pueblo. There are also pine-torch processions and katsina dances at Taos Pueblo and Basket, Buffalo, Deer, Harvest, Rainbow, and Turtle dances at Acoma, Cochiti, San Ildefonso, Santa Clara, and Taos pueblos.

**Christmas in Santa Fe** is perhaps the city's most festive time of year. During the 10 days of Las Posadas at San Miguel Mission, the story of Mary and Joseph's journey to Bethlehem is reenacted. The Feast Day of Our Lady of Guadalupe, December 12, is grandly celebrated at the Santuario de Guadalupe, and Christmas at the Palace resounds with hours of festive music emanating from the Palace of the Governors in mid-December. The traditional Christmas Eve stroll down Canyon Road, complete with snacks and costumed carolers, is *the* way to celebrate the night before Christmas when in Santa Fe.

At **Christmas on the Pecos** (☎ 505/ 887–6516) in Carlsbad, glittering backyard displays can be viewed from boats that cruise the Pecos River. Tickets usually sell out early and are available beginning in August.

➤ JAN.: During **Native American New Year's Celebrations** (☎ 505/843–7270, WEB www.indianpueblo.org) at many pueblos, Comanche, Deer, Turtle, and other traditional dances are performed.

➤ MAR.: For a $7 admission, the one-weekend **Fiery Foods Show** (☎ 505/873–8680) in Albuquerque covers everything you ever wanted to know about the international scope of New Mexico's favorite spicy food. Chile in all its incarnations, from sizzling salsas and dips to unusual beer and chocolate concoctions, is the featured spice here. The festival started in 1988 with just 35 booths and has expanded to more than 175 exhibitors from throughout the world.

In Columbus, the events surrounding Mexican revolutionary Pancho Villa's 1917 invasion of Columbus, and the subsequent return of the U.S. soldiers who hunted for him, are commemorated during **Raid Day** (☎ 505/531–2663). It takes place the weekend closest to March 9.

➤ MAR.–APR.: The **Chimayó Pilgrimage** (☎ 505/351–4889) takes place on Good Friday; thousands of New Mexicans and out-of-state pilgrims trek on foot to the Santuario de Chimayó, a small church north of Santa Fe that is believed to be the scene of miracles. People line U.S. 285 for miles en route to this sacred spot.

➤ APR.: **Frontier Days** (☎ 505/526–8911) at Fort Selden State Monument features historic displays and events commemorating the 1865 founding of this remote adobe outpost near Las Cruces. The **Taos Talking Picture Festival** (☎ 505/751–0637) has become one of the nation's most celebrated film festivals.

**Gathering of Nations Powwow** ((☎ 505/843–7270, WEB www.gatheringofnations.com), in Albuquerque, is the largest such gathering in the nation. This popular event attracts Native American dancers from across North America, who are dressed in incredible costumes and compete for large prizes. Arts-and-crafts exhibitions, traditional foods, and a beauty contest are other highlights.

During the last weekend of April, Truth or Consequences holds the **Ralph Edwards Fiesta** (☎ 505/894–3536). Residents parade and celebrate the 1950 decision to switch the town name from Hot Springs to that of a popular game show.

➤ MAY: The **Taos Spring Arts Celebration** (☎ 800/732–8267) is a two-week festival of contemporary visual arts, music, poetry readings, and dance.

The weeklong **Mescal Roast & Mountain Spirit Dances** (☎ 505/887–5516) at Carlsbad's Living Desert Zoo and Garden State Park celebrates the mystic connection Mescalero Apaches have long had with the Guadalupe Mountains of this area, where mescal plants were traditionally gathered for food.

The **New Mexico Wine and Chile War Festival** (☎ 505/646–4543) pits some of the most accomplished regional chile chefs and wine makers against each other in competitions that also offer visitors a taste of the creations. The event is held at Doña Ana County Fairgrounds, west of Las Cruces.

Mariachi music and swirling Mexican dancers are among attractions at the **Cinco de Mayo Festival** (☎ 505/525–1965), May 5, in the Old Mesilla Plaza.

➤ MID-JULY–AUG.: During **Shakespeare in Santa Fe** (☎ 505/982–2910, WEB www.shakespearesantafe.org), performances of Shakespearean plays take place several days a week. An outdoor theater on the campus of St. John's College provides a beautiful backdrop for many of the performances.

➤ JUNE: On the last weekend of the month, Albuquerque's New Mexico State Fairgrounds hosts the **New Mexico Arts and Crafts Fair** (☎ 505/884–9043, WEB www.nmartsandcrafts-fair.org), at which more than 220 artists and craftspeople come together to display their talents. Spanish, Native American, and other North American cultures are represented, and there's plenty of food and entertainment.

El Paso's annual musical drama **Viva El Paso!** (☎ 915/565–6900 or 800/915–8482, WEB www.viva-ep.org) lights up a canyon amphitheater from June through August. A diverse cast, from flamenco and ballet dancers to guitarists and actors, brings the multicultural history and legends of the region to life.

➤ LATE JUNE OR EARLY JULY–AUG.: The world-famous indoor-outdoor **Santa Fe Opera** (☎ 505/986–5900, WEB www.santafeopera.org) opens for the summer season in a beautiful facility tucked into a hillside. World premieres and classics are presented. Opening night is one of *the* social events of the year in New Mexico.

➤ JULY: For a small-town Fourth of July with a balloon rally and glorious fireworks, head to **Raton** (☎ 505/445–3689 or 800/638–6161). Age comes before youthful beauty at the **Magdalena Old-Timers Reunion** (☎ 505/854–2139), where the queen must be at least 60 years old. The reunion, held on the first weekend after the Fourth of July, includes three days of rodeo (one day a kids' rodeo), a big chuck-wagon cook-off, and outdoor dancing.

Out-of-this-world **Encounter Festival** (☎ 505/624–6860) festivities celebrate Roswell's notoriety as the home of the 1947 crash of a supposed UFO. Guest lecturers and events like alien costume competitions are part of the fun.

➤ MID–LATE JULY: The arts and crafts of Native Americans from across the country are auctioned and for sale at the **Arts and Crafts Show** (☎ 800/793–4955) at San Juan Pueblo.

**Rodeo de Santa Fe** (☎ 505/471–4300, WEB www.rodeodesantafe.org) brings a taste of the Old West, with calf roping, bull riding, and a traditional rodeo parade. World-champion rodeo competitors come from all parts of the United States and Canada to this four-decades-old event.

You can smell the burritos, tamales, and chile for blocks around the festive **Spanish Market** (☎ 505/983–4038) held on the Santa Fe Plaza during the last full weekend of July. Along with the good food, Hispanic arts and crafts are for sale. Many exhibitors are from remote villages, where outstanding works are produced.

➤ AUG.: Santo Domingo's **Corn Dance** (☎ 505/465–2214) takes place in early August when hundreds of dancers fill the plaza in thanks for the corn harvest.

The **Bat Flight Breakfast** (☎ 505/785–2232), on the second Thursday of the month, is when early risers gather at the entrance to Carlsbad Caverns to eat breakfast and watch tens of thousands of bats fly back into the cave after a night of feeding on insects.

Launched in 1922, Gallup's **Inter-Tribal Indian Ceremonial** (☎ 800/233–4528, WEB www.gallupnm.org/ceremonial) is one of the oldest Native American gatherings in the nation; the Ceremonial is an informal and festive reunion of old friends and visitors. Native American dances, a huge arts-and-crafts fair, several parades, and an all–Native American rodeo are some of the attractions of this event, held outside town in Red Rocks State Park.

Santa Fe's **Indian Market** (☎ 505/955–6200, WEB www.swaia.org/indianmrkt.html) is the world's most prestigious gathering of Native American potters, jewelers, weavers, painters, basket makers, katsina carvers, and other artists and craftspeople. At least 1,200 artists and craftspeople show their work at this event, held on the Plaza on the third weekend in August.

During **Old Lincoln Days** (☎ 505/653–4025), this Old West town's early prominence in the violent Lincoln County Wars is depicted in numerous events lasting several days, including performances of the "Last Escape of Billy the Kid" pageant.

➤ SEPT.: On Labor Day weekend, the **Bernalillo Wine Festival** (☎ 866/494–6366) brings dozens of New Mexico artists and representatives from more than 20 New Mexico wineries together in an outdoor event with music and food.

**Las Fiestas de Santa Fe** (☎ 505/988–7575, WEB www.santafefiesta.org), the city's biggest celebration, begins the first Friday after Labor Day and commemorates the reconquest of Santa Fe from the Pueblos by Don Diego de Vargas in 1692. A pet parade, dancing, religious observances, ethnic foods, fireworks, and the burning of *Zozobra* (Old Man Gloom) are all part of the event.

The **New Mexico State Fair** (☎ 505/265–1791, WEB www.nmstatefair.com) takes place at the New Mexico State Fairgrounds in Albuquerque, with arts, crafts, livestock shows, entertainment, and a rodeo.

Wagon Mound, once the pinto-bean capital of New Mexico, celebrates its heritage on **Bean Day** (☎ 505/666–2408), held on Labor Day weekend. Pitch horseshoes, watch the rodeo, and line up for the noon barbecue.

If you love pie, head to Pie Town on the second weekend in September for the **Pie Festival** (☎ 505/772–2667, WEB www.dailypie.com). Some of the participants arrive a few days early to set up operations and start rolling the crusts of their specialties.

➤ OCT.: The **Albuquerque International Balloon Fiesta** (☎ 505/821–1000, WEB www.aibf.org) is the single most popular event in the state, with about 1 million spectators viewing the mass ascensions of more than 1,000 hot-air and gas balloons. This major event in the world of ballooning—you'll never see anything like it—takes place at Balloon Fiesta Park for two weekends beginning the first full weekend in October.

The **Whole Enchilada Fiesta** (☎ 505/526–1938, WEB www.twefie.com), in Las Cruces, lasts several days and attracts thousands with food, arts and crafts, and the concoction of the world's largest enchilada—which is shared with the crowd.

At the **Lincoln County Cowboy Symposium** (☎ 505/378–4142, WEB www.zianet.com/lccs), cowboy poets, musicians, chuck-wagon cooks, and artisans congregate in Ruidoso's rugged mountain settings for festivities lasting several days.

Portales residents go nuts at harvesttime over their specialty crop, Valencia peanuts, grown in the red sandy soil of New Mexico's eastern plains. Arts-and-crafts displays along with treats made with the peanuts are featured during the **Peanut Valley Festival** (☎ 505/562–2631).

➤ NOV.: Costumed characters in the garb of the Middle Ages enliven the **Renaissance Craftfaire** (☎ 505/523–6403), singing songs and selling their wares in a Las Cruces park. The event is conducted during the first full weekend in November.

The **International Mariachi Conference** (☎ 505/525–1735, WEB www.lascrucesmariachi.org), during the second weekend of November in Las Cruces, is a celebration in song, music, and dance of the Hispanic culture and traditions.

# 1 DESTINATION: NEW MEXICO

A Land Apart

What's Where

Pleasures and Pastimes

Fodor's Choice

Great Itineraries

# A LAND APART

**A**LMOST EVERY New Mexican has a tale or two to tell about being perceived as a "foreigner" by the rest of the country. There is the well-documented case of the Santa Fe man who tried to purchase tickets to the 1996 Olympic Games in Atlanta, only to be shuffled over to the department handling international requests. Even the U.S. Postal Service occasionally returns New Mexico–bound mail to its senders for insufficient "international" postage.

Though annoying to residents, such cases of mistaken identity are oddly apt (keep an ear open to how often New Mexicans themselves refer to their state, one of the nation's poorest, as a Third World country). New Mexico is, in many ways, an anomaly: it has its own cuisine, architecture, fashion, and culture, all of these an amalgam of the designs and accidents of a long and intriguing history. In prehistoric times indigenous peoples hunted game in New Mexico's mountains and farmed along its riverbanks. Two thousand years ago Pueblo Indians began expressing their reverence for the land through flat-roofed earthen architecture, drawings carved onto rocks, and rhythmic chants and dances. The late-16th and early 17th centuries brought the Spanish explorers who, along with the Franciscan monks, founded Santa Fe as a northern capital of the empire of New Spain, a settlement that was contemporaneous with the Jamestown colony of Virginia.

Although the Spanish brutally enslaved and mistreated the Indians, during the course of several hundred years tolerance has grown and traditions have commingled. Pueblo Indians passed on their uses for chile, beans, and corn, and the Spanish shared their skill at metalwork, influencing the Indian jewelry that has become symbolic of the region. The Spanish also shared their architecture, which itself had been influenced by 700 years of Arab domination of Spain, and the acequia method of irrigation still in use in the villages of northern New Mexico.

The last of the three main cultures to make their mark was that of the Anglo (any nonindigenous, non-Hispanic person in New Mexico is considered an Anglo—even groups who don't normally identify with the Anglo-Saxon tradition). Arriving throughout the 19th century, Anglos mined the mountains for gold, other precious metals, and gemstones and uncovered vast deposits of coal, oil, and natural gas. Their contributions to New Mexican life include the railroad, the highway system, and—for better or worse—the atomic bomb.

The resulting mélange of cultures has produced a character that is uniquely New Mexican: Spanish words are sprinkled liberally through everyday English parlance; Spanish itself, still widely spoken in the smaller villages, contains numerous words from the Pueblo Indian dialects. Architectural references and culinary terms in particular tend to hew to the original Spanish: you'll admire the vigas and bancos that adorn the restaurant where you'll partake of posole or chiles rellenos. (These and other often-used words are defined in the glossary in Chapter 9.)

But beyond the linguistic quirks, gastronomic surprises, and cultural anomalies that make New Mexico unique, there remains the most distinctive feature of all—the landscape. At once subtle and dramatic, the mountains and mesas seem almost surreal as they glow gold, terra-cotta, and pink in the clear, still air of the high desert. The shifting clouds overhead cast rippling shadows across the land, illuminating the delicate palette of greens, grays, and browns that contrast with a sky that can go purple or dead black or eye-searingly blue in a matter of seconds. It's a landscape that has inspired writers (such as D. H. Lawrence and Willa Cather), painters (such as Georgia O'Keeffe), and countless poets, dreamers, and assorted iconoclasts for centuries.

Indeed, watching the ever-changing sky is something of a spectator sport here, especially during the usual "monsoons" of summer. So regular that you could almost set your watch by them, the thunderheads start to gather in late afternoon, giving visual warning before the inevitable downpour. In the meantime, the sky dazzles with its interplay of creamy-white clouds edged by charcoal, sizzling flashes of lightning, and dramatic shafts of light shooting earthward from some ethereal perch.

The mountains absorb and radiate this special illumination, transforming themselves daily according to the whims of light and shadow. The very names of the major ranges attest to the profound effect their light show had on the original Spanish settlers. The Franciscan monks named the mountains to the east of Santa Fe *Sangre de Cristo,* or "blood of Christ," because of their tendency to glow deep red at sunset. To the south, east of Albuquerque, the Sandia Mountains ("watermelon" in Spanish) also live up to their colorful name when the sun sets. Georgia O'Keeffe once joked about the Pedernal mesa in the Jemez range, "It's my private mountain, it belongs to me. God told me if I painted it enough, I could have it."

The awe-inspiring beauty of the landscape renders New Mexico's tag lines more than just marketing clichés. The state is truly a "Land of Enchantment," and Santa Fe is indisputably "the City Different." Surrounded by mind-expanding mountain views and filled with sinuous streets that promote foot over car traffic, Santa Fe welcomes with characteristic adobe warmth. Rapid growth and development have prompted many local residents to worry about becoming too much like "everywhere else," but the surfeit of trendy restaurants, galleries, and boutiques that tout regional fare and wares, both authentic and artificial, are still distinctly Santa Fean. Commercialism notwithstanding, Santa Fe's deeply spiritual aura affects even nonreligious types in surprising ways, inspiring a reverence probably not unlike that which inspired the Spanish monks to name it the City of Holy Faith. (Its full name is La Villa Real de la Santa Fe de San Francisco de Asís, or the Royal City of the Holy Faith of St. Francis of Assisi.) A kind of mystical Catholicism blended with ancient Native American lore and beliefs flourishes throughout northern New Mexico in tiny mountain villages that have seen little change through the centuries. Tales of miracles, spontaneous healings, and spiritual visitations thrive in the old adobe churches that line the High Road that leads north of Santa Fe to Taos.

I F SANTA FE IS SPIRITUAL, sophisticated, and occasionally snobby, Taos, 65 mi away, is very much an outpost despite its relative proximity to the capital. Compared with Santa Fe, Taos is smaller, feistier, quirkier, tougher, and very independent. Taoseños are a study in diverse convictions, and most anyone will share his or hers with you if you lend an ear. Rustic and comfortably unpretentious, the town contains a handful of upscale restaurants with cuisines and wine lists as innovative as what you might find in New York. It's a haven for aging hippies, creative geniuses, cranky misanthropes, and anyone else who wants a good quality of life in a place that accepts new arrivals without a lot of questions—as long as they don't offend longtime residents with their city attitudes.

Sixty miles south of Santa Fe, Albuquerque adds another distinctive perspective to the mix. New Mexico's only big city by most standards, it shares many traits with cities its size elsewhere: traffic, noise, crime, and congestion. But what sets it apart is its dogged determination to remain a friendly small town, a place where pedestrians still greet one another as they pass and where downtown's main street is lined with angle parking (a modern-day version of the hitching post). Old Town, a congenial district whose authentic historical appeal is tempered by the unabashed pursuit of the tourist buck, is a typical example of how traditional small-town New Mexico flourishes amid a larger, more demanding economy without sacrificing the heart and soul of the lifestyle. San Felipe de Neri Catholic Church, built in 1793, is still attended by local worshipers.

The unifying factor among these and other towns and the terrain around them is the appeal of the land and the people. From the stunning natural formations of Carlsbad Caverns to the oceanic sweep of the "badlands" north of Santa Fe, it's the character of the residents and respect for the land that imbue New Mexico with its enchanted spirit. First-time visitors discover the unexpected pleasures of a place where time is measured not only by linear calculations of hours, days, weeks, and years but also by the circular sweep of crop cycles, gestation periods, the rotation of generations, and the changing of seasons.

Summer is traditionally the high season, when the arts scene explodes with gallery openings, performances at Santa Fe's open-air opera house, and a variety of festivals and celebrations. In autumn, the towering cottonwoods that hug the riverbanks turn gold, days are warm and sunny, and the nights are crisp. Those beehive-shape kiva fireplaces get a workout in winter, a time when life slows down to accommodate occasional snowstorms, and the scent of aromatic firewood like piñon and cedar fill the air like an earthy incense.

Even after you leave, New Mexico will sneak into your consciousness in unexpected ways. As much a state of mind as it is a geographic entity, a place where nature can be glimpsed simultaneously at its most fragile and most powerful, New Mexico truly is a land of enchantment.

— Nancy Zimmerman

# WHAT'S WHERE

## Albuquerque
With the state's international airport, fast-growing Albuquerque is the gateway to New Mexico and the state's business, finance, education, and industry capital. Like many other areas of New Mexico, this sprawling city near the center of the state is filled with artists, writers, poets, filmmakers, and musicians. Its population, like its architecture, foods, art, and ambience, reflects the state's three primary cultures: the original Native Americans and its subsequent Hispanic and Anglo settlers.

## Northwestern New Mexico
Roads branch out west and north from Albuquerque, to the ruins of Chaco civilization and the dances and drumbeats of their descendants' ceremonies in pueblos that have survived time and change. Journey through red-rock canyons that shelter ancient hamlets or to high, fortresslike plateaus crowned by Native American villages, and you'll encounter cultures whose art, architecture, spirituality, and knowledge of nature have ensured their existence for millennia. Gallup and Farmington

are the region's two largest cities; El Morro National Monument, Chaco Canyon, Zuñi Pueblo, Aztec Ruins, and Acoma Pueblo are among the top attractions.

## Santa Fe
On a 7,000-ft-high plateau at the base of the Sangre de Cristo Mountains in north-central New Mexico, Santa Fe is one of the most visited small cities in the United States, with an abundance of museums, one-of-a-kind cultural events, art galleries, first-rate restaurants, and shops selling southwestern furnishings and cowboy gear. Among the smallest U.S. state capitals, the city is characterized by its Pueblo Revival homes and buildings, some of them constructed of adobe bricks and virtually all of the rest made to look as though they are. (Most newer houses and buildings in the region are built with cinder block or wood-frame and then filled in and covered with adobe-like stucco—to the untrained eye, it's difficult to tell the difference.) The remnants of a 2,000-year-old Pueblo civilization surround the city, and this also echoes its nearly 250 years of Spanish and Mexican rule. Other area highlights include Chimayó, a small Hispanic village famous for weaving, regional food, and the Santuario shrine; and Abiquiu, where Georgia O'Keeffe kept a studio and created hundreds of her memorable paintings.

## Taos
On a rolling mesa at the base of the Sangre de Cristo Mountains, Taos is a world-famous artistic and literary center that attracts artists and collectors to its museums and galleries. Romantic courtyards, stately elms and cottonwood trees, narrow streets, and a profusion of adobe buildings are but a few of the charms of this town of 6,500 people. Three miles northwest of the commercial center lies Taos Pueblo, and south of town is Ranchos de Taos, a farming and ranching community first settled centuries ago by the Spanish. The fabulous slopes of the Taos Valley Ski Area and Rio Grande rafting trips are yet other draws.

## Northeastern New Mexico
The brilliantly clear light of northeastern New Mexico—the area east of the Sangre de Cristo range that includes parts of Carson National Forest, a large portion of the Santa Fe Trail, and Wild West towns like Cimarron and Raton—illuminates

seemingly endless high-desert plains punctuated by windswept mesas. Hawks soar overhead and antelope gallivant across the same open landscape traversed by the Native Americans and the pioneers, cowboys, ranchers, miners, and railroaders who settled the West.

## Southeastern New Mexico

Carlsbad, just above the Texas border and along the Pecos River, is a popular destination with historic museums, 30 parks, beaches, the Living Desert Zoo and Gardens State Park, and, the main attraction, Carlsbad Caverns National Park, one of the largest and most spectacular cave systems in the world. Roswell's alien reputation draws those interested in *other*worldly things. Northwest of Carlsbad are the historic mountain towns of Lincoln County (Ruidoso, San Patricio, and Lincoln, where Billy the Kid was jailed). The high-elevation Lincoln National Forest creates a lush ecosystem above the desert brush, and in south-central New Mexico, White Sands National Monument is an surreal wonderland of shifting gypsum sand dunes.

## Southwestern New Mexico

Southwestern New Mexico has its own mystique, where shimmering mirages born of desert heat hover above mesquite-covered sand dunes. But the area isn't all desert. Near Silver City, the ore-rich mountains are dotted with old mining ghost towns. Silver City itself is establishing a reputation as an artists' haven amid the grandeur of the Gila National Forest. The Mexican-style village of Old Mesilla near Las Cruces has appealing shops and galleries occupying historic adobe buildings in the downtown plaza. Outdoor enthusiasts fish, swim, and boat along the miles of lake water at Elephant Butte Reservoir, near Truth or Consequences.

# PLEASURES AND PASTIMES

## Dining

New Mexico's cuisine is a delicious and extraordinary mixture of Pueblo, Spanish colonial, and Mexican and American frontier cooking. Recipes that came from Spain via Mexico were adapted for local ingredients—chiles, corn, pork, wild game, pinto beans, honey, apples, and piñon nuts—and have remained much the same ever since.

In northern New Mexico, babies cut their teeth on fresh flour tortillas and quickly develop a taste for *sopaipillas,* deep-fried, puff-pastry pillows drizzled with honey or stuffed with pinto beans and chicken. But it's the chile pepper, whether red or green, that is the heart and soul of northern New Mexican cuisine. The question most asked of diners in New Mexico—"red or green?"—is often responded to with the query "Which is hotter?" The answer might be either—or neither. Green is made from roasted fresh chile pods harvested beginning in late July, and red is concocted from pods of the same plant, ripened and dried. Can't decide? Order the "Christmas" combination. Like the altitude, chile may take getting used to, but once you develop a taste for it, it is addictive. For those not chile-inclined, most Mexican and New Mexican restaurants also prepare recognizable "gringo food."

You might be a bit surprised to learn that *ristras,* those strings of bright red chiles that seem to hang everywhere, are sold more for eating here than for decoration. More varieties of chiles—upward of 90—are grown in New Mexico than anywhere else in the world. Mighty wars have been waged over the spelling of chile and chili. Most New Mexicans prefer the spelling chile for the peppers and chili for the spicy dish with red chile, beans, and meat. ("If you want chili peppers, go to Texas.") *See* the glossary *in* Chapter 9 for the names of traditional New Mexican foods.

Restaurants serving New Mexican cuisine are especially popular and are almost universally inexpensive. Some serve buffalo meat (stews, steaks, and burgers), particularly in southern New Mexico—"cowboy country." Of course, there are trendy restaurants serving contemporary cuisine, particularly in Santa Fe, Taos, and Albuquerque, as well as a respectable offering of grill rooms and a growing number of Asian eateries. If you're looking for a delicious and decidedly local fast-food experience, drop by one of the state's nearly 80 Blake's Lotaburger restaurants—even famous chefs and celebrities head to Blake's when they're craving a juicy green-chile cheese-burger.

## Outdoor Activities and Sports

### BIRD-WATCHING

Bird-watchers have wonderful opportunities to spot feathered friends migrating along the Rio Grande flyway from the jungles of South America to the tundra of the Arctic Circle. The Bosque del Apache National Wildlife Refuge, 90 mi south of Albuquerque, is the winter home of tens of thousands of migrating birds, including one of only two wild flocks of the rare whooping crane. The Bitter Lake National Wildlife Refuge, north of Roswell, also serves as a stopover for migrating flocks of snow geese, sandhill cranes, and other exotic birds. If you can't spot golden eagles in northeastern New Mexico at the Maxwell Wildlife Refuge, south of Raton off I–25, dust off your binoculars!

### CANOEING AND RIVER RAFTING

You can either take it easy or challenge yourself on New Mexico's rivers. The Taos Box, a 17-mi run through the churning rapids of the Rio Grande, is one of the Southwest's most exciting rafting experiences. (Most of the hard-core river rafting is done in the Taos area.) More leisurely trips can be had aboard the sightseeing craft that ply the Rio Chama and other meandering rivers. Depending on the amount of spring runoff from snowmelts, river rafting also is popular in the Silver City area of the Gila National Forest.

### FISHING

Good fishing spots include the Rio Grande, which traverses New Mexico north to south; Abiquiu Reservoir, 55 mi northwest of Santa Fe; the 6,000-acre Heron Lake, 22 mi southwest of Chama via U.S. 64 and NM 95, which has rainbow trout, lake trout, and kokanee salmon; and Blue Water Lake, 28 mi west of Grants via NM 412. In the northwest corner of the state, especially beneath Navajo Dam, the San Juan River's high-quality water regulations make for some of the best trout fishing in the country. In northeastern New Mexico at Cimarron Canyon State Park and Lake Maloya your chances are great at pulling in your limit of browns and rainbows. Trout fisherfolk will also find pleasure in the sparkling streams of the Sangre de Cristo range, north of Santa Fe. The Pecos River and its tributaries offer excellent backcountry fishing. Anglers also can try their luck in the rivers, lakes, and streams of the Gila National Forest and Lincoln National Forest of southern New Mexico. World-class bass tournaments take place at Elephant Butte Reservoir near Truth or Consequences. Fishing on Native American reservations is not subject to state regulations but requires tribal permits.

### HIKING

New Mexico's air is clean and crisp, and its ever-changing terrain is aesthetically rewarding as well. Carlsbad Caverns National Park in the southeast has more than 50 mi of scenic hiking trails. You'll find superb hiking of all levels in northeastern New Mexico at Sugarite State Park, above Raton along quiet, wildflower-filled trails. Try the McKittrick Canyon trail in Guadalupe Mountains National Park of west Texas to view a gorgeous, tree-lined stream gurgling in the midst of desert terrain. In the Gila National Forest and Wilderness, you can explore miles of pristine country and soak sore muscles in delightful natural hot springs. The short but scenic trails at western New Mexico's El Morro National Monument make for a memorable hike. Just south of Farmington, the lunarlike terrain of the Bisti and De-Na-Zin wilderness areas are a photographer's delight. The trail at the recently christened Kasha-Katuwe Tent Rocks National Monument, off I–25 between Albuquerque and Santa Fe, cuts through a narrow box canyon, under a massive boulder, and up over a series of bizarre hoodoos shaped like teepees.

### SKIING

New Mexico contains many world-class downhill ski areas. Snowmaking equipment is used in most areas to ensure a long season, usually from Thanksgiving through Easter. The Santa Fe Ski Area averages 225 inches of dry-powder snow a year; it accommodates all levels of skiers on more than 40 trails. Within a 90-mi radius of Taos are resorts with slopes for all levels of skiers, as well as snowmobile and cross-country ski trails. With a vertical drop of more than 3,200 ft, Taos Ski Valley is the only resort in the state that's regularly ranked by *Skiing* magazine as one of the nation's top 10 facilities; it's also one of the few ski areas that still ban snowboarding. About 25 mi east of Taos, Angel Fire Resort has rapidly developed into the second-most acclaimed ski area in the state.

The Enchanted Forest near Red River, with miles of groomed trails, is the state's major Nordic ski area allowing ample cross-country access. Head to the Sangre de Cristos, the Jemez, the Sandias, or the Manzanos for other cross-country skiing terrain. There are also exciting trails north of Chama along the New Mexico–Colorado state line and in the south in the Gila wilderness and the Sacramento Mountains. Ski Apache near Ruidoso has 55 trails covering 750 acres.

## Parks and Monuments

New Mexico's outstanding parks and monuments contain outdoor recreational facilities, campgrounds, and historic exhibits. New Mexico's state-park network includes nearly four dozen parks, ranging from high-mountain lakes and pine forests in the north to the Chihuahuan Desert lowlands of the south. There are also five national forests—Carson, Cibola, Gila, Lincoln, and Santa Fe—and the Kiowa National Grasslands (part of the Cibola National Forest), as well as several state monuments and historic parks with ruins of prehistoric Native American pueblos and 17th-century mission churches. The best place to see ancient pueblos—the communities (cities, really) built by the indigenous ancestors of today's Pueblo people—is northwest New Mexico, where Aztec Ruins, Salmon Ruins, and especially Chaco Canyon stun the imagination.

There are plenty of parks and monuments close to Santa Fe and Albuquerque, the most famous being Bandelier National Monument. In southern New Mexico the biggest draws are Carlsbad Caverns National Park, White Sands National Monument, and Elephant Butte Lake State Park.

## Reservations and Pueblos

The Indian reservations of New Mexico are among the few places left in the United States where traditional indigenous culture and skills are retained in largely undiluted form. There are two general classifications of Native Americans in New Mexico: Pueblo, who established an agricultural civilization here more than seven centuries ago; and the descendants of the nomadic tribes who later came into the area—the Navajos, Mescalero Apaches, and Jicarilla Apaches.

The Jicarilla Apaches live on a reservation of three-quarters of a million acres in north-central New Mexico, the capital of which is Dulce. The terrain varies from mountains, mesas, and lakes to high grazing land, suited to cattle and horse ranching. The tribe has a well-developed tourist program that promotes fishing and camping on a 20,000-acre game preserve. Nearly all the tribe members gather at Stone Lake in mid-September for the fall festival—two days of dancing, races, and a rodeo.

A reservation of a half million acres of timbered mountains and green valleys is home to the Mescalero Apaches in southeastern New Mexico. The tribe owns and operates Ski Apache, 16 mi from Ruidoso.

The Navajo Reservation, home to the largest Native American group in the United States, covers 17.6 million acres in New Mexico, Arizona, and Utah. Many Navajos are still seminomadic, herding flocks of sheep from place to place and living in hogans (mud-and-pole houses). There are a few towns on the reservation, but for the most part it is a vast area of stark pinnacles, colorful rock formations, high desert, and mountains. The land encompasses several tribal parks, some of which include campgrounds. Navajos are master silversmiths and rug weavers, and their work is available at trading posts scattered throughout the reservation. The tribe encourages tourism.

New Mexico's pueblo cultures, each with its own reservation and distinct but overlapping history, art, and customs, evolved out of the highly civilized culture that built Chaco Canyon. Pueblos dating back centuries are located near Santa Fe, Taos, and Albuquerque; the best times to visit them are during their many year-round public dance ceremonies. Admission is free to pueblos unless otherwise indicated. Donations, however, are always welcome.

Before venturing off to visit any one of the pueblos, you might want to visit the Indian Pueblo Cultural Center in Albuquerque, which exhibits and sells the best of arts and crafts from all the New Mexico pueblos, or the Museum of Indian Arts and Culture in Santa Fe.

Fall, when the pueblos celebrate the harvest with special ceremonies, dances, and sacred rituals, is the best time to visit. The air is fragrant with curling piñon smoke. Drums throb with an insistent cadence. Dancers adorn themselves with some of the most beautiful turquoise jewelry seen anywhere. The atmosphere is light-hearted, evocative of a country fair.

The pueblos around Santa Fe—San Ildefonso, Nambé, Pojoaque, and Santa Clara—are more infused with Spanish culture than are those in other areas. Indians here also have the keenest business sense when dealing with the sale of handicrafts and art and with matters touristic. The famous Taos Pueblo is the quintessence of classic pueblo Native American culture. Sports enthusiasts from Albuquerque regularly escape urban life to fish in the well-stocked lakes and reservoirs of the nearby pueblos—Acoma ("Sky City"), Isleta, Jemez, Laguna, and Santo Domingo. The legendary Acoma Pueblo, probably the most spectacular of the pueblo communities, is 65 mi west of Albuquerque.

ETIQUETTE AND RULES

When visiting pueblos and reservations, you're expected to follow a certain etiquette. Each pueblo has its own regulations for the use of still and video cameras and video and tape recorders, as well as for sketching and painting. Some pueblos, such as Santo Domingo, prohibit photography altogether. Others, such as Santa Clara, prohibit photography at certain times, such as during ritual dances. Still others allow photography but require a permit, which usually costs from $10 to $20, depending on whether you use a still or video camera. The privilege of setting up an easel and painting all day will cost you as little as $35 or as much as $150 (at Taos Pueblo). Associated fees for using images also can vary widely, depending on what kind of reproduction rights you might require. Be sure to ask permission before photographing anyone in the pueblos; it's also customary to give the subject a dollar or two for agreeing to be photographed. Native American law prevails on the pueblos, and violations of photography regulations could result in confiscation of cameras.

Specific restrictions for the various pueblos are noted in the individual descriptions. Other rules are described below.

- Possessing or using drugs and/or alcohol on Native American land is forbidden.

- Ritual dances often have serious religious significance and should be respected as such. Silence is mandatory—that means no questions about ceremonies or dances while they're being performed. Don't walk across the dance plaza during a performance, and don't applaud afterward.

- Kivas and ceremonial rooms are restricted to pueblo members only.

- Cemeteries are sacred. They're off-limits to all visitors and should never be photographed.

- Unless pueblo dwellings are clearly marked as shops, don't wander or peek inside. Remember, these are private homes.

- Many of the pueblo buildings are hundreds of years old. Don't try to scale adobe walls or climb on top of buildings, or you may come tumbling down.

- Don't litter. Nature is sacred on the pueblos, and defacing land can be a serious offense.

- Don't bring your pet or feed stray dogs.

- Even off reservation sites, state and federal laws prohibit picking up artifacts such as arrowheads or pottery from public lands.

## Shopping

Santa Fe, Old Mesilla near Las Cruces, Taos, Madrid on the Turquoise Trail, Las Vegas, Ruidoso, and both Old Town and Nob Hill in Albuquerque are all filled with one-of-a-kind, locally owned specialty shops; national boutique chain stores are common only in Albuquerque and in some parts of Las Cruces and Santa Fe. There's plenty of opportunity to buy goods directly from their makers, be it from a pueblo jewelry maker or a chile farmer. Western wear, leather goods, handwoven shawls, Mexican imports, handcrafted items, fine arts—it's all here.

ANTIQUES

As New Mexico is one of the oldest inhabited regions of the United States, it can be great fun to browse through its antiques shops and roadside museums. You'll find everything in these shops, from early Mexican typewriters to period saddles, ceramic pots, farm tools, pioneer aviation equipment, and yellowed newspaper clippings about Kit Carson and D. H. Lawrence.

## ART

Native American art, Western art, Hispanic art, fine art, sculpture, photography, prints, ceramics, jewelry, folk art, junk art—it can all be found throughout the state. Santa Fe, with more than 150 galleries, is a leading fine arts center nationally as well as the arts capital of the Southwest. Taos, a town dense with artists, is not far behind. You'll find a small art colony in Silver City, and Old Mesilla near Las Cruces has an impressive array of galleries displaying regional talent. In autumn in northern New Mexico you can tour artists' studios.

## CRAFTS

Hispanic handcrafted furniture and artwork command high prices from collectors. Images of elongated and dour-faced *santos* (saints) come in either the form of carved wooden *bultos* sculptures or *retablos*, paintings on wood or tin. Colorful handwoven Hispanic textiles, tinwork, ironwork, and straw appliqué are also in demand. Native American textiles, rugs, katsina dolls, baskets, silver jewelry, turquoise, pottery, beadwork, ornamental shields, drums, and ceramics can be found almost everywhere in New Mexico, from Santa Fe Plaza to the Native American pueblos throughout the state. Prices range from thousands of dollars for a rare 1930s katsina doll to a few cents for hand-wrapped bundles of sage, juniper, sweet grass, and lavender that are used by Native Americans in healing ceremonies, gatherings, and daily cleansing of the home. Ignited like incense, this herbal combination gives off a sacred smoke; passing it once around the room is enough to change and charge the air. Along the High Road to Taos, Chimayó is famous for its traditional weavers, and the tiny village of Cordova for its wood-carvers. If you love Indian jewelry, head to Gallup, which has many old trading posts that sell silver, turquoise, and beadwork.

## SPICES

Roadside stands sell chile ristras, and shops carry chile powder and other spices. You'll catch the smell of chile peppers from the road; walk in a store and your eyes may water and your salivary glands begin to work. For many, especially natives of the Southwest, *picante* is the purest, finest word in the Spanish language. It means hot—spicy hot. All around you, in boxes, bags, packets, jars, and cans, there's everything picante—salsas, chile pastes, powders, herbs, spices, peppers, barbecue sauce, and fiery potions in bottles.

## Studio Tours

Northwestern New Mexico is a region of artists' colonies, and from the last weekend of September through the first weekend of December the artists and artisans in the villages of Galisteo, the Pecos Valley, El Rito, Abiquiu, Dixon, Jemez Springs, and Madrid take turns hosting studio-tour weekends. Homes and studios are open for browsing, shopping, and conversing; maps are provided to guide you to the open houses, where you'll find reasonably priced arts and crafts. Wares include everything from pottery and paintings to wreaths, ristras, and dried-flower arrangements; homemade jellies, pestos, chile sauces, and other food items; fresh produce such as garlic, chiles, and shallots; and wood carvings, religious paintings, clothing, and handmade furniture.

The quality varies, but bargains are abundant. Of course for many the real fun is the opportunity to experience village life and to get inside those charming old adobes that you can only pass by at other times of the year. Many of the villagers provide refreshments, and you're encouraged to wander at a leisurely pace.

Because studio-tour planning passes from one chairperson to another each year, there is no central number to call for information. But if you're in the Santa Fe area during the fall season, check "Pasatiempo," the Friday supplement of the *Santa Fe New Mexican,* for a report about which village is open for touring and what items are for sale. The one constant is the Dixon tour, which takes place every year on the first weekend in November. About a half hour south of Taos, Dixon was the first village to host a studio tour, and its version has the largest number of participating artists and the greatest variety of merchandise.

# FODOR'S CHOICE

## Historic Buildings

**Acoma Pueblo.** Rising out of a mesa in the northwest quadrant of the state, Acoma Pueblo's Sky City humbled the first Spanish explorers. Parts of the multistory complex are thought to be more than 1,500 years old.

**Palace of the Governors, Santa Fe.** The oldest public building in the United States, this Pueblo-style structure has served as the residence for 100 Spanish, Native American, Mexican, and American governors; it is now the state history museum.

**San Francisco de Asís Church, Ranchos de Taos.** Built in the 18th century as a spiritual and physical refuge from raiding Apaches, Utes, and Comanches, this church outside Taos is a spectacular example of adobe Mission architecture. Its simple form has inspired generations of painters and photographers, including Georgia O'Keeffe, Paul Strand, and Ansel Adams.

**San Miguel Mission, Santa Fe.** This simple, earth-hue adobe structure built in about 1625 is the oldest church still in use in the continental United States. Priceless statues and paintings are within, as well as the San José Bell, said to have been cast in Spain in 1356.

**Santuario de Chimayó, Chimayó.** Tens of thousands make pilgrimages each year to this small frontier adobe church just north of Santa Fe. Built on the site where a mysterious light is said to have come out of the ground on Good Friday night in 1810, the chapel holds a sacred *pozito* (small well). The dirt from the pozito is believed to have miraculous healing properties.

**Taos Pueblo, Taos.** For nearly 1,000 years the Taos-Tiwas have lived in or near this community, which has the largest existing multistory pueblo structure in the United States. The pueblo is a UNESCO World Heritage site.

## Dining

**Geronimo, Santa Fe.** The menu changes daily at this chic restaurant in the historic Borrego House. Enjoy such dishes as mesquite-grilled Black Angus rib eye with a spicy smoked-corn-and-tomato salsa or the superb Sunday brunch. *$$$$*

**Cafe Pasqual's, Santa Fe.** This festive, local favorite pleases with its zesty regional and Latin American dishes. Three meals a day are served, and there's a communal table for those who want to beat the lines or make acquaintances. *$$$–$$$$*

**Rancho de San Juan, Espanola.** A four-course prix-fixe dinner of some of New Mexico's finest contemporary cooking is available (by reservation only) in the intimate restaurant of this romantic hideaway in the mountains near Abiquiu. *$$$–$$$$*

**Trading Post Cafe, Taos.** Imaginative variations on Continental and other dishes have made this restaurant a town favorite. *$$$–$$$$*

**Cattleman's Steakhouse, El Paso.** Savory steak will win over experienced and inexperienced red-meat eaters alike at this ranchlike setting 20 mi east of El Paso, Texas. *$$–$$$$*

**Artichoke Cafe, Albuquerque.** Diners appreciate the excellent service and new American, Italian, and French dishes prepared at this outstanding café, whose chefs use organic produce. *$$–$$$*

**The State Line, El Paso.** Aside from its unique location directly atop the New Mexico–Texas state line near El Paso, this area favorite is noted for serving mounds of delicious barbecue with generous side dishes. *$–$$$*

**La Fonda, Artesia.** For decades, residents of both Carlsbad and Roswell have driven to this Mexican-food establishment to dine on celebrated specialties such as the Guadalajara plate of seasoned beef, cheese, and guacamole. *$–$$*

**La Posta, Old Mesilla.** Dine on authentic Mexican dishes and southwestern favorites at this old adobe structure, once a way station for the Butterfield Overland Mail and Wells Fargo stages. *$–$$*

**La Choza, Santa Fe.** Arguably the best spot for authentic New Mexican food in Santa Fe, La Choza serves delicious pork carne adovada burritos and other regional specialties. *$*

## Lodging

**Inn of the Anasazi, Santa Fe.** In the heart of the historic Plaza district, this beautifully crafted hotel has individually designed rooms, each with a beamed ceiling, kiva fireplace, four-poster bed, and handcrafted desk, dresser, and tables. *$$$$*

**Touchstone Inn, Taos.** This peaceful bed-and-breakfast overlooking the Taos Pueblo is filled with a tasteful mix of antiques and modern artworks by the talented owner, Ben Price. *$$$$*

**Ten Thousand Waves, Santa Fe.** Devotees appreciate the Zenlike atmosphere of this Japanese-style health spa and small hotel in the hills above Santa Fe. These sleek, uncluttered accommodations have fireplaces, CD stereos, and tranquil courtyards or patios. *$$$–$$$$*

**The Cottages, Silver City.** You can wander this 80-acre, forested estate in search of a lost silver mine if you're so inclined. The European-style inn also has detached cottages. *$$–$$$$*

**Hacienda del Sol, Taos.** Once a house for guests of art patron Mabel Dodge Luhan, this bed-and-breakfast contains kiva-style fireplaces, Spanish antiques, southwestern-style handcrafted furniture, and original artworks. *$$–$$$$*

**Hyatt Regency Albuquerque.** This gorgeous hotel's soaring desert-color tower climbs high above the city skyline. The Hyatt is totally modern and luxurious, from the on-site spa to the well-regarded restaurant and shopping promenade. *$$–$$$$*

**Hotel Santa Fe.** If you're looking for casual but polished comforts and more insight into Native American culture, this Picurís Pueblo-owned hotel offers attractive southwestern decor and informal talks on Native American history. *$$$*

**Fechin Inn, Taos.** Reproductions of works by iconoclastic artist Nicolai Fechin grace the rooms of this Pueblo Revival hotel on the grounds of the Fechin Institute. Relax on your balcony or take a massage after a day of skiing or hiking. *$$–$$$*

**La Posada de Albuquerque.** Zsa Zsa Gabor honeymooned at this historic downtown hotel, which overflows with southwestern charm, from its tiled lobby fountain, massive vigas, encircling balcony, and fixtures of etched glass and tin to the Native American war-dance murals behind the reception desk. *$$–$$$*

**Lundeen Inn of the Arts, Las Cruces.** Architect Gerald Lundeen seamlessly joined two 1895 adobe houses, one Mexican colonial and the other Territorial. Guest rooms are decorated in honor of western artists like Georgia O'Keeffe and Frederic Remington. *$$–$$$*

**Meson de Mesilla, Old Mesilla.** A glass-enclosed atrium and a spectacular Mesilla Valley location with lofty views of the Organ Mountains set the atmosphere of this B&B, which offers rooms from affordable to pricey. *$–$$$*

**Best Western Stevens Inn, Carlsbad.** Scenes of cavern formations and Carlsbad's historic courthouse are etched in mirrored glass and carved into wooden doors at this motel, which provides a touch of elegance at bargain prices. *$–$$*

## Outdoor Adventures

**Hot-air ballooning.** More than 1,000 balloons lift off from the Albuquerque International Balloon Fiesta, and there are year-round opportunities to soar above the city. In Taos, balloonists will thrill you with dips into the Rio Grande Gorge.

**Sand surfing, White Sands National Monument.** Wipe out on your surfboard and dive headlong into the powdery soft sand. Okay, so the New Mexico version of surfing makes landings a little hard. But you can slide plastic saucers down the dips and curves of the tall gypsum dunes and let your imagination run wild in this white landscape.

**White-water rafting, Taos.** As snows melts and water runs swift, there's no better spot for this sport than the northern Rio Grande. You can pick the degree of adventure you want, from mildly flowing water to the spectacular dips and thrills of roaring white water.

## Scenic Drives

**Enchanted Circle.** This 84-mi loop from Taos winds through alpine country, with a few colorful mining towns along the way.

**High Road to Taos.** On the old road linking Santa Fe and Taos, the stunning drive—with a rugged alpine backdrop—encompasses rolling hillsides studded with orchards and tiny picturesque villages noted for weavers and wood-carvers.

**Lake Valley National Back Country Byway.** The winding two-lane byway passes through 48 mi of forest and desert, with mountain ranges looming in the distance. The route is accessible 18 mi south of Truth or Consequences. Take the Hillsboro exit off I–25.

**Mountains to Desert.** For a dramatic ride that runs from high, cool, green mountains to hot, dry desert near White Sands National Monument, drive the stretch of U.S. 82 in south-central New Mexico that drops 6,000 ft in altitude between Cloud-croft and Alamogordo.

**Turquoise Trail.** Full of ghost towns, this old route between Albuquerque and Santa Fe ventures into backcountry, with views worth skipping the interstate for.

# GREAT ITINERARIES

In New Mexico, you can immerse yourself in a culture with ancient roots and a landscape with seemingly infinite vistas. This combination of history and natural beauty is what frames any visit to the state, and you're bound to leave with the feeling that you've been somewhere very, very far from home—without the worries of traveling in a foreign country. You can hit a few of New Mexico's high notes in a one-week trip, but don't be surprised if you find yourself dreaming of coming back for more.

## Highlights of New Mexico

*6 or 7 days*

**Albuquerque** *1 day.* If you've flown into Albuquerque, it's logical to begin your tour here. Poke through the shops of Old Town Plaza and spend some time at the New Mexico Museum of Natural History and Science. After lunch, head north to the Indian Pueblo Cultural Center and then west to Petroglyph National Monument. Return east for a sunset ride on the Sandia Peak Aerial Tramway.

☉ This tour should work any day of the week.

**Santa Fe** *2 or 3 days.* On day two, head to Santa Fe on I–25, or travel the Turquoise Trail—the beauty of it is worth the extra time it takes. Explore the adobe charms of the downtown central Plaza. Stop first at the Palace of the Governors on the plaza's north side, and then investigate the crafts and wares of Native American outdoor vendors. East of the plaza, the Romanesque-style St. Francis Cathedral is worth a look. A visit to a few of the city's spectacular museums—particularly the Museum of Fine Arts, the Museum of Indian Arts and Culture, and the Museum

of International Folk Art—is a must. head north to the Hispanic pilgrimage town of Chimayó and either San Ildefonso Pueblo or Santa Clara Pueblo.

☉ The museum at the Palace of the Governors, the Museum of Fine Arts, the Museum of Indian Arts and Culture, and the Museum of International Folk Art are closed on Monday.

**Taos** *1 day.* The following day, drive to Taos, noted for its galleries and colony of independent artists. Reserve time for Taos Pueblo, which still retains the mud-and-straw adobe walls of its original construction almost 1,000 years ago. Stay overnight in Taos or return to Santa Fe. The two routes between Santa Fe and Taos are equally scenic. Take the High Road when you can allow for a longer drive and the Rio Grande route or Low Road (NM 68) when you have less time.

☉ Some Taos art galleries are not open seven days a week.

**Carlsbad** *2 days.* It's a long drive to Carlsbad, but you should make southern New Mexico your next destination. Set aside half a day to drive the 265 mi from Santa Fe to Carlsbad (the distance will be 338 mi if you've spent the previous night in Taos). Spend some time visiting Living Desert Zoo and Garden State Park and strolling the scenic pathways along the Pecos River at Lake Carlsbad Recreation Area. Take the walking tour into the enormous caves of Carlsbad Caverns National Park; you can spend at least a half day here. On your way back to the northern part of the state, drive northwest through the mountain area of Cloudcroft and drop down to White Sands National Monument, a dazzling vista of glistening white dunes.

☉ This tour should work any day of the week.

## If You Have More Time

Follow most of the above itinerary, but plan to spend three extra days in southern New Mexico after you've reached Carlsbad. Once you've made the long journey down, you might be surprised at what you'll find in out-of-the-way corners. You can be more leisurely about visiting Carlsbad Caverns; round out your tour with a scenic drive through **Walnut Canyon** and return to the cave at sunset (if you're there during summer months) for the evening bat flight. Another day, take U.S. 62/180 south from Carlsbad to **Guadalupe Mountains National Park.** Stop over at the visitor center, and consider a short hike along a nature trail. Eat lunch or a late breakfast at delightfully ornery, middle-of-nowhere Cornudas Café; then drive on to **El Paso.** If your time is limited, drive through El Paso straight to **Las Cruces,** where you can spend the night. In the afternoon, take in the galleries and sights of **Old Mesilla,** where you can dine at one of several excellent restaurants. When you're ready to head north, take U.S. 70 northeast to **White Sands National Monument.** Proceed to **Alamogordo** and visit the Space Center if you have time. For a beautiful scenic drive take U.S. 82 east to **Cloudcroft;** then turn north onto NM 24, where you'll drive through the **Mescalero Apache Reservation** to **Ruidoso.** Spend the night and your eighth day here. Nearby is the Old West historical town of **Lincoln.** If you're in the area in colder months, consider winter sports at **Ski Apache.** If it's summer, you might want to spend some time betting on the ponies at **Ruidoso Downs.**

## If You Have 3 Days

You can still get a sense of the natural and historical wonders of New Mexico even if you are pressed for time. Start in **Albuquerque,** at **Old Town Plaza,** and drop in at the **New Mexico Museum of Natural History and Science.** You can follow up a visit the **Indian Pueblo Cultural Center** and **Petroglyph National Monument** with a sunset ride on the **Sandia Peak Aerial Tramway.** On day two, start early and drive to **Santa Fe** on I–25. Your first stop should be the **Plaza** downtown, where you can visit the **Palace of the Governors** and browse the crafts of the Native American vendors there. At the **Museum of Fine Arts** you can see works by southwestern artists, and at the **Museum of Indian Arts and Culture** you can look into New Mexico's ancient past. Give yourself time to stroll the narrow, adobe-lined streets of the charming city, and treat yourself to some fine New Mexican cuisine in the evening. On your third day, head to **Taos** to visit **Taos Pueblo.** Take in the local shops and art galleries, and try to visit at least one of the town's fine museums, perhaps the **Fechin Institute** or the **Harwood Foundation.**

# 2 ALBUQUERQUE

## WITH SIDE TRIPS
## ALONG THE TURQUOISE TRAIL

A modest and practical city with a long and
fascinating history, Albuquerque is the center
of commerce, medicine, and education in
New Mexico. Founded in 1706 as an
outpost of Spain's empire in North America,
the city has a central location that makes it
the perfect jumping-off point for excursions to
other parts of New Mexico.

Updated by
Tracy
Dingmann

**A**T FIRST GLANCE, Albuquerque appears to be a typical Sun Belt
city, spreading out in all directions with no grand design, architectural or otherwise, to hold it together. The city's growth
pattern seems as free-spirited as all those hot-air balloons that take part
in the Albuquerque International Balloon Fiesta every October. With
a bit of exploration, however, this initial impression of an asphalt
maze softens as you get a sense of Albuquerque's distinctive neighborhoods. The charms of Albuquerque may not jump out to greet you,
but the blend of Spanish, Mexican, Native American, Anglo, and
Asian influences makes this a vibrant multicultural metropolis well worth
exploring.

An unpretentious, practical city with a population nearing 700,000,
Albuquerque is the center of New Mexico's educational institutions
and financial, business, manufacturing, and medical industries. Its
people are friendly, and the state's three primary cultures rub elbows
more comfortably here than anywhere else in New Mexico. Many Albuquerqueans have descended from one or more of three groups: Native Americans, some of whom arrived more than 10,000 years ago;
17th-century Spaniards who came on horseback to conquer and convert; or the European and American trappers, fortune seekers, traders,
and merchants who made the arduous journey across the Santa Fe Trail.
From its humble beginning as a settlement of Spanish families in what
is now known as Old Town, Albuquerque grew into a trade and transportation center. It became an important station on the Spaniards' El
Camino Real, or the Royal Road, which wound from Mexico City to
Santa Fe and was for centuries New Mexico's primary link to the outside world.

Albuquerque was founded in 1706 as a farming settlement near a
bend in the Rio Grande. Named for Spain's duke of Albuquerque, then
viceroy of Mexico, it prospered, thanks to its strategic location on a
trade route and its proximity to several Native American pueblos,
which were a source of commerce and provided protection from raiding nomadic tribes. The nearby mountains and river forest yielded ample
wood. The settlers built a chapel and then a larger structure, San Felipe de Neri Catholic Church, named after a 16th-century Florentine
saint. For protection, homes were built around a central plaza like those
in other Spanish settlements. The fortresslike community could be entered from the four corners only, making it easier to defend. This four-
block area, Old Town, is the city's tourist hub, filled with shops,
galleries, and restaurants.

It would have made sense for the town to simply grow outward, expanding from its central hub. But the Rio Grande gradually changed
its course, moving farther and farther west, and Albuquerque followed. In 1880 the railroad came to central New Mexico, its tracks
missing Old Town by a good 2 mi and causing another population shift.
Old Town wasn't exactly abandoned, but New Town sprouted near
the depot and grew until it eventually enveloped Old Town.

Then came Route 66. Opened in 1926 and nicknamed "The Mother
Road" by John Steinbeck, it sparked much of Albuquerque's modern
economic development. Surging through town during the 1930s and
'40s, the route's traffic had as much impact as the railroad and the river
combined. The burgeoning city swelled around the asphalt—motels,
gas stations, diners, and truck stops formed a sea of neon that celebrated American mobility. During World War II Albuquerque flourished with the growth of a major air base, Kirtland. It and other

military-related facilities such as Sandia National Laboratory remain economic linchpins.

Albuquerque's economy continues to diversify. Intel, the world's largest computer-chip maker, has one of its biggest manufacturing centers here, across the river in Rio Rancho. Intel's presence has stimulated population and housing growth and attracted additional high-tech businesses. That the city has a substantial arts scene will be apparent the moment you step off a plane at Albuquerque International Sunport and see the works of New Mexican artists throughout the terminal. The city has significant museums and galleries and is a magnet for artists, writers, poets, filmmakers, and musicians.

Many interesting towns, parks, and Indian pueblos are just outside Albuquerque. The pueblo residents continue to preserve their customs in a changing world. Each pueblo has its own customs, history, art, and design. Visitors are generally welcome, particularly on feast days, which occur throughout the year.

# EXPLORING ALBUQUERQUE

Colorful Historic Route 66 is Albuquerque's Central Avenue, unifying, as nothing else, the diverse areas of the city—Old Town cradled at the bend of the Rio Grande, the downtown business and government centers to the east, the University of New Mexico farther east, and the Nob Hill strip of restaurants and shops following the university. The railroad tracks and Central Avenue divide the city into quadrants—Southwest, Northwest, Southeast, and Northeast. Once you understand the layout, it's easy to get around. Many attractions are a considerable distance apart. A car is a necessity, but rental rates are reasonable (about $200 per week for a compact with unlimited mileage).

Albuquerque's terrain is diverse. Along the river in the north and south valleys, the elevation hovers at about 4,800 ft. East of the river, the land rises gently to the foothills of the Sandia Mountains; their 10,678-ft summit, Sandia Crest, is a grand spot from which to view the city below. West of the Rio Grande, where much of Albuquerque's growth is taking place, the terrain rises abruptly in a string of mesas topped by five volcanic cones. The changes in elevation from one part of the city to another result in corresponding changes in temperature, as much as 10°F at any time. It's not uncommon for snow or rain to fall on one part of town while another remains sunny and dry.

*Numbers in the text correspond to numbers in the margin and on the Albuquerque and Albuquerque Old Town maps.*

## Old Town and Vicinity

### A Good Tour

Soak up the air of history in **Old Town Plaza** ①, and then cross the street and visit **San Felipe de Neri Catholic Church** ②. Cutting diagonally across the plaza, head south to the corner of San Felipe Street and Old Town Road to drop in on the **American International Rattlesnake Museum** ③. Walk south on San Felipe and west on Central Avenue to the corner of Rio Grande Boulevard, where in a strip mall you'll find the **Turquoise Museum** ④. Farther west on Central, along a historic section of Route 66 lined with shabby vintage motels, is the **Albuquerque Aquarium and Rio Grande Botanic Garden** ⑤. Leaving Old Town, take a five-minute stroll over to two of the city's cultural institutions, the **Albuquerque Museum of Art and History** ⑥ and the **New Mexico Museum of Natural History and Science** ⑦. Kids will love the **National Atomic**

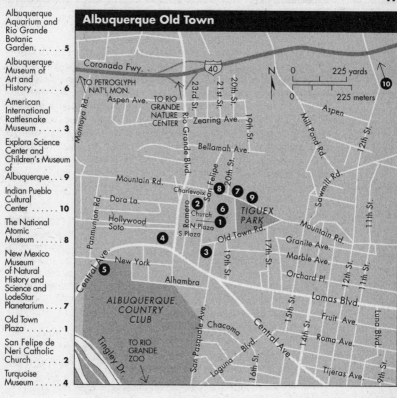

**Albuquerque Old Town**

Museum ⑧ and the **Explora Science Center and Children's Museum of Albuquerque** ⑨, which are also within walking distance. You'll need to hop in your car (or take city Bus 66) to visit the **Indian Pueblo Cultural Center** ⑩.

TIMING

The best time to begin a visit to Old Town is in the morning, before the stores open at 10 and the daily rush of activity begins. In the beaming morning light, the echoes of the past are almost palpable (and you might find parking). Plan to spend an hour and a half at the Old Town sites, an hour in the Albuquerque Museum of Art and History, and two hours in the New Mexico Museum of Natural History and Science. The Turquoise Museum is closed on Sunday, and the Albuquerque Museum of Art and History is closed on Monday. You'll need at least an hour and a half to take in all the exhibits at the Indian Pueblo Cultural Center.

## Sights to See

🖐 ⑤ **Albuquerque Aquarium and Rio Grande Botanic Garden.** A spectacular shark tank with floor-to-ceiling viewing is among the most popular of the marine exhibits here. A video follows the path of a drop of water as it forms in the Rocky Mountains, enters the upper Rio Grande, and finally spills into the Gulf of Mexico. The Spanish-Moorish garden is one of three walled gardens near the entrance of the Botanic Garden. The glass conservatory has two pavilions. The smaller one exhibits desert plants, and the larger houses the Mediterranean collection. Sharkreef Cafe (open between 7:30 and 5) serves breakfast and lunch. ✉ 2601 Central Ave., at New York Ave. NW, Tingley Park, ☎ 505/764-6200. 💵 $5. ⏰ Daily 9–5.

**⑥ Albuquerque Museum of Art and History.** This modern structure houses the largest collection of Spanish-colonial artifacts in the nation, along with relics of the city's birth and development. The centerpiece of the colonial exhibit is a pair of life-size models of Spanish conquistadors in original chain mail and armor. Perhaps the one on horseback is Francisco Vásquez de Coronado, who, in search of gold, led a small army into New Mexico in 1540—the turning point in the region's history. Among the museum's attractions are treasure chests filled with pearls and gold coins, religious artifacts, and early maps (some dating from the 15th century and showing California as an island). A multimedia presentation chronicles the development of the city since 1875. The sculpture garden contains 45 works by 20th-century southwestern artists that include Glenna Goodacre, Michael Naranjo, and Luís Jiménez. ⊠ *2000 Mountain Rd. NW, Old Town,* ☎ *505/243–7255 or 505/242–4600.* ⌨ *$2.* ☉ *Tues.–Sun. 9–5.*

**☾ ③ American International Rattlesnake Museum.** Included in this strange collection of living "rattlers" are rare and unusual specimens, such as an albino western diamondback. The museum's labels, its engaging staff, and a video will supply you with the lowdown on these venomous creatures—for instance, that they can't hear their own rattles and that the human death rate from rattlesnake bites is less than 1%. ⊠ *202 San Felipe St. NW, Old Town,* ☎ *505/242–6569.* ⌨ *$2.50.* ☉ *Weekdays noon–6, Sat. 10–6, Sun. 1–5.*

**☾ ⑨ Explora Science Center and Children's Museum of Albuquerque.** Albuquerque's cultural corridor is slated to gain another jewel in 2003, when this science museum is scheduled to move to a location across from the New Mexico Museum of Natural History and Science. The new Explora is billed as an all-ages attraction but will be especially geared to children, with hands-on exhibits about science, technology, and art. At press time, the center was located at Winrock Center. ⊠ *Louisiana at I–40, Northeast Heights,* ☎ *505/842–1537,* WEB *www.explora.mus.nm.us.* ⌨ *Call for admission prices.* ☉ *Call for hrs.*

**★ ☾ ⑩ Indian Pueblo Cultural Center.** The multilevel semicircular design at this museum was inspired by Pueblo Bonito, the prehistoric ruin in Chaco Canyon in northwestern New Mexico. Each of the state's 19 pueblos has an upper-level alcove devoted to its particular arts and crafts. Lower-level exhibits trace the history of the Pueblo people. Youngsters can touch Native American pottery, jewelry, weaving, tools, and dried corn at the Hands-on Corner and also draw petroglyph designs and design pots. Paintings, sculptures, jewelry, leather crafts, rugs, souvenir items, drums, beaded necklaces, painted bowls, and fetishes are for sale. Ceremonial dances are performed during the summer and on special holidays. ⊠ *2401 12th St. NW, Los Duranes,* ☎ *505/843–7270 or 800/766–4405,* WEB *www.indianpueblo.org.* ⌨ *$4.* ☉ *Daily 9–5:30.*

**☾ ⑧ The National Atomic Museum.** In order to be more accessible, this popular attraction has moved from the heavily restricted Kirtland Air Force Base to Old Town. Exhibits include replicas of Little Boy and Fat Man (the bombs dropped on Japan at the end of World War II), and there are children's programs and an exhibit about X-ray technology. The museum plans to mount more exhibits on the nonweapons applications of nuclear technology, such as nuclear medicine and nuclear power. In 2005 or 2006, the museum is set to change its name to the National Museum of Nuclear Science and History and to move to Balloon Fiesta Park north of town. ⊠ *1905 Mountain Rd. NW, Old Town,* ☎ *505/284–3243,* WEB *www.atomicmuseum.com.* ⌨ *$4.* ☉ *Daily 9–5.*

NEED A
BREAK?
The **Indian Pueblo Cultural Center** (✉ 2401 12th St. NW, Los Duranes, ☎ 505/843–7270) has a restaurant, the Pueblo Harvest Cafe, open for breakfast and lunch, that serves blue-corn enchiladas, *posole* (a thick soup with pork, hominy, chile, garlic, and cilantro), Native American bread pudding, and, of course, fry bread—that addictive popover-like creation that is served plain or topped with honey, beans, chile, or powdered sugar.

★ ☝ ❼ **New Mexico Museum of Natural History and Science.** The world of wonders at Albuquerque's most popular museum includes the simulated volcano (with a river of bubbling hot lava flowing beneath the see-through glass floor), the frigid Ice Age cave, and the world-class dinosaur exhibit hall. The Evolator—short for Evolution Elevator—a six-minute high-tech ride, uses video, sound, and motion to whisk you through 35 million years of New Mexico's geological history. A film in the Extreme Screen DynaTheater makes viewers feel equally involved. Arrive via the front walkway, and you'll be greeted by life-size bronze sculptures of a 21-ft-long horned pentaceratops and a 30-ft-long carnivorous albertosaur. The LodeStar Science Center features a state-of-the-art planetarium. ✉ *1801 Mountain Rd. NW, across from Albuquerque Museum of Art and History, Old Town,* ☎ *505/841–2800,* WEB *www.nmmnh-abq.mus.nm.us.* ✉ *Museum $5, combination ticket for museum and Extreme Screen DynaTheater $10, LodeStar Science Center $6.* ☽ *Daily 9–5.*

★ ☝ ❶ **Old Town Plaza.** Don Francisco Cuervo y Valdés, a provincial governor of New Mexico, laid out this small plaza in 1706. No slouch when it came to political maneuvering, he named the town after the duke of Albuquerque, viceroy of New Spain. He hoped flattery would induce the duke to waive the requirement that a town have 30 families before a charter was issued—there were only 15 families living here in 1706. The duke acquiesced. (Albuquerque is nicknamed "The Duke City," so he's hardly been forgotten.) Today the plaza is an oasis of tranquility filled with shade trees, wrought-iron benches, a graceful white gazebo, and strips of grass. Nearly 200 shops, restaurants, cafés, galleries, and several cultural sites in *placitas* (small plazas) and lanes surround Old Town Plaza. The scents of green chile, enchiladas, and burritos hang in the air. Mock gunfights are staged on Romero Street on Sunday afternoon, and during fiestas Old Town comes alive with mariachi bands and dancing señoritas. Event schedules and maps, which contain a list of public rest rooms, are available at the **Old Town Visitors Center** (✉ 303 Romero St. NW, Old Town, ☎ 505/243–3215), across the street from the San Felipe de Neri Catholic Church. The center is open daily 9–5 in summer and 9:30–4:30 the rest of the year.

❷ **San Felipe de Neri Catholic Church.** More than 2½ centuries after it first welcomed worshipers, this structure erected in 1793 is still active. The building, which replaced Albuquerque's first Catholic church, has been enlarged and expanded several times, but its adobe walls and other original features remain. Small gardens front and flank the church; the inside is dark and quiet. Next to it is a small museum that displays relics—vestments, paintings, carvings—dating from the 17th century. ✉ *2005 Plaza NW, Old Town,* ☎ *505/243–4628.* ☽ *Church open to the public 8 AM–dusk; museum Mon.–Sat. 1–4. Call ahead to confirm hrs.*

❹ **Turquoise Museum.** A novel attraction, this museum focuses on the beauty, mythology, and physical properties of turquoise, a semiprecious but widely adored gemstone that many people understandably associate with the color of New Mexico's skies. A simulated mine shaft leads to one-of-a-kind showpieces and examples from more than 60 mines

**20**

Albuquerque

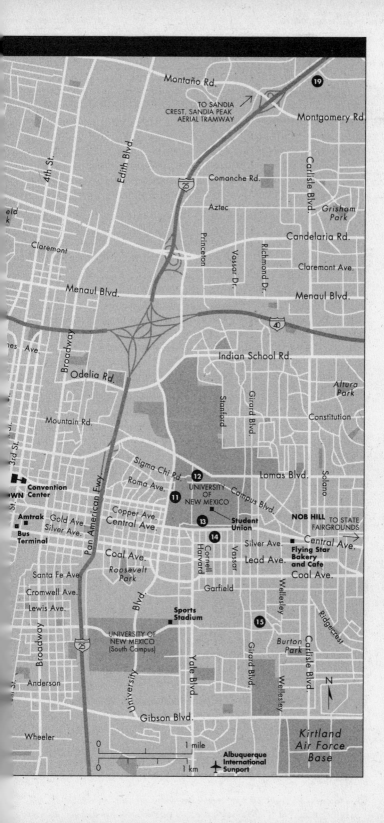

Montaño Rd.

**19**

TO SANDIA
CREST, SANDIA PEAK
AERIAL TRAMWAY

Montgomery Rd.

4th St.

Edith Blvd.

Comanche Rd.

Carlisle Blvd.

Aztec

Grisham
Park

Claremont

Candelaria Rd.

Princeton

Vassar Dr.

Richmond Dr.

Claremont Ave.

Menaul Blvd.

Menaul Blvd.

Broadway

40

Odelia Rd.

Indian School Rd.

Altura
Park

Mountain Rd.

Stanford

Girard Blvd.

Constitution

3rd St.

Sigma Chi Rd.

Lomas Blvd.

Solano

Convention
Center

Roma Ave.

**12**

UNIVERSITY
OF
NEW MEXICO

Campus Blvd.

NOB HILL    TO STATE
FAIRGROUNDS

Amtrak

Gold Ave.

**11**

Student
Union

Central Ave.

Bus
Terminal

Silver Ave.

Copper Ave.

**13**

Flying Star
Bakery
and Cafe

Central Ave.

Coal Ave.

**14**

Silver Ave.

Coal Ave.

Roosevelt
Park

Cornell

Harvard

Vassar

Lead Ave.

Santa Fe Ave.

Garfield

Wellesley

Cromwell Ave.

Pan American Fwy.

Lewis Ave.

Sports
Stadium

**15**

Ridgecrest

25

UNIVERSITY OF
NEW MEXICO
(South Campus)

Burton
Park

Carlisle Blvd.

Anderson

University

Yale Blvd.

Girard Blvd.

Wellesley

N

Wheeler

0          1 mile

0          1 km

Gibson Blvd.

Albuquerque
International
Sunport

Kirtland
Air Force
Base

on four continents. Displays show how turquoise is formed and highlight its uses by Native Americans in prehistoric times. At the education center you can learn how to distinguish the real McCoy from plastic. ✉ *2107 Central Ave. NW, Old Town,* ☎ *505/247–8650.* 🎟 *$2.* ⊙ *Mon.–Sat. 9:30–5:30.*

# The University of New Mexico

Established in 1889, the University of New Mexico is the state's leading institution of higher education, with internationally recognized programs in anthropology, biology, Latin American studies, and medicine. Its many outstanding galleries and museums are open to the public free of charge. The university's Pueblo Revival–style architecture is noteworthy, particularly the old wing of Zimmerman Library and the Alumni Chapel, both designed by John Gaw Meem, a Santa Fe–based architect who was one of the chief 20th-century proponents of the Pueblo style.

## A Good Walk

The impeccably landscaped grounds of the University of New Mexico surround a central area containing knolls, a duck pond, fountains, waterfalls, and benches. The **Maxwell Museum of Anthropology** ⑪ is in the Anthropology Building on the western edge of the campus, only a few minutes' walk from the duck pond. From the Maxwell, walk east past Alumni Chapel and turn left. At the duck pond walk north on Yale past University House. You'll come to a four-way stop at Yale and Las Lomas streets. The **Jonson Gallery** ⑫ is the second building on the northeast corner of this intersection. Walk south past the duck pond, between Zimmerman Library and Ortega Hall. Continue south under a walkway and left, past the Student Union Building, to the **University Art Museum** ⑬, in the Center for the Arts (use the Stanford Drive and Central Avenue entrance). At the corner of Central Avenue and Cornell Drive is the sales and exhibition gallery of the **Tamarind Institute** ⑭. Nine blocks south of Central along Girard Boulevard is the **Ernie Pyle Branch Library** ⑮.

### TIMING

Seeing the University of New Mexico could take the better part of a day. Spend an hour strolling the grounds, maybe catching some rays by the duck pond. Allot an hour for each subsequent stop. All facilities are open year-round, but some are closed from Saturday to Monday.

## Sights to See

⑮ **Ernie Pyle Branch Library.** After several visits to New Mexico, Ernie Pyle, a Pulitzer Prize–winning news reporter, built a house in 1940 that now contains the smallest branch of the Albuquerque Public Library. On display are photos, handwritten articles by Pyle, and news clippings about his career as a correspondent during World War II and his death from a sniper's bullet on April 18, 1945, on the Pacific island of Ie Shima. ✉ *900 Girard Blvd. SE, University of New Mexico,* ☎ *505/256–2065.* 🎟 *Free.* ⊙ *Tues.–Sat. 10–6.*

⑫ **Jonson Gallery.** The home and studio of Raymond Jonson (1891–1982) house the abstract, colorful works on paper of this Transcendentalist painter who focused on mass and form. The gallery mounts a major Jonson retrospective each summer and also exhibits works by other contemporary painters. ✉ *1909 Las Lomas Blvd. NE, University of New Mexico,* ☎ *505/277–4967.* 🎟 *Free.* ⊙ *Tues. 9–4 and 5–8, Wed.–Fri. 9–4.*

⑪ **Maxwell Museum of Anthropology.** Many of the more than 2½ million artifacts at the Maxwell, the first public museum in Albuquerque (established in 1932), come from the Southwest. Two permanent exhibitions chronicle 4 million years of human history and the lifeways, art, and cultures of 11,500 years of human settlement in the Southwest. The photographic archives contain more than 250,000 images, including some of the earliest photos of Pueblo and Navajo cultures. The museum shop sells traditional and contemporary southwestern Native American jewelry, rugs, pottery, basketry, and beadwork, along with folk art from around the world. In the children's section are inexpensive books and handmade tribal artifacts. ☒ *University of New Mexico, University Blvd., 1 block north of Grand Ave.,* ☎ *505/277–4405.* ☒ *Free.* ☉ *Tues.–Fri. 9–4, Sat. 10–4.*

OFF THE
BEATEN PATH

**NATIONAL HISPANIC CULTURAL CENTER OF NEW MEXICO –** Opened in 2001 in Albuquerque's old Barelas neighborhood as a showcase for Latino culgenealgicalture, the center contains several art galleries and performance venues, a genealogical research center and library, a restaurant, and a television studio. Exhibits include displays of photography and paintings by local artists as well as by internationally known names. The center mounts performances of flamenco dancing, bilingual theater, and traditional Spanish and New Mexican music. ☒ *1701 4th SW, Barelas (from downtown take Central Ave. west and turn south on Broadway, then turn west on Cesar Chavez Blvd., cross the Rio Grande Bridge, and drive south on 4th St.),* ☎ *505/246–2261.* ☒ *$3.* ☉ *Tues.–Sun. 10–5.*

⑭ **Tamarind Institute.** This world-famous institution played a major role in reviving the fine art of lithographic printing, which involves working with plates of traditional stone and modern metal. Tamarind certification is to a printer what a degree from Juilliard is to a musician. A small gallery within the facility exhibits prints and lithographs. Guided tours (reservations essential) are conducted on the first Friday of each month at 1:30. ☒ *108 Cornell Dr. SE, University of New Mexico,* ☎ *505/277–3901.* ☒ *Free.* ☉ *Tues.–Fri. 9–5.*

⑬ **University Art Museum.** A handsome facility, the museum holds New Mexico's largest collection of fine art. Works of old masters share wall space with the likes of Picasso and O'Keeffe, and many photographs and prints are on display. Lectures and symposia, gallery talks, and guided tours are regularly scheduled. ☒ *University of New Mexico Center for the Arts,* ☎ *505/277–4001.* ☒ *Free.* ☉ *Tues. 9–4 and 5–8, Wed.–Fri. 9–4, Sun. 1–4.*

NEED A
BREAK?

You can grab a burger or a snack or just rest your feet at the **Student Union Building** (☎ 505/277–2331), north of the university's Stanford entrance (off Central Avenue). A renovation in 2002 added a movie theater, crafts store, computer lab, and e-mail station. The coffee at **Flying Star Cafe** (☒ 3416 Central Ave. SE, Nob Hill, 1 block west of Carlisle Blvd., ☎ 505/255–6633) is brewed from beans roasted on the premises. The bakery has delectable pastries, and the café serves scrumptious soups, quiches, sandwiches, and salads. An international selection of periodicals is available for perusing while you're munching.

# Elsewhere in Albuquerque

## A Good Tour

**Cliff's Amusement Park** ⑲, **Petroglyph National Monument** ⑯, **Rio Grande Nature Center State Park** ⑰, and the **Rio Grande Zoo** ⑱ are far-flung sites usually visited separately and by car.

Each of these sites deserves a minimum of two hours.

## Sights to See

⑲ **Cliff's Amusement Park.** Drive down San Mateo Northeast in the summer and you can't help but glimpse a roller-coaster smack in the middle of the city. Cliff's Amusement Park is a clean, well-run attraction for everyone from two-year-olds on up. It features a wooden-track roller-coaster as well as rides for all ages and state fair-type games of chance. The park also has a large water-play area. Cliff's is open days and evenings from late May to mid-October, but hours vary widely, so call first. ✉ *4800 Osuna NE off San Mateo NE, Northeast Heights,* ☎ *505/881–9373.* ☞ *Park entrance $2.50, rides extra. Park plus water-play area $7.50. Discounted ride passes available.*

⑯ **Petroglyph National Monument.** Beneath the stumps of five extinct volcanoes, this park encompasses more than 15,000 ancient Native American rock drawings inscribed on the 17-mi-long West Mesa escarpment overlooking the Rio Grande valley. For centuries, Native American hunting parties camped at the base, chipping and scribbling away. Archaeologists believe the petroglyphs were carved on the lava formations between the years 1100 and 1600. Walking trails provide access to them. A paved trail at **Boca Negra Canyon** (north of the visitor center on Unser Boulevard, beyond Montaño Road) leads past several dozen petroglyphs. The trail at **Rinconado Canyon** (south of the visitor center on Unser) is unpaved. To get to the visitor center from central Albuquerque take I–40 west to the N.M. 448/Coors Road Exit north (west of the Rio Grande) and take a left on Western Trail Road. ✉ *Visitor center: 4735 Unser Blvd. NW, West Side,* ☎ *505/899–0205.* ☞ *$1 weekdays, $2 weekends.* ☉ *Daily 8–5.*

☝ ⑰ **Rio Grande Nature Center State Park.** This year-round refuge in a portion of the Bosque, the nation's largest cottonwood forest, is home to all manner of birds and migratory waterfowl. Constructed half aboveground and half below the edge of a pond, the park's Observation Room has viewing windows that provide a look at what's going on at both levels. You'll see birds, frogs, ducks, and turtles. The park has active programs for adults and children and trails for biking, walking, and jogging. ✉ *2901 Candelaria Rd. NW, North Valley,* ☎ *505/344–7240.* ☞ *$1.* ☉ *Daily 10–5.*

☝ ⑱ **Rio Grande Zoo.** An oasis of waterfalls, cottonwood trees, and naturalized animal habitats, the Rio Grande Zoo is one of the best-managed and most attractive facilities of its kind in the nation. More than 200 species of wildlife from around the world live here. In keeping with its mission of wildlife care and conservation, the zoo has established captive breeding programs for more than a dozen endangered species. Concerts are performed on the grounds during the summer. There's a café on the premises. ✉ *903 10th St. SW, Barelas,* ☎ *505/764–6200.* ☞ *$5.* ☉ *Sept.–May, daily 9–5; June–Aug., daily 9–6.*

# Sandia Peak Aerial Tramway

Rising like a wave of color poised to break on Albuquerque are the majestic Sandia Mountains, which form an ever-changing panoramic backdrop to the city. Hikers, bikers, bird-watchers, climbers, painters, skiers, and sightseers all take advantage of this wild urban refuge. An ideal way to get the lay of this spectacular land northeast of downtown is to take the tram ride up to Sandia Peak and hike along the rim.

# NEON AND NOSTALGIA

**M**ID-20TH-CENTURY AMERICAN motorists came to know their country firsthand via Route 66. Today, frequent flyers enviously wonder about the romance of the open road. Long before the prosperous age of the two-car family, the 2,400 mi of Route 66 opened in 1926 to link eight states, from Chicago to Los Angeles. It came to be known by the nickname John Steinbeck gave it—"The Mother Road." The nation's outlet for movement and change has become enveloped in nostalgia. Today in New Mexico, from the Texas to the Arizona border, it's still possible to experience vestiges of the old Route 66.

Built in part to aid rural communities and the transportation of agricultural goods, Route 66 evolved into a farmer's very escape from the Dust Bowl of the 1930s, and then a tryst for the love affair between Americans and their automobiles. The route's other nickname, "America's Main Street," was due to the fact that the road incorporated towns' main streets, and because of this, communities thrived. Along the highway that ran as vividly through the imagination as through the landscape, many discovered their ability to move on beyond the confines of their own hometown. They found places along the road that appeared to offer a better opportunity to prosper and to reinvent their destiny.

After World War II, Route 66 saw jubilant family vacationers tumble out of cars and into roadside diners and motels. The 1940s and '50s were the heyday of the highway, as Nat King Cole crooned the lyrics to Bobby Troup's song of the road. The road's adventure was overplayed in the '60s television series *Route 66*, and by 1970, nearly all of the two-laner was trumped by four-lane interstate highways. Along Route 66, the possibility of connection with America's people and places lived beyond every bend in the road. By contrast, the interstate would dampen travel with franchised monotony. Most of the bypassed Route 66 communities dried up and blew away like tumbleweeds. In many of these ghost towns, only a few crumbling buildings and fading signs remain as markers to a vanished age.

By hopping on and off I–40, it's possible to find the quieter, slower two-laner that's held on to its name. The feeling of adventure still flickers in Tucumcari at twilight, when the neon signs of the Buckaroo Motel, the Westerner Drive-In, and the Blue Swallow light up the cobalt sky. In Santa Rosa, at Joseph's Cafe, the Fat Man continues to beckon. In Albuquerque, you can drive down Central Avenue, stopping at the Route 66 Diner or the Route 66 Malt Shop and heading past the El Vado. And in Gallup, dine at Earl's Restaurant or the Eagle Cafe, and book a room at the stars of yesteryear's hotel, El Rancho Hotel. Between Albuquerque and Gallup, this ribbon of road takes you through dusty towns with names like poetry: Budville, Cubero, McCartys, Thoreau. These places also once offered the traveler the filling stations, motor courts, curio shops, and cafés that gave comfort on a long drive, and every road tripper today hopes to happen upon such an undiscovered (but really just forgotten) place.

For information on dining and lodging along Route 66, contact the **National Historic Route 66 Federation** (✉ Box 423, Tujunga, CA 91043, ☎ 818/352–7232, WEB www.national66.com). To track Route 66 through New Mexico, contact the **Route 66 Association** (☎ 505/224–2802, WEB www.rt66nm.org).

## A Good Tour

Head north from downtown on I–25 and east on Tramway Road (NM 556) to reach the base station of the **Sandia Peak Aerial Tramway.** If you have more time to spend in the area, take the Sandia Crest tour described in Side Trips from Albuquerque, *below.*

### TIMING

The tram excursion, best taken on warm, clear days and a superb experience at sunset, takes about 90 minutes round-trip. Allow more time if you want to explore the rim, stop for a picnic, or have a drink at the High Finance Restaurant. Autumn is an ideal time to view the changing colors of the aspens and scrub oaks. At any time of year, bring warm layers if you intend to spend more than a few minutes on the mountain.

## Sights to See

☪ **Sandia Peak Aerial Tramway.** Tramway cars climb 2.7 mi up the steep western face of the Sandias, giving you a close up view of red rocks and tall trees. From the observation deck at the summit you can see Santa Fe to the northeast and Los Alamos to the northwest. If you're lucky, you'll see birds of prey soaring above or mountain lions roaming the cliff sides. An exhibit room at the top surveys the wildlife and landscape of the mountain, as well as some trails. If you want to tie a meal in to the excursion, there's the pricey High Finance Restaurant above, and a new restaurant, Sandiago's, has opened at the tram's base. ⊠ *10 Tramway Loop NE, Northeast Heights,* ☎ *505/856–7325.* 🎫 *$15.* ☉ *Memorial Day–Labor Day, daily 9–9; Sept.–May 9–8.*

# DINING

Albuquerqueans love to eat out, as the city's more than 1,700 restaurants attest. Chinese, Vietnamese, Thai, Cajun, French, and Italian restaurants can all be found, along with establishments serving regional New Mexican cuisine based on the native ingredients—chile, beans, and corn—that have sustained people in this land for centuries.

The argument that Albuquerque is the Mexican food capital of the Southwest is easy to make—and tough to dispute. Fine examples of this eclectic diet, in which dishes of diverse pedigrees are doused with colorful chile sauce, can be found in paper-plate eateries and linen-tablecloth restaurants.

| CATEGORY | COST* |
|----------|-------|
| $$$$ | over $25 |
| $$$ | $18–$25 |
| $$ | $10–$17 |
| $ | under $10 |

*\* per person for a main course at dinner*

## Downtown, Old Town, and Vicinity

### Brazilian

$$$   ✕ **Tucanos Brazilian Grill.** There isn't much point in going to Tucanos if you don't love meat. Sure, they serve vegetables there, but the real focus is on the skewers of beef, chicken, and turkey that parade endlessly out of the open kitchen on the arms of eager waiters. The noisy spot just next to the new downtown Century Rio Theater is a good place to go for tropical drinks, too. Try a *caipirinha*, the lime-steeped national cocktail of Brazil. Reservations are necessary for groups of six or more. ⊠ *110 Central Ave. SW, Downtown,* ☎ *505/246–9900. AE, D, MC, V.*

## Contemporary

$$$$  ✕ **Bien Shur.** The fine food at this establishment matches the fine view of the Sandia foothills just outside. Bien Shur is part of the magnificent Sandia Casino complex but is separated from the noisy casino by a thick glass wall. The fare here ranges from grilled duck breast to steaks and seafood. Desserts are exquisite. ✉ *I–25 at Tramway to Sandia Casino, Northeast Heights,* ☎ *505/796–7788. AE, D, MC, V.*

$$$$  ✕ **High Noon Restaurant and Saloon.** Fine dining is staged in a former woodworking shop in one of Old Town's 200-year-old adobe buildings. The setting is Territorial, with viga ceilings, brick floors, handmade southwestern furniture, and New Mexican art. A skylight provides diffused light and glimpses of the stars. Among the menu highlights are bison rib eye, rack of lamb crusted in roasted pine nuts, and flame-broiled fresh salmon. From Thursday to Sunday you'll dine to the music of a flamenco guitarist. ✉ *425 San Felipe St. NW, Old Town,* ☎ *505/ 765–1455. AE, D, DC, MC, V.*

$$$$  ✕ **Seasons Rotisserie-Grill.** Upbeat yet elegant, this Old Town eatery is an easy place to have a business lunch or a dinner date, and it's conveniently near museums and shops. The kitchen serves reliable grilled specialties, like the popular spit-roasted half-chicken with garlic mashed potatoes, as well as light northern Italian pastas. Other dishes are the double-cut pork rib chop with caramelized shallot-sage sauce and grilled Atlantic salmon with lemon beurre blanc. The rooftop patio and bar provides evening cocktails and lighter meals. Reservations are recommended. ✉ *2031 Mountain Rd. NW, Old Town,* ☎ *505/766– 5100. AE, D, DC, MC, V.*

$$–$$$  ✕ **Artichoke Cafe.** Locals praise the Artichoke for its service and
★  French, new American, and Italian dishes prepared, whenever possible, with organically grown ingredients. Specialties include grilled duck, pumpkin ravioli with fresh spinach and butternut squash, and grilled chicken with five-onion risotto. The appetizers are so tasty you may want to make a meal out of them. The building is about a century old, but the decor is uptown modern. The two-tier dining room spills out into a small courtyard. ✉ *424 Central Ave. SE, Downtown,* ☎ *505/243–0200. AE, D, DC, MC, V. Closed Sun. No lunch Sat.*

## French

$$–$$$  ✕ **La Crêpe Michel.** The highlights at this intimate country-French café are its innovative chicken, beef, seafood, vegetarian, and dessert crepes. Also prepared are classic French onion soup, escargots, and fresh-baked French bread. You may notice that there is (*mon dieu!*) no wine list, which has to do with the restaurant's proximity to San Felipe de Neri Catholic Church (liquor laws prohibit alcoholic beverages from being served near a church). ✉ *Old Town Patio del Norte, 400 C-2 San Felipe St. NW, Old Town,* ☎ *505/242–1251. MC, V. Closed Mon. No dinner Sun.*

## Southwestern

$$–$$$$  ✕ **La Placita.** It's touristy and not particularly authentic, but this restaurant housed in a historic hacienda on Old Town Plaza is nothing if not convenient. Chiles rellenos, enchiladas, tacos, and sopaipillas are all on the menu, which also includes American entrées. The building dates from 1706—the adobe walls are 3 ft thick in places. For years it housed Ambrosio Armijo's mercantile store, where ladies' lace gloves sold for 10¢ a pair and gents' linen underdrawers could be purchased for $1. The six dining rooms are also art galleries—patrons dine surrounded by outstanding examples of Native American and southwestern painting, most of which may be purchased. ✉ *208 San Felipe St. NW, Old Town,* ☎ *505/247–2204. AE, D, MC, V.*

**28**

## Albuquerque Dining

$   ✕ **Barelas Coffee House.** Barelas may look like a set in search of a script, but it's the real deal: diners come from all over the city to sup in this old-fashioned chile parlor in the Hispanic Historic Route 66 neighborhood south of downtown. You may notice looks of quiet contentment on the faces of the many dedicated chile eaters as they dive into their bowls of Barelas's potent red. ✉ *1502 4th St. SW, Barelas,* ☎ *505/843–7577. Reservations not accepted. D, MC, V. Closed Sun. No dinner.*

$   ✕ **Duran's Central Pharmacy.** This expanded Old Town lunch counter with a dozen tables and a tiny patio just might serve the best tortillas in town. A favorite of old-timers who know their way around a blue-corn enchilada, Duran's is an informal place whose patrons give their food the total attention it deserves. Dinner is served only until 6 PM on weekdays and not at all on weekends. ✉ *1815 Central Ave. NW, Old Town,* ☎ *505/247–4141. No credit cards. No dinner weekends.*

$   ✕ **Garcia's Kitchen.** Authentic Mexican cooking makes the Old Town location of this local chain a good stop for smooth red chile and daily lunch specials like flautas or chicken enchiladas. Breakfast is served all day at Garcia's, whose decor might best be described as early carnival toy. ✉ *1736 Central Ave. SW, Old Town,* ☎ *505/842–0273. Reservations not accepted. AE, D, DC, MC, V.*

$   ✕ **M&J's Sanitary Tortilla Factory.** Ravenous travelers rub elbows with downtown lawyers in this large, bright, nostalgic lunchroom. The hospitable Bea Montoya, who knows her regulars by name, serves the best *carne adovada* (red chile–marinated slow-baked pork) in town. ✉ *403 2nd St. SW, Downtown,* ☎ *505/242–4890. No credit cards. Closed Sun. No dinner.*

# North of I–40

## American

$–$$   ✕ **The Range Cafe and Bakery.** Desserts are supposed to come last, but it is hard to ignore them at this Albuquerque offshoot of the popular Bernalillo eatery. Homemade pies and bread are displayed right up front at the Range, which also serves up comfort foods such as meat loaf, roast turkey sandwiches, and garlic mashed potatoes. ✉ *4200 Wyoming NE, Northeast Heights,* ☎ *505/293–2633. AE, D, MC, V.*

## Barbecue

$–$$   ✕ **Rudy's Country Store & Bar-B-Que.** At Rudy's you dine chuck-wagon style and your order comes on waxed paper so you can dive right into the Texas-style barbecue. Pork ribs, brisket, turkey, and chicken are sold by the pound and served hot. Bread, white or wheat, is served by the slice, and side dishes such as baked beans and creamed corn are available. ✉ *2321 Carlisle NE, Northeast Heights,* ☎ *505/884–5000. MC, V.*

## Contemporary

$$$$   ✕ **Restaurant Jennifer James.** The menu changes seasonally in this tiny former house in the Northeast Heights. An exposed kitchen is the highlight of the simple place, which serves such delicacies as roast duck and grilled flatiron steak seasoned with inventive North African chiles and spices from India. ✉ *2813 San Mateo NE, Northeast Heights,* ☎ *505/884–3665. AE, D, MC, V. Closed Sun.–Mon. No lunch.*

$$   ✕ **Sophia's.** The menu at Sophia's, a cheery little North Valley hideaway, is all over the map—and that's a good thing. Instead of New Mexican food, chef Dennis Apodaca serves yummy sandwiches of grilled pastrami (straight from Chicago), grilled vegetables, sliced sirloin, or fried fish on chewy fresh-baked bread. Sophia's also serves up noodle bowls with your choice of three kinds of noodles: soba, udon,

or bean thread. Side dishes done well include a vinegary potato salad and crispy shoestring fries. ✉ *6313 4th NW, North Valley,* ☎ *505/345–3935. D, MC, V. No dinner.*

### Southwestern

$$ ✗ **Casa de Benavidez.** The fajitas at this local favorite with a romantic patio are among the best in town, and the chile is faultless. This perhaps explains why many patrons return despite prices that are higher than at similar establishments. Reservations are not accepted on weekends. ✉ *8032 4th St. NW, North Valley,* ☎ *505/898–3311. AE, D, DC, MC, V. No dinner Sun.*

$$ ✗ **El Pinto.** Expect a wait on weekends at this big indoor-outdoor restaurant in the shadow of the Sandia Mountains. The food is authentic New Mexican—some of the recipes at family-owned El Pinto have been passed down three generations—as is the ambience: mariachi bands stroll through the Spanish-style setting. Homemade tortillas accompany sopaipillas, chiles rellenos, tamales, enchiladas, and other dishes; the chiles, all of which are roasted on the premises, have a sometimes undeserved reputation for mildness. ✉ *10500 4th St. NW, North Valley,* ☎ *505/898–1771. AE, D, DC, MC, V.*

$$ ✗ **Garduño's of Mexico.** Tangy margaritas, elaborate Mexican decor, and generally fine cooking are the hallmarks of Garduño's, part of a successful local chain. Some diners find the food lightweight and inconsistent, but the middle-of-the-road formula appeals to many. When the place gets crowded, which is often, it has a real party feel. ✉ *8806 4th St. NW, North Valley,* ☎ *505/898–2772. AE, D, DC, MC, V.*

$$ ✗ **Sadie's Dining Room.** Chile lovers flock to this popular eatery for such traditional New Mexican dishes as chiles rellenos and blue corn enchiladas. The service is always prompt, though sometimes there is a wait for a table. While you are waiting, try one of the excellent margaritas. ✉ *6230 4th NW, North Valley,* ☎ *505/345–5339. AE, D, MC, V.*

### Steak

$$$$ ✗ **Paul's Monterey Inn.** The decor hasn't changed since the 1970s at Paul's Monterey Inn, but that doesn't bother the steak lovers who pack the place nightly. The dimly lit Northeast Heights hideout serves buttery steaks and seafood with excellent service from an attentive staff. ✉ *1000 Juan Tabo NE, Northeast Heights,* ☎ *505/294–1461. Reservations essential. AE, D, MC, V.*

## University, Nob Hill, and Vicinity

### American Casual

$ ✗ **Kelly's Restaurant and Brew Pub.** Go to Kelly's, located on Route 66 in the historic Jones Motor Co. building, to see and be seen by tourists and locals alike. A typical summer evening finds the patio along this lively stretch jammed with people and their pets. Kelly's serves typical bar food and brews its own beers from light to dark. ✉ *3222 Central Ave. SE, Nob Hill,* ☎ *505/262–2739. AE, D, MC, V.*

$ ✗ **66 Diner.** You can satisfy your craving for a 1950s-style malt here. Besides ice cream confections and a killer jukebox, this diner serves up the best chicken-fried steak and burgers in town. ✉ *1405 Central Ave. NE, Downtown,* ☎ *505/247–1421. AE, D, MC, V.*

### Barbecue

$$–$$$ ✗ **Quarters BBQ.** All you've ever dreamed of finding in a barbecue joint awaits you when you walk into this dark den. The three-decades-old Albuquerque institution serves tender, smoky falling-off-the-bone ribs and chicken, brisket, and sausage—it's hard to know where to dive in first. You'll need a fistful of napkins, that's for sure. The sauce is more tangy than sweet, and slow smoking with a secret recipe makes for the

winning combination. Top steaks and Alaskan king crab legs are also served without barbecue sauce. ⊠ *801 Yale Blvd. SE, University of New Mexico,* ☎ *505/843–7505. AE, MC, V. Closed Sun.*

### Greek

$$–$$$  ✕ **Yanni's Mediterranean Bar & Grill.** Something of a see-and-be-seen Nob Hill spot, Yanni's is a casual, airy place serving souvlaki and gyros dinners, marinated grilled lamb chops, grilled fresh halibut, and rotisserie Greek chicken seasoned with garlic and oregano. The popular vegetarian plate includes a surprisingly good meatless moussaka, tabouli, spanakopita, and stuffed grape leaves. ⊠ *3109 Central Ave. NE, Nob Hill,* ☎ *505/268–9250. AE, D, MC, V.*

### Italian

$$$  ✕ **Scalo Northern Italian Grill.** Nob Hill trendsetters gather at this in-
★   formal eatery to experience fine Italian wines and first-rate pasta, seafood, and meat entrées. Most of the multilevel dining area looks onto the lively bar and an open kitchen, where wonders like the ravioli with spinach and ricotta cheese and the fried baby calamari with a spicy marinara and lemon aioli are created. The homemade desserts are mighty fine. ⊠ *Nob Hill Shopping Center, 3500 Central Ave. SE, Nob Hill,* ☎ *505/255–8781. AE, DC, MC, V. No lunch Sun.*

$–$$  ✕ **Il Vicino.** The gourmet pizzas at Il Vicino are baked in a European-style wood-fired oven. If a suitable combination of the 25 possible toppings eludes you, try the Pizza Rustica, a buttery cornmeal crust topped with roasted garlic, artichokes, calamata olives, and capers. Good salads, pastas, and microbrewery beers are also served here. ⊠ *3403 Central Ave. NE, Nob Hill,* ☎ *505/266–7855. Reservations not accepted. MC, V.*

### Southwestern

$  ✕ **El Patio.** A university-area hangout, this sentimental favorite has consistently great food served in the funky patio. Go for the green-chile chicken enchiladas, the best in town, or any of the heart-healthy and vegetarian selections. But watch out for the fiery green chiles served at harvesttime. ⊠ *142 Harvard St. NE, University of New Mexico,* ☎ *505/268–4245. Reservations not accepted. MC, V.*

# LODGING

Albuquerque's hotels provide a comfortable mix of modern conveniences and Old West flavor. Homier are the many bed-and-breakfast inns, some downtown in restored Victorian-era homes, others north of town in Los Ranchos and Corrales.

| CATEGORY | COST* |
| --- | --- |
| $$$$ | over $170 |
| $$$ | $120–$170 |
| $$ | $70–$120 |
| $ | under $70 |

*All prices are for a standard double room, excluding 10.8% tax.*

## Downtown, Old Town, and Vicinity

$$$–$$$$  🏨 **Doubletree Hotel.** A two-story waterfall splashes down a marble backdrop in the lobby of this 15-story downtown hotel adjoining the Albuquerque Convention Center. The pastel rooms contain custom-made southwestern furniture and complementary art. The restaurant at the foot of the waterfall is called, appropriately, La Cascada (The Cascade). Breakfast, a lunch buffet, and dinner, from fresh seafood to southwestern specialties, are served. ⊠ *201 Marquette Ave. NW, 87102,* ☎ *505/247–*

3344; 888/223–4113 *central reservations;* FAX 505/247–7025. *295 rooms. Restaurant, room service, pool, gym, bar, parking (fee). AE, D, DC, MC, V.*

**$$–$$$$** 🛏 **Böttger-Koch Mansion.** Charles Böttger, a German immigrant, built his two-story mansion in 1912. Some of the rooms in the structure, which is on the National Register of Historic Places, have original pressed-tin ceilings and roomy four-poster beds. A grassy courtyard fronted by a patio provides a quiet escape from the Old Town crowds. Breakfast might consist of stuffed French toast or perhaps burritos smothered in green chile, which you can also enjoy in your room. ✉ *110 San Felipe St. NW, 87104,* ☎ *505/243–3639 or 800/758–3639,* WEB *www.Bottger.com. 8 rooms. Free parking. AE, MC, V. BP.*

**$$–$$$$** 🛏 **Brittania & W. E. Mauger Estate B&B.** Popular with businesspeople
★ because of its downtown location, this fine B&B is in an 1897 Queen Anne Victorian, the first home in Albuquerque to have electricity. Oval windows with beveled and "feather-pattern" glass, hardwood floors, a bright redbrick exterior, and an Old West front veranda are among the noteworthy design elements. Rooms now have data ports. ✉ *701 Roma Ave. NW, 87102,* ☎ *505/242–8755 or 800/719–9189,* FAX *505/842–8855,* WEB *www.maugerbb.com. 8 rooms. In-room data ports. AE, D, DC, MC, V. BP.*

**$$–$$$$** 🛏 **Hyatt Regency Albuquerque.** Adjacent to the Albuquerque Convention
★ Center, this hotel occupies one of two soaring, desert-color towers that figure prominently in the city's skyline. The gleaming Art Deco–style interior is refined and not overbearing. The contemporary rooms in mauve, burgundy, and tan combine southwestern style with all the expected Hyatt amenities. Rooms with data ports are available. The on-site McGrath's restaurant serves steaks, chops, chicken, and seafood. ✉ *330 Tijeras Ave. NW, 87102,* ☎ *505/842–1234 or 800/233–1234,* FAX *505/766–6710,* WEB *www.hyatt.com. 395 rooms, 14 suites. Restaurant, pool, health club, 2 bars, shops, business services. AE, D, DC, MC, V.*

**$$–$$$** 🛏 **The Hotel Blue.** An Art Deco–style hotel built in 1962 lies in the heart of downtown, less than a mile from Old Town. The Ramada welcomes business travelers with conveniences like in-room data ports, two-line phones, and free local calls. The white-walled rooms are decorated with Art Deco–style prints and white furnishings trimmed with black. Rooms have king, queen or double beds. ✉ *717 Central Ave. NW, 87102,* ☎ *505/924–2400 or 877/878–4868,* FAX *505/924–2465,* WEB *www.ramadainndowntownabq.com. 125 rooms, 10 suites. Restaurant, in-room data ports, pool, gym, bar, free parking. AE, D, DC, MC, V.*

**$$–$$$** 🛏 **La Posada de Albuquerque.** Opened in 1939 by New Mexico na-
★ tive Conrad Hilton (who honeymooned here with bride Zsa Zsa Gabor), this 10-story hotel is listed on the National Register of Historic Places. The tiled lobby fountain, circular balcony, massive vigas, and Native American war-dance murals lend the place an easy southwestern charm. Ranging from small to spacious, the rooms have southwestern and Native American accents that include Hopi pottery and R. C. Gorman prints. Guests have health-club privileges at a nearby downtown health club. ✉ *125 2nd St. NW, 87102,* ☎ *505/242–9090 or 800/777–5732,* FAX *505/242–8664. 114 rooms, 4 suites. Restaurant, 2 bars, parking (fee). AE, D, DC, MC, V.*

**$$–$$$** 🛏 **Sheraton Old Town.** This modern 11-story hotel sits gracefully amid Old Town's ancient structures. A dramatic renovation has expanded the lobby and added a 14,000-square-ft ballroom. The large rooms have desert-color appointments, hand-wrought furnishings, and big bathrooms with vanities. Cristobal's is the fine dining restaurant in the hotel, featuring steaks and seafood. Cafe Plazuelas offers casual American and New Mexican food. ✉ *800 Rio Grande Blvd. NW, 87104,* ☎ *505/*

## Albuquerque Lodging

*843–6300 or 800/237–2133,* FAX *505/842–8426,* WEB *www.flalsh.net/ sheraton. 187 rooms, 22 suites. 2 restaurants, pool, hot tub, bar. AE, D, DC, MC, V.*

$$ ⊞ **Best Western Rio Grande Inn.** This member of Best Western is one of the most regionally and authentically decorated in the state. The heavy handcrafted wood furniture, tin sconces, and artwork in the rooms come from local suppliers and artisans, whose addresses are listed in a corner of the lobby. That locals are familiar with the Albuquerque Grill is a good indicator of the restaurant's value. The hotel is conveniently just off I–40 and within an easy walk of Old Town. ✉ *1015 Rio Grande Blvd. NW, 87104,* ☎ *505/843–9500 or 800/959–4726,* FAX *505/ 843–9238,* WEB *www.riograndeinn.com. 174 rooms. Restaurant, pool, outdoor hot tub, meeting room, free parking. AE, D, DC, MC, V.*

$–$$ ⊞ **Jazz Inn Bed & Breakfast.** This creatively restored 100-year-old home in the historic Huning Highland District, just off Old Route 66, is convenient to both downtown and the university. Nowhere will you find more interesting or hospitable hosts than innkeepers Sophia and Nicholas Peron. Artists and community activists, they are up on the town's music and art scene. Rooms are themed after jazz musicians like Bessie Smith and Duke Ellington and are simple, elegant, and comfortable, with decor that mixes and matches the antique with the utterly contemporary. Music lovers can browse through the music library's 4,000 CDs, tapes, and records. There's a grand piano for those who like to practice. The inn is completely handicapped accessible. Smoking is not permitted indoors. ✉ *111 Walter NE, 87102,* ☎ *505/242– 1530 or 888/529–9466,* FAX *505/224–9083,* WEB *www.jazzinn.com. 5 rooms, 2 suites. Piano. AE, D, DC, MC, V. BP.*

$–$$ ⊞ **Old Town B&B.** Part of this structure was built by local architect Leon Watson, a pioneer in the use of adobe in Pueblo Revival–style home design. The bright downstairs suite—with a viga and latilla ceiling, a kiva fireplace, and Mexican leather furniture—is stylishly southwestern without overkill. There is a bathroom with a skylight and hot tub, shared with the owner only, and a sitting room and library. The second-story room, with private bath, has views of the Sandias. ✉ *707 17th St. NW, 87104,* ☎ *505/764–9144 or 888/900–9144,* WEB *www.inn-new-mexico. com. 1 room, 1 suite with shared bath. No credit cards. BP.*

## East Side Near I–40

$$–$$$ ⊞ **Albuquerque Hilton.** A blend of contemporary sophistication and southwestern charm, the Hilton has Native American rugs, western and Native American art, arched doorways, and Santa Fe–style wooden furniture. The Ranchers Club restaurant is elegant, with a roaring fireplace. In the grill room, fish and meats are cooked over aromatic woods like piñon or mesquite. The hotel's other restaurant, Casa Chaco, serves coffee-shop breakfast and lunch fare but is transformed at night, when nouvelle southwestern cuisine is served by candlelight on crisp linen with sparkling crystal. ✉ *1901 University Blvd. NE, 87102,* ☎ *505/884–2500 or 800/274–6835,* FAX *505/889–9118,* WEB *www.hilton.com. 263 rooms, 6 suites. 2 restaurants, indoor-outdoor pool, gym, sauna, 2 bars; no-smoking rooms. AE, D, DC, MC, V.*

$–$$$ ⊞ **Albuquerque Marriott.** This 17-story luxury property takes care of the executive traveler with two concierge floors but doesn't forget the vacationer. Katsina dolls, Native American pottery, and other regional artworks decorate the elegant public areas. The rooms are traditional American, with walk-in closets, armoires, and crystal lamps, but have southwestern touches. ✉ *2101 Louisiana Blvd. NE, 87110,* ☎ *505/ 881–6800 or 800/334–2086,* FAX *505/888–2982. 411 rooms, 6 suites.*

*Restaurant, indoor-outdoor pool, gym, sauna, bar, concierge floor, business services. AE, D, DC, MC, V.*

$$ ⊞ **Barcelona Suites Uptown.** With tile floors and wrought-iron railings, this colorful three-story hotel has the feel of Old Mexico, but its southwestern-tinged furnishings are contemporary. Each suite has a galley kitchen with a wet bar and microwave. Three suites have hot tubs. ⊠ *900 Louisiana Blvd. NE, off I–40, 87110,* ☎ *505/255–5566 or 877/ 227–7848,* FAX *505/266–6644. 164 suites. Some in-room hot tubs, kitchenettes, microwaves, 2 pools, sauna. AE, D, DC, MC, V. BP.*

$ ⊞ **Midtown Econo Lodge Inn.** There's nothing special about this locally owned chain property 5 mi east of Old Town, but it is inexpensive and local calls are free, as is the cable TV. The clean rooms contain coffeemakers and queen- or king-size beds. ⊠ *2412 Carlisle Ave. NE, at I–40, 87110,* ☎ *505/880–0080; 800/553–2666 central reservations;* FAX *505/880–0053. 38 rooms, 1 suite. AE, D, DC, MC, V.*

## North Valley and Corrales

$$ ⊞ **Casita Chamisa.** In the pastoral cottonwood-shaded North Valley ★ village of Los Ranchos, 15 mi north of Old Town, this B&B consists of a handsome room in the main adobe-style house and a separate two-bedroom house with a fireplace, a kitchenette, and a greenhouse. The furnishings are a comfortable blend of local, southwestern, and Mexican materials. Casita Chamisa is on an archaeological site, with a prehistoric Native American ruin still visible. Breakfast is vegetarian-friendly: juices, coffee, breads, pancakes, coffee cake, waffles, and perhaps fruit picked from the 14 fruit trees on the grounds. The sourdough bread is made with a starter that's 120 years old. ⊠ *850 Chamisal Rd. NW, North Valley 87107,* ☎ *505/897–4644,* WEB *www.casitachamisa.com. 1 room, 1 house. Indoor pools, hot tub. AE, MC, V. BP.*

$$ ⊞ **Yours Truly.** The views are awesome from this hillside inn run by the gracious Pat and James Montgomery. Glass blocks set into the walls cast subtle light. The modern adobe rooms are not large, but they're comfortable, especially the one with a king-size bed nestled in a *banco* (adobe bench). Special touches include plush robes, afternoon wine and snacks, and fireplaces in all rooms. Pat pulls out all the stops at breakfast, which might include praline French toast or creamed gravy with sausage and green chile on biscuits. The inn is north of Albuquerque in Corrales. ⊠ *160 Paseo de Corrales [Box 2263, Corrales 87048],* ☎ *505/898–7027 or 800/942–7890,* FAX *505/898–9022,* WEB *www. yourstrulybb.com. 4 rooms. AE, MC, V. BP.*

$–$$ ⊞ **Inn at Paradise.** Near the first tee of the lush Paradise Hills Golf Club, this swank B&B resort atop the West Mesa is a golfer's dream: the 6,895 yards of bluegrass fairways and bent-grass greens challenge players of all levels. Works by local artists and craftspeople decorate the large rooms; the two suites have fireplaces. Golf packages are available. ⊠ *10035 Country Club La. NW, Albuquerque 87114,* ☎ *505/898–6161 or 800/ 938–6161,* FAX *505/890–1090,* WEB *www.innatparadise.com. 16 rooms, 2 suites, 1 apartment. Spa. AE, D, MC, V. CP.*

## Sandia Mountain Foothills

$$ ⊞ **Elaine's, A Bed and Breakfast.** This antiques-filled three-story log ★ home is set in the evergreen folds of the Sandia Mountain foothills. Four acres of wooded grounds beckon outside the back door. The top two floors have rooms with balconies and big picture windows that bring the lush mountain views indoors. The third-floor room also has cathedral ceilings and a brass bed. Breakfast, served in a plant-filled room or outside on a patio with a fountain, often includes fresh fruit,

pancakes, or waffles with sausage. ⊠ *Snowline Estate, 72 Snowline Rd. [Box 444, Cedar Crest 87008],* ☎ *505/281–2467 or 800/821–3092,* WEB *www.elainesbnb.com. 5 rooms. Hot tub. AE, D, MC, V. BP.*

# Airport Hotels

**$$$–$$$$**
★
🏨 **Wyndham Albuquerque Hotel.** Only 350 yards from the airport, this 15-story hotel provides speedy access to your flight, day or night. Rooms have Southwest accents, large work desks, data ports, and coffeemakers. ⊠ *2910 Yale Blvd. SE, 87106,* ☎ *505/843–7000 or 800/227–1117,* FAX *505/843–6307,* WEB *www.wynatabq.com. 276 rooms, 2 suites. Restaurant, in-room data ports, tennis court, pool, gym, lobby lounge, airport shuttle. AE, D, DC, MC, V.*

**$$**
🏨 **Comfort Inn.** The rooms here have uninspired but acceptable decor and furnishings. A full-service restaurant and coffee shop is adjacent to the hotel. The airport is 1 mi away. ⊠ *2300 Yale Blvd. SE, 87106,* ☎ *505/243–2244 or 800/228–5150,* FAX *505/247–2925,* WEB *www.comfortinn.com. 118 rooms. Pool, hot tub, airport shuttle. AE, D, DC, MC, V.*

**$–$$**
🏨 **Courtyard by Marriott.** Take advantage of corporate rates and amenities—available to everyone—at this haven for business travelers ½ mi north of the airport. Rooms, done in mauve and teal with Southwest-inspired paintings, have jacks for portable fax machines and modems, large desks, and long telephone cords that actually reach the work area. ⊠ *1920 Yale Blvd. SE, 87106,* ☎ *505/843–6600 or 800/321–2211,* FAX *505/843–8740. 136 rooms, 14 suites. Restaurant, in-room data ports, indoor pool, gym, lobby lounge, business services, airport shuttle. AE, D, DC, MC, V.*

**$–$$**
🏨 **Radisson Inn Albuquerque Airport.** A mere ¼ mi from the airport, this hotel has arched balconies, tan desert colors, a year-round courtyard pool, and indoor and seasonal outdoor dining. Standard rooms are comfortable; VIP executive rooms are larger and overlook the pool. Pets are welcome in some rooms. Complimentary car service is available. ⊠ *1901 University Blvd. SE, 87106,* ☎ *505/247–0512 or 800/333–3333,* FAX *505/843–7148,* WEB *www.radisson.com. 148 rooms. Restaurant, pool, gym, hot tub, bar, airport shuttle; no-smoking rooms. AE, D, DC, MC, V.*

# Camping

🛖 **Albuquerque Central KOA.** At town's edge, off Historic Route 66 in the foothills of the Sandia Mountains, this well-equipped campground has expansive views and a dog run, but only a few trees. Reservations are essential in October. ⊠ *12400 Skyline NE, Exit 166 off I–40, Northeast Heights,* ☎ *505/296–2729 or 800/562–7781,* FAX *505/296–3354. Flush toilets, full and partial hook-ups, dump station, drinking water, laundry facilities, showers, fire grates, grills, picnic tables, electricity, public telephone, general store, propane station, playground, pool. 206 sites, 100 with full hook-up.* 🏕 *$27–$38; cabins $43–$53. AE, D, MC, V.*

🛖 **Turquoise Trail Campground and RV Park.** Pine and cedar trees dot this 14-acre park in the Sandias, which has hiking trails with access to the Cibola National Forest. A museum on the premises—open to guests and nonguests for a $2.50 entrance fee—chronicles archaeological finds and contains artifacts dating from the Ice Age to the Battle of Wounded Knee. Campsite rates are calculated per person; you will need reservations in October. ⊠ *22 Calvary Rd., 5 mi north of I–40's Exit 175 in Cedar Crest, East Mountains,* ☎ *505/281–2005. Flush toilets, full and partial hook-ups, dump station, drinking water, laundry fa-*

*cilities, showers, fire grates, fire pit, grills, picnic tables, electricity, public phone, general store, ranger station nearby, propane and gas station nearby, playground. 57 sites, 45 with full hook-ups. ⊠ $11–$19; cabins $25–$50. D, MC, V.*

# NIGHTLIFE AND THE ARTS

The entertainment options in Albuquerque include theater, dance, classical and rock concerts, and film screenings. If you like to two-step to country-and-western tunes, you've come to the right place. Note that bars and lounges close by 2 AM. To find out what's going on in town, check the Friday and Sunday editions of the *Albuquerque Journal,* the Friday edition of the *Albuquerque Tribune,* or the *Weekly Alibi.* **Ticketmaster** has an event information line (☎ 505/842–5387; 505/883–7800 to purchase tickets). Try **tickets.com** (☎ 505/851–5050 or 800/905–3315 to buy tickets).

## Nightlife

### Bars and Lounges

Many of downtown Albuquerque's nightclubs, bars, pool halls, late-night dining establishments, and performance spaces are within a 10-minute walk of one another, on Central and Gold avenues between 2nd and 7th streets.

**Assets Grille & Brewing Company** (⊠ 2910 Montgomery NE, Northeast Heights, ☎ 505/881–2140) is a stylish place with 12 home-brewed beers on tap. Burgers and wood-fire pizzas are served.

**Brewster's Pub** (⊠ 312 Central Ave. SW, Downtown, ☎ 505/247–2533) is a nice neighborhood bar on busy Central Avenue that often features live alternative rock bands.

**Club Rhythm and Blues** (⊠ 3523 Central Ave. NE, Nob Hill, ☎ 505/256–0849) is open Tuesday–Saturday for live R&B.

**Martini Grill** (⊠ 4200 Central Ave. SE, Nob Hill, ☎ 505/242–4333) provides a sophisticated setting for a superlative piano bar.

**O'Neill's Pub** (⊠ 3211 Central Ave. NE, Nob Hill, ☎ 505/256–0564) serves good Mexican and American comfort food and presents jazz, bebop, and other musicians in a cheery neighborhood bar near the University of New Mexico.

**Sauce/Liquid Lounge** (⊠ 405 Central Ave. SW, Downtown, ☎ 505/242–5839) is really two bars that share a space on Central. Dark and inviting with great specialty cocktails, it also offers late-night food service.

### Live Music

The **Isleta Casino and Resort** (⊠ 1100 Broadway SE, South of Albuquerque off I–25, ☎ 505/724–3800) features oldies like Tom Jones and country-and-western acts such as Vince Gill. It's on the Isleta Indian Reservation south of Albuquerque.

The 12,000-seat **Journal Pavilion** (⊠ 5601 University Blvd. SE, Mesa del Sol, ☎ 505/452–5100 or 505/246–8742) amphitheater attracts big-name acts such as Britney Spears, Neil Young, and the Dave Matthews Band.

**Outpost Performance Space** (⊠ 210 Yale Blvd. SE, University of New Mexico, ☎ 505/268–0044) programs an eclectic slate, from local nuevo-folk to techno, jazz, and traveling East Indian ethnic.

The **Sandia Casino Amphitheatre** (✉ I–25 and Tramway NE, Northeast Heights, ☎ 505/796–7500) is a pleasant spot just outside the city to see musical acts and such comedians as Bill Cosby.

## Comedy Clubs

**Laff's Comedy Caffé** (✉ 6001 San Mateo NE, Northeast Heights, ☎ 505/296–5653) serves up the live laughs (and dinner) Wednesday–Sunday.

# The Arts

## Festivals

Every April, Albuquerque celebrates its 1706 founding by Spanish conquistadores on **Founder's Day** (✉ Tiguex Park, 17th and Mountain NW, Old Town, ☎ 505/768–3555). The festivities include a parade, an arts festival, and a two-day carnival.

At the **New Mexico Arts and Crafts Fair** (✉ New Mexico State Fairgrounds, Central Ave. and Louisiana Blvd., Northeast Heights, ☎ 505/884–9043), more than 200 Hispanic, Native American, and other North American artists come together on the last weekend in June to display handcrafted items. Food and entertainment are also part of the festival.

A series of ethnic-theme festivals called **Summerfest** (✉ Civic Plaza, 3rd and Marquette NW, ☎ 505/768–3555) bring art, music, and food to most Saturday nights from late June to mid-August. There's lots for little ones to do as well.

Just in time for the Christmas rush, the annual **Weems Artfest** (✉ New Mexico State Fairgrounds, Central and Louisiana NE, ☎ 505/293–6133) in early November is packed with art and handmade gifts. You might even see a celebrity or two—Bo Derek and Sophia Loren have exhibited and appeared in years past.

## Music

The **New Mexico Symphony Orchestra** (☎ 505/881–8999 or 800/251–6676) plays pops, Beethoven, and, at Christmas, Handel's *Messiah*. Some performances are at 2,000-seat Popejoy Hall; others are under the stars at the Rio Grande Zoo Bandshell.

**Popejoy Hall** (✉ University of New Mexico Arts Center, Central and Stanford SE, ☎ 505/277–4569 or 800/905–3315) presents concerts, from rock and pop to classical.

## Opera

**Musical Theater Southwest** (☎ 505/262–9301) is one of the largest community-based producers of musical theater in the country. Performances take place at Popejoy Hall and at the **Hiland Theater** (✉ 4804 Central Ave. SE, University of New Mexico, ☎ 505/265–9119).

## Theater

**Albuquerque Little Theater** (✉ 224 San Pasquale Ave. SW, Old Town, ☎ 505/242–4750) is a nonprofit community troupe. Its staff of professionals teams up with local volunteer talent to produce comedies, dramas, musicals, and mysteries. The company theater, across the street from Old Town, was built in 1936 and designed by John Gaw Meem. It contains an art gallery, a large lobby, and a cocktail lounge.

**KiMo Theater** (✉ 423 Central Ave. NW, Downtown, ☎ 505/764–1700), a 1927 Pueblo Deco movie palace, is one of the best places in town to see anything. Jazz, dance—everything from traveling road shows to local song-and-dance acts—might turn up here. Albuquerque native Vivian Vance of *I Love Lucy* fame once performed on the stage.

La Compania de Teatro de Albuquerque (☎ 505/242–7929), a bilingual theater company based at the KiMo Theater, performs classic and contemporary plays in English and Spanish during April, October, and December. The company also appears at the South Broadway Cultural Center.

**Rodey Theater** (✉ University of New Mexico Arts Center, Central and Stanford SE, ☎ 505/925–LOBO or 800/905–3315) stages student and professional plays and dance performances throughout the year, including the acclaimed annual Summerfest Festival of New Plays during July and the June Flamenco Festival.

# OUTDOOR ACTIVITIES AND SPORTS

Albuquerque is blessed with an exceptional setting for outdoor sports, backed by a favorable, if unpredictable, climate. Usually 10°F warmer than Santa Fe's, Albuquerque's winter days are often mild enough for most outdoor activities. The Sandias tempt you with challenging mountain adventures; the Rio Grande and its thick forest, the Bosque, provide settings for additional wilderness pursuits.

## Participant Sports

The **Albuquerque Cultural and Recreation Services Department** (✉ 400 Marquette Ave. NW, Downtown, ☎ 505/857–8669) maintains a diversified network of cultural and recreational programs. Among the city's assets are more than 20,000 acres of open space, four golf courses, 200 parks, 68 paved tracks for biking and jogging, as well as swimming pools, tennis courts, ball fields, playgrounds, and a shooting range.

### Ballooning
The Albuquerque International Balloon Fiesta is a town highlight, but if you'd like to give ballooning a try, contact one of the many outfitters that run trips; a ride will set you back about $150. **Rainbow Ryders** (✉ 11520 San Bernadino NE, Northeast Heights, ☎ 505/293–0000 or 800/725–2477). **World Balloon Corporation** (✉ 4800 Eubank Blvd. NE, Northeast Heights, ☎ 505/293–6800 or 800/351–9588).

### Bicycling
Albuquerque has miles of bike lanes and trails crisscrossing and skirting the city. Not only is Albuquerque's Parks and Recreation Department aware of bikers' needs, but bike riding is heavily promoted as a means of cutting down on traffic congestion and pollution. The elaborately detailed **Metropolitan Albuquerque Bicycle Map** can be obtained free of charge by calling 505/768–3550. For information about mountain biking in national forest land around Albuquerque call the **Sandia Ranger Station** (☎ 505/281–3304).

Bikes can be rented at several locations, including **Rio Mountainsport** (✉ 1210 Rio Grande Blvd. NW, Old Town, ☎ 505/766–9970), which is convenient to Old Town, the Rio Grande Nature Center, and the Paseo de Bosque trail.

### Bird-Watching
The Rio Grande valley, one of the continent's major flyways, attracts many migratory bird species. For details about bird-watching events and outings, contact the local chapter of the **Sierra Club** (✉ 207 San Pedro NE, Northeast Heights, ☎ 505/243–7767).

Good bird-viewing locales include the **Rio Grande Nature Center** (✉ 2901 Candelaria Rd. NW, North Valley, ☎ 505/344–7240). **Elena**

**Gallegos/Albert Simms Park** (⊠ 1700 Tramway Loop NE, Northeast Heights, ☎ 505/857–8334 or 505/873–6620) is a 640-acre reserve adjoining the Sandia Mountain Wilderness Area.

## Golf

The Albuquerque Cultural and Recreation Services Department operates four public golf courses. The two best ones are listed below. All the courses are open from sunup to sundown; special discount rates go into effect for sundown play. Each course has a clubhouse and pro shop, where clubs and other equipment can be rented. Weekday play is on a first-come, first-served basis, but reservations are taken for weekend use. The city's **Golf Management Office** (⊠ 6401 Osuna Rd. NE, Northeast Heights, ☎ 505/888–8115) can provide more information.

**Arroyo del Oso** (⊠ 7001 Osuna Rd. NE, Northeast Heights, ☎ 505/ 884–7505) has an 18-hole, par-72 course. The greens fee is $15; an optional cart costs $10. There's also a 9-hole, par-36 course here.

The 18-hole, par-71 **Los Altos Golf Course** (⊠ 9717 Copper Ave. NE, Northeast Heights, ☎ 505/298–1897), one of the Southwest's most popular facilities, has a greens fee of $15; an optional cart costs $13. The complex includes a driving range, grass tees, and a restaurant serving mainly New Mexican food.

Opened in 2000, the 18-hole, par-72 **Paa-Ko Golf Course** (⊠ Sandia Park, 1 Club House Dr., East Mountains, ☎ 505/281–6000) was voted "The Best Place to Play Golf in New Mexico" by *Golf Digest*. Golfers enjoy vistas of the mesas and the Sandia Mountains from one of five tee placements.

The University of New Mexico has two public golf courses. Both are open daily and have full-service pro shops, instruction, and snack bars. Greens fees range from $20 to $42, with higher fees, in the $70 range, for out-of-staters; optional carts cost $20. **UNM North** (⊠ 2201 Tucker Rd. NE, between Stanford Ave. and University Blvd., University of New Mexico, ☎ 505/277–4146) is a first-class 9-hole, par-36 course on campus. **UNM South** (⊠ Rio Bravo Blvd. east of I–25, Southeast Heights, ☎ 505/277–4546) has an 18-hole, par-72 championship course and a beginners' 3-hole regulation course.

## Health Clubs

A day pass ($10) at the state-of-the-art **4th Street Fitness** (⊠ 1100 4th St. NW, North Valley, ☎ 505/247–1947) entitles you to a one-on-one boxing session. Should the pummeling become too intense, you can head over to the on-site masseur for an additional fee.

**A. C. Fitness** (⊠ 5001 Montgomery Blvd. NE, Suite 147, Northeast Heights, ☎ 505/881–8500) has free weights, a cardiovascular deck, and aerobics classes. Nonmembers pay $10 per day.

**Liberty Gym** (⊠ 2401 Jefferson St. NE, Northeast Heights, ☎ 505/884– 8012) has weight-training equipment, free weights, and a cardiovascular area. The walk-in fee is $5.

## Jogging

The Albuquerque Cultural and Recreation Services Department maintains a network of Designated Recreational Trails that joggers share with bicyclists.

## Skiing

**Sandia Peak Ski Area** (⊠ N.M. 536, ☎ 505/242–9133) contains novice, intermediate, and expert downhill trails. Snowboarding is welcome on all trails, and there is cross-country terrain as well, whenever snow is available.

## Swimming

The City of Albuquerque has pools for lap and recreational swimming; the fee is $2. There are four city-run indoor pools: **Highland** (✉ 400 Jackson St. SE, Southeast Heights, ☎ 505/256–2096), **Los Altos** (✉ 10100 Lomas Blvd. NE, Northeast Heights, ☎ 505/291–6290), **Sandia** (✉ 7801 Candelaria Rd. NE, Northeast Heights, ☎ 505/291–6279), and **Valley** (✉ 1505 Candelaria Rd. NW, North Valley, ☎ 505/761–4086).

The city's outdoor pools are open from Memorial Day to mid-August: **Wilson** (✉ 6000 Anderson Ave. SE, Southeast Heights, ☎ 505/256–2095) and **Montgomery** (✉ 5301 Palo Duro NE, Northeast Heights, ☎ 505/888–8123).

**West Mesa Aquatic Center** (✉ 6705 Fortuna NW, West Side, ☎ 505/836–8718) is a public indoor-outdoor pool and fun aquatics park that's open year-round, with winding tubes and slides that provide a big splash for kids of all ages. Hours vary by season, so it is best to call ahead. Admission is 50¢ for children under age 5 and spectators, $1 for senior citizens, $2 for ages 6–12, $2.50 for teens, and $3 for adults.

## Tennis

Albuquerque's public parks contain nearly 140 courts, some of which are lighted for night play (until 10 PM). For information call the Albuquerque Cultural and Recreation Services Department. In addition, the city operates three tennis complexes.

**Albuquerque Tennis Complex** (✉ 1903 Ave. Cesar Chavez SE, Southeast Heights, ☎ 505/848–1381) consists of 16 Laykold tennis courts and two racquetball-handball courts, which may be reserved by phone or in person; reservations are taken two days ahead at 10 AM. It costs $2.10 per hour to play at the complex, which is open 8 AM –dusk weekdays.

**Jerry Cline Tennis Complex** (✉ Louisiana Blvd. at Constitution Ave., Northeast Heights, ☎ 505/256–2032) has 12 Laykold courts; 3 are lighted. There is no charge, and no reservations are needed.

**Sierra Vista Tennis Complex** (✉ 5001 Montano Rd. NW, West Side, ☎ 505/897–8819) has 10 tennis courts (2 Omni courts), 2 platform tennis courts, and an outdoor pool. Court reservations are taken two days ahead at 10 AM. It costs $2.10 per hour to play at the complex, which is open weekdays 8–8 and weekends 8–5.

For a fee, you can play tennis at a number of private clubs: **Highpoint Sports & Wellness Club** (✉ 4300 Landau Dr. NE, Northeast Heights, ☎ 505/293–5820), **Tanoan Country Club** (✉ 10801 Academy Rd. NE, Northeast Heights, ☎ 505/822–0455), and **Tennis Club of Albuquerque** (✉ 2901 Indian School Rd. NE, Northeast Heights, ☎ 505/262–1691).

# Spectator Sports

## Ballooning

Mention hot-air ballooning to an enthusiast, and Albuquerque automatically comes to mind. The city's high altitude, mild climate, and steady but manageable winds are ideal for ballooning. But it's the "Albuquerque Box," created by the city's location against the Sandia Mountains, that makes this a great place to fly.

Albuquerque's long history of ballooning dates from 1882, when Professor Park A. Van Tassel, a saloon keeper, ascended in a balloon at the

Territorial Fair. Albuquerque has become the hot-air capital of the world, partly because of the nine-day **Albuquerque International Balloon Fiesta** (⊠ 4401 Alameda NE, North Valley, ☎ 505/821–1000, WEB www.balloonfiesta.com), which began in 1972. The event, held during the first two weeks of October, is the largest hot-air-balloon gathering in the world. At the Special Shapes Rodeo, hundreds of unusual balloons, including depictions of the old lady who lived in the shoe, the pink pig, and dozens of other fanciful characters from fairy tales and popular culture, soar high above the crowds, which number more than 1 million. There are night flights, obstacle races, and many other surprising balloon events. The entrance fee to the grounds is $4. Book your hotel far in advance if you plan to attend, and note that hotel rates also rise during the fiesta. The Anderson Abruzzo International Balloon Museum is scheduled to open at Balloon Fiesta Park in 2003 and should include exhibits, a Ballooning Hall of Fame, and a ride simulator.

### Baseball
After the beloved AAA Albuquerque Dukes left town in 2000 for better digs in Portland, Oregon, Albuquerqueans voted to renovate the **former Dukes stadium** (⊠ University Ave. at Ave. Cesar Chavez, University of New Mexico, ☎ 505/843–4110) to attract a new Pacific Coast League baseball team. The as-yet-unnamed team is to begin play in spring 2003.

### Basketball
It's hard to beat the excitement of a home basketball game at the **University of New Mexico** (⊠ University Ave. at Ave. Cesar Chavez, University of New Mexico, ☎ 505/925–5627 or 800/905–3315), when 18,000 rabid fans crowd into the school's arena, "the Pit," from November to March.

### Football
The New Mexico Lobos of the **University of New Mexico** (☎ 505/925–5627 or 800/905–3315) play at 30,000-seat University Stadium in the fall.

### Hockey
The **New Mexico Scorpions** (☎ 505/881–7825) play in the Western Professional Hockey League. The home ice of the Scorps is at **Tingley Coliseum** (⊠ New Mexico State Fairgrounds, Central Ave. and Louisiana Blvd., Northeast Heights, ☎ 505/881–7825).

# SHOPPING

As is the case in other large western cities, Albuquerque's main shopping areas and malls are scattered throughout the community. Most stores are open weekdays 10–9, Saturday 10–6, and Sunday noon–6.

## Shopping Neighborhoods and Malls

**Coronado Center** (⊠ Louisiana Blvd. NE at Menaul Blvd. NE, Northeast Heights, ☎ 505/881–4600) has Macy's, JCPenney, Mervyn's, and Sears department stores, along with 160 specialty shops and a food court.

**Cottonwood Mall** (⊠ Coors Blvd. at Coors Bypass, West Side, ☎ 505/899–7467), Albuquerque's largest mall, contains such department stores as Dillard's and JCPenney. Williams-Sonoma is among the 136 specialty shops. There's a food court and a multiplex cinema.

Take in the neighborhood of **Nob Hill** (⊠ Central Ave. from Girard Blvd. to Washington St.) during the day and you will be struck by the colorful storefronts and playful signs. At night, neon-lit boutiques, galleries, and performing-arts spaces encourage foot traffic. This decidedly non-southwestern part of Albuquerque is packed full of intriguing shops and watering holes. Tucked into the **Nob Hill Business Center** (⊠ 3500 Central Ave. SE) are the funky furniture store El Paso Imports, La Montanita Natural Foods Co-op, the Aveda concept Mark Pardo Salon and Day Spa, and the quirky card and gift store Beeps. Stop for a drink at Gecko's Gallery and Grill or Il Bar, a tiny part of the fine Italian restaurant Scalo, which serves drinks and desserts. South of Central Avenue on Carlisle you'll find cool stores wrapped around the block, and along Silver are even more quirky stores to browse through.

**Old Town** (⊠ Central Ave. and Rio Grande Blvd.) has the city's largest concentration of one-of-a-kind retail shops, selling clothing, home accessories, and Mexican imports. Also here are a slew of galleries, many exhibiting Native American art.

**Winrock Center** (⊠ Louisiana Blvd. off I–40, Northeast Heights, ☎ 505/888–3038) has Dillard's and Bed, Bath and Beyond department stores, plus Oshman's SuperSports USA and 17 restaurants, from fast food to fancy fare.

## Art Galleries

**Amapola Gallery** (⊠ Old Town, 106 Romero NW, Old Town, ☎ 505/242–4311), west of the plaza near Rio Grande Boulevard, is one of the largest co-op galleries in New Mexico. It has a brick courtyard and an indoor space, both brimming with pottery, paintings, textiles, carvings, baskets, jewelry, and other items.

**Andrew Nagen** (⊠ 222 Andrews La., Corrales, ☎ 505/898–5285) has been buying, selling, and appraising antique Navajo, Mexican, Rio Grande, and Pueblo textiles since 1976. His shop is open by appointment only.

**Concetta D. Gallery** (⊠ First Plaza Galeria, 20 1st Plaza NW, Suite 29, Downtown, ☎ 505/243–5066) carries works by early Santa Fe and Taos artists, as well as contemporary regional artists such as Rod Goebel, Walter Chapman, Lincoln Fox, Don Brackett, Clifford Fragua, Ramon Kelley, Joe Horton, Carol McIlroy, Morris Ripple, and Julian Roble.

**DSG** (⊠ 3011 Monte Vista Blvd. NE, Nob Hill, ☎ 505/266–7751 or 800/474–7751), owned by John Cacciatore, handles works by leading regional artists, including Frank McCulloch, Carol Hoy, Leo Neufeld, John Rise, Jane Abrams, Nancy Kozikowski, and Angus MacPherson.

**516 Magnifico Art Space** (⊠ 516 Central Ave. SW, Downtown, ☎ 505/242–8244) exhibits all styles of art, from traditional to contemporary, in all media, with a primary focus on the work of New Mexico artists.

**Mariposa Gallery** (⊠ 3500 Central Ave. SE, Nob Hill, ☎ 505/268–6828) sells contemporary fine crafts, including jewelry, sculptural glass, works in mixed media and clay, and fiber arts. The changing exhibits focus on upcoming artists. The display of Día de los Muertos (Day of the Dead) objects in October is always worth a look. Mariposa Gallery now has two additional locations.

**Richard Levy Gallery** (⊠ 514 Central Ave. SW, Downtown, ☎ 505/766–9888) carries works on paper (including photography) and small sculpture by major regional artists, including Clinton Adams, Thomas Barrow, Ed Haddaway, Frederick Hammersley, Patrick Nagatani, Ed Ruscha, and Richard Tuttle.

**Weems Gallery** (✉ 2801-M Eubank Blvd. NE, Northeast Heights, ☎ 505/293–6133; 303 Romero St. NW, Old Town, ☎ 505/764–0302) has paintings, pottery, sculpture, jewelry, weaving, stained glass, and original-design clothes.

# Specialty Stores

## Antiques

**Antique Specialty Mall** (✉ 4516 Central Ave. SE, Nob Hill, ☎ 505/268–8080) is a center for collectibles and antiques. The emphasis is on memorabilia from the early 1880s to the 1950s. (When the set designers for the television miniseries *Lonesome Dove* needed props, they came here.) Items for sale include Art Deco and Art Nouveau objects, Depression-era glass, Native American goods, quilts and linens, vintage clothes, and western memorabilia.

**Cowboys & Indians** (✉ 4000 Central Ave. SE, Nob Hill, ☎ 505/255–4054) carries Native American and cowboy art and artifacts.

## Books

**Page One** (✉ 11018 Montgomery Blvd. NE, Northeast Heights, ☎ 505/294–2026), frequently voted the best bookstore in Albuquerque, is the largest independent bookstore in the state. Besides books of general interest, it sells technical and professional titles, maps, globes, racing forms, and 150 out-of-state and foreign newspapers. Book signings, poetry readings, and children's events are frequently scheduled.

## Clothing

**Western Warehouse** (✉ 6210 San Mateo Blvd. NE, Northeast Heights, ☎ 505/883–7161) will outfit you in western style with boots, hats, belts, and vests.

## Gifts and Toys

**Beeps** (✉ Nob Hill Shopping Center, 3500 Central Ave. SE, Nob Hill, ☎ 505/262–1900), a Nob Hill favorite, carries cards, T-shirts, and novelty items.

**Satellite Toys and Coffee** (✉ 3513 Central Ave. SE, Nob Hill, ☎ 505/256–0345) is filled with wind-up toys and collector's items for grown-ups.

## Home Furnishings

**A** (✉ 3500 Central Ave. SE, Nob Hill, ☎ 505/266–2222) is a Nob Hill stop for housewares, soaps, candles, body-care products, and jewelry.

**El Paso Import Co.** (✉ 3500 Central Ave. SE, Nob Hill, ☎ 505/265–1160) carries distressed and "peely-paint" antique-looking chests and tables loaded with character. If you love the "shabby chic" look, or want more Southwest-style in your home, head over to this Nob Hill furniture shop.

**Hey Jhonny** (✉ 3418 Central Ave. SE, Nob Hill, ☎ 505/256–9244) is an aromatic store full of exquisite candles, soaps, pillows, fountains, and other soothing items for the home.

**Moderno** (✉ 2501 Candelaria NE, Northeast Heights, ☎ 505/254–0447) stocks merchandise for contemporary living: handmade steel beds, chairs, mobiles, and modern, locally produced art, rugs, and jewelry.

**Objects of Desire** (✉ 3300 Central Ave. SE, Nob Hill, ☎ 505/232–3088) is the place to find that special lamp or table from a whimsical and worldly collection of furnishings that appeal to individualized tastes.

## Mexican Imports

**La Piñata** (✉ No. 2 Patio Market, Old Town, ☎ 505/242–2400) specializes in piñatas and papier-mâché products of all kinds.

## Music

You can't miss the distinctive spots of **Bow Wow Records** (✉ 3103 Central Ave. SE, Nob Hill, ☎ 505/256–0928), a record store painted like a Dalmatian, with a good selection of hard-to-find recordings.

**Natural Sound** (✉ 3422 Central Ave. SE, Nob Hill, ☎ 505/255–8295) is an eclectic record store with a large selection of new and used CDs.

## Native American Arts and Crafts

**Adobe Gallery** (✉ 413 Romero St. NW, Old Town, ☎ 505/243–8485) specializes in historic and contemporary art by southwestern Native Americans—Pueblo pottery, Hopi katsinas, and Navajo rugs, blankets, and paintings. The shop is in a historic *terrones* adobe (cut from the ground rather than formed from mud and dried) homestead that dates from 1878. The shop carries many books about southwestern Native Americans.

**Andrews Pueblo Pottery** (✉ 303 Romero St. NW, Suite 116, Old Town, ☎ 505/243–0414) carries a terrific selection of Pueblo pottery, fetishes, katsina dolls, and baskets for the beginning and seasoned collector.

**Bien Mur Indian Market Center** (✉ I–23 and Tramway Rd. NE, Northeast Heights, ☎ 505/821–5400) in Sandia Pueblo showcases the best of the best in regional Indian rugs, jewelry, and crafts of all kinds. You can feel very secure about what you purchase at this trading post, and prices are fair for what you get.

**Gertrude Zachary** ✉ 1501 Lomas Blvd. NW, Old Town, ☎ 505/247–4442) dazzles with its selection of Indian jewelry. This may be your best place to shop for a bargain in a good bracelet or ring. Locals buy here, too.

**Nizhoni Moses, Ltd.** (✉ 326 San Felipe St. NW, Old Town, ☎ 505/842–1808) stocks Pueblo pottery, including the black earthenware pottery of San Ildefonso, as well as the work of potters from Acoma, Santa Clara, Isleta, and Zía. Rare Zuñi and Navajo jewelry is on display, as are Navajo weavings from 1900 to the present.

**Skip Maisel Wholesale Indian Jewelry and Crafts** (✉ 510 Central Ave. SW, Old Town, ☎ 505/242–6526), in business since 1905, has been at this location since 1929. Even its exterior is a piece of art—check out the murals in the entryway alcove. Inside are quality Native American arts and crafts at wholesale prices.

**Tanner Chaney Gallery** (✉ 323 Romero St. NW, No. 5, Old Town, ☎ 505/247–2242 or 800/444–2242) is housed in the Territorial-style plaza in Old Town. The three showrooms contain Native American jewelry, sculpture, contemporary and historic pottery, baskets, incredible Navajo weavings, and many books on the Southwest.

# SIDE TRIPS FROM ALBUQUERQUE

It takes only a few minutes of driving in either direction to leave urban Albuquerque behind and experience some of New Mexico's natural and small-town beauty. Rivers, valleys, canyons, and peaks are just outside the city's limits, and amid them many villages worth a stop.

## Albuquerque Side Trips

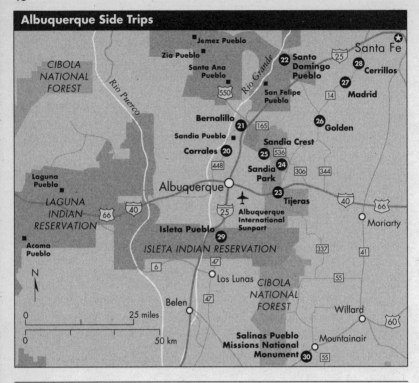

# North via I-25

The land north of Albuquerque is a little bit cooler, a little bit greener, and a lot more pastoral than the city. Drive slowly through Bernalillo and Corrales, and you're bound to see lots of horses, cows, and llamas.

## Corrales

**20** *2 mi north of Albuquerque. Take Paseo Del Norte or Alameda exits west from I-25 and head north on Coors/Corrales Road.*

Serene Corrales is an ancient agricultural community now inhabited by artists, craftspeople, and the affluent—plus a few descendants of the old families. Small galleries, shops, and places to eat dot the town, and in the fall, roadside fruit and vegetable stands open. Bordered by Albuquerque and Rio Rancho, Corrales makes a pleasant escape to winding dirt roads, fields of corn, and apple orchards. On summer weekends, visit the Corrales Farmers' Market; in October, the village holds a Harvest Festival.

## Bernalillo

**21** *17 mi north of Albuquerque via I-25.*

Once a rather tranquil Hispanic village, Bernalillo is today one of New Mexico's fastest-growing towns—it's increasingly absorbing the suburban growth northward from Albuquerque, just 17 mi south. The town holds a Wine Festival each Labor Day weekend. But the most memorable annual event is the Fiesta of San Lorenzo, which has honored the town's patron saint for nearly 400 years. On August 10, San Lorenzo Day, the entire town takes to the streets to participate in the traditional masked *matachine* dance. Matachines, of Moorish origin, were brought to this hemisphere by the Spanish. In New Mexico various versions are danced to haunting fiddle music, in both Indian pueblos and old Spanish villages at different holidays. Though interpretations of the matachines are inexact, one general theme is that of conquest. One dancer, wearing a devil's mask and wielding a whip, presides over the others. A young girl, dressed in white, is also present.

**Coronado State Monument** is named in honor of Francisco Vásquez de Coronado, the leader of the first organized Spanish expedition into the Southwest, from 1540 to 1542. The prehistoric **Kuaua Pueblo,** on a bluff overlooking the Rio Grande, is believed to have been the headquarters of Coronado and his army, who were caught unprepared by severe winter weather during their search for the legendary Seven Cities of Gold. A worthy stop, the monument has a museum in a restored kiva, with copies of magnificent frescoes done in black, yellow, red, blue, green, and white. The frescoes depict fertility rites, rain dances, and hunting rituals. The original artworks are preserved in the small visitor center. Adjacent to the monument is **Coronado State Park,** which has campsites and picnic grounds, both open year-round. In autumn the views at the monument and park are especially breathtaking, with the trees turning russet and gold. ⊠ *NM 44/U.S. 550,* ☎ *505/867–5351.* ⊠ *May–Sept. $3, Oct.–Apr. $2.* ☉ *Daily 8:30–5.*

DINING

$$$$  ✕ **Prairie Star.** Residents of Albuquerque often make the 20-minute drive to this 1940s Pueblo Revival hacienda, renowned for the sunset views from its patio. The menu combines new American, southwestern, and classical cuisine, including trout with piñon nuts, tender Greek-style rack of lamb, nightly seafood specials, and blue-corn crabcake appetizers. The breads and desserts are made on the premises. The culinary quality doesn't always live up to the fabulous setting, but this is still a safe bet for a memorable meal. ⊠ *255 Prairie Star Rd.,* ☎ *505/867–3327. AE, D, DC, MC, V.*

$–$$  ✕ **Range Cafe & Bakery.** Huevos rancheros, giant cinnamon rolls, grilled Portobello-mushroom burgers, roast-turkey sandwiches, homemade meat loaf with garlic mashed potatoes, and the signature dessert, Death by Lemon, are among the highlights at this favorite New Mexican restaurant. All the above, plus a full complement of rich, decadent Taos Cow ice cream (cinnamon is the house special flavor, available only here), is served in a refurbished mercantile building with a dead-center view of the Sandia Mountains. ⊠ *925 Camino del Pueblo,* ☎ *505/867–1700. Reservations not accepted. AE, D, MC, V.*

CAMPING

⚠ **Albuquerque North Bernalillo KOA.** Cottonwoods, pines, evergreens, and willows shade this park, where morning brings a free pancake breakfast and in summer free outdoor movies are screened. You can play badminton, basketball, croquet, horseshoes, and video games. ⊠ *555 S. Hill Rd., 87004,* ☎ *505/867–5227 or 800/562–3616. Flush toilets, laundry facilities, showers, restaurant, pool. 57 RV sites, 36 tent sites, 6 cabins.* ⊠ *$19–$34; cabins $31–$44. D, MC, V.*

SHOPPING

**Jackalope** (⊠ 834 Hwy. 44, take NM 44 exit west from I–25 N, ☎ 505/867–9813) galloped over from its famous Santa Fe location and settled down in a second home that's acres of imported pottery, crafts, table linens, jewelry, clothing, glass, tinwork, and furniture from Mexico as well as India, Eastern Europe, and China. About 20 mi north of town, this is a good place to hunt for gifts and a great place to spend an hour (at least) browsing.

### Santo Domingo Pueblo

㉒ *40 mi northeast of Albuquerque via I–25, exit on NM 22 and drive 4½ mi west.*

Santo Domingo Pueblo craftspeople sell their outstanding *heishi* (shell) jewelry and pottery, along with other traditional arts and crafts, all year long. But the Pueblo's Labor Day Arts and Crafts Fair, a three-day event, brings out artists and visitors in full force. The Corn Dance is one of the most colorful and dramatic of pueblo ceremonial events. Held in honor of St. Dominic, the pueblo's patron saint, the August 4 festivities attract more than 2,000 dancers, clowns, singers, and drummers. Painter Georgia O'Keeffe supposedly said the Corn Dance was one of the great events in her life. Santo Domingo Pueblo is not part of the Turquoise Trail. ⊠ *Off NM 22, 4½ mi west of I–25,* ☎ *505/465–2214.* ▦ *Donations encouraged. Still and video cameras, tape recorders, and sketching materials prohibited.* ☉ *Daily dawn–dusk.*

## The Turquoise Trail

A scenic drive etched out nearly a quarter century ago and still well traveled is the Turquoise Trail, which follows an old route between Albuquerque and Santa Fe that's dotted with ghost towns now being restored by writers, artists, and other urban refugees. This 70 mi of piñon-studded mountain back road is a gentle roller-coaster of panoramic views of the Ortiz, Jemez, and Sangre de Cristo mountains. It's believed that 2,000 years ago Indians mined turquoise in these hills. The Spanish took up turquoise mining in the 16th century, and the practice continued into the early 20th century, with Tiffany's removing a fair share of the semiprecious stone. In addition, gold, silver, tin, lead, and coal have been mined here. There's plenty of opportunity for picture-taking and picnicking along the way. The pace is slow, the talk is about the weather, and Albuquerque might as well be on another planet. The entire loop of this trip takes a day, the drive up the Sandia Crest a half day. Sites farther west are described *in* Chapter 6.

### Tijeras

㉓ *7½ mi from Albuquerque east on I–40 and south on NM 337.*

Begin your tour of the Turquoise Trail and the Sandia Mountains with a quick, educational stop in the Tijeras area.

☞ At the **Sandia Ranger Station** you can pick up pamphlets and maps, and—if there are enough kids in the audience—witness a fire-prevention program with a Smokey the Bear motif. Tours head to the nearby fire lookout tower and **Tijeras Pueblo ruins.** Call ahead to reserve a tour. ⊠ *11776 NM 337, south of I–40,* ☎ *505/281–3304.* ▦ *Free.* ☉ *Weekdays 8–5, weekends 8:30–noon and 12:30–5.*

### Sandia Park

㉔ *13 mi northeast of Albuquerque, 7 mi north of Tijeras. From Tijeras, take I–40 east and exit north on the Turquoise Trail (NM 14); proceed 6 mi and turn left onto NM 536.*

☞ The **Tinkertown Museum** contains a world of miniature carved-wood characters. Owner Ross Ward spent more than 35 years carving and collecting the 1,200 figures that populate this museum, including an animated miniature western village, a Boot Hill cemetery, and a circus exhibit from the 1940s. Ragtime piano music, a 40-ft sailboat, and a life-size general store are other highlights. This is one attraction guaranteed to please all ages. Don't miss the "bottle wall," made of 12,000 bottles pressed into cement. ⊠ *121 Sandia Crest Rd. (take Cedar*

*Crest exit off I–40 east and follow signs to Sandia Crest turnoff),* ☎ *505/281–5233.* 🎟 *$3.* ⊙ *Apr.–Oct., daily 9–6.*

## Sandia Crest

㉕ *25 mi from Albuquerque; east on I–40, north on NM 14, and east on NM 536.*

For awesome views of Albuquerque and half of New Mexico, take the side road to the Sandia Crest via the "backside" on NM 536, which ascends through the Cibola National Forest. At the 10,678-ft summit, explore the foot trails along the rim (particularly in summer) and take in the views, which include a close-up view of the "Steel Forest," the nearby cluster of radio and television towers. During the summer, a chairlift operates Friday through Sunday 10–4 and costs $7 round-trip. Mountain bikes may be rented at the top for $38 and a $350 deposit. Call **Sandia Ski Area** (☎ 505/242–9052) for information. Always bring an extra layer of clothing, even in summer.

If you are in need of refreshments or are searching for some inexpensive souvenirs, visit the **Sandia Crest House Gift Shop and Restaurant** (☎ 505/243–0605), on the rim of the crest.

## Golden

㉖ *25 mi northeast of Albuquerque. From the Sandia Crest, take NM 536 south to NM 14 north, the Turquoise Trail; in 20 mins or so you'll coast into Golden.*

Golden, the site of the first gold rush (in 1825) west of the Mississippi, has a rock shop and a mercantile store. The rustic adobe church and graveyard are popular with photographers. Be aware that locals are very protective of this area and aren't known to warm up to strangers. Should you have any questions about the area, **La Casita,** a gift shop at the north end of the village, serves as the unofficial chamber of commerce.

## Madrid

㉗ *37 mi northeast of Albuquerque, 12 mi northeast of Golden on NM 14.*

Totally abandoned when its coal mine closed in the 1950s, Madrid is slowly being rebuilt. The entire town was offered for sale for $250,000 back then, but there were no takers. Finally, in the early 1970s, a few artists fleeing big cities settled in and began the work of restoration. Weathered houses and old company stores have been repaired and turned into shops, some of which are definitely worth a visit. The big events here are Old Timers Days on July 4 weekend, and the Christmas open house, held weekends in December, when galleries and studios are open and the famous Madrid Christmas lights twinkle brightly. Sunday summer jazz concerts in the ball park are also popular.

☾ Madrid's **Old Coal Mine Museum** is a remnant of a once-flourishing industry. Children can explore the old tunnel, climb aboard a 1900 steam train, and poke through antique buildings full of marvelous relics. Tickets for the museum are available at the Mine Shaft Tavern out front. On weekends between Memorial Day and Labor Day you can cheer the heroes and hiss the villains of the old-fashioned melodramas performed at the **Engine House Theater.** The theater, inside a converted roundhouse machine shop, has a full-size steam train that comes chugging onto the stage. ⊠ *Old Coal Mine Museum, 2846 NM 14,* ☎ *505/ 438–3780.* 🎟 *Museum $3, melodrama $9.* ⊙ *Daily 9:30–dusk.*

DINING

$ ✕ **Java Junction.** Here's where the locals—many of whom look like and are aging hippies—congregate for their morning brew and socializing. ⊠ *2855 Hwy. 14,* ☎ *505/438–2772. D, MC, V.*

$ ✕ **Mama Lisa's No Pity Cafe.** Sit at an outdoor table and watch the world go by in the company of a fresh-baked scone, fruit pie, or healthy sandwich. The café is open 11–5. ⊠ *2859 Hwy. 14,* ☎ *no phone. No credit cards. Closed Tues.*

SHOPPING

The town of Madrid has only one street, so the shops are easy to find.

**Maya Jones Imports** (☎ 505/473–3641) stocks Guatemalan imports and one-of-a-kind creations, plus a 1934 soda fountain that pumps out phosphates, malteds, and sundaes. **Primitiva** (☎ 505/471–7904) carries handmade Mexican furniture and imports from around the world. **Tapestry Gallery** (☎ 505/471–0194) stocks hand-loomed knits and rugs, as well as wearable art and locally produced silver and turquoise jewelry.

## Cerrillos

**28** *40 mi northeast of Albuquerque, 3 mi northeast of Madrid on NM 14.*

Cerrillos was a boomtown in the 1880s—its mines brimmed with gold, silver, and turquoise, and eight newspapers, four hotels, and 21 taverns flourished. When the mines went dry the town went bust. Since then, Cerrillos has served as the backdrop for feature-film and television westerns, among them *Young Guns* and *Lonesome Dove.* Today, it might easily be mistaken for a ghost town, which it's been well on the way to becoming for decades. Time has left its streets dry, dusty, and almost deserted.

**Casa Grande** (⊠ 17 Waldo, ☎ 505/438–3008), a 21-room adobe (several rooms of which are part of a shop), has a small museum ($2) with a display of early mining exhibits. There's also a petting zoo ($2) and a scenic overlook. Casa Grande is open daily 8 AM–sunset.

Pack rats and browsers alike ought not to miss the **What-Not Shop** (⊠ 15B 1st St., ☎ 505/471–2744), a venerable secondhand/antiques shop of a half-century's standing packed floor to ceiling with Indian pottery, cut glass, rocks, political buttons, old postcards, clocks, and who knows what else.

# Pueblos South of Albuquerque

When Francisco Vásquez de Coronado arrived in what is now New Mexico in 1540, he found a dozen or so villages along the Rio Grande in the ancient province of Tiguex, between what is now Bernalillo to the north of Albuquerque and Isleta to the south. Of those, only Sandia and Isleta survive today. Santo Domingo Pueblo is covered under the Turquoise Trail side trip. The Salinas Pueblo Missions ruins, about 65 mi southeast of Albuqueruqe, remain a striking example of the Spanish penchant for building churches on sites inhabited by native people.

## Isleta Pueblo

**29** *13 mi south of Albuquerque, I–25 (to Exit 213) to NM 47 and follow signs.*

Of the pueblos in New Mexico when the Spanish first arrived, Isleta Pueblo is one of two Tiwa-speaking communities left in the middle of the Rio Grande valley. Isleta was one of the few pueblos that didn't participate in the Pueblo Revolt of 1680, during which Isleta was abandoned. Some of the residents fled New Mexico with the Spanish to El Paso, where their descendants live to this day on a reservation called Ysleta del Sur. Other members went to live with the Hopi of Arizona but eventually returned and rebuilt the pueblo.

Facing the quiet plaza is Isleta's church, **St. Augustine,** built in 1629. One of the oldest churches in New Mexico, it has thick adobe walls, a viga-crossed ceiling, and simple interior decor. Legend has it that the ground beneath the floor has the odd propensity to push church and community figures buried under the floor back up out of the ground; bodies have been reburied several times, only to emerge again.

Polychrome pottery with red-and-black designs on a white background is the specialty here. The pueblo celebrates its feast days on August 28 and September 4, both in honor of St. Augustine. The tribal government maintains picnicking and camping facilities, several fishing ponds, a casino, and an 18-hole golf course. Baking in Isleta is done in the centuries-old fashion, in beehive ovens beside adobe homes bedecked with crimson chiles. ⊠ *Tribal Rd. 40,* ☎ *505/869–3111 pueblo; 505/ 724–3800 casino; 505/869–0950 Isleta Eagle Championship Golf Course.* ☎ *Free. Camera use restricted; only church may be photographed.*

CAMPING

⚠ **Isleta Lakes and Recreation Area.** Near the pueblo on the Isleta Reservation, this area covered with cottonwoods contains three fishing lakes full of trout, bass, and catfish. You can also play basketball and softball here. ⊠ *NM 47 south of I–25's Exit 215, Isleta 87022,* ☎ *505/ 877–0370. Flush toilets, laundry facilities, showers, general store.* ☎ *$12–$15. 40 RV sites, 100 tent sites. MC, V.*

## Salinas Pueblo Missions National Monument

③⓪ *58 mi (to Punta Agua/Quarai) from Albuquerque, east on I–40 (to Tijeras Exit), south on NM 337 and NM 55; 23 mi from Punta Agua to Abó, south on NM 55, west (at Mountainair) on U.S. 60, and north on NM 513; 34 mi from Punta Agua to Gran Quivira, south on NM 55.*

Salinas Pueblo Missions National Monument is made up of three sites—**Quarai, Abó, and Gran Quivira**—each with the ruins of a 17th-century Spanish-colonial Franciscan missionary church and an associated pueblo. The sites represent the convergence of two Native American peoples, the Anasazi and the Mogollon, who lived here for centuries before the Spanish arrived. Quarai, the nearest to Albuquerque, was a flourishing Tiwa pueblo whose inhabitants' pottery, weaving, and basket-making techniques were quite refined. On the fringe of the Great Plains, all three of the Salinas pueblos were vulnerable to raids by nomadic Plains Indians. Quarai was abandoned about 50 years after its mission church, **San Purísima Concepción de Cuarac,** was built in 1630. The church's sandstone walls still rise 40 ft out of the earth. At Abó are the remains of the three-story church of San Gregorio and a large unexcavated pueblo. (The masonry style at Abó bore some similarity to that at Chaco Canyon, which has led some archaeologists to speculate that the pueblo was built by people who left the Chaco Canyon area.) A video about Salinas Pueblo can be viewed at Gran Quivira, which contains two churches and some excavated Native American structures. The monument headquarters is in the town of Mountainair. ⊠ *201 Broadway, at U.S. 60, Mountainair,* ☎ *505/847– 2585.* ☎ *Free.* ⊙ *Memorial Day–Labor Day, daily 9–7; Labor Day– Memorial Day, daily 9–5.*

# ALBUQUERQUE A TO Z

### AIR TRAVEL

The national airlines that serve Albuquerque, the major gateway to New Mexico, are America West, American, Continental, Delta, Frontier,

Northwest, Southwest, and United. Regional airlines that fly into Albuquerque are Great Plains, Mesa, Rio Grande, and Skywest. *See* Air Travel *in* Smart Travel Tips A to Z for national airline phone numbers.

➤ REGIONAL AIRLINES: **Great Plains** (☎ 866/929–8646). **Mesa** (☎ 800/637–2247). **Rio Grande** (☎ 877/435–9742). **Skywest** (☎ 800/453–9417).

## AIRPORTS AND TRANSFERS

Albuquerque International Sunport is 5 mi south of downtown. The Albuquerque Convention and Visitors Bureau maintains an information center, open daily between 9:30 and 8, on the lower level of the airport near the escalator. The trip into town from the airport takes about 10 to 15 minutes by car. Taxis, available at clearly marked stands, charge about $7 (plus 50¢ for each additional rider). Sun Tran buses stop at the sunburst signs every 30 minutes; the fare is 75¢. Some hotels provide shuttle service to and from the airport. You can also rent a limousine. The Airport Express shuttle costs less than $10 to most downtown locations.

➤ AIRPORT: **Albuquerque International Sunport** (✉ 2200 Sunport Blvd. SE, off I–25, Southeast Heights, ☎ 505/842–4366).

➤ AIRPORT SHUTTLE: **Airport Express** (☎ 505/765–1234)

## BUS TRAVEL TO AND FROM ALBUQUERQUE

Texas, New Mexico & Oklahoma Coaches, affiliated with Greyhound Lines, provides service to Albuquerque from cities in the Southwest and beyond. To get from the bus station to the center of the city, phone for a taxi or walk south on 2nd Street two blocks to catch a municipal bus.

➤ BUS SERVICE: **Bus Terminal** (✉ 300 2nd St. SW, Downtown, ☎ 505/243–4435 or 800/231–2222). **Texas, New Mexico & Oklahoma Coaches** (☎ 505/243–4435 or 800/231–2222).

## BUS TRAVEL WITHIN ALBUQUERQUE

Sun Tran buses provide good coverage of the city for residents, but the substantial distances between some of the major sights make public transportation impractical. The fare is 75¢ (exact change is required; fare box will accept a $1 bill, but no change is returned). Bus stops are well marked with the line's sunburst signs. There is no service on some major holidays.

➤ BUS SERVICE: **Sun Tran** (☎ 505/843–9200).

## CAR RENTAL

You can rent a car from one of the national agencies at Albuquerque International Sunport. *See* Car Rental *in* Smart Travel Tips A to Z for national rental-agency phone numbers.

## CAR TRAVEL

The main routes into Albuquerque are I–25 from points north and south and I–40 from points east and west. In the heart of the city, the intersection of I–25 and I–40 is known as the "Big-I." It may look complicated, but it really is fairly easy to navigate. Work in 2001 and 2002 eliminated a few exits, so be sure to have an updated city map that reflects the changes. It is still best to stay off the interstates (I–25 and I–40) during evening rush hour, which begins about 3 PM.

Albuquerque sprawls out in all directions, but getting around town is not difficult. Be warned that local drivers are notoriously casual, rarely signaling or showing consideration if you are trying to change lanes. Use extra caution at intersections, where drivers frequently scream through yellow and even red lights. A dependable east–west route through the city is Central Avenue, but you can also rely on a few one-way streets: take Coal Avenue east toward the mountains or Lead Avenue west toward the volcanoes. To go north–south, San Mateo Boulevard and Wyoming Boulevard are good bets.

Vacant parking spaces are particularly scarce in the University of New Mexico area, where even paid parking is limited, so it's best to arrive early if attending an event. Don't exceed the posted speed limit, regardless of what you see other drivers doing: police personnel have ticket quotas. You can turn right on a red light (or left at intersecting one-way streets) after coming to a complete stop unless a sign prohibiting such a turn is posted.

➤ MOTORIST INFORMATION: **New Mexico Road Conditions** (☏ 800/ 432–4269).

### EMERGENCIES
In an emergency, dial 911.
➤ HOSPITALS: **Presbyterian Hospital** (✉ 1100 Central Ave. SE, Downtown, ☏ 505/841–1111). **University Hospital** (✉ 2211 Lomas Blvd. NE, University of New Mexico, ☏ 505/272–2411).
➤ 24-HOUR PHARMACIES: **Walgreens** (✉ 6201 Central Ave. NE, Northeast Heights, ☏ 505/255–5511; ✉ 5001 Montgomery NE, Northeast Heights, ☏ 505/881–5050).

### TAXIS AND LIMOUSINES
Taxis are metered in Albuquerque, and service is around the clock. The rates run $3.80 for the first mile, $1.80 for each mile thereafter, and 50¢ for each additional passenger. Rates start at $55 to $60 per hour for standard limousines and can reach $95 per hour for stretch limos. There is usually a two-hour minimum. Call for special airport shuttle rates.
➤ CAR SERVICES: **Albuquerque Cab** (☏ 505/883–4888). **Classic Limousine** (☏ 505/247–4000). **Dream Limousine** (☏ 505/884–6464). **Imperial Limo** (☏ 505/298–9944). **Yellow Cab** (☏ 505/247–8888).

### TOURS
Gray Line of Albuquerque conducts daily tours, among them a four-hour swing through town that includes historic landmarks, downtown, Kirtland Air Force Base, and the Indian Pueblo Cultural Center. The Albuquerque Museum of Art and History leads hour-long historical walks through Old Town at 11 AM except Monday, from mid-March to mid-December. The tour is free and available on a first-come, first-served basis, so arrive early in the museum lobby.

If you are interested in exploring beyond downtown Albuquerque, you can take a Gray Line tour to Acoma Pueblo, the Anasazi cliff dwellings at Bandelier National Monument, and other Native American sites. International Universities conducts fascinating educational seminars and excursions (for groups only) that focus on the culture and history of New Mexico, including Indian pueblos, Santa Fe, and the Turquoise Trail.
➤ TOUR OPERATORS: **Albuquerque Museum of Art and History** (✉ 2000 Mountain Rd. NW, Old Town, ☏ 505/243–7255). **Gray Line of Albuquerque** (✉ 800 Rio Grande Blvd. NW, Suite 22, Old Town, ☏ 505/ 242–3880 or 800/256–8991). **International Universities** (✉ 1101 Tijeras Ave. NW, Downtown, ☏ 505/246–2233 or 800/547–5678).

### TRAIN TRAVEL
Amtrak operates the *Southwest Chief* daily between Chicago and Los Angeles. The train stops at Albuquerque Station.
➤ TRAIN SERVICE: **Albuquerque Station** (✉ 214 1st St. SW, Downtown, ☏ 505/842–9650). **Amtrak** (☏ 800/872–7245, WEB www.amtrak.com).

### VISITOR INFORMATION

The Public Lands Interpretive Association provides information related to public lands (both federal and state) and operates a bookstore carrying natural history books, guidebooks, maps, and educational books and toys.

➤ TOURIST INFORMATION: **Albuquerque Convention and Visitors Bureau** (✉ 20 1st Plaza NW, Suite 601, 87125, ☎ 505/842–9918 or 800/284–2282, WEB www.abqcvb.org). **Public Lands Interpretive Association** (✉ 6501 4th St. NW, Suite I, 87107, ☎ 877/851–8946 or 505/277–9498, WEB www.pulbiclands.org). **State Information Center** (✉ Indian Pueblo Cultural Center, 2401 12th St. NW, 87107, ☎ 505/843–7270). **University of New Mexico Information Center** (✉ 1700 Las Lomas NE, 87131, ☎ 505/277–1989).

# 3 NORTHWESTERN NEW MEXICO

Roads branch out north and west from
Albuquerque like the roots of a tree, to the
ruins of the Anasazi civilization and their
descendants' pueblos. Journey through red-
rock canyons that shelter ancient hamlets or to
high, fortresslike plateaus crowned by Native
American villages, and you'll encounter
cultures whose art, architecture, spirituality,
and knowledge of nature have allowed their
dynamic adaptation over centuries.

Updated by
Georgia de
Katona

W HEN A NEW MEXICAN SAYS HE OR SHE IS "on Indian time," the expression is usually meant as a joke. But when you leave Albuquerque or Santa Fe behind and wind your way through the red canyons of northwestern New Mexico's desert plateau, you do seem to enter a place impervious to the small demands of time-keeping. The enormous sweep of land and sky and its mysterious silence conjure the spirits of those who lived here long before recorded history. Standing on the edge of a sandstone cliff overlooking the San Juan River, entering the restored Great Kiva at the Aztec Ruins, or studying the pattern of a handwoven Navajo rug may give you insight into cultures past and present that honor conditions and cycles dictated by nature.

The stark countryside here has a unique and powerful aura that has been written about for centuries. Knowledge of the Anasazi people, who built great cities and roads in northwestern New Mexico and environs 1,000 and more years ago, has been revealed gradually through the discoveries of archaeologists. This region is today dominated by the Navajo people in the northwest and the Pueblo people—descended from the Anasazi, which translates in Navajo literally to "Ancient Enemies"—closer to the Rio Grande. From the 19th century on, generations of traders, soldiers, homesteaders, and prospectors made this area their home as well. The two largest cities, Gallup and Farmington, are the legacy of these later arrivals. Gallup remains the capital of Indian art and jewelry, and Farmington, an agricultural center for more than a century, is a hub of energy exploration.

## Pleasures and Pastimes

### Arts and Crafts

A piece of handmade Indian pottery is among the best souvenirs of a visit to northwestern New Mexico. When you tour the Acoma Pueblo you'll find vessels of all shapes and sizes displayed outside individual artists' homes. At other pueblos potters sell their works in small studios or at outdoor stalls and are usually happy to discuss the design traditions with you.

### Dining

Fast-food and familiar franchise restaurants thrive in this region, but there are some reputable homegrown establishments. As elsewhere in New Mexico, the specialty is the chile—red and green—but also western favorites like rib-eye steak and barbecue pork and chicken. Other local specialties include Navajo fry bread (not unlike a sopaipilla, served plain or topped with honey, beans, chile, or powdered sugar), tacos, and mutton stew such as you would be served at a pueblo's feast day. Delicious bread and pies, baked in beehive-shape outdoor *hornos* (ovens), are sold at roadside stands at some pueblos.

| CATEGORY | COST* |
|---|---|
| $$$$ | over $25 |
| $$$ | $18–$25 |
| $$ | $10–$17 |
| $ | under $10 |

* *per person for a main course at dinner*

### Lodging

Farmington, Grants, and Gallup are well supplied with chain motels, while Chama and Cuba have a few decent independently owned motels; there are also several appealing B&Bs in the region. You should have no problem finding a room, but book in advance if attending a special event.

| CATEGORY | COST* |
|---|---|
| $$$$ | over $170 |
| $$$ | $120–$170 |
| $$ | $70–$120 |
| $ | under $70 |

*All prices are for a standard double room, excluding 5.25–11.5% tax.*

## Outdoor Activities and Sports

No question about it, fishing is a chief lure of the Four Corners—near Farmington. The San Juan River is fishable year-round; serious fish-erfolk report some of their best experiences in winter. The large trout (up to 2 ft or more) that swim the San Juan provide exceptional catches. Hikers of all skill levels have hundreds of trails to explore, as do mountain bikers. The 3-mi hike along the San Juan River at Navajo Lake State Park is especially beautiful.

# Exploring Northwestern New Mexico

This region covers an immense territory—give yourself five to seven days for a reasonably thorough exploration. Begin by heading west out of Albuquerque on I–40, planning a night or two in the Indian Country, before heading north toward Farmington for another night in the Four Corners region. Take the next day to explore Chama and Los Ojos. Spend your last night near here or cut over to Cuba—either way, allow most of a day for touring Chaco Canyon. On your way back to Albuquerque, take an hour or so to visit the Jemez area. If you're daunted by squeezing so much into a short period, remember that it's easy to visit Acoma, Laguna, and Grants at other times as day trips from Albuquerque or Santa Fe. Some folks tackle Chaco as a day trip from the Rio Grande valley, but it's far more practical to spend the night closer by, if not in Cuba then in Abiquiu, Farmington, or even Grants or Gallup (the last two towns being relatively near Chaco's southern entrance).

## Great Itineraries

### IF YOU HAVE 2 OR 3 DAYS

The only way to tour this region adequately in two days is if you're incorporating your trip into a journey west into Arizona (via Gallup or Farmington), northwest into Utah (via Farmington), or north into Colorado (via Chama or Farmington). In just three days, however, you can make a nice loop of the region's top sites: drive west from Albuquerque on I–40, stopping in **Acoma Pueblo** ② for a couple hours before continuing west to ⛯ **Gallup** ⑦. Spend the late afternoon shopping the old trading posts there, have dinner at Earl's, and stay overnight at the atmospheric El Rancho. On day two, head north on NM 371 to ⛯ **Farmington** ⑧, stopping for a brief ramble through the **Bisti Wilderness Area.** If you like to fish or hike, head straight to the **San Juan River.** Otherwise, tour **Salmon Ruins** ⑨ and, in **Aztec** ⑩, the **Aztec Ruins National Monument and Museum.** Spend the final day at **Chaco Culture National Historical Park** ⑫.

### IF YOU HAVE 5 TO 7 DAYS

In five to seven days you can get a real sense for the past and present of northwestern New Mexico. On day one, drive west on I–40 to **Acoma Pueblo** ② and then to the museum in ⛯ **Grants** ③. The next day loop down along NM 53 for short hikes at the **Ice Cave and Bandera Volcano** ④ and **El Morro National Monument** ⑤ before stopping at ⛯ **Zuñi Pueblo** ⑥ en route to ⛯ **Gallup** ⑦. Next follow NM 371 to

# Northwestern New Mexico

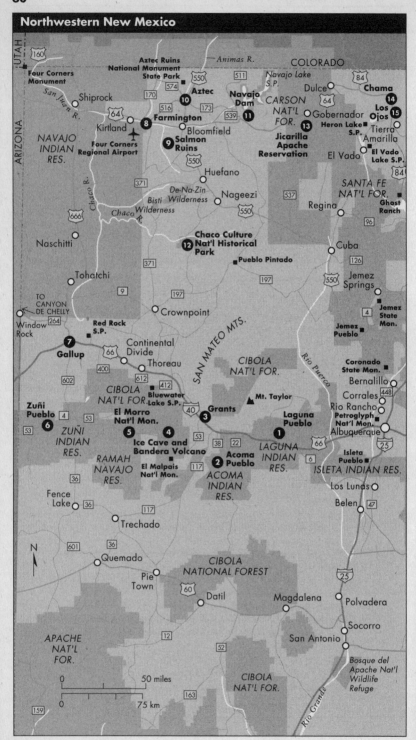

🏙 **Farmington** ⑧, visiting the **Bisti Wilderness Area** en route. After a night or two in Farmington, continue on to 🏙 **Chama** ⑭, where the next morning you can make the partial trip on the Cumbres & Toltec Scenic Railroad. That afternoon visit 🏙 **Los Ojos** ⑮, either spending the night there if you've got an extra day or in 🏙 **Cuba** if time is tight. Either way plan to spend at least a half day exploring **Chaco Culture National Historical Park** ⑫. If you've got seven days, allow yourself a full day at Chaco.

### When to Tour Northwestern New Mexico

Weatherwise, the best months to tour the ruins of Anasazi Country are from April to early June and from late August to October, but there's no bad time. The roads to Chaco Canyon are sometimes closed because of snow or mud in winter, and cold winds can make the going rough in early spring. The best seasons for attending Pueblo Indian dances are summer and fall, when harvest dances take place, and from Thanksgiving through early January. June and July are the hottest months, but by August afternoon thunderstorms begin cooling things down.

When visiting pueblos and reservations you are expected to follow a certain etiquette (☞ Pleasures and Pastimes *in* Chapter 1). Check the pueblos and monuments for dates of feast-day celebrations and fairs; some pueblos are open only on specific days.

# PUEBLO COUNTRY

The scent of smoldering piñon, the hypnotic chant of dancers, and the mood of reverence and joy that comes over a pueblo on a feast day leave lasting impressions on visitors to Pueblo country. The spirituality that pervades a pueblo like Acoma, secluded on an imposing mesa that served as a lookout for "the people of the white rock" (as the name translates in the Keresan language), is unmistakable. Though the pueblos of Pueblo country share the magnetism of so-called power spots, or vortices, the world over, they differ in a most significant way from places like Stonehenge or Machu Picchu: New Mexico's Indian pueblos are still inhabited. They are alive, their residents carrying on traditions, arts, and ways of living as vibrant today as they were centuries ago. Much but not all of Pueblo country lies within northern New Mexico. Among the region's important pueblos are Acoma, Laguna, and Zuñi. Sacred grounds include portions of El Malpais and El Morro national monuments.

## Laguna Pueblo

❶ *50 mi west of Albuquerque on I–40.*

Laguna Pueblo, which was established in 1697 by refugees from Zía, Cochiti, and Santo Domingo pueblos, is one of the youngest of New Mexico's pueblos. Scattered about the reservation are six villages, but most visitors are drawn to **Old Laguna**, capped by the eye-catching white facade of San José de Laguna Church, which is visible from I–40. The church, built in 1699, is a National Historic Landmark. In shops and artists' homes (the latter identified by signs) you can buy fine pottery decorated with geometric designs. The pueblo's villages celebrate many feast days and dances, including St. Joseph (March 19), Virgin Mary (September 8), and Sts. Margaret and Mary (October 17). All the pueblo's residents gather at Old Laguna on September 19 to honor St. Joseph with a fair. ⊠ *Off I–40,* ☎ *505/552–6654 governor's office.* 🎫 *Free.* ☼ *Daily 8–4:30, village tours by appointment. Photography rules vary; contact governor's office for information.*

## Acoma Pueblo

★ ❷   *63 mi west of Albuquerque on I–40 and NM 22 south.*

Atop a 367-ft mesa that rises abruptly from the valley floor, Acoma
Pueblo's terraced, multistory, multiunit Sky City is like no other pueblo
structure. It's one of the oldest continually inhabited spots in North
America, with portions believed to be more than 1,500 years old.
Captain Hernando de Alvarado, a member of Francisco Vásquez de
Coronado's Expedition of 1540, was the first European to see Acoma.
He reported that he had "found a rock with a village on top, the
strongest position ever seen in the world." The Spanish eventually con-
quered the Acomas and brutally compelled them to build **San Estéban
del Rey,** the immense adobe church that stands to this day. Indian la-
borers cut the massive vigas for the church's ceiling 30 mi away on
Mt. Taylor and physically carried them overland.

About a dozen families live at the pueblo full time, with most other
Acomas living on Indian land nearby and returning only in summer
and for celebrations, the primary one being the feast day of St. Stephen
(September 2), which is open to the public. Acoma's artisans are
known for their thin-walled pottery, hand-painted with intricate ge-
ometrical patterns. Visitation is by an hour-long guided tour; you're
whisked by van up a steep road from the visitor center and then led
about the mesa community on foot. Allow time to walk back down
to the visitor center via the ancient staircase carved into the side of
the mesa (ask your guide to point it out). There's no electricity or running water in the village, but you'll see cars parked outside many
homes—one wonders what it must have been like to visit Acoma before the road was constructed in 1969. Open hours vary slightly, depending on the weather. ✉ *Hwy. 22,* ☎ *505/552–6604 or 800/747–
0181,* WEB *www.puebloofacoma.org.* 🎫 *$9.* ☉ *Early Apr.–late Oct.,
daily 8–7, tours daily 8–6; late Oct.–early Apr., daily 8–4, tours daily
8–3. Closed certain periods; call first. Video cameras prohibited, still-
camera permit $10.*

## Grants

❸   *34 mi west of Laguna Pueblo, 29 mi northwest of Acoma via Hwy.
38 north and I–40 west.*

The largest community on old Route 66 between Albuquerque and
Gallup, little Grants has an intriguing museum and enough chain hotels and inexpensive restaurants to make it a good base for exploring
the eastern half of this region. The seat of Cibola County, Grants started
out as a farming and ranching center, grew into a rail transport hub,
and boomed during the 1950s when uranium was discovered in the nearby
mountains. The night skies here are said to be some of the clearest in
the world, making it a worthwhile stop for stargazers.

In the center of Grants's sleepy downtown, the small **New Mexico Mining Museum** shares quarters with the chamber of commerce off Santa
Fe Avenue. On the ground level are charts, photos, gems and minerals, and depictions of uranium-mining life in the region—this area is
free. After paying admission, you can ride the elevator down into an
amazingly realistic, re-created mine in the building's basement, where
you can make a self-guided loop of the equipment and exhibits. ✉ *100
N. Iron Ave.,* ☎ *505/287–4802.* 🎫 *Museum free, mine exhibit $3.* ☉
*Mon.–Sat. 9–4.*

Looming high above Grants to the northeast, **Mt. Taylor** rises to 11,301
ft, the highest peak in northwestern New Mexico. You can drive fairly

far up the mountain for fine views and hop out to hike on marked trails. There are also a couple of campgrounds. The annual **Mt. Taylor Winter Quadrathlon** (☎ 505/287–4802 or 800/748–2142) takes place every mid-February, when 600 unbelievably fit athletes compete in a highly challenging bicycle, foot, ski, and snowshoe race near the summit.

### Dining and Lodging

**$$–$$$**  ✕ **Monte Carlo.** A fixture in town since the 1940s, this rollicking old New Mexican eatery is best known for its *chile relleno del mar* (green chile stuffed with cheese, bay shrimp, and crabmeat). The salsas here also pack quite a punch. ✉ *721 W. Santa Fe Ave.,* ☎ *505/287–9250. MC, V.*

**$$**  🏨 **Zuni Mountain Lodge.** This contemporary lodge at the edge of the Zuni Mountain Range lies 1 mi from Bluewater Lake State Park, south of Thoreau (pronounced through). Airy, white-walled rooms with simple, attractive furnishings induce tranquility, as do views of the lake and Cibola National Forest. Surrounded by piñon and ponderosa pines at almost 8,000 ft, this is a great spot for mountain biking, hiking, or just relaxing on the covered porches. The gracious proprietor, Bob, is a wellspring of area history and suggestions for places to explore. Included in your stay are a full breakfast, with homemade baked goods and eggs cooked your way, and a delicious dinner of hearty home-style favorites. The inn also offers five-day intensive workshops on Navajo weaving and pottery in the fall. ✉ *40 Perch Dr. (Box 5114, Thoreau 87323), between Grant and Gallup; from I–40's Exit 53, head south 13 mi on NM 612,* ☎ *505/862–7769,* FAX *505/862–7616,* WEB *www.cia-g.com/žuniml. 7 rooms. Internet, some pets allowed; no room phones, no room TVS. No credit cards. MAP.*

**$–$$**  🏨 **Days Inn.** This is one of the newest and nicest of the numerous motels off Exit 85 of I–40, a reliable place for a restful stay. ✉ *1504 E. Santa Fe Ave., 87020,* ☎ *505/287–8883 or 800/544–8313,* FAX *505/287–7772. 62 rooms. Cable TV, meeting rooms. AE, D, DC, MC, V. CP.*

*En Route*  As you head toward El Morro National Monument on NM 53, you'll pass through the stark, volcanic rock–strewn **El Malpais National Monument and Conservation Area** (✉ NM 53, 23 mi south of Grants, ☎ 505/783–4774). The conservation area contains New Mexico's largest natural arch and has miles of hiking trails. The monument is popular for hiking as well as spelunking in the miles of lava tubes. Some 40 volcanoes dot 114,000 acres. There are no tourist facilities here, but a visitor center has maps and knowledgeable staff. El Malpais is not much of an attraction for the pass-through visitor but is well worth experiencing by spending a full day or two exploring the park in depth. Backcountry camping permits are available at the visitor center, though camping is *very* primitive—no facilities exist. A quick snapshot of the volcanic landscape and terrain is best gained from the Ice Cave and Bandera Volcano.

## Ice Cave and Bandera Volcano

   🖐 ❹  *25 mi southwest of Grants and 1 mi west of El Malpais via NM 53.*

Despite its unabashed commercialism, this roadside curiosity, set squarely on the Continental Divide, easily merits an hour of your time—the short trail from the 1930s trading post (with gift shop and snack bar) just off NM 53 affords unusual vistas of blackened lava fields and gnarled juniper and ponderosa stands. It's about a 20-minute moderately strenuous jaunt up to the 1,200-ft-diameter crater of **Bandera Volcano,** which last unleashed a torrent of lava 10,000 years ago. An even shorter walk leads to an old wooden staircase that descends 100 ft into the bowels of a collapsed lava tube, where the **Ice Cave** remains 31°F year-round and has a perpetual floor of blue-green ice. ⊠ *12000 Ice Caves Rd.,* ☎ *888/423–2283.* ☜ *$8.* ☉ *Memorial Day–Labor Day, daily 8–7; Labor Day–Memorial Day, daily 8–5.*

## El Morro National Monument

★ ❺ *43 mi southwest of Grants and 15 mi west of Ice Cave and Bandera Volcano via NM 53.*

When you see the imposing 200-ft-high sandstone bluff that served as a rest stop for explorers, soldiers, and pioneers, you'll understand how El Morro ("the Headlands") got its name. The bluff is the famous **Inscription Rock,** where wayfarers, beginning with Juan de Oñate in 1605, stopped to carve their names and leave messages. Petroglyphs mark the passage of travelers of earlier times. The **Inscription Trail** makes a quick ½-mi round-trip from the visitor center. While El Morro is justly renowned for Inscription Rock, try to allow an extra 90 minutes or so to venture along the spectacular, moderately strenuous 2-mi (round-trip) **Mesa Top Trail,** which meanders past the excavated edge of a massive field of pueblo ruins, cuts along the precarious rim of a deep box canyon, and affords panoramic views of the region. The monument's **museum** chronicles 700 years of human history in this region. ⊠ *Visitor center: NM 53,* ☎ *505/783–4226.* ☜ *$2, maximum of $4 per carload.* ☉ *Memorial Day–Labor Day, daily 9–7; Labor Day–Memorial Day, daily 9–5. Trails close 1 hr before monument.*

### Camping

⚠ **El Morro National Monument.** The park has a primitive campground amid the trees ¼ mi from the visitor center. Tap water is turned off during freezing weather; at those times camping is free. ⊠ *NM 53,* ☎ *505/783–4226. Pit toilets, drinking water, picnic tables, public telephone. 9 sites.* ☜ *$5. Reservations not accepted.*

## Zuñi Pueblo

❻ *35 mi west of El Morro National Monument on NM 53.*

Zuñi Pueblo has been occupied continuously since at least the year 700, and its language is unrelated to that of any other pueblo. Hawikuh, a Zuñi-speaking settlement now 12 mi south of the pueblo, was the first contacted by the Spaniards, in 1539. Francisco Vásquez de Coronado came here seeking one of the Seven Cities of Gold. He'd been tipped off by his guide, Estéban, who had seen the setting sun striking the walls of the dwellings and thought the multistoried villages were made of gold.

With a population of 8,500, Zuñi Pueblo is the largest of New Mexico's 19 Indian pueblos. You may be disappointed to find the pueblo is mostly modern housing along dusty streets. But the artists and craftspeople here are famous for their fine silversmithing and carving, Zuñi needlepoint, turquoise and silver jewelry, carved animal fetishes, pottery, and katsina dolls.

The original **Our Lady of Guadalupe Mission,** built in 1629, was destroyed during the Pueblo Revolt of 1680, when the Indians ousted the Spanish. In 1699 the mission was rebuilt, and in 1966 it was excavated and reconstructed. ⊠ *Old Mission Dr.,* ☎ *505/782–4403.* ☜ *Free.* ☉ *Weekdays 9–noon (hrs sometimes vary; call ahead).*

**A:shiwi A:wan Museum and Heritage Center,** which celebrates Zuñi history and culture, was built in harmony with traditional and environmental values of the Zuñi people. Food-preparation classes, storytelling, and other activities take place here in addition to exhibits.

Artifacts, baskets, and pottery are also on view. ✉ *1222 NM 53,* ☏
*505/782–4403.* 🔲 *Free.* ☉ *Nov.–Apr., weekdays 9–5:30; May–Oct.,*
*Mon.–Sat. 9–5:30.*

## Lodging

$$ 🏨 **Inn at Halona.** Your only opportunity to stay right in the heart of
the actual Zuñi pueblo village, this bright and cheerfully decorated inn
is filled with handwoven rugs, fine Zuñi arts and crafts, brightly col-
ored linens, and locally made furniture. An annex has a few larger rooms
in a more rustic design scheme. Outside you can relax in the tree-shaded,
enclosed flagstone courtyard or walk a short distance to the village plaza
or an art gallery. Room service is available from the neighboring gro-
cery-cum-restaurant. ✉ *23B Pia Mesa Rd. (Box 446, Zuñi 87327), off*
*NM 53,* ☏ *505/782–4118 or 800/752–3278,* 🆑 *505/782–2155,* 🆆🅴🅱
*www.halona.com. 8 rooms, 5 with bath. Room service, Internet, meet-*
*ing rooms; no smoking. MC, V. BP.*

# Gallup

❼ *42 mi north of Zuñi on NM 602, 138 mi west of Albuquerque on I–40.*

Heart of Indian Country, Indian Jewelry Capital of the World—with
more than 100 trading posts that deal in Indian jewelry, pottery, rugs,
and all manner of other arts and crafts, fine and handmade, Gallup
could be the best place to acquire that concho belt or squash-blossom
necklace you've always wanted. Prices are often better than those
you'll find in Santa Fe, and the selection is just short of overwhelm-
ing. Many of the Navajos selling their wares are from Window Rock,
Arizona, the Navajo Nation's capital, 25 mi northwest of town. As else-
where, it's buyer beware in Gallup. Generally, if a deal seems too good
to be true, it is. To assure yourself of authenticity and quality, shop at
a reputable, established dealer.

Gallup originated in the 1880s as a coal-mining town, and the rail-
road that followed encouraged a boom. Long strings of freight cars
still rumble along the tracks paralleling Historic Route 66, and train
whistles hoot regularly. During the late 1920s and '30s, Gallup became
a fabled stop along Route 66. When you drive down its neon-illumi-
nated main street, you enter a retro world of pop-culture nostalgia.

The 12-block downtown section bounded by Historic Route 66, 1st
Street, Hill Avenue, and 4th Street is best explored on foot. You can
browse through the trading posts and get a glimpse of 19th-century
architecture. The small but lively contemporary arts scene is best en-
joyed on the first Saturday of every month during the **Arts Crawl** (☏
505/863–3841) held in the evening on West Coal Avenue. Galleries such
as **Gallery 211** (✉ 211 W. Coal Ave.) and **Crashing Thunder** (✉ 226
W. Coal Ave.) open their doors with new shows, while coffee houses
and shops offer snacks and entertainment.

The 1928 Pueblo Deco **El Morro Theater** (✉ 207 W. Coal Ave., ☏ 505/
722–7469) screens Hollywood features and hosts the Gallup Film Fes-
tival—which includes a generous helping of western-theme flicks—each
October. Many of Hollywood's great westerns were filmed in this area.

NEED A
BREAK?
The **Coffee House** (✉ 203 W. Coal Ave., 1 block south of Rte. 66, ☏
505/726–0291) serves delicious coffees, teas, and Italian sodas in ad-
dition to yummy salads, sandwiches, and sweet treats. This friendly, fam-
ily-run community house of sorts is also a gallery, with exhibits of local
artists' works changing monthly. On weekend evenings you're likely to
catch a poetry reading or an open-mike night.

Clothing, furniture, tools, and typewriters are among the artifacts of the coal-mining era on display at the **Rex Museum,** operated by the Gallup Historical Society inside the former Rex Hotel. ✉ *300 W. Historic Rte. 66,* ☎ *505/863–1363.* ✆ *$2.* ☉ *Weekdays 9–3:30, Sat. 9–3 (later in summer).*

Part of the **Gallup Cultural Center,** a project of the Southwest Indian Foundation, is inside the restored 1927 Atchison, Topeka & Santa Fe Railway station, a gem of a building designed by Mary E. Coulter. Buses and trains still run in and out of the station. The cultural center includes a café (where you can lunch or sip coffee out of replicas of the china used on AT&S trains), a cinema that screens documentaries about the Southwest, and two dozen dioramas that relate the history of area native peoples, western expansion, and the building of the railroads. ✉ *201 E. Historic Rte. 66,* ☎ *505/863–4131.* ✆ *Free.* ☉ *Memorial Day–Labor Day, daily 9–9; Labor Day–Memorial Day, daily 9–4.*

During spring, summer, and early fall, wildflowers add brilliance to the landscape of **Red Rock State Park,** which has a small nature trail, and campgrounds. The park's red-rock amphitheater holds Gallup's premier event, the **Inter-Tribal Indian Ceremonial** (☎ 800/233–4528), each August. About 50,000 people come to see the dances of more than 30 tribes, watch rodeo events and parades, and stroll the marketplaces. The **Red Rocks Museum** contains exhibits of jewelry, pottery, rugs, architecture, and tools of the Anasazi, Zuñi, Hopi, and Navajo. ✉ *NM 566, Exit 31 from I–40, 7 mi east of Gallup,* ☎ *505/722–3829.* ✆ *Park free, museum $1.* ☉ *Park Nov.–Feb., daily 8–4:30; Mar.–mid-May, daily 8–6; mid-May–mid-Sept., daily 7:30 AM–10 PM; mid-Sept.–Oct., daily 7:30–6. Museum Mon.–Sat. 8:30–4:30.*

OFF THE BEATEN PATH

**CANYON DE CHELLY NATIONAL MONUMENT** – Ninety-eight miles northwest of Gallup, past Window Rock on AZ Route 264, Canyon de Chelly—pronounced de-*shay*—is well worth the drive and a day of exploring. Amid its fascinating pueblo ruins, Navajo residents farm and raise sheep in the canyon. The visitor center and museum are open all year, and from there you can book canyon tours with Navajo guides or drive the canyon rim and take the self-guided hikes. ✉ *AZ Rte. 264, 3 mi east of AZ Rte. 191, Chinle, AZ,* ☎ *520/674–5500.* ✆ *Free.* ☉ *May–Sept., daily 8–6; Oct.–Apr., daily 8–5.*

## Dining and Lodging

$–$$ ✕ **Dominic's Downtown.** This comfortable Italian eatery one block south of Route 66 serves huge salads, delicious sandwiches, pizza, and familiar Italian standards for dinner, including some very nice seafood dishes. Also on the menu are selected Mexican dishes such as tacos, burritos, and chiles rellenos. Save room for spumoni ice cream for dessert. ✉ *303 W. Coal Ave.,* ☎ *505/722–0117. AE, D, MC, V. Closed Sun.*

$–$$ ✕ **Earl's Restaurant.** If you have time for only one meal in Gallup,
★ come—as do many country-and-western stars traveling through town—to Earl's, a landmark that is Gallup's de facto dining room. The home-style rib-sticking daily specials include meat loaf and fried chicken with mashed potatoes. Another plus is some of the best green chile in all New Mexico. At Earl's it's the custom for Native American jewelry vendors to go table-to-table displaying their wares. They leave very quickly if you say you are not interested. ✉ *1400 E. Historic Rte. 66,* ☎ *505/863–4201. Reservations not accepted. AE, D, DC, MC, V.*

$ ✕ **Eagle Cafe.** For a glimpse of the past, slide into a red-vinyl booth in this 80-year-old diner, where you can watch trains chug past as you munch on mutton stew, enchiladas, or a burger. Not much has changed through the years at this tasty piece of living history. ✉ *220 W. Historic Rte. 66,* ☎ *505/722–3220. Reservations not accepted. No credit cards. Closed Sun.*

**$** ✕✉ **El Rancho.** Book a night in the Ronald Reagan, Katharine Hep-
**★** burn, or William Bendix Room—all units at this National Register historic property are named for vintage movie stars, many of whom
stayed here back when Hollywood westerns were shot in the region
(the hotel was built in 1937 by R. E. Griffith, the brother of the legendary silent-film director D. W. Griffith). A delightful combination
of nostalgic glamour, neon signage, and Old West decor, this is the pre-
mier hotel in town. The restaurant ($$), which serves decent Ameri-
can and Mexican food, is open for breakfast, lunch, and dinner. Browse
through the respected on-site art gallery for pottery, katsinas, and
sand paintings. ✉ *1000 E. Historic Rte. 66, 87301,* ☎ *505/863–9311
or 800/543–6351,* FAX *505/722–5917. 73 rooms, 3 suites. Restaurant,
bar; no-smoking rooms. AE, D, MC, V.*

**$** ✉ **Sleep Inn.** Sleep here and you'll get a reasonably priced motel room
with all the basics: chairs, a dresser, TV with remote, and a phone. ✉
*3820 E. Historic Rte. 66, 87301,* ☎ *505/863–3535 or 800/753–3746,*
FAX *505/722–3737. 61 rooms. In-room data ports, indoor pool, hot tub;
no-smoking rooms. AE, D, DC, MC, V.*

## Camping

🏕 **Canyon de Chelly National Monument.** Rustling cottonwood trees
shade campsites that serve both RVs and tents. ✉ *AZ Rte. 264, 3 mi
east of AZ Rte. 191, Chinle, AZ,* ☎ *520/674–5500,* WEB *www.nps.gov.
cach. Flush toilets, dump station, drinking water, fire pits, picnic ta-
bles, public telephone. 104 tent and RV sites.* ✉ *Free. Reservations
not accepted.*

🏕 **Red Rock State Park.** Red rocks loom 500 ft over the park's paved
campsites, which are surrounded by red sand and shady trees. ✉ *NM
566, Exit 31 from I–40, 7 mi east of Gallup,* ☎ *505/722–3829. Flush
toilets, partial hook-ups, dump station, drinking water, showers, fire
rings, picnic tables, public telephone, ranger station. 160 RV sites.* ✉
*$14 MC, V.*

## Shopping

**Kiva Gallery** (✉ 202 W. Historic Rte. 66, ☎ 505/722–5577) exhibits
art of the American Indian, including many original paintings.

At **Richardson's Trading Company** (✉ 222 W. Historic Rte. 66, ☎ 505/
722–4762), the great-granddaddy of trading posts, the wooden floors
creak under your feet as you gawk at the knockout array of Navajo
and Zuñi turquoise and silver earrings, squash blossoms, concho belts,
bracelets, natural-dye handwoven rugs, beadwork, and you name it.
Richardson's is also a veritable museum of old pawn (the often valu-
able, unclaimed items pawned by Native Americans). The fourth gen-
eration of the Tanner trading family runs **Shush Yaz Trading Co.** (✉
1304 W. Lincoln Ave., ☎ 505/722–0130), which stocks all manner of
Native American arts and crafts, including locally made Navajo squaw
skirts. The store sells traditional and contemporary jewelry and is a
great source of old pawn. The on-site restaurant serves native foods.
**Tobe Turpen's Indian Trading Post** (✉ 1710 S. 2nd St., ☎ 505/722–
3806) has been in business for more than 80 years, selling katsinas,
sand paintings, jewelry, folk art, and more. Poke around—you're likely
to make a real find here.

*En Route* Held the third Friday of every month, the **Crownpoint Rug Auction** (✉
Crownpoint Elementary School, NM 371, 26 mi north of Thoreau at
I–40, Exit 53, ☎ 505/786–7386, WEB www.crownpointrugauction.com)

is the foremost place to buy handwoven Navajo rugs—you're bidding with a mix of collectors and dealers, so prices on the some 300 to 400 rugs are sometimes well below what you'd pay at a store. Viewing begins at 3 PM, with the actual auction running from 7 PM till usually midnight or later. Keep in mind there are no overnight facilities in Crownpoint.

★ Dinosaurs used to roam the adjoining **Bisti and De-Na-Zin Wilderness areas** (✉ Bisti: NM 371, 36 mi south of Farmington; De-Na-Zin: unpaved C.R. 7500, off either NM 371 8 mi south of Bisti entrance or NM 44 at Huerfano, 34 mi south of Bloomington; ☎ 505/599–8900) when they were part of a shallow sea some 70 million years ago. Lending the 45,000 acres an eerie, lunarlike appearance are hoodoos, mushroom-shape rock formations in subtle shades of brown, gray, and white. De-Na-Zin (pronounced duh-*nah*-zen and named for a petroglyph found nearby) is the much larger and less visited of the two sections, and here you'll find hillier and more challenging terrain, plus numerous fossils and petrified logs. At Bisti (pronounced *biss*-tye), you'll encounter deeply eroded hoodoos whose striations represent layers of sandstone, shale, mudstone, coal, and silt. In many spots you'll climb over mounds of crumbly clay and silt that looks a bit like the topping of a coffee cake but gray. Both sections are ideal for photography, and in both backcountry camping is permitted. The Bureau of Land Management, which administers the land, asks that you remove nothing from either area, preserving its magical appearance for those who follow. The most fascinating terrain is 2 to 3 mi from the parking areas, and there are no trails, so bring a compass and be alert about your surrounding and where you are in relation to the sun—it's relatively easy to get lost in the vast, lonely, and barren place.

# ANASAZI COUNTRY

To gain a sense of the beauty, power, and complexity of the ancient civilizations of the Americas, you can do no better than to travel to Chaco Canyon, sometimes called the "Stonehenge of the West," and the more accessible Salmon Ruins and Aztec Ruins. Discoveries of the past 20 years, notably the Sun Dagger, which appears at a particular point in Chaco Canyon on each summer solstice, have increased interest in the science of archaeoastronomy—the study of the ways in which the ancients surveyed the skies, kept track of the movement of the planets and stars, and marked their passage within the construction of elaborate stone structures. But Anasazi Country is more than ancient ruins. Spectacular hiking, golfing, and fishing can be had here, and you can poke through small towns that are the products of northwestern New Mexico's homesteading era. The best shopping is for antiques and Native American jewelry and pottery.

## Farmington

❽ *142 mi north of Gallup via I–40 east to NM 371 north.*

A rough-edged, gritty, unpretentious town full of giant pickup trucks, with a radio dial loaded with country-and-western stations, Farmington sits in the heart of the Four Corners region, with archaeological, recreational, and scenic wonders within easy driving distance. Its central location, reasonable prices, and friendly ways make Farmington the ideal base.

The Navajo gave the name *Totah* ("among the waters") to the land around what is now Farmington, which lies at the confluence of three rivers—the Animas, La Plata, and San Juan. Homesteaders began planting farms and orchards in 1879 on this fertile land, and the "farming town" became Farmington.

The agricultural economy shifted to one based on oil and gas in the late 1940s, beginning a boom-and-bust cycle tied to the fluctuation of fuel prices. Diversification didn't come until the past decade or so, when Farmington began promoting its historic past with more gusto. Even more revitalizing was the creation of a regional shopping center, which swells the population by thousands on weekends, when Native Americans and other country people make their weekly or monthly trip to town to stock up on supplies.

You can get an inkling of what the Four Corners area was like during the trading-post days at the **Farmington Gateway Museum and Visitors Center,** in a spectacular modern sandstone building whose stonework closely resembles the Aztec and Chaco ruins. Landscaped grounds behind the building, where the Farmington Convention and Visitors Bureau is, extend down to the Animus River—an ideal spot for a picnic. The museum contains a permanent trading post exhibit and also presents art, science, Native American, and regional history exhibits throughout the year. ⊠ *3041 E. Main St.,* ☎ *505/599–1174.* ◫ *Free (except for certain exhibits).* ⊙ *Mon.–Sat. 9–5, Sun. noon–5.*

☺ If your short people start to get unruly, stop by the **E3 Children's Museum** for a break. The museum enthralls kids with a shadow room, a magnet table, giant floor puzzles, and a role-play area. It's a great spot to rest and regroup. ⊠ *302 N. Orchard,* ☎ *505/599–1425.* ◫ *Free.* ⊙ *Wed.–Fri. noon–5, Sat. 10–5.*

The **River Corridor,** a 5-mi walkway between Scott Avenue and U.S. 64 along the Animas River, winds alongside Berg Park. The corridor contains trails for walkers, runners, cyclists, and wildlife- and bird-watchers, as well as a man-made, 300-yard-long white-water course.

OFF THE
BEATEN PATH

**SHIPROCK PINNACLE –** West of Farmington, at U.S. 666 and U.S. 64, the 1,700-ft **Shiprock Pinnacle** rises from the desert floor like a massive schooner. It's sacred to the Navajo, who call it "rock with wings." No climbing or hiking is permitted. The pinnacle is composed of igneous rock flanked by upright walls of solidified lava.

**FOUR CORNERS MONUMENT –** About 30 mi west of Shiprock you'll reach the only place in the United States where you can stand in four states at the same time—at the intersection of New Mexico, Arizona, Colorado, and Utah. There's an Indian marketplace at this popular—if somewhat cheesy—attraction, which has no view to speak of. ⊠ *U.S. 160, north from U.S. 64,* ☎ *928/871–6647.* ◫ *$2.* ⊙ *May–Aug., daily 7 am–8 pm; Sept.–Apr., daily 8–5.*

## Dining and Lodging

$$$$ ✕ **K. B. Dillon's.** Fresh fish, beef, steamed vegetables, and pasta dishes are on the menu at this clubby steak house with a western-Victorian feel. There's live music some weekend nights. ⊠ *101 W. Broadway,* ☎ *505/325–0222. AE, MC, V.*

$$ ✕ **Three Rivers Eatery & Brewhouse.** In a historic downtown structure
★ with a gorgeous pressed-tin ceiling, exposed air ducts, and walls lined with historic photos, this microbrewery whips up more than 10 kinds of beer (also available to go) with names like Power Plant Porter and Chaco Nut Brown Ale. The brews go well with the enormous portions of tasty soups, salads, burgers, ribs, and other pub grub served here. It's open late most nights. ⊠ *101 E. Main St.,* ☎ *505/324–2187. Reservations not accepted. AE, D, MC, V. Closed Sun.*

$   ✕ **Bagel Conspiracy.** This urbane little bagelry and delicatessen with a bright sunny interior serves commendable fresh-baked bagels with daily-changing cream cheeses (like cranberry-orange-nut), coffees, and Italian sodas. A full range of creative sandwiches is also served. ⊠ *3554 E. Main St.,* ☎ *505/564–8888. Reservations not accepted. No credit cards. No dinner.*

$   ✕ **El Charro Cafe.** Don't be put off by El Charro's out-of-the-way location or shabby carpet. Locals who demand authentic Mexican fare head here for lunch. The pulse of life beats within the red chile. The combination plate—a tamale, an enchilada, a burrito, and guacamole, rice, and beans—won't leave you hungry. ⊠ *737 W. Main St.,* ☎ *505/327–2464. Reservations not accepted. AE, D, DC, MC, V. No dinner Sun.*

$   ✕ **The Spare Rib.** The decor here is nothing fancy, just plastic tablecloths over picnic tables, but the whole family can fill up on generous portions of delicious smoked barbecue. ⊠ *1700 E. Main St.,* ☎ *505/325–4800. Reservations not accepted. AE, D, MC, V. Closed Sun.*

$$$$   ▦ **Kokopelli's Cave.** Few accommodations in the world can claim a
★   more fascinating history and unusual setting than this fully furnished cave carved into the cliff side 250 ft above the La Plata River and an adjoining wildlife refuge. The exposed sandstone walls of this spacious one-bedroom unit trace 70 million years of erosion history. Geologist Bruce Black had the 1,650-square-ft cave blasted out in 1980, to serve as his office. It now contains a bedroom, fireplace, full kitchen (with Continental breakfast supplies included), and a romantic stone shower with a waterfall that trickles into a hot tub—there's even wall-to-wall carpeting. From the two terraces you may see the occasional ringtail cat or gray fox—a trail leads up the cliff face, some 70 vertical ft, to the parking area. The cave has two futons in the living area and accommodates up to six persons; there is a small collection of videos as well. ⊠ *206 W. 38th St., 87401,* ☎ *505/325–7855,* ☒ *505/325–9671,* WEB *www.bbonline.com/nm/kokopelli. 1 unit. No kids under 12, no smoking. AE, MC, V. CP.*

$–$$$   ▦ **Casa Blanca Bed & Breakfast Inn.** Luxury without pretension is the trademark of the innkeepers of the Mission-style Casa Blanca, which stands atop a bluff overlooking Farmington. You can relax in the southwestern-style den, watch city lights twinkle from the solarium, or zone out near the patio's fountain. One room has a double hot tub, another has a fireplace, and all receive turn-down service. Breakfast is a gourmet affair, and fresh-baked goodies are served in the afternoon. Business travelers seeking a homey atmosphere make it a point to stay here. ⊠ *505 E. La Plata St., 87401,* ☎ *505/327–6503 or 800/550–6503,* ☒ *505/326–5680. 4 rooms, 1 suite. Cable TV, Internet, meeting rooms; no smoking. AE, D, MC, V. BP.*

$–$$   ▦ **Silver River Adobe Inn.** This red-roof adobe sits on a sandstone cliff 30 ft above where the San Juan River meets the La Plata, at the west end of town. Rough-hewn timbers, fluffy quilts, and complete privacy make this rustic getaway ideal for romance or rumination. The proprietors, Diana and David, are excellent sources of information about adventures and explorations in the area. ⊠ *3151 W. Main St. (Box 3411, 87499),* ☎ *505/325–8219 or 800/382–9251,* WEB *www.cyberport.com/silveradobe. 2 rooms, 1 suite. Some kitchenettes, meeting room. AE, MC, V. BP.*

$   ▦ **Comfort Inn.** This well-run motel with warmly decorated, up-to-date rooms and a hospitable staff provides comfort indeed after a long day of sightseeing. ⊠ *555 Scott Ave., 87401,* ☎ *505/325–2626 or 800/341–1495,* ☒ *505/325–7675. 42 rooms, 18 suites. Cable TV with movies, pool, meeting rooms. AE, D, DC, MC, V. CP.*

## Nightlife and the Arts

Several of the restaurants in Farmington and Aztec are popular for cocktails, notably K. B. Dillon's and Three Rivers Eatery & Brewhouse. From
Wednesday to Saturday, regional-history and other plays are performed
at the **Outdoor Summer Theater** (⊠ Lion's Wilderness Park, College
Blvd. and Piñon Hills Blvd., ☎ 505/327–9336 or 800/448–1240) between mid-June and mid-August at 8 PM in a sandstone amphitheater.
An optional southwestern-style dinner is served prior to each performance. **San Juan College Theater** (⊠ 4601 College Blvd., ☎ 505/326–
3311 ext. 364) presents concerts, student recitals, lectures, and theatrical
performances.

## Outdoor Activities and Sports

### FISHING

**San Juan Troutfitters** (☎ 505/324–8149) conducts fly-fishing classes
and operates guided fishing trips. Call to make arrangements.

### GOLF

**Piñon Hills Golf Course** (⊠ 2101 Sunrise Pkwy., ☎ 505/326–6066),
an 18-hole, par-72 course, is one of New Mexico's best links. The greens
fee ranges from $28 to $32; an optional cart costs $16.

### WATER SPORTS

**Farmington Aquatic Center** (⊠ 1151 N. Sullivan St., ☎ 505/599–
1167), a public water wonderland, has a 150-ft-long water slide and
three pools.

## Shopping

The historic trading-post district along Main Street downtown is a good
place to look for antiques. Stores at the gargantuan **Animas Valley Mall**
(⊠ 4601 E. Main St., ☎ 505/326–5465) include Dillard's, Sears,
JCPenney, and Western Warehouse, plus specialty shops like Home Sweet
Home. The debut of the ubiquitous Gap clothing chain a few years
back was a sign of the region's steadily growing prosperity.

It's easy to while away an afternoon at the **Dusty Attic** (⊠ 111 W. Main
St., ☎ 505/327–7696), a 17,000-square-ft downtown mall where
you'll find antiques, arts, crafts, and gifts. **Fifth Generation Trading Co.**
(⊠ 232 W. Broadway, ☎ 505/326–3211), an old trading post run by
the Tanner family since 1875, has a wealth of Indian wares and is known
for sand paintings. Creaky wooden floors add to the charm of **Foutz
Indian Room** (⊠ 301 W. Main St., ☎ 505/325–9413), which sells superb Navajo folk art and old pawn. **Sentimental Journey Antiques** (⊠
218 W. Main St., ☎ 505/326–6533), a multidealer operation open
Wednesday–Friday, is crammed with interesting treasures and collectibles. About a half-hour drive west of town is the **Hogback Trading Co.** (⊠ 3221 U.S. 64, ☎ 505/598–5154), a trading post known
for fine, handwoven Navajo rugs.

# Salmon Ruins

**❾** *10 mi east of Farmington on U.S. 64.*

Salmon (pronounced *sol*-mon) Ruins, which dates from the 11th century, is a large Chacoan Anasazi apartment complex on the northern
edge of the San Juan River. A stunning example of pre-Columbian Pueblo
architecture and stonework, the site is named for a homesteader whose
family protected the ruins for nearly a century. **Heritage Park** contains
the restored Salmon Homestead and other traditional habitations of
the people of this region. ⊠ *6131 U.S. 64,* ☎ *505/632–2013.* 🖃 *$3.*
🕐 *Apr.–Oct., daily 8–5; Nov.–Mar., Mon.–Sat. 8–5, Sun. noon–5.*

## Aztec

**⑩** *14 mi northeast of Farmington on U.S. 550, 10 mi north of Bloomfield on NM 544.*

The many Victorian brick buildings and quaint outlying residential blocks give charming Aztec, the seat of San Juan County, the feeling of a picture-book hometown. Adding to the allure are the views had in the very distance of the snowcapped mountains north of Durango, Colorado, toward Telluride. The village part of the **Aztec Museum, Pioneer Village and Oil Field Exhibit** contains more than a dozen late-19th-century buildings—a blacksmith shop, a schoolhouse, a wooden oil derrick, and a log cabin, among others—that convey a sense of life as it used to be. ⊠ *125 N. Main St.,* ☎ *505/334–9829.* ☜ *Free.* ☉ *Memorial Day–Labor Day, Mon.–Sat. 9–5; Labor Day–Memorial Day, Mon.–Sat. 10–4.*

★ With the largest reconstructed Great Kiva in North America and a pueblo dwelling that once contained more than 500 rooms, **Aztec Ruins National Monument and Museum,** a World Heritage Site, dates from the early 1100s. Early homesteaders thought the dwelling was a Mexican Aztec ruin, but it actually is a section of what is known as the Chaco Phenomenon, the extensive social and economic system that reached far beyond Chaco Canyon. This pueblo was abandoned by the mid-1200s. You only need an hour or so to tour the ruin, which is less spectacular but considerably more accessible than those at Chaco. ⊠ *Near U.S. 550 and Ruins Rd.,* ☎ *505/334–6174.* ☜ *$4.* ☉ *Memorial Day–Labor Day, daily 8–6; Labor Day–Memorial Day, daily 8–5.*

### Dining and Lodging

**$–$$** ✕ **Hiway Grill.** Don't be put off by its location adjoining a package store: this is a lively restaurant with vintage car photos, a superfriendly staff, Art Deco tables, and red vinyl booths—it all has the feel of a '50s malt shop. Many of the American and New Mexican dishes—like the Mustang Melt (a burger with grilled onions and melted Swiss on rye with Thousand Island dressing) are named for classic cars. The sign outside has an actual '50s automobile stuck through it. ⊠ *401 N.E. Aztec Blvd.,* ☎ *505/334–6533. AE, D, DC, MC, V. Closed Sun.*

**$–$$** ✕🏠 **Miss Gail's Inn.** On Main Street just steps from the town's best antiquing (and the Aztec Museum), this rambling redbrick Victorian offers accommodations with character—some rooms have kitchenettes, and all are enlivened with quilts, antiques, and collectibles. You can grab lunch on weekdays and dinner on Friday and Saturday nights only (and only by advance reservation) at Giovanni's Restaurant ($$–$$$), a cheerful dining room in back with very good Italian food. ⊠ *300 S. Main St., 87410,* ☎ *505/334–3452 or 888/534–3452,* ℻ *505/334–9664. 8 rooms. Some kitchenettes. AE, D, MC, V. CP.*

**$–$$** 🏠 **Step Back Inn.** Though technically a modern motor hotel, this Victorian-style clapboard structure on the north edge of downtown offers a considerably more memorable experience than you'll have at any of the countless chain properties in nearby Farmington, and at similar prices. The public areas are inviting, and individually decorated rooms have a mix of newer pieces and reproduction antiques, floral wallpapers, and cozy chenille bedspreads. ⊠ *U.S. 550 at NM 544, 87410,* ☎ *505/334–1200 or 800/334–1255,* ℻ *505/334–9858. 40 rooms. AE, MC, V. CP.*

### Camping

⚠ **Angel Peak Recreation Area.** Get the feel of the canyon rim country and enjoy a hike through badlands formed by an ancient seabed before you pitch your tent. The last 6 mi of road leading to this primitive site is gravel. ⊠ *Rte. 7175, 20 mi south of Bloomfield,* ☎ *505/599–8900. Pit toilets, picnic tables. 7 sites.* ☒ *Free.*

# Navajo Dam

**⓫** *26 mi east of Aztec on NM 173.*

Navajo Dam is the name of a tiny town a few miles below Navajo Lake State Park and the name of the dam itself. At the base of the dam lie the legendary trout waters of the San Juan River. One of the country's top five trophy-trout streams, the San Juan has year-round fishing for rainbow, brown, and cutthroat trout. Many areas are catch and release only. The San Juan carves a scenic gorge of stepped cliffs alongside cottonwood-lined banks that attract elk, Barbary sheep, golden and bald eagles, blue herons, and not a few fly-fisherfolk in waders.

As you drive up over the dam you'll be rewarded with panoramic views down into the valley. **Navajo Lake State Park** is a popular boating and fishing spot; you can rent boats at two marinas. Short trails lead to the lakeshore, and the 3-mi-long cottonwood-shaded San Juan River Trail parallels the river down below the dam. Driving the narrow road across the top of the dam, with no guardrails, is a slightly hair-raising, memorable experience. ⊠ *1448 NM 511, off NM 173,* ☎ *505/632–2278.* ☒ *$4 per vehicle.*

## Lodging

**$$–$$$$** 🏨 **Soaring Eagle Lodge.** A haven for fly-fishers who want casual but upscale accommodations, the lodge houses guests in cabins that are fully furnished, complete with kitchenettes and rod-and-wader racks. You can step out of your cabin to a mile and a half of private river access, or take advantage of the on-site guide service and full fly shop. The food here is excellent, so the package that includes breakfast and dinner is a good choice. ⊠ *NM 511, 2 mi south of Navajo Dam, 87419,* ☎ *505/632–3721, 800/866–2719,* WEB *www.sanjuanflyfishing.com. 11 cabins. Kitchenettes, cable TV with movies, Internet, meeting rooms. MAP.*

## Camping

🏕 **Navajo Lake State Park.** At the park's three campgrounds some sites sit among piñon and juniper trees and overlook the lake. Hot showers are available at Sims Mesa and Pine campgrounds but not at Cottonwood Campground. ⊠ *1448 NM 511, off NM 173,* ☎ *505/632–2278. Flush toilets, dump stations, drinking water, fire pits, picnic tables. 200 sites.* ☒ *Tent sites $10, RV sites $14 with electricity, $18 with full hook-up.*

## Outdoor Activities and Sports

Stop by **Abe's Motel & Fly Shop/Born-n-Raised on the San Juan** (⊠ *1791 NM 173,* ☎ *505/632–2194*) to find out what flys you need to snare the wily San Juan rainbows. The lodging is a bit dodgy at Abe's, but you can pick up a cold drink and snacks or book a wade or float trip. At the revered **Rizuto's Fly Shop** (⊠ *1796 NM 173,* ☎ *505/632–3893 or 800/525–1437*), you can pick up fishing tips or book a guide.

# Chaco Culture National Historical Park

★ **⓬** *144 mi west of Abiquiu via NM 96 to NM 44/U.S. 550 to (unpaved) NM 57 south; 90 mi south of Farmington via NM 44/U.S. 550 to (unpaved) NM 57 south; 78 mi north of Grants via I–40 west to (unpaved) NM 57 north.*

The roads accessing **Chaco Canyon,** home to Chaco Culture National Historical Park, are dirt and can be impassable during inclement weather (particularly Route 57 from the south). The rough route, and the lack of gas stations, food concessions, or hotels along the way, keeps this archaeological treasure free from the overcrowding that can mar other national park visits: only about 85,000 people visit annually, compared with at least 10 times that number to Canyon de Chelly, which is just 80 mi away as the crow flies.

But persevere and you'll be rewarded with a look at an amazingly well preserved fragment of fascinating history, which is without peer in North America. Make every possible attempt to see the largest excavated ruins on the continent. The more than 2,000 sites were constructed between 900 and 1,150 years ago. Drive the paved loop road and you'll learn volumes about the sophistication, scientific knowledge, craftsmanship, and sheer ingenuity of the Anasazi, the ancestors of today's Pueblo Indians. The Anasazi built a system of 400 mi of roads radiating out in straight lines from Chaco Canyon, as well as irrigation ditches to water their cultivated fields. The complexity of the masonry and veneered walls of these dwellings, such as Pueblo Bonito, which once stood five stories tall and held 800 rooms, is astounding. Did 5,000 people once live here? Or was Chaco maintained as a ceremonial and trade center? The more that is learned about such phenomena as the Sun Dagger—a spear of light that appears in the same specific location at each summer solstice—the more questions arise about the creators of this truly marvelous place.

At the **visitor center** you can meander through a small museum on Chaco culture, peruse the bookstore, and buy bottled water (but no food). From here drive along the paved loop road to the various trailheads for the ruins; at each you'll find a small box containing a detailed self-guided tour brochure (a 50¢ donation per map is requested). Many of the 13 ruins at Chaco require a significant hike, but a few of the most impressive are just a couple hundred yards off the road. Ranger Cornucopia's hikes and campfire talks are worth sticking around for if you can.

**Pueblo Bonito** is perhaps the most brilliant of the ruins, a massive semi-circular "great house" that once stood four stories in places and encompasses many kivas and interconnected cells. The park trail runs alongside the outer mortar-and-sandstone walls, up a hill that allows a great view over the entire canyon, and then right through the ruin and several rooms. It is the most substantial of the structures—the ritualistic and cultural center of a Chacoan culture that may once have comprised some 150 settlements. Pueblo Bonito was used from AD 850 to about AD 1150, longer than any other area ruin. ⊠ *NM 57,* ☎ *505/786–7014.* ⊠ *$8 per vehicle.* ☉ *Memorial Day–Labor Day, daily 8–6; Labor Day–Memorial Day, daily 8–5.*

## Camping

⚠ **Chaco Culture National Historical Park.** Not far from the visitor center is a park service–operated campground. The site's primitiveness is its greatest asset: the nights come alive with bursts of stars, and the only noise is that of nature. The primary advantage of staying here is waking up in the canyon and having a full day to explore the ruins and perhaps hike some of the backcountry trails. Camping is limited to seven days; vehicles up to 30 ft can park here. Running water can be had at the visitor center. ⊠ *M 57,* ☎ *505/786–7014. Flush toilets, fire grates, picnic tables. 47 sites.* ⊠ *$10 Reservations not accepted.*

*En Route*  Whether you're coming or going from Chaco, **Cuba** is a good place to stop for gas and, depending on your inclination and the season, hot coffee or cold pop. There are gas stations, a convenience store, and **El Bruno's** (⊠ NM 44/U.S. 550 at NM 126, ☎ 505/289–9429), a very good Mexican restaurant that's right on the highway, plus a handful of inexpensive motels—your best bet in this regard is the **Cuban Lodge** (⊠ 6332 NM 44/U.S. 550, ☎ 505/289–3475). If you've got some time to spare, visit nearby **Pueblo Pintado** on NM 197. The village is little more than a few houses and a convenience store, but the Chacoan ruins are spectacular and easy to find.

## Jicarilla Apache Reservation

**⓭** *55 mi east of Navajo Dam on U.S. 64.*

The Spanish named the Jicarilla tribe, a group of Native Americans related to the Navajo and Apache, for the baskets they made. For centuries before the arrival of the Spanish, they were a nomadic people who roamed across northeastern New Mexico, southeastern Colorado, and the Oklahoma and Texas panhandles. Their tribe of 10,000 was decimated to 330 by 1897. The federal government relocated the tribe to this isolated area of almost a million acres a century ago. The tribe has made something of a comeback with the sale of timber, oil and gas development, casino gambling, and savvy investing.

Dulce ("sweet") on U.S. 64 is the capital of the reservation. The free **Arts & Crafts Museum** (⊠ ¼ mi west of downtown, U.S. 64, ☎ 505/759–3242 ext. 274) remains the best place to see the fine historic Jicarilla baskets, beadwork, and pottery. The **Cultural Center** (⊠ Basket La. and U.S. 64, ☎ 505/759–1343) is a small gift shop that sells mostly beadwork.

This country is known for fishing, particularly at Stone Lake, and for hunting; contact the **Game & Fish Department** (☎ 505/759–3442). You may also hike and camp. As on many other pueblos in New Mexico, the casino has become a big draw as well. Some Jicarilla celebrations are open to the public. The Little Beaver Roundup, the third weekend in July, entails a rodeo, powwow, and carnival and draws participants from Indian tribes and pueblos throughout the United States.

### Lodging

**$$** 🏨 **Best Western Jicarilla Inn.** This is the only place to stay in Dulce. The accommodations preserve the flavor of the cultural and natural setting, with dark woods, Native American art, and stone fireplaces. The restaurant, the Hill Crest, is a favorite gathering spot for celebration dinners. ⊠ *U.S. 64, 12 mi west of Jct. 84 (Box 233, Dulce 87528),* ☎ *505/759–3663 or 800/528–1234,* FAX *505/759–3170. 42 rooms. Restaurant, some kitchenettes, Internet, meeting rooms, some pets allowed. AE, D, DC, MC, V.*

# THE CHAMA VALLEY

A railroad town nestled at the base of 10,000-ft Cumbre Pass, lush and densely wooded Chama offers year-round outdoor activities, as well as a scenic railroad. From there, U.S. 84 hugs the Rio Chama and leads southward through monumental red rocks and golden sandstone spires that inspired Georgia O'Keeffe's vivid paintings of creased mountains, stark crosses, bleached animal skulls, and adobe architecture.

## Chama

**⓮** *30 mi east of Jicarilla Apache Reservation and 95 mi west of Taos on U.S. 64, 59 mi north of Abiquiu on U.S. 84.*

The booms and busts of Chama have largely coincided with the popularity of train transportation. The town's very earliest boom, which precipitated its founding, occurred in the 1880s when workers piled into town to construct the Denver & Rio Grande Railroad. In those days, narrow-gauge trains chugged over the high mountain tracks carrying gold and silver out from the mines of the San Juan Mountains, which straddle the nearby Colorado–New Mexico border. Gambling halls, moonshine stills, speakeasies, and brothels were a fixture along the main drag, Terrace Avenue. The lumber industry also thrived during the early years, and the town still has quite a few houses and buildings fashioned out of spare hand-hewn railroad ties.

Chama offers an assortment of outdoor recreation opportunities that's hard to beat. Vast meadows of wildflowers and aspen and ponderosa pines blanket the entire region. Hunters are drawn here by the abundant wildlife. There's cross-country skiing and snowmobiling in winter; camping, rafting, hiking, and fishing in summer, all in a pristine, green, high-mountain setting that feels like the top of the world.

All directions are given in terms of "the Y," the town's only major intersection (of U.S. 64/84 and NM 17). The big attraction in Chama is the historic **Cumbres & Toltec Scenic Railroad,** the narrow-gauge coal-driven steam engine that runs through the San Juan Mountains and over the Cumbres Pass. You'll chug over ancient trestles, around breathtaking bends, and high above the Los Pinos River—if the terrain looks at all familiar, you may have seen this railroad's "performance" in *Indiana Jones and the Last Crusade.* Midway through the trip you break for lunch and can switch to an awaiting Colorado-based train to complete the 64 mi to Antonito, Colorado (from which you'll be shuttled back by bus), or return from this point on the same train. Train trip packages including stays at area lodgings are available. ⊠ *15 Terrace Ave.,* ☎ *505/756–2151 or 888/286–2737.* ⊡ *$38–$58.* ☉ *Late May–mid.-Oct., daily departures at 8 AM and 10:30 AM.*

## Dining and Lodging

**$$** ✕ **Whistle Stop Cafe.** "We serve real food here," says the proprietor, meaning fresh seafood and fresh roasted turkey. The $10 dinners and $5 lunches are the big draw. Recommended are the twice-baked duck with honey-almond sauce; the blackened salmon; and halibut in lemon-dill sauce. The café is also open for breakfast. ⊠ *425 Main St., across from train station,* ☎ *505/756–1833. MC, V. Closed Nov.–Apr.*

**$$$$** ⊡ **The Lodge at Chama.** An outdoor-oriented vacation can also be luxurious. The lodge and working ranch, owned by the Jicarilla Apache tribe, is on 32,000 idyllic acres on the Colorado border, at an elevation between 9,000 and 11,000 ft, with 10 lakes. Horseback riding, trophy fishing, touring the ranch, and sitting by the huge stone fireplace ought to relax the most stressed-out executive. Meals and the bar tab are included. ⊠ *16253 U.S. 84 (Box 127, 87520),* ☎ *505/756–2133,* FAX *505/756–2519. 9 rooms, 2 suites. Restaurant, hot tub, sauna, bar, Internet, meeting rooms. D, MC, V. FAP.*

**$–$$** ⊡ **Cardin's Crossing B&B.** Fancy a cup of tea on a Victorian front porch filled with white wicker furniture? Or a stroll through a lovingly tended flower garden? At Cardin's Crossing, there's an all-out breakfast with fresh fruit and homemade cinnamon rolls, and homemade pie is served every night as a snack. The Narrow Gauge Room has a model train running overhead, and the Victorian dollhouse room has a dollhouse and canopy bed. ⊠ *551 Maple Ave. (Box 180, 87520),* ☎ *505/756–2542 or 800/852–6400. 2 rooms. Some pets allowed; no kids, no smoking. MC, V. BP.*

**$–$$** ⚏ **The Lightheart Inn.** This cozy house emphasizes the nourishment of body and soul with a massage therapist on the premises and health-conscious breakfasts. ⊠ *63 Terrace Ave. (Box 223, 87520),* ☎ *505/756–2908. 2 rooms. Hot tub. MC, V. BP.*

**$** ⚏ **River Bend Lodge.** This comfortable but not fancy lodge has one of the few hot tubs in town. It's right on the Chama River, so you can walk out your door and cast a fly, or you might come across a black bear meandering by. Management here is especially sensitive and accommodating, particularly for groups or family reunions. It also offers train packages. ⊠ *U.S. 84 (Box 593, 87520),* ☎ *505/756–2264 or 800/288–1371,* FAX *505/756–2664. 19 rooms. Cable TV with movies, hot tub, meeting room. AE, D, DC, MC, V.*

**$** ⚏ **Spruce Lodge.** So you like roughing it, but not too rough? These 12 little cabins with kitchenettes beside the Rio Chama are the perfect balance: rustic but comfortable. You know you're away from it all when you can hear the river and the wind sifting through the pines. Pets are welcome. ⊠ *U.S. 84 (Box 365, 87520),* ☎ *505/756–2593. 12 cabins. Kitchenettes. D, MC, V.*

### Nightlife and the Arts

To hear local bands on Saturday night, head for **Ben's Lounge** (⊠ NM 17, ☎ 505/756–2922). The **Chama Valley Music Festival** (☎ 505/756–2836) takes place every Friday and Saturday in July.

### Outdoor Activities and Sports

Plenty of outfitters are here to help out with equipment and tours. **Adventures** (☎ 888/660–9878) provides snowmobiles. **Chama Ski Service** (☎ 505/756–2493) rents cross-country ski equipment. **Lone Pine Hunting and Outfitting Co.** (☎ 505/756–2992 or 800/704–4087) offers horseback riding.

Looking to get on the water? You've got a few options. **Far Flung Adventures** (☎ 800/359–2627). **Los Rios** (☎ 505/776–8854 or 800/544–1181). **Canyon REO** (☎ 520/774–3377 or 800/637–4604).

### Shopping

**Local Color Gallery** (⊠ 567 Terrace Ave., ☎ 505/756–2604) carries photography and jewelry of local artisans. The sales of many goods at **Trackside Emporium** (⊠ 611 Terrace Ave., ☎ 505/756–1848) support the preservation of the railroad; here you'll find books, signs, and other memorabilia pertaining to the trains. **Chama Valley Supermarket** (⊠ 2451 U.S. 84, ☎ 505/756–2545) at the "Y" intersection sells groceries and fishing supplies.

# Los Ojos

**⑮** *13 mi south of Chama on U.S. 64/84.*

Los Ojos, midway between Tierra Amarilla and Chama, could well serve as a model for rural economic development worldwide. The little town has experienced an economic revival of sorts by returning to its ancient roots—the raising of churro sheep (the original breed brought over by the Spanish, prized for its wool) and weaving. Ganados del Valle, the community-based, nonprofit economic development corporation headquartered here, has created jobs and increased prosperity by returning to the old ways, with improved marketing. You'll also find a smattering of artists' studios, most of them in rustic buildings with corrugated metal roofs.

The cooperative **Tierra Wools** produces some of the finest original weavings in the Southwest. Designs are based on the old Rio Grande styles, and weavers make rugs and capes of superb craftsmanship entirely by hand, using old-style looms. Weaving classes are available. ⊠ *91 Main St.,* ☎ *505/588–7231.* ☉ *June–Aug., Mon.–Sat. 9–6, Sun. 10–4; Sept.–May, Mon.–Sat. 10–5.*

### Dining and Lodging

$   ✕ **Pastore's Feed and General Store.** Inside a century-old general
★   store, this funky café serves up homemade cinnamon rolls, muffins, and burritos for breakfast and gourmet sandwiches, homemade soup, and salad for lunch and early dinner. It's a fun hangout with better food than just about anything else in Chama, and everyone seems to know one another. ⊠ *100 Market St.,* ☎ *505/588–7821. No credit cards. Closed Sun.*

$   🖫 **El Vado Ranch.** This old-time hunting camp with gas-heated cabins on the river is a launch site for rafters and a favorite haunt of fishermen. They're still bragging over here about the state-record brown trout they caught in 1946. ⊠ *3150 NM 112 (Box 129, Tierra Amarilla 87575),* ☎ *505/588–7354. 9 cabins. Kitchenettes. AE, MC, V. Closed mid-Dec.– mid-Mar.*

### Camping

⚠ **El Vado RV Resort.** Tent and RV campers can plant themselves 2 mi from El Vado Lake and 5 mi from El Vado Lake State Park at this campsite among trees and sagebrush. Senior citizens are the majority here. There is a recreation room, and five RV rental units are available. ⊠ *NM 112 W (Box 89, Tierra Amarilla 87575),* ☎ *505/588– 7225. Flush toilets, full hook-ups, drinking water, laundry facilities, showers, general store, pool. 110 RV sites.* ▦ *$19. Closed mid-Oct.– mid-Apr.*

*En Route*   Heading south on U.S. 84 from Los Ojos, you will reach the small town of **Tierra Amarilla,** from which you can access two state parks. Eleven miles west of town, **Heron Lake State Park** (⊠ NM 95 and U.S. 64, ☎ 505/588–7470) is a designated "quiet lake" (powerboats may not exceed no-wake speed) ideal for sailing and trout fishing. Seventeen miles southwest of Tierra Amarilla is **El Vado Lake State Park** (⊠ NM 112, ☎ 505/588–7247), where you can water-ski, fish, and watch for bald eagles, osprey, and other birds in winter. Both parks have developed campsites. From Heron Lake, the 5½-mi Rio Chama Trail crosses the Rio Chama, winds along the south slope of the canyon, goes up to a mesa top, and descends to the shore of El Vado Lake.

# NORTHWESTERN NEW MEXICO A TO Z

### AIR TRAVEL

Most major airlines provide service to the state's main airport in Albuquerque, 145 mi east of Gallup and 185 mi southeast of Farmington. Air Canada, America West, Frontier, Mesa, and United serve Gallup City Airport and Four Corners Regional Airport in Farmington. Great Lakes Aviation flies to Farmington from Denver. *See* Air Travel *in* Smart Travel Tips A to Z for national airline phone numbers.

➤ AIRPORTS: **Four Corners Regional Airport** (⊠ 1300 W Navajo St., Farmington, ☎ 505/599–1285).**Gallup City Airport** (⊠ 2111 W. Hwy. 66, Gallup, ☎ 505/722–4896).

➤ REGIONAL AIRLINES: **Frontier** (☎ 800/432–1359, ▦ www. frontierairlines.com). **Great Lakes Aviation** (☎ 800/554–5111, ▦ www.greatlakesav.com). **Mesa Airlines** (☎ 800/637–2247, ▦ www.mesa-air.com).

## BUS TRAVEL

Texas, New Mexico & Oklahoma Coaches, affiliated with Greyhound Lines, provides service to Grants, Gallup, Farmington, and other towns in northwestern New Mexico.

➤ Bus Company: **Texas, New Mexico & Oklahoma Coaches** (☎ 505/ 325–1009 or 800/231–2222).

## CAR RENTAL

You can rent a car from Avis, Budget, or Hertz at the Farmington airport. Budget also has an office at the Gallup airport. *See* Car Rental *in* Smart Travel Tips A to Z for national rental agency phone numbers.

## CAR TRAVEL

A car is your best bet getting to and around the region. Interstate 40 heads due west from Albuquerque toward Arizona. U.S. 64 leads west from Taos into northwestern New Mexico and east from Arizona. NM 44/U.S. 550 travels to the northwest from I–25 (15 mi north of Albuquerque), intersecting with U.S. 64 at Bloomfield, 14 mi east of Farmington. Road conditions vary with the seasons. Winter can create snowy, icy roads; summer can bring ferocious thunderstorms, hailstorms, and flash flood warnings.

## EMERGENCIES

In an emergency, dial 911.

➤ Hospitals: **Rehoboth McKinley Christian Health Care Services** (✉ 1901 Red Rock Dr., Gallup, ☎ 505/863–7141). **San Juan Regional Health Center** (✉ 801 W. Maple St., Farmington, ☎ 505/325–5011).

➤ Late-Night Pharmacies: **Walgreens** (✉ Main and 30th Sts., Farmington, ☎ 505/325–1749; ✉ 1626 Historic Rte. 66, Gallup, ☎ 505/ 722–9499).

## TRAIN TRAVEL

Amtrak has daily service to between Gallup and Albuquerque on the *Southwest Chief.*

➤ Rail Service: **Amtrak** (☎ 800/872–7245, WEB www.amtrak.com).

## VISITOR INFORMATION

➤ Tourist Information: **Chama Valley Chamber of Commerce** (✉ 499 S. Terrace Ave., 87520, ☎ 505/756–2306 or 800/477–0149). **Farmington Convention and Visitors Bureau** (✉ 3041 E. Main St., 87402, ☎ 505/326–7602 or 800/448–1240, WEB www.farmingtonnm. org). **Gallup Convention and Visitors Bureau** (✉ 701 Montoya St., 87301, ☎ 505/863–3841 or 800/242–4282, WEB www.gallupnm.org). **Grants/Cibola County Chamber of Commerce** (✉ 100 N. Iron Ave., 87020, ☎ 800/748–2142, WEB www.grants.org). **Tourism Department, Jicarilla Apache Tribe**(✉ Box 507, Dulce 87528, ☎ 505/759–3242, FAX 505/759–3005). **Navajo Nation Tourism Office** (✉ Box 633, Window Rock, AZ 86515, ☎ 520/871–6436 or 520/871–7371, FAX 520/ 871–7942 or 520/871–7381).

# 4 SANTA FE

## WITH SIDE TRIPS TO AREA PUEBLOS AND HISTORIC SITES

Take a high-desert plateau with crystalline air at the foot of snowcapped peaks; layer in almost 400 years of Spanish, Mexican, and Native American influences; and sprinkle on an odd assortment of artists, writers, New Agers, and urban refugees, and you get Santa Fe, America's most un-American city.

Updated by
Andrew Collins

W ITH ITS CRISP, CLEAR AIR and bright, sunny weather, Santa
Fe couldn't be more welcoming. On a plateau at the base
of the Sangre de Cristo Mountains—at an elevation of
7,000 ft—the city is surrounded by remnants of a 2,000-year-old
Pueblo civilization and filled with reminders of almost four centuries
of Spanish and Mexican rule. The town's placid central Plaza, which
dates from the early 17th century, has been the site of bullfights, public floggings, gunfights, battles, political rallies, promenades, and public markets over the years. A one-of-a-kind destination, Santa Fe is fabled
for its rows of chic art galleries, superb restaurants, and shops selling
southwestern furnishings and cowboy gear.

La Villa Real de la Santa Fe de San Francisco de Asísi (the Royal City
of the Holy Faith of St. Francis of Assisi) was founded in the early 1600s
by Don Pedro de Peralta, who planted his banner in the name of Spain.
In 1680 the region's Pueblo people rose in revolt, burning homes and
churches and killing hundreds of Spaniards. After an extended siege
in Santa Fe, the Spanish colonists were driven out of New Mexico. The
tide turned 12 years later, when General Don Diego de Vargas returned
with a new army from El Paso and recaptured Santa Fe.

To commemorate de Vargas's victory, Las Fiestas de Santa Fe have been
held every year since 1712. The nation's oldest community celebration
takes place on the weekend after Labor Day, with parades, mariachi
bands, pageants, the burning of *Zozóbra*—also known as Old Man
Gloom—and nonstop parties. "Fiesta" (as it's referred to locally) is but
one of many annual opportunities for revelry—from the arrival of the
rodeo and the opening week of the Santa Fe Opera in summer to traditional Pueblo dances at Christmastime.

Following de Vargas's defeat of the Pueblos, the then-grand Camino Real
(Royal Road), stretching from Mexico City to Santa Fe, brought an army
of conquistadors, clergymen, and settlers to the northernmost reaches
of Spain's New World conquests. In 1820 the Santa Fe Trail—a prime
artery of U.S. westward expansion—spilled a flood of covered wagons
from Missouri onto the Plaza. A booming trade with the United States
was born. After Mexico achieved independence from Spain in 1821, its
subsequent rule of New Mexico further increased this commerce.

The Santa Fe Trail's heyday ended with the arrival of the Atchison,
Topeka & Santa Fe Railway in 1880. The trains, and later the nation's
first highways, brought a new type of settler to Santa Fe—artists who
fell in love with its cultural diversity, history, and magical color and
light. Their presence attracted tourists, who quickly became a primary
source of income for the largely poor populace.

Santa Fe is renowned for its arts, tricultural (Native American, Hispanic, and Anglo) heritage, and adobe architecture. The Pueblo people introduced adobe to the Spanish, who in turn developed the adobe
brick style of construction. In a relatively dry, treeless region, adobe
was a suitable natural building material. Melding into the landscape
with their earthen colors and rounded, flowing lines, the pueblos and
villages were hard to see from afar and thus somewhat camouflaged
from raiding nomadic tribes. The region's distinctive architecture no
longer repels visitors, it attracts them.

Among the smallest state capitals in the country, Santa Fe has no
major airport (Albuquerque's is the nearest). The city's population, an
estimated 62,000, swells to nearly double that figure in summer. In winter the skiers arrive, lured by the challenging slopes of Ski Santa Fe and

Taos Ski Valley (☞ Chapter 5). Geared for tourists, Santa Fe can put a serious dent in your travel budget. Prices are highest June–August. Between September and November and between April and May they're lower, and (except for the major holidays) from December to March they're the lowest.

# EXPLORING SANTA FE

Humorist Will Rogers said on his first visit to Santa Fe, "Whoever designed this town did so while riding on a jackass, backwards, and drunk." The maze of narrow streets and alleyways confounds motorists, but with shops and restaurants, a flowered courtyard, or an eye-catching gallery at nearly every turn they're a delight for pedestrians. The trickle of water called the Santa Fe River runs west, parallel to Alameda Street, from the Sangre de Cristo Mountains to the open prairie southwest of town, where it disappears into a narrow canyon before joining the Rio Grande. But in New Mexico there is a *dicho,* or old saying, "*agua es vida*"—"water is life"—be it ever so humble.

There are five state museums in Santa Fe, and purchasing a Museum of New Mexico pass is this most economical way to visit them all. The four-day pass costs $15 and is sold at all five of the museums, which include the Palace of the Governors, Museum of Fine Arts, Museum of Indian Arts and Culture, Museum of International Folk Art, and Museum of Spanish Colonial Art.

## Santa Fe Plaza

Much of the history of Santa Fe, New Mexico, the Southwest, and even the West has some association with Santa Fe's central Plaza, which New Mexico governor Don Pedro de Peralta laid out in 1607. The Plaza, already well established by the time of the Pueblo revolt in 1680, was the site of a bullring and of fiestas and fandangos. Freight wagons unloaded here after completing their arduous journey across the Santa Fe Trail. The American flag was raised over the Plaza in 1846, during the Mexican War, which resulted in Mexico's loss of all its territories in the present southwestern United States. For a time the Plaza was a tree-shaded park with a white picket fence. In the 1890s it was an expanse of lawn where uniformed bands played in an ornate gazebo. Particularly festive times on the Plaza are the weekend after Labor Day, during Las Fiestas de Santa Fe, and at Christmas, when all the trees are filled with lights and rooftops are outlined with *farolitos,* votive candles lit within paper-bag lanterns.

*Numbers in the text correspond to numbers in the margin and on the Downtown Santa Fe map.*

### A Good Walk

To get started, drop by the information booth at the northwest corner of the plaza, across the street from the clock, where Palace Street meets Lincoln Street (in front of the bank) to pick up a free map. From there, begin your walk around the plaza. You can get an overview of the history of Santa Fe and New Mexico at the **Palace of the Governors** ①, which borders the northern side of the Plaza on Palace Avenue. Outside, under the Palace portal, dozens of Native American craftspeople sell their wares. From the palace, cross Lincoln Street to the **Museum of Fine Arts** ②, where the works of regional masters are on display. The **Georgia O'Keeffe Museum** ③, on nearby Johnson Street, exhibits the works of its namesake, New Mexico's best-known painter.

From the O'Keeffe Museum, return to the Plaza and cut across to its southeast corner to Old Santa Fe Trail, where you can find the town's oldest hotel, **La Fonda** ④, a good place to soak up a little of bygone Santa Fe. One block east on Cathedral Place looms the imposing facade of **St. Francis Cathedral** ⑤. Across from the cathedral is the **Institute of American Indian Arts** ⑥. A stone's throw from the museum is cool, quiet **Sena Plaza** ⑦, accessible through two doorways on Palace Avenue.

TIMING

It's possible to zoom through this compact area in about five hours—two hours exploring the Plaza and the Palace of the Governors, two hours seeing the Museum of Fine Arts and the Museum of the Institute of American Indian Arts, and an hour visiting the other sites.

## Sights to See

❸ **Georgia O'Keeffe Museum.** One of many East Coast artists who visited New Mexico in the first half of the 20th century, O'Keeffe fell in love with the region and returned to live and paint here, eventually emerging as the demigoddess of southwestern art. This private museum devoted to the works of this Modernist painter opened in 1997. O'Keeffe's innovative view of the landscape is captured in *From the Plains*, inspired by her memory of the Texas plains, and *Jimson Weed*, a quintessential O'Keeffe study of one of her favorite plants. Special exhibitions with O'Keeffe's modernist peers are on view throughout the year. Unfortunately, the museum provides relatively little context for O'Keeffe's works or biographical information about her life. ⊠ 217 *Johnson St.*, ☎ *505/995–0785*, WEB *www.okeeffemuseum.org.* ⊠ *$5, free Fri. 5–8 PM.* ☉ *July–Oct., Sat.–Thurs 10–5, Fri. 10–8; Nov.–June, Thurs.–Tues. 10–5, Fri. 10–8.*

❻ **Institute of American Indian Arts Museum.** Inside the handsomely renovated former post office, this museum contains the largest collection of contemporary Native American art in the United States. The paintings, photography, sculptures, prints, and traditional crafts exhibited here were created by past and present students and teachers. The institute itself, which moved to the College of Santa Fe campus, was founded as a one-room studio classroom in the early 1930s by Dorothy Dunn, a beloved art teacher who played a critical role in launching the careers of many Native American artists. In the 1960s and 1970s it blossomed into the nation's premier center for Native American arts. Artist Fritz Scholder taught here for years, as did the sculptor Allan Houser. Among their disciples was the painter T. C. Cannon. ⊠ 108 *Cathedral Pl.*, ☎ *505/983–8900; 505/983–1777 information line;* WEB *www.iaiancad.org/museum.htm.* ⊠ *$4.* ☉ *June–Sept., Mon.–Sat. 9–5, Sun. 10–5; Oct.–May, Mon.–Sat. 10–5, Sun. noon–5.*

❹ **La Fonda.** A Santa Fe landmark, La Fonda faces the southeast corner of the Plaza. A *fonda* (inn) has stood on this site for centuries. Architect Isaac Hamilton Rapp, whose Rio Grande–Pueblo Revival structures put Santa Fe style on the map, built this hotel in 1922. The hotel was remodeled in 1926 by another luminary of Santa Fe architecture, John Gaw Meem. The hotel was sold to the Santa Fe Railway in 1926 and became one of Fred Harvey's Harvey House hotels until 1968. Because of its proximity to the Plaza and its history as a gathering place for cowboys, trappers, traders, soldiers, frontier politicians, movie stars (Errol Flynn stayed here), artists, and writers, it is referred to as "The Inn at the End of the Trail." Major social events still take place here. A great way to experience the hotel is with a drink at the fifth-floor Bell Tower

N

599

599

0        1/2 mile
0        1 km

Buckman Rd.

Paseo

W. Alameda St.

Santa Fe River

Agua Fria St.

Osage Rd.

County Road 66

Siler Rd.

14

W. San Mateo R

Llano St.

Calle Lorca

Siring

Cerrillos Rd.

TO TURQUOISE TRAIL

Av. de las Campanas

Calle Pintora

Yucca St.

Zia Rd.

TO AIRPORT

Rodeo Rd.

Vereda de Encanto

Rode

See Detail Map
Downtown Santa Fe

TO
TESUQUE,
TAOS

475

Bishop's Lodge Rd.

Valley Dr.

Hyde Park Rd.

Old Taos Hwy.

N. Guadalupe St.

Paseo de Peralta

Artist Rd.

Kearney Ave.

Washington Ave.

Old Fort
Marcy Park

N. St. Francis Dr.

San Francisco St.

W. Alameda St.

The
Plaza

E. Water St.

Old
Santa Fe
Station

Guadalupe St.

Sandoval St.

E. Alameda St.

Cathedral

Gonzales Rd.

State
Capitol

Canyon Rd.

Cerro Gordo Rd.

Santa Fe River

Peralta

Messenger
Patrick Smith
Park

Cam. Cabra

Cerrillos Rd.

Don Diego Ave.

Galisteo St.

Don Gaspar Ave.

Old Santa Fe Trail

St. Francis Dr.

Cam. del Monte Sol

Cam. de
Cruz Blanca

Cordova Rd.

Galisteo St.

Old Pecos Trail

Museum of Indian
Arts and Culture

Museum of
International
Folk Art

Wheelwrigth Museum
of the American Indian

E. San Mateo Rd.

E. Butolph Rd.

Old Santa Fe Trail

84
285

466

84
285

St. Francis Dr.

TO ALBUQUERQUE

25

TO LAS VEGAS, NM

300

# Downtown Santa Fe

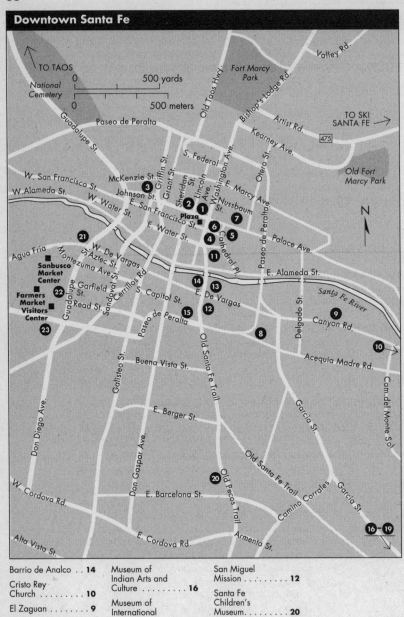

TO TAOS

National Cemetery

Paseo de Peralta

0     500 yards

0     500 meters

Fort Marcy Park

TO SKI SANTA FE

Old Fort Marcy Park

475

Valley Rd.

Old Taos Hwy.

Bishop's Lodge Rd.

Artist Rd.

Kearney Ave.

Guadalupe St.

W. San Francisco St.

W. Alameda St.

McKenzie St.

Johnson St.

E. San Francisco St.

W. Water St.

E. Water St.

Griffin St.

Grant St.

Sheridan St.

Lincoln Ave.

S. Federal

Washington Ave.

Nussbaum St.

E. Marcy Ave.

Otero St.

Plaza

Palace Ave.

Paseo de Peralta

N

W. De Vargas St.

Aztec St.

Agua Fria

Sanbusco Market Center

Farmers Market Visitors Center

Montezuma Ave.

Garfield St.

Read St.

Guadalupe St.

Sandoval St.

Cerrillos Rd.

S. Capitol St.

E. De Vargas

Cathedral Pl.

E. Alameda St.

Santa Fe River

Canyon Rd.

Acequia Madre Rd.

Delgado St.

Cam. del Monte Sol

Paseo de Peralta

Galisteo St.

Buena Vista St.

Old Santa Fe Trail

E. Berger St.

Don Gaspar Ave.

Don Diego Ave.

W. Cordova Rd.

E. Barcelona St.

E. Cordova Rd.

Alta Vista St.

Old Pecos Trail

Old Santa Fe Trail

Garcia St.

Garcia St.

Camino Corrales

Armenta St.

16 — 19

San Miguel Mission

Santa Fe Children's Museum

Santa Fe Southern Railway

Santuario de Guadalupe

SITE Santa Fe

Bar (open late spring–early fall), which offers tremendous sunset views. ⊠ *E. San Francisco St. at Old Santa Fe Trail,* ☎ *505/982–5511,*

---

NEED A
BREAK?

**Carlos' Gosp'l Cafe** (⊠ 125 Lincoln Ave., ☎ 505/983–1841) has a black-and-white checked floor and some patio chairs; it's hidden in a courtyard behind the Palace of the Governors and serves just about the best pies in town, always baked fresh daily. Great sandwiches are served, too. The gorgeous space of the **Longevity Café & Emporium** (⊠ Plaza Mercado center, 2nd floor, Water and Galisteo Sts., ☎ 505/ 986–0403), with a latilla-and-viga ceiling, leather sofas, and cool music, draws a quirky crowd and is open late. Have a cup of organic tea and a homemade dessert like pumpkin pie with ginseng-chai, or pick up holistic books and East Asian tea ware.

---

★ ❷ **Museum of Fine Arts.** Designed by Isaac Hamilton Rapp in 1917, the museum contains one of America's finest regional collections. It's also one of Santa Fe's earliest Pueblo Revival structures, inspired by the adobe structures at Acoma Pueblo. Split-cedar *latillas* (branches set in a crosshatch pattern) and hand-hewn vigas form the ceilings. The 8,000-piece permanent collection, of which only a fraction is exhibited at any given time, emphasizes the work of regional and nationally renowned artists, including the early Modernist Georgia O'Keeffe; realist Robert Henri; the "Cinco Pintores" (five painters) of Santa Fe (including Fremont Elis and Will Shuster); members of the Taos Society of Artists (Ernest L. Blumenschein, Bert G. Philips, Joseph H. Sharp, and E. Irving Couse, among others); and the works of noted 20th-century photographers of the Southwest, including Laura Gilpin, Ansel Adams, and Dorothea Lange. Rotating exhibits are staged throughout the year. Many excellent examples of Spanish-colonial-style furniture are on display. An interior *placita* (small plaza) with fountains, WPA murals, and sculpture, and the St. Francis Auditorium are other highlights. Concerts and lectures are often held in the auditorium. ⊠ *107 W. Palace Ave.,* ☎ *505/476–5072,* WEB *www.nmculture.org.* ⊡ *$7, 4-day pass $15 (good at all 5 state museums in Santa Fe), free Fri. 5–8 PM.* ☉ *Tues.–Thurs. and weekends 10–5, Fri. 10–8.*

★ ☃ ❶ **Palace of the Governors.** A humble-looking one-story adobe on the north side of the Plaza, the palace is the oldest public building in the United States. Built at the same time as the Plaza, circa 1610 (scholars debate the exact year), it was the seat of four regional governments—those of Spain, Mexico, the Confederacy, and the U.S. territory that preceded New Mexico's statehood, which was achieved in 1912. The building was abandoned in 1680, following the Pueblo Revolt, but resumed its role as government headquarters when Don Diego de Vargas successfully returned in 1692. It served as the residence for 100 Spanish, Mexican, and American governors, including Governor Lew Wallace, who wrote his epic *Ben Hur* in its then drafty rooms, all the while complaining of the dust and mud that fell from its earthen ceiling. In 2003, construction is scheduled to begin on a brand-new State History Museum, which will stand directly behind the Palace and is expected to open in 2005. Simultaneously, the palace of the Governors is slated to be renovated to a house-museum. Its rooms will contain period furnishings and exhibits that illustrate the building's myriad functions over the past four centuries.

Dozens of Native American vendors gather daily under the portal of the Palace of the Governors to display and sell pottery, jewelry, bread, and other goods. With few exceptions, the more than 500 artists and craftspeople registered to sell here are Pueblo or Navajo Indians. The merchandise for sale is required to meet Museum of New Mexico standards: all items are handmade or hand-strung in Native American households; silver jewelry is either sterling (92.5% pure) or coin (90% pure) silver; all metal jewelry bears the maker's mark, which is registered with the museum. Prices tend to reflect the high quality of the merchandise. Don't take photographs without permission.

The palace has been the central headquarters of the Museum of New Mexico since 1913, housing the main section of the **State History Museum.** Permanent exhibits chronicle 450 years of New Mexico history, using maps, furniture, clothing, housewares, weaponry, and village models. The main rooms contain rotating exhibits, such as "Jewish Pioneers of New Mexico," an exploration of the vital role Jewish immigrants played during the late 19th and early 20th centuries in the state's civic, economic, and cultural development. With advance permission, students and researchers have access to the comprehensive **Fray Angélico Chávez Library** and its rare maps, manuscripts, and photographs (more than 120,000 prints and negatives). The palace is also home to the **Museum of New Mexico Press,** which prints books, pamphlets, and cards on antique presses and hosts bookbinding demonstrations, lectures, and slide shows. There is an outstanding gift shop and bookstore. ⊠ *Palace Ave., north side of the Plaza,* ☎ *505/476–5100,* WEB *www.palaceofthegovernors.org.* ⊠ *$7, 4-day pass $15 (good at all 5 state museums in Santa Fe), free Fri. 5–8.* ☉ *Tues.–Thurs. and weekends 10–5, Fri. 10–8.*

★ ❺ **St. Francis Cathedral.** This magnificent cathedral, a block east of the Plaza, is one of the rare significant departures from the city's ubiquitous Pueblo architecture. Construction was begun in 1869 by Jean Baptiste Lamy, Santa Fe's first archbishop, working with French architects and Italian stonemasons. The Romanesque style was popular in Lamy's native home in the southwest of France. The circuit-riding cleric was sent by the Catholic Church to the Southwest to change the religious practices of its native population (to "civilize" them, as one period document puts it) and is buried in the crypt beneath the church's high altar. He was the inspiration behind Willa Cather's novel *Death Comes for the Archbishop* (1927).

A small adobe chapel on the northeast side of the cathedral, the remnant of an earlier church, embodies the Hispanic architectural influence so conspicuously absent from the cathedral itself. The chapel's *Nuestra Señora de la Paz* (Our Lady of Peace), popularly known as *La Conquistadora,* the oldest Madonna statue in the United States, accompanied Don Diego de Vargas on his reconquest of Santa Fe in 1692, a feat attributed to the statue's spiritual intervention. Every Friday the faithful adorn the statue with a new dress. Just south of the cathedral, where the parking lot meets Paseo de Peralta, is the **Archives of the Archdiocese Museum** (☎ 505/983–3811), a small museum where many of the area's historic, liturgical artifacts are on view. ⊠ *231 Cathedral Pl.,* ☎ *505/982–5619.* ☉ *Daily 8–5:45, except during mass. Mass Mon.–Sat. at 7 and 8:15 AM, 12:10, and 5:15 PM; Sun. at 6, 8, and 10 AM, noon, and 7 PM. Museum weekdays 9–noon and 1–4.*

❼ **Sena Plaza.** Two-story buildings enclose this courtyard, which can be entered only through two small doorways on Palace Avenue. Surrounding the oasis of flowering fruit trees, a fountain, and inviting benches are unique, low-profile shops. The quiet courtyard is a good place for repose. The buildings, erected in the 1700s as a single-family residence, had quarters for blacksmiths, bakers, farmers, and all manner of help. ⊠ *125 E. Palace Ave.*

# Canyon Road

Once a Native American trail and an early 20th-century route for wood-cutters and their burros, Canyon Road is now lined with art galleries, shops, and restaurants, earning it the nickname "The Art and Soul of Santa Fe." The narrow road begins at the eastern curve of Paseo de Peralta and stretches for about 2 mi at a moderate incline toward the base of the mountains.

Most establishments are in authentic, old adobe homes with undulating thick walls that appear to have been carved out of the earth. Within many are contemporary and traditional works by artists with internationally renowned names like Fernando Botero to anonymous weavers of ancient Peruvian textiles.

There are few places as festive as Canyon Road on Christmas Eve, when thousands of farolitos illuminate walkways, walls, roofs, and even trees. In May, the scent of lilacs wafts over the adobe walls, and in August red hollyhocks enhance the surreal color of the blue sky on a dry summer day.

## A Good Walk

Begin on Paseo de Peralta at the **Gerald Peters Gallery** ⑧, which has an enormous collection. Continue a half block north to Canyon Road. Turn right (east) and follow the road, which unfolds in shadows of undulating adobe walls. Street parking is at a premium, but there is a city-owned pay lot at the corner of Camino del Monte Sol, a few blocks up. Between visits to galleries and shops, take a break at one of the courtyards or fine restaurants. Be sure to stop by the beautiful gardens outside **El Zaguan** ⑨. At the intersection of Upper Canyon and Cristo Rey you'll find the massive **Cristo Rey Church** ⑩. Wear good walking shoes and watch out for the irregular sidewalks, which are built of stone and can get icy in winter.

TIMING

A tour of Canyon Road could take a whole day or as little as a few hours. If art is more than a curiosity to you, you may want to view the Gerald Peters Gallery apart from your Canyon Road tour. There is so much to see there that visual overload could hit before you get halfway up the road. Even on a cold day the walk can be a pleasure, with massive, glistening icicles hanging off roofs and a silence shrouding the side streets.

## Sights to See

⑩ **Cristo Rey Church.** Built in 1940 to commemorate the 400th anniversary of Francisco Vásquez de Coronado's exploration of the Southwest, this church is the largest Spanish adobe structure in the United States and is considered by many the finest example of Pueblo-style architecture anywhere. The church was constructed in the old-fashioned way by parishioners, who mixed the more than 200,000 mud-and-straw adobe bricks and hauled them into place. The 225-ton stone reredos (altar screen) is magnificent. ⊠ *Canyon Rd. at Cristo Rey,* ☎ *505/983–8528.* ⊙ *Daily 8–7.*

⑨ **El Zaguan.** Headquarters of the Historic Santa Fe Foundations (HSFF), this 19th-century Territorial-style house has a small exhibit on Santa Fe architecture and preservation, but the real draw is the small but stunning garden abundant with lavender, roses, and 160-year-old trees. You can relax on a wrought-iron bench and take in the fine views of the hills northeast of town. An HSFF horticulturist often gives free tours and lectures in the garden on Thursdays at 1 in summer (call to confirm). ⊠ *545 Canyon Rd.,* ☎ *505/983–2567,* WEB *www.historicsantafe.*

*com.* ✉ *Free.* ☉ *Foundations offices weekdays 9–noon and 1:30–5; gardens Mon.–Sat. 9–5.*

**❽ Gerald Peters Gallery.** While under construction, this 32,000-square-ft building was dubbed the "ninth northern pueblo," its scale rivaling that of the eight northern pueblos around Santa Fe. The suavely designed Pueblo-style gallery is Santa Fe's premier showcase for American and European art from the 19th century to the present. It feels like a museum, but all the works are for sale. Pablo Picasso, Georgia O'Keeffe, Charles M. Russell, Deborah Butterfield, George Rickey, and members of the Taos Society are among the artists represented, along with nationally renowned contemporary ones. ✉ *1011 Paseo de Peralta,* ☎ *505/954–5700,* WEB *www.gpgallery.com.* ✉ *Free.* ☉ *Mon.–Sat. 10–5.*

---

NEED A
BREAK?

A good place to rest your feet is the **Backroom Coffeebar** (✉ 616 Canyon Rd., ☎ 505/988–5323), which serves pastries and light snacks. Locals congregate in the courtyard or on the front portal of **Downtown Subscription** (✉ 376 Garcia St., ☎ 505/983–3085) a block east of Canyon Road. This café-newsstand sells coffees, snacks, and pastries, plus one of the largest assortments of newspapers and magazines in New Mexico.

---

## Lower Old Santa Fe Trail

It was along the Old Santa Fe Trail that wagon trains from Missouri rolled into town in the 1800s, forever changing Santa Fe's destiny. This area off the Plaza is one of Santa Fe's most historic.

### A Good Walk

The **Loretto Chapel** ⑪, facing the Old Santa Fe Trail, behind the La Fonda hotel, is a good place to start your walk. After visiting the chapel, head southeast on Old Santa Fe Trail to the **San Miguel Mission** ⑫. Across from the mission, on De Vargas Street, is the **Oldest House** ⑬. Up and down narrow De Vargas stretches the **Barrio de Analco** ⑭. There are a few galleries worth visiting on De Vargas Street east of Old Santa Fe Trail, and, back across Old Santa Fe Trail on the west side, check out the historic Santa Fe Playhouse. In the early art colony days, literary luminaries like Mary Austin and Witter Bynner would stage shows here. Walk farther away from downtown until you come to the **New Mexico State Capitol** ⑮, which contains some interesting artwork.

TIMING

Plan on spending a half hour at each of the churches and the New Mexico State Capitol and an hour exploring the Barrio de Analco. The entire walk can easily be done in about 3½ hours.

### Sights to See

**⑭ Barrio de Analco.** Along the south bank of the Santa Fe River, the barrio—its name means "district on the other side of the water"—is one of America's oldest neighborhoods, settled in the early 1600s by the Tlaxcalan Indians (who were forbidden to live with the Spanish near the Plaza) and in the 1690s by soldiers who had helped recapture New Mexico after the Pueblo Revolt. Plaques on houses on East De Vargas Street will help you locate some of the important structures. Check the performance schedule at the **Santa Fe Playhouse** on De Vargas Street, founded by writer Mary Austin and other Santa Feans in the 1920s.

**⑪ Loretto Chapel.** A delicate Gothic church modeled after Sainte-Chapelle in Paris, Loretto was built in 1873 by the same French architects and Italian stonemasons who built St. Francis Cathedral. The chapel is known for the "Miraculous Staircase" that leads to the choir loft. Legend has it that the chapel was almost complete when it became obvious that there wasn't room to build a staircase to the choir loft. In answer to the prayers of the cathedral's nuns, a mysterious carpenter arrived on a donkey, built a 20-ft staircase—using only a square, a saw, and a tub of water to season the wood—and then disappeared as quickly as he came. Many of the faithful believed it was St. Joseph himself. The staircase contains two complete 360-degree turns with no central support; no nails were used in its construction. The chapel closes for services and special events. Adjoining the chapel are a small museum and gift shop. ⊠ *211 Old Santa Fe Trail,* ☎ *505/982–0092,* WEB *www.lorettochapel.com.* ✉ *$2.50.* ⊙ *Mid-Oct.–mid-May, Mon.–Sat. 9–5, Sun. 10:30–5; mid-May–mid-Oct., Mon.–Sat. 9–6, Sun. 10:30–5.*

⓯ **New Mexico State Capitol.** The symbol of the Zía Pueblo, which represents the Circle of Life, was the inspiration for the Capitol, also known as the Roundhouse. Doorways at opposing sides of this 1966 structure symbolize the four winds, the four directions, and the four seasons. Throughout the building are artworks from the outstanding collection of the Capitol Art Foundation, historical and cultural displays, and handcrafted furniture. The **Governor's Gallery** hosts temporary exhibits. Six acres of imaginatively landscaped gardens shelter outstanding sculptures. ⊠ *Old Santa Fe Trail at Paseo de Peralta,* ☎ *505/986–4589.* ✉ *Free.* ⊙ *Mid-May–Aug., Mon.–Sat. 8–7; Sept.–mid-May, weekdays 8–7; tours by appointment.*

⓭ **The Oldest House.** More than 800 years ago, Pueblo people built this structure out of "puddled" adobe (liquid mud poured between upright wooden frames). This house, which contains a gift shop, is said to be the oldest in the United States. ⊠ *215 E. De Vargas St.*

★ ⓬ **San Miguel Mission.** The oldest church still in use in the United States, this simple earth-hue adobe structure was built in the early 17th century by the Tlaxcalan Indians of Mexico, who came to New Mexico as servants of the Spanish. Badly damaged in the 1680 Pueblo Revolt, the structure was restored and enlarged in 1710. On display in the chapel are priceless statues and paintings and the San José Bell, weighing nearly 800 pounds, which is believed to have been cast in Spain in 1356. In winter, the church sometimes closes before its official closing hour. Mass is held on Sunday at 5 PM. Next door in the back of the Territorial-style dormitories of the old St. Michael's High School, a **Visitor Information Center** can help you find your way around northern New Mexico. ⊠ *401 Old Santa Fe Trail,* ☎ *505/983–3974.* ✉ *$1.* ⊙ *Mission Mon.–Sat. 10–4, Sun. 3–4:30.*

## Upper Old Santa Fe Trail

### A Good Tour

This museum tour begins 2 mi south of the Plaza, an area best reached by car or via one of the city buses that leave hourly from near the Plaza. Begin at the **Museum of Indian Arts and Culture** ⓰, which is set around **Milner Plaza,** an attractively landscaped courtyard and gardens with outdoor art installations. Many days the Plaza hosts Native American dances, jewelry-making demonstrations, kids' activities, and other interactive events; there's also a Museum Hill Cafe, which is open for lunch and run by the same talented team that runs the O'Keeffe Cafe. To get here from downtown, drive uphill on Old Santa Fe Trail to Camino Lejo. Across Milner Plaza is the **Museum of International Folk Art** ⓱. From Milner Plaza, a bike-pedestrian path leads a short way to the new **Museum of Spanish Colonial Art** ⓲. Return to Milner Plaza, from which a different bike-pedestrian path leads a short way to the **Wheel-**

**wright Museum of the American Indian** ⑲. To reach the **Santa Fe Children's Museum** ⑳ you'll need to drive back down the hill or ask the bus driver to let you off near it.

Set aside a half to full day to see all the museums on the Upper Santa Fe Trail. Kids usually have to be dragged from the Children's Museum, even after an hour or two.

## Sights to See

★ ⑯ **Museum of Indian Arts and Culture.** An interactive, multimedia exhibition tells the story of Native American history in the Southwest, merging contemporary Native American experience with historical accounts and artifacts. The collection has some of New Mexico's oldest works of art: pottery vessels, fine stone and silver jewelry, intricate textiles, and other arts and crafts created by Pueblo, Navajo, and Apache artisans. You can also see art demonstrations and a video about the life and work of Pueblo potter Maria Martinez. ⊠ *710 Camino Lejo,* ☎ *505/476–1250,* WEB *www.miaclab.org.* ➿ *$7, 4-day pass $15 (good at all 5 state museums in Santa Fe).* ☺ *Tues.–Sun. 10–5.*

★ ⑰ **Museum of International Folk Art.** Everywhere you look in this facility, the premier institution of its kind in the world, you'll find amazingly inventive handmade objects—a tin Madonna, a devil made from bread dough, and all kinds of rag dolls. Florence Dibell Bartlett, who founded the museum in 1953, donated its first 4,000 works. In the late 1970s Alexander and Susan Girard, major folk-art collectors, gave the museum 106,000 items. The Hispanic Heritage Wing contains art dating from the Spanish-colonial period (in New Mexico, 1598–1821) to the present. The 5,000-piece exhibit includes religious works—particularly *bultos* (carved wooden statues of saints) and *retablos* (holy images painted on wood or tin). The objects in the Neutrogena Wing are exhibited by theme rather than by date or country of origin—you might, for instance, find a sheer Eskimo parka alongside a Chinese undergarment made of bamboo and cotton webbing. Lloyd's Treasure Chest, the wing's innovative basement section, provides a behind-the-scenes look at more of this collection. You can rummage about storage drawers, peer into microscopes, and, on occasion, speak with conservators and other museum personnel. ⊠ *706 Camino Lejo,* ☎ *505/476–1200,* WEB *www.moifa.org.* ➿ *$7, 4-day pass $15 (good at all 5 state museums in Santa Fe).* ☺ *Tues.–Sun. 10–5.*

⑱ **Museum of Spanish Colonial Art.** Opened in July 2002, this 5,000-square-ft adobe museum occupies a building designed in 1930 by acclaimed architect John Gaw Meem. The Spanish Colonial Art Society formed in Santa Fe in 1925 to preserve traditional Spanish-colonial art and culture. The museum, which sits next to the Museum of New Mexico complex, displays the fruits of the society's labor—one of the most comprehensive collections of Spanish-colonial art in the world. The Hale Matthews Library contains a 1,000-volume collection of books relating to this important period in art history. Objects here, dating from the 16th century to the present, include retablos, elaborate santos, tinwork, straw appliqué, furniture, ceramics, and ironwork. There's also a fine collection of works by Hispanic artists of the 20th century. ⊠ *750 Camino Lejo,* ☎ *505/982–2226,* WEB *www.spanishcolonial.org/museum.shtml.* ➿ *$6, 4-day pass $15 (good at all 5 state museums in Santa Fe).* ☺ *Daily 10–5.*

⑳ **Santa Fe Children's Museum.** Stimulating hands-on exhibits, a solar greenhouse, oversize geometric forms, and a simulated 18-ft mountain-climbing wall all contribute to the museum's popularity with kids. Puppeteers and storytellers occasionally perform. ⊠ *1050 Old Pecos Trail,* ☏ *505/989–8359,* WEB *www.santafechildrensmuseum.org.* ⊠ *$3.* ⊙ *Sept.–May, Thurs.–Sat. 10–5, Sun. noon–5; June–Aug., Wed.–Sat. 10– 5, Sun. noon–5.*

⑲ **Wheelwright Museum of the American Indian.** A private institution in a building shaped like a traditional octagonal Navajo hogan, the Wheelwright opened in 1937. Founded by Boston scholar Mary Cabot Wheelwright and Navajo medicine man Hastiin Klah, the museum originated as a place to house ceremonial materials. Those items are not on view to the public. What is displayed are 19th- and 20th-century baskets, pottery, sculpture, weavings, metalwork, photography, and paintings, including contemporary works by Native American artists. The Case Trading Post on the lower level is modeled after the trading posts that dotted the southwestern frontier more than 100 years ago. It carries an extensive selection of books and contemporary Native American jewelry, katsina dolls, weaving, and pottery. ⊠ *704 Camino Lejo,* ☏ *505/982–4636 or 800/607–4636,* WEB *www.wheelwright.org.* ⊠ *Free.* ⊙ *Mon.–Sat. 10–5, Sun. 1–5; gallery tours Mon.–Tues. and Fri. at 2, Sat. at 11.*

## Historic Guadalupe Railroad District

The historic warehouse district of Santa Fe is commonly referred to as the Railyard or Guadalupe District. After the demise of the train route through town, the low-lying warehouses were converted to artist studios and antiques shops, and bookstores, specialty shops, and restaurants have sprung up. The restored scenic train line puts the town's old depot to use. The local farmers' market turns the depot parking lot into a colorful outdoor fiesta.

### A Good Walk

From the Plaza, head west on San Francisco Street, and then take a left onto Guadalupe Street toward **Santuario de Guadalupe** ㉑, a short way farther on your right. After you visit the Santuario, take your time browsing through the shops and eating lunch in one of the restaurants farther down Guadalupe Street or around the corner at the **Sanbusco Market Center,** a massive warehouse. Check out the innovative shops and the photographic history on the walls near the market's main entrance. Back on Guadalupe, head south past the historic Gross Kelly Warehouse, one of the earliest Santa Fe–style buildings. You'll pass two huge murals on buildings facing Guadalupe Street depicting the magical-realism that flavors so much of New Mexico culture. Note Santa Fe's two train depots—one is now the site of the touristy Tomasita's Restaurant; the other, set farther back, is the Santa Fe Depot, where the **Santa Fe Southern Railway** ㉒ departs and where the **Santa Fe Farmers Market** is held. Continue a short distance south on Guadalupe until you reach **SITE Santa Fe** ㉓ gallery and performance space, set inside a former bottling warehouse.

TIMING

A visit to the Santuario de Guadalupe can take 15 minutes to an hour, depending on whether or not there's an art show in progress. If you like shopping, you might spend hours in this neighborhood.

### Sights to See

㉒ **Santa Fe Southern Railway.** For a leisurely tour across the Santa Fe plateau and into the vast Galisteo Basin, where panoramic views extend for up to 120 mi, take a nostalgic ride on the antique cars of the Santa Fe Southern Railway. The train once served a spur of the Atchison, Topeka & Santa Fe Railway. Today the train takes visitors on 36-

mi round-trip scenic trips to Lamy, a sleepy village with the region's only Amtrak service, offering picnics under the cottonwoods (bring your own or buy one from the caterer that meets the train) at the quaint rail station. Aside from day trips, the railway offers special events such as a Friday-night "High Desert High Ball" cash bar with appetizers and a "Sunset Run," on which a barbecue, a campfire, and live entertainment await you at the Lamy depot. Trains depart from the Santa Fe Depot, rebuilt in 1909 after the original was destroyed in a fire. There's talk of eventually opening a regional transportation and rail museum here. ⊠ *410 S. Guadalupe St.,* ☎ *505/989–8600 or 888/ 989–8600,* WEB *www.sfsr.com. Reservations essential.* 🎫 *Day trips from $25, "Sunset Run" from $45, High Desert High Ball from $40.* ⊙ *Call for schedule.*

㉑ **Santuario de Guadalupe.** A humble adobe structure built by Franciscan missionaries between 1776 and 1795, this is the oldest shrine in the United States to Our Lady of Guadalupe, patron saint of Mexico. The sanctuary, now a nonprofit cultural center, has adobe walls nearly 3 ft thick. Among the sanctuary's religious art and artifacts is a priceless 16th-century work by Venetian painter Leonardo de Ponte Bassano that depicts Jesus driving the money changers from the Temple. Also of note is a portrait of Our Lady of Guadalupe by the Mexican colonial painter José de Alzíbar. Other highlights are the traditional New Mexican carved and painted altar screen, an authentic 19th-century sacristy, a pictorial-history archive, a library devoted to Archbishop Jean Baptiste Lamy that is furnished with many of his belongings, and a garden with plants from the Holy Land. ⊠ *100 Guadalupe St.,* ☎ *505/988–2027.* 🎫 *Donation suggested.* ⊙ *Mon.–Sat. 9–4.*

㉓ **SITE Santa Fe.** The events at this nexus of international contemporary art include lectures, concerts, author readings, performance art, and gallery shows. The facility hosts a biennial exhibition every odd-numbered year. There are always provocative exhibitions here, however, and the immense, open space is ideal for taking in the many larger-than-life installations. ⊠ *1606 Paseo de Peralta,* ☎ *505/989–1199,* WEB *www.sitesantafe.org.* 🎫 *$5, free Fri.* ⊙ *Wed.–Thurs. and weekends 10–5, Fri. 10–7.*

# DINING

Dining is a serious sport in Santa Fe, and both locals and visitors love to debate which restaurant serves the spiciest green-chile stew or freshest margarita and which of each season's inevitable half dozen new hot spots will last more than a year. Several very high-profile chefs helm restaurants here, and quite a few divey, locals joints serve highly acclaimed food. People sometimes complain about the steep restaurant prices (as much as 50% greater than elsewhere in the state)—indeed, a meal at any of the better eateries will set you back about what you'd pay in New York or San Francisco. Nevertheless, if you look around a bit, you can find some great bargains. And, with certain notable exceptions, most of the high-end restaurants do serve food and provide service that's commensurate with the lofty prices.

So-called Santa Fe–style cuisine has so many influences that the term is virtually meaningless. Traditional, old-style Santa Fe restaurants serve New Mexican fare, which combines both Native American and Hispanic traditions and differs markedly from most Americanized Mexican cooking. Many of the better restaurants in town serve a contemporary regional style of cooking that blends New Mexican ingredients and preparations with those of interior and coastal Mexico, Latin

# Downtown Santa Fe Dining

| | | | |
|---|---|---|---|
| Anasazi Restaurant . . . . . . . **15** | El Encanto . . . . . . . **31** | Los Mayas . . . . . . . . **4** | Santacafé . . . . . . . **13** |
| Andiamo . . . . . . . . **35** | El Farol . . . . . . . . . **27** | Maria's New Mexican Kitchen . . . . . . . . . **37** | Santa Fe Baking Company . . . . . . . . **38** |
| Atomic Grill . . . . . . **20** | El Mesón . . . . . . . **14** | Masa Sushi . . . . . . . **1** | The Shed . . . . . . . . **16** |
| Cafe Paris . . . . . **9** | Four & Twenty Blackbirds . . . . . . **34** | O'Keeffe Cafe . . . . **8** | 315 . . . . . . . . . . **22** |
| Cafe Pasqual's . . . . **19** | Geronimo . . . . . . **26** | Old House . . . . . . . **7** | Vanessie . . . . . . . . . **3** |
| Cafe San Estevan . . . . . . **30** | Guadalupe Cafe. . . **24** | Paul's . . . . . . . . . **12** | Whistling Moon Cafe . . . . . . **2** |
| The Compound . . . . **25** | Il Piatto . . . . . . . . **11** | Pink Adobe . . . . . . **23** | Zia Diner . . . . . . . . **32** |
| Cowgirl Hall of Fame . . . . . **33** | Il Vicino . . . . . . . . **6** | Plaza Restaurant . . . **10** | |
| Coyote Cafe and Rooftop Cantina . . . **21** | India Palace . . . . . . **18** | Ristra . . . . . . . . . . **28** | |
| | Kasasoba . . . . . . . **29** | Rociada . . . . . . . . **5** | |
| | La Casa Sena: . . . . **17** | | |
| | La Choza . . . . . . . . **36** | | |

America, the Mediterranean, East Asian, and varied parts of the United States. There are several high-caliber Italian restaurants in town, and a growing number of commendable Asian eateries, but all in all the city's culinary diversity is limited.

Keep in mind that some of the city's best eateries, at least in terms of food if not necessarily ambience, are outside of downtown, sometimes even out amid the dreary shopping centers along Cerrillos Road and St. Michael's Drive. Dress is informal but neat just about everywhere, and waits for a table are very common on weekends and even some weekdays during the busy summer season; it's a good idea to call ahead even when reservations are not accepted, if only to get a sense of the waiting time.

| CATEGORY | COST* |
| --- | --- |
| $$$$ | over $25 |
| $$$ | $18–$25 |
| $$ | $10–$17 |
| $ | under $10 |

*per person for a main course at dinner*

# American/Casual

**$–$$   ✕ Bobcat Bite.** This divey grill in a tiny house a 15-minute drive south of town serves steaks and chops but is famous for one thing: the biggest and juiciest burgers in town. Locals prefer them topped with cheese and green chiles. The hours vary and can be a bit limited, so call ahead. ⊠ *Old Las Vegas Hwy., 4½ mi south of the Old Pecos Trail exit off I–25,* ☎ *505/983–5319. Reservations not accepted. No credit cards.*

**$–$$   ✕ Cowgirl Hall of Fame.** A rollicking and fanatically popular bar and grill with several atmospheric rooms overflowing with Old West memorabilia, Cowgirl deserves kudos for its reasonably priced and nearly always quite tasty southwestern, Tex-Mex, barbecue, and southern fare. Highlights include sizzling barbecue, bourbon-glazed pork chops, and salmon tacos with a kicky tomatillo salsa. So what's the drawback? Consistently subpar service. Nevertheless, knock back a few drinks and catch one of the nightly music acts—usually rock or blues—and you're likely to leave smiling. Grab a seat on the spacious patio in warm weather. ⊠ *319 S. Guadalupe St.,* ☎ *505/982–2565. AE, D, MC, V.*

**$–$$   ✕ Zia Diner.** This slick diner with a low-key, art deco–style interior serves comfort food prepared with the occasional nouvelle twist. Stop in for a full meal (ask about the night's blue-plate special, like Friday's fish Vera Cruz style) or just a thick slice of fresh strawberry-rhubarb pie. Service is fast and friendly, and the food is fresh. There's a cheerful patio. ⊠ *326 S. Guadalupe St.,* ☎ *505/988–7008. AE, MC, V.*

**$   ✕ Atomic Grill.** Burgers, salads, pizzas, sandwiches, and other light munchies are served at this tiny late-night café a block off the Plaza. The food is decent and the service brusque but usually okay. The best attributes are the comfy patio overlooking pedestrian-heavy Water Street, the huge list of imported beers, and the late hours (it's open til 3 most nights)—an extreme rarity in Santa Fe. You'll be glad this place exists when the bars let out and you're famished. ⊠ *103 Water St.,* ☎ *505/820–2866. MC, V.*

**$   ✕ Tesuque Village Market.** A favorite spot for a snack or a full meal ★ before heading to the opera or after a shopping at the Tesuque Pueblo Flea Market, this epicurean grocery and people-watching café has a tiny but lovely patio and a less atmospheric indoor seating area. The kitchen serves up tasty American and New Mexican fare—pork chops verde, *posole* stew (soup made with lime hominy, pork, chile, and garlic), French toast, Frito pie. Save room for a fresh-baked brownie or cookie. ⊠ *NM 599 at Bishop's Lodge Rd., Tesuque, 5 mi north of Santa Fe,* ☎ *505/ 988–8848. Reservations not accepted. MC, V.*

## Cafés

$–$$ ✕ **O'Keeffe Cafe.** This swanky café at the Georgia O'Keeffe Museum turns out some of the best lunch fare in Santa Fe. The spinach-chevre salad with jícama, avocado, pine nuts, and a sage vinaigrette scores high marks, as does an entrée of seared salmon with a cilantro-lime dressing served over mashed potatoes with an ancho-chile mole. The management also operates the Museum Hill Cafe at Milner Plaza, outside the folk and Indian art museums. ⊠ *217 Johnson St.,* ☎ *505/992– 1065. AE, MC, V. Closed Sun.–Mon. No dinner.*

$ ✕ **Four and Twenty Blackbirds.** Set in a tiny converted 1920s grocery
★ store (it still contains the original deli counter and refrigerator), this café is most famous for its savory and sweet pies, from chicken to gooseberry to coconut cream. But you can drop in at lunchtime to sample such exquisite sandwiches as roast beef with vine-ripened tomatoes and blue-cheese cole slaw. There's also a wide selection of kitchen goods, gourmet foods, and fun knick knacks. Parking is at the vintage Texaco station a few doors down. ⊠ *620 Old Santa Fe Trail,* ☎ *505/983- 7676. No dinner. MC, V.*

$ ✕ **Santa Fe Baking Company.** Breakfast tends to be a big social affair in Santa Fe, and several very good bakeries vie heavily for the morning crowd. Although it's located at a strip shopping center just south of town, Santa Fe Baking prepares some of the best food—massive breakfast burritos, fluffy French toast, and blue-corn pancakes. At lunch, it's great for copious deli sandwiches. Order at the counter and grab a seat in the high-ceilinged, light-filled dining room. ⊠ *504 W. Cordova Rd.,* ☎ *505/988–4292. Reservations not accepted. AE, MC, V. No dinner.*

## Chinese

$–$$ ✕ **Chow's.** A pleasing alternative to the many Americanized Chinese restaurants in town, Chow's occupies a modest but cheerful space in a shopping center a few miles south of the Plaza. The kitchen conjures up imaginative Chinese dishes, including a knockout starter of fried wontons stuffed with crab and Parmesan cheese and tossed with an orange-ginger glaze. A worthy entrée is scallops wok-fried with red-chile rings, bok choy, and coconut milk. Green-tea ice cream makes a nice dessert. ⊠ *720 St. Michael's Dr.,* ☎ *505/471–7120. AE, MC, V. Closed Sun.*

## Contemporary

$$$$ ✕ **Anasazi Restaurant.** Soft light illuminates the Chaco Canyon–inspired sandstone walls and adobe interior of this restaurant, which became a Santa Fe fixture the day it opened. The kitchen combines New Mexican and Native American ingredients to produce such exotic fare as buffalo carpaccio with parsley-sage oil and blackberry–whole grain mustard as well as blue corn–dusted diver scallops with chile-dipped shrimp, corn puree, and blood-orange coulis. The large dining room has wooden tables and *bancos* (benches built into the plastered walls) upholstered with handwoven textiles from Chimayó. The Sunday brunch is excellent. ⊠ *113 Washington Ave.,* ☎ *505/988–3236. AE, D, DC, MC, V.*

$$$$ ✕ **The Compound.** Three decades ago, this handsome adobe tucked down
★ an alley off Canyon Road epitomized white-glove fine dining. Its fortunes waxed and waned over the years before acclaimed restaurateurs

Brett Kemmerer and Mark Kiffin rescued it from oblivion and transformed it into one of the state's culinary darlings. It's still a fancy place, but dress is a cut below formal, and the staff highly attentive but also easy-going. From the oft-changing menu consider a starter of cockle risotto with peas, parsley, reggiano parmagiano, and chorizo broth. Memorable entrées include "forever-braised" bone-in pork leg with mustard greens, roasted apples, small turnips, and fresh horseradish; or buttermilk roast chicken with creamed fresh spinach and foie gras pan gravy. ⊠ *653 Canyon Rd.,* ☎ *505/982–4353. AE, D, DC, MC, V. No lunch weekends.*

**$$$$**   ✕ **Coyote Cafe and Rooftop Cantina.** Touristy, bold, and presided over by celebrity chef Mark Miller, this is the restaurant lots of people love to bad-mouth. Say what you will, Coyote Cafe manages to produce superbly original Southwest cooking, and the service is surprisingly pleasant considering the high expectations and sometimes overwhelming crowds. Try wild-boar tamale with *huitlacoche* (a type of mushroom) sauce, or the fillet of tea-smoked salmon slow-roasted with fennel and star anise. The open dining room can be loud and obnoxiously showy. On the wine list are more than 500 vintages. Inventive, delicious, mostly under-$10 fare is served on the open-air Rooftop Cantina April through October—it's highly underrated and is an excellent lunch option. ⊠ *132 W. Water St.,* ☎ *505/983–1615. Reservations essential. AE, D, DC, MC, V.*

**$$$$**   ✕ **Geronimo.** Chef Eric DiStefano changes the menu frequently at this
   ★   restaurant in the Borrego House, which dates from 1756. A typical meal might start with an appetizer of cold-water lobster tail on angel hair pasta. Entrées are artful, like mesquite-grilled elk tenderloin with smoked bacon and chestnut strudel, or red-corn relleno with duck and black-bean sauce. The Sunday brunch is also impressive. The intimate, white dining rooms have beamed ceilings, wood floors, fireplaces, and cushioned bancos. In summer you can dine under the front portal; in winter the bar with fireplace is inviting. ⊠ *724 Canyon Rd.,* ☎ *505/982–1500. AE, MC, V. No lunch Mon.*

**$$$–$$$$**   ✕ **Cafe Pasqual's.** This cheerful cubbyhole dishes up southwestern and
   ★   Nuevo Latino specialties for breakfast, lunch, and dinner. Don't be discouraged by lines out in front—it's worth the wait. The culinary muse behind it all is Katharine Kagel, who for more than 20 years has been introducing specialties like buttermilk biscuits with sage-bacon gravy, homemade sausage, and poached eggs to diners. Dinner is a more formal affair: the free-range chicken mole enchilada with plantain rice, fresh corn torte, and mango-jícama salad is a pleasure; the kicky starter of spicy Vietnamese squid salad with tamarind, garlic, and lime over baby spinach is also fantastic. Mexican folk art and colorful tiles and murals by Oaxacan artist Leo Vigildo Martinez create a festive atmosphere. Try the communal table if you want to be seated in a hurry. ⊠ *121 Don Gaspar Ave.,* ☎ *505/983–9340. AE, MC, V.*

**$$$–$$$$**   ✕ **Old House.** Chef Martín Rios changes the menu every Thursday at his fashionably casual restaurant inside the equally fashionable Eldorado Hotel. Entrées have included lavender-honey-glazed Muscovy duck breast and leg confit with creamy white polenta, baby carrots, and natural dark jus. More than two dozen of the impressive wines are served by the glass. A separate dining room has a slightly more refined interior than the hotel-hacienda ambience of the main dining room. ⊠ *Eldorado Hotel, 309 W. San Francisco St.,* ☎ *505/988–4455. AE, D, DC, MC, V. No lunch.*

**$$$–$$$$**   ✕ **Ristra.** This unprepossessing restaurant in the up-and-coming Guadalupe District presents a first-rate menu of southwestern-influenced country French cooking. You might start with a lobster brioche tartlette layered with tomatoes, leeks, caviar, and a lobster sauce;

achiote elk tenderloin with morel barley, glazed shallots, baby gold beets, and red wine sauce is a tempting main dish. The wines are well selected and the service is swift and courteous. Navajo blankets hang on stark white walls, and Pueblo pottery adorns the handful of niches. ⊠ *548 Agua Fria St.,* ☎ *505/982–8608. AE, MC, V. No lunch.*

$$$–$$$$ ✕ **Santacafé.** Minimalist elegance marks the interior of Santacafé, one
★ of Santa Fe's vanguard "food as art" restaurants, two blocks north of the Plaza in the historic Padre Gallegos House. Seasonal ingredients are included in the inventive dishes, which might include serrano-wrapped cod with white beans, sun-dried tomatoes, and grilled sweet peppers. Poblano chowder makes a terrific starter, as does the sublime crispy-fried calamari with a snappy lime dipping sauce. The patio is a joy in summer, and the bar makes a snazzy spot to meet friends for drinks just about any time of year. If you're on a tight budget, consider the reasonably priced lunch menu. ⊠ *231 Washington Ave.,* ☎ *505/984–1788. AE, MC, V.*

$$–$$$ ✕ **Paul's.** Whimsical painted Oaxacan figurines line a few shelves of
★ this otherwise simple storefront café with a small but well-trained staff. The pumpkin bread stuffed with pine nuts, corn, and green chiles with queso blanco, red-chile sauce, and caramelized apples is a classic specialty, but don't overlook baked salmon with a pecan-herb crust and sorrel sauce. The blue-crab cakes with a tomato-orange-chipotle sauce star among the starters. ⊠ *72 W. Marcy St.,* ☎ *505/982–8738. AE, D, DC, MC, V. Closed Mon.*

## Continental

$$$$ ✕ **La Casa Sena.** The southwestern-accented and Continental fare served at La Casa Sena is rich and beautifully presented. Weather permitting, get a table on the patio surrounded by hollyhocks, flowering shrubs, and centuries-old adobe walls. If you order the *trucha en terracotta* (fresh trout wrapped in corn husks and baked in clay), ask your waiter to save the clay head for you as a souvenir. Finish dinner with the wonderful citrus mascarpone tart with orange sauce and Grand Marnier–soaked berries. Weekend brunch dishes are equally elegant. For a musical meal (evenings only), sit in the restaurant's adjacent Cantina, where the talented staff belt out Broadway show tunes. Meals in the Cantina are less expensive, and less exciting. Reservations are essential in summer. ⊠ *Sena Plaza, 125 E. Palace Ave.,* ☎ *505/988–9232. AE, D, DC, MC, V.*

## Eclectic

$$–$$$ ✕ **Cafe San Estevan.** This place is perfect when you're seeking a restaurant with exceptional New Mexican and Continental fare, all of it prepared simply but with ultrafresh ingredients and superb presentation. The small and rather noisy dining room is charming nonetheless, with some tables facing a corner fireplace. The chiles rellenos here are exceptional, stuffed with cheese and onions and served with rice and *calabacitas* (a kind of squash)—nothing here is greasy or overwrought. Also top-notch are the spaghettini with chicken, cream sauce, and fresh peas. Chef-owner Estevan Garcia puts on a great show. ⊠ *428 Agua Fria St.,* ☎ *505/995–1996. AE, D, MC, V. Closed Mon.*

$$–$$$ ✕ **Pink Adobe.** Rosalea Murphy opened her restaurant back in 1944, and the place still seems to reflect a time when fewer than 20,000 people lived in town. The intimate, rambling rooms of this late-17th-century house have fireplaces and artwork and are filled with conversation made over special-occasion meals. The ambience of the restaurant, rather than the food, accounts for its popularity. The steak Dunigan, smothered in green chile and mushrooms, and the savory shrimp Louisianne—

fat and deep-fried crispy—are among the Continental, New Orleans creole, and New Mexican dishes served. The apple pie drenched in rum sauce is a favorite. Particularly strong margaritas are mixed in the adjacent Dragon Room bar. ⊠ *406 Old Santa Fe Trail,* ☎ *505/983–7712. AE, D, DC, MC, V. No lunch weekends.*

**$–$$** ✕ **Harry's Roadhouse.** This quirky, always-packed adobe compound
★ consists of several inviting rooms, from a diner-style space with counter seating to a cozier nook with a fireplace—there's also an enchanting courtyard out back with juniper trees and flower gardens. The varied menu of contemporary diner favorites, pizzas, New Mexican fare, and bountiful salads is supplemented by a long list of daily specials. Favorites include Moroccan vegetable stew over couscous with harissa; and grilled-fish tacos with tomatillo salsa and black beans. Breakfast is a favorite meal here—try the blueberry buckwheat pancakes. ⊠ *Old Las Vegas Hwy., 1 mi south of the Old Pecos Trail exit off I–25,* ☎ *505/989–4629. AE, D, MC, V.*

**$–$$** ✕ **Plaza Restaurant.** Run with homespun care by the Razatos family
★ since 1947, this café has been a fixture on the Plaza since 1918. The decor—red leather banquettes, black Formica tables, tile floors, a coffered tin ceiling, and a 1940s-style service counter—hasn't changed much in the past half century. The food runs the gamut, from cashew mole enchiladas to New Mexico meat loaf to Mission-style burritos, but the ingredients tend toward southwestern. You'll rarely taste a better or spicier tortilla soup. You can cool it off with an old-fashioned ice cream treat from the soda fountain. All in all, it's a good stop for breakfast, lunch, or dinner. ⊠ *54 Lincoln Ave.,* ☎ *505/982–1664. Reservations not accepted. AE, D, MC, V.*

## French

**$$–$$$$** ✕ **Rociada.** Country French cooking is the bill of fare at this intimate bistro with soft lighting and a pressed-tin ceiling. Fresh ingredients are used for the Provençale specialties, including crayfish and escargots with a smoked-tomato saffron cream, and steak au poivre with spinach-mashed potatoes and Roquefort. The list of French wines is extensive. ⊠ *304 Johnson St.,* ☎ *505/983–3800. AE, D, MC, V. Closed Sun. No lunch.*

**$$$** ✕ **Cafe Paris.** This tiny, bright bistro sits down a redbrick alley beside the Lensic Theater—it could just as easily be down a Parisian side street. The decor, paintings, and staff are French, and simple French classics like shrimp Provençale and filet mignon with a green peppercorn sauce are served without fanfare but with great affection. It's a pleasant lunch option, too. ⊠ *31 Burro Alley,* ☎ *505/986–9162. MC, V. Closed Mon.*

**$$$** ✕ **315.** As if it were on a thoroughfare in Paris rather than on Old Santa Fe Trail, 315 has a Continental, white-tablecloth sophistication, but the offbeat wall art gives it a contemporary feel. Chef-owner Louis Moskow prepares refreshingly uncomplicated, Provençale-inspired fare using organic vegetables and locally raised meats. Seasonal specialties on the ever-evolving menu might include veal scallopini with chestnut sauce, and steak frites with béarnaise sauce and herb butter. The garden patio opens onto the street scene. There's an exceptional wine list. ⊠ *315 Old Santa Fe Trail,* ☎ *505/986–9190. AE, MC, V. Closed Sun.*

## Indian

**$–$$** ✕ **India Palace.** Even seasoned veterans of East Indian cuisine have been
★ known to rate this deep-pink, art-filled restaurant among the best in

the United States. The kitchen prepares fairly traditional recipes—tandoori chicken, lamb vindaloo, *saag paneer* (spinach with farmer's cheese), shrimp *biryani* (tossed with cashews, raisins, almonds, and saffron rice)—but the presentation is always flawless and the ingredients fresh. Meals are cooked as hot or mild as requested. Try the Indian buffet at lunch. ⊠ *227 Don Gaspar Ave. (enter from parking lot on Water St.),* ☎ *505/986–5859. AE, D, MC, V.*

## Italian

**$$–$$$** ✕ **Andiamo.** Produce from the farmers' market across the street adds to the seasonal surprises of this intimate northern Italian restaurant set inside a romantic cottage. Start with the crispy polenta with rosemary and Gorgonzola sauce; move on to the calamari pizza with fontina cheese, grilled onions, and bacon; and consider such hearty entrées as lasagna Bolognese or penne with merguez sausage, tomatoes, spinach, and roasted peppers. ⊠ *322 Garfield St., near the Railyard,* ☎ *505/995–9595. AE, DC, MC, V. No lunch.*

**$$** ✕ **Il Piatto.** Creative pasta dishes like risotto with duck, artichoke, and truffle oil and homemade pumpkin ravioli with pine nuts and brown sage butter grace the menu here. Entrées include roasted garlic–and–basil–stuffed duck breast with toasted almond jus. It's a crowded but nevertheless enjoyable trattoria with informal ambience and a snug, urbane bar; the windows are dressed in frilly valances, and a mural of the Italian countryside lines one wall. ⊠ *95 W. Marcy St.,* ☎ *505/984–1091. AE, MC, V. No lunch weekends.*

## Japanese

**$–$$** ✕ **Masa Sushi.** Its linoleum floor, acoustic-tile ceilings, and a small dining room in a shopping center a short drive west of downtown might not raise your expectations that Masa serves the best sushi and Japanese fare in Santa Fe, but dig into a spicy scallop roll or fresh sea eel or sea urchin sushi, and you'll believe it. Shrimp tempura and *gyoza* (pork dumplings) are favorites from the "cooked" side of the menu. There's karaoke many weeknights. ⊠ *Solana Center, 927 W. Alameda St.,* ☎ *505/982–3334. MC, V. Closed Sun. No lunch Sat.*

## Latin

**$$–$$$** ✕ **Los Mayas.** Owners Fernando Antillas and Reyes Solano brought the spirit of Latin America with them when they opened this restaurant. They've transformed a nondescript building into a cozy, tile-floored space with a patio. The menu mixes New Mexican, Latin American, and South American recipes. Try the enchiladas banana (rolled corn tortillas stuffed with plantains and topped with mole sauce) or the grilled shrimp with garlic and rice. There is music every night. ⊠ *409 W. Water St.,* ☎ *505/986–9930. AE, D, MC, V. No lunch.*

## Mediterranean

**$–$$** ✕ **Whistling Moon Cafe.** Unusual spices scent the inspired, mostly ★ Mediterranean fare at this cozy spot, where specialties include chicken tagine, lamb shawarma, artichoke–grilled onion pizzas, and homemade walnut-mushroom ravioli. The coriander-cumin fries are irresistible, as is the homemade Moroccan-vanilla crème brûlée. Although the small ocher dining room with red Moroccan weavings is a touch noisy, the food and prices more than make up for it. ⊠ *402 N. Guadalupe St.,* ☎ *505/983–3093. MC, V. No lunch weekends.*

# Mexican

**$$-$$$** ✕ **El Encanto.** A classy addition to the Guadalupe District, El Encanto was opened late in 2001 by the owner of Bert's la Taqueria, but here you'll generally find more upscale renditions of interior Mexican fare, including a full list of creative moles. The restaurant occupies a thick-walled adobe with a warren of romantic dining rooms hung with local art. Specialties include yellowfin tuna grilled with an agave-wine sauce and grilled pork loin baked with a pumpkin-seed salsa. ✉ *416 Agua Fria St.,* ☎ *505/988–5991. AE, MC, V. Closed Sun.*

**$-$$$** ✕ **Bert's la Taqueria.** Salsa fans love this upbeat spot where chips are
★ served with six varieties of the hot stuff. The noisy dining room is filled with vintage Mexican movie posters and closely spaced tables that look back toward an open grill. The menu mixes the expected Mexican fare—enchiladas, soft tacos—with more unusual regional recipes. ✉ *1620 St. Michael's Dr.,* ☎ *505/474–0791. AE, MC, V. Closed Sun.*

**$$** ✕ **Old Mexico Grill.** For a taste of Old Mexico in New Mexico, sample dishes like *arracheras* (the traditional Mexican name for fajitas) and tacos *al carbón* (shredded pork cooked in a mole sauce). Start the meal with a fresh ceviche appetizer and a cool lime margarita. It's a cozy spot with tile floors and wooden tables, a bit more charming than its shopping-center locale might suggest. ✉ *2434 Cerrillos Rd., College Plaza South,* ☎ *505/473–0338. Reservations not accepted. D, MC, V. No lunch weekends.*

# Pan-Asian

**$$-$$$** ✕ **Zen World Cuisine.** If you don't mind the slightly odd location at the planned residential community of El Dorado, about a 15-mi drive southeast of Santa Fe, Zen can be counted on for a delicious meal at quite reasonable prices. The funky dining room overlooks an open kitchen—it's very informal, and mostly locals eat here—not an exciting space, but all the better to focus on the highly exciting East-meets-West food, such as lime-grilled turkey medallions with jasmine rice, green curry, and crispy leek; or red-bean paste and sesame-seared salmon with apple-macadamia tart Tatin. ✉ *7 Ave. Vista Grande, El-dorado, 1½ mi south of I–25, off U.S. 285,* ☎ *505/466–3700. MC, V. Closed Sun.–Mon.*

**$$** ✕ **Mu Du Noodles.** This warm and cozy eatery on an unfortunately busy stretch of Cerrillos Road excels both in its friendly and helpful staff and its superb pan-Asian fare. Book ahead on weekends—this place fills up fast. You can count on some great dinner specials each night, too. Sample shrimp pad Thai, tofu green curry, or house-marinated pork with rice vermicelli. ✉ *1494 Cerrillos Rd.,* ☎ *505/988–1411. AE, MC, V. No lunch.*

**$-$$** ✕ **Kasasoba.** Maybe the best all-around Asian restaurant in Santa Fe,
★ this intimate, classy eatery behind the Sanbusco Center has just a handful of tables and specializes in both Japanese and Chinese noodle dishes. The *zaru soba* (cold buckwheat noodles with nori, wasabi, spring onions, and a dashi-shoyu dipping sauce) with tempura vegetables and shrimp is heavenly, as is the yellowfin tuna sashimi starter. Ramen and udon noodle specialties round out the menu, and there's a short but well-chosen wine list. ✉ *544 Agua Fria St.,* ☎ *505/984–1969. AE, MC, V. No lunch Sat.–Mon.*

# Pizza

**$** ✕ **Il Vicino.** This slick space a couple of blocks west of the Plaza, part of a local chain, serves exceptionally tasty wood-fired pizza, plus impressive salads, panini sandwiches, and a robust house-microbrewed ale, Wet Mountain I.P.A. Costs are low, in part because service is limited: you order your meal at the front desk, and they bring it out to you. The Angeli (roasted chicken, Portobello mushrooms, artichoke hearts, Gorgonzola, and balsamic marinara) is a winner among the 15 creatively topped pies. ⊠ *321 W. San Francisco St., ☎ 505/986–8700. AE, D, MC, V.*

## Southwestern

**$$–$$$** ✕ **Gabriel's.** A great option near Pojoaque, perfect before the opera or on your way back to Santa Fe from points north, Gabriel's offers one of the best restaurant settings in the area: a spacious dining room with a Spanish-colonial theme, and a large flower-filled patio with candlelit tables. The main event here is the guacamole, prepared with great fanfare table-side. The margaritas are also stellar. Main dishes—steak fajitas, crab enchiladas—are less memorable but still usually quite good, and service is friendly but uneven. ⊠ *U.S. 285/84, just north of Camel Rock Casino, 15 mi north of Santa Fe, ☎ 505/455–7000. AE, D, DC, MC, V.*

**$$–$$$** ✕ **Maria's New Mexican Kitchen.** Maria's is proud to serve a whopping 100 kinds of margarita. All but six of the tequilas are 100% agave. This is also an excellent source of authentic New Mexican fare, including chiles rellenos, blue-corn enchiladas, and green-chile tamales. Strolling guitarists serenade the crowds most nights. ⊠ *555 W. Cordova Rd., ☎ 505/983–7929. AE, D, DC, MC, V.*

**$–$$$** ✕ **The Shed.** The lines at lunch attest to the status of this downtown New Mexican eatery. The rambling adobe dating from 1692 is decorated with folk art, and service is downright neighborly. Even if you're a devoted green chile fan, try the locally grown red chile the place is famous for. Specialties include red-chile enchiladas, green-chile stew with potatoes and pork, posole, and charbroiled Shedburgers. The homemade desserts are fabulous. There's a full bar, too. ⊠ *113½ E. Palace Ave., ☎ 505/982–9030. AE, DC, MC, V. Closed Sun. No dinner Mon.–Wed.*

**$–$$** ✕ **Guadalupe Cafe.** Come to this informal café for hefty servings of New Mexican favorites like enchiladas and quesadillas, topped off with *sopaipillas* (fluffy fried bread) and honey. The seasonal raspberry pancakes are one of many breakfast favorites. Service can be brusque and the wait for a table considerable. ⊠ *422 Old Santa Fe Trail, ☎ 505/982–9762. Reservations not accepted. AE, D, DC, MC, V. Closed Mon. No dinner Sun.*

**$** ✕ **La Choza.** The far-less touristy, harder-to-find, and less expensive ★ sister to the Shed, La Choza arguably serves even better New Mexican fare. Chicken or pork *carne adovada* burritos, white-clam chowder spiced with green chiles, huevos rancheros, and wine margaritas are specialties. The dining rooms are dark and cozy, with vigas set across the ceiling and local art on the walls. The staff is friendly and competent, perhaps happy not to be contending with the hordes of tourists who frequent restaurants around the Plaza. ⊠ *905 Alarid St., near Cerrillos Rd. at St. Francis Dr., ☎ 505/982–0909. AE, DC, MC, V. Closed Sun.*

## Spanish

**$$$–$$$$** ✕ **El Farol.** In this crossover-cuisine town, owner David Salazar sums up his food in one word: "Spanish." Order a classic entrée like paella or make a meal from the nearly 30 different tapas—from tiny fried squid to wild mushrooms. Dining is indoors and out. Touted as the oldest continuously operated restaurant in Santa Fe, El Farol (built in 1835) has a relaxed ambience, a unique blend of the western frontier and

**104**

**Greater Santa Fe Dining & Lodging**

contemporary Santa Fe. People push back the chairs and start dancing at around 9:30. The restaurant books outstanding live entertainment, mostly blues and jazz, and there's usually a festive flamenco performance weekly. ⊠ *808 Canyon Rd.,* ☎ *505/983–9912. D, DC, MC, V.*

**$$–$$$** ✕ **El Mesón.** This place is as fun for having drinks or catching live music (from tango nights to Sephardic music) as for enjoying a full meal. The dignified dining room with an old-world feel has simple dark-wood tables and chairs, white walls, and a wood-beam ceiling—unpretentious yet elegant. Tapas include serrano ham and fried red potatoes with garlic aioli. Among the more substantial entrées are a stellar paella as well as cannelloni stuffed with veal, smothered with béchamel sauce, and served with manchego cheese au gratin. ⊠ *213 Washington Ave.,* ☎ *505/983–6756. AE, MC, V. Closed Mon. No lunch.*

## Steak

**$$–$$$$** ✕ **Vanessie.** This classy, lodgelike space with high ceilings and a tremendously popular piano cabaret serves hefty portions of well-prepared chops and seafood. New Zealand rack of lamb, Australian cold-water rock lobster, and dry-aged steaks are among the specialties. There's lighter fare—burgers, onion loaf, salads—served in the piano bar, where noted musicians Doug Montgomery and Charles Tichenor perform classical and Broadway favorites well into the evening (no cover). ⊠ *434 W. San Francisco St.,* ☎ *505/982–9966. AE, DC, MC, V. No lunch.*

# LODGING

In Santa Fe you can ensconce yourself in quintessential Santa Fe style or anonymous hotel-chain decor, depending on how much you want to spend. Cheaper motels and hotels are on Cerrillos (pronounced sah-*ree*-yos) Road, which south of St. Francis Drive becomes a dreadfully traffic-clogged strip of could-be-anywhere fast-food and lodging chains. Quality varies greatly out on Cerrillos, but some of the best-managed and most attractive properties are (from most to least expensive) the Doubletree, the Courtyard Marriott, and the Motel 6. You'll pay a great deal more the closer you are to the Plaza, but for many visitors it's worth it to be within walking distance of many attractions. Some of the best deals are offered by B&Bs—many of those near the Plaza, while not cheap, still offer much better values than the big and inevitably touristy hotels. Rates drop considerably from November to April (excluding Thanksgiving and Christmas).

| CATEGORY | COST* |
| --- | --- |
| **$$$$** | over $220 |
| **$$$** | $160–$220 |
| **$$** | $100–$160 |
| **$** | under $100 |

*All prices are for a standard double room, excluding 11.5% tax.*

## Downtown Vicinity

**$$$$** ▥ **Eldorado Hotel.** The city's largest property sometimes gets a bad rap because it's the closest thing Santa Fe has to a convention hotel, but this is actually a highly inviting property with individually decorated rooms, a gracious staff, and some of the best mountain views of any downtown hotel. Rooms are stylishly furnished with carved south-western-style desks and chairs, large upholstered club chairs, and art prints; many have terraces or kiva-style fireplaces. The rooftop pool and gym are great fun. The Old House restaurant is highly rated.

# Downtown Santa Fe Lodging

Alexander's Inn . . . . **15**

Dancing Ground
of the Sun . . . . . . . **12**

Don Gaspar Inn . . . **21**

Dunshee's . . . . . . . **23**

Eldorado Hotel . . . . . **4**

El Farolito . . . . . . **19**

Garrett's
Desert Inn . . . . . . . **11**

Grant Corner
Inn . . . . . . . . . . . . **3**

Hotel St. Francis . . . **6**

Hotel Santa Fe . . . . **17**

Inn at Loretto . . . . . **10**

Inn of the
Anasazi . . . . . . . . . . **8**

Inn of the
Governors . . . . . . . **7**

Inn on the Paseo . . . . **5**

Inn of the
Turquoise Bear . . . . **22**

Inn on the
Alameda . . . . . . . . **16**

La Fonda . . . . . . . . . **9**

La Posada de
Santa Fe Resort
and Spa . . . . . . . . **13**

The Madeleine . . . . **14**

Pueblo Bonito
B&B Inn . . . . . . . . . **20**

Radisson
Santa Fe . . . . . . . . . . **1**

Santa Fe
Budget Inn . . . . . . . **18**

Water Street Inn . . . . **2**

There's music nightly, from classical Spanish guitar to piano, in the comfortable lobby lounge. Nearby, the inn rents out about 50 fully furnished apartments and condos with kitchens and as many as three bedrooms—these are ideal for longer stays or when traveling with friends or family. ⊠ *309 W. San Francisco St., 87501,* ☎ *505/988–4455 or 800/955–4455,* ℻ *505/995–4555,* ⌨ *www.eldoradohotel.com. 201 rooms, 18 suites, 41 apartments, 10 condos. 2 restaurants, pool, health club, hot tub, massage, sauna, bar, lounge, shops, concierge, meeting rooms, parking (fee). AE, D, DC, MC, V.*

$$$$ 🏨 **Inn at Loretto.** This plush, oft-photographed, ancient pueblo–inspired property attracts a loyal clientele, many of whom swear by the friendly staff and high decorating standards. The lobby opens up to the gardens and pool, and leather couches and high-end architectural details make the hotel a pleasure to relax in. Rooms are among the largest of any downtown property and contain vibrantly upholstered handcrafted furnishings and sumptuous slate-floor bathrooms. The restaurant, Nellie's, serves estimable, creative southwestern fare. The Loretto opened a swank spa in summer 2002. Spa Blue offers a wide range of treatments, from desert sage massages to Decleor skin-care facials. ⊠ *211 Old Santa Fe Trail, 87501,* ☎ *505/988–5531; 800/727–5531 outside New Mexico;* ℻ *505/984–7988;* ⌨ *www.hotelloretto.com. 140 rooms, 5 suites. Restaurant, pool, lounge, shops, meeting rooms, parking (fee). AE, D, DC, MC, V.*

$$$$ 🏨 **Inn of the Anasazi.** Although it looks unassuming from the outside,
★ this first-rate boutique hotel is one of Santa Fe's finest, with superb craftsmanship in every architectural detail. Each room has a beamed ceiling, kiva-style fireplace, antique Indian rugs, handwoven fabrics, and organic toiletries (including sunblock). Other amenities include full concierge services, twice-daily maid service, exercise bikes upon request, and a library with books on New Mexico and the Southwest. An especially nice touch in this desert town are the humidifiers in each guest room. A few deluxe rooms have balconies. The staff is thoroughly on top of things, and while this is an old building, it's been totally renovated. The restaurant is sublime, and hotel guests can dine in the romantic, candlelighted library. ⊠ *113 Washington Ave., 87501,* ☎ *505/988–3030 or 800/688–8100,* ℻ *505/988–3277,* ⌨ *www.innoftheanasazi.com. 59 rooms. Restaurant, in-room safes, minibars, in-room VCRs, bar, library, parking (fee), some pets allowed (fee). AE, D, DC, MC, V.*

$$$$ 🏨 **La Fonda.** A rich history and charm are more prevalent in this sole Plaza-front hotel than first-class service and amenities. The present structure, built in 1922 and enlarged many times, captures the essence of authentic Santa Fe style—the pueblo-inspired architecture that defines the town today. Antiques and Native American art decorate the tiled lobby, and each room has hand-decorated wood furniture, wrought-iron light fixtures, and beamed ceilings. Some of the suites have fireplaces. The 14 rooftop rooms are the most luxurious and include Continental breakfast and private concierge services; there's also an exercise room, garden, and outdoor hot tub up here. There are plans to add a spa in 2003. La Plazuela Restaurant, with its hand-painted glass tiles, is a joy to sit in and serves quite good and creative southwestern food. Folk and Latin jazz bands rotate nightly in the bar. ⊠ *100 E. San Francisco St., 87501,* ☎ *505/982–5511 or 800/523–5002;* ℻ *505/988–2952,* ⌨ *www.lafondasantfe.com. 143 rooms, 24 suites. Restaurant, pool, gym, 3 hot tubs, massage, 2 bars, laundry service, meeting rooms, parking (fee). AE, D, DC, MC, V.*

$$$$ 🏨 **La Posada de Santa Fe Resort and Spa.** In 1999 new owners undertook a massive renovation, transforming the Posada ("shelter") into an upscale, valet-parking-only hotel. Rooms here vary greatly in look and feel, from cozy and colorful to luxurious and high-ceilinged to dark

and bare. Many rooms have fireplaces, beamed ceilings, and Native American rugs. Most of the accommodations are in a rambling adobe complex surrounding the main building; those in the older casitas, though authentic to their origins, seem cold and shabby and are the least desirable. The main building contains a handful of Victorian rooms with ceilings, marble accents in the bathrooms, and an old-world feel. The real stars here are the bar, the spa, and the common areas, including the wonderfully atmospheric Staab House Lounge off the lobby. The hotel's location, on a shaded stretch of Palace just blocks from the Plaza, is also ideal. Fuego restaurant specializes in world-beat contemporary fare. The resort and spa amenities are top-notch—$35 day passes are available for use of the spa, with individual treatments extra. ⊠ *330 E. Palace Ave., 87501,* ☎ *505/986–0000 or 800/727–5276,* FAX *505/982–6850,* WEB *www.laposadadesantafe.com. 120 rooms, 38 suites. Restaurant, pool, health club, hot tub, spa, steam rooms, bar, parking (fee). AE, D, DC, MC, V.*

**$$$–$$$$** 🏨 **Inn on the Alameda.** Near the Plaza and Canyon Road is one of the
★ Southwest's best small hotels. Alameda means "tree-lined lane," and this one perfectly complements the inn's location by the gurgling Santa Fe River. The adobe architecture and enclosed courtyards strewn with climbing rose vines combine a relaxed New Mexico country atmosphere with the luxury and amenities of a top-notch hotel. Rooms have a southwestern color scheme, handmade armoires and headboards, and ceramic lamps and tiles—many have patios and kiva fireplaces. The solicitous staff is first-rate. ⊠ *303 E. Alameda St., 87501,* ☎ *505/984–2121 or 800/289–2122,* FAX *505/986–8756,* WEB *www.innonthealameda. com. 59 rooms, 10 suites. Some refrigerators, gym, 2 hot tubs, massage, bar, library, laundry facilities, concierge, parking (free), meeting rooms, some pets allowed (fee). AE, D, DC, MC, V. CP.*

**$$–$$$$** 🏨 **Grant Corner Inn.** The surrounding small garden and Victorian porch shaded by a huge weeping willow make this downtown Victorian B&B feel private. Antique Spanish and American country furnishings share space with potted greens and knickknacks. Room accents include old-fashioned fixtures, quilts, and Native American blankets. The ample breakfast, which is open to the public, includes home-baked breads and pastries, jellies, and blue-corn waffles. A separate nearby two-room hacienda can sleep seven. ⊠ *122 Grant Ave., 87501,* ☎ *505/983–6678 or 800/964–9003,* FAX *505/983–1526,* WEB *www.grantcornerinn.com. 9 rooms, 1 hacienda. Dining room, free parking; no kids under 8, no smoking. DC, MC, V. BP.*

**$$$** 🏨 **El Farolito.** All the beautiful southwestern and Mexican furniture in this small, upscale compound is custom-made, and all the art and photography original. Rooms are spacious with fireplaces and and separate entrances; some are in their own little buildings. El Farolito has a peaceful downtown location, just steps from the Capitol and a few blocks from the Plaza, and rooms are spacious and pleasant. Some have CD players. The same owners run the smaller Four Kachinas inn, which is close by and has one handicapped-accessible room (rare among smaller Santa Fe properties). ⊠ *514 Galisteo St., 87501,* ☎ *505/988–1631 or 888/634–8782,* WEB *www.farolito.com. 7 rooms, 1 suite. Some in-room VCRs; no smoking. AE, D, MC, V. CP.*

**$$$** 🏨 **Hotel Santa Fe.** Picurís Pueblo maintains the controlling interest in
★ this handsome Pueblo-style three-story hotel on the edge of the Guadalupe District and a short walk from the Plaza. The light and airy rooms and suites are done in traditional southwestern style, with locally handmade furniture, wooden blinds, and Pueblo paintings; many have balconies overlooking the city lights. The hotel gift shop, the only tribally owned store in Santa Fe, has lower prices than many nearby retail stores. The Corn Dance Cafe serves contemporary southwestern

fare with many Native American ingredients and preparations—braised venison with sage and juniper in red wine is a specialty. Guests can learn about Native American history and culture from informal talks held in the lobby, and Native American dances take place May–October. ⊠ *1501 Paseo de Peralta, 87505,* ☎ *505/982–1200 or 800/825–9876;* FAX *505/984–2211;* WEB *www.hotelsantafe.com. 40 rooms, 91 suites. Restaurant, some microwaves, pool, outdoor hot tub, massage, bar, laundry service, meeting rooms, concierge, free parking. AE, D, DC, MC, V.*

**$$$**   🏨 **Inn of the Governors.** It looks like a glorified motor lodge from the outside, but this rambling hotel by the Santa Fe River has surprisingly characterful rooms and a young, enthusiastic staff. Rooms have a Mexican theme, with bright colors, hand-painted folk art, feather pillows, southwestern fabrics, and handmade furnishings; deluxe rooms also have balconies and fireplaces. New Mexican dishes and lighter fare like wood-oven pizzas are served in the restaurant, Mañana, which also books first-rate entertainers. ⊠ *101 W. Alameda St., 87501,* ☎ *505/982–4333 or 800/234–4534,* FAX *505/989–9149,* WEB *www.innofthegovernors.com. 100 rooms. Restaurant, room service, refrigerators, pool, bar, free parking, meeting rooms. AE, D, DC, MC, V. FP.*

**$$–$$$**   🏨 **Dancing Ground of the Sun.** This relatively new compound of 1930s adobe casitas and guest rooms has saltillo-tile floors and handsome, locally made furnishings—aspen-and-willow chairs, Native American drums, and driftwood tables are among the many pieces that recall the region's Native American and Hispanic legacy. The casitas have fully stocked kitchens, and many other units have refrigerators, microwaves, and coffeemakers; many rooms have fireplaces. The inn is on the curve of a busy road that loops around the historic center of town—somewhat noisy, but ideal for access to both the Plaza and Canyon Road. ⊠ *711 Paseo de Peralta, 87501,* ☎ *505/986–9797 or 800/745–9910,* FAX *505/986–8082,* WEB *www.dancingground.com. 6 rooms, 5 casitas. Some kitchens; no smoking AE, MC, V. CP.*

**$$–$$$**   🏨 **Don Gaspar Inn.** One of the city's best-kept secrets, this exquisitely
★      landscaped and decorated compound is on a pretty residential street a few blocks south of the Plaza. Its three historic houses have three distinct architectural styles: Arts and Crafts, Pueblo Revival, and Territorial. Floral gardens and aspen and cottonwood trees shade the tranquil paths and terraces, and both Southwest and Native American paintings and handmade furnishings enliven the sunny rooms and suites. The Arts and Crafts main house has two fireplaces, two bedrooms, and a fully equipped kitchen. Considering the setting and amenities, it's a great value. ⊠ *623 Don Gaspar Ave., 87505,* ☎ *505/ 986–8664 or 888/986–8664,* FAX *505/986–0696,* WEB *www.dongaspar. com. 4 rooms, 5 suites, 1 cottage. Some in-room hot tubs, some kitchens, refrigerators; no smoking. AE, MC, V. CP.*

**$$–$$$**   🏨 **Hotel St. Francis.** Listed in the National Register of Historic Places, this three-story building, parts of which were constructed in 1923, has walkways lined with turn-of-the-20th-century lampposts and is just one block south of the Plaza. The simple and elegant rooms with high ceilings, casement windows, brass-and-iron beds, marble and cherry antiques, and original artworks suggest a refined establishment, but the service has been known to fall short. Afternoon tea, with scones and finger sandwiches, is served daily (not complimentary) in the huge lobby, which rises 50 ft from a floor of blood-red tiles. The hotel bar is among the few places in town where you can grab a bite to eat until midnight. ⊠ *210 Don Gaspar Ave., 87501,* ☎ *505/983–5700 or 800/ 529–5700,* FAX *505/989–7690,* WEB *www.hotelstfrancis.com. 83 rooms. Restaurant, room service, bar, laundry service, free parking. AE, D, DC, MC, V.*

**$$–$$$** ★ ⊞ **Inn of the Turquoise Bear.** In the 1920s, poet Witter Bynner played host to an eccentric circle of artists and intellectuals, as well as some wild parties in his mid-19th-century Spanish–Pueblo Revival home, which is now a B&B. Rooms are simple but have plush linens. The inn's style preserves the building's historic integrity, and there's plenty of ambience and a ranchlike lobby where you can stretch out or converse with other guests. You might sleep in the room where D. H. Lawrence and Frieda slept, or perhaps Robert Oppenheimer's room. The terraced flower gardens provide plenty of places to repose, away from the traffic on Old Santa Fe Trail, which borders the property. This is the quintessential Santa Fe inn. ⊠ *342 E. Buena Vista, 87501,* ☎ *505/983–0798 or 800/396–4104,* FAX *505/988–4225,* WEB *www.turquoisebear.com. 8 rooms, 2 with shared bath; 2 suites. In-room VCRs, library. AE, D, MC, V. CP.*

**$$–$$$** ⊞ **Radisson Santa Fe.** With the right management, this could be a first-rate hotel—rooms have pleasant if uninspired southwestern furnishings and earth-tone fabrics, and the pool grounds are attractive. Higher-end condo units have full kitchens and one or two bedrooms. Nonetheless, the staff is inadequately trained. What sets the Radisson apart is its hilltop location just off St. Francis Drive, with spectacular views east toward the Sangre de Cristo Mountains and south toward the Sandias. Many rooms don't have views, so ask when reserving. The Plaza is a 5-minute drive (and a manageable 20-minute walk), the Santa Fe Opera just a bit farther. Las Mañanitas restaurant serves decent Spanish and southwestern fare, and the adjacent cabaret is home to the city's outstanding flamenco dancer, Maria Benitez. Guests have free access to the Santa Fe Spa next door, which has a full health club. ⊠ *750 N. St. Francis Dr., 87501,* ☎ *505/992–5800 or 800/333–3333,* FAX *505/ 992–5865,* WEB *www.radisson.com/santafenm. 160 rooms, 4 suites. Restaurant, pool, hot tub, bar, meeting rooms, free parking. AE, D, DC, MC, V.*

**$$–$$$** ⊞ **Water Street Inn.** The large rooms in this restored adobe 2½ blocks from the Plaza are decorated with reed shutters, antique pine beds, hand-stenciled artwork, and a blend of cowboy, Hispanic, and Native American art and artifacts. Most have fireplaces. Afternoon hors d'oeuvres are served in the living room. A patio deck is available for relaxing. The one drawback is that the inn overlooks a parking lot. ⊠ *427 W. Water St., 87501,* ☎ *505/984–1193 or 800/646–6752,* WEB *www. waterstreetinn.com. 8 rooms, 4 suites. In-room VCRs, outdoor hot tub, free parking. AE, DC, MC, V. CP.*

**$–$$$** ★ ⊞ **Alexander's Inn.** This two-story 1903 Craftsman-style house in the Eastside residential area, a few blocks from the Plaza and Canyon Road, exudes the charm of an old country inn. Rooms are cozy and warm, with American country–style wooden furnishings, family heirlooms, hand-stenciled walls, and dried-flower arrangements. The grounds are dotted with tulips, hyacinths, and lilac and apricot trees. There's also a pair of two-story cottages with kitchens. The owners also run the seven-room Hacienda Nicholas ($$–$$$), a small adobe house done in southwestern style and with a more upscale look. Several of the Nicholas's pleasant rooms with a mix of Provençal and Mexican furnishings open onto a courtyard with fireplaces. ⊠ *529 E. Palace Ave., 87501,* ☎ *505/986–1431 or 888/321–5123,* WEB *www.alexanders-inn. com. 5 rooms, 2 with shared bath; 2 cottages. Outdoor hot tub, free parking, some pets allowed (fee); no TV in some rooms, no kids under 12 (except in cottages). D, MC, V. CP.*

**$–$$$** ⊞ **Inn on the Paseo.** This inn is on a busy road, but at least this stretch of Paseo de Peralta is just two lanes wide and is in a semi-residential neighborhood a short walk from the Plaza. Rooms are fairly simple but very clean and light, some with hardwood floors and all with pleasing southwestern furnishings and color schemes. The staff is laid-back and friendly. Try to get a room away from the road to avoid traffic noise. The two historic main buildings are joined by a modern lobby with a pitched ceiling, where Continental breakfast is served—in warm weather you can dine on the sundeck. ⊠ *630 Paseo de Peralta, 87501,* ☎ *505/984–8200 or 800/457–9045,* ℻ *505/989–3979,* WEB *www.innonthepaseo.com. 18 rooms. Free parking; no kids under 8, no smoking. MC, V. CP.*

$$    🖼 **Pueblo Bonito B&B Inn.** Rooms in this adobe compound built in 1873 have handmade and hand-painted furnishings, Navajo weavings, sand paintings and pottery, locally carved *santos,* and western art. All have kiva fireplaces and private entrances, and many have kitchens. Breakfast is served in the main dining room. Afternoon tea also offers complimentary margaritas. The Plaza is a five-minute walk away. ⊠ *138 W. Manhattan Ave., 87501,* ☎ *505/984–8001 or 800/461–4599,* ℻ *505/984–3155,* WEB *www.pueblobonitoinn.com. 13 rooms, 7 suites. Dining room, some kitchens, hot tub, laundry facilities. AE, DC, MC, V. CP.*

$-$$    🖼 **Garrett's Desert Inn.** This sprawling, U-shape motor court may surround a parking lot and offer relatively little in the way of ambience, but it's well maintained and has an outstanding location just a few blocks from the Plaza, smack in the middle of historic Barrio de Analco. The clean, no-frills rooms are done in earthy tones with a smattering of Southwest touches, and there's a pleasant pool and patio. ⊠ *311 Old Santa Fe Trail, 87501,* ☎ *505/982–1851 or 800/888–2145,* WEB *www.garrettsdesertinn.com. 82 rooms. Pool, billiards, lounge, car rental, free parking. AE, DC, MC, V. CP.*

$-$$    🖼 **The Madeleine.** Carolyn Lee, who owns Alexander's Inn, has named her successful establishments after her children. The Madeleine is the only Queen Anne–style house in the city, three blocks east of the Plaza in a quiet garden setting. The public rooms in this 1886 building are open and sunny, with genuine Queen Anne style. This is arguably the most romantic of Lee's inns, at least if Victoriana is your thing. Four of the rooms have fireplaces; the third-floor room has wonderful mountain views and a spiral staircase to the garden. Other touches include stained-glass windows, lace curtains, and fresh-cut flowers. You'll feel as if you've made a genteel step back in time. ⊠ *106 Faithway St., 87501,* ☎ *505/986–1431 or 888/321–5123,* WEB *www.madeleineinn.com. 6 rooms, 2 with shared bath; 2 cottages. No kids under 12 (except in cottages), no smoking. AE, D, MC, V. BP.*

$    🖼 **Santa Fe Budget Inn.** On the southern edge of the Railyard District, this inn offers affordable low-frills comfort and standard southwestern decor within walking distance of the Plaza (six blocks). Special packages are available for three- and four-day stays during peak-season events. ⊠ *725 Cerrillos Rd., 87501,* ☎ *505/982–5952,* ℻ *505/984–8879,* WEB *www.santafebudgetinn.com. 160 rooms. Restaurants, pool, free parking. AE, DC, MC, V. CP.*

## Lower Cerrillos Road

$-$$    🖼 **El Rey Inn.** The tree-shaded, whitewashed El Rey has been a Santa Fe landmark motel for 65 years. Rooms are decorated in southwestern, Spanish colonial, and Victorian style. Some have kitchenettes and fireplaces. The largest suite, with seven rooms, sleeps six and has antique furniture, a full kitchen, a breakfast nook, and two patios. Service is friendly. ⊠ *1862 Cerrillos Rd., 87505,* ☎ *505/982–1931 or 800/521–1349,* ℻ *505/989–9249. 79 rooms, 8 suites. Some kitchenettes, pool, 2 hot tubs, sauna, playground, laundry facilities. AE, DC, MC, V. CP.*

# North of Santa Fe

**$$$$** 🏨 **Bishop's Lodge Resort and Spa.** This resort established in 1918 is
★ in a bucolic valley at the foot of the Sangre de Cristo Mountains and
yet only a five-minute drive from the Plaza. Behind the main building
is an exquisite chapel that was once the private retreat of Archbishop
Jean Baptiste Lamy. Outdoor activities include hiking, horseback riding, organized trail riding (with meals) into the adjacent national forest, skeet-shooting, and trapshooting. The two lodge buildings have
antique southwestern furnishings—shipping chests, tinwork from Mexico, and Native American and western art; most of the rooms, in other
buildings scattered around the property, have less character, though some
rooms have fireplaces. The lodge has a state-of-the-art spa and good
fitness facilities. The restaurant, specializing in inventive Nuevo Latino
fare, serves a bountiful Sunday brunch, probably the best in Santa Fe.
Although Bishop's is among the priciest hotels in town, the off-season
discounts are as steep as 65%. ⊠ *Bishop's Lodge Rd., 2½ mi north of
downtown, 87501,* ☎ *505/983–6377 or 800/732–2240,* FAX *505/989–
8739,* WEB *www.bishopslodge.com. 92 rooms, 19 suites. 2 restaurants,
some refrigerators, 4 tennis courts, pool, gym, hot tub, massage, spa,
fishing, hiking, horseback riding, bar, children's programs (ages 4–12),
business services, meeting rooms, airport shuttle, free parking. AE, D,
MC, V.*

**$$$$** 🏨 **Hacienda del Cerezo.** Stop reading here if $600 is more than you
★ want to spend on a room. Keep in mind that the rate includes three
meals for two people prepared by a master chef; dinner is a five-course
candlelit affair in the great room or in the courtyard, looking out onto
the vanishing-edge pool and the desert beyond. The inn sits on a splen-
didly isolated patch of land 25 minutes northwest of downtown.
Rooms are subtly executed in prints, ornaments, carvings on the beams
of the viga ceilings, and etchings in the glass shower doors. Each room
has a king-size bed, a generous sitting area, a kiva fireplace, an enclosed
patio, and a view of the mountains. Service is gracious and understated.
⊠ *100 Camino del Cerezo, 87501,* ☎ *505/982–8000 or 888/982–8001,*
FAX *505/983–7162,* WEB *www.haciendadelcerezo.com. 10 rooms. Restaurant, tennis court, pool, outdoor hot tub, hiking, horseback riding, free
parking; no kids. AE. FAP.*

**$$$–$$$$** 🏨 **Ten Thousand Waves.** Devotees appreciate the Zenlike atmosphere
★ of this Japanese-style health spa and small hotel above town. Eight cozy
hillside cottages tumble down a piñon-covered hill below the first-rate
spa, which is tremendously popular with day visitors. The sleek, un-
cluttered accommodations have marble or stone wood-burning fire-
places, CD stereos, fine woodwork, low-slung beds or futons, and
courtyards or patios; two come with full kitchens. The facility has pri-
vate and communal indoor and outdoor hot tubs and spa treatments.
Private tubs run from $20 per hour, communal tubs from $14 for an
unlimited time; massage and spa treatments cost from $45 to $205.
Overnight guests can use the communal tubs for free. The snack bar
serves sushi and other healthful treats. ⊠ *3451 Hyde Park Rd., 4 mi
from the Plaza (Box 10200, 87501),* ☎ *505/982–9304,* FAX *505/989–
5077,* WEB *www.tenthousandwaves.com. 8 cottages. Snack bar, some
kitchens, refrigerators, some in-room VCRs, 9 outdoor hot tubs, mas-
sage, spa, shop, some pets allowed (fee), free parking; no TV in some
rooms. D, MC, V.*

# Camping

🏕 **Los Campos RV Resort.** The only full-service RV park in town lies
between a car dealership on one side and open vistas on the other. Poplars
and Russian olive trees, a dry riverbed, and mountains rise in the

background. ⌧ *3574 Cerrillos Rd.,* ☎ *505/473–1949 or 800/852–8160.
Flush toilets, full hook-ups, dump station, drinking water, electricity,
laundry, grills, picnic tables, public phone, playground, pool. 95 sites.
⌸ $25–$33. MC, V.*

▲ **Rancheros de Santa Fe Campground.** This 22-acre camping park
is on a hill in the midst of a piñon forest. Bring your tent or RV, or
rent a cabin. You can get LP gas service here. An Internet station and
cable TV hook-ups were added in 2002; other amenities include nightly
movies in summer, a hiking trail, and a recreation room. ⌧ *Old Las
Vegas Hwy. (Exit 290 from I–25, 10½ mi south of the Plaza),* ☎ *505/
466–3482 or 800/426–9259,* WEB *www.rancheros.com. Flush toilets,
full hook-ups, dump station, drinking water, laundry facilities, showers, grills, picnic tables, electricity, public telephone, general store,
playground, pool. 37 tent sites, 95 RV sites, 5 cabins.* ⌸ *Tent sites $15–
$17, water and electric hook-ups $19–$23, full hook-ups $22–$27, cab-
ins $30–$33. MC, V.* ☉ *Mid-Mar.–Oct.*

▲ **Santa Fe KOA.** In the foothills of the Sangre de Cristo Mountains,
20 minutes southeast of Santa Fe, this large campground with tent sites,
RV sites, and cabins is covered with piñons, cedars, and junipers. Internet access is available; activities include basketball, ring toss, video
games, and free movies. ⌧ *Old Las Vegas Hwy. (Box 95-A, 87505),*
☎ *505/466–1419 or 800/562–1514,* WEB *www.koa.com/where/nm/
31159.htm. Flush toilets, partial hook-ups (electric), drinking water,
laundry facilities, showers, fire grates, fire pits, picnic tables, electricity, public phone, general store. 44 RV sites, 26 tent sites, 10 cabins.
⌸ Tent sites $22–$25, RV sites $26–$31, cabins $38–$40. D, MC, V.*
☉ *Mar.–Oct.*

# NIGHTLIFE AND THE ARTS

Santa Fe ranks among America's most cultured small cities. Gallery
openings, poetry readings, plays, and dance concerts take place year-
round, not to mention the famed opera and chamber-music festivals.
Check the arts and entertainment listings in Santa Fe's daily newspaper,
the *New Mexican* (www.sfnewmexican.com), particularly on Friday,
when the arts and entertainment section, "Pasatiempo," is included,
or check the weekly *Santa Fe Reporter* (www.sfreporter.com) for shows
and events. Activities peak in the summer.

## Nightlife

Culturally endowed though it is, Santa Fe has a pretty mellow nightlife
scene, its key strength being live music, which is presented at numerous bars, hotel lounges, and restaurants. Austin-based blues and country groups and other acts wander into town, and members of blockbuster
bands have been known to perform unannounced at small clubs while
vacationing in the area. But on most nights your best bet might be quiet
cocktails beside the flickering embers of a piñon fire or under the stars
out on the patio.

**Catamount Bar** (⌧ 125 E. Water St., ☎ 505/988–7222) is popular with
the post-college set; jazz and blues/rock groups play on weekends and
some weeknights. The dance floor isn't great—too small, and with bright
lights.

**Dragon Room** (⌧ 406 Old Santa Fe Trail, ☎ 505/983–7712), at the
Pink Adobe restaurant, has been the place to see and be seen in Santa
Fe for decades; flamenco and other light musical fare entertain at the
packed bar.

**El Cañon Lounge** (✉ Hilton Santa Fe, 308 W. San Francisco St., ☎ 505/ 986–6417) may be attached to the bland Hilton hotel and its upscale Piñon Restaurant, but this is a terrific hangout with dark lighting, a long bar, lots of comfy seating, and an all-around cool vibe. It's just down from the Plaza, and the kitchen serves a nice little range of bar snacks, from oyster stew to bratwurst with sauerkraut.

**Eldorado Court and Lounge** (✉ 309 W. San Francisco St., ☎ 505/988– 4455), in the lobby of the classy Eldorado Hotel, is a gracious lounge where classical guitarists and pianists perform nightly. It has the largest wines-by-the-glass list in town.

**El Farol** (✉ 808 Canyon Rd., ☎ 505/983–9912) restaurant is where locals like to hang out. The roomy, somewhat ramshackle bar area has an old Spanish-western atmosphere, but you can order some fine Spanish brandies and sherries. On most nights you can listen to live flamenco, country, folk, or blues. Dancers pack the floor on weekend nights in summer.

**Evangelo's** (✉ 200 W. San Francisco St., ☎ 505/982–9014) is an old-fashioned, smoky street-side bar, with pool tables, 200 types of imported beer, and rock bands on many weekends.

The city's largest dance club, **Paramount/Bar B** (✉ 331 Sandoval St., ☎ 505/982–8999), has a snappy theme for each night of the week. The interior is contemporary and well lit and the dance floor is large. It's a good place to meet people, and it draws a gay-straight mix many evenings. There's also a Latin dance night, trash disco, and, on Friday, live music. In back, swanky Bar B is a cozy and somewhat quieter nook that usually has its own musical theme (and DJ). Cover charge varies.

**Rodeo Nites** (✉ 2911 Cerrillos Rd., ☎ 505/473–4138) attracts a country-western crowd, and lots of singles on the make. It can get a bit rough in the wee hours, so get there on the early side for line dancing and some very hot two-stepping.

**Second Street Brewery** (✉ 1814 2nd St., ☎ 505/982–3030), a short drive south of downtown, packs in an eclectic, somewhat collegiate bunch for microbrewed ales, pretty good pub fare, and live rock and folk. There's an expansive patio, and the staff is friendly.

**Swig** (✉ 135 W. Palace Ave., Level 3, ☎ 505/955–0400), a trendy upscale lounge that opened in spring 2002, has developed a loyal following for its chichi postmodern decor, rooftop patio, and well-dressed crowd. Drinks are expensive by Santa Fe standards, but that hasn't deterred many people.

# The Arts

The performing arts scene in Santa Fe blossoms in summer. Classical or jazz concerts, Shakespeare on the grounds of St. John's campus, experimental theater at Santa Fe Stages, or flamenco—"too many choices!" is the biggest complaint. The rest of the year is a bit more quiet, but an increasing number of off-season venues have developed in recent years.

## Concert Venues

Just a 10-minute drive north of town, **Camel Rock Casino** (✉ U.S. 285/ 84, ☎ 800/GO–CAMEL, WEB www.camelrockcasino.com) presents relatively inexpensive pop and rock (Neil Sedaka, Pat Benatar, etc.) concerts.

Santa Fe's vintage downtown movie house was fully restored and converted into the 850-seat **Lensic Performing Arts Center** (✉ 211 W. San

Francisco St., ☎ 505/988–1234, WEB www.lensic.com) in 2001. The grand 1931 building, with Moorish and Spanish Renaissance influences, hosts the Santa Fe Symphony, theater, classic films, lectures and readings, noted pop and jazz musicians, and many other noteworthy events.

The **St. Francis Auditorium** (✉ Museum of Fine Arts, northwest corner of the Plaza) is the scene of cultural events such as theatrical productions and varied musical performances.

## Dance

The esteemed **Aspen Santa Fe Ballet** (☎ 505/988–1234, WEB www. aspensantafeballet.com) presents several ballet performances throughout the year at the Lensic Performing Arts Center.

Fans of Spanish dance should make every effort to see **Maria Benitez Teatro Flamenco** (✉ Radisson Santa Fe, 750 N. St. Francis Dr., ☎ 505/ 955–8562 or 888/435–2636, WEB www.mariabenitez.com), who performs from late June through August at the Radisson Santa Fe. Maria Benitez is one of the world's premier flamenco dancers, and her performances often sell out well in advance.

## Film

**Cinematheque** (✉ 1050 Old Pecos Trail, ☎ 505/982–1338) screens foreign and independent films.

The intimate **Jean Cocteau** (✉ 418 Montezuma Ave., by the Sanbusco Center, ☎ 505/988–2711) shows art films and has a pleasant little café.

## Music

The acclaimed **Santa Fe Chamber Music Festival** (☎ 505/982–1890, WEB www.sfcmf.org) runs July through August, with performances nearly every night at either the Lensic Performing Arts Center or the St. Francis Auditorium. There are also free youth-oriented concerts given on several summer mornings.

**Santa Fe Opera** (☎ 505/986–5900 or 800/280–4654, WEB www. santafeopera.org) performs in a strikingly modern structure—a 2,126-seat, indoor-outdoor amphitheater with excellent acoustics and sight lines. Carved into the natural curves of a hillside 7 mi north of the city on U.S. 285/84, the opera overlooks mountains, mesas, and sky. Add some of the most acclaimed singers, directors, conductors, musicians, designers, and composers from Europe and the United States, and you begin to understand the excitement that builds every June. John Crosby directs the company, which presents five works in repertory each summer—a blend of seasoned classics, neglected masterpieces, and world premieres. Many evenings sell out far in advance, but inexpensive standing-room tickets are often available on the day of the performance.

The **Santa Fe Symphony** (☎ 505/983–1414 or 800/480–1319, WEB www. sf-symphony.org) performs eight concerts each season (from September to May) in the Lensic Performing Arts Center.

Orchestra and chamber concerts are given at St. Francis Auditorium and the Lensic Performing Arts Center by the **Santa Fe Pro Musica** (☎ 505/988–4640 or 800/960–6680, WEB www.santafepromusica.com) from September through April. Baroque and other classical compositions are the normal fare; the annual Christmas and April's Bach Festival performances are highlights.

On the campus of the Santa Fe Indian School, the **Paolo Soleri Outdoor Amphitheater** (✉ 1501 Cerrillos Rd., ☎ 505/989–6300) hosts concerts spring–fall.

## Theater

The **Greer Garson Theatre Center** (✉ College of Santa Fe, 1600 St. Michael's Dr., ☎ 505/473–6011 or 800/456–2673, WEB www.csf.edu) stages student productions of comedies, dramas, and musicals from October to May.

The oldest extant theater company west of the Mississippi, the **Santa Fe Playhouse** (✉ 142 E. De Vargas St., ☎ 505/988–4262) occupies a converted 19th-century adobe stable and has been presenting an adventurous mix of avant-garde pieces, classical drama, and musical comedy since 1922. The Fiesta Melodrama—a spoof of the Santa Fe scene—runs late August–mid-September.

Internationally renowned **Santa Fe Stages** (☎ 505/982–6683, WEB www.santafestages.org) presents theater, dance, and music from late June to August; the company also presents shorter series from time to time. Performances are at the Lensic Performing Arts Center and **Firestone Plaza** (✉ 100 N. Guadalupe St.).

Several evenings and a few afternoons per week from mid-July through late August, **Shakespeare in Santa Fe** (☎ 505/982–2910, WEB www.shakespearesantafe.org) presents performances of the Bard's finest at both the Lensic and in the courtyard of the John Gaw Meem Library at **St. John's College** (✉ 1160 Camino Cruz Blanca). When at St. John's campus, which occupies a magical setting in the city's east-side foothills, a performance of Renaissance music begins at 6, followed by the play at 7:30. It's best to get tickets in advance. Bring a picnic basket or buy food at the concession stand. It can get cold and the performers have been known to keep the show going in light rain. Tickets cost $15–$32. At St. John's, you can also opt to sit in the grass and watch for free; a $5 donation is suggested.

# OUTDOOR ACTIVITIES AND SPORTS

The Santa Fe National Forest is right in the city's backyard and includes the Dome Wilderness (5,200 acres in the volcanically formed Jemez Mountains) and the Pecos Wilderness (223,333 acres of high mountains, forests, and meadows at the southern end of the Rocky Mountain chain). The 12,500-ft Sangre de Cristo Mountains (the name translates as "Blood of Christ," for the red glow they radiate at sunset) fringe the city's east side, constant and gentle reminders of the mystery and power of the natural world. To the south and west, sweeping high desert is punctuated by several less formidable mountain ranges. The dramatic shifts in elevation and topography around Santa Fe make for a wealth of outdoor activities. Head to the mountains for fishing, camping, and skiing; to the nearby Rio Grande for kayaking and rafting; and almost anywhere in the area for bird-watching, hiking, and biking.

## Participant Sports

For a report on general conditions in the forest, contact the **Santa Fe National Forest Office** (✉ 1474 Rodeo Rd., 87505, ☎ 505/438–7840, WEB www.fs.fed.us/r3/sfe). For a one-stop shop for information about recreation on public lands, which includes national and state parks, contact the **New Mexico Public Lands Information Center** (✉ 1474 Rodeo Rd., 87505, ☎ 505/438–7542, FAX 505/438–7582, WEB www.publiclands.org). It has maps, reference materials, licenses, permits—just about everything you need to plan an adventure in the New Mexican wilderness.

Opened in 2001, the impressive **Genoveva Chavez Community Center**
(✉ 3221 Rodeo Rd., ☎ 505/955–4001) is a reasonably priced (adults
$4 per day), top-notch facility with a regulation-size ice rink, an enor-
mous gymnasium, indoor running track, 50-m pool, leisure pool with
water slide and play structures, aerobics center, state-of-the-art fitness
room, two racquetball courts, and a child-care center.

## Bicycling

You can pick up a map of bike trips—among them a 30-mi round-trip
ride from downtown Santa Fe to Ski Santa Fe at the end of NM 475—
from the New Mexico Public Lands Information Center.

**Bike N' Sport** (✉ 1829 Cerrillos Rd., ☎ 505/820–0809) provides
rentals and information about guided tours. **Sun Mountain** (✉ 107 Washington Ave., ☎ 505/820–2902) rents mountain bikes and offers a
wide range of bike tours. The shop will also deliver to your hotel, any
day, year-round.

## Bird-Watching

At the end of Upper Canyon Road, at the mouth of the canyon as it
wends into the foothills, the 135-acre **Randall Davey Audubon Center**
harbors diverse birds and other wildlife. Guided nature walks are
given many weekends; there are also two major hiking trails that you
can tackle on your own. The home and studio of Randall Davey, a prolific early Santa Fe artist, can be toured on Monday afternoons in summer. A nature bookstore was added in 2002. ✉ *Upper Canyon Rd.,*
☎ *505/983–4609,* WEB *www.audubon.org/chapter/nm/nm/rdac.* 🎟 *$2,*
*house tour $5.* ☉ *Weekdays 9–5, weekends 10–4; grounds daily dawn–*
*dusk.*

## Fishing

There's excellent fishing spring through fall in the Rio Grande and the
mountain streams that feed into it, as well as a short drive away along
the Pecos River. **High Desert Angler** (✉ 435 S. Guadalupe St., ☎ 505/
98–TROUT or 888/98–TROUT) is a superb fly-fishing outfitter and
guide service. This is your one-stop for equipment rental, fly-fishing
tackle, licenses, and advice.

## Golf

**Marty Sanchez Links de Santa Fe** (✉ 205 Caja del Rio Rd., off NM
599 [the Santa Fe Relief Route], ☎ 505/955–4400), an outstanding
municipal facility with beautifully groomed 18- and 9-hole courses, sits
on high prairie west of Santa Fe with fine mountain views. It has driving and putting ranges, a pro shop, and a snack bar. The greens fee is
$49 for nonresidents on the 18-hole course, $30 on the par-3 9-holer.

The 18-hole, par-72 **Pueblo de Cochiti Golf Course** (✉ 5200 Cochiti
Hwy., Cochiti Lake, ☎ 505/465–2239), set against a backdrop of
steep canyons and red-rock mesas, is a 45-minute drive southwest of
the city. Cochiti, one of the top public golf courses in the state, has a
greens fee of $27 on weekdays and $35 on weekends and holidays.

The **Towa Golf Resort** (✉ Cities of Gold Casino Resort, 17746 U.S.
285/84, Pojoaque, ☎ 505/455–9000 or 877/465–3489), 15 mi north
of Santa Fe, was designed by pro legend Hale Irwin and sits in the foothills
of the Sangre de Cristos, with stunning views of the Santa Fe ski basin
and the Jemez Mountains over Los Alamos. The challenging 18-hole
course opened in 2001; another 18 holes were slated to open in fall
2002. The greens fee is $49.

## Hiking

Hiking around Santa Fe can take you into high-altitude alpine country or into lunaresque high desert as you head south and west to lower

elevations. For winter hiking, the gentler climates to the south are less likely to be snow-packed, while the alpine areas will likely require snow-shoes or cross-country skis. In summer, wildflowers bloom in the high country and the temperature is generally at least 10 degrees cooler than in town. The mountain trails accessible at the base of the Ski Santa Fe area (end of NM 475) stay cool on even the hottest summer days. Weather can change with one gust of wind, so be prepared with extra clothing, rain gear, food, and lots of water. Keep in mind that the sun at 10,000 ft is very powerful, even with a hat and sunscreen.

For information about specific hiking areas, contact the New Mexico Public Lands Information Center. The **Sierra Club** (✉ 621 Old Santa Fe Trail, ☎ 505/983–2703, WEB riogrande.sierraclub.org/santafe/home. html) organizes group hikes of all levels of difficulty.

**Aspen Vista** is a lovely hike along a south-facing mountainside. Take Hyde Park Road (NM 475) 13 mi, and the trail begins before the ski area. After walking a few miles through thick aspen groves you'll come to panoramic views of Santa Fe. The path is well marked and gently inclines toward Tesuque Peak. The trail becomes shadier with elevation—snow has been reported on the trail as late as July. In winter, after heavy snows, the trail is great for intermediate-advanced cross-country skiing. The round-trip is 12 mi, but it's just 3½ mi to the spectacular overlook. The hillside is covered with golden aspen trees in late September.

**Tsankawi Trail,** pronounced sank-ah-*wee,* will take you through the ancient rock trails of the Pajarito Plateau. The Pueblo people created the trails in the 1400s as they made their way from their mesa-top homes to the fields and springs in the canyon below. In the 1½-mi loop you'll see petroglyphs and south-facing cave dwellings. Wear good shoes for the rocky path and a climb on a 12-ft ladder that shoots between a crevasse in the rock and the highest point of the mesa. This is an ideal walk if you don't have time to explore Bandelier National Monument in depth but want to get a taste of it. It's on the way to Los Alamos, about a 35-minute drive from Santa Fe. ✉ *25 mi northwest of Santa Fe (take U.S. 285/84 north to the Los Alamos exit for NM 502; go west on 502 until the turnoff for White Rock, Hwy. 4; continue for several mi to the sign for Tsankawi on the left; the trail is clearly marked),* ☎ 505/672–3861.

**Kasha-Katuwe Tent Rocks National Monument** is a great choice if you have time for only one hike. The sandstone rock formations look like stacked tents in a stark, water- and wind-eroded box canyon. Located 45 minutes south of Santa Fe, near Cochiti Pueblo, Tent Rocks is excellent hiking year-round, although it can get hot in summer, when you should bring extra water. The drive to this magical landscape is equally awesome, as the road heads west toward Cochiti Dam and through the cottonwood groves around the pueblo. It's a good hike for kids. The round-trip hiking distance is only 2 mi, about 1½ hours, but it's the kind of place where you'll want to hang out for a while. Take a camera. ✉ *I–25 south to Cochiti exit 264 (follow NM 16 for 8 mi, turning right onto NM 22; continue approximately 3½ more mi past Cochiti Pueblo entrance; turn right on NM 266 "Tent Rocks" and continue 5 mi to the "WELCOME TO TENT ROCKS" sign; the last stretch of road is jarring, washboarded gravel),* ☎ 505/761–8700, WEB *www.nm. blm.gov/www/aufo/tent_rocks/tent_rocks.html.* 🎫 *$5 per vehicle.*

## Horseback Riding

New Mexico's rugged countryside has been the setting for many Hollywood westerns. Whether you want to ride the range that Gregory Peck and Kevin Costner rode or just head out feeling tall in the saddle, you can do so year-round. Rates average about $20 an hour.

**Bishop's Lodge** (✉ Bishop's Lodge Rd., ☎ 505/983–6377) provides rides and guides year-round. Call for reservations. Rides with **Broken Saddle Riding Co.** (✉ off NM 14, Cerrillos, ☎ 505/424–7774) take you around the old turquoise and silver mines the Cerrillos area is noted for. On a Tennessee Walker or a Missouri Fox Trotter you can explore the Cerrillos hills and canyons, 23 mi southeast of Santa Fe. This is not the usual nose-to-tail trail ride.

**Galarosa Stable** (✉ NM 41, Galisteo, ☎ 505/466–4654, WEB www. galarosastables.com) provides rentals by the half- or full day south of Santa Fe in the panoramic Galisteo Basin. In the heart of Carson National Forest, about an hour north of Santa Fe, **Vallecitos Stables** (✉ Hwy. 250, off NM 111, north of Ojo Caliente, Vallecitos, ☎ 505/582–4221 or 80/797–7261, WEB www.vallecitosstables.com) conducts trail rides through this scenic high-mountain forest on Andalusian, Tennessee Walker, and American Saddlebred horses.

## Jogging

Because of the city's altitude (7,000–7,500 ft), you may feel heavy-legged and light-headed if you start running shortly after you arrive. Once you've become acclimated, though, you'll find that this is a great place to run. There's a jogging path along the Santa Fe River, parallel to Alameda, and another at Fort Marcy on Washington Avenue. The winding roads and paths up near the scenic campus of St. John's College are also ideal, although the terrain is quite hilly. Pick up gear and running advice at **Running Hub** (✉ 333 Montezuma Ave., No. 6, ☎ 505/820–2523); the store sponsors informal group runs many days—these are open to anybody.

## River Rafting

If you want to watch birds and wildlife along the banks, try the laid-back Huck Finn floats along the Rio Chama or the Rio Grande's White Rock Canyon. The season is generally between April and September. Most outfitters have overnight package plans, and all offer half- and full-day trips. Be prepared to get wet, and wear secure water shoes. For a list of outfitters who guide trips on the Rio Grande and the Rio Chama, write the **Bureau of Land Management (BLM), Taos Resource Area Office** (✉ 224 Cruz Alta Rd., Taos 87571, ☎ 505/758–8851, WEB www.nm.blm.gov/www/tafo/rafting/commercial.html), or stop by the BLM visitor center along NM 68 several miles south of Taos.

**Kokopelli Rafting Adventures** (✉ 541 Cordova Rd., ☎ 505/983–3734 or 800/879–9035, WEB www.kokopelliraft.com) specializes in trips through the relatively mellow White Rock Canyon as well as white water. **New Wave Rafting** (✉ 103 E. Water St., Suite F, ☎ 505/984–1444 or 800/984–1444, WEB www.bass-station.com/nwr) conducts full-day, half-day, and overnight river trips, with daily departures from Santa Fe. **Santa Fe Rafting Company and Outfitters** (✉ 1000 Cerrillos Rd., ☎ 505/988–4914 or 800/467–7238) customizes rafting tours. Tell them what you want—they'll do it.

## Skiing

To save time during the busy holiday season you may want to rent skis or snowboards in town the night before hitting the slopes, or early in the morning so you don't waste any time paid for by your pricey lift ticket. **Alpine Sports** (✉ 121 Sandoval St., ☎ 505/983–5155) rents downhill and cross-country skis and snowboards. **Cottam's Ski Rentals** (✉ Hyde Park Rd., 7 mi northeast of downtown, toward Ski Santa Fe, ☎

505/982–0495) rents the works, including snowboards, sleds, and snowshoes.

**Ski Santa Fe** (✉ end of NM 475, 18 mi northeast of downtown, ☎ 505/982–4429; 505/983–9155 conditions; WEB www.skisantafe.com), open roughly from late November through early April, is a fine, mid-size operation that receives an average of 225 inches of snow a year and plenty of sunshine. It's one of America's highest ski areas—the 12,000-ft summit has a variety of terrain and seems bigger than its 1,650 ft of vertical rise and 500 acres. There are some great powder stashes, tough bump runs, and many wide, gentle cruising runs. The 43 trails are ranked 20% beginner, 40% intermediate, and 40% advanced; there are seven lifts. Snowboarders are welcome, and there's the Norquist Trail for cross-country skiers. Chipmunk Corner provides day care and supervised kids' skiing. The ski school is excellent. Rentals, a good restaurant, a ski shop, and Totemoff Bar and Grill round out the amenities.

**Pajarito Mountain Ski Area** (✉ off NM 501, just west of downtown Los Alamos, ☎ 505/662–5725; 888/662–SNOW conditions; WEB www.skipajarito.com), a small, low-key area near Los Alamos, has some excellent long runs and a good selection of wide-open, intermediate mogul runs. There's no artificial snowmaking, so the slopes are barely open during dry winters and the season runs according to conditions (usually about mid-December through April). But there's never a wait in lift lines.

## Tennis

Santa Fe has more than two dozen public tennis courts available on a first-come, first-served basis. For information, call the **City Parks Division** (☎ 505/473–7236).

There are several major private tennis facilities with indoor, outdoor, and lighted courts. A favorite is **Sangre De Cristo Racquet Club** (✉ 1755 Camino Corrales, ☎ 505/983–7978), which has seven outdoor courts and one indoor. **Santa Fe Country Club** (✉ Airport Rd., ☎ 505/471–3378) has three outdoor courts. **Shellaberger Tennis Center** (✉ College of Santa Fe, St. Michael's Dr., ☎ 505/473–6144) is quite affordable and has seven outdoor courts.

# SHOPPING

Santa Fe has been a trading post for eons. A thousand years ago the great pueblos of the Chacoan civilizations were strategically located between the buffalo-hunting tribes of the Great Plains and the Indians of Mexico. Native Americans in New Mexico traded turquoise, which was thought to have magical properties, and other valuables with Indians from Mexico for metals, shells, parrots, and other exotic items. After the arrival of the Spanish and the subsequent development of the West, Santa Fe became the place to exchange silver from Mexico and natural resources from New Mexico—including hides, fur, and foodstuffs—for manufactured goods, whiskey, and greenbacks from the United States. With the building of the railroad in 1880, Santa Fe had access to all kinds of manufactured goods as well as those unique to the region via the old trade routes.

The trading legacy remains, but now downtown Santa Fe caters almost exclusively to those looking for handcrafted goods. Sure, T-shirt outlets and major retail clothing shops have moved in, but shopping in Santa Fe consists mostly of one-of-a-kind independent stores.

Santa Fe is a great place to window shop, perhaps because of the high visual standards such an artistic community commands. It is a town where color, texture, and pattern make a brave stand for diversity rather than uniformity. Canyon Road, where art galleries lie within a short distance of one another, is the perfect place to find one-of-a-kind gifts and collectibles. The downtown district, around the Plaza, has unusual gift shops, clothing, and shoe stores that range from theatrical to conventional, curio shops, and art galleries. The funky Guadalupe District, on the southwest perimeter of downtown, includes the Sanbusco Market Center. It's a laid-back neighborhood with a burgeoning restaurant and shopping scene, and it's far less touristy than the Plaza.

Farther out on Cerrillos Road, a traffic-jammed strip of shopping centers and chain motels, a new clutch of modern superstores has sprung up alongside Santa Fe's rather ordinary Villa Linda shopping mall. All the usual suspects are out here, around the intersection with Rodeo Road. On Cerrillos out by the I–25 exit, the inevitable **Santa Fe Premium Outlets** (⊠ 8380 Cerrillos Rd., at I–25, ☎ 505/474–4000) contains about 35 shops, including Donna Karan, Coach, Bose, Dansk, and Brooks Brothers.

## Art Galleries

The following are only a few of the nearly 200 galleries in greater Santa Fe—with the best of representational, nonobjective, Native American, Latin American, cutting-edge, photographic, and soulful works that defy categorization. The Santa Fe Convention and Visitors Bureau (☞ Visitor Information *in* Santa Fe A to Z, *below*) has a more extensive listing. *The Wingspread Collectors Guide to Santa Fe and Taos* is a good resource and is available in hotels and at some galleries, as well as on the Web at www.collectorsguide.com. Check the "Pasatiempo" pullout in the *Santa Fe New Mexican* on Friday for a preview of gallery openings.

**Andrew Smith Gallery** (⊠ 203 W. San Francisco St., ☎ 505/984–1234) is a significant photo gallery dealing in works by Edward S. Curtis and other 19th-century chroniclers of the American West. Other major figures are Ansel Adams, Eliot Porter, Laura Gilpin, Dorothea Lange, Alfred Stieglitz, Annie Liebowitz, and regional artists like Barbara Van Cleve.

**Bellas Artes** (⊠ 653 Canyon Rd., ☎ 505/983–2745), a sophisticated gallery and sculpture garden, has ancient ceramics and represents internationally renowned artists like Judy Pfaff, Phoebe Adams, and Olga de Amaral.

**Charlotte Jackson Fine Art** (⊠ 200 W. Marcy St., ☎ 505/989–8688) focuses primarily on monochromatic "radical" painting. Florence Pierce, Joe Barnes, Anne Cooper, and Joseph Marioni are among the artists producing minimalist works dealing with light and space.

**Dewey Galleries** (⊠ Catron Building, 53 Old Santa Fe Trail, ☎ 505/982–8632) shows historic Navajo textiles and jewelry, Pueblo pottery, and antique Spanish-colonial furniture, as well as paintings and sculpture (notably that of Allan Houser).

**Gerald Peters Gallery** (⊠ 1011 Paseo de Peralta, ☎ 505/954–5700) is Santa Fe's leading gallery of American and European art from the 19th century to the present. It has works by Max Weber, Albert Bierstadt, the Taos Society, the New Mexico Modernists, and Georgia O'Keeffe, as well as contemporary artists.

# THE ART OF SANTA FE

**T**HE **ARTISTIC ROOTS** of Santa Fe stretch back to the landscape and the devotion of those who roamed and settled here long before the Santa Fe Trail transplanted goods and people from the East. The intricate designs on Native American pottery and baskets, the embroidery on the ritual dancewear, the color and pattern on Rio Grande weavings, and the delicate paintings and carvings of devotional images called santos all contributed to the value and awareness of beauty that Santa Fe holds as its cultural birthright. The rugged landscape, the ineffable quality of the light, and the community itself continue to draw to Santa Fe a plethora of musicians, writers, and visual artists. The spell of beauty is so powerful here that some people call the town "Fanta Se," but for those who live in Santa Fe the arts are very real (as are economic realities; most artists hold additional jobs—ask your waiter). The painter and part-time Santa Fe resident Robert Henri once said, "There are moments in our lives, there are moments in a day, when we seem to see beyond the usual." Santa Fe is alive with those moments, and many artists draw their inspiration from them.

With wide-eyed enchantment, visitors often buy paintings in orange, pink, and turquoise that are perfect next to the adobe architecture, blue sky, and red rocks of the New Mexican landscape. When they get home, however, the admired works sometimes end up in a closet simply because it's so hard to integrate the southwestern look with the tone of the existing furnishings and artwork. Taking the risk is part of the experience. Rather than suffering from buyer's remorse, those who make the aesthetic leap can take the spirit of northern New Mexico home with them. Although it may shake up the home decor, the works are a reminder of a new way of seeing and of all the other values that inspire one to travel in the first place.

Most galleries will send a painting (not posters or prints) out on a trial basis for very interested clients. If looking at art is new to you, ask yourself if your interest is in bringing home a souvenir that says "I was there" or in art that will live in the present and inspire the future, independent of the nostalgia for the "land of enchantment." Santa Fe has plenty of both to offer—use discrimination while you look so you don't burn out on the first block of Canyon Road.

**S**ANTA FE, while holding strong in its regional art identity, emerged in the late 1990s as a more international art scene. Native American and Hispanic arts groups now include the work of contemporary artists who have pressed beyond the bounds of tradition. Bold color and the oft-depicted New Mexico landscape are still evident, but you're just as likely to see mixed-media collages by a Chinese artist currently living in San Francisco. A few Santa Fe outlets, such as the Riva Yares Gallery and evo gallery, are dedicated to representing artists with Latin American roots. "The world is wide here," Georgia O'Keeffe once noted about northern New Mexico. And just as Santa Fe welcomed early Modernist painters who responded to the open landscape and the artistic freedom it engendered, contemporary artists working with edgier media, such as conceptual, performance, and installation art, are finding welcoming venues in Santa Fe, specifically at Plan B and SITE Santa Fe.

**LewAllen Contemporary** (✉ 129 W. Palace Ave., ☎ 505/988–8997) is a leading center for a variety of contemporary arts by both southwestern and other acclaimed artists, among them Judy Chicago; sculpture, photography, ceramics, basketry, and painting are all shown in this dynamic space.

**Nedra Matteucci Galleries** (✉ 1075 Paseo de Peralta, ☎ 505/982–4631; ✉ 555 Canyon Rd., ☎ 505/983–2731) exhibits works by California regionalists, members of the early Taos and Santa Fe schools, and masters of American Impressionism and Modernism. Spanish-colonial furniture, Indian antiquities, and a fantastic sculpture garden are other draws of this well-respected establishment.

**Niman Fine Arts** (✉ 125 Lincoln Ave., ☎ 505/988–5091) focuses on the prolific work of contemporary Native American artist—Hopi painter Dan Namingha.

**photo-eye Gallery** (✉ 376 Garcia St., ☎ 800/227–6941) shows contemporary photography that includes the beautiful and sublime; there's also a stellar bookstore.

**Plan B Evolving Arts** (✉ 1050 Old Pecos Trail, ☎ 505/982–1338) showcases young artists, with an emphasis on cutting-edge and avant-garde works, and presents provocative performance pieces.

**Riva Yares Gallery** (✉ 123 Grant St., ☎ 505/984–0330) specializes in contemporary artists of Latin American descent. There are sculptures by California artist Manuel Neri, color field paintings by Esteban Vicente, and works by Santa Feans Elias Rivera, Rico Eastman, and others.

**Shidoni Foundry and Galleries** (✉ Bishop's Lodge Rd., Tesuque, 5 mi north of Santa Fe, ☎ 505/988–8001) casts work for accomplished and emerging artists from all over North America. On the grounds of an old chicken ranch, Shidoni has a rambling sculpture garden and a gallery. Self-guided tours are permitted Saturdays 9–5 and weekdays noon–1.

**Wyeth Hurd Gallery** (✉ 839 Paseo de Peralta, ☎ 505/989–8380) carries the work of the multigenerational arts family that includes N. C. Wyeth; his children Andrew, Carolyn, Ann, and Henriette Wyeth; Peter Hurd, Henriette's husband; Michael Hurd, son of Henriette and Peter; Jamie Wyeth, Andrew's son; and Peter de la Fuente, Henriette and Peter's grandson. Works include the landscape of the Delaware River valley that so inspired the Wyeth family and the New Mexico landscapes of Peter Hurd, who grew up in Roswell.

## Specialty Stores

### Books
More than 20 stores in Santa Fe sell used books, and a handful of high-quality shops carry the latest releases from mainstream and small presses.

**Allá** (✉ 102 W. San Francisco St., upstairs, ☎ 505/988–5416) is one of Santa Fe's most delightful small bookstores. It focuses on hard-to-find Spanish-language books and records, including limited-edition handmade books from Central America. It also carries Native American books and music, as well as English translations.

**Collected Works Book Store** (✉ 208B W. San Francisco St., ☎ 505/988–4226) carries art and travel books, including a generous selection of books on southwestern art, architecture, and general history, as well as the latest in contemporary literature.

**Garcia Street Books** (✉ 376 Garcia St., ☏ 505/986–0151) is an outstanding independent shop strong on art, architecture, cookbooks, literature, and regional southwestern works—it's just a block from the Canyon Road galleries.

**Nicholas Potter** (✉ 211 E. Palace Ave., ☏ 505/983–5434) specializes in used, rare, and out-of-print books. The quixotic shop also stocks used jazz and classical CDs.

**Photo-eye Books** (✉ 376 Garcia St., ☏ 505/988–5152) stocks new, rare, and out-of-print photography books.

## Clothing

Women have been known to arrive here in Liz Claiborne and leave in a broomstick skirt and Navajo velvet shirt. Men who swore they never would don silver *bolo* ties. Function dictates form in cowboy fashions. A wide-brimmed hat is essential in open country for protection from heat, rain, and insects. Cowboy hats made by Resistol, Stetson, Bailey, and other leading firms cost between $30 and $500, and hats made of fur and other exotic materials can fetch four figures.

The pointed toes of cowboy boots slide easily in and out of stirrups, and high heels help keep feet in the stirrups. Tall tops protect ankles and legs on rides through brush and cactus country and can protect the wearer from a nasty shin bruise from a skittish horse.

Some western fashion accessories were once purely functional. A colorful bandanna protected an Old West cowboy from sun- and windburn and served as a mask in windstorms, when riding drag behind a herd or, on occasions far rarer than Hollywood would have us believe, when robbing trains. A cowboy's sleeveless vest enhanced his ability to maneuver during roping and riding chores and provided pocket space that his skintight pants—snug to prevent wrinkles in the saddle area—didn't. Belt buckles are probably the most sought-after accessories—gold ones go for as much as $1,000.

**Back at the Ranch** (✉ 235 Don Gaspar, ☏ 505/989–8110 or 888/962–6687) is a musty old shop stocked with handmade cowboy boots, from red leather to turquoise snakeskin, along with funky furniture, 1950s-blanket coats, jewelry, and buckles. Some things get better with age, especially cowboy boots.

**Jane Smith** (✉ 550 Canyon Rd., ☏ 505/988–4775) sells extraordinary handmade western wear for women and men, from cowboy boots and sweaters to Plains Indians–style beaded tunics.

**Mirá** (✉ 101 W. Marcy St., ☏ 505/988–3585) clothing for women is slick, eclectic, and funky, combining the adventurous spirit of Mexico with global contemporary fashion. The shop has accessories and collectibles from Latin America, hemp apparel, and knockout vintage-inspired dresses.

**Montecristi Custom Hat Works** (✉ 322 McKenzie St., ☏ 505/983–9598) is where the smart set goes for custom-made straw hats so snug they're all but guaranteed to stay on, even in an open convertible.

**Origins** (✉ 135 W. San Francisco St., ☏ 505/988–2323) borrows from many cultures, carrying pricey women's wear like antique kimonos and custom-dyed silk jackets. One-of-a-kind accessories complete the spectacular look that Santa Fe inspires.

## Home Furnishings

**Artesanos** (✉ 222 Galisteo St.; 1414 Maclovia St.; ☏ 505/471–8020) is one of the best Mexican-import shops in the nation, with everything from leather chairs to papier-mâché *calaveras* (skeletons used in Day of the Dead celebrations), tinware, and Talavera tiles.

In the Guadalupe District, **Cookworks** (⊠ 322 S. Guadalupe St., ☎ 505/988–7676) is really three excellent culinary shops in one: the first has cookware, the second cookbooks, and the third gourmet gifts and fancy prepared foods.

The **Design Center** (⊠ 418 Cerrillos Rd.,) is a minimall of a dozen high-quality antiques shops (all with their own phone numbers).

**Doodlet's** (⊠ 120 Don Gaspar Ave., ☎ 505/983–3771) has an eclectic collection of stuff: pop-up books, bizarre postcards, tin art, hooked rugs, and stringed lights. Wonderment is in every display case, drawing the eye to the unusual.

**Foreign Traders** (⊠ 202 Galisteo St., ☎ 505/983–6441), a Santa Fe institution founded as the Old Mexico Shop in 1927 and still run by the same family, stocks handicrafts, antiques, and accessories from Mexico and other parts of the world.

**Galisteo Home Furnishings** (⊠ 132 E. Marcy St., ☎ 505/992–3300) sells the sort of cushy lodge-inspired furnishings you'll see in those classic Santa Fe–style homes throughout town—great wrought-iron chandeliers and lamps, dark-wood tables and armoires, and plush sofas with classic western fabrics.

**Jackalope** (⊠ 2820 Cerrillos Rd., ☎ 505/471–8539), a legendary if somewhat overpriced bazaar, sprawls over 7 acres, incorporating several pottery barns, a furniture store, endless aisles of knickknacks from Latin America and Asia, and a huge greenhouse. There's a lunch counter, barnyard animals, and a prairie-dog village.

**Montez Gallery** (⊠ Sena Plaza Courtyard, 125 E. Palace Ave., ☎ 505/982–1828) sells Hispanic works of religious art and decoration, including retablos, bultos, furniture, paintings, pottery, weavings, and jewelry.

**Pachamama** (⊠ 223 Canyon Rd., ☎ 505/983–4020) carries Latin American folk art, including small tin or silver *milagros,* the stamped metal images used as votive offerings. The shop also carries weavings and Spanish-colonial antiques.

## Jewelry
**Karen Melfi Collection** (⊠ 225 Canyon Rd., ☎ 505/982–3032) sells high-quality yet moderately priced handmade jewelry and other wearable art.

**Ornament of Santa Fe** (⊠ 209 W. San Francisco, ☎ 505/983–9399) is full of cosmopolitan jewelry and unique hair accessories. Precious and semiprecious stones set in gold and silver push the envelope of tradition without being trendy.

## Native American Arts and Crafts
**Cristof's** (⊠ 420 Old Santa Fe Trail, ☎ 505/988–9881) has a large selection of pottery, sculpture, and contemporary Navajo weavings and sand paintings.

**Joshua Baer & Co.** (⊠ 116½ E. Palace Ave., ☎ 505/988–8944) carries superb historic Navajo textiles and rare antique Pueblo weavings.

**Morning Star Gallery** (⊠ 513 Canyon Rd., ☎ 505/982–8187) is a veritable museum of Native American art and artifacts. An adobe shaded by a huge cottonwood tree houses antique basketry, pre-1940 Navajo silver jewelry, Northwest Coast Native American carvings, Navajo weavings, and art of the Plains Indians.

**Packard's on the Plaza** (✉ 61 Old Santa Fe Trail, ☎ 505/983–9241), the oldest Native American arts-and-crafts store on Santa Fe Plaza, sells Zapotec Indian rugs from Mexico and original rug designs by Richard Enzer, old pottery, saddles, katsina dolls, and an excellent selection of coral and turquoise jewelry. Prices are quite high, but so are the standards.

The **Rainbow Man** (✉ 107 E. Palace Ave., ☎ 505/982–8706), established in 1945, does business in the remains of a building that was damaged during the 1680 Pueblo Revolt. The shop carries early Navajo, Mexican, and Chimayó textiles, along with photographs by Edward S. Curtis, vintage pawn jewelry, and katsinas.

**Relics of the Old West** (✉ 402 Old Santa Fe Trail, ☎ 505/989–7663) stocks eclectic crafts and artifacts from cowboy-and-Indian days, as well as high-end Navajo textiles, old and new. Navajo weavers are on-site demonstrating their craft during the summer.

**Trade Roots Collection** (✉ 411 Paseo de Peralta, ☎ 505/982–8168) sells Native American ritual objects, such as fetish jewelry and Hopi rattles. The store is a good source of crafts materials.

## Markets

**Tesuque Pueblo Flea Market** (✉ U.S. 285/84, 7 mi north of Santa Fe, ☎ 505/995–8626) was once considered the best flea market in America by its loyal legion of bargain hunters. The Tesuque Pueblo took over the market in the late '90s and raised vendor fees, which increased the presence of predictable, often pricey goods brought in by professional flea-market dealers. It remains a big shopping to-do, however, and you can still find everything from a half-wolf puppy or African carvings to vintage cowboy boots, fossils, or a wall clock made out of an old hubcap. The 12-acre market is next to the Santa Fe Opera and is open Friday–Sunday, mid-March–December.

Browse through the local produce, meat, flowers, honey, and cheese—much of it organic—at the **Santa Fe Farmers Market** (✉ Guadalupe St. by the Railyard, ☎ 505/983–4098), which is held Tuesday and Saturday mornings from 7 'til noon, late April–November. It's a great people-watching event, and there's storytelling for kids.

# SIDE TRIPS FROM SANTA FE

You can hardly grasp the profundity of New Mexico's ancient past or its immense landscape without journeying into the hinterland. Each of the excursions below can be accomplished in a day or less, but in the cases of Abiquiu and Los Alamos it's worth considering an overnight. The High Road to Taos is a very full day, so start early or plan on spending the night near or in Taos.

## Pueblos near Santa Fe

This trip will take you to several of the state's 19 pueblos, including San Ildefonso, one of the state's most picturesque, and Santa Clara, whose lands harbor a dramatic set of ancient cliff dwellings. Between the two reservations sits the ominous landmark called Black Mesa, which you can see from NM 30 or NM 502. The solitary butte has inspired many painters, including Georgia O'Keeffe. Plan on spending one to three hours at each pueblo, and leave the day open if you are there for a feast day, when dances are set to an organic rather than mechanical clock. Pueblo grounds and hiking areas do not permit pets.

## Santa Fe Side Trips

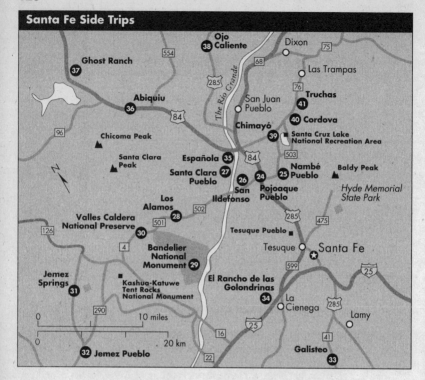

### Pojoaque Pueblo

**24** *17 mi north of Santa Fe on U.S. 285/84.*

There is not much to see in the pueblo's plaza area, which hardly has a visible core, but the state visitor center and adjoining **Poeh Cultural Center and Museum** on U.S. 285/84 are worth a visit. The latter is an impressive complex of traditional adobe buildings, including the three-story Sun Tower, which contains a museum, a cultural center, and artists' studios. There are frequent demonstrations by artists, exhibitions, and, on Saturday from May through September, traditional ceremonial dances. By the early 20th century the pueblo was virtually uninhabited, but the survivors eventually began to restore it. Pojoaque's feast day is celebrated with dancing on December 12. The visitor center is one of the friendliest and best stocked in northern New Mexico, with free maps and literature on hiking, fishing, and the area's history. The crafts shop in the visitor center is one of the most extensive among the state's pueblos; it carries weaving, pottery, jewelry, and other crafts by both Pojoaque and other indigenous New Mexicans. The pueblo also operates the adjacent **Cities of Gold Resort,** which comprises a casino, 124-room hotel, sports bar and simulcast, Towa Golf Resort, and several shops and restaurants. ⊠ *U.S 285/84, 17 mi north of Santa Fe,* ☎ *505/455–3460,* WEB *www.citiesofgold.com.* ✉ *Free.* ⊙ *Apr.–Dec., Mon.–Sat. 9–6, Sun. 10–4; Jan.–Mar., Mon.–Sat. 9–5:30, Sun. 10–4. Sketching, cameras, and video cameras prohibited, except during Sat. Native American dances.*

### Nambé Pueblo

**25** *4 mi east of Pojoaque on NM 503, 20 mi north of Santa Fe.*

Nambé Pueblo has no visitor center, so the best time to visit is during a ceremonial feast-day celebration on October 4, the feast day of St. Francis, or during the very popular 4th of July celebration. If you want to explore the landscape surrounding the pueblo, take the drive past the pueblo until you come to **Nambé Falls Recreational Area** (☎ 505/455–2304). There's a shady picnic area and a large fishing lake that's open March–November. The waterfalls are about a 15-minute hike in from the parking and picnic area along a rocky, clearly marked path. The water pours over a rock precipice—a loud and dramatic sight given the modest size of the river. ⊠ *Nambé Pueblo Rd. off NM 503,* ☎ *505/455–2036.* 🎟 *$2.*

### San Ildefonso Pueblo

**26** *23 mi north of Santa Fe via U.S. 285/84 to NM 502 west.*

Maria Martinez, one of the most renowned Pueblo potters, lived here. She first created her exquisite "black on black" pottery in 1919 and in doing so sparked a major revival of all Pueblo arts and crafts. She died in 1980, and the 26,000-acre San Ildefonso Pueblo remains a major center for pottery and other arts and crafts. Many artists sell from their homes, and there are trading posts, a visitor center, and a museum where some of Martinez's work can be seen on weekdays. San Ildefonso is also one of the more visually appealing pueblos, with a well-defined plaza core and a spectacular setting beneath the Pajarito Plateau and Black Mesa. The pueblo's feast day is January 23, when unforgettable buffalo, deer, and Comanche dances are performed from dawn to dusk. Cameras are not permitted at any of the ceremonial dances but may be used at other times with a permit. ⊠ *NM 502,* ☎ *505/455–3549.* 🎟 *$3 per vehicle, still-camera permit $10, video recorder permit $20, sketching permit $15.* ⊙ *Daily 8–4.*

### Santa Clara Pueblo

**27** *27 mi northwest of Santa Fe, 10 mi north of San Ildefonso Pueblo via NM 30.*

Santa Clara Pueblo, southwest of Española, is the home of a historic treasure—the awesome **Puyé Cliff Dwellings** (open June–August, daily 8–7), believed to have been built in the 13th to 14th centuries. They can be seen by driving 9 mi up a gravel road through a canyon, south of the village off NM 502. The pueblo also contains four ponds, miles of stream fishing, and picnicking and camping facilities. You can tour the cliff dwellings, topped by the ruins of a 740-room pueblo, on your own or with a guide. Permits for the use of trails, camping, and picnic areas, as well as for fishing in trout ponds, are available at the sites; recreation areas are open April–October, dawn–dusk.

Shops in the village sell burnished red pottery, engraved blackware, paintings, and other arts and crafts. All pottery is made via the coil method, not with a pottery wheel. Santa Clara is known for its carved pieces, and Avanyu, a water serpent that guards the waters, is the pueblo's symbol. Other typical works include engagement baskets, wedding vessels, and seed pots. The pueblo's feast day of St. Claire is celebrated on August 12. ⊠ *Off NM 502 on NM 30, Española,* ☎ *505/753–7326.* 🎟 *Pueblo free, cliff dwellings $5, video and still-camera permits $15.* ⊙ *Daily 8–4:30.*

## Jemez Country

In the Jemez region, the 1,000-year-old Anasazi ruins at Bandelier National Monument present a vivid contrast to Los Alamos National Laboratory, birthplace of the atomic bomb. You can easily take in part of Jemez Country in a day trip from Santa Fe.

On this tour you can see terrific views of the Rio Grande valley, the Sangre de Cristos, the Galisteo Basin, and, in the distance, the Sandias.

There are places to eat and shop for essentials in Los Alamos and a few roadside eateries along NM 4 in La Cueva and Jemez Springs. There are also numerous turnouts along NM 4, several which have paths leading down to the many excellent fishing spots along the Jemez River.

The 48,000-acre Cerro Grande fire of May 2000 burned much of the pine forest in the lower Jemez Mountains, as well as more than 250 homes in Los Alamos. Parts of the drive are still scarred with charcoaled remains, but a considerable amount of vegetation has returned.

## Los Alamos

**28** *35 mi from Santa Fe via U.S. 285/84 north to NM 502 west.*

Look at old books on New Mexico and you'll rarely find a mention of Los Alamos, now a busy town of 18,500 that has the highest per capita income in the state. Like so many other communities in the Southwest, Los Alamos was created expressly as a company town; only here the workers weren't mining iron, manning freight trains, or hauling lumber—here, for at least the first two decades, most residents were busy toiling at America's foremost nuclear research facility, Los Alamos National Laboratory (LANL). The facility still employs some 10,000 area workers.

Just a few miles from ancient cave dwellings, scientists led by a morally conflicted J. Robert Oppenheimer built Fat Man and Little Boy, the atom bombs that in August 1945 decimated Hiroshima and Nagasaki, respectively. LANL was created in 1943 under the auspices of the intensely covert Manhattan Project, whose express purpose it was to expedite an Allied victory during World War II. Indeed, Japan surrendered—but a full-blown Cold War between Russian and the United States ensued for another 4½ decades.

LANL works hard today to promote its broader platforms, including "enhancing global nuclear security" but also finding new ways to detect radiation, fighting pollution and environmental risks associated with nuclear energy, and furthering studies of the solar system, biology, and computer sciences. Similarly, the town of Los Alamos now strives to be more well rounded, better understood, and tourist-friendly.

The **Bradbury Science Museum** is Los Alamos National Laboratory's public showcase, and its exhibits offer a surprisingly balanced and provocative examination of such thorny topics as atomic weapons and nuclear power. You can experiment with lasers; witness research in solar, geothermal, fission, and fusion energy; learn about DNA fingerprinting; and view exhibits about World War II's Project Y (the Manhattan Project, whose participants developed the atomic bomb). ⊠ *Los Alamos National Laboratory, 15th St. and Central Ave.,* ☎ *505/667-4444,* WEB *www.lanl.gov/external/museum.* ⊡ *Free.* ☉ *Tues.–Fri. 9–5, Sat.–Mon. 1–5.*

The New Mexican architect John Gaw Meem designed the **Fuller Lodge,** a short drive up Central Avenue from the Bradbury Science Museum. The massive log building was erected in 1928 as a dining and recreation hall for a small private boys' school. In 1942 the federal government purchased the school and made it the base of operations for the Manhattan Project. Part of the lodge is an art center that shows the works of northern New Mexican artists; there's a picturesque rose garden on the grounds. ⊠ *2132 Central Ave.,* ☎ *505/662–9331,* WEB *www.losalamos.org/flac.html.* ⊡ *Free.* ☉ *Mon.–Sat. 10–4.*

The **Los Alamos Historical Museum,** in a log building adjoining Fuller Lodge, displays exhibits on the once-volatile geological history of the volcanic Jemez Mountains, the 700-year history of human life in this area, and more on—you guessed it—the Manhattan Project. It's rather jarring to observe ancient Anasazi potsherds and arrowheads in one display and photos of an obliterated Nagasaki in the next. ✉ *1921 Juniper St.,* ☎ *505/662–4493,* WEB *www.losalamos.com/historicalsociety/ museum.asp.* ☷ *Free.* ☉ *Oct.–Apr., Mon.–Sat. 10–4, Sun. 1–4; May– Sept., Mon.–Sat. 9:30–4:30, Sun. 11–5.*

## DINING AND LODGING

**$–$$** ✕ **Hill Diner.** With a friendly staff and clientele, this large diner serves some of the finest burgers in town, along with chicken-fried steaks, homemade soups, and heaps of fresh vegetables. ✉ *1315 Trinity Dr.,* ☎ *505/ 662–9745. AE, D, DC, MC, V.*

**$** ✕🏨 **Los Alamos Inn.** Rooms in this one-story hotel have modern southwestern decor and sweeping canyon views. Tommy's, the inn's restaurant and bar, serves American and southwestern regional specialties; the Sunday brunch is popular. ✉ *2201 Trinity Dr., 87544,* ☎ *505/662– 7211 or 800/279–9279,* FAX *505/661–7714,* WEB *www.losalamosinn.com. 115 rooms. Restaurant, pool, some refrigerators, some kitchenettes, business services, bar, meeting room. AE, D, DC, MC, V.*

**$** 🏨 **Best Western Hilltop House Hotel.** Minutes from the Los Alamos National Laboratory, this hotel hosts both vacationers and scientists. All the rooms are furnished in modern southwestern style; deluxe ones have kitchenettes. ✉ *400 Trinity Dr. (Box 250, 87544),* ☎ *505/662–2441 or 800/462–0936,* FAX *505/662–5913,* WEB *www.bestwesternlosalamos. com. 87 rooms, 13 suites. Restaurant, room service, refrigerators, indoor pool, gym, hot tub, lounge, laundry facilities, meeting rooms. AE, D, DC, MC, V. CP.*

**$** 🏨 **Renata's Orange Street Bed & Breakfast.** Linda Hartman is the proprietor of this B&B. In an unremarkable 1948 wood-frame house in a quiet residential neighborhood, rooms are furnished in southwestern and country style. The public area has cable TV and a VCR, and you can use the kitchen and the laundry; rooms also have high-speed DSL access. ✉ *3496 Orange St., 87544,* ☎ FAX *505/662–2651 or 800/ 662–3180,* WEB *www.losalamos.com/orangestreetinn. 6 rooms, 2 with bath; 3 suites. In-room data ports, some refrigerators, laundry facilities, business services. AE, D, DC, MC, V. BP.*

## Bandelier National Monument

**㉙** *40 mi from Santa Fe, north on U.S. 285/84, west on NM 502, south on NM 501 (W. Jemez Rd.) to "T" intersection with NM 4; turn left (east) and drive 6 mi to monument's entrance.*

Seven centuries before the Declaration of Independence was signed, compact city-states existed in the Southwest. Remnants of one of the most impressive of them can be seen at **Frijoles Canyon** in Bandelier National Monument. At the canyon's base, beside a gurgling stream, are the remains of cave dwellings, ancient ceremonial kivas, and other stone structures that stretch out for more than a mile beneath the sheer walls of the canyon's tree-fringed rim. For hundreds of years the Anasazi people, relatives of today's Rio Grande Pueblo Indians, thrived on wild game, corn, and beans. Suddenly, for reasons still undetermined, the settlements were abandoned.

Wander through the site on a paved, self-guided trail. If you can climb steep wooden ladders and squeeze through narrow doorways, you can explore some of the cave dwellings and cell-like rooms.

Bandelier National Monument, named after author and ethnologist Adolph Bandelier (his novel *The Delight Makers* is set in Frijoles Canyon), contains 23,000 acres of backcountry wilderness, waterfalls, and wildlife. Sixty miles of trails traverse the park. A small museum in the visitor center focuses on the area's prehistoric and contemporary Native American cultures, with displays of artifacts from 1200 to modern times. ☎ *505/672–0343*, WEB *www.nps.gov/band.* ☜ *$10 per vehicle, good for 7 days.* ☉ *Summer, daily 8–6; spring and fall, daily 8–5:30; winter, daily 8–4:30.*

## Valles Caldera National Preserve

**⑳** *15 mi southwest of Los Alamos via NM 4.*

A high-forest drive brings you to the awe-inspiring Valle Grande, which at 14 mi in diameter is one of the world's largest calderas and which became Valles Caldera National Preserve in summer 2000. You can't imagine the volcanic crater's immensity until you spot what look like specks of dust on the lush meadow floor and realize they're cows. Presently the Santa Fe National Forest is administering this 89,000-acre preserve; plans are for a board of trustees to assume control by 2004. Their focus will be developing a comprehensive usage and management policy that will make this stunning tract available to visitors for hiking, cross-country skiing, limited camping, and photographing wildlife. Until then, you can still take in a tremendous view across the caldera from a few roadside parking areas along NM 4. ✉ *NM 4 (contact: Jemez Ranger District),* ☎ *505/829–3535,* WEB *www.fs.fed.us/r3/sfe/valles/index.html.*

## Jemez Springs

**㉛** *20 mi west of Valle Caldera on NM 4.*

The funky mountain village of Jemez Springs draws outdoorsy types for hiking, cross-country skiing, and camping in the nearby U.S. Forest Service areas. The town's biggest tourist draws are Jemez State Monument and Soda Dam, but many people come here for relaxation at the town's bathhouse.

The geological wonder known as **Soda Dam** was created over thousands of years by travertine deposits—minerals that precipitate out of geothermal springs. With its strange mushroom-shape exterior and caves split by a roaring waterfall, it's no wonder the spot was considered sacred by Native Americans. In summer, it's popular for swimming. ✉ *NM 4, 1 mi north of Jemez State Monument.*

**Jemez State Monument** contains impressive Spanish and Native American ruins. About 600 years ago ancestors of the people of Jemez Pueblo built several villages in and around the narrow mountain valley. One of the villages was Guisewa, or "Place of the Boiling Waters." The Spanish colonists built a mission church beside it, San José de los Jemez, which was abandoned in 1630. ✉ *NM 4, Jemez Springs,* ☎ *505/829–3530,* WEB *www.nmculture.org.* ☜ *$3.* ☉ *Daily 8:30–5.*

The original structure at the **Jemez Spring Bath House** was erected in the 1870s near a mineral hot spring. Many other buildings were added over the years, and the complex was completely renovated into an intimate Victorian-style hideaway in the mid-1990s. It's a funky, low-key spot that's far less formal and fancy than the several spa resorts near Santa Fe. You can soak in a mineral bath for $9 (30 minutes) or $14 (60 minutes). Massages cost between $30 (30 minutes) and $75 (90 minutes). An acupuncturist is available with advance notice. Beauty treatments include facials, manicures, and pedicures. The Jemez Package ($79) includes a half-hour bath, an herbal blanket wrap, and a one-hour massage. It's best to make reservations for services. You can stroll down a short path behind the house to see where the steaming-hot springs feed into the Jemez River. ✉ *NM 4,* ☎ *505/829–3303,* WEB *www.jemez.com/baths.* ☉ *Memorial Day–Labor Day, daily 9–9; Labor Day–Memorial Day, daily 10–7:30.*

**Arts of the Jemez** (☎ contact the Walatowa Visitor Center, 505/834–7235, WEB www.jemezsprings.org/arts.htm) sponsors open houses and tours of the nearly 20 arts-and-crafts studios set throughout the Jemez Valley. These events are held for three weekends in the fall, and then again for the two weekends that bracket Thanksgiving. From late September through early January, previews of area artists' works are exhibited at the Walatowa Visitor Center at the Jemez Pueblo. Elsewhere during the year, many of the Jemez Valley studios are open by chance.

DINING AND LODGING

$ ✕🔲 **Laughing Lizard Inn and Cafe.** Consisting of a simple four-room motel-style inn and a cute adobe-and-stone café with a corrugated-metal roof, the Laughing Lizard makes for a sweet and cheerful diversion—it's right in the center of the village. Rooms are cozy and simple with white linens, dressers, books, and porches that look out over the rugged mesa beyond the river valley. Healthful, eclectic fare—apple-walnut sandwiches, raspberry-chipotle-chicken burritos, herbal teas, homemade desserts—is served in the homey café (limited hours off-season; call first), which has a saltillo-tile screened porch and an open-air wooden deck. ✉ *NM 4, 87025,* ☎ *505/829–3108,* WEB *www.thelaughinglizard.com. 4 rooms. Café. D, MC, V.*

$$ 🔲 **Riverdancer Inn.** On 6 acres along the Jemez River beneath towering mesas, this light-filled, contemporary adobe inn has rooms with cove ceilings, tile floors, and Native American arts and crafts. All open onto a courtyard with a natural spring. Wellness packages include massage, acupuncture, and aromatherapy. ✉ *16445 NM 4, 87025,* ☎ *505/ 829–3262 or 800/809–3262,* WEB *www.riverdancer.com. 6 rooms, 1 suite. Some kitchens, massage, hiking. BP. D, MC, V.*

## Jemez Pueblo

㉜ *12 mi south of Jemez Springs via NM 4; 85 mi west of Santa Fe via U.S. 285/84 and NM 4; 75 mi west of Santa Fe via I-25, U.S. 550, and NM 4.*

As you continue southwest along NM 4 the terrain changes from a wooded river valley with high mesas on either side to an open red-rock valley, the home of the Jemez Pueblo, which is set along the Jemez River. After Pecos Pueblo (☞ Chapter 6) was abandoned in the 1838, Jemez was the state's only pueblo with residents who spoke Towa (different from Tiwa and Tewa). The Jemez Reservation encompasses 88,000 acres, with two lakes, Holy Ghost Springs and Dragonfly Lake (off NM 4), open for fishing by permit only, April to October on weekends and holidays. The only part of the pueblo open to the public is the **Walatowa Visitor Center,** a fancy new incarnation of which opened in 2000; it contains a small museum, an extensive crafts shop, a short nature walk, and rotating art and photography exhibits. The pueblo is sometimes open to the public for special events, demonstrations, and ceremonial dances—call for details. On weekends April–mid-October (10–6) when weather permits, arts and crafts and traditional foods are sold across the street at the **Jemez Red Rocks Open-air Market.** The pueblo is noted for its polychrome pottery. The Walatowa gas and convenience store, on NM 4 next to the visitor center, is one of the few such establishments between Los Alamos and Bernalillo. Interesting group educational tours and demonstrations can be arranged in advance; call for information. ✉ *7413 NM 4,* ☎ *505/834–7235,* WEB *www.jemezpueblo. org.* ▣ *Free.* ☉ *Daily 10–4. Photographing, sketching, and video recording prohibited.*

## Galisteo

**❸❸** *25 mi south of Santa Fe via I–25 and to U.S. 285 to NM 41 south.*

South of Santa Fe lie the immense open spaces of the sublime Galisteo Basin and the quintessential New Mexican village of Galisteo—a harmonious blend of multigenerational New Mexicans and recent migrants who protect and treasure the bucolic solitude of their home. The drive from Santa Fe takes about 30 minutes and offers a panoramic view of the surreal, sculpted landscape of the Galisteo Basin, which is an austere contrast to the alpine country of the Sangre de Cristos. It's a good place to go for a leisurely lunch or a sunset drive to dinner, maybe with horseback riding or a day of lounging and having body treatments at the local spa, Vista Clara Ranch.

Founded as a Spanish outpost in 1614 and built largely with rocks from nearby Pueblo ruins, Galisteo is a village with many artists and equestrians (trail rides and rentals are available at local stables). Cottonwood trees shade the low-lying pueblo-style architecture, a premier example of vernacular use of adobe and stone. The small church is open only for Sunday services. The excellent gallery **Linda Durham Contemporary Art** (☎ 505/466–6600) exhibits sculpture and paintings from mainly New Mexican artists. Aside from the inn, spa-resort, and the gallery, a *tiendita*, a small store that sells bare essentials, constitutes the commercial center of Galisteo.

DINING AND LODGING

**$$$$** ✕⊡ **Vista Clara Ranch Resort and Spa.** On the edge of Galisteo, this
★ hideaway on 80 acres combines modern spa amenities and treatments with ancient healing arts. The southwestern-style accommodations are charming and serene. The spa and beauty treatments include herbal and aroma wraps, salt glows, massage, facials, pedicures, and even all-natural hair coloring. Daily guided hikes head to petroglyph-inscribed rock formations. You can ride horseback and visit an authentic Native American sweat lodge. Vista Clara is upscale but unpretentious. Round-trip transportation from Santa Fe–area hotels can be arranged for day-trippers, and there are also multiday packages. A three-course prix-fixe dinner is served Monday–Saturday by 24-hour advance reservation—even if you're not staying or taking treatments here, the dining experience is worth the trip. Vista Clara donates all of its profits to charities ⊠ *NM 41 (HC 75, Box 111, Galisteo 87540)*, ☎ *505/466–4772 or 888/663–9772*, 𝖥𝖠𝖷 *505/466–1942*, 𝖶𝖤𝖡 *www.vistaclara.com. 10 rooms. Restaurant, pool, health club, spa, laundry service; no smoking. MC, V.*

**$$–$$$** ✕⊡ **The Galisteo Inn.** In the center of Galisteo, this rambling old
★ adobe hacienda has been deftly transformed into an idyllic inn. Thick adobe walls, wide-plank pine floors worn with age and rich in patina, and vistas and patios from which to enjoy them add to the privacy and romance of this refuge. The restaurant ($$$) is acclaimed for its innovative American cuisine (reservations essential). The menu changes often and might feature roasted veal chop stuffed with prosciutto, sage, and fresh mozzarella with a port-wine glaze. ⊠ *9 La Vega (HC 75, Box 4, Galisteo 87540)*, ☎ *505/466–8200*, 𝖥𝖠𝖷 *505/466–4008*, 𝖶𝖤𝖡 *www.galisteoinn.com. 12 rooms. Restaurant, pool, hot tub, sauna; no kids under 10, no smoking. D, MC, V. BP.*

## El Rancho de las Golondrinas

**❸❹** *15 mi south of Santa Fe off I–25's Exit 276 in La Cienega.*

The "Williamsburg of the Southwest," El Rancho de las Golondrinas ("the ranch of the swallows") is a reconstruction of a small agricultural village. Originally a *paraje*, or stopping place, on El Camino Real, the village has buildings from the 17th to 19th century. Travelers would stop at the ranch before making the final leg of the journey north on El Camino Real, a half-day ride from Santa Fe in horse-and-wagon time. By car, the ranch is only a 25-minute drive from the Plaza. From Interstate 25, the village is tucked away from view, frozen in time. Owned and operated by the Paloheimo family, direct descendants of those who owned the ranch when it functioned as a paraje, the restored grounds of this living museum maintain an authentic character without compromising history for commercial gain. Even the gift shop carries items that reflect life on the ranch and the cultural exchange that took place there.

Guided tours (April–October) survey Spanish-colonial lifestyles in New Mexico from 1660 to 1890: you can view a molasses mill, threshing grounds, and wheelwright and blacksmith shops, as well as a mountain village and a *morada* (meeting place) of the order of Penitentes (a religious fraternity known for its reenactment during Holy Week of the tortures suffered by Christ). Farm animals roam through the barnyards on the 200-acre complex. Wool from the sheep is spun into yarn and woven into traditional Rio Grande–style blankets, and the corn grown is dried and used to feed the animals. During the spring and harvest festivals, on the first weekends of June and October, respectively, the village comes alive with Spanish-American folk music, dancing, and food and crafts demonstrations. ⊠ *334 Los Pinos Rd.,* ☎ *505/471–2261,* WEB *www.golondrinas.org.* ⌨ *$5.* ⊙ *Wed.–Sun. 10–4.*

## Georgia O'Keeffe Country

It's just a 20-minute drive north of Santa Fe to reach the Española Valley, which leads to the striking mesas, cliffs, and valleys that so inspired the artist Georgia O'Keeffe—she lived in this area for the final 50 years of her life. You'll first come to the small, workaday city of Española, a major crossroads from which roads lead to Taos, Chama, and Abiquiu. The other notable community in this area is tiny Ojo Caliente, famous for its hot-springs spa retreat.

### Española
**㉟** *20 mi north of Santa Fe via U.S. 285/84.*

This small but growing city midway along the Low Road from Santa Fe to Taos is a little rough around the edges—it was founded in the 1880s as a stop on the Denver and Rio Grande Railroad, and it lacks the colonial charm of either Santa Fe or Taos. Española is rather busy today and has many cheap restaurants, a few chain motels, but few reasons to stick around for more than a quick meal. One of the city's modern trademarks are lowriders, which you'll see cruising the streets. They're mostly classic cars that have been retrofitted with lowered chassis and hydraulics that often allow the cars to bump and grind; the cars are often painted with spectacular murals, from religious art to scenes of the region's landscape.

All of the main arteries converge in the heart of town in a confusing, unpleasant maze of drab shopping centers, so watch the signs on the south side of town. Traffic moves slowly, especially on weekend nights when cruisers bring car culture alive.

**DINING AND LODGING**

**$–$$**  ✕ **El Paragua Restaurant.** With a dark, intimate atmosphere of wood
**★** and stone, this historic place started out as a lemonade–cum–taco stand in the late 1950s but is now known for some of the state's most authentic New Mexican and regional Mexican cuisine. Steaks and

fish are grilled over a mesquite-wood fire; other specialties include chorizo enchiladas, panfried breaded trout Amadine, and menudo. ✉ *603 Santa Cruz Rd. (NM 76 just east of NM 68),* ☎ *505/753–3211 or 800/ 929–8226. AE, DC, MC, V.*

**$$$–$$$$** ✕⌨ **Rancho de San Juan.** Well north of Española's bustle and a great
★ choice if you're visiting Abiquiu or Ojo Caliente, this secluded 225-acre Relaix & Châteaux compound hugs the base of Black Mesa. Many of the rooms at the understated and very romantic inn are self-contained suites, some set around a central courtyard and others farther out amid the wilderness. All rooms have museum-quality southwestern furnishings, CD stereos, and local artwork; some rooms have fireplaces, Jacuzzi tubs, and full kitchens. A four-course prix-fixe dinner of some of New Mexico's finest contemporary cooking is available (by reservation only) in the intimate restaurant ($$$$), Wednesday through Sunday. Guests can hike up to a serene hand-carved sandstone shrine on a bluff high above the property. Spa and massage services are also available. ✉ *U.S. 285, 3½ mi north of U.S. 84 (Box 4140, Española, 87533),* ☎ *505/753– 6818 or 800/726–7121,* WEB *www.ranchodesanjuan.com. 9 rooms, 8 suites. Restaurant, some kitchens, hiking. AE, D, DC, MC, V.*

## Abiquiu

**36** *24 mi northwest of Española via U.S. 84.*

This tiny, very traditional Hispanic village was home to *genízaros,* people of mixed tribal backgrounds with Spanish surnames. The surnames came from Spanish families who used Indians as servants. Many descendants of original families still live in the area, although since the late 1980s Abiquiu and its surrounding countryside have become a nesting ground for those fleeing big-city lifestyles, among them actresses Marsha Mason and Shirley MacLaine. A feeling of insider versus outsider and old-timer versus newcomer still prevails. Newcomers or visitors may find themselves resented; it's best to observe one very important local custom: no photography is allowed in and around the village.

You can visit **Georgia O'Keeffe's home** through advance reservation (four months recommended) with the **Georgia O'Keeffe Foundation** (☎ 505/685–4359, WEB www.abiquiuinn.com/tour.html), which conducts one-hour tours Tuesday, Thursday, and Friday, April–November, for $22. In 1945 Georgia O'Keeffe bought a large, dilapidated late-18th-century Spanish-colonial adobe compound just off the Plaza. Upon the 1946 death of her husband, photographer Alfred Stieglitz, she left New York City and began dividing her time permanently between this home, which figured prominently in many of her works, and the one in nearby Ghost Ranch. She wrote about the house, "When I first saw the Abiquiú house it was a ruin . . . As I climbed and walked about in the ruin I found a patio with a very pretty well house and a bucket to draw up water. It was a good-sized patio with a long wall with a door on one side. That wall with a door in it was something I had to have. It took me 10 years to get it—three more years to fix the house up so I could live in it—and after that the wall with the door was painted many times." The patio is featured in *Black Patio Door* (1955) and *Patio with Cloud* (1956). O'Keeffe died in 1986 at the age of 98 and left provisions in her will to ensure that the property's houses would never be public monuments.

**Bode's** (✉ U.S. 84, ☎ 505/685–4422) across from the Abiquiu post office, is much more than a gas station. It's a popular stop for newspapers, quirky gifts, cold drinks, supplies, and excellent green chile stew and sandwiches. The station serves as general store and exchange post for news and gossip.

The **Dar al Islam** (✉ Hwy. 155 at sign 42A, ☎ 505/685–4515) adobe mosque was built by Egyptian architect Hassan Fathy, and visitors are welcome. The annual North American Muslim Powwow is held here each June. To reach the mosque from Bode's, drive ¼ mi north, turn right onto unpaved County Road 155, and proceed 3 mi, making a left at the main entrance sign.

DINING AND LODGING

$–$$ ✕▦ **Abiquiu Inn and Cafe Abiquiu.** Deep in the Chama Valley, the inn has a secluded, exotic feel—almost like an oasis—with lavishly decorated rooms, including several four-person casitas, with woodstoves or fireplaces and tiled baths. Middle Eastern and Mediterranean cuisine is on the menu at the café ($–$$). The inn is owned and operated by the Dar al-Islam mosque and is the departure point for tours of the O'Keeffe home. It has an exceptional art gallery, crafts shop, and gardens. ✉ U.S. 84 (Box 120, Abiquiu, 87510), ☎ 505/685–4378 or 800/447–5621, ℻ 800/447–5621 ext. *2, ⓦ www.abiquiuinn.com. 19 rooms, 5 casitas. Restaurant, shops. AE, D, DC, MC, V.

## Ghost Ranch
③⑦ 10 mi northwest of Abiquiu on U.S. 84.

For art historians, the name Ghost Ranch brings to mind Georgia O'Keeffe, who lived on but a small parcel of this 20,000-acre dude and cattle ranch. The ranch's owner in the 1930s—conservationist and publisher of Nature Magazine Arthur Pack—first invited O'Keeffe here to visit in 1934; Pack soon sold the artist the 7-acre plot on which she lived summer through fall for most of the rest of her life.

In 1955, Pack donated the rest of the ranch to the Presbyterian Church, which continues to use Pack's original structures and about 55 acres of land as a conference center.

The **Ghost Ranch Conference Center** (✉ U.S. 84, ☎ 505/685–4333 or 800/821–5145, ⓦ http://plazaresolana.org), open year-round, is busiest in summer, when dozens of workshops take place. Subjects range from poetry and literary arts to photography, horseback riding, and every conceivable traditional craft of northern New Mexico. Guests camp or stay in semi-rustic cottages or casitas. After registering at the main office, you may come in and hike high among the wind-hewn rocks so beloved by O'Keeffe (but her original house is closed to the public).

The **Florence Hawley Ellis Museum of Anthropology** contains Indian tools, pottery, and other artifacts excavated from the Ghost Ranch Gallina digs. Pioneer anthropologist Florence Hawley Ellis conducted excavations at Chaco Canyon and at other sites in New Mexico. Adjacent to the Ellis Museum, the **Ruth Hall Museum of Paleontology** exhibits the New Mexico state fossil, the coelophysis, also known as "the littlest dinosaur," originally excavated near Ghost Ranch. ✉ Ghost Ranch, ☎ 505/685–4333. ⊟ Donation $2. ☉ Tues.–Sat. 9–noon and 1–5, Sun. 1–5.

OFF THE BEATEN PATH
**MONASTERY OF CHRIST IN THE DESERT** – Designed by a Japanese monk, this remote rock-and-adobe church can be visited for Sunday mass at 9:15, on holidays, and for silent overnight retreats (if requested in advance by mail or e-mail); there are basic accommodations for up to 16 guests. ✉ Guestmaster, Christ in the Desert (Box 270, Abiquiu 87510); pass Ghost Ranch Visitor's Center and turn left on Forest Service Rd. 151; follow dirt road 13 mi to monastery (road is impassable during rainy weather), ☎ no phone, ⓦ www.christdesert.org.

*En Route*   The best and most interesting way to reach Ojo Caliente from Ghost Ranch is to return down U.S. 84 just past Abiquiu and then make a left turn (north) onto NM 554 toward El Rito, 12 mi away. This small, rural community known for its crafts making (especially weaving) has a funky general store and the **El Farolito** (⊠ Main St., ☎ 505/581–9509), a minuscule dinner restaurant on the town's tree-shaded Main Street that serves State Fair blue-ribbon chili and other New Mexican specialties at its eight tables. The ride here offers a stunning view back east toward the Sangre de Cristos.

## Ojo Caliente

③⑧ *28 mi northeast of Abiquiu by way of El Rito via NM 554 to NM 111 to U.S. 285; 50 mi north of Santa Fe on U.S. 285.*

Ojo Caliente is the only place in North America where five different types of hot springs—iron, lithia, arsenic, salt, and soda—are found side by side. The town was named by Spanish explorer Cabeza de Vaca, who visited in 1535 and believed he had stumbled upon the Fountain of Youth. He recorded his excitement in his journal:

"The greatest treasure I have found these strange people to possess are some hot springs which burst out of the foot of a mountain that gives evidence of being an active volcano. So powerful are the chemicals contained in this water that the inhabitants have a belief that the waters were given to them by their gods after weeping many tears. From the effect of the waters upon my remaining men, I am inclined to believe that the waters will do many things that our doctors are not capable of doing . . . I believe I have found the Fountain of Youth."

Modern-day visitors draw similar conclusions about the restorative powers of the springs. The spa itself, built in the 1920s (no one knows the exact date), is a no-frills establishment that has seen better days; it comprises a hotel and cottages, a restaurant, a gift shop, massage rooms, men's and women's bathhouses, a chlorine-free swimming pool, and indoor and outdoor mineral-water tubs. The hotel, one of the original bathhouses, and the springs are all on the National Register of Historic Places, as is the adjacent Round Barn, from which visitors can take horseback tours and guided hikes to ancient Pueblo dwellings and petroglyph-etched rocks. Spa services include wraps, massage, facials, and acupuncture. The setting at the foot of sandstone cliffs topped by the ruins of ancient Indian pueblos is nothing short of inspiring.

LODGING

$$–$$$   🏨 **Ojo Caliente Mineral Springs Spa and Resort.** Accommodations at this spa are decidedly spartan, with down comforters on the beds and rudimentary bathrooms without showers or tubs—you've come for the mineral springs, after all, and that's where the bathing takes place. Lodgers have complimentary access to the mineral pools and milagro (miracle) wraps, and the bathhouse is equipped with showers. Some cottages have kitchenettes. Horseback tours of the area must be prearranged, so notify the office in advance. Poppy's Cafe serves New Mexican specialties. ⊠ *50 Los Baños Dr. (Box 68, 87549), off U.S. 285, 30 mi north of Española,* ☎ *505/583–2233 or 800/222–9162,* FAX *505/583–2464,* WEB *www.ojocalientespa.com. 19 rooms, 19 cottages, 2 3-bedroom houses. Restaurant, some kitchenettes, some refrigerators, massage, spa, meeting rooms; no room phones, no TV in some rooms. AE, D, DC, MC, V.*

# The High Road to Taos

The main highway to Taos along the Rio Grande gorge (NM 68) provides dramatic close-ups of the river and rocky mountain faces (☞ Low

Road to Santa Fe *in* Side Trips *in* Chapter 5), but if you have an extra hour or two, the High Road to Taos is worth choosing for its views of sweeping woodlands and traditional Hispanic villages. The High Road follows U.S. 285 north to NM 503 (a right turn just past Pojoaque), to County Road 98 (a left toward Chimayó), to NM 76 northeast to NM 75 east, to NM 518 north. The drive through the rolling foothills and tiny valleys of the Sangre de Cristos, dotted with orchards, pueblos, and picturesque villages, is stunning. In mid-April the orchards are in blossom; summer turns the valleys into lush green oases; and in fall, the smell of piñon adds to the sensual overload of golden leaves and red-chile ristras hanging from the houses. In winter, the fields are covered with quilts of snow, and the lines of homes, fences, and trees stand out like bold pen-and-ink drawings against the sky. But the roads can be icy and treacherous—if in doubt, stick with the "low road" to Taos. If you decide to take the High Road just one way between Santa Fe and Taos, you might want to save it for the return journey—the scenery is best enjoyed when traveling north to south.

## Chimayó

**39** *28 mi north of Santa Fe, 10 mi east of Española on NM 76.*

From U.S. 285/84 north of Pojoaque, scenic NM 503 winds past horse paddocks and orchards in the narrow Nambé Valley, then ascends into the red-sandstone canyons with a view of Truchas Peaks to the northeast before dropping into the bucolic village of Chimayó. Nestled into hillsides where gnarled piñons seem to grow from bare bedrock, Chimayó is famed for its weaving, its red chiles, and its two chapels.

The **Santuario de Chimayó,** a small frontier adobe church, has a fantastically carved and painted wood altar and is built on the site where, believers say, a mysterious light came from the ground on Good Friday in 1810 and where a large wooden crucifix was found beneath the earth. The chapel sits above a sacred *pozito* (a small hole), the dirt from which is believed to have miraculous healing properties. Dozens of abandoned crutches and braces placed in the anteroom—along with many notes, letters, and photos—testify to this. The Santuario draws a steady stream of worshipers all year long—Chimayó is considered the Lourdes of the Southwest. During Holy Week as many as 50,000 pilgrims come here. The shrine is a National Historic Landmark. It's also surrounded by commercialism in the way of small adobe shops selling every kind of religious curio imaginable. Mass is celebrated on Sunday. ⊠ *Signed lane off C.R. 98,* ☎ *505/351–4889.* 🖾 *Free.* 🕐 *Daily 9–5.*

A smaller chapel just 200 yards from El Santuario was built in 1857 and dedicated to **Santo Niño de Atocha.** As at the more famous Santuario, the dirt at Santo Niño de Atocha's chapel is said to have healing properties in the place where the *Santo Niño* was first placed. The little boy saint was brought here from Mexico by Severiano Medina, who claimed Santo Niño de Atocha had healed him of rheumatism. San Ildefonso pottery master Maria Martinez came here for healing as a child. Tales of the boy saint's losing one of his shoes as he wandered through the countryside helping those in trouble endeared him to the people of northern New Mexico. It became a tradition to place shoes at the foot of the statue as an offering. 🖾 *Free.* 🕐 *Daily 9–5.*

### DINING AND LODGING

**$$** ✕ **Rancho de Chimayó.** In a century-old adobe hacienda tucked into the mountains, with whitewashed walls, hand-stripped vigas, and cozy dining rooms, the much-hyped Rancho de Chimayó is still owned and operated by the family that first occupied the house. There's a roaring fireplace in winter and, in summer, a terraced patio shaded by catalpa trees. Good, if predictable New Mexican fare is served, but the ambience is the real draw here. You can take an after-dinner stroll on the grounds' paths. Reservations are essential in summer. ⌧ *C.R. 98,* ☎ *505/351–4444. AE, D, DC, MC, V. Closed Mon. Nov.–mid-May.*

$ ✕ **Léona's Restaurante.** This fast-food-style burrito and chile stand under a massive catalpa tree at one end of the Santuario de Chimayó parking lot has only a few tables, and in summer it's crowded. The specialty is flavored tortillas—everything from jalapeño to butterscotch. Her business became so successful that owner Léona Tiede opened a tortilla factory in Chimayó's Manzana Center and now does a thriving mail-order business. ⌧ *Off C.R. 98, behind Santuario de Chimayó,* ☎ *505/351–4569 or 888/561–5569. AE, D, DC, MC, V. Closed Tues. Nov.–Apr. No dinner.*

$–$$ ☷ **Casa Escondida.** Intimate and peaceful, this adobe inn has sweeping views of the Sangre de Cristo range. The setting makes it a great base for mountain bikers. Chopin on the CD player and the scent of fresh-baked strudel waft through the rooms. Rooms are decorated with antiques and Native American and other regional arts and crafts. Ask for the Sun Room, in the main house, which has a private patio, viga ceilings, and a brick floor. The separate one-bedroom Casita Escondida has a kiva-style fireplace, tile floors, kitchenette, and a sitting area. A large hot tub is hidden in a grove behind wild berry bushes. ⌧ *Off NM 76 at C.R. 0100 (Box 142, 85722),* ☎ *505/351–4805 or 800/643–7201,* FAX *505/351–2575,* WEB *www.casaescondida.com. 7 rooms, 1 house. Some kitchenettes, outdoor hot tub. MC, V. BP.*

$–$$ ☷ **Hacienda de Chimayó.** This authentic adobe house is furnished with antiques, and each room has a private bath and fireplace. The inn sits directly on Chimayó's main road and is conveniently across from the lovely Rancho de Chimayó restaurant and within walking distance of the Santuario. ⌧ *C.R. 98 (Box 11, Chimayó 87522),* ☎ *505/351–2222,* WEB *www.ranchodechimayo.com. 6 rooms, 1 suite. AE, D, DC, MC, V. CP.*

$ ☷ **La Posada de Chimayó.** New Mexico's first B&B is a peaceful place whose two suites have fireplaces, Mexican rugs, handwoven bedspreads, and comfortable regional furniture. The entire guest house can be rented by the week and the minimum stay is two nights. Views are somewhat obscured and the house is set close to the dirt road. ⌧ *279 Rio Arriba, C.R. 0101 (Box 463, 87522),* ☎ FAX *505/351–4605,* WEB *www.laposadadechimayo.com. 2 suites. Some pets allowed; no kids under 12, no smoking. No credit cards. BP.*

### SHOPPING

**Centinela Traditional Arts-Weaving** (⌧ NM 76, 1 mi east of junction with C.R. 98, ☎ 505/351–2180 or 877/351–2180) continues the Trujillo family weaving tradition, which started in northern New Mexico more than seven generations ago. Irvin Trujillo and his wife, Lisa, are both award-winning master weavers, creating Rio Grande–style tapestry blankets and rugs, many of them with natural dyes that authentically replicate early weavings. Most designs are historically based, but the Trujillos contribute their own designs as well. The shop and gallery carries these heirloom-quality textiles, with a knowledgeable staff on hand to demonstrate or answer questions about the weaving technique.

**Ortega's Weaving Shop** (⌧ NM 76 at C.R. 98, ☎ 505/351–4215 or 877/351–4215) sells Rio Grande– and Chimayó-style textiles made by the family whose Spanish ancestors brought the craft to New Mexico in the 1600s. The Galeria Ortega, next door, sells traditional New Mexican and Hispanic and contemporary Native American arts and crafts. The shop is closed on Sunday.

## Cordova

**40** *4 mi east of Chimayó via NM 76.*

A minuscule mountain village with a small central plaza, a school, a post office, and a church, Cordova is the center of the regional wood-carving industry. The town supports more than 30 full-time and part-time carvers. Most of them are descendants of José Dolores López, who in the 1920s created the village's signature unpainted "Cordova style" of carving. Most of the *santeros* (makers of religious images) have signs outside their homes indicating that santos are for sale. The pieces are expensive, ranging from several hundred dollars for small ones to several thousand for larger figures. There are also affordable and delightful small carvings of animals and birds. The St. Anthony of Padua Chapel, which is filled with handcrafted retablos and other religious art, is worth a visit.

## Truchas

**41** *4 mi northeast of Cordova via NM 76.*

Truchas (Spanish for "trout") is where Robert Redford shot the movie *The Milagro Beanfield War* (based on the much better novel written by Taos author John Nichols). This village is perched on the rim of a deep canyon beneath the towering Truchas Peaks, mountains high enough to be almost perpetually capped with snow. The tallest of the Truchas Peaks is 13,102 ft, the second-highest point in New Mexico. There are a few galleries and a small market in this town, which feels like an outpost just waking up from the colonial days. Continue 7 mi north on NM 76, toward Taos, and you'll come to the marvelous San Tomás Church in the village of Trampas. It dates from at least 1760.

SHOPPING

The most notable of the colorful shops and galleries in Truchas is **Cordovas Handweaving Workshop** (⊠ village center, ☎ 505/689–2437).

# SANTA FE A TO Z

### AIR TRAVEL

Most major airlines provide service to the state's main airport in Albuquerque, about an hour's drive from Santa Fe. There is no air service between Albuquerque and Santa Fe. Great Lakes Aviation flies daily from Denver to Santa Fe; round-trip fares are usually around $250. *See* Air Travel *in* Smart Travel Tips A to Z for national airline phone numbers.

➤ REGIONAL AIRLINE: **Great Lakes Aviation** (☎ 800/554–5111).

### AIRPORTS AND TRANSFERS

Tiny Santa Fe Municipal Airport offers limited services, although there's some talk of expanding the facility and its runways to help lure additional airlines. The airport is 9 mi southwest of downtown.

➤ AIRPORT: **Santa Fe Municipal Airport** (⊠ Airport Rd. and Hwy. 599, ☎ 505/955–2908).

### BUS TRAVEL TO AND FROM SANTA FE

Bus service on Texas, New Mexico & Oklahoma Coaches, affiliated with Greyhound Lines, is available to Santa Fe from major cities and towns through the region.

➤ BUS INFORMATION: **Greyhound/Texas, New Mexico & Oklahoma Coaches** (☎ 505/243–4435 or 800/231–2222, WEB www.greyhound.com).

## BUS TRAVEL WITHIN SANTA FE

The city's bus system, Santa Fe Trails, covers seven major routes through town and is useful for getting from the Plaza to some of the outlying attractions. Route 10 is most useful for visitors, as it runs from downtown to the museums on Old Santa Fe Trail south of town (still a car is a much more practical way to get around). A daily pass costs $1. Buses run about every 30 minutes on weekdays, every hour on weekends. Service begins at 6 AM and continues until 10 PM on weekdays and until 8 PM on Saturday. There is no bus service on Sunday.

➤ BUS SERVICE: **Santa Fe Trails** (☎ 505/438–1464).

## CAR RENTAL

Santa Fe is served by several national rental car agencies, including Avis, Budget, and Hertz. Additional agencies with locations in Santa Fe include Advantage, Classy Car Rentals (which specializes in luxury and sports vehicles), Enterprise, Sears, and Thrifty. *See* Car Rental *in* Smart Travel Tips A to Z for national rental agency phone numbers.

➤ RENTAL AGENCIES: **Advantage** (☎ 505/983–9470). **Classy Car Rentals** (☎ 505/690–3296). **Enterprise** (☎ 505/473–3600). **Sears** (☎ 505/984–8038). **Thrifty** (☎ 505/474–3365 or 800/367–2277).

## CAR TRAVEL

South–north–running I–25 passes actually curves in almost a west–east direction as it cuts just south of Santa Fe, which is 62 mi northeast of Albuquerque. U.S. 285/84 runs north–south through the city. The Turquoise Trail (☞ Side Trips *in* Chapter 2) is a scenic, two-lane approach to Santa Fe from Albuquerque. The NM 599 bypass, also called the Santa Fe Relief Route, cuts around the city from I–25's Exit 276, southwest of the city, to U.S. 285/84, north of the city; it's a great shortcut if you're heading from Albuquerque to Española, Abiquiu, Taos, or other points north of Santa Fe.

Parking in Santa Fe is difficult, but public and private lots can be found throughout the city. Parking meters are well monitored. There are parking garages near the Plaza on San Franscisco and Water streets. On weekends, you can park for free in the lots of some of the government buildings near the Capitol, which is within walking distance of the Plaza (check signs carefully for specific parking rules).

## EMERGENCIES

In an emergency, dial 911.

➤ HOSPITAL: **St. Vincent Hospital** (✉ 455 St. Michael's Dr., ☎ 505/983–3361).

➤ 24-HOUR PHARMACY: **Walgreens** (✉ 1096 St. Francis Dr., ☎ 505/982–4643).

## LODGING

In addition to the usual array of inns and hotels here, Santa Fe has a wide range of long- and short-term vacation rentals, some of them available through property management companies, including the Management Group, Santa Fe Vacation Rental, and Southwestern Exclusives. Rates generally range from $100 to $300 per night for double-occupancy units, but better values can be found at some of the two- to four-bedroom properties, which can be a great deal when several guests are splitting the fee. Most of the places have fully stocked kitchens.

Another route is to rent a furnished condo or casita at one of the several compounds in town geared toward travelers seeking longer stays. The best of these is the luxurious Campanilla Compound ($1,300–$2,000/wk in summer), which sits on a hill just north of downtown.

➤ LOCAL AGENTS: **Campanilla Compound** (☎ 505/988–7585 or 800/

828–9700, WEB www.campanillacompound.com). **Management Group** (☎ 505/982–2823, WEB www.santafe-rentals.com). **Santa Fe Vacation Rental** (☎ 888/340–2883, WEB www.staabvr.com). **Southwestern Exclusives** (☎ 505/995–0777 or 800/358–8133, WEB www.southwesternexclusives. com).

## TAXIS

Capital City Cab Company controls all the cabs in Santa Fe. The taxis aren't metered; you pay a flat fee based on how far you're going, usually $4–$8 within the downtown area. There are no cab stands; you must phone to arrange a ride.

➤ CONTACT: **Capital City Cab Company** (☎ 505/438–0000).

## TOURS
### GENERAL-INTEREST

Aboot About has been walking groups through the history, art, and architecture of Santa Fe since the late 1970s. Tours ($10) leave daily at 9:30 and 1:30 from the Eldorado Hotel and at 9:45 and 1:45 from the Hotel St. Francis. Tours take about 90 minutes. No reservations are required. Great Southwest Tours conducts guided mountain hikes and 7- to 35-passenger van and bus excursions to Bandelier, Abiquiu, Taos, and elsewhere in the region; it also provides a shuttle service to and from downtown hotels and the Santa Fe Opera. Santa Fe Detours conducts bus, river, rail, horseback, and walking tours and organizes rafting and ski packages. This is an excellent choice if you're looking for a general overview of the city and some of the nearby attractions.

Rojo Tours designs specialized trips—to view wildflowers, pueblo ruins and cliff dwellings, galleries and studios, Native American arts and crafts, and private homes—as well as adventure activity tours. Afoot in Santa Fe Tours conducts a two-hour close-up look at the city. The tours ($10) leave from the Inn at Loretto from Monday to Sunday at 9:30. Afoot offers open-air trolley tours ($12) several times daily, April–October.

There are also more than 20 independent tour guides based in Santa Fe who are members of the New Mexico Guides Association. Many of these individuals have particular specialties. For example, Kay Lewis's tours emphasize regional art; Stefanie Beninato can give customized ghost, Jewish legacy, or garden walks; Chip Conway's rambles explore the cultures of New Mexico's indigenous peoples, and former Smithsonian docent Barbara Harrelson offers tours that focus on Southwest literature and authors. Other guides specialize in everything from German-language narration to all-women adventures to Georgia O'Keeffe.

➤ CONTACTS: **Aboot About** (☎ 505/988–2774). **Afoot in Santa Fe Tours** (☎ 505/983–3701). **Great Southwest Tours** (☎ 505/455–2700, WEB www.swadventures.com). **New Mexico Guides Association** (☎ 505/ 466–4877, WEB www.nmguides.com/members.html). **Rojo Tours** (☎ 505/ 474–8333, WEB www.rojotours.com). **Santa Fe Detours** (☎ 505/983– 6565 or 800/338–6877, WEB www.sfdetours.com).

### LEARNING EXPERIENCES

Art Adventures in the Southwest takes you into the New Mexico landscape for outdoor art classes with Jane Shoenfeld. All materials are supplied, as are all levels of experience. Santa Fe Art Institute is housed in the Visual Arts Center designed by Mexican architect Ricardo Legorreta (a Modernist break from Santa Fe style). The institute (not part of the College of Santa Fe) offers weeklong workshops that have been led by such renowned artists as Phoebe Adams and Richard Diebenkorn.

Dormitory quarters are available and studio space is provided. Workshops are offered year-round.

Santa Fe Photographic Workshops offers workshops in photographic processes including digital imaging, platinum, and travel photography. The workshops have an excellent reputation, and many instructors return year after year. Santa Fe School of Cooking holds night and day classes in regional New Mexican fare.

➤ CONTACTS: **Art Adventures in the Southwest** (☎ 505/986–1108, FAX 505/986–3845, WEB skyfields.net). **Santa Fe Art Institute** (✉ 1600 St. Michael's Dr., College of Santa Fe campus, ☎ 505/424–5050, WEB www.sfai.org). **Santa Fe Photographic Workshops** (☎ 505/983–1400, WEB www.santafeworkshops.com). **Santa Fe School of Cooking** (☎ 505/983–4511, WEB www.santafeschoolofcooking.com).

### TRAIN TRAVEL
Amtrak's *Southwest Chief* stops in Lamy, a short drive south of Santa Fe, on its route from Chicago to Los Angeles via Kansas City; other New Mexico stops include Raton, Las Vegas, Albuquerque, and Gallup daily.

➤ TRAIN INFORMATION: **Amtrak** (☎ 800/872–7245, WEB www.amtrak. com).

### VISITOR INFORMATION
➤ TOURIST INFORMATION: **Española Valley Chamber of Commerce** (✉ 417 Big Rock Center [Box 190, Española 87532], ☎ 505/753–2831, WEB www.espanola.com/chamber). **Los Alamos Meeting and Visitor Bureau** (✉ Fuller Lodge, 2132 Central Ave. [Box 460 VG, Los Alamos 87544], ☎ 505/662–8105 or 800/444–0707, WEB www.visit.losalamos. com). **New Mexico Department of Tourism visitor center** (✉ Lamy Bldg., 491 Old Santa Fe Trail, 87503, ☎ 505/827–7400 or 800/733–6396 ext. 0643, WEB www.newmexico.org). **Santa Fe Convention and Visitors Bureau** (✉ 201 W. Marcy St. [Box 909, 87501], ☎ 505/955–6200 or 800/777–2489, WEB www.santafe.org).

# 5 TAOS

WITH THE ENCHANTED CIRCLE
AND TAOS SKI VALLEY

The essence of Taos lies in the easy rapport
of its Native American, Hispanic, and Anglo
inhabitants, a reality vividly illustrated by this
small town's effusive cultural spirit and eclectic
architecture. The diversity, physical beauty,
and Old West feel of Taos have lured
authors, painters, and other artists since the
early 20th century. More recently, outdoors
enthusiasts have discovered the area's world-
class ski slopes and rushing rivers.

Updated
by Holly
Hammond

**T**AOS CASTS A LINGERING SPELL. Majestic Taos Mountain presides over the valley, where the air smells of piñon smoke and sagebrush. The two-centuries-old Plaza and old adobe buildings testify to the town's Native American and Spanish origins. Many roads and lanes around town remain unpaved and rutted, and vacation homes take their place among farmsteads handed down from Spanish-colonial days.

With a population of about 6,500, Taos, on a rolling mesa at the base of the Sangre de Cristo Mountains, is actually three towns in one. The first is the low-key business district of art galleries, restaurants, and shops that recalls the Santa Fe of a few decades ago. The second area, 3 mi north of the commercial center, is Taos Pueblo, home to Tiwa-speaking Native Americans. Life at the Taos Pueblo long predates the arrival of the Spanish in America in the 1500s. Unlike many nomadic Native American tribes that were forced to relocate to government-designated reservations, the residents of Taos Pueblo have inhabited their land (at present 95,000 acres) at the base of the 12,282-ft-high Taos Mountain for centuries.

The third part of Taos, 4 mi south of town, is Ranchos de Taos, a farming and ranching community settled by the Spanish. Ranchos is best known for the San Francisco de Asís Church, whose buttressed adobe walls shelter significant religious artifacts and paintings. Its massive exterior and *camposanto* (graveyard) are among the most photographed in the country.

That so many 20th-century painters, photographers, and literary figures—among them Georgia O'Keeffe, Ansel Adams, and D. H. Lawrence—have been drawn to the earthy spirit of Taos has only heightened its appeal. Bert Phillips and Ernest Blumenschein, traveling from Denver on a planned painting trip into Mexico in 1898, stopped in Taos to have a broken wagon wheel repaired. Enthralled with the landscape, earth-hue adobe buildings, piercing light, and clean mountain air, they abandoned their plan to journey farther south. They returned to the Taos area often, speaking so highly of it that other East Coast artists followed them west. By 1915, the Taos Society of Artists had been established. Blumenschein and Phillips, with Joseph Henry Sharp and Eanger Irving Couse, all graduates of the Paris art school Académie Julian, formed the core of the group.

The persuasive hospitality of transplanted socialite Mabel Dodge Luhan also drew cultural luminaries here. Some of the early Taos artists spent their winters in New York or Chicago teaching painting or illustration to earn enough money to summer in New Mexico. Others became full-time New Mexicans. Living conditions were primitive then: no running water, electricity, or even indoor plumbing. But these painters happily endured such inconveniences to indulge their fascination with Native American customs, modes of dress, and ceremonies. Eventually, they co-opted the Native architecture and dress and presumptuously fancied that they "knew" Indian culture. The Society of Artists disbanded in 1927, but Taos continued to attract artists. Several galleries opened and, in 1952, local painters joined together to form the Taos Artists' Association, forerunner to today's Taos Art Association. At present, several dozen galleries and shops display art, sculpture, and crafts, and about 1,000 artists live in town or nearby. No mere satellite of Santa Fe, Taos is an art center in its own right.

# Pleasures and Pastimes

### Arts and Crafts

If your idea of fun is museum-going and gallery-hopping, you'll love Taos. The creative spirit is strong here, and it's contagious. Even if you begin by just browsing, you might find that you can't go home without a certain painting or pot that captures the unique enchantment of the place. It's easy to visit a lot of galleries in a short time; many are side by side on a few streets around the Plaza. Southwestern landscapes and Native American themes are frequent subjects. Look for outstanding weaving, jewelry, tin work, and other crafts, too. Studio tours are held every fall, when you can visit with working artists in the area.

### Dining

Taos is a great place for New Mexican fare, prepared with locally grown chiles and homemade tortillas, but the town also draws raves for outstanding contemporary restaurants with award-winning wine lists. Pan-Asian and Middle Eastern flavors are also influences in the increasingly sophisticated cuisines finding their way to this small town with a big attitude.

| CATEGORY | COST* |
|---|---|
| $$$$ | over $25 |
| $$$ | $18–$25 |
| $$ | $10–$17 |
| $ | under $10 |

*per person for a main course at dinner

### Lodging

If you want to enter into the mood of northern New Mexico, stay at a B&B in a refurbished old adobe, with a view of the desert and mountains. With their kiva fireplaces, beamed *viga* ceilings, and thick, hand-shaped walls, these lodgings exude warmth and comfort as well as a fascinating slice of southwestern Americana. And you don't have to give up luxury: many hostels offer spa facilities and sumptuous meals as well as a glimpse into the past.

| CATEGORY | COST* |
|---|---|
| $$$$ | over $170 |
| $$$ | $120–$170 |
| $$ | $70–$120 |
| $ | under $70 |

*All prices are for a standard double room, excluding 11.32 % tax.

### Outdoor Activities and Sports

The glorious landscape around Taos draws serious athletes as well as those who just want to wander under the huge skies and gaze at the mountains. Cycling is popular, with rallies and races held in late summer. The vast Carson National Forest is an excellent spot for most any outdoor pursuit. The rivers and lakes are excellent for trout fishing; you can arrange for outings with local expert guides. The waters also invite rafters, especially when spring runoff fills the rivers with white water. There are innumerable trails for hiking for all levels of fitness, up into alpine reaches and down into rocky gorges. And of course winter brings skiers from all over to the world-class slopes of Taos Ski Valley and the four other resorts nearby.

# EXPLORING TAOS

Taos is small and resolutely rustic, and the central area is highly walkable. Sociable Taoseños make the town a welcoming place to explore.

## Close-Up

# HOSTESS OF TAOS

**MABEL DODGE LUHAN,** a progressive-minded socialite from Buffalo, New York, arrived on the scene in 1917, fell in love with Taos, and stayed. In the high-desert landscape and in the Taos Pueblo culture she found a purpose and unity that she firmly believed ought to be extended to American society at large. When she walked away from her "old, mythical life," aiding her as soul mate and spiritual mainstay was a statuesque Taos Pueblo man, Antonio Luhan, who became her fourth, and last, husband. In the house they built together next to Pueblo land, they hosted many of the era's great artists, writers, philosophers, psychologists, anthropologists, and social reformers. Mabel's friends and acquaintances included Martha Graham, Aldous Huxley, and Carl Jung. Mabel wrote to D. H. Lawrence many times and even tried to send him psychic messages until finally he, too, came to Taos and was profoundly affected by what he found. Although he stayed less than two years all together, some of his finest writing, including *The Plumed Serpent* and several novelettes, essays, and poems, grew out of his experiences in Taos and Mexico. Mabel herself penned several books; *Edge of Taos Desert: An Escape to Reality* (1937) is a part of her autobiography that vividly describes her life in Taos. She and her beloved Tony died within months of each other in 1970. Their house is now a conference center and B&B.

You'll need a car to reach the Enchanted Circle, the Rio Grande Gorge, Taos Ski Valley, and other places of interest beyond Taos proper. Traffic can be heavy in the peak summer and winter seasons; ask locals about back roads that let you avoid the busy Paseo del Pueblo.

The Museum Association of Taos includes seven properties. Among them are the Harwood Museum, the Fechin Institute, the Millicent Rogers Museum, and the Van Vechten–Lineberry Taos Art Museum, as well as those in the Kit Carson Historic Museum consortium: the Blumenschein Home and Museum, the Kit Carson Home and Museum, and La Hacienda de los Martínez. Each of the museums charges $4 or $5 for admission, but you can opt for a combination ticket—$20 for all seven, valid for one year, or buy a $10 joint ticket to the three Kit Carson museums.

*Numbers in the text correspond to numbers in the margin and on the Taos map.*

### Great Itineraries

IF YOU HAVE 1 DAY

Begin by strolling around **Taos Plaza** ①, taking in the galleries and Native American crafts shops. Take Ledoux Street south from the west Plaza and go two blocks to visit the **Harwood Foundation** ③. Walk back to the Plaza and cross over to Kit Carson Road, where you'll find more shops and galleries as well as the **Kit Carson Home and Museum** ④. Continue north on Paseo del Pueblo to the **Fechin Institute** ⑨. In the afternoon, get in the car and head north on Paseo del Pueblo to the traffic light, where you'll turn left on U.S. 64. to the **Rio Grande Gorge**

**Bridge** ⑮. If you're feeling peppy, you can climb down to the river, or just gaze down into the breathtaking chasm from the bridge. Return the way you came, turning right at the light, and drive the short distance to Millicent Rogers Road. Turn right and proceed to the **Millicent Rogers Museum** ⑭, where you can easily spend the rest of the afternoon. If you are in town for the evening, stop in at the **Adobe Bar** at the Taos Inn for music and people-watching.

IF YOU HAVE 3 DAYS

Spend the first day doing the one-day tour above. On the second day, drive out to the **Taos Pueblo** ⑬ in the morning and tour the ancient village while the day is fresh. Return to town and go to the **Blumenschein Home and Museum** ② and the **Van Vechten-Lineberry Taos Art Museum** ⑩. Lunch at the nearby **Dragonfly Café**. After lunch, drive out to **La Hacienda de los Martinez** ⑪ for a look at early life in Taos and then to **Ranchos de Taos** ⑫ to see the beautiful **San Francisco de Asís Church**. If it's dinnertime, eat at **Joseph's Table** or the **Trading Post Café**. If it's still early, drive back to town and browse in the shops on Bent Street and the adjacent John Dunn House Shops. On the third day, drive the **Enchanted Circle** to get a sense of the surrounding landscape.

## When to Tour Taos

Each season brings its own beauty to Taos. Spring means blue skies, pleasant temperatures, with occasional rain. Summers can get hot, but frequent afternoon thunderstorms bring relief. In a sky this big, you can often see rain falling in one place, sun shining in another, and a rainbow arcing the two. In the autumn the chamisa and sunflowers bloom yellow along the roadsides and the weather is dry. Winters are snowy with cold nights, but the days are often bright; if you like to ski, this is the time to visit.

# Downtown Taos

More than four centuries after it was laid out, Taos Plaza remains the center of commercial life in Taos. Bent Street, where New Mexico's first American governor lived and died, is an upscale shopping area and gallery enclave.

## A Good Walk

Begin at the gazebo in the middle of **Taos Plaza** ①. After exploring the Plaza, head south from its western edge down the small unmarked alley (its name is West Plaza Drive). The first cross street is Camino de la Placita. Across it, West Plaza Drive becomes Ledoux Street. Continue south on Ledoux to the **Blumenschein Home and Museum** ② and, a few doors farther south, the **Harwood Foundation** ③. (If you're driving, the parking area for the Harwood Foundation is at Ledoux and Ranchitos Road.)

From the Harwood Foundation, walk back north on Ranchitos Road a few blocks, make a left on Camino de la Placita, and go right onto Don Fernando Road. Follow it east along the north side of the Plaza to Paseo del Pueblo Norte (NM 68), which is the main street of Taos. As you cross NM 68, Don Fernando Road changes to Kit Carson Road. On the north side of Kit Carson Road is the **Kit Carson Home and Museum** ④. After visiting the home, head back to Paseo del Pueblo Norte and walk north past the Taos Inn and **Stables Art Center** ⑤ to browse through Bent Street's shops, boutiques, and galleries.

In a tiny plaza is the **Governor Bent Museum** ⑥, the modest home of the first Anglo governor of the state. Across the street is the John Dunn House. Once the homestead of a colorful and well-respected Taos gambling and transportation entrepreneur, the Dunn House is now a

**150**

Taos

small shopping plaza. At the western end of Bent Street, head north on Camino de la Placita. In about 2½ blocks you'll come to the Taos Volunteer Fire Department building, which doubles as a fire station and the **Firehouse Collection** ⑦ exhibition space.

Head east on Civic Plaza and cross Paseo del Pueblo Norte. To the north will be **Kit Carson Memorial Park** ⑧ and the **Fechin Institute** ⑨, named for the iconoclastic artist Nicolai Fechin. On 10 handsome acres north of the Fechin Institute stands the **Van Vechten–Lineberry Taos Art Museum** ⑩.

### TIMING

The entire walk can be done in a half day, a whole day if you stop to lunch along the way and browse in the shops and galleries. The Fechin Institute is closed Monday and Tuesday. Hours vary by season, but visits by appointment are welcomed. Some museums are closed on the weekend, so you may want to do this walk on a Wednesday, Thursday, or Friday. You'll be able to tour each of the museums in less than an hour.

## Sights to See

❷ **Blumenschein Home and Museum.** For an introduction to the history of the Taos art scene, start with Ernest L. Blumenschein's residence, which provides a glimpse into the cosmopolitan lives led by the members of the Taos Society of Artists, of which Blumenschein was a founding member. One of the rooms in the adobe-style structure dates from 1797. On display are the art, antiques, and other personal possessions of Blumenschein and his wife, Mary Greene Blumenschein, who also painted, as did their daughter Helen. Several of Ernest Blumenschein's vivid oil paintings hang in his former studio, and also on display are works by other early Taos artists. ⊠ *222 Ledoux St.,* ☎ *505/ 758–0505.* ☞ *$5 (or use Kit Carson Historic Museums of Taos joint ticket).* ☉ *Apr.–Oct., daily 9–5; Nov.–Mar., daily 10–4.*

★ ❾ **Fechin Institute.** The interior of this extraordinary adobe house, built between 1927 and 1933 by Russian émigré and artist Nicolai Fechin, is a marvel of carved Russian-style woodwork and furniture that glistens with an almost golden sheen. Fechin constructed it to showcase his daringly colorful paintings. Fechin's daughter Eya oversees her father's architectural masterpiece—she loves talking about him and life "back then" (she arrived in Taos with her father when she was 12). Listed on the National Register of Historic Places, the Fechin Institute hosts exhibits and special workshops devoted to the artist's unique approach to learning, teaching, and creating. Open hours are often in flux, so call ahead. ⊠ *227 Paseo del Pueblo Norte,* ☎ *505/758–1710.* ☞ *$4.* ☉ *Wed.–Sun. 10–2.*

☝ ❼ **Firehouse Collection.** More than 100 works by well-known Taos artists like Joseph Sharp, Ernest L. Blumenschein, and Bert Phillips hang in the Taos Volunteer Fire Department building. The exhibition space adjoins the station house, where five fire engines are maintained at the ready and an antique fire engine is on display. ⊠ *321 Camino de la Placita,* ☎ *505/758–3386.* ☞ *Free.* ☉ *Weekdays 9–4:30.*

☝ ❻ **Governor Bent Museum.** In 1846, when New Mexico became a U.S. possession as a result of the Mexican War, Charles Bent, a trader, trapper, and mountain man, was appointed governor. Less than a year later he was killed in his house by an angry mob protesting New Mexico's annexation by the United States. Governor Bent was married to María Ignacia, the older sister of Josefa Jaramillo, the wife of mountain man Kit Carson. A collection of Native American artifacts, western Americana, and family possessions is squeezed into five small rooms of the adobe building where Bent and his family lived. ⊠ *117 Bent St.,* ☎ *505/758–2376.* ▦ *$1.* ☉ *Daily 10–5.*

★ ❸ **Harwood Foundation.** The Pueblo Revival former home of Burritt Elihu "Burt" Harwood, a dedicated painter who studied in France before moving to Taos with his public-spirited wife, Lucy, in 1916, is adjacent to a museum dedicated to the works of local artists. Traditional Hispanic northern New Mexican artists, early art-colony painters, post–World War II Modernists, and contemporary artists such as Larry Bell, Agnes Martin, Ken Price, and Earl Stroh are represented. Mabel Dodge Luhan, a major arts patron, bequeathed many of the 19th-century and early 20th-century works in the Harwoods' collection, including *retablos* (painted wood representations of Catholic saints) and *bultos* (three-dimensional carvings of the saints). In the Hispanic Traditions Gallery upstairs are 19th-century tinwork, furniture, and sculpture. Downstairs, among early 20th-century art-colony holdings, look for E. Martin Hennings's *Chamisa in Bloom.* A tour of the ground-floor galleries shows that Taos painters of the era, notably Oscar Berninghaus, Ernest Blumenschein, Victor Higgins, Walter Ufer, Marsden Hartley, and John Marin, were fascinated by the land and the people linked to it. An octagonal gallery exhibits works by Agnes Martin. Martin's seven large canvas panels (5 ft by 5 ft) are studies in white, their precise lines and blocks forming textured grids. Operated by the University of New Mexico since 1936, the Harwood is the second-oldest art museum in the state. ⊠ *238 Ledoux St.,* ☎ *505/758–9826.* ▦ *$5.* ☉ *Tues.–Sat. 10–5, Sun. noon–5.*

👋 ❹ **Kit Carson Home and Museum.** Kit Carson bought this low-slung 12-room adobe home in 1843 for his wife, Josefa Jaramillo, the daughter of a powerful, politically influential Spanish family. Three of the museum's rooms are furnished as they were when the Carson family lived here. The rest of the museum is devoted to gun and mountain-man exhibits, such as rugged leather clothing and Kit's own Spencer carbine rifle with its beaded leather carrying case, and early Taos antiques, artifacts, and manuscripts. ⊠ *Kit Carson Rd.,* ☎ *505/758–0505.* ▦ *$5 (or use Kit Carson Historic Museums of Taos joint ticket).* ☉ *Apr.–Oct., daily 9–5; call for winter hrs.*

---

NEED A BREAK?     Let the coffee aroma draw you into the tiny **World Cup** (⊠ 102 Paseo del Pueblo Norte, ☎ 505/737–5299).

---

👋 ❽ **Kit Carson Memorial Park.** The noted pioneer is buried in the park that bears his name. His grave is marked with a *cerquita* (a spiked wrought-iron rectangular fence), traditionally used to outline and protect burial sites. Also interred here is Mabel Dodge Luhan, the pioneering patron of the early Taos art scene. The 20-acre park has swings and slides for recreational breaks. It's well marked with big stone pillars and a gate. ⊠ *Paseo del Pueblo Norte at Civic Plaza Dr.,* ☎ *505/758–8234.* ▦ *Free.* ☉ *Memorial Day–Labor Day, daily 8–8; Labor Day–Memorial Day, daily 8–5.*

❺ **Stables Art Center.** It was in the stables in back of this house that the Taos Artists' Association first began showing the works of members and invited nonmember artists from across northern New Mexico. In 1952 the association purchased the handsome adobe building, which is now the visual arts gallery of the Taos Art Association. All the work on exhibit is for sale. ⊠ *133 Paseo del Pueblo Norte,* ☎ *505/758–2036.* ▦ *Free.* ☉ *Daily 10–5.*

❶ **Taos Plaza.** The first European explorers of the Taos Valley came here with Captain Hernando de Alvarado, a member of Francisco Vásquez de Coronado's expedition of 1540. Basque explorer Don Juan de Oñate arrived in Taos in July 1598 and established a mission and trading arrangements with residents of Taos Pueblo. The settlement developed into two plazas: the Plaza at the heart of the town became a thriving business district for the early colony, and a walled residential plaza was constructed a few hundred yards behind. It remains active today, home to a throng of gift and coffee shops. The covered gazebo was donated by heiress and longtime Taos resident Mabel Dodge Luhan. On the southeastern corner of Taos Plaza is the **Hotel La Fonda de Taos.** Some infamous erotic paintings by D. H. Lawrence that were naughty in his day but are quite tame by present standards can be viewed ($2 entry fee) in the former barroom beyond the lobby.

NEED A BREAK? To fuel your walk, grab a pick-me-up at **trans-fu'sion** (⊠ 204 Paseo del Pueblo Norte, ☎ 505/758–5842), a coffee bar that serves smoothies and an array of herbal tonic drinks as well as java.

🔟 **Van Vechten–Lineberry Taos Art Museum.** This privately run museum shows the works of painter Duane Van Vechten, the late wife of Edwin C. Lineberry. Her former studio is the entrance to the museum, whose collection of 130 works by more than 50 Taos artists includes pieces of varying quality by the founders of the Taos Society of Artists. The museum's signature piece is *Our Lady of Gualadupe* (1929) by Van Vechten. On a par with the exhibits are the museum grounds, a 10-acre walled park, and the building itself, which was the home of the artist and Mr. Lineberry, who maintains the museum with his wife, Novella. ⊠ *501 Paseo del Pueblo Norte,* ☎ *505/758–2690.* 🎟 *$6.* ⊙ *Wed.–Fri. 10–5, Sat. 1–5, Sun. 1–4.*

NEED A BREAK? Join the locals at the north or south location of the **Bean** (⊠ 900 Paseo del Pueblo Norte, ☎ 505/758–7111; ⊠ 1033 Paseo del Pueblo Sur, ☎ 505/758–5123). The Bean roasts its own coffee, and the south-side location offers breakfast and lunch.

# South of Taos

The first Spanish settlers were farmers who faced raids by non–Pueblo Indians like the Comanches. Aspects of this history come alive on this meandering drive south through fields and farmland to a restored hacienda and into a former farming village with its famous, fortresslike church.

### A Good Drive

Head south 3 mi on NM 240 (also known as Ranchitos Road) to **La Hacienda de los Martínez** ⑪. As you pass by the adobe cottages and modest homes dotting the landscape, you'll get a sense of the area's rural roots. From the hacienda continue south and east another 4 mi to NM 68 and the small farming village of **Ranchos de Taos** ⑫. Watch for signs for **San Francisco de Asís Church,** which is on the east side of NM 68. The small plaza here contains several galleries worth checking out. Off the beaten path from Ranchos de Taos is the **Picurís Pueblo.**

TIMING

Set aside about two hours to tour the hacienda, a bit of Ranchos de Taos, and San Francisco de Asís Church. You'll need to make a day of this tour if you continue on to Picurís Pueblo.

### Sights to See

⑪ **La Hacienda de los Martínez.** Spare and fortlike, this adobe structure built between 1804 and 1827 on the bank of the Rio Pueblo served as

# FESTIVALS OF TRADITION

**S**EVERAL YEARLY FESTIVALS CELEBRATE the Native American and Hispanic roots of Taos. During the last weekend in September, La Hacienda de los Martínez hosts the **Old Taos Trade Fair,** a reenactment of autumn gatherings of the 1820s, when Plains Indians and trappers came to Taos to trade with the Spanish and the Pueblo Indians. The two-day event includes demonstrations of blacksmithing, weaving, and other crafts, a chili cook-off, native foods, music, and dancing.

The **Wool Festival** (www.taoswoolfestival.org), held in early October in Kit Carson Memorial Park, commemorates the long tradition of wool growing and weaving begun in the 16th century, when Spanish settlers brought the tough little churro sheep to northern New Mexico. Every aspect of the craft "from sheep to shawl" is demonstrated, including shearing, spinning, and weaving. Handmade woolen items are for sale, and you can taste favorite lamb dishes.

During the second weekend of July, the **Taos Pueblo Powwow** attracts Native Americans from many Indian nations. Visitors are welcome to watch the traditional drumming and dancing, shop at the arts-and-crafts market, and partake of fry bread, mutton, green chile, and other local delicacies.

a community refuge during Comanche and Apache raids. Its thick walls, which have few windows, surround two central courtyards. Don Antonio Severino Martínez was a farmer and trader; the hacienda was the final stop along El Camino Real (the Royal Road), the trade route the Spanish established between Mexico City and New Mexico. The restored period rooms here contain textiles, foods, and crafts of the early 19th century. There's a working blacksmith's shop, and weavers create beautiful textiles on reconstructed period looms. During the last weekend in September the hacienda hosts the Old Taos Trade Fair (☞ Festivals of Tradition, *below*). ✉ *Ranchitos Rd. (NM 240),* ☎ *505/ 758–0505.* ⊠ *$5 (or use Kit Carson Historic Museums of Taos joint ticket).* ☉ *Apr.–Oct., daily 9–5; Nov.–Mar., daily 10–4.*

OFF THE BEATEN PATH **PICURÍS PUEBLO –** The Picurís (Keresan for "those who paint") Native Americans once lived in six- and seven-story dwellings similar to those still standing at the Taos Pueblo, but these were abandoned in the wake of 18th-century Pueblo uprisings. Relatively isolated about 30 mi south of Taos, Picurís, one of the smallest pueblos in New Mexico, is surrounded by the timberland of the Carson National Forest. The 270-member Tiwa-speaking Picurís tribe is a sovereign nation and has no treaties with any country, including the United States. You can tour the village and 700-year-old ruins of kivas (ceremonial rooms) and storage areas, which were excavated in 1961. The exhibits in the pueblo's museum include pottery and some ruins. The Hidden Valley Restaurant also has a gift shop. Fishing, picnicking, and camping are allowed at nearby trout-stocked Pu-Na and Tu-Tah lakes. Fishing and camping permits can be obtained at the restaurant (no state fishing license is required). The pueblo honors its patron saint, San Lorenzo, with a festival on August 9 and 10. An example of the Picurís people's enterprising spirit is their majority interest in the lovely Hotel Santa Fe in the state's capital city; many pueblo members commute to work there. ✉ NM 75, Peñasco *(from Ranchos de Taos head south on NM 518, east on NM 75, and turn right at signs for village; from NM 68 head east on NM 75 and make a left into village)*, ☎ 505/587–2519, WEB www.picurispueblo. com. ✎ *Museum free, self-guided walking or driving tour $1.75, still-camera permit $5 (includes $1.75 fee for camera holder), video camera or sketching permit $10 (includes $1.75 tour fee).* ☉ *Daily 8–5, but call ahead especially Labor Day–Memorial Day, when the pueblo is sometimes closed.*

⑫ **Ranchos de Taos.** A few minutes' drive south of the center of Taos, this village still retains some of its rural atmosphere despite the highway traffic passing through. Huddled around its famous adobe church and dusty plaza are cheerful, remodeled shops and galleries standing shoulder to shoulder with crumbling adobe shells. This ranching, farming, and budding small-business community was an early home to Taos Native Americans before being settled by Spaniards in 1716. While many of the adobe dwellings have seen better days, the shops, modest galleries, taco stands, and two fine restaurants point to an ongoing revival.

The massive bulk of **San Francisco de Asís Church** (✉ NM 68, 500 yards south of NM 518, Ranchos de Taos, ☎ 505/758–2754) is an enduring attraction. The Spanish Mission–style church was erected in 1815 as a spiritual and physical refuge from raiding Apaches, Utes, and Comanches. In 1979 the deteriorated church was rebuilt with traditional adobe bricks by community volunteers. Every spring a group gathers to re-mud the facade. The earthy, clean lines of the exterior walls and supporting bulwarks have inspired generations of painters and photographers. The late-afternoon light provides the best exposure of the heavily buttressed rear of the church—though today's image-takers face the challenge of framing the architecturally pure lines through rows of parked cars and a large, white sign put up by church officials; morning light is best for the front. Bells in the twin belfries call Taoseños to services on Sunday and holidays. From Monday through Saturday from 9 to 4 you can step inside. In the parish hall nearby a 15-minute video presentation every half hour describes the history and restoration of the church and explains the mysterious painting, *Shadow of the Cross,* on which each evening the shadow of a cross appears over Christ's shoulder. Scientific studies made on the canvas and the paint pigments cannot explain the phenomenon. ✉ *Paseo del Pueblo Sur (NM 68), about 4 mi south of Taos Plaza.*

NEED A
BREAK? The storefront **Ranchos Coffee Company** (✉ 1574 Paseo del Pueblo Sur, ☎ 505/751–0653) has fresh coffee, tea, pastries, and sandwiches.

## Taos Pueblo to Rio Grande Gorge

### A Good Drive

Drive 2 mi north on Paseo del Pueblo Norte (NM 68), and keep your eyes peeled for the signs on the right, beyond the post office, directing you to **Taos Pueblo** ⑬. To reach the **Millicent Rogers Museum** ⑭ next, return to NM 68 to head north and make a left onto County Road BA030. If you find yourself at the intersection with U.S. 64 and 150, you've gone too far. Continue down the county road to the big adobe wall; the sign for the museum is on the right. This rural road eventually connects back onto Upper Ranchitos Road. After exploring the museum, return to NM 68 north; then make a left on U.S. 64 west to the **Rio Grande Gorge Bridge** ⑮, a stunning marriage of natural wonder and human engineering. Bring along sturdy hiking shoes and plenty of water and snacks for an invigorating walk down into the gorge. But remember, what goes down must come up, and it's an arduous path.

TIMING

Plan on spending 1½ hours at the pueblo. Taos can get hot in summer, but if you visit the pueblo in the morning, you'll avoid the heat and the crowds. Winters can be cold and windy, so dress warmly. If your visit coincides with a ceremony observance, set aside several hours, because the ceremonies, though they are worth the wait, never start on time. Two hours should be enough time to take in the museum and the grandeur of the Rio Grande Gorge Bridge.

## Sights to See

⑭ **Millicent Rogers Museum.** More than 5,000 pieces of Native American and Hispanic art, the core of Standard Oil heiress Millicent Rogers's private collection, are on exhibit here: baskets, blankets, rugs, jewelry, katsina dolls, carvings, paintings, and rare religious and secular artifacts. Of major importance are the pottery and ceramics of Maria Martinez and other potters from San Ildefonso Pueblo. Docents conduct guided tours by appointment, and the museum hosts lectures, films, workshops, and demonstrations. ⊠ *1504 Millicent Rogers Rd. (from Taos Plaza head north on Paseo del Pueblo Norte and left at the sign for C.R. BA030—also called Millicent Rogers Rd. or Museum Rd.),* ☎ *505/758–2462,* WEB *www.millicentrogers.com.* ⊡ *$6.* ☉ *Apr.–Sept., daily 10–5; Nov.–Mar., Tues.–Sun. 10–5.*

⑮ **Rio Grande Gorge Bridge.** It's a breathtaking experience to see the Rio Grande flowing 650 ft underfoot. The bridge is the second-highest expansion bridge in the country. Hold on to your camera and eyeglasses when looking down, and watch out for low-flying planes. The Taos Municipal Airport is close by, and daredevil private pilots have been known to challenge one another to fly under the bridge. Shortly after daybreak, hot air balloons fly above and even inside the gorge. ⊠ *U.S. 64, 12 mi west of town.*

★ ☾ ⑬ **Taos Pueblo.** For nearly 1,000 years the mud-and-straw adobe walls of Taos Pueblo have sheltered Tiwa-speaking Native Americans. A United Nations World Heritage Site, this is the largest multistory pueblo structure in the United States. The two main buildings, Hlauuma (north house) and Hlaukwima (south house), separated by a creek, are believed to be of a similar age, probably constructed between 1000 and 1450. The dwellings have common walls but no connecting doorways—the Tiwas gained access only from the top, via ladders that were retrieved after entering. Small buildings and corrals are scattered about.

The pueblo today appears much as it did when the first Spanish explorers arrived in New Mexico in 1540. The adobe walls glistening with mica caused the conquistadors to believe they had discovered one of the fabled Seven Cities of Gold. The outside surfaces are continuously maintained by replastering with thin layers of mud, and the interior walls are frequently coated with thin washes of white clay. Some walls are several feet thick in places. The roofs of each of the five-story structures are supported by large timbers, or *vigas,* hauled down from the mountain forests. Pine or aspen *latillas* (smaller pieces of wood) are placed side by side between the vigas; the entire roof is then packed with dirt.

Even after 400 years of Spanish and Anglo presence in Taos, inside the pueblo the traditional Native American way of life has endured. Tribal custom allows no electricity or running water in Hlauuma and Hlaukwima, where varying numbers (usually fewer than 100) of Taos Native Americans live full-time. About 2,000 others live in conventional homes on the pueblo's 95,000 acres. The crystal-clear Rio Pueblo de Taos, originating high above in the mountains at the sacred Blue Lake, is the primary source of water for drinking and irrigating. Bread is still baked in *hornos* (outdoor domed ovens). Artisans of the Taos Pueblo produce and sell (tax-free) traditionally handcrafted wares, such as mica-flecked pottery and silver jewelry. Great hunters, the Taos Native Americans are also known for their work with animal skins and their excellent moccasins, boots, and drums.

Although the population is about 80% Catholic, the people of Taos Pueblo, like most Pueblo Native Americans, also maintain their native religious traditions. At Christmas and other sacred holidays, for instance, immediately after Mass, dancers dressed in seasonal sacred garb proceed down the aisle of St. Jerome Chapel, drums beating and rattles shaking, to begin other religious rites.

The pueblo **Church of San Geronimo,** or St. Jerome, the patron saint of Taos Pueblo, was completed in 1850 to replace the one destroyed by the U.S. Army in 1847 during the Mexican War. With its smooth symmetry, stepped portal, and twin bell towers, the church is a popular subject for photographers and artists (though the taking of photographs inside is discouraged).

The public is invited to certain ceremonial dances held throughout the year: January 1, Turtle Dance; January 6, Buffalo or Deer Dance; May 3, Feast of Santa Cruz Foot Race and Corn Dance; June 13, Feast of San Antonio Corn Dance; June 24, Feast of San Juan Corn Dance; second weekend in July, Taos Pueblo Powwow; July 25–26, Feast of Santa Ana and Santiago Corn Dance; September 29–30, Feast of San Geronimo Sunset Dance; December 24, Vespers and Bonfire Procession; December 25, Deer Dance or Matachines. While you're at the pueblo, respect the RESTRICTED AREA signs that protect the privacy of residents and native religious sites; do not enter private homes or open any doors not clearly labeled as curio shops; do not photograph tribal members without asking permission; do not enter the cemetery grounds; and do not wade in the Rio Pueblo de Taos, which is considered sacred and is the community's sole source of drinking water. ⊠ *Head to the right off Paseo del Pueblo Norte just past Best Western Kachina Lodge,* ☎ *505/758–1028,* WEB *www.taospueblo.com.* 🎫 *Tourist fees $10. Guided tours by appointment. Still-camera permit $10 (note: cameras that may look commercial, such as those with telephoto lenses, might be denied a permit); video-camera permit $20. Commercial photography, sketching, or painting only by prior permission from governor's office (505/758–1028); fees vary; apply at least 10 days in advance.* ☉ *Apr.–Nov., daily 8–4; Oct.–Mar., daily 8:30–4. Closed for funerals, religious ceremonies, and for a 2-month "quiet time" in late winter or early spring, and the last part of Aug.; call ahead before visiting at these times.*

NEED A BREAK?

Look for signs that read FRY BREAD on dwellings in the pueblo: you can enter the kitchen and buy a piece of fresh bread dough that is flattened and deep-fried until puffy and golden brown and then topped with honey or powdered sugar.

# DINING

For a place as remote as Taos, the dining scene is surprisingly varied. You can find the usual coffee shops and Mexican-style eateries but also

Taos Dining

restaurants serving creatively prepared Continental, Italian, and south-western cuisine.

## Downtown Taos

### American

$$ ✗ **Ogelvie's Bar and Grill.** On the second floor of an old two-story adobe building, Ogelvie's is the perfect spot for people-watching from on high, especially from the outdoor patio in summer. You won't find any culinary surprises here, just dependable meat-and-potato dishes. The sure bets are Angus beef, lamb sirloin, and meat or cheese enchiladas. ⊠ *East side of Taos Plaza, ☎ 505/758–8866. Reservations not accepted. AE, DC, MC, V.*

### American/Casual

$ ✗ **Eske's Brew Pub.** This casual dining and quaffing pub is favored by off-duty ski patrollers and river guides. The menu mostly covers hearty sandwiches with soup and salad. The microbrewery downstairs produces everything from nutty, dark stout to light ales. There's live music on weekends. ⊠ *106 Des Georges La., ☎ 505/758–1517. MC, V.*

$ ✗ **Michael's Kitchen.** This casual, homey restaurant serves up a bit of everything—you can order a hamburger while your friend who can't get enough chile can order another enchilada. Brunch is popular with the locals, and amusing asides to the waitstaff over the intercom contribute to the energetic buzz. Breakfast, lunch, and dinner are served daily, but be sure to order dinner by 8:30 PM. ⊠ *304 Paseo del Pueblo Norte, ☎ 505/758–4178. Reservations not accepted. AE, D, MC, V.*

### Cafés

$ ✗ **Dragonfly Café.** This breakfast and lunch café bakes its own bread and serves large and tasty omelets, Swedish pancakes, Vietnamese chicken salad, and panini sandwiches. You can sit out front when it's warm and watch the tourists go by. ⊠ *402 Paseo del Pueblo Norte, ☎ 505/737–5859. MC, V.*

### Contemporary

$$$–$$$$ ✗ **Apple Tree.** Named for the large tree in the umbrella-shaded courtyard, this is a great lunch and dinner spot in a historic adobe a block from the Plaza. Among the well-crafted dishes are barbecued duck fajitas and mango chicken enchiladas. The restaurant has received regular awards for its wine selection, which includes many options by the glass. Sunday brunch is served from 11 to 3. Expect about a 15-minute wait if you don't have a reservation. ⊠ *123 Bent St., ☎ 505/758–1900. AE, D, DC, MC, V.*

$$–$$$$ ✗ **Doc Martin's.** The restaurant of the Taos Inn takes its name from the building's original owner, a local physician who performed operations and delivered babies in rooms that are now the dining areas. Try the piñon-crusted salmon and the Aztec chocolate mousse with roasted-banana sauce. The wine list has won awards from *Wine Spectator* and other organizations. ⊠ *Taos Inn, 125 Paseo del Pueblo Norte, ☎ 505/758–1977. MC, V.*

$$–$$$$ ✗ **Lambert's of Taos.** The signature dishes at this restaurant 2½ blocks south of the Plaza include curried crab cakes and pepper-crusted lamb. California's finest vintages receive top billing on the wine list. ⊠ *309 Paseo del Pueblo Sur, ☎ 505/758–1009. AE, DC, MC, V. No lunch.*

$$$ ✗ **Byzantium.** Off a grassy courtyard near the Blumenschein and Harwood museums, this restaurant offers an eclectic menu with touches of Asia, the Middle East, and Europe in dishes such as Asian seafood cakes, duck curry, and vegetable potpie. ⊠ *Ledoux St. and La Placita, ☎ 505/751–0805. AE, MC, V. Closed Tues.–Wed. No lunch.*

$$-$$$   ✕ **La Luna.** In a colorful two-level space with a mural along one wall, the former New Yorkers who own the place have attracted a local clientele fond of the pasta dishes (like penne with cilantro-citrus sauce), the daily fish specials, and pizza from the wood-fired oven. Also for sale: the house apple-balsamic vinaigrette and salsa. ☒ *225 Paseo del Pueblo Sur,* ☏ *505/751–0023. AE, D, MC, V. No lunch Sun.*

$–$$   ✕ **Bravo!** This restaurant and full bar inside an upscale grocery store and beer and wine shop is a great stop for gourmet picnic fixings or an on-site meal. You can feast on anything from a turkey sandwich to Louisiana crawfish—and there's a children's menu to boot. The beer and wine selection is formidable. ☒ *1353A Paseo del Pueblo Sur,* ☏ *505/758–8100. Reservations not accepted. MC, V. Closed Sun.*

## Deli

$$   ✕ **Bent Street Deli.** Great soups, sandwiches, salads, and desserts are the trademarks of the unassuming Bent Street Deli, which serves beer, wine, and gourmet coffees. Reubens are on the menu for East Coasters and others who can't live without a dose of pastrami. Dinners are a little fancier: fresh salmon, pork loin with red wine mushroom glaze, and shrimp in pesto sauce. Breakfast is served until 11 AM. ☒ *120 Bent St.,* ☏ *505/758–5787. MC, V. Closed Sun.*

$   ✕ **Taos Wrappers.** Owner-chefs Kim Wever and Greg Payton have a loyal clientele for take-out lunch, and a small eat-in space with tiny tables. Pesto chicken, roasted veggies, and curried tuna are among the healthful ingredients inside flavored tortilla wraps. There are soups, salads, and desserts, too. ☒ *616 Paseo del Pueblo Sur,* ☏ *505/751–9727. No credit cards.*

## Hawaiian

$–$$   ✕ **Island Coffees & Hawaiian Grill.** If you're tired of burritos, stop in at Island Coffees for Maui crab cakes or mango coconut chicken. Lots of noodle dishes and stir fries are on the menu, along with Kona coffees. You can even check your e-mail or surf the Web. Breakfast is available from 6:30 AM. ☒ *1032 Paseo del Pueblo Sur,* ☏ *505/758–7777. MC, V. Closed Sun.*

## Middle Eastern

$   ✕ **Sheva Café.** Delectable falafel, eggplant salad, and stuffed grape leaves served with homemade pita bread have made this vegetarian café a local favorite. The friendly Israeli staff will make you feel at home. ☒ *812B Paseo del Pueblo Norte,* ☏ *505/737–9290. No credit cards. No dinner Fri.–Sat.*

## Southwestern

$   ✕ **Guadalajara Grill.** Tasty Mexican cuisine is the feature here, served quickly from the open, spotless kitchens and popular enough with local patrons that there is one on each end of town. You'll hear Spanish banter across the kitchen counter while you watch your burritos or enchiladas being prepared. ☒ *822 Paseo del Pueblo Norte,* ☏ *505/737–0816;* ☒ *1384 Paseo del Pueblo Sur,* ☏ *505/751–0063. MC, V.*

$   ✕ **Orlando's.** This family-run local favorite features authentic-tasting *carne adovada* (red chile–marinated pork), blue-corn enchiladas, and an innovative shrimp burrito, among other offerings. Eat in the cozy dining room or call ahead for takeout. ☒ *114 Don Juan Valdez La., off Paseo del Pueblo Norte,* ☏ *505/751–1450. No credit cards. Closed Sun.*

# South of Taos

## American

$$$–$$$$   ✕ **Stakeout Grill and Bar.** On Outlaw Hill in the foothills of the Sangre de Cristo Mountains, this old adobe homestead has 100-mi-long

views and sunsets that dazzle. The sturdy fare includes New York strip steaks, Alaskan crab legs, swordfish steaks, duck, chicken, and daily pasta specials. The restaurant's decor will take you back to the days of the Wild West, even though the owners hail from northern Italy. ⊠ *Stakeout Dr., 8½ mi south of Taos Plaza, east of NM 68 (look for cowboy sign)*, ☎ *505/751–3815. AE, D, DC, MC, V.*

### Contemporary

$$$–$$$$ ✕ **Joseph's Table.** Widely acclaimed Joseph's is a rustic, dramatic
★ stage for carefully prepared fare like grilled corn chipotle aioli with cotija cheese, duck breast on corn pudding, and pepper steak with garlic-mashed red potatoes. The first-rate desserts are more ornate. ⊠ *4167 Paseo del Pueblo Sur (NM 68), Ranchos de Taos*, ☎ *505/751–4512. AE, D, DC, MC, V.*

$$$–$$$$ ✕ **Trading Post Cafe.** A western ambience, impeccable service, and an
★ imaginative menu have made the Trading Post a popular dining spot in Ranchos. The marinated salmon gravlax appetizer is exceptional, and the paella is a bounty for two. Try the homemade raspberry sorbet or the flan. To park, turn east onto Hwy. 518 (Talpa Road) just north of the restaurant, and then walk back along Talpa Road to get to the entrance. ⊠ *4179 Paseo del Pueblo Sur (NM 68), Ranchos de Taos*, ☎ *505/758–5089. D, DC, MC, V. Closed Sun.*

## North of Taos

### Cafés

$ ✕ **Abe's Cantina y Cocina.** Have your breakfast burrito, rolled tacos, or homemade tamales at one of the small tables crowded next to the canned goods, or take it on a picnic. You never know when the place might be closed for golf outings. ⊠ *Taos Ski Valley Rd. (C.R. 150), Arroyo Seco*, ☎ *505/776–8643. No credit cards. Closed Sun.*

$ ✕ **Taos Cow.** A.k.a. Casa Vaca, this is headquarters for ice cream made from growth-hormone-free cows (featured in area health food stores). They also serve coffee, chai, breakfast, and lunch. Favorites among the three-dozen ice cream flavors are cherry ristra, piñon caramel, and the true test—vanilla. ⊠ *482 NM 150, Arroyo Seco*, ☎ *505/776–5640. MC, V.*

### Contemporary

$$$$ ✕ **Momentitos de la Vida.** Chef Chris Maher's restaurant brings an am-
★ bitious, worldly focus to dining out in the area. Outstanding food and wine are served in elegant surroundings. An evening's entrée might be apricot-glazed Cornish hen or pistachio-encrusted rack of lamb, but save room for desserts, which change nightly. There's live music in the piano bar several nights a week. Sunday brunch allows those on a tighter budget to enjoy the food and atmosphere. ⊠ *Taos Ski Valley Rd. (State Rd. 150)*, ☎ *505/776–3333. AE, MC, V. Closed Mon. No lunch.*

### Italian

$$$ ✕ **Villa Fontana.** Entering this restaurant, which serves northern Ital-
★ ian cuisine, is like walking into a sophisticated Italian country inn: warm coral walls, candlelight, gleaming hardwood tables, starched linens, and courtly service. Notable dishes include cream of wild mushroom soup, osso buco, and fresh fish and game. Lunch is served in the garden. ⊠ *NM 522, 5 mi north of Taos Plaza, Arroyo Hondo*, ☎ *505/758–5800. AE, D, DC, MC, V. Closed Sun. No lunch Nov.–May.*

### Southwestern

$$–$$$ ✕ **Old Blinking Light.** Just past the landmark "old blinking light" (now a regular stoplight), this rambling adobe is known for its steaks, ribs, and margaritas. In summer you can sit out in the walled garden and

take in the spectacular mountain view. There's a wine shop on the premises. ⊠ *Ski Valley Rd., El Prado,* ☎ *505/776–8787. AE, MC, V.*

# LODGING

The hotels and motels along NM 68 (Paseo del Pueblo Sur and Norte) suit every need and budget; rates vary little between big-name chains and smaller establishments. Make advance reservations and expect higher rates during the ski season (usually from late December to early April) and in the summer. Skiers have many choices for overnighting, from accommodations in the town of Taos to spots snuggled up right beside the slopes.

The best deals in town are the bed-and-breakfasts. Mostly family-owned, they provide personal service, delicious breakfasts, and many extras that hotels charge for. The B&Bs are often in old adobes that have been refurbished with style and flair.

## Downtown Taos

$$$$    ⊡ **Touchstone Inn.** D. H. Lawrence visited this house when Miriam De-
★       Witt owned it in 1929. The inn's owner, Taos artist Bren Price, has filled the rooms, named after famous Taos literary figures, with tasteful antique and modern pieces. The grounds overlook part of the Taos Pueblo lands, and this makes for a quiet stay within a mile of Taos Plaza. Some suites have fireplaces. Early morning coffee is poured in the living room, and breakfasts with inventive presentations are served in the glassed-in patio. ⊠ *110 Mabel Dodge La. (Box 1885, 87571),* ☎ *505/758–0192 or 800/758–0192,* ℻ *505/758–3498,* WEB *www.touchstoneinn.com. 8 suites. In-room VCRs, hot tub. MC, V. BP.*

$$$–$$$$   ⊡ **Casa de las Chimeneas.** Tile hearths, French doors, and traditional
★       viga ceilings grace the House of Chimneys B&B, 2½ blocks from the Plaza and secluded behind thick walls. Each room in the 1912 structure has a private entrance, a fireplace, handmade New Mexican furniture, and a bar stocked with complimentary beverages. All rooms overlook the gardens. Two-course breakfasts are served, and late-afternoon hors d'oeuvres are generous enough to be a light meal. ⊠ *405 Cordoba Rd. (Box 5303, 87571),* ☎ *505/758–4777 or 877/758–4777,* ℻ *505/758–3976,* WEB *www.visittaos.com. 8 rooms, 2 suites. Minibars, in-room VCRs, outdoor hot tub, gym, sauna, laundry service; no smoking. AE, MC, V. BP.*

$$$–$$$$   ⊡ **Inn on La Loma Plaza.** The walls surrounding this Pueblo Revival
★       building date from the early 1800s; the inn itself is listed on the National Register of Historic Places. The rooms have kiva fireplaces and Mexican-tile bathrooms; the living room has a well-stocked library with books on Taos and art. Owners Jerry and Peggy Davis provide helpful advice about the area and serve a generous breakfast, afternoon snacks, and evening coffee. Guests have privileges at the nearby health club (but there's an outdoor hot tub here too). ⊠ *315 Ranchitos Rd. (Box 4159, 87571),* ☎ *505/758–1717 or 800/530–3040,* ℻ *505/751–0155,* WEB *www.vacationtaos.com. 5 rooms, 2 studios. Some kitchenettes, hot tub, library. AE, D, MC, V. BP.*

$$–$$$$   ⊡ **Hacienda del Sol.** Art patron Mabel Dodge Luhan bought this
★       house in the 1920s and lived here with her husband, Tony Luhan, while building their main house. It was also their private retreat and guest house for visiting notables; Frank Waters wrote *People of the Valley* here. Most of the rooms contain kiva fireplaces, southwestern handcrafted furniture, and original artwork. The secluded outdoor hot tub has a stunning view of Taos Mountain. Breakfast is a gourmet affair. ⊠ *109 Mabel Dodge La. (Box 177, 87571),* ☎ *505/758–0287,* ℻ *505/*

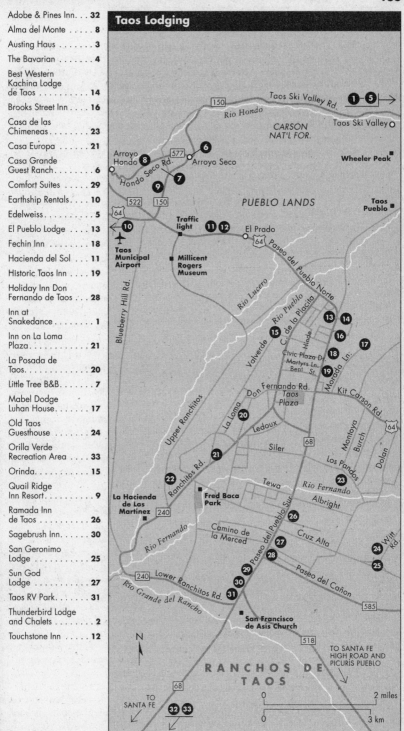

**Taos Lodging**

758–5895, WEB *www.taoshaciendadelsol.com. 11 rooms. Outdoor hot tub. MC, V. BP.*

$$$ ⬛ **Earthship Rentals.** "Earthships" are passive solar homes, built partly underground, that exist "off the grid," with self-sustaining energy, water, and waste systems. Three of these uniquely charming structures are available, by the night or week, on the mesa northwest of Taos, so you can experience for yourself the home of the future. ✉ *Solar Survival, Box 1041, 87571,* ☎ *505/751–0462,* FAX *505/751–1005,* WEB *www.earthship.org. 3 houses. Kitchens; no room phones, no TV in some rooms. AE, MC, V.*

$$$ ⬛ **Ramada Inn de Taos.** More Taos than Ramada, the two-story adobe-style hotel welcomes you with a lobby fireplace, desert colors, western art, and Native American pottery. The rooms have an inviting southwestern flavor; some have fireplaces. ✉ *615 Paseo del Pueblo Sur, 87571,* ☎ *505/758–2900 or 800/659–8267,* FAX *505/758–1662. 124 rooms. Dining room, indoor pool, hot tub, lounge, meeting rooms. AE, D, DC, MC, V.*

$$–$$$ ⬛ **Fechin Inn.** This graceful Pueblo Revival structure on the grounds
★ of the Fechin Institute (to which guests have free admission) is adjacent to Kit Carson Memorial Park. Painter Nicolai Fechin's daughter, Eya, participated in the planning; Fechin reproductions adorn the rooms, and the woodwork in the lobby is based on the artist's designs. Breakfast is available, as are cocktails in the evening. Rooms are comfortable, if nondescript; most have private balconies or patios. Pets are welcome and ski storage is available. ✉ *227 Paseo del Pueblo Norte, 87571,* ☎ *505/751–1000 or 800/811–2933,* FAX *505/751–7338,* WEB *www.fechin–inn.com. 71 rooms, 14 suites. Gym, massage, meeting rooms. AE, D, DC, MC, V. CP.*

$$–$$$ ⬛ **Little Tree B&B.** In a real adobe house in the open country between
★ Taos and the Ski Valley, Little Tree's rooms are built around a garden courtyard and have spectacular views of Taos Mountain. Some have kiva fireplaces and Jacuzzis, and all are decorated in true southwestern style. A full breakfast and afternoon refreshments are served. ✉ *Hondo-Seco Rd. (PO Drawer ii, 87571),* ☎ *505/776–8467 or 800/334–8467,* WEB *www.littletreebandb.com. 4 rooms. Some in-room hot tubs; no TV in some rooms. AE, D, MC, V. BP.*

$$–$$$ ⬛ **Mabel Dodge Luhan House.** This National Historic Landmark was once the home of the heiress who drew the literati to the area. Guests included D. H. Lawrence, Georgia O'Keeffe, and Willa Cather. The main house, which has kept its simple, rustic feel, has nine guest rooms; there are eight more in a modern building, as well as a two-bedroom cottage. You can sleep in Mabel's own hand-carved bed or stay in the O'Keeffe Room or Ansel Adams Room. The inn is frequently used for artistic, cultural, and educational workshops. ✉ *240 Morada La. (Box 558, 87571),* ☎ *505/751–9686 or 800/846–2235,* FAX *505/737–0365,* WEB *www.mabeldodgeluhan.com. 15 rooms, 2 with shared bath; 1 cottage. Meeting rooms. AE, MC, V. BP.*

$$–$$$ ⬛ **La Posada de Taos.** A couple of blocks from Taos Plaza, this provincial adobe has beam ceilings, a portal, and the intimacy of a private hacienda. Five guest rooms are in the main house; the sixth is a separate cottage with a queen-size four-poster bed, a sitting room, and a fireplace. The rooms have mountain views or face a flowering courtyard; all but one of the rooms have adobe, kiva-style fireplaces. Breakfasts are hearty. ✉ *309 Juanita La. (Box 1118, 87571),* ☎ *505/758–8164 or 800/645–4803,* FAX *505/751–4694,* WEB *www.laposadadetaos.com. 5 rooms, 1 cottage. Some in-room hot tubs, hot tub. AE, MC, V. BP.*

$$–$$$ ⬛ **Orinda.** Built in 1947, this adobe estate has spectacular views and country privacy. The one- and two-bedroom suites have separate entrances, kiva-style fireplaces, traditional viga ceilings, and Mexican-

tile baths. Two rooms share a common sitting room. One suite has a Jacuzzi. The hearty breakfast is served family-style in the soaring two-story sun atrium amid a gallery of artworks, all for sale. ⊠ *461 Valverde (Box 4451, 87571),* ☎ *505/758–8581 or 800/847–1837,* ⨳ *505/751–4895,* WEB *www.orindabb.com. 5 suites. Some in-room hot tubs; no smoking. AE, MC, V. BP.*

$$–$$$ 🛏 **Sagebrush Inn.** A tad run-down but still charming, this Pueblo Mission–style 1929 adobe 3 mi south of the Plaza contains authentic Navajo rugs, rare pottery, southwestern and Spanish antiques, and paintings by southwestern masters. Georgia O'Keeffe once lived and painted in one of the third-story rooms. Many of the bedrooms have kiva-style fireplaces; some have balconies looking out to the Sangre de Cristo Mountains. There's country-western music nightly. The Sagebrush Village offers condominium family lodging, too. ⊠ *1508 Paseo del Pueblo Sur (Box 557, 87571),* ☎ *505/758–2254 or 800/428–3626,* ⨳ *505/758–5077,* WEB *www.sagebrushinn.com. 68 rooms, 32 suites. 2 restaurants, in-room data ports, pool, 2 hot tubs, bar, lounge, meeting rooms. AE, D, DC, MC, V.*

$$–$$$ 🛏 **San Geronimo Lodge.** On a small street off Kit Carson Road, this lodge built in 1925 sits on 2½ acres that front majestic Taos Mountain and back up to the Carson National Forest. A balcony library, attractive grounds, many rooms with fireplaces, two rooms designed for people with disabilities, and a room for guests with a pet are among the draws. A full breakfast is served, and the hotel staff will arrange ski packages. ⊠ *1101 Witt Rd., 87571,* ☎ *505/751–3776 or 800/894–4119,* ⨳ *505/751–1493,* WEB *www.sangeronimolodge.com. 18 rooms. Pool, hot tub, massage, some pets allowed. AE, D, DC, MC, V.*

$–$$$ 🛏 **Sun God Lodge.** Though inexpensive, this motel has old adobe charm with basic amenities; some rooms have kitchenettes and fireplaces. Right on the main highway, the Sun God is convenient to restaurants and historic sites. ⊠ *919 Paseo del Pueblo Sur, 87571,* ☎ *505/758–3162 or 800/821–2437,* ⨳ *505/758–1716,* WEB *www.sungodlodge.com. 55 rooms. Hot tub, laundry room. AE, D, MC, V.*

$$ 🛏 **Best Western Kachina Lodge de Taos.** Just north of Taos Plaza, this two-story Pueblo-style adobe carries the theme of the katsina (a figure representing a masked ancestral spirit) throughout. Guest rooms sustain the Native American motif, with handmade and hand-painted furnishings and colorful bedspreads. From Memorial Day to Labor Day a troupe from Taos Pueblo performs nightly ritual dances outside by firelight. ⊠ *413 Paseo del Pueblo Norte (Box NN, 87571),* ☎ *505/758–2275 or 800/522–4462,* ⨳ *505/758–9207,* WEB *www.kachinalodge.com. 113 rooms, 5 suites. Restaurant, coffee shop, pool, hot tub, bar, shops, meeting rooms. AE, D, DC, MC, V.*

$$ 🛏 **Brooks Street Inn.** An elaborately carved corbel arch, the handiwork of Japanese carpenter Yaichikido, spans the entrance to a shaded, walled garden. Fluffy pillows, fresh flowers, and paintings by local artists are among the grace notes in the rooms; some have fireplaces. Blue-corn pancakes with pineapple salsa, stuffed French toast with an apricot glaze, and other home-baked delights are served at breakfast. ⊠ *119 Brooks St. (Box 4954, 87571),* ☎ *505/758–1489 or 800/758–1489,* WEB *www.brooksstreetinn.com. 6 rooms. No smoking. AE, MC, V. BP.*

$$ 🛏 **Casa Europa.** This 17th-century estate on 6 acres, with views of pastures and mountains, is furnished with European antiques and southwestern pieces. The two main guest areas are light and airy, with comfortable chairs to relax in while the fireplace crackles. Breakfasts are elaborate, and complimentary homemade afternoon pastries are served, except during ski season, when they're replaced by evening hors d'oeuvres. ⊠ *840 Upper Ranchitos Rd. (HC 68, Box 3F, 87571),* ☎

*888/758–9798,* ☎ FAX *505/758–9798,* WEB *www.casaeuropa.com. 5 rooms, 2 suites. Hot tub, sauna, 2 lounges. AE, MC, V. BP.*

$$ ⊞ **Comfort Suites.** Each unit at this complex contains a living room with a sofa bed, a bedroom with a king- and a queen-size bed, a television in both rooms, a microwave oven, a coffeemaker, and a refrigerator. ⊠ *1500 Paseo del Pueblo Sur (Box 1268, 87571),* ☎ *505/751–1555 or 888/751–1555,* WEB *www.taoswebb.com/taoshotels/comfortsuites. 60 suites. In-room data ports, refrigerators, pool, hot tub. AE, D, DC, MC, V. BP.*

$$ ⊞ **El Pueblo Lodge.** This low-to-the-ground, pueblo-style adobe a few blocks north of Taos Plaza has practical in-room amenities and guest laundry rooms. The traditional southwestern furnishings and fireplaces in some rooms lend a homey feel. ⊠ *412 Paseo del Pueblo Norte (Box 92, 87571),* ☎ *505/758–8700 or 800/433–9612,* FAX *505/758–7321,* WEB *www.elpueblolodge.com. 61 rooms. Some kitchenettes, refrigerators, pool, hot tub, laundry facilities. AE, D, MC, V. CP.*

$$ ⊞ **Historic Taos Inn.** Mere steps from Taos Plaza, this hotel is listed on the National Register of Historic Places. The guest rooms are pleasant and comfortable, and in summer there's dining alfresco on the patio. The lobby, which also serves as seating for the Adobe Bar, is built around an old town well from which a fountain bubbles forth. Many shops and eateries are within walking distance of the inn, and its own restaurant, Doc Martin's, is quite popular itself. ⊠ *125 Paseo del Pueblo Norte, 87571,* ☎ *505/758–2233 or 800/826–7466,* FAX *505/758–5776,* WEB *www.taosinn.com. 36 rooms. Restaurant, bar, lounge, library. AE, DC, MC, V.*

$$ ⊞ **Holiday Inn Don Fernando de Taos.** The accommodations at this hotel with a Pueblo-style design are grouped around central courtyards and connected by walkways. Appointed with hand-carved New Mexican furnishings, some rooms have kiva-style fireplaces. There's a free shuttle to take guests to the town center. ⊠ *1005 Paseo del Pueblo Sur, 87571,* ☎ *505/758–4444 or 800/759–2736,* FAX *505/758–0055,* WEB *www.holiday-taos.com. 124 rooms. Restaurant, in-room data ports, some refrigerators, tennis court, indoor pool, hot tub, bar, lounge. AE, D, DC, MC, V.*

$$ ⊞ **Old Taos Guesthouse.** Once a ramshackle adobe hacienda, this homey B&B has been completely and lovingly outfitted with the owners' hand-carved doors and furniture, western artifacts, and antiques. Some rooms have the smallest bathrooms you'll ever encounter but have private entrances, and some have fireplaces. There are 80-mi views from the outdoor hot tub, and it's just a five-minute drive to town. The owners welcome families. Breakfasts are healthy and hearty. ⊠ *1028 Witt Rd. (Box 6552, 87571),* ☎ *800/758–5448,* ☎ FAX *505/758–5448,* WEB *www.oldtaos.com. 9 rooms. Hot tub. MC, V. BP.*

## Ranchos de Taos

$$–$$$$ ⊞ **Adobe & Pines Inn.** Native American and Mexican artifacts decorate the main house of this B&B, which has expansive mountain views. Part of the main building dates from 1830. The rooms contain Mexican-tiled baths, kiva fireplaces, fluffy goose-down pillows, and comforters. A separate cottage and two equally handsome casitas also house guests. The owners serve gourmet breakfasts in a sunny glass-enclosed patio. ⊠ *NM 68 and Llano Quemado (Box 837, Ranchos de Taos 87557),* ☎ *505/751–0947 or 800/723–8267,* FAX *505/758–8423,* WEB *www.adobepines.com. 5 rooms, 1 cottage, 2 casitas. 5 hot tubs, sauna; no smoking. AE, MC, V. BP.*

## Arroyo Seco

**$$$–$$$$**    ▢ **Alma del Monte.** Mountain views abound from the rooms and the courtyard of this B&B on the high plain between Taos and the ski valley. Heated saltillo-tiled floors, kiva fireplaces, whirlpool baths, Victorian antiques, generous breakfasts, and afternoon wine with hors d'oeuvres make it a hard place to leave, even for skiing. Children must be 16 or older. ✉ 372 Hondo Seco Rd. (Box 1434, Taos 87571), ☎ 505/776–2721 or 800/273–7203, FAX 505/776–8888, WEB www. almaspirit.com. 5 rooms. In-room hot tubs, hot tub. MC, V. BP.

**$$–$$$$**    ▢ **Casa Grande Guest Ranch.** Watch the stars and the lights of Taos twinkle as you soak in the hot tub of this B&B; morning views stretch for miles. Three comfortable rooms are integrated into the family home built not far from the property's historic hacienda on the flanks of El Salto Mountain. Breakfast burritos with all the trimmings will see you through a horseback ride up to the waterfalls. Children must be 18 and over. ✉ 75 Luis O. Torres Rd., Arroyo Seco 87514, ☎ 888/ 236–1303, FAX 505/776–2177, WEB www.guestranch.com. 3 rooms. Hot tub. AE, MC, V. BP.

**$$–$$$$**    ▢ **Quail Ridge Inn Resort.** On the way to Taos Ski Valley, this large resort has one- and two-story modern adobe bungalows that are comfy and efficient. Some suites have kitchens; all have fireplaces. The resort provides a host of recreational amenities, from organized trail rides to hot-tub soaks. Skiing, tennis, rafting, mountain-biking, and fly-fishing packages are available for groups or individuals. ✉ Taos Ski Valley Rd. (C.R. 150; Box 707, Taos 87571), ☎ 505/776–2211 or 800/624–4448, FAX 505/776–2949, WEB www.taoswebb.com/hotel/quailridge. 50 rooms, 60 suites. Restaurant, in-room data ports, 8 tennis courts, pool, gym, hot tub, racquetball, squash, volleyball, lounge, meeting rooms. AE, D, DC, MC, V.

## Camping

▵ **Orilla Verde Recreation Area.** You can hike, fish, and picnic at this area along the banks of the Rio Grande, 10 mi south of Ranchos de Taos, off NM 68 at NM 570. As for paying the camping fee, leave cash in an envelope provided, drop it in a tube, and the rangers will collect it. ✉ Bureau of Land Management, Cruz Alta Rd., Taos 87571, ☎ 505/758–8851. Flush toilets, drinking water, fire grates, picnic tables. 70 tent sites. 💲 $10. No credit cards. Closed mid-Oct.–Apr.

▵ **Taos RV Park.** The sites are grassy, with a few small trees, in this park 3½ mi from Taos Plaza near the junction of NM 68 and NM 518. A recreation room has video games, TV, and a pool table. Some RV supplies are for sale. There are horseshoes, billiards, and a kitchen area. ✉ 1800 Paseo del Pueblo Sur, next to the Budget Host Inn (Box 729F, Ranchos de Taos 87557), ☎ 505/758–2524 or 800/323–6009, WEB www.newmex.com/rv. Flush toilets, full hook-ups, drinking water, showers, picnic tables, electricity, public telephone, general store, playground. 62 RV sites, 28 tent sites. 💲 RV sites $24–$27, tent sites $18. D, MC, V.

# NIGHTLIFE AND THE ARTS

Evening entertainment is modest in Taos. Some motels and hotels present solo musicians or small combos in their bars and lounges. Everything from down-home blues bands to Texas two-step dancing blossoms on Saturday and Sunday nights in winter. In summer things heat up during the week as well. For information about what's going on around town pick up Taos Magazine. The weekly Taos News, pub-

lished on Thursday, carries arts and entertainment information in the
"Tempo" section. The arts scene is much more lively, with festivals every
season for nearly every taste.

# Nightlife

## Bars and Lounges

The **Adobe Bar** (⊠ Taos Inn, 125 Paseo del Pueblo Norte, ☎ 505/758–
2233), a local meet-and-greet spot known as "Taos's living room," books
talented acts, from solo guitarists to small folk groups and, two or three
nights a week, jazz musicians. **Fernando's Hideaway** (⊠ Holiday Inn,
1005 Paseo del Pueblo Sur, ☎ 505/758–4444) occasionally presents
live entertainment—jazz, blues, hiphop, R&B, salsa, vocals, and country music. Saturday is reserved for karaoke. Lavish complimentary happy-
hour buffets are laid out on weekday evenings.

## Cabaret

The **Kachina Lodge Cabaret** (⊠ 413 Paseo del Pueblo Norte, ☎ 505/
758–2275) brings in headline acts, such as Arlo Guthrie and the Dirty
Dozen Brass Band, on a regular basis and has dancing.

## Coffeehouse

**Caffe Tazza** (⊠ 122 Kit Carson Rd., ☎ 505/758–8706) presents free
evening performances throughout the week—folk singing, jazz, blues,
poetry, and fiction readings.

## Country-and-Western

The **Sagebrush Inn** (⊠ 1508 Paseo del Pueblo Sur, ☎ 505/758–2254)
hosts musicians and dancing in its lobby lounge. If you hear that South
by Southwest is playing, check out the three-man band. There's no cover
charge, and if you show up on a Thursday, you can learn to two-step.

## Jazz and Dance Clubs

**Alley Cantina** (⊠ 121 Teresina La., ☎ 505/758–2121) has jazz, folk,
and blues—as well as shuffleboard and board games for those not moved
to dance. The piano bar at **Momentitos de la Vida** (⊠ C.R. 150, Arroyo Seco, ☎ 505/776–3333) often presents jazz and bossa nova.
**Thunderbird Lodge** (⊠ 3 Thunderbird Rd., ☎ 505/776–2280) in the
Taos Ski Valley has free jazz nights and country-and-western swing dancing. **Western Sky Café** (⊠ 1398 Weimer Rd., ☎ 505/751–7771) offers evenings of blues and jazz standards.

# The Arts

Long a beacon for visual artists, Taos is also becoming a magnet for
touring musicians, especially in the summer, when performers and au-
diences are drawn to the heady high desert atmosphere. Festivals celebrate the visual arts, music, poetry, and film.

The **Taos Art Association** (⊠ 133 Paseo del Pueblo Norte, ☎ 505/758–
2052) has information about art-related events in Taos.The **Taos Community Auditorium** (⊠ 145 Paseo del Pueblo Norte, ☎ 505/758–4677)
presents plays, dance, concerts, and movies.

The **Taos Spring Arts Festival** (☎ 505/758–3873 or 800/732–8267, WEB
www.taosguide.com), held throughout Taos during the month of May,
is a showcase for the visual, performing, and literary arts of the community and allows you to rub elbows with the many artists who call
Taos home. The Mother's Day Arts and Crafts weekend during the festival always draws a crowd.

The **Taos Fall Arts Festival** (☎ 505/758–3873 or 800/732–8267, WEB
www.taosguide.com), from late September to early October, is the

major arts gathering, when buyers are in town and many other events, such as a Taos Pueblo feast, take place.

The **Taos Poetry Circus** (WEB www.poetrycircus.org) comes to town for a week every June, presenting a performance series that includes readings, seminars, slams, and the World Heavyweight Championship Poetry Bout. It includes events at Taos Pueblo with young Native American poets.

### Film
**Taos Talking Picture Festival** (☎ 505/751–0637 or 800/267–0104, WEB www.ttpix.org) is a multicultural celebration of cinema artists, with a focus on Native American film and video makers. The mid-April festival presents independent films, documentaries, animation, and some classic cinema.

### Music
From mid-June to early August the Taos School of Music and the International Institute of Music fill the evenings with the sounds of chamber and symphonic orchestras at the **Taos Chamber Music Festival** (☎ 505/776–2388). Nearly four decades old, this is America's oldest chamber music summer program and possibly the largest assembly of professional musicians in the Southwest. Concerts are presented every Saturday evening, and every other Friday evening from mid-June to August, at the Taos Community Auditorium. Tickets cost $15. The events at Taos Ski Valley are free.

The Taos School of Music gives free weekly summer concerts and recitals from mid-June to early August at the **Hotel Saint Bernard** (☎ 505/776–2251), at the mountain base (near the lifts) of Taos Ski Valley.

**Music from Angel Fire** (☎ 505/758–4667 or 505/377–3233) is a series of classical and jazz concerts presented at the Taos Community Auditorium and the Angel Fire Community Auditorium in the town center from late August to early September. Tickets cost about $12 per concert.

Solar energy was pioneered in this land of sunshine, and each year in late June the flag of sustainability is raised at the three-day **Taos Solar Music Festival** (WEB www.solarmusicfest.com). Top-name acts appear, and booths promote alternative energy, permaculture, and other eco-friendly technologies.

# OUTDOOR ACTIVITIES AND SPORTS

Whether you plan to cycle around town, jog along Paseo del Pueblo Norte, or play a few rounds of golf, keep in mind that the altitude in Taos is over 7,000 ft. It's best to keep physical exertion to a minimum until your body becomes acclimated to the altitude—a full day to a few days, depending on your constitution. With the decreased oxygen and humidity, you may experience some or all of the following symptoms: headache, nausea, insomnia, shortness of breath, diarrhea, sleeplessness, and tension. If you are planning to engage in physical activity, avoid alcohol and coffee (which aggravate "high-altitude syndrome") and drink a lot of water and juice. Some locals also recommend taking aspirin in the morning and afternoon.

## Participant Sports
### Ballooning
**Paradise Balloons** (☎ 505/751–6098) and **Pueblo Balloons** (☎ 505/751–9877) conduct balloon rides over and into the Rio Grande gorge at sunrise or by moonlight. The cost is $195 plus gratuities.

## Bicycling

Taos-area roads are steep and hilly, and none have marked bicycle lanes, so be careful while cycling. The West Rim Trail offers a fairly flat but view-studded 9-mi ride that follows the Rio Grande canyon's west rim from the Rio Grande Gorge Bridge to near the Taos Junction Bridge.

**"Gearing Up" Bicycle Shop** (✉ 129 Paseo del Pueblo Sur, ☎ 505/751–0365) is a full-service bike shop that also has information about tours and guides. **Native Sons Adventures** (✉ 1033A Paseo del Pueblo Sur, ☎ 505/758–3392 or 800/753–7559) offers guided tours on its mountain bikes.

## Fishing

Carson National Forest (☞ Side Trips, *below*) has some of the best trout fishing in New Mexico. Its streams and lakes are home to rainbow, brown, and native Rio Grande cutthroat trout.

In Taos, **Los Rios Anglers** (✉ 226C Paseo del Pueblo Norte, ☎ 505/758–2798 or 800/748–1707) offers free one-hour fly-casting clinics, weekly between May and August. **Solitary Angler** (✉ 204B Paseo del Pueblo Norte, ☎ 505/758–5653 or 866/502–1700) guides fly-fishing expeditions that search out uncrowded habitats. Well-known area fishing guide **Taylor Streit** (☎ 505/751–1312) takes individuals or small groups out for fishing and lessons.

## Golf

The greens fee at the 18-hole, PGA-rated, par-72 championship course at **Taos Country Club** (✉ Hwy. 570, Ranchos de Taos, ☎ 505/758–7300 or 888/826–7465) ranges between $25 and $42; optional carts cost $22.

## Health Clubs and Fitness Centers

The **Northside Health & Fitness Center** (✉ 1307 Paseo del Pueblo Norte, ☎ 505/751–1242) is a spotlessly clean facility with indoor and outdoor pools, a hot tub, tennis courts, and aerobics classes. Nonmembers pay $9 per day; passes for a week or longer are also available. The center provides paid child care with a certified Montessori teacher. About 3 mi south of the Plaza, **Taos Spa & Tennis Club** (✉ 111 Doña Ana Dr., ☎ 888/758–1981) has tennis and racquetball courts, indoor and outdoor pools, fitness equipment, saunas, steam rooms, and hot tubs, as well as baby-sitting and massage services. Nonmembers pay $10 per day. The **Taos Youth and Family Center** (✉ 1005 Camino de Colores, ☎ 505/758–4160) has an outdoor Olympic-size ice arena, where rollerblading, volleyball, and basketball take place in summer. Other scheduled activities are open to the public.

## Jogging

The track around the football field at **Taos High School** (✉ 134 Cervantes St., ☎ 505/758–5230) isn't officially open to the public, but no one seems to object when nonstudents jog there. The paved paths and grass of **Kit Carson Memorial Park** make for a pleasant run. The mountain roads north of Taos present a formidable challenge.

## River Rafting

The Taos Box, at the bottom of the steep-walled canyon far below the Rio Grande Gorge Bridge, is the granddaddy of thrilling white water in New Mexico and is best attempted by experts only—or on a guided trip—but the river also offers more placid sections such as through the Orilla Verde Recreation Area. Spring runoff is the busy season, from mid-April through June, but rafting companies conduct tours March to November. Shorter two-hour options usually cover the fairly tame section of the river. The **Bureau of Land Management, Taos Resource**

**Area Office** (✉ 226 Cruz Alta, ☎ 505/758–8851) has a list of registered river guides and information about running the river on your own.

**Big River Raft Trips** (☎ 505/758–9711 or 800/748–3760) offers dinner float trips and rapids runs. **Far Flung Adventures** (☎ 505/758–2628 or 800/359–2627) operates half-day, full-day, and overnight rafting trips along the Rio Grande and the Rio Chama. **Los Rios River Runners** (☎ 505/776–8854 or 800/544–1181) will take you to your choice of spots—the Rio Chama, the Lower Gorge, or the Taos Box. **Native Sons Adventures** (✉ 715 Paseo del Pueblo Sur, ☎ 505/758–9342 or 800/ 753–7559) offers several trip options on the Rio Grande. **Rio Grande River Tours** (☎ 505/758–0762 or 800/525–4966) runs trips through Pilar Canyon and the Lower Rio Grande gorge.

### Skiing

The five ski resorts within 90 mi of Taos have beginning, intermediate, and advanced slopes and snowmobile and cross-country skiing trails. All the resorts have fine accommodations and safe child-care programs at reasonable prices. Only Taos Ski Valley prohibits snowboarding. For information on Angel Fire, Red River, or Taos Ski Valley, *see* Side Trips, *below*.

**Sipapu Lodge and Ski Area** (✉ NM 518, Vadito, ☎ 505/587–2240 or 800/587–2240, WEB www.sipapunm.com) is open from mid-December to the end of March.

**Ski Rio** (✉ NM 196 off NM 522, Costillo, ☎ 505/758–7707), north of Taos Ski Valley, opens for daily business from mid-December to early April. The resort has 83 runs and makes its own snow.

### Swimming

The **Don Fernando Municipal Swimming Pool** (✉ 120 Civic Plaza Dr., ☎ 505/737–2622) is open on weekdays 1–4:30 and on weekends 1– 5. Admission is $2.

### Tennis

**Kit Carson Memorial Park** (✉ Paseo del Pueblo Norte at Civic Plaza Dr.) and **Fred Baca Park** (✉ 301 Camino de Medio) has free public tennis courts, available on a first-come, first-served basis. The **Quail Ridge Inn and Tennis Ranch** (✉ Taos Ski Valley Rd./State Rd. 150, ☎ 800/624–4448) has eight Laykold tennis courts (two indoor). Outdoor courts are free to guests; indoor courts cost $15 per hour, $30 per hour for visitors. **Taos Spa & Tennis Club** (✉ 111 Doña Ana Dr., ☎ 888/ 758–1981) has tennis and racquetball courts; nonmembers pay $10 per day.

## Spectator Sports

Sporting events in the Taos area include the **Rodeo de Taos,** which takes place at the Taos County Rodeo Fairgrounds in mid-June, and the **Taos Mountain Balloon Rally,** held in a field south of downtown during the last week in October. Contact the Taos County Chamber of Commerce (☞ Visitor Information *in* Taos A to Z, *below*) for more information.

# SHOPPING

Retail options in Taos Plaza consists mostly of T-shirt emporiums and souvenir shops that are easily bypassed, though a few stores, like Blue Rain Gallery, carry quality Native American artifacts and jewelry. The more upscale galleries and boutiques are two short blocks north on Bent Street, including the John Dunn House Shops. Kit Carson Road, also known as U.S. 64, has a mix of the old and the new. There's metered municipal parking downtown, though the traffic can be daunt-ing. Some shops worth checking out are in St. Francis Plaza in Ran-chos de Taos, 4 mi south of the Plaza near the San Francisco de Asís Church.

## Art Galleries

For at least a century, artists have been drawn to Taos by its special light, open space, and natural grandeur. The result is a vigorous art community with some 80 galleries, a lively market, and an estimated 1,000 residents producing art full- or part-time. Many artists explore themes of the western landscape, Native Americans, and adobe ar-chitecture; others create abstract forms and mixed-media works that may or may not reflect the Southwest. Some local artists grew up in Taos, but many—Anglo, Hispanic, and Native Americans—are adopted Taoseños.

**Blue Rain Gallery** (⊠ 117 S. Plaza, ☎ 505/751–0066) carries some of the finest examples of Pueblo pottery and Hopi katsina dolls to be found anywhere, ranging in price from several hundred to several thousand dollars. The owner, Leroy Garcia, takes time to explain the materials and traditions. The gallery also sells Indian-made jewelry and art.

**Clay and Fiber Gallery** (⊠ 201 Paseo del Pueblo Sur, ☎ 505/758–8093) has exhibited first-rate ceramics, glass, pottery, and hand-painted silks and weavings by local artists for the past quarter century.

**Fenix Gallery** (⊠ 228B Paseo del Pueblo Norte, ☎ 505/758–9120) is a showcase for contemporary art, exhibiting paintings, sculpture, ce-ramics, and lithography by established Taos artists.

**Gallery Elena** (⊠ 111 Morada La., ☎ 505/758–9094) shows the works of Veloy, Dan, and Michael Vigil.

**Inger Jirby Gallery** (⊠ 207 Ledoux St., ☎ 505/758–7333) displays the landscapes and interiors of colorist Jirby.

**Las Comadres** (⊠ 228A Paseo del Pueblo Sur, ☎ 505/737–5323) is a women's cooperative gallery showing arts and crafts.

**Leo Weaver Jewelry Galleries** represents 50 local jewelry artists at two locations (⊠ 62 St. Francis Plaza, Ranchos de Taos, ☎ 505/751–1003; ⊠ Historic Taos Inn, 125 Paseo del Pueblo Norte, ☎ 505/758–8171). You'll find contemporary and traditional designs in silver, gold, and precious stones, as well as beautiful silver disk concha belts.

**Lumina Gallery** (⊠ 239 Morada La., ☎ 505/758–7282) exhibits paint-ings by artists who have worked in New Mexico for at least 20 years, as well as sculpture, photography, and antiques. Artists represented in-clude Joe Waldrun and Chuck Henningsen. The gallery is in the for-mer adobe home of Victor Higgins, one of the original members of the Taos Society of Artists. The outdoor sculpture garden is a serene oasis.

**Michael McCormick Gallery** (⊠ 106C Paseo del Pueblo Norte, ☎ 505/758–1372) is home to the sensual, stylized female portraits by Miguel Martinez and the architectural paintings of Margaret Nes. The adja-cent JD Challenger studio and gallery displays the artist's paintings of Native Americans.

**Mission Gallery** (⊠ 138 E. Kit Carson Rd., ☎ 505/758–2861) carries the works of early Taos artists, early New Mexico Modernists, and im-portant contemporary artists. The gallery is in the former home of painter Joseph H. Sharp.

**Navajo Gallery** (✉ 210 Ledoux St., ☎ 505/758–3250) shows the works of owner and Navajo painter and sculptor R. C. Gorman, well known for his ethereal interpretations of Indian imagery.

**New Directions Gallery** (✉ 107B N. Plaza, ☎ 505/758–2771 or 800/658–6903) displays works by contemporary Taos artists such as Larry Bell, Ted Egri, and Maya Torres in a light-filled room.

**Parks Gallery** (✉ 140 Kit Carson Rd., ☎ 505/751–0343) specializes in contemporary paintings, sculptures, and prints. Mixed-media artist Melissa Zink shows here, as well as painter Jim Wagner.

**R. B. Ravens Gallery** (✉ St. Francis Plaza, Ranchos de Taos, ☎ 505/758–7322) exhibits paintings by the founding artists of Taos, pre-1930s weavings, and ceramics.

**Shriver Gallery** (✉ 401 Paseo del Pueblo Norte, ☎ 505/758–4994) handles drawings and etchings, traditional bronze sculptures, and paintings, including oils, watercolors, and pastels.

**Six Directions** (✉ 129B N. Plaza, ☎ 505/758–5844) has paintings, alabaster and bronze sculpture, Native American artifacts, silver jewelry, and pottery. Bill Rabbit and Robert Redbird are among the artists represented here.

**Spirit Runner Gallery** (✉ 303 Paseo del Pueblo Norte, ☎ 505/758–1132) exhibits colorful acrylic and gold-leaf paintings by Taos native Ouray Meyers.

# Specialty Stores

## Books

**Brodsky Bookshop** (✉ 226B Paseo del Pueblo Norte, ☎ 505/758–9468) has new and used books—contemporary literature, southwestern classics, children's titles—piled every which way, but the amiable proprietor will help you find what you need.

**Fernandez de Taos Book Store** (✉ 109 N. Plaza, ☎ 505/758–4391) carries magazines, major out-of-town newspapers, and many books on southwestern culture and history.

**G. Robinson Old Prints and Maps** (✉ John Dunn House, 124D Bent St., ☎ 505/758–2278) stocks rare books, Edward Curtis photographs, and maps and prints from the 16th to 19th century.

**Inspirations** (✉ 114 Doña Luz, ☎ 505/751–0959) stocks spiritual and new-age books and tapes and offers tarot readings.

**Merlin's Garden** (✉ 127 Bent St., ☎ 505/758–0985) is a funky repository of metaphysical books and literature from Ram Dass to Thomas More. The shop also carries tapes, incense, crystals, and jewelry.

**Moby Dickens** (✉ John Dunn House, 124A Bent St., ☎ 505/758–3050), great for browsing, is a bookstore for all ages. It carries many books on the Southwest as well as a large stock of general-interest books.

**Mystery Ink** (✉ 121 Camino de la Placita, ☎ 505/751–1092) specializes in high-quality used books, especially murder mysteries. The shop also carries some foreign-language literature.

**Taos Book Shop** (✉ 122D Kit Carson Rd., ☎ 505/758–3733), the oldest bookshop in New Mexico, founded in 1947, specializes in out-of-print and southwestern books. The founders, Genevieve Janssen and Claire Morrill, compiled the reminiscences of their Taos years in *A Taos Mosaic* (University of New Mexico Press).

## Clothing

**La Lana Wools** (✉ 136 Paseo del Pueblo Norte, ☎ 505/758–9631) carries exquisite handwoven and hand-knit wearables, as well as plant-dyed yarns.

**Overland Sheepskin Company** (✉ NM 522, 100-A McCarthy Plaza, ☎ 505/758–8822, ☎ 505/758–5150) carries high-quality sheepskin coats, hats, mittens, and slippers, many with Taos beadwork.

**Taos Moccasin Co. Factory Outlet** (✉ 216B Paseo del Pueblo Sur, ☎ 800/747–7025) sells moccasins made in the building next door—everything from booties for babies to men's high and low boots—at great discounts.

## Collectibles

**Horse Feathers** (✉ 109B Kit Carson Rd.,, ☎ 505/758–7457) is a fun collection of cowboy antiques and vintage western wear—boots, hats, buckles, jewelry, and all manner of paraphernalia.

## Home Furnishings

**Abydos** (✉ 7036 S.R. 518, Talpa, ☎ 505/758–0483) sells fine handmade New Mexican–style furniture.

**Alhambra** (✉ 124 Paseo del Pueblo Sur, ☎ 505/758–4161) carries a lovely collection of antiques, Oriental rugs and textiles, and South Asian artifacts.

**Camino Real Imports** (✉ 1305A Paseo del Pueblo Norte, ☎ 505/758–7999), 2½ mi north of the Taos Plaza, has rooms full of Mexican artifacts, like serapes, clay pots, tin ornaments, knitwear, ponchos, blankets, and handpainted tiles and sinks.

**Casa Cristal Pottery** (✉ 1306 Paseo del Pueblo Norte, ☎ 505/758–1530), 2½ mi north of the Taos Plaza, has a huge stock of stoneware, serapes, clay pots, Native American ironwood carvings, fountains, sweaters, ponchos, clay fireplaces, Mexican blankets, tiles, piñatas, and blue glassware from Guadalajara.

**Casa Del Sol** (✉ 1638 Paseo del Pueblo Norte, ☎ 505/758–7496), north of town near the intersection of NM 150, is a warehouse of Mexican imports like straw and tin ornaments, clay pots, shawls, ponchos, clay fireplaces, blankets, tiles, and piñatas.

**Country Furnishings of Taos** (✉ 534 Paseo del Pueblo Norte, ☎ 505/758–4633) sells folk art from northern New Mexico, handmade furniture, metalwork lamps and beds, and colorful accessories.

**Flying Carpet** (✉ 208 Ranchitos Rd., ☎ 505/751–4035) carries colorful rugs and kilims from Turkey, Kurdistan, Persia, and elsewhere. Owner Bill Eagleton, who wrote a book about Kurdish carpets, and his wife, Kay, have a keen eye for quality and design.

**Franzetti Metalworks** (✉ 120G Bent St., ☎ 505/758–7872) displays owner Pozzi Franzetti's whimsical steelwork designs—from switch plate covers to wall hangings in animal and western motifs.

**John Bosshard Tribal and Traditional Arts** (✉ 112C Camino de la Placita, ☎ 505/751–9445) stocks antiques and artworks from the Southwest and around the world.

**La Unica Cosa** (✉ 117 Paseo del Pueblo Norte, ☎ 505/758–3065) has a striking collection of Zapotec Indian rugs and hangings.

**Lo Fino** (✉ 201 Paseo del Pueblo Sur, ☎ 505/758–0298) carries the works—hand-carved beds, tables, chairs, *trasteros* (free-standing cupboards), and benches—of the 10 top southwestern furniture and lighting designers, as well as some Native American alabaster sculpture, basketry, and pottery.

**Los Ancestros** (✉ 66 St. Francis Plaza, Ranchos de Taos, ☎ 505/737–5053) stocks Spanish-colonial reproductions and accessories.

**Taos Blue** (✉ 101A Bent St., ☎ 505/758–3561) carries jewelry, pottery, and contemporary works by Native Americans (masks, rattles, sculpture), as well as Hispanic *santos* (*bultos* and *retablos*).

The **Taos Company** (✉ 124K Bent St., ☎ 800/548–1141) sells magnificent Spanish-style furniture, chandeliers, rugs, and textiles; Mexican *equipal* (wood and leather) chairs; and other accessories.

**Taos Tinworks** (✉ 1204D Paseo del Pueblo Norte, ☎ 505/758–9724) sells handcrafted tinwork such as wall sconces, mirrors, lamps, and table ornaments by Marion Moore.

**Weaving Southwest** (✉ 216B Paseo del Pueblo Norte, ☎ 505/758–0433) represents 25 tapestry artists who make beautiful rugs, blankets, and pillows. The store also sells supplies for weavers.

## Native American Arts and Crafts

**All One Tribe** (✉ Taos, ☎ 800/442–3786) is a co-op of Native American master drum makers who sell hand-painted, signed instruments.

**Buffalo Dancer** (✉ 103A E. Plaza, ☎ 505/758–8718) buys, sells, and trades Native American arts and crafts, including pottery, belts, katsina dolls, hides, and silver-coin jewelry.

**Don Fernando Curios and Gifts** (✉ 104 W. Plaza, ☎ 505/758–3791), which opened in 1938 (it's the oldest Native American arts shop on the Taos Plaza), sells good turquoise jewelry, katsinas, straw baskets, and colorful beads.

**El Rincón** (✉ 114 E. Kit Carson Rd., ☎ 505/758–9188) is housed in a large, dark, cluttered century-old adobe. Native American items of all kinds are bought and sold here: drums, feathered headdresses, Navajo rugs, beads, bowls, baskets, shields, beaded moccasins, jewelry, arrows, and spearheads. The packed back room contains Indian, Hispanic, and Anglo Wild West artifacts.

**Southwest Moccasin & Drum** (✉ 803 Paseo del Pueblo Norte, ☎ 505/758–9332 or 800/447–3630) has a large selection of native moccasins and drums, many painted by local artists.

**Taos Drums** (✉ Santa Fe Hwy./NM 68, ☎ 505/758–9844 or 800/424–3786) is the factory outlet for the Taos Drum Factory. The store, 5 mi south of Taos Plaza (look for the large tepee), stocks handmade Pueblo log drums, leather lamp shades, and wrought-iron and southwestern furniture.

**Taos General Store** (✉ 223C Paseo del Pueblo Sur, ☎ 505/758–9051) stocks a large selection of furniture and decorative items from around the world, as well as American Indian pots, rugs, and jewelry.

## Sporting Goods

**Cottam's Ski and Outdoor** (✉ 207A Paseo del Pueblo Sur, ☎ 505/758–2822) carries hiking and backpacking gear, maps, fishing licenses and supplies, and ski equipment.

**Los Rios Anglers** (✉ 226C Paseo del Pueblo Norte, ☎ 505/758–2798 or 800/748–1707) is a fly-fisherman's haven for fly rods, flies, clothing, books, instruction, and guide service to local streams.

**Mudd 'n' Flood Mountain Shop** (✉ 134 Bent St., ☎ 505/751–9100) has gear and clothing for rock climbers, backpackers, campers, and backcountry skiers.

**Taos Mountain Outfitters** (✉ 114 S. Plaza, ☎ 505/758–9292) has supplies for kayakers, skiers, climbers, and backpackers, as well as maps, books, and handy advice.

# SIDE TRIPS FROM TAOS

## The Enchanted Circle

The Enchanted Circle is an 84-mi loop north from Taos and back to town (U.S. 64 to NM 522 to NM 38 back to U.S. 64). The drive rings Wheeler Peak, New Mexico's highest mountain, and takes you through glorious panoramas of alpine valleys and the towering mountains of the lush Carson National Forest. You can see all the major sights in one day, or take a more leisurely tour and stay overnight.

*Numbers in the text correspond to numbers in the margin and on the Taos Environs and the Enchanted Circle map.*

### A Good Drive

Traveling east from Taos along U.S. 64, you'll soon be winding through Taos Canyon, climbing your way toward 9,000-ft Palo Flechado Pass. On the other side of the pass, in about 25 mi you'll come to **Angel Fire** ⑯, a ski resort. Continue east on U.S. 64 about 14 mi to tiny **Eagle Nest** ⑰, an old-fashioned ski-resort village. Next take NM 38 going northwest and head over Bobcat Pass, a tad under 10,000 ft in elevation, about 16 mi from **Red River** ⑱. From Red River the Enchanted Circle heads west about 12 mi to scenic **Questa** ⑲. The **Red River Hatchery** ⑳ is about 5 mi south of Questa on NM 522. Continue south on NM 522 and keep an eye out for the sign on the left that points to the **D. H. Lawrence Ranch and Memorial** ㉑. You can visit the memorial, but the other buildings on the ranch are closed to the public. From here, Taos is about 15 mi south via NM 522 to U.S. 64.

TIMING

Leave early in the morning and plan to spend the entire day on this trip. During ski season, which runs from late November to early April, you may want to make it an overnight trip and get in a day of skiing. In spring, summer, and fall your drive should be free of snow and ice. A sunny winter day will yield some lovely scenery (but if it's snowy, don't forget your sunglasses).

### Sights To See

⑯ **Angel Fire.** Named for its blazing sunrise and sunset colors by the Ute Indians, who gathered here each autumn, Angel Fire is known these days primarily as a ski resort. In the summer there are arts and music events as well as hiking, river rafting, and ballooning. A prominent landmark is the **DAV Vietnam Veterans Memorial**, a 50-ft-high wing-shape monument built in 1971 by D. Victor Westphall, whose son David was killed in Vietnam. ✉ *U.S. 64, 25 mi east of Taos,* ☎ *505/377–6900 or 800/446–8117,* WEB *angelfirenm.com.*

㉑ **D. H. Lawrence Ranch and Memorial.** The influential and controversial English writer David Herbert Lawrence and his wife, Frieda, arrived in Taos at the invitation of Mabel Dodge Luhan, who collected famous writers and artists the way some people collect butterflies. Luhan provided them a place to live, Kiowa Ranch, on 160 acres in the mountains. Rustic and remote, it's known as the D. H. Lawrence Ranch, though Lawrence never actually owned it. Lawrence lived in Taos on

## Taos Environs and the Enchanted Circle

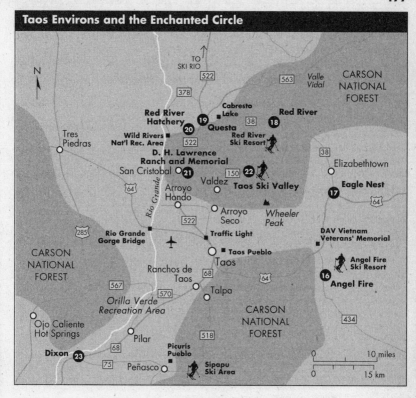

and off for about 22 months during a three-year period between 1922 and 1925. He wrote his novel *The Plumed Serpent* (1926), as well as some of his finest short stories and poetry, while in Taos and on excursions to Mexico. The houses here, owned by the University of New Mexico, are not open to the public, but you can go in the small cabin where Dorothy Brett, the Lawrences' traveling companion, stayed. You can also visit the D. H. Lawrence Memorial, a short walk up Lobo Mountain. A white shedlike structure, it's simple and unimposing. The writer fell ill while in France and died in a sanatorium there in 1930. Five years later Frieda had Lawrence's body disinterred and cremated and brought his ashes back to Taos. Frieda Lawrence is buried, as was her wish, in front of the memorial. ⊠ *NM 522 (follow signed dirt road from the highway), San Cristobal,* ☎ *505/776–2245.* 🎟 *Free.* ☉ *Daily dawn–dusk.*

**🅐 Eagle Nest.** Thousands of acres of national forest surround this rustic village, population 189, elevation 8,090 ft. The shops and other buildings here evoke New Mexico's mining heritage, while a 1950s-style diner, Kaw-Lija's, serves up a memorable burger. ⊠ *NM 38, 14 mi north of Angel Fire,* ☎ *505/377–2420 or 800/494–9117,* WEB *www. eaglenestnm.com.*

**🅑 Questa.** Literally "hill," in the heart of the Sangre de Cristo Mountains, Questa is a quiet village about 12 mi from the town of Red River, nestled against the Red River itself and amid some of the most striking mountain country in New Mexico. **St. Anthony's Church,** built of adobe with 5-ft-thick walls and viga ceilings, is on the main street. Questa's **Cabresto Lake,** in Carson National Forest, is about 8 mi from town. Follow NM 563 to Forest Route 134, then 2 mi of a primitive road (134A)—you'll need a four-wheel-drive vehicle. You can trout fish and boat here from about June to October.

**⑱** **Red River.** Home of a major ski resort, elevation 8,750 ft, Red River came into being as a miners' boomtown during the 19th century, taking its name from the river whose mineral content gives it a rosy color. When the gold petered out, Red River died, only to be rediscovered in the 1920s by migrants escaping the dust storms in the Great Plains. An Old West flavor remains: Main Street shoot-outs, an authentic melodrama, and square dancing and two-stepping are among the diversions here. Because of its many country dances and festivals, Red River is affectionately called "The New Mexico Home of the Texas Two-Step." The bustling little downtown area contains shops and sportswear boutiques. There is good fishing to be had in the Red River itself, and excellent alpine and Nordic skiing in the surrounding forest. ✉ *Off NM 38,* ☎ *505/774–2366 or 800/348–6111,* WEB *www.redrivernm.com.*

NEED A BREAK?   In Red River stop by the **Sundance** (✉ High St., ☎ 505/754–2971) for Mexican food. **Texas Red's Steakhouse** (✉ Main St., ☎ 505/754–2922) has steaks, chops, burgers, and chicken.

**⑳** **Red River Hatchery.** Freshwater trout are raised here to stock waters in Questa, Red River, Taos, Raton, and Las Vegas. You can feed them and learn how they're hatched, reared, stocked, and controlled. The visitor center has displays and exhibits, a fishing pond, and a machine that dispenses fish food. The self-guided tour can last anywhere from 20 to 90 minutes, depending on how enraptured you become. There's a picnic area and camping on the grounds. ✉ *NM 522, 5 mi south of Questa,* ☎ *505/586–0222.* ✑ *Free.* ☉ *Daily 8–5.*

## Camping

The country around Taos provides a wealth of camping opportunities, from organized campgrounds to informal roadside campsites and sites that require backpacking in. If mountains, pines, and streams are your goal, stake out sites in Carson National Forest along the Rio Hondo or Red River; if you prefer high-desert country along the banks of the Rio Grande, consider Orilla Verde or Wild River recreation area.

**Carson National Forest.** Within the forest are dozens of campsites along 400 mi of cool mountain trout streams and lakes. You may also choose your own site, anywhere along a forest road. Rest rooms are provided. Contact the U.S. Forest Service for the latest camping information. ✉ *Forest Service Building, 208 Cruz Alta Rd., Taos 87571,* ☎ *505/758–6200.* ✑ *Free–$7.*

**Enchanted Moon Campground.** In Valle Escondido, off U.S. 64 near Angel Fire, this wooded area with a trout pond has views of the Sangre de Cristos. ✉ *7 Valle Escondido Rd., Valle Escondido 87571,* ☎ *505/758–3338,* WEB *www.emooncampground.com. Flush toilets, full hook-ups, drinking water, showers, picnic tables, electricity, public telephone, playground. 44 RV sites, 25 tent sites.* ✑ *RV sites $19, tent sites $13. MC, V.*

**Questa Lodge.** This RV park is on the Red River off the Enchanted Circle, just off NM 522. There are areas for basketball, croquet, and volleyball. ✉ *Lower Embargo Rd. (Box 155, Questa 87556),* ☎ *505/586–0300. Flush toilets, drinking water, laundry facilities, showers, fire grates, picnic tables, playground. 26 RV sites.* ✑ *$20. Closed mid-Oct.–Mar.*

**Roadrunner Campground.** The Red River runs right through this woodsy mountain campground. There is a tennis court and an area with video games. ✉ *NM 578 (Box 588, Red River 87558),* ☎ *505/*

754–2286 or 800/243–2286, WEB *www.redrivernm.com/roadrunnerrv.*
*Flush toilets, full hook-ups, drinking water, laundry facilities, show-*
*ers, picnic tables, electricity, public telephone, general store, play-*
*ground. 155 RV sites.* ☎ *$27. Closed early spring–mid-Dec.*

⚠ **Wild River Recreation Area.** This area at the confluence of the Rio
Grande and the Red River near Questa (about 35 mi north of Taos,
off NM 522 and NM 378) has a visitor center and rim-top campsites,
as well as less-developed river sites that require a hike in. You can fish,
hike, and bicycle here. ✉ *Bureau of Land Management, Cruz Alta Rd.,
Taos 87571,* ☎ *505/758–8851. Flush toilets, drinking water, grills, picnic tables. 10 sites.* ☎ *Rim-top sites $7, riverside sites $5.*

## Outdoor Activities and Sports

**Carson National Forest** surrounds Taos and spans almost 200 mi across
northern New Mexico encompassing mountains, lakes, streams, villages, and much of the Enchanted Circle. Hiking, cross-country skiing, horseback riding, mountain biking, backpacking, trout fishing,
boating, and wildflower viewing are among the popular activities here.
The forest is home to big-game animals and many species of smaller
animals and songbirds. You can drive into the forest land via Hwys.
522, 150, 38, and 578. Contact the Carson National Forest for maps,
safety guidelines, and conditions (it's open weekdays 8–4:30). ✉ *Forest Service Building, 208 Cruz Alta Rd., Taos 87571,* ☎ *505/758–6200.*

### BIKING

The **Enchanted Circle Bike Tour** (☎ 800/384–6444) takes place in mid-
September. The rally loops through the entire 84-mi Enchanted Circle, through Red River, Taos, Angel Fire, Eagle Nest, and Questa, past
a brilliant blaze of fall color. During the summer, you can head up the
mountainside via ski lift in Red River, Angel Fire, and Sipapu.

### GOLF

The 18-hole, par-72 course at the **Angel Fire Country Club** (✉ Country Club Dr. off NM 434, Angel Fire, ☎ 505/377–3055), one of the
highest in the nation, is open from May to mid-October. The greens
fee is $35; an optional cart costs $12.50 per person.

### HIKING

Carson National Forest has hundreds of miles of trails that wind
through diverse terrain. Strenuous trails lead to Wheeler Peak, the highest point in New Mexico, at 13,161 ft. Gentler paths head up other
piney and meadow-filled mountains like Gold Hill or past old mining
camps. For canyon climbing, head into the rocky Rio Grande gorge.
The best entry point into the gorge is at the Wild River Recreation Area
in Cerro, 35 mi north of Taos.

If you're coming from a lower altitude, you should take time to accli-
matize, and all hikers should follow basic safety procedures. Wind, cold,
and wetness can occur any time of year, and the mountain climate produces sudden storms. Dress in layers and wear sturdy footwear; carry
water, food, sunscreen, hat, sunglasses, and a first-aid kit. Contact the
Forest Service for maps of hiking trails. The **Bureau of Land Management, Taos Resource Area Office** (✉ 226 Cruz Alta, Taos, ☎ 505/758–
8851) can help with hiking information.

### SKIING

**Angel Fire Resort** is a busy ski destination, with 68 runs for all levels
of skiers, 5 lifts, and a snowboarding slope. ✉ *N. Angel Fire Rd. off
NM 434, Angel Fire,* ☎ *505/377–6401; 800/633–7463 outside New
Mexico;* WEB *www.angelfireresort.com.* ☎ *$43 a day.* ☾ *Mid-Dec.–early
Apr.*

At the **Enchanted Forest Cross-Country Ski Area,** 24 mi of groomed trails loop from the warming hut through meadows and pines in Carson National Forest, 3 mi east of Red River. ✉ *417 W. Main St. (Red River 87558),* ☎ *505/754–2374 or 800/966–9381,* WEB *www.enchantedforestxc.com.* 🎫 *$10 a day.* ☉ *Late Nov.–Easter.*

The **Red River Ski Area** is in the middle of the historic gold-mining town of Red River, with lifts within walking distance of restaurants and hotels. Slopes for all levels of skiers make the area popular with families, and there's a snowboarding park. ✉ *Pioneer Rd. off NM 38, Red River,* ☎ *505/754–2323,* WEB *www.redriverskiarea.com.* 🎫 *$43 a day.* ☉ *Thanksgiving–Easter.*

## Taos Ski Valley

**㉒** *C.R. 150, 22 mi northeast of Taos.*

A trip to Taos Ski Valley begins at the traffic light where you turn right onto NM 150 (Taos Ski Valley Road) from U.S. 64. Along the way, the hamlet of Arroyo Seco, some 5 mi up NM 150 from the traffic light, is worth a stop for lunch or ice cream and a look at crafts and antiques shops. Beyond Arroyo Seco the road crosses a high plain, then plunges into the Rio Hondo Canyon to follow the cascading brook upstream through the forest to Taos Ski Valley, where NM 150 ends. (It does not continue to Red River, as some disappointed motorists discover.)

Skiers from around the world return to the slopes and hospitality of the Village of Taos Ski Valley every year. This world-class area is known for its alpine village atmosphere, perhaps the finest ski school in the country, and the variety of its 72 runs. The valley also attracts outdoor enthusiasts with good hiking in summer and fall. Some of the best trails in Carson National Forest begin at the Village of Taos Ski Valley and go though dense woodland up to alpine tundra. There aren't many summer visitors, so you can have the trails up to Bull-of-the-Woods, Gold Hill, Williams Lake, Italianos, and Wheeler Peak nearly all to yourself. Easy nature hikes are organized by the Bavarian hotel, guided by Shar Sharghi, a botanist and horticulturist. Special events like barn dances and wine tastings occur throughout the nonskiing seasons.

### Dining and Lodging

In winter, an espresso stand on the top level of the base lodge complex pours courage in a cup to those about to tackle the mountain.

**$$–$$$** ✕ **Rhoda's Restaurant.** Rhoda Blake founded Taos Ski Valley with her husband, Ernie. Her slope-side restaurant serves pasta, burgers, and sandwiches for lunch. Dinner fare is fancier, like veal medallions with pancetta and seafood chile rellenos. There's also a kids' menu. ✉ *Resort Center, on the slope,* ☎ *505/776–2005. AE, MC, V.*

**$** ✕ **Tim's Stray Dog Cantina.** This good spot for lunch at the ski area is known for New Mexican food such as chiles rellenos. ✉ *Sutton Pl.,* ☎ *505/776–2894. MC, V.*

**$$$$** ✕▦ **The Bavarian.** This luxurious, secluded re-creation of a Bavarian ★ lodge has the only mid-mountain accommodations in the Taos Ski Valley. The King Ludwig suite has a dining room, kitchen, marble bathroom, and two bedrooms with canopied beds. Three suites have whirlpool tubs, and there's a three-bedroom, three-bath apartment. The restaurant serves Bavarian cuisine. Summer activities include hiking, touring with the resident botanist, horseback riding, rafting, and fishing. Seven-night ski packages are offered. ✉ *Twining Rd. off C.R. 150, Village of Taos Ski Valley 87525,* ☎ *505/776–8020,* FAX *505/776–5301,* WEB *www.thebavarian.net. 4 suites. Restaurant, kitchenettes, in-room VCRs, fishing, hiking, horseback riding. AE, MC, V. Closed May and early Nov. BP.*

**$$$–$$$$** ✕🖼 **Inn at Snakedance.** This modern resort hotel is right on the slopes. The inn has a handsome library where guests can enjoy an après-ski coffee or after-dinner drink next to a fieldstone fireplace. Some rooms have fireplaces. In summer the hotel offers weeklong vacation packages, including a cooking school and fitness adventure courses. The restaurant is a six-time winner of the *Wine Spectator* Award of Excellence. ✉ *Off Taos Ski Valley Rd. (C.R. 150; Box 89, Village of Taos Ski Valley 87525),* ☎ *505/776–2277 or 800/322–9815,* 𝐅𝐀𝐗 *505/776–1410,* 𝐖𝐄𝐁 *www.innsnakedance.com. 60 rooms, 1 condo. Minibars, refrigerators, gym, hot tub, massage, sauna, library. AE, DC, MC, V. Closed mid-Apr.–Memorial Day.*

**$$$** ✕🖼 **Thunderbird Lodge and Chalets.** This two-story wood-frame inn is only 150 yards from the main lifts, on the sunny side of Taos Ski Valley. A large conference room has board games and a library. There are supervised children's activities during holiday seasons. Lodge rooms are cozy and functional; chalet rooms are larger and have king-size beds. Sumptuous breakfast buffets and family-style dinners are served in the pine-paneled dining room. Reservations are recommended for dinner. Ski-week packages are available. ✉ *3 Thunderbird Rd., off Taos Ski Valley Rd. (C.R. 150; Box 87, Village of Taos Ski Valley 87525),* ☎ *505/776–2280 or 800/776–2279,* 𝐅𝐀𝐗 *505/776–2238,* 𝐖𝐄𝐁 *www.thunderbird-taos.com. 32 rooms. Restaurant, hot tub, massage, sauna, bar, library, recreation room, library, meeting room. AE, MC, V.*

**$$$$** 🖼 **Austing Haus.** Owner Paul Austing constructed much of this hand-
★ some building, 1½ mi from Taos Ski Valley, along with many of its furnishings. The breakfast room has large picture windows, stained-glass paneling, and an impressive fireplace. Aromas of fresh-baked goods such as Paul's apple strudel come from the kitchen. Guest rooms are pretty and quiet with harmonious, peaceful colors; some have four-poster beds and fireplaces. During the winter the inn offers weeklong ski packages. ✉ *Taos Ski Valley Rd. (State Rd. 150; Box 8, Village of Taos Ski Valley 87525),* ☎ *505/776–2649 or 800/748–2932,* 𝐅𝐀𝐗 *505/776–8751,* 𝐖𝐄𝐁 *www.taoswebb.com/hotel/austinghaus. 22 rooms, 3 chalets. Hot tub, meeting rooms. AE, DC, MC, V. BP.*

**$$$–$$$$** 🖼 **Edelweiss.** Put your skis on at the back door of this intimate lodge, and glide down to the lift. Breakfasts, lunches, and afternoon hors d'oeuvres are served in the dining room overlooking the bunny slope. The rooms upstairs have polished antique chests, bookshelves, and gable-framed views. One suite has a large Jacuzzi in the bedroom nook. There is a three-night minimum. Ski-week packages are available. ✉ *106 Sutton Pl., Village of Taos Ski Valley 87525,* ☎ *505/776–2301 or 800/458–8754,* 𝐅𝐀𝐗 *505/776–2533,* 𝐖𝐄𝐁 *www.newmex.com/edelweiss. 8 suites. Some in-room hot tubs, outdoor hot tub, ice-skating; no smoking. MC, V. Closed mid-Apr.–Nov. BP.*

## Shopping

**Andean Softwear** (✉ 118 Sutton Pl., ☎ 505/776–2508) carries exotic clothing, textiles, and jewelry. Note the deliciously soft alpaca sweaters from Peru. You can bring your ski boots up to the pros at the **Boot Doctor** (✉ 103 Sutton Pl., ☎ 505/776–2489)—if anyone can make 'em fit, they can; if not, they'll find a pair that does. A demo program lets you try skis out. Ski clothing and accessories fill out the store in winter, and in summer you can get hiking clothing, sandals, and clogs.

## Outdoor Activities and Sports

### HIKING

**Wheeler Peak** is a designated wilderness area of Carson National Forest, where travel is restricted to hiking or horseback riding. Part of the Sangre de Cristo Mountains, the 13,161-ft-high peak is the highest point in New Mexico. The 8-mi trail to the peak begins at the Village of Taos Ski Valley. Only experienced hikers should tackle this strenuous trail. Dress warmly even in summer, take plenty of water and food, and pay attention to *all* warnings and instructions distributed by the forest rangers. ⊠ *Twining Campground (next to the ski area parking lot),* ☎ *505/ 758–6200.*

### SKIING

With 72 runs and an average of 323 inches of annual snowfall, **Taos Ski Valley** is justly popular. The slopes offer something for every level of skier: 51% (e.g. the ridge chutes, Al's Run, Inferno) are for experts, 25% (e.g. Honeysuckle) are for intermediate skiers, and 24% (e.g. Bambi, Porcupine) are for beginners. There's no snowboarding. ⊠ *Village of Taos Ski Valley,* ☎ *505/776–2291,* WEB *www.skitaos.org.* ☜ *$49.* ☉ *Late Nov.–early Apr.*

## Low Road to Santa Fe

Traveling south out of town, Paseo del Pueblo Sur becomes NM 68, and wide-open views abound—from picture-perfect mountains on the east to the distant western horizon across the plain. The jagged slash cut into the land a few miles west was carved over many millennia by the Rio Grande. The highway also winds down from the high plateau into the rocky canyon of the Rio Grande. But before you reach the "Big River," watch for another river rushing in from the east about 20 mi south of Taos. This is the Embudo River, and 2 mi east across it on NM 75 lies the pretty hamlet of Dixon. New Mexico 68 continues south and begins to parallel the Rio Grande just before the Embudo Station restaurant and microbrewery, seen across a bridge on the right bank. Farther south the river canyon widens into a valley with farmers' fields and orchards near Velarde, where fruit and vegetable stands tempt travelers from both sides of the road.

### Dixon

**㉓** *20 mi south of Taos.*

The small village of Dixon and its surrounding country lanes are home to a surprising number of artists. Artistic sensibility, as well as generations of dedicated farmers, accounts for the community's well-tended fields, pretty gardens, and fruit trees—a source of produce for restaurants and farmers' markets such as the one in Santa Fe. It's simple to find your way around; there's only one main road. The Dixon Arts Association lists some four dozen members, many represented in a cooperative showroom in the village center, **Casa de Piedra Gallery** (⊠ State Rd. 75, ☎ 505/579–4111). You can taste award-winning wines at **La Chiripada Winery** (⊠ State Rd. 75, ☎ 505/579–4437 or 800/ 528–7801), whose name means "stroke of luck."

### DINING AND LODGING

**$$–$$$**  ✕ **Embudo Station.** The restaurant's emphasis is on locally grown produce and house-brewed beers. Lunch and dinner are served in the casual indoor dining room or outside on the riverside patio. Try the roasted rainbow trout served on a cedar plank or a hearty sandwich of turkey cured in the smokehouse next door. ⊠ *Hwy. 68, Embudo,* ☎ *505/852– 4707 or 800/852–4707,* FAX *505/852–2479. AE, MC, V. Closed mid-Nov.–early Apr. and Mon.*

**$$**  ▥ **Rock Pool Gardens.** The two-bedroom suite has a kitchenette stocked with breakfast items; a bathroom connects the bedrooms, each of which has its own access and patio. A second suite has one bedroom and full kitchen. The rustic walls and willow twig furniture lend a country air. You can use the Jacuzzi under the trees and the heated pool set in natural rock. ⊠ *State Rd. 75, Dixon 87527,* ☎ *505/579–4602,* FAX *505/579–9182. 2 suites. Kitchens, refrigerator, pool, hot tub. No credit cards.*

# TAOS A TO Z

### AIR TRAVEL
Rio Grande Air offers several round-trips daily between Albuquerque, Los Alamos, and Taos.
➤ REGIONAL AIRLINE: **Rio Grande Air** (☎ 877/435–9742).

### AIRPORTS AND TRANSFERS
Albuquerque International Sunport is the nearest (130 mi) major airport to Taos. Taos Municipal Airport is 12 mi west of the city.

Faust's Transportation operates radio-dispatched taxis between Taos Municipal Airport and town ($20) and between the Albuquerque airport and Taos ($40 one-way, $75 round-trip). They also go to Taos Ski Valley, Angel Fire, and Red River. Twin Hearts Express charges $40 one-way and $75 round-trip to the Albuquerque airport and also has service to Taos Ski Valley, Red River, Questa, and Santa Fe.
➤ AIRPORTS: **Albuquerque International Sunport** (⊠ 2200 Sunport Blvd. SE, off I–25, ☎ 505/842–4366). **Taos Municipal Airport** (⊠ U.S. 64, ☎ 505/758–4500).
➤ AIRPORT TRANSFERS: **Faust's Transportation** (☎ 505/758–3410 or 888/830–3410). **Twin Hearts Express** (☎ 505/751–1201 or 800/654–9456).

### BUS TRAVEL TO AND FROM TAOS
Texas, New Mexico & Oklahoma Coaches, a subsidiary of Greyhound Lines, runs buses twice a day from Albuquerque to Taos. Buses stop at the Taos Bus Station.
➤ BUS COMPANY: **Texas, New Mexico & Oklahoma Coaches** (☎ 800/231–2222, WEB www.greyhound.com).
➤ BUS STATION: **Taos Bus Station** (⊠ 1008 Paseo del Pueblo Sur, ☎ 505/758–1144).

### BUS TRAVEL WITHIN TAOS
The town of Taos transit department's Chile Line bus service has two lines. The Green Line circles around town, while the Red Line runs between Taos Pueblo and the Ranchos de Taos post office. Tickets are 50¢, all-day passes $1.
➤ BUS INFORMATION: **Chile Line** (☎ 505/751–4459).

### CAR RENTAL
Cottam Walker rents cars by the day, week, and month. Dollar Rent a Car will deliver vehicles to the Fechin Inn.
➤ RENTAL AGENCIES: **Cottam Walker** (⊠ 1320 Paseo del Pueblo Sur, ☎ 505/751–3200). **Dollar Rent a Car** (⊠ Taos Municipal Airport, ☎ 505/751–1000).

### CAR TRAVEL
The main route from Santa Fe to Taos is NM 68, also known as the Low Road, which winds between the Rio Grande and red-rock cliffs before rising to a spectacular view of the plain and river gorge. You can also take the wooded High Road to Taos (☞ Side Trips from Santa Fe *in* Chapter 4) from Santa Fe. From points north of Taos, take NM 522; from points east or west, take U.S. 64.

The altitude in Taos will affect your car's performance, causing it to "gasp" because it's getting too much gas and not enough air. If a smooth ride matters, you can have your car tuned up for high-altitude driving.

Major hotels have ample parking. Metered parking areas are all over town; in peak seasons—summer and winter—traffic and parking can be a headache. There's a metered parking lot between Taos Plaza and Bent Street and a free lot on Kit Carson, two blocks east of Paseo del Pueblo.

➤ HIGHWAY INFORMATION: **New Mexico Road Conditions** (☎ 800/432–4269).

### EMERGENCIES
In an emergency, dial 911.

➤ HOSPITAL: **Holy Cross Hospital** (✉ 630 Paseo del Pueblo Sur, ☎ 505/758–8883).

➤ PHARMACIES: **Raley's Pharmacy** (✉ 1100 Paseo del Pueblo Sur, ☎ 505/758–1203). **Taos Pharmacy** (✉ Piñon Plaza, 622A Paseo del Pueblo Sur, ☎ 505/758–3342). **Wal-Mart Discount Pharmacy** (✉ 926 Paseo de Pueblo Sur, ☎ 505/758–2743).

➤ POLICE: **New Mexico state police** (☎ 505/758–8878). **Taos Police** (☎ 505/758–2216).

### LODGING
Several organizations can help you find accommodations in and around Taos.

➤ RESERVATIONS: **Taos Central Reservations** (✉ Box 1713, Taos 87571, ☎ 505/758–9767 or 800/821–2437, WEB www.taoscentralreservations.com). **Taos Lodging** (✉ Box 1101, Taos 87571, ☎ 505/751–1771 or 800/954–8267, WEB www.taoslodging.com). **Taos Ski Central** (✉ Box 696, Village of Taos Ski Valley 87525, ☎ 800/238–2829, WEB www.taosskicentral.com). **Traditional Taos Inns Association** (☎ 505/776–8840, WEB www.taos.lodging.com).

### TAXIS
Taxi service in Taos is sparse, but Faust's Transportation, based in nearby El Prado, has a fleet of radio-dispatched cabs.

➤ TAXI COMPANY: **Faust's Transportation** (☎ 505/758–3410 or 505/758–7359).

### TOURS
#### ORIENTATION TOUR
Historic Taos Trolley Tours conducts two three-hour narrated tours of Taos daily, including stops at the San Francisco de Asís Church, Taos Pueblo, La Hacienda de los Martínez, and a Taos drum shop. Tours run from May to October and cost $25 each.

#### SPECIAL-INTEREST TOURS
All Aboard guide service conducts 1½-horr walking tours in town ($10 per person). Native Sons Adventures organizes biking, backpacking, rafting, snowmobiling, and horseback and wagon expeditions. Roadrunner Tours, run by Nancy and Bill Burch, rents out cars, jeeps, skis, and horses and offers snowmobile tours and sleigh rides from the Elkhorn Lodge near Angel Fire. Taos Indian Horse Ranch conducts two-hour trail rides, as well as old-fashioned horse-drawn sleigh rides through the Taos Pueblo backcountry—winter weather permitting—complete with brass bells, a Native American storyteller, toasted marshmallows, and green-chile roasts. Escorted horseback tours and hayrides are run through Native American lands during the remainder of the year. Tours are by reservation only; no alcohol is permitted. The ranch closes for 42 to 48 days each year to observe the Taos Pueblo Sweats Ceremony; call the Taos Pueblo Governor's Office for the exact dates.

Taos Studio Tours offers individual or small group tours to galleries and artists' studios, Saturday mornings June–September or by appointment all year.

➤ ORIENTATION TOUR: **Historic Taos Trolley Tours** (☎ 505/751–0366, WEB www.taostrolleytours.com).

➤ SPECIAL-INTEREST TOURS: **All Aboard** (☎ 505/758–9368). **Native Sons Adventures** (✉ 715 Paseo del Pueblo Sur, Taos, ☎ 505/758–9342 or 800/753–7559). **Roadrunner Tours** (☎ 505/377–6416). **Taos Indian Horse Ranch** (✉ 1 Miller Rd., Taos Pueblo, ☎ 800/659–3210). **Taos Pueblo Governor's Office** (☎ 505/758–9593). **Taos Studio Tours** (☎ 505/751–1965, WEB www.taostours.com).

## VISITOR INFORMATION

➤ TOURIST INFORMATION: **Taos County Chamber of Commerce** (✉ 1139 Paseo del Pueblo Sur [Drawer I, Taos 87571], ☎ 505/758–3873 or 800/ 732–8267, WEB www.taosguide.com). **Village of Taos Ski Valley Visitors & Conference Bureau** (✉ Box 91, Village of Taos Ski Valley 87525, ☎ 800/992–7669, WEB www.skitaos.org or www.taosskivalley.com).

## WORKSHOPS

Taos Art School offers educational field trips and workshops from May to October in painting, sculpture, weaving, photography, creativity, Native American pottery making, Pueblo culture, and other topics. Taos Institute of Arts holds its weeklong intensive classes in ceramics, fiber arts, jewelry making, painting, photography, and writing, among others, at Mountain Village, 20 mi south of Taos, from June to October. Fechin Art Workshops presents hands-on sessions June to October—in photography, painting, drawing, and sculpture—at the Donner Ranch 18 mi north of Taos.

The German Summer School allows no English during its five-week language-learning session for teachers and students of German, held in June and July at the Thunderbird Lodge in Taos Ski Valley. UNM's Taos Summer Writers' Conference, held in July at the Sagebrush Inn in Taos, conducts a variety of weekend and weeklong workshops from fiction to poetry to screenwriting.

➤ WORKSHOP INFORMATION: **Fechin Art Workshops** (✉ Box 220, San Cristobal 87564, ☎ 505/776–2622). **German Summer School** (✉ Dept. of Foreign Language and Literature, Ortega Hall 347A, University of New Mexico, Albuquerque 87131, ☎ 505/277–7367). **Taos Art School** (✉ Box 2588, Taos 87571, ☎ 505/758–0350, WEB www. taosartschool.org). **Taos Institute of Arts** (✉ 108 Civic Plaza Dr., ☎ 505/758–2793 or 800/822–7183, WEB www.tiataos.com). **UNM's Taos Summer Writers' Conference** (✉ English Dept., University of New Mexico, Albuquerque 87131, ☎ 505/277–6248).

# 6  NORTHEASTERN NEW MEXICO

The brilliantly clear light of northeastern New Mexico illuminates seemingly endless high-desert plains. Hawks soar overhead and antelope gallivant across the same open landscape traversed by the Native Americans and the cowboys, ranchers, miners, and railroaders who settled the West.

Updated
by Holly
Hammond

Y**OU'LL BATTLE NEITHER CROWDS NOR HYPE** in northeastern New Mexico, one of the best-kept secrets in the state. You can have a wildflower-strewn trail through alpine meadows and forests of aspen and ponderosa pine all to yourself, or step back in time in small towns that treasure their past but do not exploit it. The sheer variety of terrain and climate, and the combination of natural and social history, make the region an ideal destination, whether as a short side trip or part of a journey from New Mexico toward the Plains states.

In 1908 an African-American cowboy named George McJunkin found arrowheads embedded in a bison bone. Archaeologists determined that the arrowheads had been made by ancient hominids, now known as Folsom Man, who inhabited northeastern New Mexico at least 10,000 years ago. In more recent centuries, Apaches, Utes, Comanches, and other Plains Indians hunted and camped here.

The opening of the Santa Fe Trail in the first half of the 19th century and the arrival of the railroad in the 1870s and '80s brought streams of people and goods into northeastern New Mexico, as did the coal mines. Italians, Mexicans, Greeks, Slavs, Spaniards, and Irish all headed to Raton to harvest coal in mines that first opened in 1879. German-Jewish merchants opened shops in the town of Las Vegas to serve the miners, the railroads, and the local Hispanic population.

During the railroad heyday, Civil War veterans homesteaded in the region, some working for Lucien Maxwell, onetime mountain man and fur trader who came to control the largest landholding (1,714,765 acres) in the western hemisphere. Many of New Mexico's large ranches date from the era of the Maxwell Land Grant, territory awarded to the father of Maxwell's wife and another man by the Mexican government in 1841. Modern-day land baron Ted Turner now owns an enormous chunk of open land in these parts.

History is very much alive in northeastern New Mexico, in the stories of the people who live here and their way of life, in the architecture, and in the landscape itself. Exploring this land of vast plains, rugged mesas, and wild, crystalline streams may well be the best way to immerse yourself in the American West.

## Pleasures and Pastimes

### Dining

| CATEGORY | COST* |
|---|---|
| $$$$ | over $25 |
| $$$ | $18–$25 |
| $$ | $10–$17 |
| $ | under $10 |

* per person for a main course at dinner

### Fishing

Whether you prefer lake or stream fishing, gray hackle peacocks or PowerBait, some of your greatest fishing dreams might just come true in northeastern New Mexico. Idyllic clear mountain streams and alpine lakes are regularly stocked with rainbows; in Cimarron Canyon State Park you can catch your limit on German browns. Numerous operators arrange fishing trips.

## Lodging

| CATEGORY | COST* |
|---|---|
| $$$$ | over $170 |
| $$$ | $120–$170 |
| $$ | $70–$120 |
| $ | under $70 |

*All prices are for a standard double room, excluding 5.25–11.5% tax.*

## Viewing Wildlife

Early morning and late afternoon are the best times to grab your binoculars and head out to spot wildlife—elk, deer, wild turkey, bears, and bobcats—in the Raton area, or on the road to Sugarite Canyon State Park, Yankee Canyon, or York Canyon. But it's possible to catch a glimpse of antelope any time of day, especially on the open range.

# Exploring Northeastern New Mexico

Interstate 25 heading north from Santa Fe is the fastest route through the region, but try to sample as many local roads as possible to catch the area's true flavor. The destinations below are arranged in a loop from Pecos via I–25 north to Las Vegas, Springer, and Raton (with an optional side loop over Johnson Mesa to Folsom, Capulín, and Clayton). Either way, the tour continues by heading west to Cimarron and then along U.S. 64 west through Cimarron Canyon; past Eagle Nest Lake and Angel Fire (☞ Chapter 5); and then south on Hwy. 434 through stunning Guadalapita Canyon to Mora. Here you can either continue south toward Santa Fe back through Las Vegas or opt for the more dramatic mountain route, skirting over the east face of the Sangre de Cristo range.

## Great Itineraries

IF YOU HAVE 2 DAYS

Stroll around the Plaza and Bridge Street in **Las Vegas** ②. After you've walked the town, drive north on I–25 to ⊡ **Raton** ⑥ and visit the **Raton Museum** and **Historic First Street.** Take a picnic up to **Lake Maloya** in **Sugarite Canyon State Park** and hike or go fishing. The next day, drive west on U.S. 64 to ⊡ **Cimarron** ⑨, exploring the heart of yesteryear's Wild West. Spend the night in the allegedly haunted **St. James Hotel.** In the morning continue west on U.S. 64, stopping off to fish or walk along the Cimarron River in Cimarron Canyon, and then head south on Hwy. 434 at Angel Fire, stopping off for a visit to Victory Ranch in **Mora** ⑩, before continuing back toward Santa Fe.

IF YOU HAVE 4 TO 5 DAYS

The main routes through northeastern New Mexico follow the path of the original Santa Fe Trail and its shortcut, the Cimarron Route (which passed near Clayton and Springer), enabling you to retrace the steps of the pioneers. Begin at **Pecos National Historic Park** ① before heading north to ⊡ **Las Vegas** ②, where you should stay at the **Plaza Hotel.** Detour for an hour or two to **Fort Union National Monument** ③. Back at I–25, continue north to ⊡ **Raton** ⑥. On day three head east on Hwy. 72 over starkly captivating Johnson Mesa and visit **Capulin Volcano National Monument.** After viewing four states from the rim of the volcano, have lunch at the **Capulin Country Store,** at the junction of U.S. 64/87 and Hwy. 325. If you have an extra day, head east to ⊡ **Clayton** ⑧ to view the dinosaur tracks at **Clayton Lake State Park.** Have dinner at the **Eklund Hotel Dining Room & Saloon** and spend the night at the **Best Western.** The following day drive west on U.S. 56 toward Springer, detouring first to **Dorsey Mansion. Springer** ⑤ is a good place to have lunch and browse in the antiques shops downtown. With or without the Clayton detour, continue west to ⊡ **Cimarron** ⑨ (via U.S.

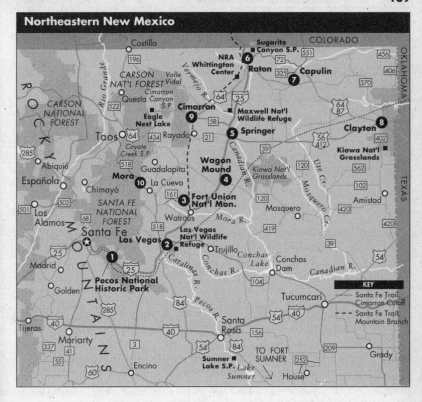

**Northeastern New Mexico**

64 from Capulin, or Hwy. 58 from Springer), and from here repeat the last day of the two-day itinerary given above.

### When to Tour Northeastern New Mexico

In a region where the weather is close to perfect, the only months to avoid are March and April, when "Texas blows through" and you'll find yourself dodging tumbleweeds in the highway. From late spring, when the wildflowers begin to bloom, into late summer is a wonderful time to visit—an occasional afternoon thunderstorm, often followed by a rainbow, punctuates days that are mostly sunny. Fall brings the gold of aspens and some of the best fishing and hiking. Temperatures can remain mild through Thanksgiving, and a crisp winter with good snow is a blessing for cross-country skiers. The wide vistas on snowy days are unforgettable. Roads are well maintained throughout the year, but be alert to storm warnings.

# SANTA FE TRAIL COUNTRY

Comanche, Apache, and other Native American peoples of the Great Plains and Southwest lived in northeastern New Mexico. Throughout the region you'll find reminders of them and the pioneers who traveled the Santa Fe Trail, two sections of which passed through the area. The Mountain Route entered New Mexico from southeastern Colorado, crossed through Raton Pass, and passed Cimarron and Rayado before heading on to Fort Union. Because it was so arduous, this route was less subject to Indian attack, mostly from the Comanches and Apaches, whose land was being usurped. The quicker, flatter Cimarron Route (aka Cimarron Cutoff), entering New Mexico from Oklahoma and passing across the dry grasslands, left travelers much more vulnerable. The Mountain Route, which William Becknell followed 900 mi from Franklin, Missouri, during his first successful navigation, also provided an excellent source of water—the Arkansas River. The Cimarron Route was deathly dry.

## Pecos National Historic Park

❶ *25 mi east of Santa Fe on I–25.*

Pecos was the last major encampment that travelers on the Santa Fe Trail reached before Santa Fe. Today the little village is mostly a starting point for exploring the Pecos National Historic Park, the centerpiece of which is the **ruins of Pecos,** once a major Pueblo village with more than 1,100 rooms. Twenty-five hundred people are thought to have lived in this structure, as high as five stories in places. Pecos, in a fertile valley between the Great Plains and the Rio Grande valley, was a trading center centuries before the Spanish conquistadors visited in about 1540. The Spanish later returned to build two missions.

The Pueblo was abandoned in 1838, and its 17 surviving occupants moved to the Jemez Pueblo (☞ Chapter 4). Anglo travelers on the Santa Fe Trail observed the mission ruins with a great sense of fascination (and relief—for they knew it meant their journey was nearly over). A couple of miles from the ruins, **Andrew Kozlowski's Ranch** served as a stage depot, where a fresh spring quenched the thirsts of horses and weary passengers. The ranch now houses the park's law-enforcement corps and is not open to the public. You can view the mission ruins and the excavated pueblo on a ¼-mi self-guided tour in about two hours.

The pivotal Civil War battle of Glorieta Pass took place on an outlying parcel of park land in late March 1862; a victory over Confederate forces firmly established the Union army's control over the New Mexico Territory. The Union troops maintained headquarters at Kozlowski's Ranch during the battle. Check out the park visitor center to go on guided park tours (in summer only) and to see exhibits on the region's checkered history. Major wildfires in spring of 2000 burned some of the wilderness within the park, but none of the ruins were touched. ✉ *Hwy. 63, off I–25 at Exit 307, Pecos,* ☎ *505/757–6414,* WEB *www.nps.gov/peco.* ✉ *$3.* ☉ *Memorial Day–Labor Day, daily 8–6; Labor Day–Memorial Day, daily 8–5.*

## Las Vegas

❷ *40 mi east of Pecos on I–25.*

The antithesis of the Nevada city that shares its name, Las Vegas is a town of 16,000 that time appears to have passed by. Once an oasis for stagecoach passengers en route to Santa Fe, it became, for a brief period after the railroad arrived in the late 19th century, New Mexico's major center of commerce. The seat of San Miguel County, Las Vegas, elevation 6,470 ft, lies where the Sangre de Cristo Mountains meet the high plains of New Mexico, and its name, meaning "the meadows," reflects its scenic setting. Bookstores, western-wear shops, boutiques, and coffeehouses line the streets near the downtown Plaza and Bridge Street.

More than 900 structures here are listed on the National Register of Historic Places, and the town has nine historic districts, many with homes and commercial buildings of ornate Italianate design (a welcome relief if you're experiencing adobe overload). History lives in the doorways of this once rough-and-tumble stop on the Santa Fe Trail—the nearest to Santa Fe. Butch Cassidy is rumored to have tended bar here, Doc Holiday practiced dentistry, and German-Jewish merchants ran mercantile establishments. Long a popular film location, Las Vegas is where Tom Mix shot his vintage westerns. Contemporary films with a Las Vegas background include *Wyatt Earp, The HiLo Country,* and *All the Pretty Horses*; episodes of *Walker, Texas Ranger* have been filmed here as well.

To gain an appreciation of the town's architecture, try some of the walking tours described in brochures available at the **Las Vegas Chamber of Commerce** (✉ 727 Grand Ave., ☎ 505/425–8631 or 800/832–5947). Best bets include Stone Architecture of Las Vegas; the Carnegie Park Historic District; and the business district of Douglas/Sixth Street and Railroad Avenue, which includes the famous Harvey House hotel of the railroad chain, La Casteneda, where the grand lobby and dining room are still intact and you can still order a drink at the bar.

**Las Vegas City Museum & Rough Riders Memorial** houses historical photos, medals, uniforms, and memorabilia from the Spanish-American War, documents pertaining to the city's history, and Native American artifacts. Theodore Roosevelt recruited many of his Rough Riders—the men the future president led into battle in Cuba in 1898—from northeastern New Mexico, and their first reunion was held here. ✉ *725 Grand Ave.,* ☎ *505/454–1401 ext. 283.* ☞ *Free.* ☉ *Weekdays 9–noon and 1–4, Sat. 10–3.*

A favorite fishing hole for rainbow and German brown trout is **Storrie Lake State Park.** The 1,200-acre lake also draws water-skiers, sailboarders, and windsurfers. You can camp in the area. ✉ *Hwy. 518, 4 mi north of Las Vegas,* ☎ *505/425–7278,* WEB *www.emnrd.state.nm.us.* ☞ *$4 per vehicle.*

**Las Vegas National Wildlife Refuge** has the best birding around, with 271 known species—including eagles, sandhill cranes, hawks, and prairie falcons—that travel the Central Flyway to this 18,750-acre area of marsh, wetlands, native grasslands, and timber. Here the Sangre de Cristo Mountains meet the Great Plains. A nature trail winds beside sandstone cliffs and ruins. Get oriented by dropping by the visitor center. ✉ *Rte. 1 (Box 399, Las Vegas 87701), 1 mi east of Las Vegas on Hwy. 104, then 4 mi south on Hwy. 281,* ☎ *505/425–3581.*

Las Vegas is the home of **New Mexico Highlands University** (✉ 901 University Ave., ☎ 800/338–6648, WEB www.nmhu.edu), which puts on concerts, plays, sporting events, and lectures. Its tree-shaded campus of largely Spanish colonial and Romanesque Revival buildings anchors the eastern side of downtown. It houses Depression-era murals by painter Lloyd Moylan.

About 5 mi northwest of town in Montezuma, students from around the world study language and culture at the **Armand Hammer United World College of the American West** (✉ Hwy. 65, ☎ 505/454–4200, WEB www.uwc-usa.org). Looming over the school property is the fantastically ornate, vaguely Queen Anne–inspired Montezuma Castle, a former resort hotel developed by the Santa Fe Railroad and designed by the famous Chicago firm of Burnham and Root. The structure that stands today was the third incarnation of the Montezuma Hotel, which opened in 1886. Weekly tours of the castle are available, and you can wander the school's majestic, rolling grounds. Check in with the guard booth at the campus entrance.

Continue another ½ mi north of the campus on Hwy. 65, and you'll see the signs to the right for the **hot springs** that inspired Montezuma's tourist boom in the 1880s. You can freely bathe in the several warm springs, which overlook the castle, if you follow a few basic posted rules (no nude bathing, no alcohol, open 5 AM–midnight). The trip from the Las Vegas Plaza up to Montezuma is a favorite of mountain bikers—you'll understand the appeal once you dip into these muscle-relaxing waters.

OFF THE
BEATEN PATH
**MADISON VINEYARDS & WINERY –** Proud producers of some very fine New Mexico wines, Madison has picked up quite a few awards over the years. The tasting room in El Barranco is open Monday–Saturday 10–5, Sunday noon–5. ⊠ *Hwy. 3, 6 mi south of I–25, Exit 323, 23 mi southwest of Las Vegas,* ☎ *505/421–8028.*

## Dining and Lodging

**$–$$$** ✕ **El Rialto Restaurant & Lounge.** The perfectly blended margaritas will put you in the right mood for fried oyster dinners, huge steaks, stuffed sopaipillas, and great tamales. American dishes, seafood, and the salad bar are other options. The attached Rye Lounge is a fun spot for drinks. ⊠ *141 Bridge St.,* ☎ *505/454–0037. AE, D, MC, V. Closed Sun.*

**$–$$** ✕ **Estella's Restaurant.** An old-fashioned storefront café with a high
★ pressed-tin ceiling, vintage photos, and a Formica counter with swivel stools, Estella's serves simple, spicy New Mexican fare—huevos rancheros, green-chile enchiladas—plus a few American favorites like burgers and chile cheese fries. It's a great spot for people-watching. ⊠ *148 Bridge St.,* ☎ *505/454–0048. No credit cards. Closed Sun. No dinner Mon.–Wed.*

**$** ✕ **Murphey's Drugs.** A Las Vegas institution, Murphey's is the place to sit at an old-fashioned soda fountain, order a lime rickey or cherry Coke, sip a milk shake, or savor a homemade dessert. ⊠ *600 Douglas Ave.,* ☎ *505/425–6811. No credit cards. No dinner.*

**$** ✕⌷ **Plaza Hotel.** Rooms at this three-story Italianate hotel balance
★ the old and the new—not fancy, but very nice. In addition to plenty of space, rooms have painted trim and borders, high stamped-tin ceilings, a sprinkling of antiques, modern baths, coffeemakers, TVs, and phones. Continental breakfast is served. Reasonably priced packages include dinner at the Landmark Grill ($$–$$$), which serves filet mignon, piñon-crusted trout, and Mexican food. ⊠ *230 Old Town Plaza, 87701,* ☎ *505/425–3591 or 800/328–1882,* ℻ *505/425–9659,* ᴡᴇʙ *www.lasvegasnewmexico.com/plaza. 32 rooms, 4 suites. Restaurant, room service, cable TV, bar, Internet, meeting rooms, some pets allowed (fee). AE, D, DC, MC, V.*

**$$** ⌷ **Pendaries Village.** The mood here is Holiday Inn meets Kit Carson, but the standard motel-room decor in no way detracts from the thrill of high-altitude golfing. The **Pendaries Golf Course** (☎ 505/425–8890) begins at 7,500 ft with a par 73, set smack at the eastern edge of the Sangre de Cristo Mountains. Special golf packages are offered. Greens fees are $32 weekdays, $40 weekends; optional golf cart rental is $22. The rustic lodge has a restaurant usually crowded with locals who come for the steaks, southwestern food, and pastas. Pendaries is in the tiny mountain hamlet of Rociada, an exquisite place to relax. ⊠ *1 Lodge Rd. (Box 820, Rociada 87742), off Hwy. 105, 26 mi northwest of Las Vegas,* ☎ *505/425–3561 or 800/733–5267,* ℻ *505/425–3562,* ᴡᴇʙ *www.pendaries.net. 18 rooms. Restaurant, 18-hole golf course, bar, meeting rooms. MC, V.*

**$–$$** ⌷ **Inn on the Santa Fe Trail.** David and Lavinia Fenzi and a friendly staff run this well-kept, hacienda-style motel. The grounds are well manicured, there's a nice pool area, and the unfussy rooms have TVs with premium cable and well-chosen southwestern furnishings created by area artisans. Guests have privileges at a nearby health club. ⊠ *1133*

*N. Grand Ave., 87701, ☎ 505/425–6791 or 888/448–8438, FAX 505/425–0417, WEB www.innonthesantafetrail.com. 28 rooms, 2 suites. Restaurant, in-room data ports, pool, hot tub, business services. AE, D, DC, MC, V. CP.*

**$** 🏠 **Carriage House B&B.** This dramatic three-story 1893 house lies in the eastern half of the town's colorful historic district, a short drive from the downtown Plaza. Rooms are homey and inviting, abundant with frilly Victoriana, stuffed animals, delicate fabrics, and a smattering of antiques. Continental breakfast is included. ⊠ *925 6th St., 87701, ☎ 505/454–1784 or 888/221–9689, WEB www.newmexicocarriagehouse.com. 3 rooms. D, MC, V. CP.*

### Camping

⚠ **Las Vegas New Mexico KOA.** Five miles south of Las Vegas you can camp and cook out near a piñon-juniper hillside with beautiful views. There is a recreation room, volleyball, and horseshoes. ⊠ *I–25, Exit 339, at U.S. 84, HCR 31, Box 1, Las Vegas 87701, ☎ 505/454–0180 or 800/562–3423, WEB www.koa.com. Flush toilets, full hook-ups, drinking water, laundry facilities, showers, picnic tables, general store, playground, pool. 5 cabins, 50 tent sites, 54 hook-ups. 🚐 RV sites $24–$29, tent sites $20–$24, cabins $35–$39. D, MC, V.*

⚠ **Pecos River Campground.** Wagon-wheel ruts of the Santa Fe Trail run through the park where this appealing campground is situated. You'll find abundant wildflowers, nearby fishing, a national forest, and a meteor crater. Cabin and trailer rental is available. ⊠ *I–25, Exit 319, 24 mi west of Las Vegas, HCR 73, Box 30, San Jose 87565, ☎ 505/421–2211 or 888/421–2211, WEB www.elvalle.com/prc.html. Flush toilets, full hook-ups, drinking water, laundry facilities, showers, picnic tables, electricity, public telephone, general store. 42 RV sites, 10 tent sites. 🚐 RV sites $10–$18, tent sites $10, cabins $35, trailers $50. No credit cards.*

### Outdoor Activities and Sports

**Brazos River Ranch** (☎ 505/425–1509) can take you on jeep tours, trail rides, and hunting and fishing trips. Arrange for backcountry horseback riding and wilderness pack trips with **Tererro Riding Stables** (☎ 505/757–6193).

### Shopping

Shops are located mainly on Bridge Street, off the Plaza. **New Moon Fashions** (⊠ 132 Bridge St., ☎ 505/454–0669) has a well-chosen selection of western and imported women's clothing. **Rough Rider Trading Co.** (⊠ 158 Bridge St., ☎ 505/425–0246) sells western wear, handcrafted furniture, hand weaving, and rustic wood and metal crafts. **Tome on the Range** (⊠ 116 Bridge St., ☎ 505/454–9944) is a well-appointed bookstore with good southwestern and kids' sections. **Plaza Antiques** (⊠ 1805 Old Town Plaza, ☎ 505/454–9447) contains several dealers offering a wide range of antiques from different periods; it's in a stunningly restored hip-roof adobe 1870s Victorian. **Meadowland Antiques and Spice Co.** (⊠ 131 Bridge St., ☎ 505/425–9502) sells gourmet foods, candies, a huge selection of spices, and distinctive furnishings and has a little espresso bar in back.

## Fort Union National Monument

❸ *26 mi from Las Vegas, north on I–25 and (past Watrous) northwest on Hwy. 161; 94 mi northeast of Santa Fe on I–25.*

The ruins of New Mexico's largest American frontier–era fort sit on an empty windswept plain that still echoes with the isolation surely felt by the soldiers stationed here between 1851 and 1890. The fort was established to protect travelers and settlers along the Santa Fe Trail.

It became a military supply depot for the Southwest, but with the "taming" of the West it was abandoned. The visitor center provides historical background about the fort and the Santa Fe Trail. Talks on the Santa Fe Trail and Fort Union are given daily, and guided tours are available by reservation. Sunset programs feature period music. Call for schedule and details. ⊠ *Off Hwy. 161, Watrous,* ☎ *505/425–8025,* WEB *www.fortunion.areaparks.com.* ⚏ *$3.* ☉ *Labor Day–Memorial Day, daily 8–5; Memorial Day–Labor Day, daily 8–6.*

## Wagon Mound

❹ *40 mi north of Las Vegas on I–25.*

As you drive up I–25 from Las Vegas and Fort Union, the high prairie unfolds before you to the east, an infinite horizon of grassland that's quite breathtaking when the sun sets. Soon interrupting this view is a butte shaped like a covered wagon that was a famous Santa Fe Trail landmark, Wagon Mound. The butte is where travelers crossed over from the Cimarron Cutoff to journey south to Fort Union. Local lore tells of mysterious lights, ghosts, and murders committed on top of the butte. The town serves a free barbecue at noon on Labor Day to celebrate its bean-growing heritage. Other events—horseshoe tournaments, a rodeo, and a parade—take place that same weekend in this otherwise sleepy village.

### Dining

$–$$    ✕ **Santa Clara Cafe.** The cattle brands of local ranchers decorate this café, which serves delectable pies—among them walnut-raisin and a knockout four-fruit cobbler. Dishes include slow-cooked roast beef, mashed potatoes, and other home-cooked vittles. The café is in a century-old building on the actual Santa Fe Trail. ⊠ *709 Railroad Ave.,* ☎ *505/666–2011. D, MC, V.*

## Springer

❺ *25 mi north of Wagon Mound on I–25.*

A stroll under the shady oaks of Springer's main street is a journey into the past. Add vintage cars, and you'd think Harry Truman were still president. More than a few locals here still seem a bit rankled about losing the title of county seat to Raton—in 1897. The main industry of this town of 1,262 is the Springer Boys School, an incarceration facility for minors. Long a shipping center for cattle, sheep, and mining machinery, Springer was founded in 1870 when land baron Lucien Maxwell deeded 320 acres to his lawyer, Frank Springer, for handling the sale of the Maxwell Land Grant to the Dutch East India Company.

Crammed with everything you'd expect to find at a five-and-dime, **Springer Drug** is a local hangout and site of an ongoing gabfest. The highlight is the old (not old-fashioned, this is the original article) soda fountain, where you can order a sundae, malt, shake, or cone. The root-beer float comes in a glass so big you could dive into it. In winter, home-made chili is served on Wednesday. ⊠ *825 4th St.,* ☎ *505/483–2356.*

When Springer was the Colfax County seat, the 1883 structure that houses the **Santa Fe Trail Museum** served as a courthouse. The museum has a curious jumble of documents, maps, memorabilia, and other artifacts. The setup is not particularly sophisticated—it takes a bit of patience to wade through the assorted bits and pieces of the past. ⊠ *606 Maxwell St.,* ☎ *505/483–2998.* ⚏ *$2.* ☉ *Memorial Day–Labor Day, Mon.–Sat. 9–4; limited hrs early fall and late spring (call ahead).*

OFF THE
BEATEN PATH

**DORSEY MANSION –** In the middle of nowhere (about 35 mi northeast of Springer) stands this curious 36-room log-and-masonry castle built in 1880 by Stephen Dorsey, a U.S. senator from Arkansas. Its grand furnishings include a cherrywood staircase from Chicago, gargoyles depicting Dorsey family members, a dining room that seats 60, and a swank billiard room. It was once a social gathering place for the rich and powerful. The career of the ambitious senator, who owned the mansion for 15 years, dissolved in a mail-fraud scandal. You must make reservations by phone to visit the mansion. ⊠ *Off U.S. 56, 25 mi east of Springer; turn north (left) at the rest stop at Mile Marker 24 and take the dirt road 12 mi,* ☎ *505/375-2222,* WEB *www.dorseymansion.com.* ▢ *$3.* ☉ *Daily, by appointment.*

**MAXWELL NATIONAL WILDLIFE REFUGE –** More than 300 species of migratory waterfowl, including many geese and ducks in fall and winter, stop for a spell at this low-key 2,800-acre prairie refuge 12 mi north of Springer. Sightings of great blue herons are not uncommon in mid-winter, and bald eagles are fairly plentiful at this time. Sandhill cranes usually drop by in early fall, Canada geese around December. Deer, prairie dogs, long-tailed weasels, jackrabbits, coyotes, bears, and elk live here. The fishing season (Lake 13 is a fabled spot to catch rainbows) is between March and October. You can camp (no fee, no facilities) near the fishing areas. ⊠ *Off I–25 (take Maxwell Lakes exit at Mile Marker 426; follow Hwy. 445 north ¾ mi, then Hwy. 505 west 2½ mi to unmarked gravel road to refuge),* ☎ *505/375-2331.* ▢ *Free.* ☉ *Daily.*

## Dining and Lodging

$$ ✕ **El Taco.** Just about everybody in town drops by this distinctive eatery at least once a week to enjoy a good meal, to shoot pool, or to yuk it up at the carved century-old bar. The kitchen turns out excellent New Mexican fare, prepared with vegetable oils and fresh ingredients. The red chile that accompanies the huevos rancheros could substitute for rocket fuel, and Mama Sofia's El Taco combination is gargantuan. The sopaipillas are light and perfect. Breakfast is served. ⊠ *704 Maxwell Ave.,* ☎ *505/483–0402. D, MC, V. Closed Sun.*

$ ✕🏠 **Brown Hotel & Cafe.** Granny's parlor circa 1924 is the best way to describe the Brown Hotel, where the lobby furnishings include a rocking chair by the fireplace and hooked rugs and doilies. Antiques decorate the basic rooms, some of which have chenille-covered beds. The café's claims to fame include the baked goods and made-from-scratch soups; both New Mexican and standard American dishes are on the menu. ⊠ *302 Maxwell Ave., 87747,* ☎ *505/483–2269. 11 rooms. Café. MC, V. BP.*

## Shopping

**Jespersen's Cache** (⊠ 403 Maxwell Ave., ☎ 505/483–2349), a pack rat's paradise, is a place to get lost for a morning or afternoon. The sheer mass of stuff is astounding—boxed Barbies, railroad lanterns, Depression-era glass, carousel horses. If you've got a collector's eye, you could make your lucky find here.

# Raton

❻ *39 mi north of Springer on I–25, 100 mi northeast of Taos on U.S. 64.*

Vastly underrated as a destination, Raton occupies an appealing spot at the foot of a lush mountain pass, offering wide-open views of stepped mesas and sloping canyons from the higher points in town. Midway between Albuquerque and Denver, it's an ideal base for exploring northeastern New Mexico. Because Raton was a racetrack town from the 1940s through the early '90s, motels are plentiful. There's some talk today of bringing back horse racing.

As it has for more than a century, Raton (population 8,500), the seat of Colfax County, runs on ranching, railroading, and the industry for which it's most famous, mining. In the early 1900s there were about 35 coal camps around Raton, most of them occupied by immigrants from Italy, Greece, and Eastern Europe. It was hard living in these camps and a tough road out, but a familial, close-knit interdependence grew out of mining life—a spirit that still prevails in Raton today. People here are genuinely friendly and have great pride in their town.

Originally a Santa Fe Trail forage station called Willow Springs, Raton was born in 1880 when the Atchison, Topeka & Santa Fe Railway established a repair shop at the bottom of Raton Pass. The town grew up around 1st Street, which paralleled the railroad tracks. Much of the Raton Downtown Historic District, which has 70-odd buildings on the National Register of Historic Places, lies along Historic First Street, which consists of several restored blocks of antiques shops, galleries, and everyday businesses.

The Historic 1st Street area provides a fine survey of western architecture from the 1880s to the early 1900s. In the early 20th century the **Mission Santa Fe Depot** (⊠ 1st St. and Cook Ave.), a 1903 Spanish Mission Revival structure, serviced several dozen trains daily (Amtrak still stops here). The **Wells Fargo Express Building** (⊠ 145 S. 1st St.), also designed in the Spanish Mission Revival style, was erected in 1910. The building houses the **Old Pass Gallery** (☎ 505/445–2052), which presents exhibits of regional art, books, and jewelry. Garlands and female figureheads adorn the 1906 **Abourezk Building** (⊠ 132 S. 1st St.), originally a drugstore, later a dry-goods and grocery store, and now the home of the Heirloom Shop.

The tiny **Raton Museum,** inside the 1906 Coors Building (the beer manufacturer used it as a warehouse), brims with artifacts of the coal camps, railroading, ranch life, and the Santa Fe Trail. The museum, which has a large and interesting photo collection, is a good first stop on a visit to the area. The docents enjoy explaining local history. ⊠ *218 S. 1st St.,* ☎ *505/445–8979.* ▧ *Free.* ◐ *May–Sept., Tues.–Sat. 10– 5; Oct.–Apr., Thurs.–Sat. 10–3.*

Just down a couple of blocks from the train station, the **Scouting Museum** opened in 1999 and is a must-see for anyone planning a visit to Philmont Scout Ranch in Cimarron. Amiable curator Dennis Downing has amassed an exhaustive collection of scouting-related books, badges, films of old jamborees, buttons, and *Boys Life* magazines. ⊠ *400 S. 1st St.,* ☎ *505/445–1413.* ▧ *Free.* ◐ *June–Aug., daily 10–7, or by appointment.*

More retro 1930s and '40s than Victorian, 2nd Street—Raton's main commercial drag—also has a number of handsome old buildings. The pride and joy of the neighborhood is the **Shuler Theater** (⊠ 131 N. 2nd St.), a 1915 European rococo–style structure whose lobby contains WPA murals depicting local history. The Shuler is one of the few remaining stages hand-operated with hemp rope and wooden pulleys. On weekdays between 8 and 5 the staff will happily take you on a free tour.

Southern California may have its HOLLYWOOD sign, but northeastern New Mexico has its RATON sign—and this neon-red beauty is completely accessible. From the north end of 3rd Street, head west on Moulton Avenue to Hill Street and follow signs along the twisting road to the parking area at Goat Hill. Here you can walk around the sign, take in

270-degree views of the countryside, or picnic while contemplating the history of Raton Pass—the original Santa Fe Trail ran up Goat Hill clear into Colorado.

★ ⓒ **Sugarite Canyon State Park,** a gem of a park near the Colorado state line, has some of the state's best hiking, camping, wildflower viewing, fishing, and bird-watching ("sugarite" is a corruption of the Comanche word *chicorica,* meaning "an abundance of birds," and is pronounced shug-ur-*eet*). The road to Sugarite twists and turns high up into the canyon to Lake Maloya, a trout-stocked body of water from which a spillway carries overflow down into the canyon. From its 7,500-ft elevation, hills rise up the eastern and western canyon walls where miners once dug for ore; you can still see gray slag heaps and remnants of the coal camp, which thrived here from 1910 to 1940, along portions of the park road near the visitor center (the former coal-camp post office) and down near the base of the canyon. The center contains exhibits on the mining legacy, and from here you can hike 1½ mi to the original camp.

Hikes elsewhere in the park range from the easy ½-mi Grande Vista Nature Trail to the pleasant 4-mi jaunt around Lake Maloya to the challenging Opportunity Trail. "Caprock" is the name given to the park's striking basaltic rock columns, which were formed millions of years ago when hot lava from a nearby volcano created the 10- to 100-ft-thick rocks. Climbing is permitted on these sheer cliffs. ⊠ *Hwy. 526, 7 mi northeast of Raton via Hwy. 72,* ☎ *505/445–5607,* ⟨WEB⟩ *www.emnrd.state.nm.us.* ⊠ *$4 per vehicle.* ⊙ *Daily 6 AM–9 PM.*

The vast wilderness west of Raton comprises **Vermejo Park Ranch** (⊠ Drawer E, Raton 87740, ☎ 505/445–3097, ⟨WEB⟩ www.vermejoparkranch.com), a 588,000-acre property owned by CNN media mogul Ted Turner—the single largest private owner of New Mexico land. Elevations within this ranch, which spans just about every Southwest ecosystem, range from 6,400 to 13,000 ft. For an enormous fee you can stay at the ranch's ultraprivate resort, where your own private guide will take you fishing among 21 stocked lakes or hunting for turkeys, mule deer, and elk. For his part, Turner has removed miles of barbed wire, reintroduced American buffalo and other indigenous flora and fauna, and made every effort to return this land—which he purchased in 1996 from the Pennzoil Company for a plum $80 million—to its original, pristine state.

## Dining and Lodging

$$–$$$$ ✕ **Pappas' Sweet Shop Restaurant.** You'll feel pampered at this restaurant, whose antiques and collectibles exude a sense of history and a pleasant nostalgia for the Greek candy maker who founded the place in the 1920s. It's no longer a sweets shop today but serves familiar American fare, like Alaskan king crab legs, porterhouse steak, shrimp fettuccine, and a few surf-and-turf combos. ⊠ *1201 S. 2nd St.,* ☎ *505/445–9811. AE, D, DC, MC, V. Closed Sun. in winter.*

$$–$$$ ✕ **The Grapevine.** Arguably the best place to eat in Raton, this cheery Italian restaurant prepares tasty thin-crust pizzas (try the Rustica, a white pesto pie with fresh tomatoes, garlic, mozzarella, and ricotta), calzones, and eggplant dishes. A specialty is chicken with artichokes, fresh tomatoes, and basil in a marinara sauce. Amaretto cheesecake is a favorite dessert. ⊠ *120 N. 2nd St.,* ☎ *505/445–0969. AE, D, DC, MC, V. Closed Sun.*

$–$$$ ✕ **Domingo's.** It's a bit of a gimmick, but kids especially love eating in the cavelike restaurant with faux stalagmites and stalagtites that recall Carlsbad Caverns (well, if it had a waterfall), plus a game room and live music on weekends. Standard Mexican and American fare is served. Domingo's has a gift shop with salsas, sopaipilla mix, and such. ⊠ *1903 S. Cedar St., off U.S. 64/87, just east of I–25,* ☎ *505/445–2288. AE, D, DC, MC, V.*

$   ✕ **Eva's Bakery.** In a cheerful storefront across from the Shuler Theater, this inviting sit-down bakery has fabulous chocolate-cake doughnuts and oatmeal-raisin cookies and attracts old-timers who gather here to keep up with town gossip and political intrigue. Chile fries, burgers, and frito pies are big sellers. ⊠ *134 N. 2nd St.,* ☎ *505/445–3781. Reservations not accepted. No credit cards. Closed Sun. No dinner.*

$   ✕ **Hot Dog Depot.** Cute, clean, and blessedly smoke-free, this café inside a bright turquoise Victorian house serves hearty breakfasts, homemade chili and soup, and salads. The coffee is only 49¢ a cup. ⊠ *100 S. 3rd St.,* ☎ *505/445–9090. Reservations not accepted. MC, V. Closed Sun.*

$$   ⊞ **Hearts Desire Inn Bed & Breakfast.** Gregarious host Barbara Riley, who grew up on a ranch south of Springer, has filled the rooms of her inn with Victorian antiques and collectibles (many for sale). This 1885 former boardinghouse is steps from downtown dining and the historic district. The top-floor hunting-and-fishing-theme suite has a full kitchen, TV and VCR, and two twin beds. In addition to a full breakfast, snacks are served in the evening. ⊠ *301 S. 3rd St., 87740,* ☎ *505/445–1000. 5 rooms, 1 suite. Some kitchenettes, some in-room VCRs. MC, V. BP.*

$$   ⊞ **Holiday Inn Express.** Brand-new with clean rooms, many with fine views east to Johnson Mesa and the vast grasslands, this pleasant franchise lies just south of downtown. An extensive Continental breakfast buffet is included. ⊠ *101 Card Ave., 87740, I–25, Exit 450,* ☎ *505/445–1500 or 800/465–4329,* FAX *505/445–7650. 50 rooms. In-room data ports, pool, hot tub, laundry facilities; no-smoking rooms. AE, D, DC, MC, V. CP.*

$–$$   ⊞ **Best Western Sands.** Some of the good-size rooms at this 1950s-style motel have refrigerators, and all have coffeemakers, queen or king beds, and TVs with premium cable. The Sands provides free transportation to and from Raton's bus depot and Amtrak station. ⊠ *300 Clayton Rd. (Hwy. 87/U.S. 64), 87740,* ☎ *505/445–2737 or 800/528–1234,* FAX *505/445–4053. 50 rooms. Restaurant, in-room data ports, some refrigerators, cable TV, pool, hot tub, playground, business services; no-smoking rooms. AE.*

$   ⊞ **El Portal.** This eccentric, if a bit ragged, hostelry occupies a restored 1885 downtown building. The antiques-filled lobby has a working fireplace and a vintage Royal typewriter. Expect old beds, unmodernized bathrooms, no room phones, and somewhat musty accommodations, but for the price of the cheapest chain motel you'll be treated to an authentic Old West experience. Adjoining the hotel are 39 apartments leased both short- and long-term. ⊠ *101 N. 3rd St., 87740,* ☎ *505/445–3631. 23 rooms. Some kitchenettes, some pets allowed; no room phones. MC, V.*

## Camping

⚠ **Sugarite Canyon State Park.** Arrive early for the best choice among the fully developed sites at either of the park's two campgrounds, Lake Alice and Soda Pocket. Follow park warnings regarding the resident brown bears at Soda Pocket. ⊠ *Hwy. 526 (HCR 63, Box 386, 87740), 6 mi northeast of Raton,* ☎ *505/445–5607,* WEB *www.emnrd. state.nm.us. Flush toilets, full hook-ups, dump station, drinking water, showers, picnic tables, electricity. 41 tent and RV sites, 12 with hook-ups.* 🚏 *$7–$11. No credit cards.*

## Nightlife and the Arts

**Shuler Theater** (⊠ 131 N. 2nd St., ☎ 505/445–4746) presents late-summer concerts, Music at Angel Fire, and productions by the Creede

Repertory Theater. Children's theater, local college productions, and traveling dance, folk dance, and vocal evenings are scheduled throughout the year. The beautiful **El Raton Theatre** (✉ 115 N. 2nd St., ☎ 505/445–5528) dates to the 1940s and shows first-run movies. For the better part of this century, locals have popped into the rollicking **White House Saloon** (✉ 133 Cook Ave., ☎ 505/445–9992) for drinks after work and late into the evening.

## Outdoor Activities and Sports

Raton's playground is **Sugarite Canyon State Park.** Sugarite's alpine **Lake Maloya** (✉ Hwy. 526, 10 mi northeast of Raton, ☎ 505/445–5607) is generously stocked with rainbow trout. The profusion of wildflowers and flocks of bluebirds make the lake a joy to hike around. Boating and ice-fishing are popular as well.

## Shopping

**Cloth Caravan** (✉ 148 S. 1st St., ☎ 505/445–2441 or 877/445–2761) sells quilting and needlework supplies and fabrics. Hattie Sloan, the proprietor of the **Heirloom Shop** (✉ 132 S. 1st St., ☎ 505/445–8876), was one of the key figures involved in the restoration of Historic 1st Street. Hattie knows her antiques and has packed her highly browsable shop with beautiful selections, from rhinestone necklaces to quilts, china, and linens. Given the quality of some of the merchandise, the prices at **Santa Fe Trail Traders** (✉ 100 S. 2nd St., ☎ 505/445–2888 or 800/286–6975) are reasonable. Items include earrings, sand paintings, dream catchers, Nambé hand-cast bowls, Navajo rugs old and new, beadwork, and katsinas (many by well-known artists).

**Rubin's Family Clothiers** (✉ 113 S. 2nd St., ☎ 505/445–9492) sells Pendleton shirts, woolen skirts, and well-made shoes. Its owners, Kathryn and Leon Rubin, can tell you a thing or two about local history—their store has been in the family for almost a century. You can enter **Solano's Boot & Western Wear** (✉ 101 S. 2nd St., ☎ 505/445–2632) a city slicker and exit a cowboy or cowgirl. The enormous space, an experience as much as a store, is full of fashionable, practical western garb. Check out the collection of cowboy hats.

*En Route* To reach Capulin from Raton, skip U.S. 64 and instead take **Hwy. 72** past Sugarite Canyon State Park, a stunning road that climbs up over Johnson Mesa, from which you have amazing 100-mi views north over the mesa into the plains of eastern Colorado. It's bare and flat up here, as though you're driving across a table straddling the Colorado–New Mexico border. About halfway across the mesa (15 mi from Raton), note the **old stone church** to your right, which was built by the early farmsteaders and has since been abandoned—it's a beautiful, lonely little building with a presence that illustrates the life of solitude the mesa's settlers must have endured.

Farther along on the right, a **historical marker** details the 1908 discovery of Folsom Man by George McJunkin, which established the existence of indigenous inhabitants in the area dating back some 10,000 years. The road trails down the eastern side of the mesa and leads into tiny Folsom. Here make a right turn south on Hwy. 325 to reach Capulin Volcano, 6 mi away.

# Capulin

❼ *46 mi east of Raton via Hwy. 72 and Hwy. 325.*

Tiny Capulin has a gas station, a campground, and—well—little else. If you're in luck, lunch will be on at the delightful **Capulin Country Store,** which in addition to fine food sells crafts and gifts (like candlesticks made of elk antlers and dolls sewn from old quilts), snacks, maps, and cold drinks.

From the crest of **Capulin Volcano National Monument,** elevation 8,182 ft, you can see four states: Colorado, New Mexico, Texas, and Oklahoma. To the southeast is the vast section of the Santa Fe Trail that includes the Cimarron Cutoff; to the west are the snowcapped Sangre de Cristo Mountains. Unlike much of the dry surrounding territory, Capulin has enough water to support an oasis of trees, shrubs, and wildflowers. A narrow 2-mi paved road (no trailers, towed vehicles, bicycles, or pedestrians allowed) leads to the rim of the volcano; from there you can walk the final ⅓ mi into the extinct, and rather uninteresting, crater vent. (An easy-to-hike 1-mi trail circles the rim, so you can see it from different angles.) The cone of Capulin (the word is Spanish for "chokecherry") rises more than 1,300 ft from its base. The visitor center has books, a brief video about the site, and interpretive exhibits. On busy summer weekends, you may have a short wait to enter the paved road. ⊠ *Hwy. 325, 3 mi north of Capulin off U.S. 64,* ☎ *505/ 278–2201,* WEB *www.nps.gov/cavo.* 🎫 *$5 per vehicle.* ☉ *Memorial Day– Labor Day, daily 7:30–6:30; Labor Day–Memorial Day, daily 8–4.*

### Dining

$–$$  ✕ **Capulin Country Store.** From May to December, seven days a week, lunch is the big meal (and big deal) of the day at the Capulin Country Store, where Jenny Lee Pugh sets the tables with chicken-fried steak with mashed potatoes, the volcano burger (smothered in chili and cheese), and excellent desserts. Sunday dinner buffets served on holiday weekends only are not to be missed, as the ranchers who drive from miles in every direction will tell you. ⊠ *U.S. 64 at Hwy. 325,* ☎ *505/ 278–3900. Reservations not accepted. AE. No lunch weekdays Jan.– Apr.*

*En Route*   Should you decide to skip Clayton and drive back west to Cimarron, take U.S. 64 west via Raton, which passes through ranch country underneath the biggest, bluest skies imaginable. Antelope herds graze alongside cattle. This is the classic West, with old windmills jutting into the sky of the rimrock country. The 29-mi stretch from Capulin passes through the **Raton-Clayton volcano field,** where the cones of quiet volcanos break the flat, green landscape.

## Clayton

❽ *43 mi east of Capulin on U.S. 64/87; 83 mi east of Springer on U.S. 56.*

Clayton, which lies flat on the high prairie at an elevation of 5,000 ft, seemingly grew up out of nothing. Downtown is sleepy and sunny, with the old-fashioned retro-veneer typical of little western towns. It's nowhere near an interstate and so lacks the scads of ubiquitous chain properties found in Las Vegas and Raton; mom-and-pop-owned shops dominate. The town bills itself as the carbon-dioxide capital of the world, but the carbon dioxide here isn't hanging in the air but rather underground, embedded in sandstone southwest of town. Cattle graze on the many ranches around Clayton.

The friendly locals here may look at you cockeyed when they learn you've come to sightsee, but Clayton does have a few notable landmarks. The guest rooms of the 1892 **Eklund Hotel Dining Room & Saloon** have been closed since the 1970s, but the splendid Victorian dining room, which is still open, is furnished with crystal chandeliers, apricot tufted-velvet booths, gilt-flocked wallpaper, and marble fireplaces. The atmosphere in the saloon is quite different but no less authentic. Here you'll find a large raw-rock fireplace, wooden booths, and mounted heads of elk and buffalo, plus historic photos and clippings of Clayton's past. The town's biggest character, Black Jack Ketchum, the notorious train robber, was hanged just out front. His last words were "I had breakfast in Clayton, but I'll have dinner in hell!" Put your boot up on the brass rail at the bar (won in a poker game) and order a cold one.

★ ☺ More than 500 fossilized dinosaur tracks can be observed along the ½-mi wooden **Dinosaur Trackway at Clayton Lake State Park,** making this one of the few sites of its kind in the world. The tracks, estimated to be 100 million years old, were made when the area was the shore of a prehistoric sea. Eight species of dinosaurs, vegetarian and carnivorous, lived here. The sparkling lake that gives the state park its name is ideal for camping, hiking, and fishing. ⊠ *Hwy. 370, 12 mi north of Clayton,* ☎ *505/374–8808,* WEB *www.emnrd.state.nm.us/ nmparks.* ☒ *$4 per vehicle.* ☉ *Daily 6 AM–9 PM.*

There are few better places in New Mexico to soak in wide-open prairie vistas, clear skies, and fresh air than in the 136,000-acre **Kiowa National Grasslands.** One section of the grasslands is near Clayton and spreads east into Oklahoma and Texas. The other is about 80 mi west of Clayton, closer to Springer, south of U.S. 56. In the section near Clayton, if you look carefully, you can see ruts made by the wagons that crossed on the Old Santa Fe Trail. The land was drought-stricken during the Dust Bowl of the 1920s and '30s, when homesteaders abandoned their farms. After that, the government purchased the land and rehabilitated it to demonstrate that it could be returned to grassland agriculture.

For an enjoyable loop drive through the grasslands, head east out of Clayton on U.S. 56; at Hwy. 406 head north to just past Seneca, to where Hwy. 406 makes a sharp turn to the east. Take the county gravel road west 3 mi and north 1 mi, noting the interpretive sign about the Santa Fe Trail. Continue a little farther north to the green gate that leads to the trail (following the limestone markers), where you can see ancient wagon ruts. Except for the occasional house or windmill, the view from the trail is not much different from what the pioneers saw. ⊠ *Off U.S. 56 (administrative office: 714 Main St., Clayton 88415,* ☎ *505/374–9652), north and south of Clayton.* ☒ *Free.*

### Dining and Lodging

$$–$$$ ✕ **Eklund Hotel Dining Room & Saloon.** American standards and Mexican and New Mexican fare (good sopaipillas) are served in both the dining room and saloon. Hand-cut steaks are the house specialty, and you can order hamburgers, beef stew, chicken-fried steak, and a decent club sandwich. ⊠ *15 Main St.,* ☎ *505/374–2551,* WEB *www.theeklund. com. MC, V. No lunch Mon.–Sat. in dining room.*

$ 🏨 **Best Western Kokopelli Lodge.** When locals have out-of-town guests they can't put up for the night, they send them to the southwestern-style Best Western, where the rooms are spacious and pets are allowed (by prior arrangement). ⊠ *702 S. 1st St., 88415,* ☎ *505/374–2589 or 800/392–6691,* FAX *505/374–2554. 44 rooms. Pool, some pets allowed. AE, D, DC, MC, V.*

## Cimarron

❾ *108 mi from Clayton via U.S. 56/412 west to Springer, I–25 north, and Hwy. 58 west; 42 mi southwest of Raton on U.S. 64.*

As you approach Cimarron from the south or east, you can't help but notice a rock projection over the town. Known as the **Tooth of Time,** it indicated to Santa Fe Trail travelers that their journey was nearing an end, for Santa Fe was only seven days away by wagon. Today the Tooth of Time is the emblem of the Philmont Scout Ranch, where 25,000 Boy Scouts assemble each summer.

In a land that was once home to Jicarilla Apaches and Utes, Cimarron later became a refuge for gamblers and outlaws and a stopping point for soldiers, gold seekers, and mountain men. (Its name means "untamed" in Spanish.) Founded in the early 1840s, it was the home of land baron Lucien Maxwell. These days, sleepy Cimarron (population 900) is a trove of Old West artifacts and lore, as well as a base from which to head out for great fishing. Don't be surprised to find deer grazing on the edge of town or encounter a herd of elk crossing the road.

With 27 bullet holes in the tin dining-room ceiling, resident ghosts profiled on the TV show *Unsolved Mysteries*, and a guest book signed by Jesse James, the **St. James Hotel** epitomizes the Wild West. Every notable outlaw of the late 19th century is said to have visited the place. Chef to presidents Lincoln and Grant, Frenchman Henri Lambert opened the St. James first as a saloon in 1872 and then eight years later developed it into a hotel. The lobby is filled with western Victoriana: overstuffed sofas; stuffed heads of bison, elk, deer, and bear on the walls; and fringe on the lamp shades. Tours of the hotel are $2.

★ The workers who toiled inside the sturdy stone building that holds the **Old Mill Museum** once processed 300 barrels of flour a day for the Maxwell Ranch and the Jicarilla Apache reservation. Now the mill houses four floors of vintage photos, clothing, tools, and memorabilia depicting life in Colfax County from the 1860s into the 20th century. ⊠ *220 W. 17th St., 1 block north of St. James Hotel,* ☎ *505/376-2417.* ☞ *$2.* ◷ *Memorial Day–Labor Day, Mon.–Wed. and Fri.–Sat. 9–5, Sun. 1–5; May and Labor Day–end of Sept., Sat. 9–5, Sun. 1–5.*

The largest scouting venue in the world, 137,000-acre **Philmont Scout Ranch** sees nearly 30,000 young visitors every summer—on any given day about 3,000 of them are out plying the property's miles of rugged trails. Phillips Petroleum magnate and Boy Scouts of American benefactor Waite Phillips established the mountainous ranch. The museums of the Philmont Scout Ranch include **Villa Philmonte,** the restored 1927 Spanish-Mediterranean summer home of Waite Phillips, furnished with European and southwestern antiques and Native American and southwestern art. Tours of the mansion are conducted in July and August. Scouting cofounder Ernest Thompson Seton donated most of the holdings of the **Philmont Museum & Seton Memorial Library,** among them New Mexican art and artifacts and books on natural history and the history of the Southwest. ⊠ *Hwy. 21, 4 mi south of Cimarron,* ☎ *505/376-2281.* ☞ *Museum free, villa tour $4.* ◷ *Museum Sept.–May, weekdays 8–5; June–Aug., daily 8–6. Villa tours July–Aug., daily 8–11 and 12:30–4:30; by appointment rest of yr.*

☾ Also here is the **Kit Carson Museum,** where costumed reenactments of life in 19th-century New Mexico and period crafts demonstrations take place in the adobe-style buildings, which include a working horno oven, blacksmith shop, and a trading post stocked as it might have been during Santa Fe Trail days. ⊠ *Hwy. 21, 11 mi south of Cimarron,* ☎ *505/376-2281.* ☞ *Free.* ◷ *June–Aug., daily 8–5.*

OFF THE      **VALLE VIDAL –** One of New Mexico's great scenic routes heads north-
BEATEN PATH  west from U.S. 64 toward the town of Costillo (44 mi north of Taos on
             Hwy. 522), affording great opportunities for sighting elk, deer, wild
             turkeys, and many other birds. The roughly 80-mi road is dirt and re-

quires several hours of driving to complete—it's okay for non–four-wheel-drive vehicles in summer and fall (assuming there hasn't been a major rainfall in a couple days and you're comfortable driving on some pretty rough roads). The trip passes through high-mountain grasslands, ponderosa, aspen, and sandstone cliffs. The fishing (season is July–December) in Valle Vidal is mighty fine—one rare trout species is found only here—and there are two campgrounds. The western section of the road is closed May through June for elk-calving season, and the eastern section is closed to protect the elks January through March. ⊠ *Off U.S. 64, turnoff is 8 mi east of Cimarron,* ☎ *505/758–6200.*

## Dining and Lodging

**$–$$**   ✕ **Colfax Tavern.** Also known as Cold Beer, New Mexico, this little
★   red roadhouse continues a tradition from the Prohibition era. An ongoing card game, excellent green-chile burgers, Shiner Bock on tap, spaghetti Mondays, brisket Wednesdays, Saturday-night dances, and a winter *Jeopardy!* tournament are among the joint's trademarks. Visitors can walk into this hangout and feel right at home. Wear your cowboy boots. ⊠ *U.S. 64, Colfax, 11 mi east of Cimarron,* ☎ *505/376–2229. Reservations not accepted. MC, V.*

**$–$$**   ✕▥ **St. James Hotel.** Lace curtains and Victorian-era antiques adorn the 12 rooms (there are also 10 modern but less distinctive motel rooms) at this landmark lodging. There's a bit of a chill in the air, and the rooms aren't well soundproofed or especially luxurious—just what you'd expect in an allegedly haunted hotel. The restaurant, Lambert's ($$–$$$), with a ceiling full of bullet holes from the old days, serves steaks and pastas, and the café, Sweetwater's ($–$$), serves American and Mexican standards. ⊠ *Hwy. 21 at 17th St., 87714,* ☎ *505/376–2664 or 800/748–2694,* ℻ *505/376–2623. 21 rooms, 1 suite. Restaurant, café, lounge. AE, MC, V.*

**$$–$$$**   ▥ **Casa del Gavilan.** On the Santa Fe Trail and directly below the Tooth
★   of Time and 10,242 Trail Peak, this 1912 white adobe compound (the name means "house of the hawk") on 225 acres is a romantic hideaway of the first order. The original owner, industrialist J. J. Nairn, used to entertain artists and other creative types here. The furnishings—artworks of various origins and southwestern antiques—have been carefully selected. You can enjoy breakfast in the dining room or out on the patio. ⊠ *Hwy. 21 (Box 518, 87714), 6 mi south of Cimarron,* ☎ *505/376–2246 or 800/428–4526,* ℻ *505/376–2247,* ᴡᴇʙ *www.casadelgavilan.com. 5 rooms. No room TVs, no smoking. AE, D, MC, V. BP.*

**$**   ▥ **Kit Carson Inn.** This serviceable motel is nothing special, but it'll do the job if you're after shelter and a hot shower. The Kit Carson Restaurant serves a decent chicken quesadilla and primo fried onions. ⊠ *31039 U.S. 64, 87714,* ☎ *505/376–2288 or 800/578–7878. 38 rooms. Restaurant, lounge. AE, D, DC, MC, V.*

## Shopping

The **Cimarron Art Gallery** (⊠ 337 E. 9th St., ☎ 505/376–2614) sells southwestern jewelry, art, and artifacts, and there's a 1930s soda fountain where you can purchase sodas, ice cream cones, and coffee drinks. **Tracy's Blue Moon Eclectics** (⊠ 333 E. 9th St., ☎ 505/376–9040) stocks handmade pottery at very reasonable prices and has other handmade gift items such as candles, jewelry, and edibles.

*En Route*   One of the most breathtaking stretches of highway in the state is U.S. 64 west from Cimarron through **Cimarron Canyon State Park** (☎ 505/377–6271, ᴡᴇʙ www.emnrd.state.nm.us/nmparks; ▨ $4 per vehicle). The road passes through a steep and lush canyon banked by 400-ft crenellated granite palisades. Paralleling the road is the sparkling

Cimarron River, which is known for its superb trout fishing. Wildlife (including elk, deer, and bear), granite cliff formations, a natural spring, an abandoned mine, and a visitor center are further draws. The park also has a campground. West of Cimarron Canyon State Park, U.S. 64 passes over a high bald ridge, from which you'll be awarded a magnificent view over **Eagle Nest Lake,** the Moreno Valley, and the eastern slope of the Sangre de Cristo Mountains in the distance. Continue down through Eagle Nest Lake village toward Angel Fire (☞ Chapter 5), making a left turn (south) onto Hwy. 434, which passes little Black Lake, offering one final view of the valley before narrowing sharply and plummeting into dark, deep, ponderosa pine–shrouded Guadalapita Canyon. Drive slowly: the road twists and turns and crosses several one-lane bridges over Coyote Creek.

The Rincon Mountains rise to 9,500 ft to the west of Hwy. 434, and to the east (a left turn off the highway) you can stop for a ramble at **Coyote Creek State Park** (☎ 505/387–2328; ☒ $4), which also has exceptionally good trout fishing and some campsites. South of Coyote Creek State Park on Hwy. 434, you'll pass through a pair of tiny, insular, agricultural villages, **Guadalapita** and **El Turquillo.** Here the highway widens as it opens into a broad sunny valley—to the east you'll spy the red-rock cliffs that form the face of Black Mesa, the land barrier between here and the eastern grasslands. In El Turquillo stands a pretty yellow chapel with a corrugated metal roof and red belfry. As you come around a bend in Hwy. 434 heading from El Turquillo toward Mora, behold the Sangre de Cristo range, specifically the east side of **Trampas and Truchas peaks,** from an angle few tourists ever see. Just before Mora and the intersection with Hwy. 518 is an intricate network of irrigation ditches that farmers employ to keep this region so fertile.

## Mora

**❿** *72 mi south from Cimarron on U.S. 64 west to Eagle Nest Lake and Hwy. 434 south via Angel Fire; 30 mi northwest of Las Vegas on Hwy. 518; 85 mi northeast of Santa Fe via the High Road to Taos north to Peñasco and then Hwy. 518 south.*

Mora is a reasonably sized, mostly Hispanic farming village where you can get gas, pick up snacks, and get your bearings. Especially if you've ⟲ got animal-loving kids with you, stop by **Victory Ranch,** a working 1,100-acre alpaca farm. You can pet and feed the high altitude–loving creatures as well as visit the gift shop for alpaca wool sweaters, hats, and gloves. The ranch is handicapped accessible. ☒ *Hwy. 434, 1 mi north of Hwy. 518,* ☎ *505/387–2254,* WEB *www.victoryranch.com.* ☒ *$2.* ☉ *Thurs.–Mon. 10–4.*

At the junction of Hwy. 434 and Hwy. 518, make a right and head a couple of miles north to **Cleveland Mill,** a fixture in Mora Valley, which served as the region's main flour mill in the late 1800s. Milling demonstrations are held over Labor Day weekend, and in the summer you can visit the artists cooperative, where craftspersons sell their sculpture, weaving, jewelry, and other fine arts. ☒ *Hwy. 518,* ☎ *505/387–2645.* ☒ *$2.* ☉ *Memorial Day–late Oct., daily 10–5.*

*En Route*   From Cleveland Mill you can either return via Hwy. 518 to Las Vegas (about 30 mi) or continue north on Hwy. 518 over the gorgeous eastern face of the Sangre de Cristo range. You'll eventually come to Peñasco, on the High Road to Taos, from which you can either go south to Santa Fe or north to Taos. A relatively untraveled route, **the drive from Mora to Peñasco** offers some spectacular mountain views and passes by old farmsteads.

As you head south on Hwy. 518 toward Las Vegas, be sure to stop in the curious **La Cueva Historic District.** In the 1850s, pioneer Vicente Romero established his legendary ranch and stone-wall mill here to supply the soldiers of Fort Union. La Cueva means "the cave," and it's said Romero slept in caves while he built the ranch. His mill generated electricity for the area until 1950. The original ranch is now known as Salmon Ranch, where you can pick raspberries early to mid-fall or buy fresh berries, raspberry jam and vinegar, and dried flowers and herbs at the original La Cueva Ranch store. Brilliantly colored wildflower gardens, homemade tamales, and raspberry sundaes draw families out for weekend excursions. The town's San Rafael Church, dating from the 1870s, is also worth a look. Call ahead for the ranch's hours. ⊠ *Hwy. 518 at Hwy. 442, 10 mi south of Mora, 20 mi north of Las Vegas,* ☎ *505/387–2900.*

# NORTHEASTERN NEW MEXICO A TO Z

### AIR TRAVEL
The two closest airports to northeastern New Mexico are Albuquerque (ABQ) and Amarillo, Texas (AMA). Albuquerque is closer to Las Vegas, Cimarron, Mora, and Springer. Amarillo is closer to Clayton and Capulin. Raton is about equidistant from both. Albuquerque International Sunport is served by American, America West, Continental, Delta, Frontier, Great Lakes, Mesa, Northwest, Rio Grande Air, Skywest, Southwest, and United airlines. Amarillo International Airport is served by American, Continental, Delta, Southwest, and United airlines. *See* Air Travel *in* Smart Travel Tips A to Z for national airline phone numbers.
➤ REGIONAL AIRPORTS: **Great Lakes Aviation** (800/554–5111). **Mesa Airlines** (800/637–2247). **Rio Grande Air** (877/435–9742).
➤ AIRPORTS: **Albuquerque International Sunport** (⊠ 2200 Sunport Blvd. SE, Albuquerque, ☎ 505/842–4366, WEB www.cabq.gov/airport). **Amarillo International Airport** (⊠ 10801 Airport Blvd. (take I–40 to Airport Blvd. exit), Amarillo, TX, ☎ 806/335–1671, WEB www.amarillo-cvb.org/airport.html).

### BUS TRAVEL
Texas, New Mexico & Oklahoma Coaches, affiliated with Greyhound Lines, makes daily runs between Albuquerque and Raton and between Taos and Raton, with stops in Las Vegas, Springer, Cimarron, and Maxwell.
➤ BUS COMPANY: **Texas, New Mexico & Oklahoma Coaches** (☎ 505/445–9071 in Raton; 800/231–2222).

### CAR RENTAL
You can rent a car from one of the majors at Amarillo International Airport and Albuquerque International Sunport. *See* Car Rental *in* Smart Travel Tips A to Z for national rental agency phone numbers.

### CAR TRAVEL
Interstate 25 is the main route into northeastern New Mexico from Santa Fe. U.S. 64 heads east into the region from Taos and west into the region from Oklahoma. U.S. 56/412 heads west from Oklahoma toward Springer, where it connects with I–25.

### EMERGENCIES
In case of emergency dial 911.
➤ HOSPITAL: **Northeastern Regional Hospital** (⊠ 1235 8th St., Las Vegas, ☎ 505/425–6751).

## TRAIN TRAVEL

Amtrak operates the *Southwest Chief* between Chicago and Los Angeles; Las Vegas and Raton are the train's stops in northeastern New Mexico.

➤ CONTACT: **Amtrak** (☎ 800/872–7245, WEB www.amtrak.com).

## VISITOR INFORMATION

➤ CONTACT: **Cimarron Chamber of Commerce** (✉ 104 N. Lincoln Ave., 87740, ☎ 505/376–2417 or 800/700–4298, WEB www.cimarronnm. com). **Clayton Chamber of Commerce** (✉ 1103 S 1st St., 88415, ☎ 505/374–9253 or 800/390–7858, WEB www.claytonnewmexico.org). **Las Vegas Chamber of Commerce** (✉ 727 Grand Ave. [Box 128, 87701], ☎ 505/425–8631 or 800/832–5947, WEB www.lasvegasnewmexico.com). **New Mexico Department of Tourism** (WEB www.nenewmexico.com). **Raton Chamber of Commerce** (✉ 100 Clayton Rd., 87740, ☎ 505/445–3689 or 800/638–6161, WEB www.raton.com). **Springer Chamber of Commerce** (✉ 606 Maxwell St., 87747, ☎ 505/483–2998).

# 7 SOUTHEASTERN NEW MEXICO

## INCLUDING WHITE SANDS NATIONAL MONUMENT AND TEXAS'S GUADALUPE MOUNTAINS

There is beauty in simplicity—in the graceful curve of a stark white-sand dune or the smooth dome of a stalagmite millions of years in the making. Even the desert's seemingly barren hills are rich in shadow, light, and color during sunset. In higher elevations, fragrant pines and cold mountain streams are oblivious to the summer heat below. Southeastern New Mexico was one of the country's last frontiers, and uncivilized charm lingers in its patches of unspoiled wilderness.

Revised
by Marilyn
Haddrill

**B**URSTING WITH GEOLOGICAL CONTRAST, southeastern New Mexico transforms before your eyes as you drive from one ecological zone to the next. Parched red earth that musters up little more than scrub oak leads to the blindingly white gypsum dunes of White Sands National Monument. From nearby Alamogordo, you can double your altitude in a 19-mi climb through Lincoln National Forest to the cool air of Cloudcroft (8,600 ft). Mule deer, with their large, curious ears, can be spotted in either the Lincoln National Forest's juniper and pines or among sand dunes along the Pecos River farther east. The Chihuahuan desert, a seemingly monotonous landscape left behind by a long-vanished ocean, holds the underground wonderland of Carlsbad Caverns, the hulking El Capitán peak, and, in Guadalupe Mountains National Park, pure, bubbling streams and prickly cactus.

For all its beauty, the area can seem harsh to strangers. Spanish settlers quickly bypassed the region in favor of the more friendly environs of the Rio Grande area in the western and northern portions of New Mexico. Yet, it was in this very region—at Black Water Draw near what is now Portales and Clovis—that evidence of some of the earliest inhabitants of North America was unearthed. Primitive hunters and gatherers lived here as long as 11,000 years ago. Artifacts prove their coexistence with such fantastic creatures as the monstrous wooly mammoth.

Native Americans lived here for hundreds of years before the eventual Spanish encroachment. Though some Hispanic settlers had established scattered communities, the area was seen primarily as the homeland of Mescalero Apaches and other tribes. In the mid-1800s, Fort Sumner and Fort Stanton became symbols of a determined U.S. takeover, offering protection for miners and Anglo settlers during intensified skirmishes with tribes. Near Ruidoso, in what is left of their traditional homeland in the Sacramento Mountains, the Mescalero Apaches now own a luxury resort and ski area that attracts tens of thousands of visitors annually.

The grasslands in southeastern New Mexico came to be ruled by cattle kings such as John Chisum, who moved from Texas in 1872 to ranch near what is now Roswell. During the first half of 1878, baby-face outlaw Billy the Kid (Henry McCarty) became a living legend during the infamous Lincoln County War, waged by rival entrepreneurs. Even the toughest of Texans referred to this neighboring corner of New Mexico as the "badlands" for its hostile terrain and notoriety as a hideout for outlaws (you'll find many "Billy the Kid was here" references in the area). In the vanished town of Seven Rivers, between Carlsbad and Artesia, shoot-outs were said to be so common that one source claimed "you could read your newspaper by the light of the gunfire." Many thought the accounts were exaggerated, until the old Seven Rivers Cemetery was moved in the early 1980s to make way for Brantley Dam and reservoir. Bullets, knife blades, and crushed bones were found with the young cowboys buried there.

The discovery of valuable minerals in the early 1900s—including oil, gas, and potash—attracted roughnecks and miners who tackled the formidable task of forcing the land to surrender its wealth. As reminders of this effort, grasshopper-like pumping jacks slurp oil from below dunes and plains. Potash mine refineries are scattered near Carlsbad, though many are closing as the ore—used primarily as a fertilizer ingredient—is depleted. The Pecos River merely trickles in places as precious water has been diverted to cultivate crops such as alfalfa and cotton. But local springs still feed the river in downtown Carlsbad, where a watery oasis provides a haven for waterfowl and those who swim, boat, or fish.

More than any other corner of the state, southeastern New Mexico retains a delicious feeling of wildness. The nearest interstate is generally as far as 200 mi away. Stargazing is no idle pastime here—no lights from strip malls or urban sprawl pollute the heavens. The Milky Way splashes across a sky so dark that if you had the time to count them, you'd swear you could see billions of stars. Scientists built one of the largest solar observatories in the world in Cloudcroft, owing to the clean view. The town of Alamogordo below it has special lights to reduce any glare. Despite the clear skies, this corner is the home of Roswell and the unending debate over an unidentified flying object (UFO) that passed through the night sky in July 1947.

# Pleasures and Pastimes

## Dining
Leave the fancy duds at home, because you're unlikely to find a formal dining room to strut into. Much of southeastern New Mexico is cowboy country: thick steaks and barbecue make the meal. The dress code is casual at all the restaurants reviewed below, with the possible exception of evening meals at the elegant Dan-Li-Ka Restaurant near Ruidoso. While you wouldn't be out of place in dressy clothes here, informal attire also is welcome.

| CATEGORY | COST* |
|---|---|
| $$$$ | over $25 |
| $$$ | $18–$25 |
| $$ | $10–$17 |
| $ | under $10 |

*per person for a main course at dinner

## Lodging
Southeastern New Mexico has the usual chain motels, and your best choice for a luxury resort, quaint cabin, or B&B would be in the Sacramento Mountains (Ruidoso and Lincoln), which is primarily a resort area. Otherwise, you'll find most communities offer the type of practical, comfortable lodging meant for business travelers.

| CATEGORY | COST* |
|---|---|
| $$$$ | over $170 |
| $$$ | $120–$170 |
| $$ | $70–$120 |
| $ | under $70 |

*All prices are for a standard double room, excluding 8–12% tax.

## Outdoor Activities and Sports
Fishing, hiking, and boating on the Pecos River and in Brantley Lake State Park are among the popular activities in southeastern New Mexico. Except on certain lakes operated by the Mescalero Apaches, who charge separate fees and set their own catch limits, you'll need a fishing license. Clerks at most sporting-goods shops can inform you of fishing regulations, which can vary. If you're hiking, be aware that trails in arid and even mountainous regions seldom have water available. Always carry water with you if you plan an excursion of more than a mile. Before you pack simply a purifier, call the administrators of the area in which you'll be hiking and find out about water sources. You might have to pack in all the water you need.

# Exploring Southeastern New Mexico

The wildly rugged Guadalupe and Sacramento mountain ranges cut through the south-central portion of the state, dividing the Pecos River valley to the east from the Mesilla River valley to the west. Make the Carlsbad Caverns National Park and White Sands National Monument on opposite sides of these mountains a top priority: they are truly among the world's greatest natural wonders.

## Great Itineraries

You can explore a cross section of the southeast's attractions in three days by moving quickly. If you start your trip from El Paso, Texas, swing through Guadalupe Mountains and Carlsbad Caverns national parks first. If you're dropping down from Albuquerque, reverse the itinerary and make cities such as Ruidoso and Roswell your first stops before traveling on to the national parks.

### IF YOU HAVE 3 DAYS

It's best to start from the gateway of El Paso, Texas, and make **Guadalupe Mountains National Park** ① your first rest stop. Just north of the mountains, over the Texas state line, is **Carlsbad Caverns National Park** ②. Take the Big Room Tour in the late morning or early afternoon, and in warmer months, be sure to catch the spectacular evening bat exodus out of the cave's mouth. Afterward, you can drop by Granny's Opera House in **White's City** ③ for a live melodrama performance and overnight in ⊡ **Carlsbad** ④. On the morning of day two, stop by **Living Desert Zoo and Gardens State Park** before heading north to **Roswell** ⑤ to learn about alleged alien visitors at the **International UFO Museum and Research Center** and view the impressive collections of the **Roswell Museum and Art Center,** including the Goddard rocketry display and paintings by southwestern artists. Push on to overnight in ⊡ **Lincoln** ⑧. You'll awaken in a town of 70, where the ghosts of past gunslingers loom large. Make time for some outdoor activities in the mountains surrounding **Ruidoso** ⑩. A ski resort is open in the winter, while horse racing takes place at **Ruidoso Downs** in summer. Arrange your schedule so that you'll have at least an hour for **White Sands National Monument,** which is open during the summer until 9 PM.

### IF YOU HAVE 5 DAYS

Spend most of your first day at **Guadalupe Mountains National Park** ① in Texas. At **McKittrick Canyon** are three trails of varying lengths. On your first evening, view the bat flight at **Carlsbad Caverns National Park** ② and spend the night in ⊡ **White's City** ③.

On the morning of day two, return to Carlsbad Caverns to take the Natural Entrance Route into the depths of the cavern, after which you can loop through the interior, and then take the Big Room Tour. That afternoon, visit **Living Desert Zoo and Gardens State Park** in ⊡ **Carlsbad** ④. In the evening, consider strolling some of the scenic walkways along the Pecos River at the **Lake Carlsbad Recreation Area.**

On day three, drive north on U.S. 285 to **Roswell** ⑤, where you can stop at the **Roswell Museum and Art Center** and **International UFO Museum and Research Center.** Continue to ⊡ **Lincoln** ⑧ on U.S. 70/380 west and take in a bit of the Wild West before settling down for the night. Spend day four perusing the museums and galleries of ⊡ **Ruidoso** ⑩ and **Ruidoso Downs.** In the morning take your post-breakfast hike in **Cloudcroft** ⑬ before examining the space ware at the **Space Center** in **Alamogordo** ⑫. Close your day and finish up the last roll of film at **White Sands National Monument.**

### When to Tour Southeastern New Mexico

Winters tend to be gentle in the desert regions, but between May and early September blistering heat is not uncommon. Even the mountainous areas can be uncomfortably warm during a hot spell. Plan summer outdoor excursions for early morning or late evening. Spring is cooler, but it's often accompanied by nasty, dust-laden winds. One of the best times to visit is between late September and early November, when skies are clear blue and the weather is usually balmy. In winter months, keep in mind that the higher elevations of Ruidoso can accumulate some hefty snows.

# THE SOUTHEAST CORNER

Some folks refer to the southeast as "Little Texas," and geographically and in other ways it is indeed an extension of its neighbor to the east. The biggest attraction—Carlsbad Caverns National Park—is just above the state line. Cattle and sheep roam miles of arid pastures, reminiscent of days when livestock growers challenged a harsh, defiant land that didn't yield easily to civilization. During the past two decades a steady migration of newer residents—many of them retirees leaving crowded metropolitan areas for wide-open spaces and clean air—has introduced a more rounded mix of cultures and viewpoints.

## Guadalupe Mountains National Park

★ ❶ *U.S. 62/180, 110 mi northeast of El Paso, Texas; 40 mi southwest of Carlsbad Caverns National Park.*

The vast Guadalupe Mountains jut out of the desert, and El Capitán peak, a lordly symbol of the mountains themselves, is visible for miles in all directions. The mountains provide sanctuary for diverse populations of vegetation and wildlife, including hundreds of mule deer and the occasional mountain lion. Fossils left over from an ancient sea are part of a geological terrain popular with students and researchers.

This national park is relatively new, created by Congress in 1966 and formally established in 1972. The heart of the acreage is from a gift of 5,632 acres given to the federal government by the Wallace Pratt family. Pratt had worked as a geologist for Humble Oil, later known as Exxon, when he first viewed and later acquired the wildly beautiful McKittrick Canyon area of the park in 1921. Most of the remaining acreage was added in a purchase of 70,000 acres from the J. C. Hunter Ranch.

These untamed foothills and canyons have never been tapped for development because of a general lack of water. If you don't have time for a hike, you can pull into the **visitor center** to view exhibits and a slide show that can give you a quick introduction to what this 86,416-acre park is all about. You'll see panoramic vistas and glimpses of wildflowers. But photos just can't do justice to the real thing. There are 80 mi of hiking trails, from short excursions to grueling adventures. Take your pick. But try not to leave without giving one of the trails a try.

About 1 mi northeast of the visitor center, turn west off U.S. 62/180 to see the **Pinery Butterfield Station Ruins.** This was one of the stops along the old Butterfield Overland Mail Coach route in the mid-1800s, where passengers en route from St. Louis or San Francisco could pause for rest and refreshment. There is a paved ⅔-mi round-trip trail. At the **Frijole Ranch History Museum** you can view cultural exhibits representing the Guadalupe Mountains area. Turn west off U.S. 62/180, about 2 mi northeast of the visitor center.

## Southeastern New Mexico

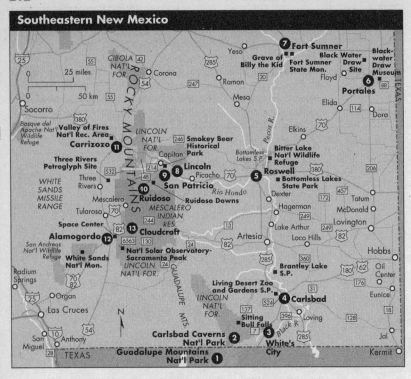

The **McKittrick Canyon** gate opens from 8 until 4:30 daily in winter months and from 8 through 6 when daylight saving time is in effect (closed Christmas Day). In this day-use area you can hike almost 1 mi on a nature loop or take a 4½-mi round-trip excursion to the Pratt Lodge (now vacant). Another option is a 6¾-mi round-trip to the Grotto picnic area. Turn west off U.S. 62/180 6 mi northeast of the visitor center and travel 4 mi to McKittrick Canyon Visitor Center, where the trails begin. ⊠ *Guadalupe Mountains National Park (HC60, Box 400, Salt Flat, TX 79847), off U.S. 62/180 55 mi southwest of Carlsbad and 110 mi northeast of El Paso,* ☎ *915/828–3251.* 🖅 *Free.*

## Camping

⚠ **Cornudas High Desert RV Park & Motel.** This pit stop in the middle of nowhere is on your way to the Guadalupe Mountains, 63 mi east of El Paso. A six-room hotel decorated with a western storefront is a virtual oasis in the midst of utter isolation. Owner May Carson makes a great green-chile burger. ⊠ *Off U.S. 62/180, 50 mi southwest of Guadalupe Mountains National Park visitor center,* ☎ *915/964–2409. Flush toilets, restaurant, electricity, public telephone, general store, service station. 8 RV sites with full hook-up, 6 motel rooms.* 🖅 *RV sites $17, motel $34. AE, D, DC, MC, V.*

⚠ **Dog Canyon Campground.** This campground is a little tricky to find—as well as remote—but well worth the effort. On the north side of Guadalupe National Park, it can be accessed by turning west on County Road 408 off U.S. 62/180, about 9 mi south of Carlsbad. Drive 23 mi on this county road; then turn south on Hwy. 137. Travel 43 mi through Lincoln National Forest until the road dead-ends just at the park boundary, at the New Mexico–Texas state line. Here, you'll find a very well-maintained camping area in a coniferous forest, where hiking trails are available. ⊠ *Guadalupe Mountains National Park, off*

*Rte. 137, 65 mi southwest of Carlsbad, ☎ 505/981–2418. Flush toilets, drinking water, picnic tables, public telephone, ranger station. 4 RV sites, 9 tent sites.* ⌨ *$8. AE, D, DC, MC, V.*

⚠ **Pine Springs Campground.** You'll be snuggled amid piñon and juniper trees at the base of a tall mountain peak at this site behind the Guadalupe Mountains National Park visitor center. Wood and charcoal fires are prohibited, although camp stoves are allowed. Shade here can be a bit sparse in the intense summer heat. ⊠ *Guadalupe Mountains National Park, off U.S. 62/180, ☎ 915/828–3251. Flush toilets, drinking water, picnic tables, public telephone, ranger station. 20 tent sites, 18 RV sites, 1 wheelchair-accessible site, 2 group sites.* ⌨ *$8. Advance reservations accepted for group sites only; call to determine availability of other sites. AE, D, DC, MC, V.*

## Dining

$ ✕ **Cornudas Café.** Your first thought when you see the colorful flags ★ flapping outside this remote roadside café will be "How did this get here?" Food has been served at this site for almost a century, dating from the construction of the first roadway through the area. Try the café's famous green chile hamburgers, and enjoy the quirky, ornery ambience. Levi-clad cowboy legs with boots hold up the tables. Visitors leave everything from caps to license plates to business cards to add to the clutter. Owner May Carson never throws any of it away. Mexican imports are for sale in the gift shop. The annual Cornudas Chile Cook-off takes place in September. ⊠ *Off U.S. 62/180, 63 mi east of El Paso, Texas, and 103 mi southwest of Carlsbad, ☎ 915/964–2409. AE, D, DC, MC, V.*

# Carlsbad Caverns National Park

★ ❷ *167 mi east of El Paso, Texas, on U.S. 62/180; 320 mi southeast of Albuquerque.*

Hundreds of thousands of people come each year to Carlsbad Caverns National Park to view its subterranean chambers, fantastic rock formations, and delicate mineral sculptures, which have evocative names like Hall of the White Giant, the Kings Palace, the Devils Den, the Caveman, and Iceberg Rock. In this setting you can feel insignificant and yet connected to eternity itself. Near the Rock of Ages stalagmite, a now abandoned tradition called for visitors to sit in the utter darkness during the singing of the hymn *Rock of Ages*.

The park is in the Chihuahuan Desert, which extends north from Mexico into southwestern Texas and southeastern New Mexico. Pictographs near the main cave entrance indicate that pre-Columbian Native Americans took shelter here more than 1,000 years ago, though archaeologists doubt that they ventured far inside. It wasn't until the 19th century that nearby settlers rediscovered the caverns, their attention captured by the smokelike swirling columns of bats leaving the caverns each night to feed on insects. Area caves were mined for bat dung, which was used as fertilizer for many years. No one was interested in the caves for any other reason until the early 1920s, after cowboy Jim White had explored them for two decades. White finally secured a photographer, Ray Davis, to bear witness to his extravagant claims about this amazing underground environment. Davis's photos sparked interest in the caverns. White turned tour operator, taking people down 170 ft in a bucket left over from the days of mining bat guano. The federal government got wind of this natural wonder, and in 1923 President Calvin Coolidge designated the caverns a national monument; in 1930 the area was upgraded to the status of national park.

The origins of Carlsbad Caverns go back 250 million years, when the 300-mi-long Capitán Reef formed around the edge of the warm, shallow sea that once covered this region. The sea evaporated and the reef was buried until a few million years ago, when a combination of erosion and earthquakes brought parts of it back aboveground. Rainwater seeping down through the reef's cracks gradually enlarged them into cavities, which eventually collapsed, forming huge rooms. For eons the evaporated limestone deposited on the cave ceilings grew into great hanging stalactites, which in turn dripped onto the floor. In time massive stalagmites grew up to meet them, and other more fragile formations such as cave pearls, draperies, popcorn, and lily pads were formed.

Don't give in to the temptation to touch the cave's walls and jutting rock formations. Oil from the human hand forms a type of waterproofing that inhibits the natural water seepage. You also shouldn't leave the guided pathways; if you do, you not only risk serious injury but can damage the cave.

The temperature inside Carlsbad Cavern remains at a constant 56°F. It's damp, so bring a sweater and comfortable shoes with rubber soles—because of the moisture, the paved walkways can get slippery. The cavern is well lighted, and park rangers provide assistance and information. Electronic signals along the way trigger the CD-ROM audio guide—recorded commentary by park rangers, geologists, and cavers—for the Natural Entrance and Big Room trails. Exhibits at the visitor center describe park history and geology and the lives of bats. You can eat aboveground at the visitor center or at an underground lunchroom. ⊠ *Carlsbad Caverns National Park, 3225 National Parks Hwy., Carlsbad 88220,* ☎ *505/785–2232 recorded information and direct contact; 800/967–2283 reservations (central National Park Service number);* WEB *www.nps.gov/cave.* 🎟 *General entrance $6, CD-ROM audio guide $3 additional; see individual cave descriptions below for additional fees and hrs of operation.* ☉ *Visitor center Memorial Day–mid-Aug., daily 8–7; mid-Aug.–Memorial Day, daily 8–5:30.*

There are two self-guided routes into Carlsbad Cavern: the **Natural Entrance Route and the Big Room Route.** If you take the Natural Entrance Route, you'll proceed on foot along a paved walkway that winds into the caverns' depths for about a mile, passing through underground rooms and descending slowly to a depth of about 750 ft. It takes about one hour to complete; the trail can be slick and the grades are fairly steep, so be prepared for a strenuous hike. The Big Room Route is less difficult. A high-speed elevator from the visitor center carries you down 750 ft to an underground lunchroom where you can begin your exploration. This mile-long route also takes about an hour to walk. A portion of the main cavern is accessible to visitors using wheelchairs. In both cases you'll visit the Big Room, large enough to hold 14 football fields; the highest part of the ceiling reaches 255 ft. 🎟 *Combined ticket to Natural Entrance Route and Big Room Route $6.* ☉ *Natural Entrance Route Memorial Day–mid-Aug., daily 8:30–3:30 (last entry to the caverns); mid-Aug.–May, daily 8:30–2 (last entry to the caverns). Big Room Route Memorial Day–mid-Aug., daily 8:30–5 (last elevator down); mid-Aug.–Memorial Day, daily 8:30–3:30 (last elevator down).*

A third option for exploring the caverns is the ranger-led **Kings Palace Tour** through the Kings Palace, the Queens Chamber, the Papoose Room, and the Green Lake Room. The tour covers about a mile, including an uphill 80-ft climb on a switchback trail, and takes about 1½ hours to complete. 🎟 *$8 (in addition to $6 general entrance fee to caverns).* ☉ *Early Sept.–early Mar., daily at 10 and 2; mid-Mar.–Memorial Day,* *daily at 9, 11, 1, and 3; Memorial Day–early Sept., daily 9–11 and 1–3 on the hr.*

A few other **off-trail tours** are available within Carlsbad Caverns. Lefthand Tunnel is in an undeveloped part of the caverns and contains clear pools and ancient reef fossils. Lower Cave, billed as a "moderately strenuous" tour, involves climbs on 50 ft of vertical ladders. Children younger than six are not allowed on this tour. Hall of the White Giant is a strenuous tour that requires squirming long distances on your hands and knees through tight passageways into a remote chamber with glistening white formations. The tour of "wild" Spider Cave takes you through the park's backcountry and involves tight crawlways; avoid this one if you're squeamish. Reservations are essential for the special tours. The minimum age for visitors to the Hall of the White Giant and the Spider Cave is 12. ☎ *505/785–2232; 800/967–2283 reservations.* ✉ *In addition to general entrance fee to cavern: Lefthand Tunnel $7, Lower Cave $20, Hall of the White Giant $20, Spider Cave $20.* ☉ *Lefthand Tunnel, daily at 9 AM; Lower Cave, weekdays at 1; Hall of the White Giant, Sat. at 1; Spider Cave (separate from main cavern), Sun. at 1.*

**Slaughter Canyon Cave,** 25 mi from the main cavern, is much less accessible. Millions of years old, the cave was discovered by Tom Tucker, a local goatherd, in 1937. The cave consists primarily of a 1,140-ft-long corridor with numerous side passages. The total extent of the surveyed passage is 1¾ mi, and the lowest point is 250 ft below the surface. Outstanding formations are the Christmas Tree, the Monarch, the Tear Drop, and the China Wall.

Rangers lead groups of 25 on a two-hour lantern tour of the cave. Children under age six are not permitted. The cave temperature is a constant 62°F, and the humidity is a clammy 90%. You'll need to bring along your own flashlight, hiking boots or good walking shoes (sneakers aren't recommended), and drinking water. Photographs are permitted, but no tripod setups are allowed because the group moves along at a relatively brisk pace. Unless you're in great physical shape and have a long attention span, Slaughter Canyon Cave may be more cave viewing than you bargained for. But it's a great adventure if you want to experience what cave exploration is really like, minus paved pathways and electric lighting.

Make reservations at least a day ahead of your visit; in summer it's recommended you reserve a place at least two weeks ahead. The last few miles of the road to the cave are gravel. The mouth is at the end of a ½-mi path up a 500-ft rise. Allot sufficient time to complete the drive and climb or you might arrive late for the tour. ☎ *505/785–2232; 800/967–2283 reservations.* ✉ *$15.* ☉ *Tours Memorial Day–Labor Day, daily at 10 and 1; early Sept–early Mar.; weekends at 10; mid-Mar.–Memorial Day, weekends at 8 and 11.*

The newest discovery in Carlsbad Caverns National Park is **Lechuguilla Cave,** the deepest limestone cave in the United States. Scientists began mapping the cave network in 1986, and though they've located more than 106 mi of caverns extending to a depth of more than 1,570 ft, much more of this area along the park's northern border remains to be investigated. Lechuguilla is not open to the public, but an exhibit describing it can be viewed at the visitor center.

Every evening between late May and mid-October at about sunset, Mexican free-tailed bats swirl by the tens of thousands out of the cavern's ★ entrance to scout for flying insects. Watching the nightly **bat flights** has been one of the greatest attractions at Carlsbad Caverns since 1929.

(No scientist has yet figured out how a bat hanging upside down in a dark cave knows when the sun has set outside.) The population of bats varies even daily but is estimated to be several hundred thousand. Collectively, the bats consume more than 3 tons of bugs per night. Prior to the exodus, which begins at dusk, a park ranger gives an informative talk about these much-maligned creatures. The time of the bat flights varies, so ranger lectures are flexible as well; the time is posted at the visitor center. The bats leave for the warmer climates of Mexico in winter. ⊠ *Bat Flight Amphitheater (near visitor center).* ☞ *Free.*

The scenic 9½-mi **Walnut Canyon Desert Drive** begins ½ mi from the visitor center and travels along the top of the ridge to the edge of Rattlesnake Canyon and back down through upper Walnut Canyon to the main entrance road. The backcountry scenery on this one-way gravel loop is stunning; go late in the afternoon or early in the morning to enjoy the full spectrum of changing light and dancing colors. You might also spot some of the many inquisitive mule deer that inhabit the park. The self-guided, partially wheelchair-accessible Desert Nature Walk, about ½ mi long, begins near the cavern's entrance.

Trees shade the picnic and recreation area at **Rattlesnake Springs,** near the Black River—don't let the name scare you; you wouldn't find any more rattlesnakes here than at any other similar site in the Southwest. A favorite of bird-watchers, the springs were a source of water for Native Americans hundreds of years ago. Today it's the main source of water for the park. Overnight camping and parking are not allowed.

## Camping

Backcountry camping is by permit only in Carlsbad Caverns National Park; free permits can be obtained at the visitor center, where you can also pick up a map of areas closed to camping. You'll need to hike to campsites. There are no vehicle or RV camping areas in the park.

Nearby Brantley Lake State Park (in the town of Carlsbad) and Dog Canyon Campground (in Guadalupe Mountains National Park) in Lincoln National Forest have camping facilities. Commercial sites can be found in White's City and Carlsbad.

## Outdoor Activities and Sports

### BIRD-WATCHING

From turkey vultures to golden eagles, more than 200 species of birds have been identified in Carlsbad Caverns National Park. The best place to bird-watch in the park, if not the entire state, is Rattlesnake Springs. Ask for a checklist at the visitor center and then start looking for red-tailed hawks, red-winged blackbirds, white-throated swifts, northern flickers, pygmy nuthatches, yellow-billed cuckoos, roadrunners, mallards, American coots, and green- and blue-winged teal.

### HIKING

Hiking in Carlsbad Caverns National Park can be exhilarating—the desert terrain is stark and awe-inspiring—but few trails are marked. A topographical map, available at the visitor center, is helpful for finding some of the old ranch trails. Permits aren't required except for overnight backpacking, but all hikers are requested to register at the information desk at the visitor center. Bring water; there's none available. No pets or guns are permitted.

# White's City

❸ *7 mi east of Carlsbad Caverns National Park on Hwy. 7, at junction with U.S. 62/180.*

At the turnoff from the highway to Carlsbad Caverns, the one-road town of White's City contains motels, restaurants, a saloon, a campground, a grocery store, a post office, a gas station, souvenir shops, a museum, a water park for registered guests, and even a place to take in staged melodramas—all along a simple, western-style boardwalk. The town is one of the few privately owned towns in the country. The owners, the White family, live in a cluster of homes above the hotel properties.

Early American memorabilia and artifacts—antique dolls and dollhouses, guns and rifles, music boxes, old cars, and a 6,000-year-old mummified Native American (or so the label says)—fill the homespun **Million Dollar Museum.** Thirty-two mostly German dollhouses made between the late 19th and mid-20th centuries are also on display. ⊠ *21 Carlsbad Caverns Hwy., off White's City boardwalk,* ☎ *505/785–2291.* 🎟 *$3.50.* ⊙ *Mid-May–mid-Sept., daily 7 AM–10 PM; mid-Sept.–mid-May, daily 7–6.*

★ **Granny's Opera House** is the place to go if you're ready to shed your inhibitions and whoop it up. During the hour-long old-fashioned melodramas, you can boo at the villain, throw popcorn, cheer on the heroes, tune up your vocal cords for a sing-along, and be pulled on stage. ⊠ *13 Carlsbad Caverns Hwy.,* ☎ *505/785–2291.* 🎟 *$7.50 (includes popcorn).* ⊙ *June–Sept., Fri.–Sun. at about 7:30 PM, depending on when bats fly at Carlsbad Caverns National Park.*

## Dining and Lodging

$$ ✕ **Velvet Garter Restaurant and Saloon.** This eatery dishes up steaks, chicken, shrimp, and Mexican food in an Old West atmosphere, although a newly added Italian menu with pasta and luscious sauces has proven to be a hit. Food prices are old-style, too. A 10-ounce rib-eye steak costs $16.95, and all the entrées come with soup and salad. ⊠ *26 Carlsbad Caverns Hwy.,* ☎ *505/785–2291. AE, D, MC, V.*

$ ✕ **Jack's.** A good spot to have a hearty breakfast before heading off to the caverns, this fast-food favorite shares an adobe-style building with the Velvet Garter Restaurant. Grab a booth and order eggs, a burger, Mexican food, or pizza. ⊠ *26 Carlsbad Caverns Hwy.,* ☎ *505/785– 2291. No credit cards.*

$$ 🏨 **Best Western Cavern Inn.** This Territorial-style, two-story motor inn just outside the entrance leading to Carlsbad Caverns has rooms with southwestern decor. Under the same ownership next door is the hacienda-style Best Western Guadalupe Inn, with the same rates and southwestern furnishings. The Guadalupe Inn has 42 rooms. Many tour groups and families stay at both hotels, which share facilities. All guests are free to use the water park, open May through September. The high-desert landscaping includes piñon pines, ocotillo cacti, and yucca plants. Mule deer often amble down from their protected haven at Carlsbad Caverns National Park. ⊠ *17 Carlsbad Caverns Hwy. (look for large registration sign on south side of road), 88268,* ☎ *505/785– 2291 or 800/228–3767,* 🖷 *505/785–2283,* 🕸 *www.whitescity. caverns.com. 63 rooms. In-room data ports, pool, spa, playground, some pets allowed (fee). AE, D, DC, MC, V.*

# Lincoln National Forest

*Access via Hwy. 137 (turn southwest off U.S. 285 12 mi northwest of Carlsbad), U.S. 82 west from Artesia, U.S. 70 west from Roswell, U.S. 82 east from Alamogordo, U.S. 70 east from Tularosa, and U.S. 380 east from Carrizozo. Numerous other gravel or dirt roads lead into the forest.*

Covering 1.1 million acres of Eddy, Otero, Chaves, and Lincoln counties, this magnificent forest is distinguished by a diversity of plant and animal life. It encompasses two distinct regions, ranging from arid, lower elevations near Carlsbad to the towering pines and mountain peaks of the Ruidoso area. The forest's southernmost portion of piñon and juniper stretches through the Guadalupe Mountains to connect with the Carlsbad Caverns and Guadalupe Mountains national parks. The forest land has many caves, some of which can be accessed free by permit. Call the **Guadalupe Ranger District** (☎ 505/885–4181) for permit information. These caves are not developed, so be prepared for primitive conditions. The only private development you'll find other than scattered ranches is at **Queen** (49 mi southwest of Carlsbad, on Hwy. 137). This site consists of a small mobile-home community, restaurant, store, gas station, and church camp. This forested area is hugely popular with hunters lured by ample populations of mule deer.

Water sources in the southernmost forest are virtually nonexistent, except for livestock catchments maintained by ranchers. Coming upon
★ **Sitting Bull Falls,** you'll think you've wandered onto a Hollywood movie set of an oasis. Water cascades off a 150-ft-high cliff face to create clear, sparkling pools below. A 1-mi hike from the parking lot over a paved trail takes you to a desert riparian area with ferns, watercress, and cottonwoods. At the parking lot, the forest service provides rock ramadas for picnic areas. Viewing decks are also available, along with rest rooms. Swimming is permitted, and 16 mi of hiking trails lace the area. The park is open for day use only. If you want to camp overnight, drive southwest on Hwy. 137 until you reach the New Mexico–Texas state line and Dog Canyon Campground in Guadalupe Mountains National Park. ⊠ *From Carlsbad take U.S. 285 north about 12 mi, then turn west on Hwy. 137 for 27 mi,* ☎ *no phone.* ⊡ *$5 per vehicle, free Wed.* ⊙ *Daily dawn–dusk.*

The northernmost portion of the Lincoln forest, surrounding the resort community of Ruidoso, has some of the more traditional evergreen attributes of snowy mountain peaks, lakes, and gurgling mountain streams. Development has capitalized on this beauty, so the forest becomes part of the ambience of cabins, resorts, church camps, condos, and ski runs. Still, there are many miles of pristine areas. Hiking trails often thread wilderness that is free from civilization's encroachment.

More than 25 camping sites are scattered throughout Lincoln National Forest. While fishing lakes and streams are available on private, municipal, or tribal lands, there is very little opportunity for the sport on public forest land. To obtain more information about hiking, camping, hunting, and other recreation, contact the forest service's main headquarters in Alamogordo (☎ 505/437–6030).

## Carlsbad

❹ *27 mi northeast of Carlsbad Caverns National Park, east on Hwy. 7 and north on U.S. 60/180; 20 mi north of White's City on U.S. 62/180.*

On the Pecos River, with 2¾ mi of beaches and many picturesque riverside pathways, Carlsbad, population 25,000, seems suspended between the past and the present. The Territorial town square, a block from the river, encircles a Pueblo-style country courthouse designed by New Mexican architect John Gaw Meem, who also designed many of the buildings on the University of New Mexico campus in Albuquerque. Some of the city's fanciest houses occupy quiet residential areas along the riverbanks.

A boat parade and evening fireworks attract thousands of visitors to the Lake Carlsbad Recreation Area for Fourth of July festivities. The ★ hugely popular **Christmas on the Pecos** (☎ 505/887–6516, WEB www. christmasonthepecos.com) features dazzling Christmas displays that decorate backyards and lots along a 2½-mi stretch on the Pecos River. Demand has created 12 tours nightly from Thanksgiving to New Year's Eve (excluding Christmas Eve). Internet ticket sales now are available year-round. Prices for boat tours vary ($5 Monday–Wednesday, $7 Sunday and Thursday, $9 Friday–Saturday). The night breeze blowing across the water can be chilly, so dress warmly. Boats leave from the **Pecos River Village** (✉ 710 N. Muscatel Ave.), once an amusement park and now a convention center.

The **Carlsbad Museum and Arts Center** houses Pueblo pottery, Native American artifacts, and early cowboy and ranch memorabilia along with exhibitions of contemporary art. The real treasure, though, is the McAdoo Collection, with works by painters of the Taos Society of Artists. ✉ 418 W. Fox St., ☎ 505/887–0276. 🎟 Free. ⊗ Mon.–Sat. 10–5.

★ ☾ Atop Ocotillo Hills on the northwest edge of Carlsbad, **Living Desert Zoo and Gardens State Park** contains impressive plants and animals native to the Chihuahuan Desert. The Desert Arboretum has hundreds of exotic cacti and succulents, and the Living Desert Zoo—more a reserve than a traditional zoo—is home to mountain lions, deer, elk, wolves, buffalo, rattlesnakes, and other indigenous species. Nocturnal exhibits and dioramas let you in on the area's nighttime wildlife. Though there are shaded rest areas, rest rooms, and water fountains, in hot weather try to visit during the early morning or early evening, when it's cooler. In spring the Living Desert hosts the four-day Annual Mescal Roast and Mountain Spirit Dances demonstrated by members of the Mescalero Apache Indian tribe. Tribal members once harvested the revered desert plant, mescal, for food. ✉ 1504 Miehls Dr., off U.S. 285, ☎ 505/887–5516. 🎟 $4. ⊗ Memorial Day–Labor Day, daily 8–8; Labor Day–Memorial Day, daily 9–5; last admission 1½ hrs before closing.

## Dining and Lodging

$–$$ ✕ **Bamboo Garden Restaurant.** Possibly the best Chinese food in ★ southern New Mexico can be found right here in cowboy country. Kung Pao chicken, a dish with vegetables and peanuts stir-fried in chile pepper sauce, is among menu items that include standard favorites such as sweet-and-sour pork and cashew shrimp. Surroundings are pleasant but not elegant, with Asian decor. The food is fresh, crisp, and skillfully prepared. ✉ 1511 N. Canal St., ☎ 505/887–5145. AE, D, MC, V. Closed Mon.

$ ✕ **Furr's Cafeteria.** For a chain establishment, the food at roomy Furr's is exceptionally good. The fare includes fried chicken, roast beef, and lasagna. ✉ 901 S. Canal St., ☎ 505/885–0430. AE, D, MC, V.

$ ✕ **Lucy's Mexicali Restaurant & Entertainment Club.** "The best margaritas and hottest chile in the world" is the motto of this family-owned oasis of great Mexican food. All the New Mexican standards are prepared here, along with some not-so-standard items such as chicken fajita burritos, Tucson-style chimichangas, and brisket *carnitas* (meat sautéed with chiles and seasonings). Low-fat and fat-free Mexican dishes and 12 microbrewery beers are served. Live entertainment is offered on weekends. ✉ 701 S. Canal St., ☎ 505/887–7714. AE, D, DC, MC, V.

$ ✕ **Red Chimney.** If you hanker for sweet and tangy barbecue, try this restaurant, which has log-cabin decor and an Early American atmosphere. Sauce from an old family recipe is slathered on chicken, pork, beef, turkey, and ham. Fried catfish and other home-style dishes are also served. ⊠ *817 N. Canal St.,* ☎ *505/885–8744. MC, V. Closed weekends.*

**$$**  ✕🏠 **Holiday Inn Carlsbad Downtown.** The rugs, paintings, and room
**★**  decor of this two-story lodge harmonize with the building's Territo-
rial theme. Children under 19 stay free if they're in a room with their
parents. The hotel's Phenix Bar & Grill is a pub that earned its name
and quirky spelling from a rip-roaring Old West town that once flour-
ished a few miles away. ⊠ *601 S. Canal St., 88220,* ☎ *505/885–8500
or 800/742–9586,* 𝖥𝖠𝖷 *505/887–5999. 100 rooms, 5 suites. Restaurant,
in-room data ports, cable TV, pool, gym, hot tub, lounge, playground,
laundry service, meeting room, airport shuttle, some pets allowed.
AE, D, DC, MC, V. BP.*

**$–$$**  🏠 **Best Western Stevens Inn.** Scenes of cavern formations and Carlsbad's
**★**  historic courthouse are etched in mirrored glass and carved into wooden
doors at this motel, which provides a touch of elegance. Prints of western landscapes decorate the spacious rooms, which have voice mail. Prime
rib and steaks are served in the evening at the motel's Flume Room Restaurant and Coffee Shop, which opens for continuous service beginning at
5:30 AM daily. ⊠ *1829 S. Canal St. (Box 580, 88220),* ☎ *505/887–2851
or 800/730–2851,* 𝖥𝖠𝖷 *505/887–6338,* 𝖶𝖤𝖡 *www.carlsbadnm.com. 202
rooms. Restaurant, some in-room data ports, some kitchenettes, some
microwaves, some refrigerators, cable TV, pool, wading pool, hot tub,
bar, playground, laundry facilities, meeting rooms, airport shuttle, some
pets allowed (fee). AE, D, DC, MC, V.*

**$**  🏠 **Days Inn.** Rooms at this motel on the south side of town have
southwestern decor, king-size beds, and sofa beds. ⊠ *3910 National
Parks Hwy., 88220,* ☎ *505/887–7800; 800/329–7466 central reservations;* 𝖥𝖠𝖷 *505/885–9433. 42 rooms, 8 suites. Cable TV, indoor pool,
airport shuttle, some pets allowed (fee). AE, D, DC, MC, V. CP.*

**$**  🏠 **Carlsbad Super 8.** This three-story motel 2 mi from the regional air-
port and one block from Carlsbad's convention center has rooms in
southwestern tones with generic furnishings and coffeemakers. Outdoor grills are available, and nearby is a fast-food restaurant that's open
24 hours. The outdoor pool is heated. ⊠ *3817 National Parks Hwy.,
88220,* ☎ *505/887–8888; 800/800–8000 central reservations;* 𝖥𝖠𝖷 *505/
885–0126. 60 rooms. Some microwaves, some refrigerators, cable TV,
pool, hot tub. AE, D, DC, MC, V. CP.*

**$**  🏠 **Continental Inn.** This inn is south of Carlsbad, about 30 minutes
from Carlsbad Caverns. The simple rooms have typical matching curtains and bedspreads in southwestern patterns. The small grounds are
well kept. ⊠ *3820 National Parks Hwy., 88220,* ☎ *505/887–0341 or
877/887–0341,* 𝖥𝖠𝖷 *505/885–1186. 57 rooms, 3 suites. Some microwaves, some refrigerators, cable TV, pool, airport shuttle, some pets
allowed. AE, D, DC, MC, V.*

**$**  🏠 **Quality Inn.** One mile from the municipal airport, this two-story stone-
face inn surrounds a landscaped patio with a pool and a sundeck
about as large as an aircraft hangar. Rooms are comfortable, with nondescript modern furnishings. The Cafe in the Park serves free Continental breakfasts to guests. ⊠ *3706 National Parks Hwy., 88220,* ☎
*505/887–2861 or 800/321–2861,* 𝖥𝖠𝖷 *505/887–2861. 120 rooms.
Restaurant, cable TV, pool, hot tub, bar, shop, laundry service, airport
shuttle, some pets allowed. AE, D, DC, MC, V. CP.*

**$**  🏠 **Stagecoach Inn.** A family-style motor inn, the Stagecoach has basic
rooms at affordable rates (which go up during holiday periods). On
the premises is a tree-shaded park with a playground and a picnic area.
⊠ *1819 S. Canal St., 88220,* ☎ 𝖥𝖠𝖷 *505/887–1148. 55 rooms. Restaurant, kitchenettes, microwaves, refrigerators, pool, wading pool, hot
tub, playground, laundry service, some pets allowed (fee). AE, D, DC,
MC, V.*

## Camping

⚠ **Brantley Lake State Park.** Thirteen miles north of Carlsbad, the campground in this state park is shaded with Afghan pines, Mexican elders, and desert plants. Some camping and picnic sites have views of the 3,000-acre lake and dam—an inviting haven in this upper Chihuahuan desert region. Unsupervised swimming also is allowed, along with boating and fishing for largemouth bass, bluegill, crappie, and walleye pike. ⊠ *U.S. 285 (Box 2288, 88221),* ☎ *505/457–2384; 877/664–7787 reservations;* FAX *505/457–2385. Flush toilets, 3 full hook-ups, 48 partial hook-ups, dump station, drinking water, showers, fire grates, grills, picnic tables, electricity, public telephone, ranger station, playground, lake. 51 RV sites, unlimited primitive sites.* 🍴 *Full hook-up $18, partial hook-up $14, primitive sites $8. No credit cards.*

⚠ **Carlsbad RV Park & Campgrounds.** This tree-filled, full-service campground inside the city limits has level gravel sites and an indoor swimming pool. Camping cabins with heating and air-conditioning also are available. Other facilities include phone hook-ups and a meeting room. Reservations are recommended in summer. A professional RV service is next door. ⊠ *4301 National Parks Hwy., 88220,* ☎ *505/885–6333,* FAX *505/885–0784,* WEB *www.carlsbadrvpark.com. Flush toilets, full hook-ups, partial hook-ups, dump station, drinking water, laundry facilities, showers, grills, picnic tables, electricity, public telephone, general store, playground, pool. 96 RV sites, 41 tent sites.* 🍴 *Full hook-up $20, partial hook-up $19, tent sites $15. D, MC, V.*

## Nightlife and the Arts

Like many other small towns, Carlsbad tends to fold up at night—you're pretty much limited to special events and the lounge circuit. **Lucy's Mexicali Restaurant & Entertainment Club** has bands on the weekend. On Saturday, popular country-and-western bands play at the **Silver Spur Lounge** in the Best Western Stevens Inn, a favored local hangout where dancing takes place all week long.

# Artesia

*36 mi north of Carlsbad on U.S. 285, 40 mi south of Roswell on U.S. 285, 110 mi west of Alamogordo on U.S. 82.*

Artesia got its name from the artesian wells that were dug in the late 1800s to tap the plentiful supply of water just below the ground's surface. The underground bounty includes more than clear liquid, however. Oil and gas were discovered in the 1920s; today there are more than 20,000 oil and 4,000 natural-gas wells in the area. Pumping jacks cover the dunes and fields to the east. The Navajo Oil Refinery, alongside U.S. 285, is a major employer for this city of about 12,000.

A Federal Law Enforcement Training Center took over the abandoned campus of a private liberal arts college in 1989. Thousands of law-enforcement employees from agencies such as the U.S. Bureau of Land Management and U.S. Customs Service train at its driving and shooting ranges. Other than grabbing a meal, there isn't much to do here. On football-season Fridays you can't miss the array of orange banners and bulldog emblems touting the local high-school team, the Bulldogs, in this highly sports-conscious town.

## Dining

$–$$ ✕ **La Fonda.** While en route to or from Carlsbad Caverns, consider
★ stopping at this popular restaurant known for its milder style of Mexican cuisine. Try the house special, the Guadalajara, for a palate-pleasing blend of seasoned beef, cheese, and guacamole served on a corn

tortilla. Plants and bright southwestern scenes decorate the dining room. ⊠ *210 W. Main St.,* ☎ *505/746–9377. AE, D, MC, V.*

*En Route*  If you would like a closer look at some of the irrigated farmland and dairies of the Pecos Valley, veer northeast off the main highway (U.S. 285) just north of Artesia and take Alt. U.S. 285. This 40-mi route meanders through quaint farming villages of Lake Arthur, Dexter, and Hagerman and will rejoin the main highway at Roswell. If you want to view one of the valley's little-known but fascinating attractions, turn east onto Hatchery Road in Dexter. One mile's journey will take you to the **Dexter National Fish Hatchery & Technology Center** (⊠ 7116 Hatchery Rd., Dexter, ☎ 505/734–5910) a facility with the noble mission of studying, propagating, and possibly salvaging endangered species of warm-water fish such as the Colorado squawfish (once common to the Colorado River). You can view live exhibits and read all about the center's activities at a small visitor center on site. A guide will accommodate tour groups if requests are made in advance.

# Roswell

⑤  *40 mi north of Artesia on U.S. 285; 205 mi southeast of Albuquerque, south on I–25 and east on U.S. 380; 78 mi southwest of Fort Sumner, via Hwy. 20 and U.S. 285.*

It's not surprising that the true town of Roswell has been lost in the waves of Unidentified Flying Object (UFO) debates. Rather than being exclusively the hotbed of UFO activity, Roswell is in reality a conservative city with an economy based on manufacturing, agriculture, oil, and gas. The population of around 50,000 grew out of a farming community founded in the fertile Pecos Valley about a century ago; artesian wells still provide the water used to irrigate crops like alfalfa, hay, and cotton. That most visitors come only in search of UFOs elicits a few heavy sighs from residents. The town's notoriety may chagrin the locals a little, but they've learned to have fun with it—and also cash in on the tourist trade.

★ ℭ  Depending on your point of view, the **International UFO Museum and Research Center** will be a folly of only-in-America kitsch or an opportunity to examine UFO documentation and other phenomena involving extraterrestrials. This homespun, nonprofit facility is surprisingly low-tech—some of the displays look like they've seen previous duty on B-movie sets (the museum is, coincidentally, inside an old movie house). The blowups of newspaper stories about the Roswell crash, its fallout, and 1950s UFO mania make interesting reading, and you can view the videotaped recollections of residents who say they saw the Roswell crash. Dummies used in movies about the Roswell incident are also on exhibit. The gift shop sells all manner of souvenirs depicting wide-eyed extraterrestrials, along with books and videos. Though some of the exhibits are whimsical, the portion of the museum devoted to research accumulates serious written collections and investigations of reported UFOs. ⊠ *114 N. Main St.,* ☎ *505/625–9495.* ⊡ *Free.* ☉ *Daily 9–5.*

Roswell's **Encounter Festival** (☎ 505/625–9495) takes place during the first week in July, with lectures about UFOs, science-fiction writers workshops, and events such as alien-costume competitions.

The impressive **Roswell Museum and Art Center** often gets overlooked next to the alien hoopla. It holds a good survey of southwestern artists, highlighted with works by Georgia O'Keeffe, Henriette Wyeth, Peter Hurd, and Luis Jimenez. The extensive Rogers Aston Collection has displays of Plains Indian cultures, Spanish armor, and the gear of those

# UFO OVER ROSWELL

**O**F ALL THE SIGHTINGS of Unidentified Flying Objects in the world, it's the one that took place more than 50 years ago outside Roswell, New Mexico, that remains most credible in people's minds. Rumors of alien bodies and silenced witnesses are the real-life happenings that inspired fantastical entertainment like the TV series *The X-Files* and *Roswell*. The most likely reason so many people refuse to dismiss the Roswell Incident is the undisputed fact that in July 1947 *something* fell from out of the sky. To the exasperation of the U.S. military—which itself helped spark the original rumors of a spacecraft—its explanations of what made up the glittering silver debris at a ranch northwest of Roswell have never totally convinced the public. Roswell's International UFO Museum and Research Center keeps visitors informed of the latest research on the Roswell Incident, and the annual UFO Encounter festival in July provides a forum for enthusiasts.

On July 8, 1947, officers at Roswell Army Airfield announced to the *Roswell Daily Record* that the military had retrieved wreckage of a UFO nearby. The next day, Army Air Force officials retracted the story, saying it was in fact a weather balloon that had crashed. Over the years, theories of a cover-up and suspicions that the military had also recovered alien bodies linked the town of Roswell with aliens as strongly as Loch Ness is with its monster. Backing up the alien-bodies theory is the testimony of people like mortician Glen Dennis, who today works with Roswell's International UFO Museum and Research Center. He maintains that a nurse at the military hospital passed him sketches of aliens and that the military called him in 1947 to ask odd questions about embalming bodies.

In the 1990s a flood of information, including books like *UFO Crash at Roswell* and accounts from eyewitnesses who claim they were silenced, rekindled the conspiracy theories. The air force responded in 1994 with a report revealing that fragments mistaken for a flying saucer came not from a weather balloon but from an air force balloon used in the top-secret Project Mogul. The true nature of the balloon had to be concealed in 1947, because its purpose was to monitor evidence of Soviet nuclear tests.

As this new explanation didn't address the alien-bodies issue, the air force issued a 231-page report, "The Roswell Report, Case Closed," in 1997. This document explains that from 1954 to 1959, life-size dummies were used in parachute drop experiments. That this time frame postdates the 1947 Roswell Incident is immaterial to the air force, which claims people have simply confused dates in their memories.

The holes in every story, whether from the military or eyewitnesses, have allowed the Roswell UFO legend to mushroom extravagantly. It now incorporates tales of captured aliens (alive and dead) that further feed our imaginations, thanks in part to the capitalizing media. You'll see depictions of slender, doe-eyed aliens, known as the "Grays," all over storefronts and souvenir shops in Roswell. These spooky, diminutive creatures might even be called the New Mexico version of leprechauns, with only the rare treasure seeker truly hoping to encounter one.

who settled the land. Robert H. Goddard's collection exhibits the inventions and journals of the rocketry genius, who conducted some of his early experiments near Roswell. The **Robert H. Goddard Planetarium** presents star talks and multimedia programs. ⊠ *100 W. 11th St.,* ☎ *505/624–6744.* 🎫 *Free.* ☉ *Mon.–Sat. 9–5, Sun. 1–5. Planetarium shows 1 wk each month, Aug.–May, and daily June–July; call for schedule.*

The lakes at **Bottomless Lakes State Park** are sinkholes created when dissolved salt and gypsum deposits dissolved. With a bathhouse and other structures newly renovated in 2002, you'll find modern showers and rest rooms at the main Lea Lake facility. Paddleboats and paddleboards can be rented from Memorial Day to Labor Day. During the peak season, interpretive lectures are given in the evenings. ⊠ *Off U.S. 380 (12 mi east of Roswell, turn south on Hwy. 409 and continue 3 mi),* ☎ *505/624–6058.* 🎫 *$4 per vehicle.* ☉ *Daily 6 AM–9 PM.*

From the viewing platforms along the 8½-mi self-guided tour at the **Bitter Lake National Wildlife Refuge,** you can watch for snow geese, sandhill cranes, and other exotic birds, along with more familiar species. ⊠ *4065 Bitter Lakes Rd. (from Roswell, head north on U.S. 285, then turn east on Pine Lodge Rd. for 7 mi),* ☎ *505/622–6755.* 🎫 *Free.* ☉ *Daily dawn–dusk.*

## Dining and Lodging

$$–$$$$ ✕ **Cattle Baron.** Grilled meats and spicy sauces distinguish this restaurant, which specializes in steaks and seafood. The dark wood of the furnishings and rooms is offset by ample windows and a skylight. The ingredients at the salad bar are fresh and the salads ample. ⊠ *1113 N. Main St.,* ☎ *505/622–2465. AE, D, DC, MC, V.*

$–$$ ✕ **El Toro Bravo.** Next to the International UFO Museum and Research Center, this Mexican restaurant makes itself at home with matador paintings, piñatas, and wrought-iron wall lamps. A singing duet performs classics and oldies on Thursday, Friday, and Saturday evenings. Owner Artie Acevas uses family recipes in the preparation of ethnic favorites such as fajitas, enchiladas, tacos, and burritos. Cold beer and wine help cool the fire of spicy chile dishes. ⊠ *102 S. Main St.,* ☎ *505/622–9280. AE, D, MC, V.*

$$ 🏨 **Best Western Sally Port Inn & Suites.** The red-tile roof and white walls of this motel match those of the nearby New Mexico Military Institute, which inspired the name Sally Port—a passageway in military quarters. The standard rooms are large, and there are executive suites with business-oriented amenities. ⊠ *2000 N. Main St., 88220,* ☎ *505/622–6430,* 🖷 *505/623–7631. 99 rooms, 25 suites. Restaurant, in-room data ports, some in-room hot tubs, cable TV, indoor pool, gym, hair salon, hot tub, sauna, video games, meeting rooms, some pets allowed (fee). AE, D, MC, V.*

$–$$ 🏨 **Ramada Inn.** Large, contemporary rooms and convenient access to U.S. 70 from west Roswell are provided at this comfortable, updated inn. ⊠ *2803 W. 2nd St., 88220,* ☎ *505/623–9440,* 🖷 *505/622–9708. 61 rooms. Restaurant, cable TV, pool, meeting room, airport shuttle, some pets allowed. AE, MC, V.*

## Camping

🛆 **Bottomless Lakes State Park.** The park's main campground, at Lea Lake, has lots of amenities. This a desert environment, so don't expect much natural shade, but all camp sites have sheltered picnic tables. There is also a small developed area with 10 tent sites at the park's north end. ⊠ *Off U.S. 380 (12 mi east of Roswell, turn south on Hwy. 409 and continue 3 mi),* ☎ *877/664–7787. Flush toilets, pit toilets, full hookups, partial hook-ups (electric and water), dump station, drinking* *water, showers, grills, picnic tables, electricity, public telephone, ranger station, playground, lake. 32 RV sites, 27 tent sites. ☎ Tent sites $10, partial hook-up $14, full hook-up $18. No credit cards.*

# EAST-CENTRAL OUTPOSTS

Vast herds of pronghorn (commonly, but erroneously, called antelope) graze alongside roadways in this wide-open area, known as the Eastern Plains of New Mexico. When rains have been generous to this usually parched area, green grass and wildflowers adorn rolling hills more reminiscent of Wyoming. Ordinarily, however, the grasslands struggle to survive the burning heat of the New Mexico summer and take on a golden brown hue. The many miles of uninhabited prairie create a convenient cattle range, helping the many ranchers in this area continue a century-old tradition. Cattle graze in pastoral scenes that stretch for miles.

People in these rural agricultural and oil communities are busy making a living. You won't find many "cute" touristy stops or shops along highways. But the purity of the rural life seen here is part of its charm. A note of warning: don't be caught out on the highway in winter during a heavy snowstorm. Blinding, blizzardlike conditions can prevail, creating heaps of snow.

## Portales

**❻** *From Roswell, take U.S. 285 north 5 mi and U.S. 70 east 92 mi. Or, if you want a nice drive through sand dunes and rural farmland, from Artesia, take U.S. 82 east 65 mi to Lovington and S.R. 206 north to Portales 109 mi.*

Along with neighboring Clovis, this farming and ranching community bills itself as the world's top producer of Valencia peanuts, a specialty crop ideally suited to red, sandy soil. In October, Portales hosts a peanut festival where nuts are sold in raw form or cooked up in candies and other delicacies. Portales also is home to Eastern New Mexico University, a four-year college.

**☾** The nation's largest **windmill collection** is found on Portales's Kilgore Street (you can't miss it). Resident Bill Dalley has collected the 85 windmills in his own backyard. Since he's the past president of the International Windmillers' Trade Fair Association, meetings of the group are sometimes conducted here.

In the early 1930s, archaeologists in eastern New Mexico unearthed remnants of prehistoric animals like mammoths, camels, and saber-tooth tigers. More importantly, this was the first site in the contiguous United States that provided conclusive evidence that humans lived here at least 11,300 years ago. The culture and artifacts associated with these earliest inhabitants take their name from the nearby city of Clovis. The

**★** **Black Water Draw Museum** contains photographs of early excavations, along with artifacts from Clovis, Folsom, and later Native American civilizations. The museum looks a little lonely on the side of U.S. 70, 8 mi northeast of Portales, but its interior certainly shows considerable tender loving care. The exhibits are very informative and well presented. The museum also contains a "touch and feel" table for children.

The **Black Water Draw Archaeological Site** remains active and is open at regular hours to visitors during the summer and on weekends in spring and fall. Self-guided tours on developed trails are well worth the effort for the privilege of viewing work in progress at a major archaeological site. Stay strictly on the trails. Wear a hat, use sunscreen, and carry water for these excursions, particularly on hot summer days. An exhibit building offers a fascinating look at ongoing excavations of pre-historic animal bones, with many additional bones exposed during recent excavations. An ancient, hand-dug well also can be viewed near the exhibit building. A proposed master plan calls for building a major interpretive and research complex at the Black Water Draw site itself, though lack of funding has stalled progress. ⊠ *West side of Hwy. 467, 5 mi north of Portales (turn at Mile Marker 5),* ☎ *505/356–5235.* ▨ *Site and museum $2.* ☉ *Site and museum Memorial Day–Labor Day, Mon.–Sat. 10–5, Sun. noon–5. Museum Labor Day–Memorial Day, Tues.–Sat. 10–5, Sun. noon–5. Site Labor Day–Oct., Sat. 10–5, Sun. noon–5; Mar.–Memorial Day, Sat. 10–5, Sun. noon–5.*

## Dining and Lodging

$–$$$  ✕ **Cattle Baron.** This Portales steak house in the heart of cattle coun-
★      try was the founding establishment for the popular chain that now extends into Roswell, Ruidoso, and Las Cruces. Prime rib is the specialty, and the trademark salad bar never disappoints with its fresh greens, crisp veggies, and homemade soups. The interior is decorated with plenty of wooden accents and skylights. ⊠ *1600 S. Ave. D,* ☎ *505/356–5587. AE, D, DC, MC, V.*

$–$$  ✕ **Mark's Restaurant & Catering.** Tasty breakfast omelets, steaks, and sandwiches attract the hungry college crowd from nearby Eastern New Mexico University. Try the house specialty, a chicken-fried steak dinner. This diner-style hangout has a fun atmosphere. The tables are inlaid with tile, the chairs are covered with brightly colored vinyl, and there are a few exotic parrot decorations. All food is prepared fresh. ⊠ *1126 W. 1st St., across from airplane display next to Eastern New Mexico University,* ☎ *505/359–0857. D, MC, V.*

$    ▤ **Morning Star Bed & Breakfast & Gifts.** Antiques and brass highlights accent the fresh, bright decor of this adobe-style bed-and-breakfast in downtown Portales. The rooms have color themes—violet, blue, and peach. The bridal suite is a two-bedroom apartment with its own bath and kitchen. The other three rooms share a common area, which has a refrigerator. Guests are greeted with soft drinks. ⊠ *620 W. 2nd St., 88130,* ☎ *305/356–2994. 3 rooms, 1 suite. Some refrigerators, pool; no room phones, no kids. AE, MC, V. CP.*

$    ▤ **Super 8.** Decorated with contemporary furnishings and pastel colors, this motel has large rooms and bathrooms. It's one of the nicest lodging options in the city and offers convenient access to Portales businesses and Eastern New Mexico University. ⊠ *1805 W. 2nd St., 88130,* ☎ *505/356–8518, ℻ 505/359–0431. 45 rooms. Cable TV, hot tub. AE, D, DC, MC, V.*

## Camping

⚠ **Oasis State Park.** Six miles north of Portales via U.S. 70 and Hwy. 467, you can hike, bird-watch, and fish at a 3-acre lake stocked with rainbow trout and catfish, though boating and swimming are prohibited. Horseback riding also is allowed on the premises. This truly is an oasis surrounded by large cottonwood and elm trees. Since the park is off the beaten track, you'll very likely find a shady place to roost here even during peak holiday or tourist seasons. ⊠ *Off N.M. 467, 6 mi north of Portales,* ☎ *505/356–5331; 877/665–7787 for reservations. Flush toilets, pit toilets, partial hook-ups (electric and water), dump station, drinking water, showers, grills, picnic tables, electricity, ranger station, playground. 13 RV sites, 10 tent sites.* ▨ *$10 tent sites, $14 for electrical hook-ups, $18 for electrical and water hook-ups. No credit cards.*

# Fort Sumner

**❼** *70 mi northwest of Black Water Draw Museum, north on U.S. 70 and west on U.S. 60/84; 85 mi northeast of Roswell, north on U.S. 285 and northeast on Hwy. 20; 159 mi southeast of Albuquerque, east on I–40 and south on U.S. 84.*

Besides its historic significance as one of the area's earliest military outposts and the place where on-the-run Billy the Kid was killed, the town of Fort Sumner has other solid credentials like farming and ranching. The National Aeronautics and Space Administration uses the Fort Sumner Air Park for launching balloons used in scientific research. Nearby Sumner Lake provides both irrigation water and boating and fishing opportunities. In June, the De Baca County Chamber of Commerce hosts the annual Old Fort Days here with living-history demonstrations and mock shoot-outs.

Artifacts and photographs at **Fort Sumner State Monument** illustrate the history of the fort, which was established in 1862 on the east bank of the Pecos River. From 1863 to 1868 it was the headquarters for a disastrous attempt to force the Navajo people and some Apache bands—after their defeat on various battlefields in the Southwest—to farm the inhospitable land. Natural disasters destroyed crops, wood was scarce, and even the water from the Pecos proved unhealthy. Those who survived the harsh treatment and wretched conditions (3,000 didn't) were allowed to return to reservations elsewhere in 1868. The post was then sold and converted into a large ranch. This is the same ranch where, in 1881, Sheriff Pat Garrett gunned down Billy the Kid, who's buried in a nearby cemetery. His headstone was secured in a barred cage after it was stolen and recovered. ⊠ *Billy the Kid Rd. (from town of Fort Sumner, head east on U.S. 60/84 and south on Billy the Kid Rd., parts of which are signed Hwy. 212),* ☎ *505/ 355–2573.* ▣ *$3.* ◉ *Wed.–Tues. 8:30–5.*

The small **Old Fort Museum**, next to Fort Sumner, has displays about Billy the Kid and ranch life. ⊠ *Billy the Kid Rd.,* ☎ *505/355–2942.* ▣ *$3.* ◉ *Daily 9–5 daily (hrs can vary; call ahead to verify).*

The **Billy the Kid Museum** houses 17,000 square ft of exhibits about the young scofflaw, as well as antique wagon trains, guns, household goods, and other artifacts of the frontier era. ⊠ *1601 Sumner Ave./U.S. 60/84,* ☎ *505/355–2380.* ▣ *$4.* ◉ *Mid-May–Sept., daily 8:30–5; Oct.–Dec. and mid-Jan.–mid-May, Mon.–Sat. 8:30–5, Sun. 11–5.*

At **Sumner Lake State Park** you can boat, fish, camp, picnic, hike, sightsee, swim, and water-ski. Fishing opportunities vary, since the lake is periodically drained for irrigation. A boat ramp and dock offer convenient access to water sports. ⊠ *10 mi north of Fort Sumner on U.S. 84, then west on Hwy. 203 for 6 mi,* ☎ *505/355–2541.* ▣ *$4 per vehicle.*

## Camping

⚠ **Sumner Lake State Park.** The choices at this popular recreational site range from primitive, shoreline camping with no facilities to developed or partially developed sites. Shading in this desert location varies. ⊠ *10 mi north of Fort Sumner on U.S. 84, then west on Hwy. 203 for 6 mi,* ☎ *505/355–2541; 877/665–7787 for reservations. Flush toilets, pit toilets, partial hook-ups (electric and water), dump station, drinking water, showers, fire grates, grills, picnic tables, electricity, ranger station, playground, lake. 40 developed sites, 18 sites with partial hook-up, 50 primitive sites.* ▤ *Tent sites $8; extra fees for hook-ups. No credit cards.*

*En Route*   To continue touring southeastern New Mexico, the easiest route (132 mi) is to backtrack to Roswell via Hwy. 20 to U.S. 285 and head west on U.S. 70/380 toward Lincoln County. Look for the many pronghorn grazing alongside roadways in the flat eastern plains, which are the ideal habitat for these delicate creatures. If you count the number of pronghorn spotted, the total can sometimes surpass 100 along even short stretches of road, when rains have made grassland abundant.

A more adventurous route (178 mi) to Lincoln County would be a loop west from Fort Sumner on U.S. 60. At the town of Vaughn head south on U.S. 54 and travel through the southernmost region of Cibola National Forest to the fringes of the Lincoln National Forest. These areas are mountainous but semiarid, as evidenced by sparse hillsides dotted with brush and junipers. On this route you'll pass through **Corona,** near where the Roswell UFO is said to have crashed. No signs designate the site. At Carrizozo head east on U.S. 380. You'll pass the towns of Capitan and Lincoln before you reach U.S. 70. Cut back west on U.S. 70 to get to San Patricio.

# HEADING TO HIGH COUNTRY

From the hub city of Roswell, U.S. 70 shoots out of the flatlands west toward mountain peaks. The route's slow climb in elevation is apparent beginning near San Patricio. Here, in an area known as the Hondo Valley, the shrubs and scattered forest dotting the otherwise naked hillsides provided inspiration for many of the late artist Peter Hurd's stunning landscapes.

Onward and upward, the pines thicken and grow taller. The Rio Ruidoso (Spanish for "river of noisy water") dances alongside the highway as the air grows cooler and fragrant. Imagine this majestic land as it was when outlaws, Indians, merchants, ranchers, and lawmen battled each other for control of the frontier. Consider a solitary horseback ride or hike on a wilderness trail, or try lake fishing on reservation land controlled by the Mescalero Apaches. Near the town of Ruidoso, more modern diversions are skiing, shopping, horse racing, and casino gambling.

## Lincoln

★ **8**   *12 mi east of Capitan on U.S. 380; 47 mi west of Roswell on U.S. 70/ 380 to Hondo, then 10 mi northwest on U.S. 380 to Lincoln.*

It may not be as well known as Tombstone, Arizona, or Deadwood, South Dakota, but Lincoln ranks right up there with the toughest of the tough old towns of the Old West. Mellowing with age, the notorious one-street town has become a National Historic Landmark and a state monument. Its well-preserved museums and historic houses are managed by the state and Ruidoso's Hubbard Museum of the American West, and a single ticket ($6) grants entry to all attractions.

The violent, gang-style Lincoln County War flared up more than a century ago, as two factions, the Tunstall-McSween and the Murphy-Dolan groups, clashed over lucrative government contracts to provide food for the U.S. Army at Fort Stanton and area Indian reservations. The local conflict made national news, and President Hayes ordered Lew Wallace, governor of New Mexico, to settle the conflict. One of the more infamous figures to emerge from the bloodshed was a short, slight, sallow young man with buck teeth, startling blue eyes, and curly reddish-brown hair. His name was Billy the Kid.

He is said to have killed 21 men (probably an exaggeration), including Lincoln County's sheriff William Brady—for whose murder Billy the Kid was convicted in 1881 and sentenced to hang. Billy managed to elude the gallows, however. On April 28, 1881, though manacled and shackled, he made a daring escape from the old Lincoln County Courthouse, gunning down two men and receiving cheers from townspeople who supported his group, the Tunstall-McSweens. Three months later a posse led by Sheriff Pat Garrett tracked down Billy at a home in Fort Sumner, surprised him in the dark, and finished him off with two clean shots. One of the West's most notorious gunmen, and ultimately one of its best-known folk legends, was dead at age 21.

☙ The **Historic Lincoln Center,** on the eastern end of town, serves as an information center and has a 12-minute video about Lincoln and exhibits devoted to Billy the Kid, the Lincoln County War, cowboys, Apaches, and Buffalo Soldiers. The center's guides and attendants dress in period costumes and lead a walking tour through town on the hour, vividly describing each building's role as a setting in the Lincoln County War. ✉ *Main St./U.S. 380,* ☎ *505/653–4025.* ✆ *$6 pass grants access to all historic buildings.* ⏱ *Daily 8:30–4:30.*

Lincoln was first settled by Spanish settlers in the 1840s. The short, round **Torreon** fortress served as protection from Apache raids. The building would come in handy during the Lincoln County War, too. José Montaño ran a saloon and boardinghouse within his **Montaño Store** for more than 30 years after the Civil War. Governor Lew Wallace stayed here when trying to arrange a meeting with Billy the Kid. On view today are written displays about adobe making and Lincoln's Hispanic community. **Dr. Wood's House** was once occupied by a country doctor specializing in tuberculoses treatments. ✉ *Main St./U.S. 380,* ☎ *no phone.* ✆ *$6 pass grants access to all historic buildings.* ⏱ *Daily 9–4:30.*

☙ Nothing has changed much at the **Tunstall Store Museum,** the rival store to L. G. Murphy & Co. (which now houses the Lincoln County Courthouse Museum). John Chisum and Alexander McSween had law offices here as well. When the state of New Mexico purchased the store in 1957, boxes of unused stock dating from the late 19th and early 20th centuries were discovered. The clothes, hardware, butter churns, kerosene lamps, and other items are displayed in the store's original cases. ✉ *Main St./U.S. 380,* ☎ *505/653–4049.* ✆ *$6 pass grants access to all historic buildings.* ⏱ *Daily 9–4:30.*

☙ The **Lincoln County Courthouse Museum** is the building from which Billy the Kid made his famous escape. You can walk in the room where Billy was imprisoned and view a hole in the wall that just might have been caused by the gun he fired during his escape. Display cases contain historical documents. You can read one of Billy's handwritten, eloquent letters to Governor Lew Wallace, defending his reputation. The Lincoln State Monument office is here. ✉ *Main St./U.S. 380,* ☎ *505/653–4372.* ✆ *$6 pass grants access to all historic buildings.* ⏱ *Daily 8:30–4:30.*

When church services, weddings, funerals, and other regularly scheduled functions are not taking place here, Lincoln's historic **Iglesia de San Juan Bautista** originally built in 1887 can be viewed free. The tiny church was built and restored entirely from local materials. Roof beams and other wood elements including latillas and vigas were dragged by oxcart from the nearby Capitan Mountains. ✉ *Main St./U.S. 380,* ☎ *505/257–7067.* ✆ *Free.* ⏱ *Daily 8:30–4:30.*

## Dining and Lodging

**$$–$$$** ✕▦ **Ellis Store Country Inn.** Listed for sale in 2002 (be aware this can
★ lead to changes), this B&B has a rich history dating from 1850, when it was a modest two-room adobe in a territory where settlers and Mescaleros clashed. During the Lincoln County War, Billy the Kid was

known to frequent the place. Rooms in the main house are decorated with antiques. Behind the main house is the Mill House, which has four guest rooms and a large common room and is ideal for families. Casa Nueva has two suites with reproduction antiques and a country-French feeling. Owner Jinny Vigil, who's won *New Mexico* magazine's chef-of-the-month award more than once, cooks six-course gourmet meals in the evening (by reservation only), served in a wood-panel dining room. Vigil's well-manicured garden is becoming increasingly popular for June weddings. ⊠ *U.S. 380, Mile Marker 98 (Box 15, 88338),* ☎ *505/653–4609 or 800/653–6460,* ℻ *505/653–4610. 10 rooms (4 share 2 baths), 2 suites. Restaurant; no smoking. AE, D, DC, MC, V. BP.*

$   ✕⊞ **Wortley Pat Garrett Hotel.** This ranch-style inn relives the past by shedding the modern distractions of phones, faxes, and televisions. Rooms are named after characters in the Lincoln County War, and antiques and old newspaper accounts are displayed throughout the inn. Historical field trips and classes are part of the experience. For leisurely chats, rocking chairs are set up on the front porch. Rebuilt after a fire in 1935, the inn is on the site of the real thing, where Deputy U.S. Marshal Bob Olinger ate his last meal at noontime on April 28, 1881. As the lawman consumed roast beef and mashed potatoes, he heard gunfire from the courthouse down the street. He ran outside, becoming a casualty after meeting up with one of Billy the Kid's bullets during the outlaw's famous escape. In the **Wortley Dining Room** (☎ 505/653–4438), open Wednesday–Sunday 8–6, the town's Irish-American heritage is honored with a menu featuring old-time favorites such as corned beef and cabbage. Reservations are required for steak dinners, served at 6 PM. ⊠ *U.S. 380, 88338,* ☎ *505/653–4300 or 877/967–8539,* ℻ *505/653–4686,* ⅦⅢ *www.lincolnnewmexico.com. 7 rooms. Restaurant (no credit cards). AE, MC, V. Lodge and restaurant closed Nov.–Apr.*

$$   ⊞ **Casa de Patrón Bed-and-Breakfast.** This B&B is in the former
★    adobe home of Juan Patrón, an early settler and father of three who was gunned down at age 29 in the violence that swept Lincoln County. Billy the Kid really did sleep here, as a guest of Juan Patrón, and while being held by the sheriff under protective custody. The main house has high viga ceilings and Mexican-tile baths; the adjacent Old Trail House has two large rooms—one decorated in Hispanic-cowboy style and the other in a garden motif—with fireplaces. With vigas and portals, the two small adobe casitas have a traditional New Mexican flavor (Casa Bonita has cathedral ceilings). All rooms are furnished with antiques and collectibles, and one is wheelchair accessible. Full country breakfasts are served to guests staying in the main house, Continental breakfasts to those in the casitas. ⊠ *U.S. 380 (Box 27, 88338),* ☎ *505/653–4676 or 800/524–5202,* ℻ *505/653–4671,* ⅦⅢ *www.casapatron.com. 5 double rooms, 2 casitas. Some kitchens, some microwaves, some refrigerators, meeting rooms; no smoking. MC, V. BP, CP.*

# San Patricio

❾ *14 mi south of Lincoln, 45 mi west of Roswell on U.S. 70/380*

Ranchers, farmers, artists, and others who appreciate the pastoral pleasures of the Hondo Valley live in San Patricio and the nearby villages of Tinnie and Hondo. The Rio Ruidoso flows into the Rio Hondo here, a boon to farmers and wildlife alike. During the harvest, fresh cider and produce are sold at roadside stands.

★    The late artist Peter Hurd lived in the Hondo Valley on the Sentinel
Ranch, which is still owned by his son, Michael Hurd. The **Hurd–La Rinconada Gallery** displays Peter Hurd's landscapes and portraits.

The artist is famous for western scenes but gained some notice when a portrait he painted of Lyndon B. Johnson displeased the president, who refused to hang it in the White House. Also on display are the works of Hurd's late wife, Henriette Wyeth (Andrew Wyeth's sister), and Michael Hurd, who runs the ranch. Michael is an amiable host who has established an international reputation with a series of paintings he calls "The Road West," his vision of the lonely desert scenery surrounding his home. Michael's sister Carole Hurd Rogers and her husband, Peter Rogers, also an artist, live near the ranch as well. Paintings by Jamie Wyeth, father Andrew Wyeth, and grandfather N. C. Wyeth round out the impressive presentation at the gallery. Signed reproductions and some original paintings are for sale. ⊠ *U.S. 70, Mile Marker 281,* ☎ *505/653–4331.* ⊘ *Mon.–Sat. 9–5.*

## Lodging

$$$–$$$$  🏨 **Hurd Ranch Guest Homes.** Modern and western furnishings and paint-
★ ings, sculpture, and Native American artifacts decorate the adobe casitas on the Sentinel Ranch. Peter Hurd made them available to friends and to customers who needed accommodations while he painted their portraits. The rooms have washing machines and dryers, fully equipped kitchens, and fireplaces. The newest one is named after actress Helen Hayes, who was a family friend and frequent visitor. A wing of the Hurd–La Rinconada Gallery has a spacious apartment with an enclosed patio for rent. Facilities also are available for weddings and conferences. ⊠ *U.S. 70 (Box 100, 88348),* ☎ *505/653–4331 or 800/658–6912,* FAX *505/653–4218. 4 casitas, 1 apartment. Some in-room hot tubs, kitchens, microwaves, refrigerators, cable TV, in-room VCRs, laundry facilities. AE, D, MC, V.*

# Ruidoso

⑩ *20 mi west of San Patricio on U.S. 70*

A sophisticated year-round resort town on the eastern slopes of the pine-covered Sacramento Mountains, Ruidoso retains a certain rustic charm. Shops, antiques stores, bars, and restaurants line its main street, and in winter, skiers flock to nearby Ski Apache. **Ruidoso Downs** is so close to Ruidoso you won't realize it's a separate township, but its Ruidoso Downs Racetrack and museums are the area's huge draws. The summer horse-racing season keeps the 9,800 or so permanent residents entertained after the snow and ski bunnies disappear.

**Ruidoso Downs Racetrack & Casino,** the self-proclaimed Home of the World's Richest Quarter Horse Race, has a fabulous mountain vista as the setting for cheering the ponies. On Labor Day the track is the site of the All-American Quarter Horse Futurity, with a total purse of as much as $2.5 million. Twenty percent of revenues from the **Billy the Kid Casino,** with some 300 slot machines, boosts purses for the races. Casino gambling allowed at horse racing tracks is credited with reviving the sport in New Mexico by attracting quality horses and competition. The casino is decorated with murals suggesting nearby historic Lincoln, where Billy the Kid once hung out. The facility also offers year-round, full card simulcasting from the nation's largest tracks. ⊠ *U.S. 70, Ruidoso Downs,* ☎ *505/378–4431.* 🎫 *Racetrack open seating free, reserved seating $4.50 and up; Turf Club $9.50 (higher on special weekends).* ⊘ *Racing late May–Labor Day, Thurs.–Sun. and Mon. holidays (post time 1 PM on weekends and holidays, 3:30 PM on weekdays). Casino Mon.–Thurs. 11–11, Fri. noon–midnight, Sat. noon–1 AM, Sun. 11–10.*

★ ☞ About ½ mi east of the racetrack you can pay further respects to horses at the **Hubbard Museum of the American West.** The museum houses the **Anne C. Stradling Collection** of more than 10,000 artworks and objects related to the horse—paintings, drawings, and bronzes by master artists; saddles from Mexico, China, and the Pony Express; carriages and wagons; a horse-drawn grain thresher; and clothing worn by Native Americans and cowboys. The **Racehorse Hall of Fame** celebrates accomplished horses and jockeys and screens rare and contemporary video footage. Activities at the children's interactive center include pony rides, horse demonstrations, and puzzles. Youngsters can don Old West attire and have their photos taken in a jockey outfit. In front of the museum is a bronze sculpture of eight galloping horses—*Free Spirits at Noisy Water.* Not only beautiful, the monument represents a minor feat of engineering, since of the eight horses only nine hooves actually touch the ground. The museum also operates many of the exhibits in the nearby historic town of Lincoln. ✉ *U.S. 70 E, Ruidoso Downs,* ☎ *505/378–4142.* 🎫 *$6.* ☉ *Daily 10–5.*

The **Mescalero Apache Indian Reservation,** bordering Ruidoso to the west, is inhabited by more than 2,500 Mescalero Apaches, most of whom work in tourism-related enterprises. One of the state's most elegant resorts, the Apache-owned and -operated **Inn of the Mountain Gods** has been demolished and is being rebuilt, due to reopen in 2004. Also on the reservation are a general store, a trading post, and a museum that has clothing and crafts displays and screens a 12-minute video about life on the reservation. Regular talks survey the history and culture of the Mescalero Apaches. There are also campsites (with hook-ups at Silver and Eagle lakes only) and picnic areas. Ritual dances are occasionally performed for the public, the most colorful of which is on the Fourth of July. ✉ *Tribal Office, U.S. 70, Mescalero,* ☎ *505/671–4494.* 🎫 *Free.* ☉ *Reservation and tribal museum weekdays 8–4:30.*

## Dining and Lodging

$$–$$$$ ✕ **Cattle Baron.** This southern New Mexico franchise serves up steaks, scampi, and more exotic dishes such as mustard grilled pork chops, while offering the chance to graze a generous salad bar. Succulent prime rib is the house specialty. Ample greenery and tile floors add a pleasant country ambience. ✉ *657 Sudderth Dr.,* ☎ *505/257–9355. AE, D, DC, MC, V.*

$$–$$$$ ✕ **La Lorraine.** The colonial French decor with flower arrangements and chandeliers sets the perfect mood for traditional French cuisine—chateaubriand, veal chop, duck breast, and the like. Owner Kathy Garber presents a comprehensive wine list enabling selections of your favorite. ✉ *2523 Sudderth Dr.,* ☎ *505/257–2954. AE, D, DC, MC, V. Closed Sun. No lunch Mon.–Tues.*

$–$$ ✕ **Pub 48.** This happening place for hip families is operated by the Sierra Blanca Brewing Co. An adobe brick fireplace, wooden ceilings, and a play station for kids help create a cozy, mountain cabin atmosphere. Try some of the excellent microbeers, such as the nut brown ale served from a copper bar, while sampling pizzas or steaks and seafood. ✉ *441 Mechem Dr./Hwy. 48,* ☎ *505/257–9559. AE, D, MC, V.*

$ ✕ **Lincoln County Grill.** The locals come here for quick service and good, inexpensive food. Step up to the counter to order hearty Texas chili, old-fashioned hamburgers, or chicken-fried steak. At breakfast you can grab eggs served with fluffy, homemade "Lincoln County" biscuits. Vinyl-covered tables are decorated with old coffee, tea, and tobacco tin images. This is a great stop for families in a hurry and on a budget. ✉ *2717 Sudderth Dr.,* ☎ *505/257–7669. AE, D, MC, V.*

$–$$$ ✕▥ **Park Inn Swiss Chalet.** With a sweeping view of the forest, this property is 16 mi from the Ski Apache slopes. Common spaces have

Swiss and German touches like cowbells, an alpenhorn, and cuckoo clocks, but otherwise, guest-room decor is basic with some painted headboards and furnishings. The restaurant serves no-nonsense German and American cuisine—try the Wiener schnitzel or the three-sausage platter. The cozy bar, which has a small fireplace, is a convivial place to decompress after a day of skiing. On the walkways and decks facing the forest, you can relax near the fragrant pines. ⊠ *1451 Mechem Dr., 88345,* ☎ *505/258-3333 or 800/477-9477,* FAX *505/258-5325,* WEB *www.ruidoso.net/swisschalet. 82 rooms. Restaurant, in-room data ports, indoor pool, hot tub, sauna, hiking, bar, laundry facilities, meeting rooms. AE, D, DC, MC, V. BP.*

$$–$$$$ 🏨 **Ruidoso Lodge Cabins.** In the heart of Ruidoso's gorgeous, tree-filled
★ Upper Canyon, owners Judy and Kurt Wilkie oversee a placid retreat of 1920s, knotty-pine abodes. The immaculate one- and two-bedroom cabins are decorated in western and southwestern decor. Some have hot tubs, and all have fireplaces and decks with gas grills offering serene views. The cabins are fully equipped with kitchen utensils and dishes—but no phones. Prices vary widely depending on the season. You can trout fish here, right along the Rio Ruidoso, but arrange for your own gear. Hiking trails lead off from the property. ⊠ *300 Main St., 88345 (take Sudderth Dr. north from U.S. 70 through downtown Ruidoso and continue west through Upper Canyon, where Sudderth turns into Main St.),* ☎ *505/257-2510 or 800/950-2510,* WEB *www.ruidoso.net/ ruicabins. 10 cabins. Some in-room hot tubs, kitchenettes, microwaves, refrigerators, cable TV, in-room VCRs, fishing, hiking; no room phones. D, MC, V.*

$$$ 🏨 **Riverside Cottages.** These cozy cabins snuggled amid tall pines right
★ next to a bubbling stream are billed as a romantic getaway for couples. Rustic decor (lots of wood and plaid) combined with modern amenities such as indoor hot tubs and gas fireplaces create a luxurious country feel. The renovated cabins are just across the Rio Ruidoso from the Ruidoso Lodge Cabins, operated by the same owners (Judy and Kurt Wilkie). Kitchenettes are stocked with cooking utensils and dishes. The original cabins, formerly known as the Cowan Cabins, and the secluded location were acquired several years ago. Since privacy is highly valued at this particular site, visitors are not allowed. Discounts may be offered in the off-season, while prices may go up during peak demand. ⊠ *300 N. Main St. (office), 88345,* ☎ *505/257-4753 or 800/ 497-7402,* WEB *www.ruidoso.net/river. 8 cabins. In-room hot tubs, kitchenettes, microwaves, refrigerators, cable TV, in-room VCRs, fishing, hiking; no room phones. D, MC, V.*

$$–$$$ 🏨 **Shadow Mountain Lodge.** Designed for couples, this lodge is on the west side of town in the unique Upper Canyon. Room amenities include hair dryers and irons. Each suite has a fireplace with pressed wood that is either complimentary or offered for purchase, depending on the season. You can enjoy views of tall pines and the landscaped gardens from the front veranda. Outside in the gazebo you can take a relaxing soak in the hot tub. In late 2002, construction of four new detached cabins (each with its own indoor hot tub) was scheduled for completion. ⊠ *107 Main Rd., 88345,* ☎ *505/257-4886 or 800/441-4331,* FAX *505/257-2000,* WEB *www.shadowmountainlodge.com. 19 suites, 4 cabins. In-room data ports, some in-room hot tubs, some kitchenettes, some microwaves, refrigerators, cable TV, in-room VCRs, outdoor hot tub, laundry facilities. AE, D, DC, MC, V.*

$–$$$ 🏨 **Sierra Blanca Cabins.** Log cabin–style abodes tucked between the pines alongside the Rio Ruidoso offer a gorgeous outdoor setting within walking distance of downtown shops and other attractions. This is an affordable option for families. Discounts are offered for area food outlets and ski rentals. Each cabin has a fireplace, outdoor grill, and picnic area. ✉ *215–217 Country Club Rd. (west on Sudderth Dr. to Country Club Rd.), 88345,* ☎ *505/257–2103 or 866/262–2103,* WEB *www.sierrablancacabins.com. 9 cabins. Kitchenettes, cable TV, playground, some pets allowed (fee). AE, D, MC, V.*

$$ 🏨 **Hawthorn Suites Golf and Convention Resort.** Opened in 2001, Ruidoso's newest luxury resort is next door to one of New Mexico's top-rated golf courses (The Links at Sierra Blanca) and to the Ruidoso Convention Center. A dramatic, inlaid rock kiva fireplace is the centerpiece of the expansive lobby area. The complimentary full breakfast is served in a dining area that has views of the golf course and the mountains. Rooms are typical but spacious chain accommodations. ✉ *107 Sierra Blanca Dr., 88345,* ☎ *505/258–5500,* FAX *505/258–2419,* WEB *www.ruidosohawthorn.com. 117 rooms. In-room data ports, some in-room hot tubs, cable TV, in-room VCRs, indoor pool, gym, hot tub, laundry service. AE, D, DC, MC, V. BP.*

$$ 🏨 **Park Place Bed & Breakfast.** Guests at this cozy lodge are blessed
★ with both hospitality and privacy. Three rooms updated with new carpet and tile in 2002 are available, accessible through a private entrance leading into a slant-roof hallway. Each room has a VCR and access to a video library. You can choose seclusion in your own luxurious space or stroll into an inviting lobby where you might meet up with other guests for conversation or games in front of a toasty fireplace. Friendly owners Eddie and Donna Parker discreetly entertain by stepping in from their portion of the house, connected through the kitchen and dining area. Eddie will cook you up a breakfast that might include fruit, muffins, and green chile omelets. Outside, you can enjoy the hot tub, play volleyball, or watch the deer feed in the evenings. The more expensive Parker's Room has its own private Jacuzzi. ✉ *137 Reese Dr., 88345 (turn off U.S. 70 north onto Sudderth Dr., left on Thomas St., then right on Reese Dr. to cross the river),* ☎ *505/257–4638 or 800/687–9050,* FAX *505/630–0127,* WEB *www.ruidoso.net/parkplace. 3 rooms. In-room VCRs, tennis court, outdoor hot tub, fishing, croquet, horseshoes, volleyball. AE, MC, V.*

$–$$ 🏨 **Days Inn Ruidoso Downs.** This standard, contemporary lodge is next to the Sierra Blanca Mountain foothills and only ½ mi from the Ruidoso Downs Racetrack. Some rooms have balconies. Rates can rise drastically if you happen to roll into town during peak demand, so check first. The next-door restaurant is open for breakfast and lunch. ✉ *2088 Hwy. 70 W, Ruidoso Downs 88346,* ☎ FAX *505/378–4299. 50 rooms. In-room data ports, microwaves, refrigerators, cable TV, indoor pool, hot tub, laundry facilities, Internet. AE, D, DC, MC, V. CP.*

## Nightlife and the Arts

A 512-seat venue hosting top-tier performances from jazz musicians to international ballet dancers can be found in the **Spencer Theater for the Performing Arts** (✉ Hwy. 220 [off Hwy. 48, take Hwy. 220 north], ☎ 505/336–4800 or 888/818–7872; 800/905–3315 ticket orders; FAX 505/336–0010; WEB www.spencertheater.com). The white, templelike building looms majestically amid mountain vistas just north of Ruidoso and is one of the state's cultural icons. Tickets run $20–$40, and free tours are given Tuesday and Thursday, 10–2. Professionals often train local children to act in special free summer performances. Children's theater and outdoor summer concerts also are offered at the site.

## Outdoor Activities and Sports

Run by the Mescalero Apaches on 12,003-ft Sierra Blanca, **Ski Apache** (✉ Ski Run Rd./Hwy. 532, ☎ 505/336–4356; 505/257–9001 snow report) has powder skiing for all skill levels on 55 trails and 750 acres. One of Ski Apache's distinctions is its high mountain elevation surrounded by desert. This unique climate can produce mounds of snowfall (averaging about 15 ft each winter) followed by days of pleasant, sunny weather. With the largest lift capacity in New Mexico, this huge resort can transport more than 16,500 people hourly. Ski Apache also has the state's only gondola. The season typically runs from Thanksgiving through Easter, and the snowmaking system is able to cover a third of the trails. Lift operations are open daily from 8:45 AM to 4 PM; the ski area charges adults $45 for a full day with lift tickets and $31 for a half day. Multiday discounts are offered. Snowboarding is allowed on all trails. Families should check out the Kiddie Korral Program for children ages four to six. While there are no overnight accommodations at the resort, day lodges have two cafeterias, three snack bars, and two outdoor hamburger stands. From Ruidoso take Hwy. 48 6 mi, and turn west on Hwy. 532 for 12 mi.

## Capitan

*22 mi north of Ruidoso on Hwy. 48, 12 mi west of Lincoln on U.S. 380.*

Capitan is famous as the birthplace and final home of Smokey Bear, the nation's symbol of wildfire prevention. The original bear concept was created in 1944, and the poster bear is still seen in public service announcements issued by the Ad Council. After a devastating 1950 forest fire in the Capitan Mountains, a bear cub was found badly burned and clinging to a tree. Named Smokey after the poster bear, he lived in the National Zoo in Washington until his death in 1976, when he was returned home for burial.

Displays at the **Smokey Bear Historical Park** visitor center explain forest-fire prevention and fire ecology. A theater with informational films is offered at the 3-acre park, which also contains a picnic area. Capitan's original train depot is adjacent to the museum and gift shop. The site hosts special events for youngsters, such as an Easter egg hunt, Halloween night, and Smokey's Christmas at the Park. ⊠ *118 Smokey Bear Blvd., off Hwy. 380,* ☎ *505/354–2748.* ⊠ *$1.* ☉ *Daily 9–5.*

## Carrizozo

*37 mi northwest of Capitan on U.S. 380, 58 mi north of Alamogordo on U.S. 54.*

Back when railroad crews began using this site as a supply center, the community that rose up was named after *carrizo,* the reedlike grass growing in the area. The extra "-zo" appeared when the carrizo grew so thick a ranch foreman added it to the town's name for emphasis. The ranching community incorporated in 1907 and in 1912 became the county seat of Lincoln County. About 1,000 residents live in this charming, isolated town at the junction of U.S. 54 and U.S. 380.

The **Sierra Blanca Brewing Co.,** modestly hidden on a back street of Carrizozo, is the largest brewery in New Mexico (and officially the 113th largest in the nation), with a maximum capacity of 3,800 beer barrels annually. The high-tech brewing process is reflected in the smooth taste of creations such as pale ale, which you can sample free on the premises. Free tours also are offered. ⊠ *503 12th St.,* ☎ *505/648–6606.* ☉ *Free tours daily 9–4.*

Near Carrizozo is the **Valley of Fires Recreation Area,** operated by the Bureau of Land Management. According to Indian legend, a volcanic eruption about 1,000 years ago created a valley of fire here. When the lava cooled, a dark, jagged landscape remained. A ¾-mi trail penetrates the lava-flow area, which looks like a *Star Trek* backdrop and covers 44 mi (it's 5 mi wide in some places). Crevices and bowls trapping precious water nurture ocotillo and blooming cactus, creating natural land-scaping along the well-maintained trail. The visitor center has a gift shop with souvenirs and books. Caving is allowed with the proper permits. ⊠ *U.S. 380, 4 mi west of Carrizozo,* ☎ *505/648–2241.* ⊑ *$3 per individual; $5 per carload.* ☉ *Information center daily 8–4.*

### Dining and Lodging

$   ✕ **Outpost Bar & Grill.** Rural restaurants in southern New Mexico have a long-standing rivalry over who makes the best green-chile hamburgers in the region. Many fans will tell you that the winner is right here. Besides cooking awesome burgers, this bar and grill has a wacky hunting-lodge decor full of animal heads, snakeskins, and painted cow skulls. The massive antique wooden bar is the centerpiece of the establishment. ⊠ *U.S. 54 S,* ☎ *505/648–9994. No credit cards.*

$   ⊞ **Rainbow Inn.** Relatively new furnishings and modern amenities such as remote-control TVs are generally unusual in small rural motels such as this one. Yet you can find most of the comforts of a major establishment here, including refrigerators and microwaves in rooms. The motel is also adjacent to a restaurant. ⊠ *Intersection of U.S. 308 and U.S. 54 (Box 873, Carrizozo 88301),* ☎ *505/648–4006,* ℻ *505/648–2989,* 🕸 *http://townofcarrizozo.org. 11 rooms. Microwaves, refrigerators, cable TV, some pets allowed. AE, D, DC, MC, V.*

$   ⊞ **Sands RV Park & Motel.** Under new ownership as of 2001, this motel has nicely maintained, newly refurbished rooms with extras including access to satellite television. An RV park ($10) with extra wide spaces and full hook-ups and showers is also on the premises. ⊠ *U.S. 54 S (Box 873, Carrizozo 88301),* ☎ ℻ *505/648–2989,* 🕸 *http://townofcarrizozo. org. 9 rooms. Microwaves, refrigerators, cable TV, showers, laundry facilities, some pets allowed. AE, D, DC, MC, V.*

### Camping

⚠ **Valley of Fires Recreation Area.** This small campground sits atop an island of sandstone surrounded by lava. Continuous improvements, such as paving and updated facilities, are being made. ⊠ *U.S. 380, 4 mi west of Carrizozo,* ☎ *505/648–2241. Flush toilets, pit toilets, partial hook-ups (electric and water), dump station, drinking water, showers, fire grates, grills, picnic tables, electricity, public telephone, ranger station. 20 RV sites with partial hook-ups, 5 tent sites.* ⊑ *Primitive camping $5, developed camping $7, RV sites $11.*

*En Route*   Twenty-eight miles south of Carrizozo, take C.R. B-30 east off U.S.
★   54 and in 5 mi you'll come to **Three Rivers Petroglyph Site,** one of the Southwest's most comprehensive and fascinating examples of prehistoric rock art. The 21,000 sunbursts, lizards, birds, hand prints, plants, masks, and other symbols are thought to represent the nature-worshiping religion of the Jornada Mogollon people, who lived in this region between AD 900 and 1400. Symbols were pinpointed and identified through extensive work of two members of the Archaeological Society of New Mexico's Rock Art Recording Field School. Fragrant desert creosote and mesquite can be found here, along with cacti that blossom brilliant colors in early summer. A rugged trail snakes for 1 mi, and from its top you can see the Tularosa Basin to the west and the Sacramento Mountains to the east. A short trail leads to a partially excavated prehistoric village. You can camp at the site, and there are 10 covered shelters with picnic tables, barbecue grills, rest rooms, and water. ⊠ *C.R. B-30 east off U.S. 54,* ☎ *505/525–4300.* ⊑ *$2 per vehicle.*

## Alamogordo

⑫   *58 mi south of Carrizozo on U.S. 54, 46 mi southwest of Ruidoso; 68 mi northeast of Las Cruces on U.S. 70.*

Defense-related activities are vital to the town of Alamogordo and to
Otero County, which covers much of the Tularosa Basin desert. Look
up and you might see the dark, bat-shape outline of a Stealth fighter
swooping overhead—Holloman Air Force Base is home to these high-
tech fighter planes. Many residents work at White Sands Missile Range,
where the nation's first atomic bomb exploded at Trinity Site on July
12, 1945. If you find U.S. 70 closed temporarily, it's due to test launches
(locals have grown accustomed to this). South of Alamogordo, huge
military exercises involving both U.S. and foreign troops are conducted at the Fort Bliss Military Reservation along Route 54. It's not
all that surprising that flying objects can be mistaken for Unidentified
Flying Objects in this state.

�馬 The multistory structure that houses the **New Mexico Museum of
Space History** gleams metallic gold when the sun hits it at certain angles. The facility formerly known as the Space Center underwent a name
change in 2001, partially to avoid confusion with its famous counter-
part of the same name in Houston. Its centerpiece is the **International
Space Hall of Fame,** into which astronauts and other space-exploration
celebrities are routinely inducted. A simulated red Mars landscape is
among the indoor exhibits. Outside, the **Stapp Air and Space Park** displays a rocket sled from the 1950s and other space-related artifacts.
The scenic **Astronaut Memorial Garden** has a view of White Sands National Monument. The **Clyde W. Tombaugh IMAX Dome Theater and
Planetarium** screens films and presents planetarium and laser light
shows. Weeklong annual space-shuttle camps for children take place
from the first week in June through the first week in August. ⊠ *At top
of Hwy. 2001 (from U.S. 70 take Indian Wells Rd. to Scenic Dr.; from
U.S. 54 take Florida Ave. to Scenic Dr.),* ☎ *505/437–2840.* ▣ *Museum $2.50, IMAX show (1 film) $5.50, IMAX show (2 films) $9,
evening IMAX film $6.50 (film and show fees sometimes vary).* ☉ *In-
ternational Space Hall of Fame daily 9–5. Tombaugh IMAX Dome Theater and Planetarium Memorial Day–Labor Day, shows daily on the
hr 10–4 and at 7; Labor Day–Memorial Day, shows weekdays at
noon, 2, and 4; weekends at 11, noon, 2, 3, and 4; Fri.–Sat. evening
shows at 7.*

☆ A narrow-gauge train at the **Toy Train Depot** rumbles along a 2½-mi
track through Alamogordo's Alameda Park. The depot, built in 1898,
also displays toy trains in five rooms, with elaborate layouts including one that depicts the Alamogordo area's train era for the past century. Displays include live steam engines and active model train layouts.
Whistles and rumbles from nearby heavy freight trains (these are real)
help set the scene, since the attraction is only 50 yards from the Union
Pacific main line. If you make advance reservations, you can take a guided
tour of the abandoned Alamogordo and Sacramento Railway roadbed
and trestles. ⊠ *1991 N. White Sands Blvd. (Alameda Park),* ☎ *505/
437–2855.* ▣ *Train $2, displays $2.* ☉ *Wed.–Sun. 12:30–4:30.*

Tasty nuts are the crop at **Eagle Ranch Pistachio Groves,** where you
can buy nut meats in varieties of forms from chocolate candies to cran-
berry biscotti or linger in the coffee shop or art gallery. George and
Marianne Schweers own the family farm, which in 1972 diversified
into pistachios, an unusual crop for New Mexico. The ranch now has
12,000 pistachio trees, the largest such grove in the state. Ask for permission at the store to camp at the picnic area—there's no charge for
self-contained vehicles. ⊠ *7288 Hwy. 54/70, 4 mi north of White
Sands Mall, Alamogordo,* ☎ *800/432–0999.* ▣ *Farms tours free.* ☉
*Mon.–Sat. 8–6, Sun. 9–6. Farm tours Sept.–May, weekdays at 1:30;
June–Aug., weekdays at 10:30 and 1:30.*

★ ☾ **White Sands National Monument,** with shifting sand dunes 60 ft high, encompasses 145,344 acres and the largest deposit of gypsum sand in the world. The monument, one of the few landforms recognizable from space, has displays in its **visitor center** that describe how the dunes were formed. A 17-minute introductory video that's very helpful if you intend to hike among the dunes is screened at the visitor center, where there's a gift shop, snack bar, and bookstore.

A 16-mi round-trip car ride takes you into this eerie wonderland of gleaming white sand. You can climb to the top of the dunes for a photograph, then tumble or surf down on a sled sold at the visitor center. As you wade barefoot in the gypsum crystals you'll notice the sand is not hot, and there's even moisture to be felt a few inches below the surface. Gypsum is one of the most common minerals on earth, and unlike the silica sand on beaches, gypsum is finer and used for making Sheetrock and plaster of paris. A walk on the 1-mi **Big Dune Trail** will give you a good overview of the site; other options are the 4½-mi **Alkali Flat Trail** and the 600-yard **Boardwalk.** The **Nature Center in the Dunes** museum has exhibits and other information. The picnic area has shaded tables and grills. Backpackers' campsites are available by permit, obtainable at the visitor center, but there aren't any facilities. Once a month from May to September, White Sands celebrates the full moon by remaining open until 11 PM, allowing you to experience the dunes by lunar light. Call for information and reservations for monthly auto caravans to **Lake Lucero,** the source of the gypsum sand deposit. In summer rangers lead tours daily at sunset. ⊠ *Off U.S. 70, 15 mi southwest of Alamogordo, Holloman AFB,* ☎ *505/679–2599,* WEB *www.nps.gov/whsa.* 🎫 *$3.* ☉ *Memorial Day–Labor Day, daily 7 AM– 9 PM; visitor center 8–7. Labor Day–Memorial Day, daily 7 AM–dusk; visitor center 8–5.*

OFF THE
BEATEN PATH

**WHITE SANDS MISSILE RANGE MUSEUM & MISSILE PARK –** Here you can see outdoor displays of more than 50 rockets and missiles along with indoor exhibits honoring historic contributions of scientists including rocketry genius and inventor Werner Von Braun. The museum also contains accounts of early Native American inhabitants who occupied the surrounding Tularosa Basin. ⊠ *White Sands Missile Range (turn east off U.S. 70, 45 mi southwest of Alamogordo or 25 mi northeast of Las Cruces; take access road 5 mi to gate and stop to obtain visitor's pass [you must have current driver's license and insurance to enter, as well as photo identification for all passengers]),* ☎ *505/678–8824.* 🎫 *Free.* ☉ *Museum weekdays 8–4:30, weekends 10–3; Missile Park daily dawn–dusk.*

## Dining and Lodging

$–$$ ✕ **Compass Rose Brewpub.** Patterned after a Bavarian-style tavern, this unusual establishment has wooden bench seating and cozy surroundings along with selections of cheese, meat, bread, and salads. Hot sandwiches and stews also are served, and you can eat on an outdoor patio during balmy weather. The tasty food is a change of pace from southwestern fare and might be a reflection of the presence of German air force troops training at nearby Holloman Air Force Base. ⊠ *2203 E. 1st St.,* ☎ *505/434–9633. AE, D, MC, V.*

$–$$ ✕ **Margo's.** *Chalupas* (beans, meat, and cheese served on crisp tortillas) is the specialty Mexican dish at family-owned Margo's. In winter, *menudo,* made of hominy and tripe, is served hot and steaming. The southwestern decor includes colorful blankets. ⊠ *504 1st St.,* ☎ *505/ 434–0689. AE, D, MC, V.*

**$** ⊡ **Days Inn.** Contemporary rooms with standard furnishings expected of a chain lodging, but stays are pleasant here because of extra touches such as hair dryers in every room. ⊠ *907 S. White Sands Blvd., 88310,* ☎ *505/437–5090,* FAX *505/434–5667. 40 rooms. Refrigerators, microwaves, cable TV, pool, gym. AE, D, DC, MC, V. CP.*

## Camping

⚠ **Alamogordo KOA Kampground.** Motel-style amenities, such as a lounge and a recreation room, are available at this facility, where patches of green lawn and trees make the outdoors inviting. ⊠ *412 24th St., 1 block east of U.S. 70/54,* ☎ *505/437–3003. Flush toilets, full hook-ups, showers, laundry facilities, grills, picnic tables, general store, playground, pool. 67 RV sites, 10 tent sites, 2 cabins.* ⌨ *Tent sites $19–$21, RV sites $25–$27, cabins $33–$35. D, MC, V.*

# Cloudcroft

⑬ *19 mi east of Alamogordo on U.S. 82.*

Cloudcroft is a quiet mountain resort town with cabins and church camps tucked into secluded woods. Longtime weekenders don't mind telling you that they hope their haven remains a secret. A low-key version of Ruidoso, Cloudcroft has a small stretch of specialty shops and some log cabin–style restaurants and lodgings. The headquarters of the **Lincoln National Forest Sacramento Ranger District** (⊠ 61 Curlew St., off U.S. 82, ☎ 505/682–2551) has maps showing area hiking trails.

The **National Solar Observatory–Sacramento Peak,** 12 mi south of Cloudcroft on the Sunspot Highway at elevation 9,200 ft, is designated for observations of the sun. The observatory, established in 1947, has four telescopes, including a 329-ft Vacuum Tower that resembles a pyramid. One observation point has a majestic view of White Sands and the Tularosa Basin. During the day you can inspect the telescopes on a self-guided tour and watch live filtered television views of the sun. This is a working community of scientists—not a tourist attraction— so you're pretty much on your own. About half of the 60 people who work at the site also live here amid lofty aspen trees. A continuous, 45-minute informational movie plays in the visitor center, where displays of photographs can also be viewed. ⊠ *Sunspot Hwy., Sunspot,* ☎ *505/434–7000.* ⌨ *Free.* ☉ *Visitor center Mar.–Dec., daily 10–6; Jan–Feb., weekends 10–4. Self-guided tours daily dawn–dusk; May– Sept, guided tours Sat. at 2 PM.*

## Dining and Lodging

For cabin rental information, call the Cloudcroft Chamber of Commerce, or try **Cabins at Cloudcroft** (☎ 505/682–2396; 800/248–7967 within New Mexico; WEB www.cloudcroftnm.com). Rates are $75– $170 for one- to four-bedroom cabins.

**$$–$$$$** ✕⊡ **The Lodge.** The Mexican revolutionary Pancho Villa and Holly-
★ wood celebrities Judy Garland and Clark Gable are among the past guests at this Victorian lodge, originally a retreat owned by the Alamogordo and Sacramento Mountain Railway. The Lodge was originally built in 1899, burned down in 1909, and was rebuilt in about 1911. The Bavarian-style interior seems right out of a gothic novel. Rooms have comforters, period antiques, and ceiling fans. Rebecca's restaurant is named after a flirtatious redheaded ghost who is said to haunt the hallways in search of a new lover, but more important, executive chef Timothy Wilkins has won many gold medals in New Mexico culinary competitions for his southwestern and classical cuisine. While steam heaters in the rooms once added to the classical charm, they were very difficult to control—so modern air-conditioning and heating systems

have (thankfully) replaced this antiquated system. Affiliated with the
lodge is the off-premises **Lodge Pavilion,** a rustic 10-room B&B. On
the premises is a private, historic "minilodge," the **Retreat Suites,**
which has three one-bedroom suites and one two-bedroom suite. A huge
common area includes a large table and kitchen facilities. ⌧ *1 Corona
Pl. (Box 497, 88317),* ☎ *505/682–2566 or 800/395–6343,* FAX *505/
682–2715,* WEB *www.thelodgeresort.com. 61 rooms. Restaurant, some
in-room data ports, some kitchens, some microwaves, some refrigerators, 9-hole golf course, pool, gym, some hot tubs, outdoor hot tub,
sauna, croquet, horseshoes, volleyball, cross-country skiing, snowmobiling, lounge, some pets allowed (fee). AE, D, DC, MC, V.*

# SOUTHEASTERN NEW MEXICO A TO Z

### AIR TRAVEL
Albuquerque International Sunport is 380 mi north of Carlsbad and
295 mi north of Roswell. El Paso International Airport in Texas is the
main gateway to southern New Mexico. The major airlines with scheduled service to the airport are America West, American, Continental,
Delta, Frontier, Southwest, and Azteca Airlines (specializing in flights
to and from Mexico). *See* Air Travel *in* Smart Travel Tips A to Z for
national airline phone numbers.

The municipal airports in Carlsbad and Roswell have daily shuttle-flight
service on Mesa Airlines. Roswell is southeastern New Mexico's major
flight hub, offering the most daily flights and scheduling options.
➤ AIRLINES: **Azteca Airlines** (☎ 800/445–9820). **Mesa Airlines** (☎ 800/
637–2247, WEB www.mesa-air.com).
➤ AIRPORTS: **Albuquerque International Sunport** (⌧ 2200 Sunport
Blvd. SE, Albuquerque, ☎ 505/842–4366). **El Paso International Airport** (⌧ 6701 Convair Dr., El Paso, TX, ☎ 915/772–4271). **Sierra Blanca
Regional Airport** (⌧ 1 Airport Rd., Ruidoso, ☎ 505/336–8111).

### BUS TRAVEL
Texas, New Mexico & Oklahoma Coaches, which is affiliated with
Greyhound Lines, provides bus service to Carlsbad, White's City, and
other destinations in southern New Mexico. Silver Stage Lines operates van service to Carlsbad Caverns National Park from any point on
the Carlsbad–El Paso route.
➤ BUS COMPANIES: **Silver Stage Lines** (☎ 800/522–0162). **Texas, New
Mexico & Oklahoma Coaches** (☎ 505/887–1108 in Carlsbad; 800/
231–2222 for all other destinations).

### CAR RENTAL
You can rent a car at El Paso International Airport and Albuquerque
International Sunport. Auto dealerships in some southeastern New Mexico cities rent cars. Your best bet for finding car rentals in smaller communities, such as Roswell and Carlsbad, is at municipal airports. Both
Avis and Hertz rent cars at the Roswell airport, while Hertz has a site
at Carlsbad's airport. Enterprise in downtown Ruidoso will deliver rental
cars to the Sierra Blanca Airport upon request. *See* Car Rental *in* Smart
Travel Tips A to Z for national rental-agency phone numbers.

### CAR TRAVEL
To get to Roswell and other points in southeastern New Mexico, drive
east from Albuquerque on I–40 for about 60 mi, exit on U.S. 285 heading south, and continue for 140 mi to Roswell. From Roswell take U.S.
285 to Carlsbad, about 75 mi away (320 mi from Albuquerque). From
El Paso, Texas, take U.S. 62/180 east and north 154 mi to Carlsbad
Caverns (187 mi to Carlsbad).

The major highway south through southeastern New Mexico is U.S. 285, accessible from I–40 at the Clines Corner exit, 59 mi east of Albuquerque. If you're destined for Roswell or Carlsbad from southwestern New Mexico, the best route is U.S. 70 east from Las Cruces or U.S. 62/180 east from El Paso, Texas.

The quality of the roadways in southeastern New Mexico varies widely, particularly in remote rural areas. Drive with caution on the region's narrow highways, which particularly in mountainous areas have no shoulders. On minor roadways, even if paved, be alert for curves, dips, and steep drop-offs.

### EMERGENCIES
In case of emergency dial 911.

Some Walgreens pharmacies in Roswell, Carlsbad, and other southeastern communities have late-night or 24-hour pharmacies. Wal-Mart and large grocery chain stores including Albertson's also have pharmacies.

➤ HOSPITALS: **Carlsbad Medical Center** (✉ 2430 W. Pierce, Carlsbad, ☎ 505/887–4100). **Eastern New Mexico Medical Center** (✉ 405 W. Country Club Rd., Roswell, ☎ 505/622–8170).

### TOURS
Around and About Tours offers excursions of several days to a week from El Paso, Texas, into New Mexico. Gray Line of Albuquerque guides group sightseeing tours to Carlsbad Caverns National Park by special request.

➤ TOUR OPERATORS: **Around and About Tours** (✉ 6716 Mesa Grande Ave., El Paso, TX, ☎ 915/833–2650). **Gray Line of Albuquerque** (✉ 300 2nd St. SW, Albuquerque, ☎ 866/242–2998, 505/244–9258).

### VISITOR INFORMATION
➤ TOURIST INFORMATION: **Alamogordo Chamber of Commerce** (✉ 1301 N. White Sands Blvd., 88310, ☎ 505/437–6120 or 800/826–0294, WEB www.alamogordo.com). **Capitan Chamber of Commerce** (✉ Box 441, 88316, ☎ 505/354–2273). **Carlsbad Chamber of Commerce** (✉ 302 S. Canal St., 88220, ☎ 505/887–6516, WEB www.chamber.caverns. com). **Carrizozo Chamber of Commerce** (✉ Box 567, 88301, ☎ 505/ 648–2732). **Cloudcroft Chamber of Commerce** (✉ Box 1290, 88317, ☎ 505/682–2733, WEB www.cloudcroft.net). **Lincoln State Monument** (✉ U.S. 380 [Box 36, 88338], ☎ 505/653–4372). **Portales Chamber of Commerce** (✉ 200 E. 7th St., 88130, ☎ 800/635–8036, WEB www. portales.com). **Roswell Chamber of Commerce** (✉ 121 W. 2nd St., ☎ 505/623–5695, WEB www.roswellnm.org). **Ruidoso Valley Chamber of Commerce** (✉ 720 Sudderth Dr., 88345, ☎ 505/257–7395, WEB www. ruidoso.net/chamber).

# 8 SOUTHWESTERN NEW MEXICO

## INCLUDING EL PASO, TEXAS, AND CIUDAD JUÁREZ, MEXICO

Lakes along the Rio Grande reflect serene clouds, dust devils dance across the plains, a distant horseback rider searches for a calf lost from a cattle herd. In the far southwestern corner's wilderness of pines and sheer canyons, wild creatures find refuge from encroaching civilization. Of the Old West, adobe sanctuaries and cobbled plazas are surviving remnants.

Updated by
Marilyn
Haddrill

W IDELY DIVERSE CULTURES mingle in southwestern New Mexico, and their respective art, architecture, and ethnic foods beckon the traveler in search of adventure. The precursor to this rich variety, however, was frequent and ongoing power struggles. Apache Indians and the Spanish threatened each other for three centuries; the Apache leader Geronimo would close out his life battling Anglo encroachment. Once the United States secured the lands for its own in the mid-1800s, ranchers and the infighting of lawmen and outlaws would create a unique American West mythology.

Where caravans of horses and wagons from Mexico's interior once snaked cautiously, urban development booms in the borderland of New Mexico, west Texas, and Mexico. More than 400 years ago, the vast desert area in south-central New Mexico was known as the "Pass of the North," a vital pathway for Spanish explorers in North America. Cabeza de Vaca led the first Spanish expedition into the area in 1593. Five years later Juan de Oñate brought 500 colonists from Mexico across the Rio Grande into what is now New Mexico. Trade between the eventual northern colonial outposts and old Mexico followed El Camino Real (The Royal Road), a route that for the most part traveled parallel to the Rio Grande. The portion of the trek north of Las Cruces and east of the Rio Grande became known as Jornada del Muerto (Journey of Death) because of the physical hardship and Indian attacks travelers often endured. Conquistadors left behind armor, helmets, and other relics leading to many stories of lost treasure.

El Paso, Texas, named after the Spanish explorers' route, is the area's largest city and most convenient gateway. But the nerve center of southern New Mexico is Las Cruces (The Crosses), with a population of about 75,000. The Organ Mountains overlooking the city dominate the landscape and the works of area painters and photographers. Sunset can color the jagged peaks a brilliant magenta, called "Las Cruces purple." Nearby Old Mesilla once served as the Confederate territorial capital of New Mexico and Arizona.

Parched Spanish sojourners of the 16th century would be shocked to witness the agrarian lifestyle in the fertile Mesilla Valley, just north of El Paso. Miles of lush fields and pecan orchards track the path of the Rio Grande. The huge Elephant Butte reservoir is the source of much of the water that irrigates some of the country's most prolific pecan and chile farms. As New Mexico's largest body of water, Elephant Butte Lake is a mecca for water sports and fishing. At nearby Truth or Consequences you can soak at bargain prices in natural hot springs.

Outdoor enthusiasts also head to the Gila National Forest and Gila Wilderness areas, where quaint old mining towns are the relics of fevered quests for silver, copper, and other minerals once found abundantly in the ore-rich hills. Area museums contain comprehensive displays of locally found minerals, along with colorful pottery created by early Native American inhabitants. The mountainous area where both Geronimo and Billy the Kid lived provides breathtaking vistas.

North of Gila National Forest, Hwy. 60 runs east–west through ranching communities whose lifestyles and isolation evoke a simpler past. In this lonely landscape you'll find the gleaming white, dish-shape radio telescope antennas of the Very Large Array, focusing its attention a billion light-years away.

## Southwestern New Mexico

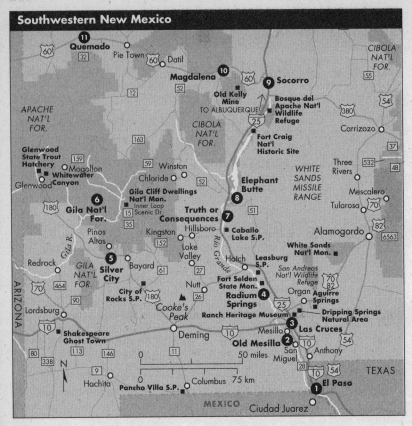

## Pleasures and Pastimes

### Dining

The cost of a meal in this area is extremely reasonable. The Mexican restaurants in the Mesilla Valley and Las Cruces rival those in Santa Fe except in price. Almost any Mexican-style eatery in the valley is sure to please, especially if you're a fan of the locally grown green chiles. Barbecue joints and steak houses are just as popular as Mexican restaurants.

| CATEGORY | COST* |
|---|---|
| $$$$ | over $25 |
| $$$ | $18–$25 |
| $$ | $10–$17 |
| $ | under $10 |

*per person for a main course at dinner*

### Lodging

The Las Cruces area has two fine bed-and-breakfasts—Meson de Mesilla in Old Mesilla and Lundeen Inn of the Arts. The Cottages in Silver City, is highly recommended as is Casitas de Gila, where you can enjoy sublime isolation at the edge of the Gila Wilderness. You can also check out guest ranches and the standard chain motels.

| CATEGORY | COST* |
|---|---|
| $$$$ | over $170 |
| $$$ | $120–$170 |
| $$ | $70–$120 |
| $ | under $70 |

*All prices are for a standard double room, excluding 8–12% tax.*

## Outdoor Activities and Sports

Outdoor opportunities abound in this corner of New Mexico. Elephant Butte Lake near Truth or Consequences offers world-class competition fishing for monstrous striped bass, though other varieties such as catfish are also abundant. All sorts of water sports take advantage of the lake's miles of surface. Elephant Butte is on a flat, open plain and can get pretty toasty during summer months. The Gila National Forest and mountains near Silver City provide a cooler environment for trout fishing or hiking, but don't expect large streams or lakes here: this forest land is dryer than what you would find in higher elevations. The mountains are still immense and fun to explore, either on foot or via scenic drives. Camping is another popular activity in this area. Birdwatchers will be busy just about anywhere they go along the Rio Grande, Gila National Forest, Elephant Butte Lake, or Bosque del Apache Wildlife Refuge.

# Exploring Southwestern New Mexico

The Rio Grande carves through the fertile Mesilla Valley, known for its plump green chiles and acres of thick, shaded pecan groves. Try leaving I–10 and follow the green agriculture fields along Hwy. 28, which begins just north of El Paso and ends at Old Mesilla. You must stop in the shops and restaurants in Old Mesilla's historic plaza; its adobe structures appear much as they did a century ago. From Las Cruces, take Hwy. 185 north through the farm valley on a route that leads to Hatch. During the fall harvest the valley is scented with the aroma of roasting chiles.

Surrounding the old mining town of Silver City is the vast and scenic Gila National Forest, which includes the Black Range mountains. New Mexico's largest lake, Elephant Butte, begins at Truth or Consequences and tracks north for miles alongside I–25. The Bosque del Apache Wildlife Refuge near Socorro provides a haven for many species of waterfowl. Another opportunity to leave the beaten path awaits at Socorro, where you can turn west on U.S. 60 to explore tiny rural villages such as Magdalena and Datil. On the Plains of San Augustin, look for the awesome array of giant, gleaming white radio antennas that are part of the National Radio Astronomy Observatory.

## Great Itineraries

In this highly diverse region, you can balance a mix of historical, cultural, and outdoor experiences. Adjust your schedule to your own tastes, but be open to a little adventure. This is an ideal opportunity to leave behind urban pleasures for those of a quiet rural inn or remote forest trail. The Old West city of El Paso, Texas, serves as the gateway to southern New Mexico, which is why it is included here.

IF YOU HAVE 3 DAYS

Spend your first day exploring the history and Spanish missions of ⊞ **El Paso** ①. On day two, travel north on Hwy. 28 through shady pecan orchards to **Old Mesilla** ② and visit the galleries, shops, and restaurants. In the afternoon, take U.S. 70 northeast to **White Sands National Monument** (☞ Chapter 7). Return to ⊞ **Las Cruces** ③ to spend the night, and if you're in Las Cruces on a Wednesday or Saturday morning, stop by the open-air downtown farmers' market. Next take I–10 west 61 mi to **Deming,** and turn northwest onto U.S. 180 to drive 51 mi to ⊞ **Silver City** ⑤. If there's still time, you can hike, fish, or visit ghost towns in the **Gila National Forest** ⑥.

IF YOU HAVE 7 DAYS

Follow the three-day itinerary above and spend your fourth day on a scenic drive east on Hwy. 152 through **Hillsboro** to ⛰ **Truth or Consequences** ⑦ and **Elephant Butte Lake State Park.** Spend part of your fifth day in the area before continuing north on I–25 to **Bosque del Apache National Wildlife Refuge** and overnighting in ⛰ **Socorro** ⑨. On day six, take U.S. 60 west to investigate the **Very Large Array,** and **Datil,** among other small towns, and overnight at one of the small places along U.S. 60. Spend your seventh day making your way back south along I–25 to El Paso, stopping at one of the forts, or Hatch for some chiles to bring home.

## When to Tour Southwestern New Mexico

Winters tend to be gentle in the desert regions of southern New Mexico, but between May and early September the days can be blisteringly hot. Even the mountainous areas can be uncomfortably warm during a hot spell. Plan summer outdoor excursions for early morning or late evening. Wear sunscreen, sunglasses, and hats in the midday sun, and carry plenty of water. Spring is cooler, but it's often accompanied by nasty, dust-laden winds. One of the best times to visit is between late September and early November, when skies are clear blue and the weather is usually balmy.

# BORDERLAND

Lines drawn on a map do little to divide the inhabitants of two countries and three states who share an ancestry dating back to the arrival of Spanish colonists. In the small border cities of Columbus, New Mexico, and Las Palomas, Mexico, families live and do business on both sides of the international boundary line. Housing and commercial developments along I–10 are quickly joining Las Cruces, New Mexico, to El Paso, Texas. The city of Anthony marks a midway point, straddling the two states. This "Borderland" of New Mexico, Texas, and the Mexican state of Chihuahua also draws transplants from the eastern and western United States, who come to take advantage of the mild weather and placid way of life.

You might be surprised to find U.S. Border Patrol checkpoints on all major highways leading away from the El Paso area to destinations such as Carlsbad, Deming, Truth or Consequences, and Alamogordo. Uniformed officers will simply ask your citizenship, though trained dogs sometimes circle vehicles in searches for illegal drugs. The stops are routine, and law-abiding citizens should encounter no difficulty.

## El Paso, Texas

❶ *267 mi south of Albuquerque, I–25 to I–10.*

Yes, El Paso *is* in Texas—but just barely. At one time, the city along the now streamlike Rio Grande was part of the New Mexico Territory. One glance at a map will explain why this area has become the transportation hub for southern New Mexico.

In April 1598, Spanish explorer Don Juan de Oñate dubbed the entire Rio Grande valley Paso del Rio del Norte ("the pass through the river of the north")—from which El Paso derives its name. Oñate was so grateful that the expedition of about 500 ragged colonists had reached the Rio Grande that he ordered his people to don their best clothes for a feast of thanksgiving—a celebration that preceded the arrival of the pilgrims in Massachusetts by nearly a quarter century. On that feast day, April 30, Oñate issued a formal proclamation of *La Toma*, claiming the land for the King of Spain.

Today El Paso is most strongly associated with Anglo-America's Old West tales of cattle drives and gunfighters. Between the southern end of the Rockies and the northern terminus of Mexico's Sierra Madre, the city was a major stopping point on the way west during the California gold rush. The downtown area in about 1850 was sparsely settled, with a dirt trail leading to the Rio Grande. Adobes began to appear along an established roadway about eight years later. San Jacinto Plaza soon became the official town square. The arrival of the railroad, the real life giver to towns, came in 1888.

Many of El Paso's downtown buildings date from the early 20th century, when architect Henry C. Trost produced his finest work, from the pillars and stained glass of the grandiose Camino Real Paso del Norte to the sturdy, reinforced concrete of the Mills Building. Trost, whose influences were many—from adobe to Frank Lloyd Wright—received much acclaim for his buildings at the University of Texas at El Paso. Based on Bhutanese structures, the campus buildings have an almost monastic design. Unfortunately, many downtown gems, like the historically protected Plaza Hotel (one of Conrad Hilton's first hotels), stand empty. During the 1950s hotels could be filled, sometimes with Hollywood stars and the wealthy heading for a cheap and easy divorce in Ciudad Juárez across the border. Adding to the town's bravado were live alligators in the plaza pond (a sculpture of writhing alligators has replaced the real reptiles, which ended their residency in the 1960s).

The **El Paso Museum of Arts** has an American collection that includes Southwest artists Tom Lea, Frederic Remington, Henrietta Wyeth, and native son Luis Jimenez. In the Spanish Viceroyal and Mexican folk *retablos* room is striking religious art. Drawings and prints by masters like Picasso, Goya, and Rivera, and works by contemporary artists are other museum highlights. ⊠ *One Arts Festival Plaza*, ☎ *915/532–1707.* ▦ *Free.* ☉ *Tues.–Sat. 9–5, Sun. noon–5.*

**Magoffin Home State Historical Park,** a Territorial-style adobe homestead near downtown El Paso, was erected in 1875 by an early El Paso pioneer, Joseph Magoffin. The home's traditional design includes thick adobe walls and an enclosed patio. Paintings and furniture belonging to the original owners lie within, including an imposing 13-ft-tall half-canopy bed with rose-color silk upholstery. The bed is part of a five-piece bedroom set purchased at the 1884 World's Fair in New Orleans. ⊠ *1120 Magoffin St. (follow signs off I–10; westbound traffic takes Cotton St. exit, eastbound traffic takes Downtown exit to Kansas St.),* ☎ *915/533–5147.* ▦ *$2.* ☉ *Daily 9–4.*

In the lower valley outside El Paso are some of the Southwest's earliest Spanish missions and other historic structures. The **Mission Trail Association** (☎ 915/534–0630, WEB www.missiontrail.com) has information about them. Also, the **El Paso–Juárez Trolley Co.** (☎ 915/544–0061) or **All Seasons Tours & Receptive Services** (☎ 915/877–3002), owned by Jo Ann Shaw, conducts custom mission tours upon request. To start your own mission trail tour, take the Zaragosa exit off I–10 just east of El Paso southwest for 4 mi, and then turn south onto Socorro Road and follow the mission trail signs.

★ Spanish refugees from Santa Fe's Pueblo Revolt of 1680 established the **Mission Ysleta** (*ysleta* means "small island") circa 1681. The clergy converted members of the Tigua tribe who had accompanied the refugees on their southern flight. The thick-walled adobe structure has a small door, which the settlers hoped would leave them less vulnerable to attacks by hostile Native Americans. Like the other old missions in the area, this structure remains an active church. A guide from the Mission Trail Association is available to conduct free tours from Friday through Sunday, depending on church schedules. ✉ *Old Pueblo Rd. at Zaragosa and Alameda (take Zaragosa exit off I–10, east of El Paso)*, ☎ *915/859–9848.* 🖵 *Free.* ⊙ *Mon.–Sat. 9–5; Sun. openings vary with church schedules.*

Adjacent to Mission Ysleta is the **Tigua Indian Reservation** (✉ 119 S. Old Pueblo Rd., ☎ 915/859–7913), home of the oldest ethnic group in Texas. Tigua pottery, jewelry, art, and replicas of ancient Native American homes are sold here. The **Speaking Rock Casino & Entertainment Center** (✉ Tigua Indian Reservation, 122 Old Pueblo Rd., ☎ 915/860–7777), was closed in early 2002 following a years-long court battle over its legality under Texas state law. While federal courts ultimately sided with the state of Texas, tribal officials were attempting to convince state legislators to pass a bill that would authorize the casino to reopen. In the meantime, visitors could dine at the on-site restaurant, visit the lounge, and participate in legal games such as pool.

**Socorro Mission,** to the south of the Tigua Indian Reservation, is famed for its fine vigas—the carved ceiling beams that support adobe architecture. Because it is so small, the building is used only for special occasions such as weddings and funerals. The Mission Trail Association has a free tour guide here in the morning, Friday through Sunday, unless it conflicts with services. The church structure, weakened by rains, will be undergoing major renovations through about 2005, so openings may be a little iffy during this time. ✉ *328 S. Nevares Rd.,* ☎ *915/859–7718.* 🖵 *Free.* ⊙ *Weekdays 9–5.*

**Presidio Chapel San Elceario** in San Elizario (yes, the two spellings conflict) is 6 mi south of the Socorro Mission. The 1789 Spanish fortress provided settlers protection from raiding Comanches and Apaches. After fire damaged the chapel in 1936, a bell tower and stained glass were added. It was near this site that the expedition of Spanish explorer Don Juan de Oñate stopped to conduct a thanksgiving celebration in 1598. ✉ *1556 San Elizario Rd.,* ☎ *915/851–2333.* 🖵 *Free.* ⊙ *Daily 10–4 (generally).*

The **San Elizario County Jail** is thought to have been built as a private residence in the early 1800s, but at some point the adobe structure transitioned into El Paso County's first courthouse and jail. Outlaw Billy the Kid is said to have helped break a friend out of one of the iron cages here, though the story cannot be verified. The account is included in a book written by former Lincoln County sheriff Pat Garrett, who ultimately tracked down and shot Billy the Kid. In the same vicinity, you'll find other historic structures including Los Portales, originally built in the 1850s as a private residence. ✉ *San Elizario Plaza,* ☎ *915/851–1682 San Elizario Genealogy and Historical Society.* 🖵 *Free guided tours of jail and plaza beginning at the Los Portales building.* ⊙ *Daily 10–2 (variable).*

A major expansion completed in late 2001 doubled the capacity of a casino that now offers 600 slot machines at **Sunland Park Racetrack & Casino** (✉ 101 Futurity Dr., Sunland Park, ☎ 505/589–1131). Race days are Friday–Sunday and Tuesday from November through early April. Post time is 12:35 PM November through January and 1:05 PM February through April. It's an attractive facility, enhanced by an artificial lake in the middle of the track. A restaurant, lounge, snack bar, special promotions, and live entertainment on weekends are offered.

The casino stays open year-round, from noon to midnight. From El Paso, take Sunland Park exit off I–25 near the northern city limits.

## Dining and Lodging

**$$–$$$$**  ✕ **Cattleman's Steakhouse.** What the owners describe as "Dakota-style
★  badland bluffs" signal your arrival at this restaurant and attraction, and a cowboy on horseback greets you in the parking lot. Cattleman's is pretty much in the middle of nowhere—20 mi east of El Paso—but it's worth the trip, as much for the fun ambience as for the terrific steaks. The succulent slabs are so tender they almost melt in your mouth. A zoo, deer display, playground, party facilities, a lake walk, and an Old West are among the nonculinary diversions. Free hayrides are given on Sunday. Cattleman's is part of Indian Cliffs Ranch, which provided the backdrop for scenes in the movie *Courage Under Fire.* Open hours are weekdays 4:30–10, Saturday 12:30–10, and Sunday 12:30–9. ✉ *Off I–10, Exit 49 (follow signs), Fabens,* ☎ *915/544–3200. Reservations not accepted. AE, D, MC, V.*

**$–$$$**  ✕ **The State Line.** The best barbecued ribs and smoked chicken in the
★  region can be found in northwestern El Paso (near Sunland Park Race-Track). Bring an appetite, because the trimmings include generous help-ings of potato salad, coleslaw, and beans. For dessert try the ultrarich brownie. Drinks are served in an outdoor courtyard, where you can wait for your table. ✉ *1222 Sunland Park Dr. (Sunland Park exit off I–10),* ☎ *915/581–3371. Reservations not accepted. AE, D, MC, V.*

**$–$$**  ✕ **La Norteña y Cafe Deluxe.** The after-work and singles crowd pack into this casual, hip meeting point for Mexican cuisine and pool shoot-ing. Behind the long bar, cooks dish up staple dishes and surprises like a shark and potato taco, and quail. Breakfast here is a good bet, too. Booths and tables fill the cavernous space, which served as a jail and Chinese laundry in its past lives. Beer and alcohol logos are painted on the brick walls. The eatery is close to the Greyhound terminal and in walking distance from the civic center and Camino Real Hotel. ✉ *212 W. Overland,* ☎ *915/533–0533. AE, MC, V.*

**$**  ✕ **Leo's.** You'll not be disappointed at any of this El Paso establish-ment's five locations. The Mexican food is repeatedly voted an ethnic favorite by locals in annual newspaper polls. Enchiladas, tacos, com-bination plates, and fluffy sopaipillas are served in helpings that will leave you stuffed—that is, if you can elbow your way through the crowds and get a table. ✉ *2285 Trawood St.,* ☎ *915/591–2511;* ✉ *5103 Mon-tana St.,* ☎ *915/566–4972;* ✉ *5315 Hondo Pass,* ☎ *915/757–9025;* ✉ *315 Mills Ave.,* ☎ *915/544–1001;* ✉ *8001 N. Mesa St.,* ☎ *915/ 833–1189. AE, D, MC, V.*

**$$**  ✕▥ **Camino Real Hotel, El Paso.** This towering, redbrick downtown hotel is listed on the National Register of Historic Places and has a great location across from the art museum and civic center. The guest rooms are quite large, if a bit ordinary. The jewel of the hotel is the high-ceil-ing Dome Bar, surrounded by marble and beneath a 1912 Tiffany stained-glass dome of rich blues. In the days when the hotel was the Hotel Paseo del Norte, cattlemen filled the bar with smoke as they cut their deals. Today, locals sink into deep chairs while enjoying the evening musical entertainment. The Dome Restaurant offers fine din-ing, and brunch is popular at the more casual Azulejo. ✉ *101 S. El Paso St., 79901,* ☎ *915/534–3000 or 800/769–4300,* ℻ *915/534–3024,* ᴡᴇʙ *www.caminoreal.com. 359 rooms. 2 restaurants, coffee shop, room service, cable TV, pool, gym, sauna, meeting rooms, airport shuttle, parking, some pets allowed (fee). AE, D, DC, MC, V.*

**$$**  ▥ **Hilton El Paso Airport.** Just 200 yards from the El Paso International Airport, this modern hotel offers luxury as well as convenience for air travelers. More than half the rooms can be converted into two-room suites. Two restaurants on the premises provide a choice of continental fare (Magnim) or northern Italian dishes (Canarozzos). The pool here has a 200-ft water slide. ⊠ *2027 Airway Blvd., 79925,* ☎ *915/778–4241,* FAX *915/772–6871. 272 rooms. 2 restaurants, some in-room hot tubs, some microwaves, some refrigerators, cable TV, pool, hot tub, spa, meeting rooms, airport shuttle, parking, some pets allowed. AE, D, DC, MC, V.*

**\$\$**  🖭 **Holiday Inn Sunland Park.** Outdoor courtyards contribute to the atmosphere of this Holiday Inn, on a hill with 6½ acres near Sunland Park RaceTrack. The southwestern-style rooms have ironing boards, hair dryers, and coffeemakers. Breakfast buffets are served in the Sierra Grille Restaurant, and a Sunday brunch is available from 11 to 3. ⊠ *900 Sunland Park Dr., 79922,* ☎ *915/833–2900 or 800/658–2744,* FAX *915/833–6338,* WEB *www.holidayinnsunland.com. 178 rooms. Restaurant, in-room data ports, pool, hot tub, lounge, meeting rooms; no pets. AE, D, DC, MC, V.*

### Nightlife and the Arts

Locals drink to free musical entertainment on weekends at the **Camino Real Hotel** (⊠ 101 S. El Paso St., ☎ 915/534–3000) Dome Bar. The year's highlight for the city is the annual **Viva El Paso!** (☎ 915/565–6900 or 800/915–8482), a musical celebrating the El Paso region's history and legendary characters with music, dance, and drama. It takes place at the outdoor McKelligon Canyon Amphitheater in the Franklin Mountains, June through August, Thursday through Saturday. You can opt to take in the barbecue dinner served prior to the show, but make reservations for that, too. The **El Paso–Juárez Trolley Co.** (☎ 915/544–0062) provides a shuttle service to Viva El Paso! from downtown and airport hotels. By car, take I–10 east to Route 54 north. Take the Fred Wilson Road exit, turn left on Fred Wilson Road and left on Alabama Street, and you'll shortly arrive at the canyon's entrance on McKelligon Canyon Road.

### Shopping

El Paso has some delightful specialty outlets reflecting the tastes of economy-minded residents. Colorful blankets, leather goods, ceramics, tile for home building, and household decorative items are among the most popular Mexican imports. At the **Butterfield Trading Post** (⊠ I–10 and Airway Blvd., ☎ 915/771–7723) you'll find an open-air market and bargains such as \$5 Mexican blankets. Handcrafted wooden furniture with southwestern flourishes is sold at **Casa Rustica** (⊠ 6600 Montana Ave., ☎ 915/771–9096), along with exotic imports such as African masks. If you really want to immerse yourself in cowboy trappings, visit **El Paso Saddleblanket Co.** (⊠ 601 N. Oregon St., downtown Exit 19 off I–10, ☎ 915/544–1000). You'll find saddles, cowhides, skulls, horns, Indian pottery, and cowboy antiques such as branding irons in this 36,000-square-ft wholesale warehouse.

El Paso is *big* on cowboy boots and has several factory outlet stores. Even though the boots stocked are discontinued styles or irregular, the **Tony Lama Factory Stores** (⊠ 5040 N. Desert Blvd., ☎ 915/581–8192; ⊠ 12151 Gateway West, ☎ 915/858–0124; ⊠ 7156 Gateway East, ☎ 915/772–4327) carry a most prestigious name, and the boots are handcrafted in El Paso. If your boots were made for riding, not walking, check out **Barnett Harley-Davidson** (⊠ 8272 I–10, between Lomaland and Lee Trevino, ☎ 915/592–5804 or 800/736–8173), the world's largest dealership for the famed motorcycles. New, used, and rare bikes are showcased, and parts and accessories are also for sale.

# Ciudad Juárez, Mexico

*Across the Rio Grande border from El Paso.*

Just across the shallow Rio Grande lies the Mexican city that at one time made up a single Spanish settlement with El Paso. Juárez is a city of tremendous contrast, from residential districts of handsome, hacienda-style mansions to outlying colonias with tiny makeshift residences and dirt streets. Numerous *maquiladora* factories—"twin" plants operated by U.S. companies—have boosted the city's population to more than 1,700,000. Workers in maquiladoras assemble electronic and automobile components that are then shipped to the United States for further assembly.

In addition to other safety concerns, driving here is not recommended. You can park in El Paso near the Santa Fe Street Bridge and walk to Juárez, or catch a ride with the **El Paso–Juárez Trolley Co.** Border Jumper (✉ One Civic Center Plaza, El Paso, ☎ 915/544–0062), which leaves hourly from 10 to 5. For a $12.50 ticket, you'll have a day's worth of transportation along the route that weaves through Juárez shopping areas and restaurants. The trolley also enables you to escape many of the hassles of getting through vehicle customs checks on both sides of the border, though you still might get snagged in backed-up traffic while awaiting border crossings. Trolleys make hourly stops at the designated points, and drivers provide narration and border-incident stories along the way. The trolley company also provides free shuttle transportation to and from participating El Paso hotels. Juárez is a sprawling city, and although there are sidewalks, there are dull stretches past graffiti-covered storefronts, parking lots, and strip malls. Distances between points of interest can be great, so it's best to catch the next trolley coming through.

Juárez became an official settlement with the building of its first church, **Nuestra Señora de Guadalupe Misión** (Our Lady of Guadalupe Mission), which was completed in 1668. The church and the **Juárez Cathedral** (✉ corner of Avda. 16 de Septiembre and Mariscal, ☎ 52/656–155505) next door still have an active congregation. The downtown **Mercado** (Old City Market; ✉ Avda. 16 de Septiembre) is where most day-trippers spend their time shopping. For a better view of local life, walk down Calle Francisco I. Madero from the mercado, and you'll reach a **park** centered by a statue of Benito Juárez.

## Dining

$–$$  ✕ **Viva Mexico.** Entertainers in colorful Mexican garb swirl, dance, and sing in the circular stage area of Viva Mexico, where family-style performances take place Wednesday through Sunday. You can dine on authentic Mexican dishes along with standard steak and seafood fare. Tables are strategically arranged in the plaza-style ground floor and balcony area. Breakfast and lunch buffets also are served here (executive menus designed for working folks are available in the afternoons Monday through Friday). ✉ *Centro Comercio Pueblito Mexicano, Avdas. Lincoln and Zempoala,* ☎ *52/656–629–0156 or 52/656–629–0165. AE, D, DC, MC, V.*

## Shopping

In a city of nearly 2 million, shops are numerous, but you're best off sticking to tourist-oriented locales. On the street you'll be approached by insistent vendors; watch out for these street entrepreneurs, or you might end up purchasing a cassette tape that turns out to be a fuzzy recording of a radio broadcast. Be extra alert to your safety west of Avenida de Juárez. Many stores in Juárez are closed on Sunday. Your most reliable shopping options in town are spots such as the **Mercado**

# SACRED GROUND

**S**YMBOLS OF CATHOLICISM seem to be a hallmark of New Mexico, and visitors seek out adobe churches to photograph and colorful religious icons and minishrines to buy as souvenirs. More intimate and poignant expressions of New Mexicans' deep religiosity are found in homemade shrines and centuries-old churches of healing.

Alongside the state's roadways are small memorials of flowers and crosses known in Spanish as *descansos*, or resting places, for those who have died in automobile accidents. The monuments are erected by family or friends to honor the memory of the dead and on narrow, curving roads and steep embankments serve as chilling reminders to the living not to take safe passage for granted.

Some historians say the custom of highway shrines was introduced to the Western hemisphere four centuries ago by the first Spanish explorers, who experienced so many losses of life that their trails were strewn with crosses marking the fallen. Las Cruces, New Mexico, is thought to have obtained its name, "The Crosses," after one such site where Spanish explorers were slaughtered in an Indian ambush. Tragedy along the famous trade route Camino Real in south-central New Mexico was so common for early Spanish explorers, merchants, and missionaries that one segment was known as Jornada del Muerto, or Journey of Death.

In modern times, those of Hispanic descent and others practicing the Southwest's shrine tradition have seen their custom thwarted elsewhere in the country. State highway departments in more densely populated regions order the roadside shrines to be removed because of the problems they present for road maintenance crews.

But in New Mexico, road department officials go out of their way to honor the shrines held so sacred by the loved ones who maintain them. If the shrines need to be temporarily moved for mowing or other maintenance, crews work with families to make sure the monuments are returned to their original spots.

**C**ROSSES in general are a revered symbol in this state, where they often can be seen high atop a barren hill where religious treks are made. The crosses are placed either by a community or, as in Lincoln (☞ Chapter 7), by a single, devout individual. New Mexico also is known for a variety of spontaneous shrines, created by those who report experiencing miracles or religious visions. One woman in Lake Arthur, near Artesia in southeastern New Mexico, saw the image of Christ in a tortilla she was cooking. She built her own shrine surrounding the tortilla, complete with flickering candles, and the faithful and curious can make pilgrimages to it.

In an awesome display of religious faith during Holy Week, thousands of people journey miles by foot to reach Chimayó in northern New Mexico. They seek the blessing and healing of the holy soil found in the town's Santuario (sanctuary) church. The ground's sacredness dates from 1810, when a man discovered a crucifix glowing in the dirt. Though several attempts were made to relocate the cross, legend says the crucifix always reappeared where it was first found. Today the cross hangs above the altar, and the holy dirt can be taken from a sacred *pozito* (a small hole) in the floorboards of an adjoining room. Those seeking healing or giving thanks leave small photographs or tokens of their faith within an anteroom.

(⊠ Avda. 16 de Septiembre). Merchants hawk wares in a labyrinth of booths carrying piñatas (papier-mâché animals stuffed with candy), wooden figurines, belts, and jewelry. You're expected to barter. Don't hesitate to quibble or you'll be snickered at behind your back for paying the first asking price. **Avenida de Juárez** has many small individual shops where you can purchase items such as handwoven shawls and serapes.

## Old Mesilla

★ ❷   *2 mi south of Las Cruces on Hwy. 28.*

Historians disagree about the origins of Mesilla (today, Old Mesilla), which in Spanish means "little table." Some say the town occupies the exact spot that Don Juan de Oñate declared "the first pueblo of this kingdom." Other historians say Oñate instead meant the entire Mesilla Valley. Still, the reference to a "little table" does imply a small area. Village residents might be correct when they refer to their town as the first place in New Mexico officially proclaimed Spanish territory by Oñate. Old Mesilla is often referred to simply as Mesilla, and another town named Mesilla Park exists nearby.

Native Americans very likely lived here before the Spanish and other Europeans, though over the years signs of earlier habitation were erased by bulky adobe structures that date back as much as 150 years. As elsewhere in New Mexico, the thick walls served as sturdy residences or businesses but also as fortification against frequent Apache Indian attacks.

By some accounts, residents determined to escape U.S. rule built Mesilla in the early 1850s in Mexican territory on the Rio Grande's west side. Mesilla and Las Cruces coexisted on opposite sides of the international boundary line until the river changed its course in 1865—leaving both villages east of the Rio Grande. By this time Mesilla had already been officially annexed by the United States—the area was among 30,000 square mi purchased from Mexico in 1854. Mesilla was the largest station between El Paso and Los Angeles along the east–west Butterfield Stage Line in the mid-1800s. For a brief time in 1861, Mesilla was the Confederate territorial capital of an area that included Arizona and western New Mexico. In 1881 the Santa Fe Railroad extended its line into Las Cruces, bypassing Mesilla and establishing Las Cruces as the area's major hub of commerce and transportation.

A notorious event took place on August 27, 1871, when an argument between opposing political factions erupted into a bloodbath. The riot began after Republicans and Democrats staged political rallies in Mesilla's plaza on the same day—a terrible idea as it turned out. A Republican candidate for probate judge was clubbed over the head and died. Gunfire broke out, and eight people were killed before troops finally stormed the village to restore order. Another milestone was the trial of Billy the Kid, at which a Mesilla jury convicted the outlaw for the murder of Matthew Brady, the sheriff of Lincoln County. The Kid was transferred to the Lincoln County Courthouse (☞ Lincoln *in* Chapter 7) to be hanged for the crime but briefly staved off the inevitable by escaping.

Shops, galleries, and restaurants line the cobbled streets of Old Mesilla. With a Mexican-style plaza and gazebo where many weddings and fiestas take place, the village retains the charm of bygone days. The **San Albino Church** (⊠ Old Mesilla Plaza) was established in 1851. The present building of adobe and stained glass was erected in 1906 on the foundation of an earlier church.

OFF THE
BEATEN PATH

**STAHMANN FARMS –** Pecan trees cover about 4,000 acres at one of the largest pecan orchards in the world. You can take a shaded drive through the trees and drop by the farm's store to sample pecan products. ☒ *Hwy. 28, 8 mi south of Old Mesilla, San Miguel,* ☎ *505/526–8974 or 800/654–6887.* ☉ *Store Mon.–Sat. 9–6, Sun. 11–5.*

## Dining and Lodging

$$–$$$$   ✕ **Double Eagle.** Chandeliers, century-old wall tapestries, and gold-leaf ceilings are among the noteworthy design elements of this restaurant inside an 1848 mansion on Old Mesilla's plaza. Some say that ghosts, including one of a young man who incurred his mother's wrath by falling in love with a servant girl, haunt the structure. Continental cuisine, steaks, and flambé dishes are served in the main restaurant. The fare at Pepper's, the adjoining southwestern-style café-bar, includes borderland chile dishes, shark fajitas, and green-chile cheese wontons. The Double Eagle Sunday champagne brunch is worth a stop. ☒ *308 C. de Guadalupe,* ☎ *505/523–6700. AE, D, DC, MC, V.*

$–$$$   ✕ **Lorenzo's.** A hand-painted mural of the Mesilla Valley decorates this
   ★   intimate restaurant, where red tablecloths and bottles of imported oil set an appropriately Italian mood. The pueblo-style building and outdoor courtyard provide a quiet, relaxing setting for a leisurely lunch or dinner. The pizzas, pasta, sandwiches, and salads served at Lorenzo's are based on old Sicilian recipes, distinguished by excellence in homemade sauces, pasta, and breads. Lorenzo's is such a local favorite that it has expanded to occupy three area locations (two are in nearby Las Cruces). ☒ *Oñate Plaza, 2000 Hwy. 292,* ☎ *505/525–3170. AE, D, MC, V.*

$–$$   ✕ **La Posta.** Once a way station for the Butterfield Overland Mail and
   ★   Wells Fargo stages, the adobe restaurant has hosted celebrities including comedian Bob Hope and Mexican revolutionary Pancho Villa. Some of the Mexican entrées follow recipes dating back more than a century; other fare includes southwestern favorites like chiles rellenos and red or green enchiladas. Exotic birds and tropical fish inhabit the lushly planted atrium. ☒ *2410 C. de San Albino,* ☎ *505/524–3524. AE, D, DC, MC, V. Closed Mon.*

$–$$   ✕ **Old Mesilla Pastry Cafe.** Melt-in-your-mouth baked goods and occasional specialty items like grilled buffalo and ostrich meat make this café a good stop for breakfast or lunch. The savory pizzas include one made with green chiles and chicken. The restaurant recently expanded hours to include dinner served Friday and Saturday evenings. ☒ *2790 Avda. de Mesilla,* ☎ *505/525–2636. AE, MC, V. Closed Mon.–Tues.*

$   ✕ **Chope's Bar & Cafe.** About 15 mi south of Old Mesilla, this earthen-color adobe establishment in La Mesa looks unremarkable from the outside. But the fiery southwestern-style food served inside is highly popular with the locals. The bar is a favorite watering hole. ☒ *Hwy. 28, La Mesa,* ☎ *505/233–9976 bar; 505/233–3420 restaurant. No credit cards in bar. MC, V in restaurant.*

$–$$$   ✕🖫 **Meson de Mesilla.** Folks drive to Mesilla from all over southern
   ★   New Mexico and west Texas to enjoy this inn's Continental cuisine ($$–$$$; reservations recommended). Dishes like fresh Atlantic salmon, chateaubriand for two, and filet mignon are standard house specials. For inn guests only, a gourmet breakfast is served in a glass-enclosed atrium. The views of the jagged Organ Mountains and lower mesas from the back patio and second-floor balcony are additional lures. Rooms are done in Southwest tones and furnished with light-wood furniture and some antiques. They also have TVs, clock radios, and ceiling fans. The lower-priced single rooms are a good option for businesspeople on a budget. ☒ *1803 Avda. de Mesilla, 88046, off I–10, Exit 140, and ¾ mi west into Mesilla,* ☎ *505/525–9212 or 800/732–6025,* 🆀🆇 *505/527–4196. 15 rooms. Restaurant, in-room data ports, some refriger-*

*ators, cable TV, pool, lounge, some pets allowed (fee); no smoking. AE, D, DC, MC, V. BP.*

## The Arts

Foreign films are shown and amateur theater productions take place in one of Mesilla's historic buildings, the **Fountain Theater** (✉ 2468 C. de Guadalupe, ½ block off plaza, ☎ 505/524–8287), named for one of Mesilla's early pioneering families.

## Shopping

High-quality Native American jewelry and crafts are surprisingly economical, making shopping even more pleasing in the authentic adobe ambience of the **Old Mesilla Plaza.** The Farmers Market in the plaza offers homegrown produce such as watermelons and green chiles (in season), as well as handcrafted souvenirs and jewelry, noon–4 Sunday and 11–4 Thursday year-round. **El Platero** (✉ 2350 C. de Principal, ☎ 505/523–5561) offers jewelry, souvenirs, southwestern gift items and post cards.

An interior-design firm and art gallery, **Charles Inc.** (✉ 1885 W. Boutz St., corner of Avda. de Mesilla, ☎ 505/523–1888) has an extensive collection of fine works, such as bronze and marble pieces by master stone carver Jesús Mata. Custom designs with a southwestern flair can be found in handcrafted furniture, doors, and cabinets at **Mesilla Woodworks** (✉ 1802 Avda. de Mesilla, ☎ 505/523–1362).

# Las Cruces

❸  *45 mi north of El Paso on I–10.*

A mixture of old and new, Las Cruces is a casual city of diverse neighborhoods. The ones with adobe structures near the downtown area date back more than a century, though some sadly are crumbling into ruin. For about the last decade, the city has been revamping its downtown, open-air pedestrian district by replacing outdated shops and abandoned buildings with museums, a performing arts center, and a renovated old movie house. The transformation is a work in progress, but the downtown area is assuming a cohesive identity vastly improved from the old hodgepodge of bygone days. Take note of beautifully crafted, life-size bronze statues that represent different generations of travelers along the ancient Camino Real trade route.

The city and surrounding area represent one of the fastest-growing metropolitan areas in the United States (the second largest in New Mexico), with an economy closely linked to the border factories of El Paso, Texas, and Ciudad Juárez, Mexico; defense and commercial activities at White Sands Missile Range; and a major land-grant college, New Mexico State University.

Increasing commitment to the fine arts is represented in various city-owned downtown sites known as the **Cultural Complex,** which operates from headquarters at the Branigan Cultural Center. The center itself is the hub of educational activities, arts conferences, and traveling exhibits honoring different crafts such as quilting. The **Museum of Fine Arts And Culture,** open Wednesday–Friday 10–2, Saturday 9–2, features works of regional artists with an eclectic mix of styles, including emphasis on the Southwest and desert earth tones. The **Log Cabin Museum** is an original structure transferred from southern New Mexico's Black Range Mountains. Hands-on displays include a cider press and butter churn. Free admission can be obtained by inquiring at the cultural center headquarters. The city plans to open the **New Mexico Railroad and Transportation Museum,** converted from an abandoned

Santa Fe Railroad Depot several blocks west of the downtown strip. ⊠ *500 N. Water St.,* ☎ *505/541–2155,* WEB *www.lascruces-culture.org.* 🎫 *Free.* ◎ *Weekdays 9–5, Sat. 9–3.*

♻ The handsomely designed **New Mexico Farm and Ranch Heritage Museum** documents 3,000 years of agriculture in New Mexico and the Southwest. One exhibit re-creates a Mogollon pit house—an early farmhouse—from 1,200 years ago. (The Mogollon were the first people in what is now New Mexico to cease being nomadic.) Longhorn cattle, churro sheep, and some of the dairy cows are among the heritage breeds—descendants of animals the Spanish brought from Mexico—raised here. Unusual breeds of animals include burros called Jerusalem donkeys for the crosslike markings on their backs. At calf-feeding time (11 AM and 3 PM), you can learn about the history of dairy production in New Mexico and pet a calf. Chuck-wagon cooking demonstrations are offered throughout open hours Sunday. ⊠ *4100 Dripping Springs Rd. (from Las Cruces head east on University Ave., which becomes Dripping Springs Rd.; ranch is 1½ mi east of I–25),* ☎ *505/522–4100.* 🎫 *$3.* ◎ *Tues.–Sat. 9–5, Sun. noon–5.*

## Dining and Lodging

**$$–$$$$** ✕ **Cattle Baron.** Part of a regional chain, this restaurant serves prime rib, steaks, seafood, and pastas and has a well-stocked salad bar. The plant-filled, skylit dining room is done in brass and wood. The outdoor patio has city views. ⊠ *790 S. Telshor Blvd.,* ☎ *505/522–7533. AE, D, MC, V.*

**$$–$$$** ✕ **Lemongrass.** One of the newer and more elegant eateries in Las Cruces
★ is this Thai establishment. The decor includes pastel colors and lush green carpeting, and gentle Asian music plays in the background. Dishes are authentic, such as Gang Dang Gai, featuring a scrumptious combination of green chile curry simmered in coconut milk with chicken and vegetables. ⊠ *2540 El Paseo Rd. (Hadley Center),* ☎ *505/ 523–8778. AE, D, DC, MC, V.*

**$–$$$** ✕ **Lorenzo's.** Convenient to New Mexico State University, this is the
★ largest of the three Lorenzo's locations in the Las Cruces area. Grilled fish and chicken are served along with Sicilian sandwiches, pizzas, pastas, and salads. The smaller outlet on North Alameda Street is open only for lunch Monday through Friday and is used for catering. The third and newest establishment is near Old Mesilla (Hwy. 292)—see the listing under Old Mesilla. ⊠ *University Plaza, 1753 E. University Ave.,* ☎ *505/521–3505;* ⊠ *2000 Hwy. 292,* ☎ *505/525–3170;* ⊠ *741 N. Alameda St.,* ☎ *505/524–2850. AE, D, MC, V.*

**$–$$** ✕ **My Brother's Place.** *Tostadas compuestos* (a concoction of red or
★ green chile, meat, pinto beans, and cheese in a crispy tortilla cup) and other southwestern dishes are served with flair at this exceptional Mexican restaurant, where you can order pitchers of beer or margaritas to wash down the fire. Try an *empanada* (Mexican pastry) or crème caramel flan for dessert. The upstairs lounge is a pleasant watering hole decorated with brightly colored chairs and piñatas. Several varieties of Mexican beer are served here. (Try Negra Modelo or Tecate.) ⊠ *334 S. Main St.,* ☎ *505/523–7681. AE, D, DC, MC, V.*

**$–$$** ✕ **Si Señor Restaurant.** Popular with businesspeople, this immaculate restaurant has spacious rooms with southwestern decor and paintings. Mexican entrées emphasize three distinct chile sauce types—Las Cruces green (mild and flavorful), Deming red, and a variety described as "smoke," known as Hatch green. Friendly service and a pleasant atmosphere make for a relaxing meal. ⊠ *1551 E. Amador,* ☎ *505/527–0817. AE, D, MC, V.*

$ ✕ **The Durango Bagel.** The Durango caters to a college crowd. Conversation usually flows with the gourmet coffee and specialty bagels like apple-walnut and cranberry-orange. Muffins, cookies, and sandwiches are also served. ⊠ *2460 S. Locust St.,* ☎ *505/522–3397. No credit cards.*

$ ✕ **Mesilla Valley Kitchen.** Sidle up to the counter and order a gourmet sandwich, breakfast special, or beef burger accompanied by spud chips. Homemade baked goods in this southwestern-style eatery include cinnamon rolls, cookies, and muffins. ⊠ *Arroyo Plaza, 2001 E. Lohman Ave.,* ☎ *505/523–9311. AE, D, DC, MC, V.*

$ ✕ **Nellie's.** It's tough to find seating in the tiny Mexican diner, but that's because the food is incredible. You wouldn't give this place a second look if you judged it only by its plain appearance, but locals eat here in droves. The restaurant has gained national recognition for its mouth-watering dishes, such as chiles rellenos and combinations of enchiladas and tacos. ⊠ *1226 Hadley Ave.,* ☎ *505/524–9982. No credit cards.*

$ ✕ **Red Mountain Café.** This café serves a booming business district on the northeast side of Las Cruces. The variety of food here runs from standard deli sandwiches to imported fare and vegetarian pita pockets stuffed with smoked cheeses or hummus. The quaint setting has a European air. Table service has replaced the old counter service, adding an additional touch of elegance. ⊠ *1120 Commerce Dr., Suite A (Commerce Plaza), off Telshor Blvd.,* ☎ *505/522–7584. AE, D, MC, V. Closed Sun.*

$ ✕ **Scoopy's.** Within a former hamburger stand at its original location, Scoopy's offers all manner of delectable sundaes and sodas using home-made, custard-style ice cream. The low-fat treats can be supplemented with specialty hot dogs, mesquite-smoked turkey sandwiches, or prime rib on a sourdough bun. Order from the window, and eat in your car or on the outside benches. In early 2002, a second Scoopy's opened on the city's east side (Roadrunner Parkway) in a sparkling new purple-and-maroon building that looks good enough to eat. ⊠ *590 S. Valley Dr.,* ☎ *505/647–5066;* ⊠ *131 N. Roadrunner Pkwy.,* ☎ *505/521–1161. No credit cards.*

$$–$$$ 🏠 **Lundeen Inn of the Arts.** You'll think you've accidentally detoured
★ to Santa Fe at this art-filled B&B, but you'll luckily be paying Las Cruces prices. Architect Gerald Lundeen seamlessly joined two 1895 adobe houses, one Mexican colonial and the other Territorial. Linda, his wife, runs the impressionist gallery on the premises. Guest rooms pay homage to western artists like Georgia O'Keeffe and Frederic Remington. Five rooms have balconies, and all the accommodations are furnished with a whimsical mix of antiques and newer handcrafted pieces. One suite has spectacular views of the Organ Mountains. Gourmet breakfasts might include French toast with apple-and-raisin frosting, sweet-potato pancakes, or pumpkin waffles. You can work it off at a local health club, where membership is extended free to guests. The Lundeens also offer crafts and art classes, which guests can attend. ⊠ *618 S. Alameda Blvd., 88005,* ☎ *505/526–3326,* FAX *505/647–1334,* WEB *www.innofthearts.com. 18 rooms, 2 suites, 2 casitas. No-smoking rooms. AE, D, MC, V. BP.*

$ 🏠 **Teakwood Inn & Suites.** Formerly associated with Days Inn, this privately owned establishment is tidy and relatively inexpensive—rooms start at $59 for a single. The two-story motel is near I–10 and convenient to New Mexico State University and Old Mesilla. ⊠ *2600 S. Valley Dr., 88005, off I–10, Exit 142,* ☎ *505/526–4441 or 800/829–7466,* FAX *505/526–1980. 131 rooms. Microwaves, refrigerators, cable TV, indoor pool, sauna, laundry facilities, Internet, meeting rooms, some pets allowed (fee). AE, D, DC, MC, V. BP*

## Camping

⚠ **Aguirre Springs.** This exceptionally beautiful high-elevation spot is tucked alongside the towering spires of the Organ Mountains, giving you an expansive view of the Tularosa Basin. During drought conditions, fires may be restricted or prohibited. ⊠ *Off U.S. 70 (from Las Cruces take U.S. 70 northeast 12 mi, then head south at the road marked Aguirre Springs an additional 5 mi),* ☎ 505/525–4300. Pit toilets, fire grates, fire pits, grills, picnic tables. 54 sites. ⬚ *Free with $3 day use fee. Reservations not accepted. No credit cards.*

## Nightlife and the Arts

**New Mexico State University** (⊠ Corbett Center, University Park, ☎ 505/646–4411 information center; 505/646–1420 special events office) presents lectures, concerts, and other special events. Good ol' country-and-western music and dancing are found Wednesday through Saturday nights at **Rodeo USA** (⊠ 170 W. Picacho, ☎ 505/524–5872). The locally based **Tierra del Encanto Ballet Folklorico** performs folk dances of Mexico at the annual weekend **International Mariachi Festival** (☎ 505/534–0360) in November.

## Outdoor Activities

**Aguirre Springs** is beneath the towering spires of the Organ Mountains in a juniper-oak woodland zone. Trails lead into the upper regions of the ponderosa pines, including **Pine Tree Trail** (4-mi loop) and **Baylor Pass National Recreation Trail** (6 mi one-way), two developed paths. During drought conditions, fires may be restricted or prohibited. ⊠ *Off U.S. 70 (from Las Cruces take U.S. 70 northeast 12 mi, then head south at the road marked Aguirre Springs an additional 5 mi),* ☎ 505/525–4300. ⬚ $3. ☉ Apr.–Oct., daily 8–8; Nov.–Mar., daily 8–6.

At the **Dripping Springs Natural Area** is an abandoned mountain resort built in the 1870s and converted decades later into a sanatorium for tuberculosis patients. Also here is **Hermit's Peak,** a hill where a local legend—Agostini Justiniani, an Italian nobleman—lived in solitude during the 19th century. Agostini was rumored to have miraculous healing powers and treated sick people with his abundance of herbs. He was found murdered at the site in 1869. Trails lead from the area to the Organ Mountains. This site is for day use only. ⊠ *Dripping Springs Rd. (from Las Cruces head east on University Ave. 10 mi),* ☎ 505/522–1219. ⬚ $3 per vehicle. ☉ Daily 8 AM–dusk.

## Shopping

At the **outdoor market** on North Main Street, approximately 200 vendors sell produce, handcrafted items, and baked goods on Wednesday and Saturday between 8:30 AM and 12:30 PM. The upscale **Glenn Cutter Gallery** (⊠ 2640 El Paseo Rd., ☎ 505/524–4300) has regional and historic scenes from artists such as Fred Chilton, and fine jewelry as well. The small gallery (closed on Monday), run by **Mesilla Valley Fine Arts, Inc.** (⊠ Mesilla Valley Mall, 700 N. Telshor Blvd., ☎ 505/522–2933), exhibits the works of regional artists and photographers and carries note cards, bookmarks, and limited-edition prints.

# Radium Springs

❹ *13 mi north of Las Cruces on I–25.*

Fort Selden was established in 1865 to protect Mesilla Valley settlers and travelers. The flat-roof adobe brick buildings at **Fort Selden State Monument** are arranged around a drill field. Several units of Buffalo Soldiers, the acclaimed African-American cavalry troops, were stationed here. Indians thought the soldiers' hair resembled that of a buffalo and gave the regiments their name. Knowing the respect the Apaches held for the animal, the soldiers interpreted the comparison as a show of admiration by their enemy and did not take offense. Buffalo Soldiers were also stationed at Fort Bayard, near Silver City, and Fort Stanton, in Lincoln County, to shield miners and travelers from Apache Indian attacks.

In the early 1880s, Capt. Arthur MacArthur was appointed post commander of Fort Selden. His young son spent several years on the post and grew up to become World War II hero General Douglas MacArthur. A permanent exhibit called "Fort Selden: An Adobe Post on the Rio Grande" depicts the roles of officers, enlisted men, and women on the American frontier during the Indian Wars. Camping facilities can be found at Leasburg State Park. ⊠ *Off I–25's Radium Springs exit 19, 13 mi north of Las Cruces,* ☎ *505/526–8911,* WEB *www. museumofnewmexico.org.* ☞ *$3.* ☉ *Wed.–Mon. 8:30–5.*

Originally built along the Rio Grande in 1908, Leasburg Dam retains irrigation water for Mesilla Valley farmland with the bonus of creating a popular recreation known as **Leasburg State Park.** You're likely to see kayakers and anglers enjoying the pooled water. Simmering hot days attract swimmers in droves as they bob in waist-deep currents from cool water spilling over the dam. ⊠ *Hwy. 157 west of I–25.* ☞ *Day use $4 per vehicle.* ☉ *Daily 7 AM–sunset.*

## Camping

🏕 **Leasburg State Park Campground.** A nicely developed camping area draws locals as well as out-of-state visitors. Reservations are essential during peak times (weekends, holidays, and summer). ⊠ *Hwy. 157 west of I–25,* ☎ *505/524–4068 reservations,* WEB *www.emnrd. state.nm.us/nmparks. Flush toilets, partial hook-ups (electric and water), dump station, drinking water, showers, fire grates, fire pits, grills, picnic tables, electricity, public telephone, ranger station, playground, swimming (river). 18 RV sites, 6 developed tent sites, 3 primitive sites.* ☞ *$8–$14. No credit cards.*

# Deming

*60 mi west of Las Cruces on I–10.*

In the 1800s Deming was considered so out of control that Arizona outlaws were sent here (with one-way stage tickets) as punishment. A stop on the Butterfield Stage Trail, Deming received an economic boost when the Atchison, Topeka & Santa Fe Railway met up with the Southern Pacific line here in 1881. Farming and small industry are now the main sources of income for the town's roughly 15,000 residents.

OFF THE BEATEN PATH

**PANCHO VILLA STATE PARK –** Early on the morning of March 9, 1916, Francisco "Pancho" Villa, a revolutionary from Mexico, crossed into New Mexico to attack the town of Columbus and nearby Camp Furlong, a U.S. military outpost. This was the first time since the War of 1812 that the United States had experienced an armed invasion. A general who later would be commander of Allied forces in World War I—General John Joseph "Black Jack" Pershing—led 10,000 troops into Mexico for a grueling but futile search for Villa that lasted almost a year. This park on the site of Camp Furlong has exhibits depicting the raid, along with a 20-minute documentary film. The park recently added a small replica of the "Jenny" airplane, associated with early 1900s barnstorming. Plans also were in the works for displaying a Dodge model antique car of the type found in the area during Pancho Villa's raid. ⊠ *Hwy. 11, 35 mi south of Deming,* ☎ *505/531–2711,* WEB *www.newmexico.org.* ☞ *$4 per vehicle.* ☉ *Visitor center daily 8–5.*

**SHAKESPEARE GHOST TOWN** – In the heart of a real working ranch 50 mi west of Deming, portions of this settlement have been preserved as they were in Shakespeare's heyday as a gold and silver mining town in the late 1800s. Founded in 1856, the ghost town has been designated a National Historic Site. You can see original structures such as homes, saloons, and stables on regularly scheduled tours; townspeople from nearby Lordsburg periodically mount historic re-enactments. You'll find no snack shops or other tourist amenities in Shakespeare, as owner Janaloo Hill (who grew up on the ranch) has vowed not to compromise the authenticity of this genuine piece of the Old West. ⊠ *2.5 mi southwest of Lordsburg, south of I–10 at exit 22, Box 253, Lordsburg, NM 88045,* ☎ *506/542–9034.* ⬜ *$3 ($4 special events).* ⊙ *Tours: Mar.– Dec., one weekend each month at 10 and 2, or by special appointment; call ahead.*

### Dining and Lodging

$–$$  ✕ **Si Señor Restaurant.** Tasty, spicy Mexican food in various combinations is served at Si Señor. Also on the menu are steaks and other standard American fare. This family-owned restaurant isn't fancy, but the food's good and the prices are reasonable. ⊠ *200 E. Pine St.,* ☎ *505/546–3938. AE, D, MC, V.*

$  ▦ **Holiday Inn Deming.** Since rural communities tend to have sparse lodging options, this motel is a standout as the most luxurious in at least a 60-mi radius. It's also very accessible from the interstate (I–10). The spacious rooms have southwestern and contemporary accents. Room amenities include irons and ironing boards. ⊠ *Off I–10's Exit 85 east, 88031,* ☎ *505/546–2661. 116 rooms. Restaurant, refrigerators, cable TV, pool, gym, bar, dry cleaning, laundry facilities, some pets allowed. AE, D, DC, MC, V.*

### Camping

⚠ **Pancho Villa State Park Campground.** This campground on the Mexican border is a comfortable place to stop for the night. You may think you are in the middle of nowhere, but there is a general store and a service station next door. ⊠ *Hwy. 11, 35 mi south of Deming,* ☎ *505/ 531–2711,* ⬛ *www.newmexico.org. Flush toilets, partial hook-ups (electric and water), dump station, drinking water, showers, fire grates, fire pits, grills, picnic tables, electricity, public telephone, ranger station, playground. 61 RV sites, 5 primitive sites.* ⬜ *$10 RV sites (plus $4 for electrical hook-up), tent sites $8.*

# GILA NATIONAL FOREST

Cliff dwellings, ghost towns, and sprawling ranches interspersed among miles of unspoiled forests are the legacy of the hearty individualists who have inhabited this remote area over the centuries. The desert and alpine terrain is gouged with deeply carved canyons, and the jagged scenery ranges from tall timber to sparser juniper forests. The early cliff dwellers mysteriously disappeared sometime after the year 1000, leaving behind the ruins and relics of a culture replaced half a millennium later by Spanish explorers, roving bands of Apaches, and occasional trappers. In the 1800s Apache leaders including Cochise, Geronimo, and Victorio waged war against the encroaching Mexican and American settlers. For a time, the sheer ruggedness of the mountains provided refuge for the Apaches. The area changed forever, though, when in the late 1800s the mineral-laden mountains lured crazed but stalwart prospectors determined to make their fortunes in gold, silver, and copper. Scenic drives lead to several ghost towns, including the old gold-mining settlement of Mogollon.

# Silver City

**➎** *53 mi northwest of Deming; 115 mi northwest of Las Cruces, west on I–10 and northwest on U.S. 180.*

Silver City sprouted as a tough and lawless mining camp in 1870, struggling to become a more respectable—and permanent—settlement. Henry McCarty spent part of his boyhood here, perhaps learning some of the ruthlessness that led to his later infamy under his nickname—Billy the Kid. Other mining towns in the area sparked briefly and then died, but Silver City flourished and became the area's most populated city (now with 12,000 residents). Even today the Silver City area remains aloof and beautiful, which is part of its charm. Its privacy is buffered by the Gila National Forest and vast Gila Wilderness.

Thanks to efforts of preservationists, Silver City's origins are evident in the many distinctive houses and storefronts that have been salvaged. A stroll through the historic downtown district, a haven for artists, will take you by many of the town's three dozen or so art galleries. With the area's copper ore fast being depleted, the town's traditional ties to mining are being upstaged with newcomers. New agers drive around in retro Volkswagen vans alongside sports utility vehicles owned by the newly retired or outdoor enthusiasts.

In the historic district, the **Murray Ryan Visitor's Center** (✉ 201 N. Hudson St., ☎ 800/548–9378; 800/290–8330 Old West information line) also houses the Silver City Grant County Chamber of Commerce. If you're traveling north on Hwy. 90, the highway turns into Hudson Street. If you're traveling on U.S. 180, it turns into Silver Heights Boulevard within the city limits and intersects Hudson Street.

The Ailman House, built in 1881, serves as headquarters for the **Silver City Museum,** whose backlit painting of the mining and ranching community circa 1882 provides a good overview of the area's colorful history. Displays include pottery and other relics from the area's Mimbres and Mogollon Native American cultures. From the museum's upper level you can catch a glimpse of Silver City's three historic districts. Self-guided walking tours with maps are sold in the museum's store, which carries southwestern gifts and books. Free guided walking tours of the neighboring historic district are offered on Memorial Day and Labor Day. The museum also features a local-history research library. ✉ *312 W. Broadway,* ☎ *505/538–5921.* 🎟 *Free.* ☉ *Tues.–Fri. 9–4:30, weekends 10–4.*

The **Western New Mexico University Museum** contains the world's largest permanent collection of Mimbres pottery, basketry, and other artifacts. Delicate artistry on pottery includes finely drawn black-and-white geometric designs along with animal symbols representing an ancient Native American civilization that once dominated the area. Mimbres designs have influenced modern artisans throughout the world. Exhibits also include the famous, intricately decorated Casas Grandes pottery from northern Mexico. The museum's fourth floor displays photos and other memorabilia of the university, which is more than a century old. From this lofty height, you also can see a 360-degree view of Silver City. Quite unusual are the antique urinals in the men's rest room. ✉ *1000 W. College Ave. (on campus, west end of 10th St.),* ☎ *505/538–6386.* 🎟 *Free.* ☉ *Weekdays 9–4:30, weekends 10–4.*

OFF THE BEATEN PATH

**CITY OF ROCKS STATE PARK –** About 30 mi southeast of Silver City is this aptly named park with wondrous temples and towers of stone, spewed forth from an ancient volcano. Abrasive action of winds and sand then sculpted the monoliths. To appreciate these natural marvels in the 680-

acre park you'll need to don a pair of good walking shoes and penetrate the interior. You can't help but imagine yourself in a bizarre city as you peer down "streets" and "alleyways" lined with all shapes and sizes of solid-rock structures. The park has a large developed campground ($10–$14) with some RV hook-ups, flush toilets, and showers. ⊠ *Off U.S. 180, Faywood,* ☎ *505/536–2800.* ☞ *$4 per vehicle.*

## Dining and Lodging

**$–$$$** ✕ **Diane's Restaurant.** Fresh flowers grace wooden tables brightly lit
★ by wholesome New Mexico sunshine that beams through the windows of this quaint eatery. Chef-owner Diane Barrett serves gourmet items including rack of lamb or blackened pork loin with apple bourbon demiglace and potatoes. Imported beer and specialty wines also are available in casual surroundings. Diane still offers fabulous sandwiches on bread she bakes. All her baked goods are light and exceptionally tasty, but her cinnamon rolls are knockouts. ⊠ *510 N. Bullard St.,* ☎ *505/538–8722. AE, D, MC, V. Closed Mon.*

**$–$$$** ✕ **Vicki's Eatery.** Vegetarian dishes along with specialty items such as seafood ravioli marinara represent plenty of options for those interested in health as well as great taste. An outdoor patio is open in summer. ⊠ *107 W. Yankie St.,* ☎ *505/388–5430. AE, MC, V.*

**$–$$** ✕ **Jalisco's.** George and Cecilia Mesa, along with son Michael Mesa,
★ own this family restaurant noted for such Mexican dishes as enchiladas and chiles rellenos based on old family recipes. Imports from nearby Palomas, Mexico, help brighten the restaurant, which exhibits colorful paintings of Mexican marketplaces by local artist Mark Wilson. ⊠ *103 S. Bullard St.,* ☎ *505/388–2060. MC, V. Closed Sun.*

**$** ✕ **A.I.R. Espresso, Art, Ice Cream.** A.I.R. stands for Artist-In-Residence, which is exactly what owner Jacqueline Shaw is. While painting her own masterpieces, she operates this ice cream and coffee shop, where her peers often gather for long chats. Relax on a plump sofa or enjoy the mountain breeze while lounging on the rear patio. Shaw specializes in mochas and cappuccinos, along with hot chocolate, truffles, and toffee. Waffle cones, gourmet ice cream, and frozen yogurt are also served along with a few pastries. In early 2002, new partner Sharifa Renfro joined the business. She jokingly calls herself the resident coffee roaster. ⊠ *112 W. Yankie St.,* ☎ *505/388–5952. D, MC, V.*

**$** ✕ **Gregorio's Kountry Kitchen.** Though small and informal, this diner serves huge helpings of southwestern food. If you're just plain hungry and not choosy about atmosphere, drop in. The restaurant is attached to the Maxwell House building, which contains a clothing and jewelry store. ⊠ *1500 N. Hudson St.,* ☎ *505/388–4512. MC, V. Closed Sun.*

**$$–$$$$** ⊟ **The Cottages.** Virgin forests, a friendly wild fox, and a lost silver
★ mine add to the romantic allure of this modern inn with detached country French–style cottages and B&B-style rooms. Water from hot mineral springs is piped directly into the private baths. For extra warmth, you can light up your own fireplace. Owners Robert "Mike" and Colleen Michael operate this 80-acre estate, which has access to miles of pristine trails (you're invited to wander them in search of the silver mine). The detached cottages are stylishly furnished and supplied with cooking utensils and staples like eggs, milk, and fresh fruit, along with snacks and frozen items for lunch or dinner. Upon arrival, you're likely to be greeted with an evening treat such as Colleen's homemade peach pie. ⊠ *2037 Cottage San Rd. (Box 2562, 88062),* ☎ *505/388–3000 or 800/938–3001,* WEB *www.zianet.com/cottages. 2 suites, 3 cottages. In-room data ports, in-room hot tubs, some kitchens, some kitchenettes, microwaves, refrigerators, in-room VCRs, hiking; no pets, no kids (some exceptions), no smoking. AE, D, MC, V.*

**$$$** ⊞ **Bear Mountain Lodge.** Owned and operated by the Nature Conservancy, this serene, isolated haven offers luxury accommodations for bird-watchers and nature lovers. You have immediate access to 178 acres of Gila National Forest land, where you can spot bird species such as the Gila woodpecker, vermilion flycatcher, and red-faced warbler. The tidy, mission-style lodge has a naturalist available to answer questions and conduct regular activities for guests. Ordinarily, you must book for a minimum two-night stay. ⊠ *Cottage San Rd., 3 mi off Alabama St. (3 mi north of Silver City, take U.S. 180 west and turn north onto Alabama), 88062,* ☎ *505/538–2538,* WEB *www.bearmountainlodge. com. 11 rooms. In-room data ports, hiking, Internet; no room TVs. AE, MC, V. BP.*

**$$** ⊞ **Holiday Inn Express.** Just 2 mi from Silver City's historic downtown district, this inn provides bright, contemporary decor in a modern atmosphere (this is one of the area's newest motels). ⊠ *1103 Superior St., 88061,* ☎ *505/538–2525. 63 rooms. In-room data ports, refrigerators, cable TV, gym, hot tub, meeting rooms, pets allowed (some); no-smoking rooms. AE, D, DC, MC, V. CP.*

**$** ⊞ **Comfort Inn.** This modern motel contains southwestern-style rooms with good views of Silver City. ⊠ *1060 E. Hwy. 180, 88061,* ☎ *505/534–1883; 800/228–5150 central reservations;* FAX *505/534–0778. 52 rooms, 2 suites. Cable TV, indoor pool, some in-room hot tub, laundry facilities, meeting rooms, some pets allowed. AE, D, DC, MC, V. CP.*

**$** ⊞ **Econo Lodge Silver City.** This lodge on a mesa overlooking Silver City has economy accommodations and contemporary decor. ⊠ *1120 Hwy. 180 E, 88061,* ☎ *505/534–1111; 800/553–2666 central reservations;* FAX *505/534–2222;* WEB *www.econolodgesilvercity.com. 62 rooms. In-room data ports, microwaves, refrigerators, pool, gym, hot tub, laundry facilities, meeting rooms, some pets allowed. AE, D, DC, MC, V. CP.*

**$** ⊞ **Palace Hotel.** Owners Nancy and Cal Thompson have replicated the intimacy of a small European hotel at the Palace, a grand structure that was a first-class lodging when it opened in 1900. It saw less fabulous times as an apartment building before the Thompsons took over and renovated it in the late 1980s. Some rooms have western furnishings, others a distinctly Victorian decor. The upstairs garden room provides solitude for playing games or reading. ⊠ *106 W. Broadway, 88061,* ☎ *505/388–1811,* WEB *www.zianet.com/palacehotel. 11 rooms, 7 suites. Cable TV; no pets. AE, D, DC, MC, V. CP.*

**$** ⊞ **Super 8.** A forest of piñon and juniper trees surrounds this two-story motel. Most of the rooms have double beds; five business minisuites have extra amenities. ⊠ *1040 E. U.S. 180, 88061,* ☎ *505/388–1983; 800/800–8000 central reservations;* FAX *505/388–1983. 64 rooms. Some in-room data ports, some refrigerators, cable TV, some pets allowed (fee). AE, D, DC, MC, V. CP*

## Shopping

**Hester House Candy & Gifts** (⊠ 316 N. Bullard St., ☎ 505/388–1360) sells highly edible homemade fudge, chocolates, and truffles, along with porcelain dolls, Tiffany-style lamps, wind chimes, jewelry, bath products, and garden art. The shop is open daily except Sunday. A family-owned clothing and jewelry store, the **Maxwell House** (⊠ 1500 N. Hudson St., ☎ 505/388–1573) offers a unique selection of hand-picked designs at economical prices.

Cool off with an ice cream cone and visions of Santa as you inspect Christmas ornaments or sample other treats at **Pretty Sweet Emporium** (⊠ 312 N. Bullard St., ☎ 505/388–8600). At **O'Keefe Bookshop** (⊠ 102 W. Broadway, ☎ 505/388–3313), mostly used books represent a whopping selection of Southwest folklore and history topics. Vendors at the **Silver City Trading Co.'s Antique Mall** (⊠ 205 W. Broadway, ☎ 505/388–8989) stock antiques, collectibles, and Navajo katsina dolls; works of area artists also are displayed. It's also the only place in the area where you can buy the Sunday *New York Times*. A local cooperative representing 36 artists runs **Yankie Creek Gallery** (⊠ 300 N. Bullard St., ☎ 505/538–5232 or 505/388–4775), where gourd art and stained-glass items can be found in addition to paintings.

## Gila National Forest

❻  *8 mi northeast of Silver City via Hwy. 15 to Pinos Altos range and Gila Cliff Dwellings portion of Gila National Forest; 60 mi northwest of Silver City via U.S. 180 to western portions of forest. From I–25 eastern edge of forest can be accessed via Hwy. 152: 62 mi north of Las Cruces take Hwy. 152 west toward Hillsboro; 91 mi north of Las Cruces take Hwy. 52 west through Winston and Chloride.*

The Gila National Forest covers 3.3 million acres—about 65 mi by 100 mi—and includes the nation's first land designated (in 1924) as wilderness by the U.S. Forest Service. About 1,500 mi of hiking trails lace the forest. Open camping is permitted, and there are 18 developed campgrounds (7 have toilets and potable water). The forest roads are ideal for mountain biking, but the trails are often too rough for bicycles. White-water rafting usually begins in April, and you can fish (there are trout aplenty) in streams, rivers, and three lakes. About a quarter of the forest is designated wilderness and closed to vehicular traffic, but much of the rest remains open for touring.

The gorgeous **Inner Loop Scenic Drive** circles 75 mi around part of the forest. Though the roads are paved, some turns are sharp, narrow, and steep—it's best not to take large RVs on this route. Starting from Silver City, take Hwy. 15 north to Gila Cliff Dwellings National Monument. From the monument backtrack on Hwy. 15 to Hwy. 35 heading southeast to Hwy. 152, which leads west back to Silver City.

About 700 years ago the Mogollon Indians built the 42 rooms of stone and mud that compose the **Gila Cliff Dwellings National Monument.** The visitor center has a small museum and books and other materials about the wilderness and the Mogollon Indians. A 1-mi loop trail that's steep in parts (wear sturdy footwear) leads to the dwellings; along the wheelchair-accessible Trail to the Past you can view pictographs. ⊠ *Off Hwy. 15, 44 mi north of Silver City,* ☎ *505/536–9461 or 505/536–9344.* ➣ *$3.* ☉ *Monument Memorial Day–Labor Day, daily 8–6; Labor Day–Memorial Day, daily 9–4. Visitor center Memorial Day–Labor Day, daily 8–5; Labor Day–Memorial Day, daily 8–4:30.*

U.S. 180 leads west about 50 mi from Silver City to Glenwood and
★  the Whitewater Canyon. The **Catwalk** (⊠ Catwalk Rd. [Hwy. 174]; turn east 5 mi off U.S. 180), a 250-ft-long metal walkway drilled into the sides of massive rock cliffs, was built originally in 1935 as an access route to the canyon to establish water lines extending 3 mi into Whitewater Canyon. It's so remote here that famous outlaws including Butch Cassidy, the Wild Bunch, and others all have used this massive canyon for hideouts. You need to be in reasonably good physical condition to scramble up some steep stairways, but the 2.2-mi round-trip trail is well maintained and worth the exertion for a breathtaking view of mountain stream water cascading over huge boulders. Admission is $3.

Several miles north of the Catwalk on U.S. 180 is the **Glenwood State Trout Hatchery** (⊠ U.S. 180, ☎ 505/539–2461), where there are picnic tables and a fishing pond. Rocky Mountain bighorn sheep graze nearby. East of the Glenwood State Trout Hatchery on Hwy. 159 is **Mogollon.** The gold-mining town, established in the 1880s, was a ghost town but has been revived by a dozen or so residents who open art galleries and conduct tours during the summer.

As you drop down into **Pinos Altos** 7 mi north of Silver City on Hwy. 15, check out the **Log Cabin Museum** (⊠ 33 Main St., off Hwy. 15, ☎ 505/388–1882), where you'll find a structure originally built in 1865 by George Shafer. The property still remains in the family. Dusty artifacts tell the story of more than a century of occupation. You'll find another diverse gallery along this tiny town's Main Street at **Silver Winds Gallery** (⊠ 29 Main St., ☎ 505/388–5202), featuring Native American and southwestern art.

On the eastern edge of the Gila National Forest, Hwy. 52 leads west from I–25 to **Winston** and **Chloride,** two fascinating mining towns about 35 mi northwest of Truth or Consequences. Prospectors searching for silver in the nearby ore-rich mountains founded the towns in the late 1800s; abandoned saloons and pioneer relics remain from the mining days. Though the communities are designated ghost towns, the 50 or so residents of each place dispute the moniker. ⊠ *Gila National Forest Headquarters, 3005 E. Camino del Bosque, Silver City,* ☎ *505/388–8201.*

## Dining and Lodging

**$$–$$$$**  ✕ **Buckhorn Saloon and Opera House.** Mosey up to the wooden bar
★  at this genuine 1800s saloon and slug down a taste of the Old West. Dance-hall girl "Debbie deCamp"—a life-size doll—strikes a sultry pose on a balcony overlooking the saloon. After visiting the bar (which opens at 3 PM), order up a steak or other entrée in the adjoining dining room and from Wednesday to Saturday listen to folk singers croon their mellow tunes. Food served here is all homemade, fresh and without preservatives. The kitchen excels at homemade salad dressings and desserts. Reservations are recommended. This complex also includes the Opera House, where melodramas are performed (on Friday and Saturday at 8), and Pinos Altos Mercantile, a business founded in the 1860s that's now an ice cream parlor and soda shop. ⊠ *32 Main St., Pinos Altos, 7 mi north of Silver City on Hwy. 15,* ☎ *505/538–9911; 505/388–3848 opera house. MC, V. Closed Sun. No lunch.*

**$–$$**  ✕ **Carmen's.** If you're driving on Hwy. 12 just northwest of the Gila National Forest through Reserve, New Mexico (population about 300), you don't want to zip past this tidy little restaurant with cheery purple curtains. You'll enjoy the spicy enchiladas. (Owners Johnny and Carmen De La O are known for their authentic Mexican recipes.) Eat now, because once you leave Reserve headed northeast, travel is slow and there are no other towns for about 70 mi. ⊠ *Hwy. 12 at Hwy. 435,* ☎ *505/533–6990. MC, V.*

**$**  ✕ **The Chuck Wagon Cafe.** Originally built in the early 1900s, the barn-like building that houses a comfy diner-style eatery has been everything from a church to a skating rink to a wrestling arena. The restaurant (which is said to have its own friendly ghost) is now owned by locals Jody Wilson Kipp and Ruth Pelletier Perry. Wooden floors and cattle brands on the wall make this a down-home country place, offering tasty chicken-fried steak as a popular option. ⊠ *30 mi northwest of Silver City on U.S. 180,* ☎ *505/535–4100. No credit cards.*

**$$$–$$$$**  🛏 **Casitas de Gila.** Private casitas with artful themes such as "Little
★  House of the Sun and Moon" nestle alongside the vast New Mexico Gila Wilderness. The sky, absent artificial light, is the darkest of dark except for billions of twinkling stars and the bright splash of the Milky

Way from horizon to horizon. You can savor the profound solitude and quiet amid comfortable elegance enhanced by antiques, kiva fireplaces, and handcrafted Mexican furnishings. Kitchens are stocked with supplies. The nearby Double E Guest Ranch offers horseback riding, hiking trails allow exploration of about 70 acres, and telescopes and spotting scopes magnify sky viewing. You can even pan for gold in the nearby creek. ⊠ *310 Hooker Loop (Box 325, Gila 88038),* ☎ *505/535–4455,* ℻ *505/535–4456,* WEB *www.casitasdegila.com. 5 casitas. Picnic area, kitchens, microwaves, refrigerators, outdoor hot tub, hiking; no room TVs. AE, D, DC, MC, V.*

**$$–$$$**    ⚄ **Bear Creek Motel & Cabins.** Gold panning, hiking, and fishing are among the activities that take place at this mountain getaway, one of the better accommodations in the Silver City area. A ponderosa pine forest surrounds the well-kept A-frame cabins, half of which have kitchens, cookware, and fireplaces. ⊠ *Hwy. 15 (Box 53082, Pinos Altos 88053), 6 mi north of Silver City,* ☎ *505/388–4501,* ℻ *505/538–5583,* WEB *www.BearCreekCabins.com. 15 cabins. In-room data ports, some kitchenettes, some refrigerators, hiking, some pets allowed (fee). AE, D, DC, MC, V.*

**$–$$$**    ⚄ **Los Olmos Guest Ranch.** Tall trees shade this San Francisco Valley ranch, whose stone cabins sleep from two to six people. The cabins are furnished with contemporary pieces, and though there are minimal amenities (no phones or TVs), you can count on maximum seclusion. Guests sign up from Wednesday to Sunday for optional gourmet dinners—chicken, lamb, pastas, trout, steaks, and vegetarian entrées. The ranch is near the Glenwood State Trout Hatchery and within hiking distance of Whitewater Canyon and the Catwalk. ⊠ *U.S. 180 and Catwalk Rd., Glenwood 88039,* ☎ *505/539–2311,* ℻ *505/539–2312,* WEB *www.gilanet.com/losolmos. 14 cabins. Dining room, pool, hot tub, billiards, hiking, horseback riding, horseshoes, volleyball, playground, some pets allowed. AE, D, MC, V. BP.*

## Lake Valley National Back Country Byway

★    *From Silver City: head east on U.S. 180/Hwy. 152 to junction with Hwy. 27. From Hatch: head west on Hwy. 26 and north on Hwy. 27.*

The 48-mi Lake Valley National Back Country Byway provides an exciting link to the Wild West. This remote drive (there are no gas stations)—Hwy. 27 between Nutt and Hillsboro (31 mi) and Hwy. 152 east from Hillsboro to Truth or Consequences (17 mi)—follows part of the route taken by the Kingston Lake Valley Stage Line, which operated in a region terrorized by Apache leaders like Geronimo and outlaw bands led by Butch Cassidy and other notorious figures. A Lake Valley–area landmark, west of Hwy. 27, is Cooke's Peak, where the first wagon road through the Southwest to California was opened in 1846.

Not much is going on these days in the old silver mining town of **Lake Valley**—the last residents departed in the mid-1990s—but it once was home to 4,000 people. Its mine produced 2.5 million ounces of pure silver and gave up one nugget weighing several hundred pounds. You can visit the schoolhouse (which later served as a saloon) and walk around the chapel, the railroad depot, and some old homes. At the junction of Hwy. 152 and Hwy. 27 is another mining-era boomtown, **Hillsboro,** where gold was discovered as well as silver (about $6 million worth of the two ores was extracted). The town has a small museum and some shops, restaurants, and galleries.

**Caballo Lake State Park** provides a nesting ground for golden and bald eagles, often sighted as they glide aloft searching for prey. Activities at the lake include fishing and various water sports. Hiking trails lead through desert areas. Late March or early April, when prickly pears and other succulents bloom, is a good time to visit. ⊠ *Take state park exit off I–25, about 58 mi north of Las Cruces and 16 mi south of Truth or Consequences,* ☎ *505/743–3942,* 𝖥𝖠𝖷 *505/743–0031.* ⊛ *$4 per vehicle.* ☉ *Visitor center 7:30–4:30 (later in summer).*

### Lodging

**$–$$**  ☷ **Black Range Lodge Bed & Breakfast.** Built from the ruins of an old casino and saloon that date from the 1880s, this getaway has sturdy log beam ceilings and rock walls. Don't expect the ruffles and flourishes of your typical B&B. The payoff is an informal, rustic atmosphere, indoors and out, which particularly appeals to families. The outdoor experience is enhanced by a hot tub and nearby freshwater creek with a hiking trail. A two-bedroom guest house has full kitchens in each section, along with a deck, satellite TV, indoor hot tub, and spectacular views. ⊠ *119 Main St./Hwy. 152 (Star Rte. 2, Box 119, Kingston 88042),* ☎ *505/895–5652,* 𝖥𝖠𝖷 *505/895–3326,* 𝖶𝖤𝖡 *www.zianet.com/ blackrange/lodge. 7 rooms, 3 suites, 1 guest house. Some in-room hot tubs, some kitchens, some microwaves, some refrigerators, cable TV, outdoor hot tub, billiards, hiking, video game room, Internet, meeting rooms, some pets allowed (fee); no smoking. D, MC, V. BP.*

### Camping

⚠ **Caballo Lake State Park.** Three camping areas offer views of the lake, which is within walking distance of each site. Cottonwoods and other trees shade two sites; the other has desert landscaping. The tent sites ($8) are lakeside. You can stock up on goods at a grocery store, bait shop, and gasoline station 3 mi from the park. Developed sites for RVs cost $10–$14 (some have sewer). ⊠ *Take state park exit off I– 25, about 58 mi north of Las Cruces and 16 mi south of Truth or Consequences,* ☎ *505/743–3942,* 𝖥𝖠𝖷 *505/743–0031. 136 sites. Flush toilets, full hook-ups, partial hook-ups, dump station, drinking water, showers, fire grates, fire pits, grills, picnic tables, electricity, public telephone, ranger station, playground, lake.* ⊛ *RV sites $10–$14, tent sites $8. No credit cards.*

# ALONG THE CAMINO REAL

Four centuries ago, caravans of Spanish colonists and traders made the desolate 1,200-mi journey from Mexico City to Santa Fe via El Camino Real. As they came up from what is now El Paso and were nearing the Las Cruces area, they veered away from the Rio Grande to avoid its treacherous passages. The hostile, arid terrain they traversed is visible east off I–25, which traces this part of El Camino Real. Hazards such as frequent attacks from hostile Native Americans led to a chilling nickname for this stretch of road—Jornada del Muerto, or Journey of Death. Portions of the well-worn path still can be spotted from the air and ground, but there is no formal designation or access to the route from the highway. Interstate 10 heads west at Las Cruces, at which point I–25 continues north more or less parallel to El Camino Real. East of I–25, Elephant Butte Lake now covers part of the Jornada del Muerto route, and visible tracks are inaccessible on private land. Funding has been made available to establish a $7.3 million El Camino Real International Heritage Center off I–25, just south of Exit 115 between Socorro and Truth or Consequences. The center and interpretive exhibits were scheduled for completion in late 2002.

# Truth or Consequences

❼ *72 mi north of Las Cruces on I–25, 140 mi south of Albuquerque on I–25.*

Truth or Consequences really did get its name from the game show of the same name. The show's producer, Ralph Edwards, suggested that a town adopt the name to honor the production's 10th anniversary, in 1950. The community that had been known as Hot Springs accepted the challenge, earning national publicity for the stunt. A portion of the community rebelled, though, withdrawing from T or C (as the town is sometimes called) and incorporating as Williamsburg. T or C's name remains a sore spot in some circles.

The area's earliest Native American inhabitants believed the natural hot springs found here had magical healing properties long before modern settlements were built or names were changed. Bathhouses tapping into the soothing mineral waters were established near the downtown district in the 1930s. About a half dozen of those still operate at bargain prices (as low as $4 for a half hour). The facilities are clean but modest. Healers at the springs practice natural methods such as massage, Reiki, reflexology, and Ayurvedic science. In late 2001, the classy Sierra Grande Lodge & Spa (owned by New York City's Raoul's) opened in a remodeled historic downtown hot springs building.

**Hay-Yo-Kay Hot Springs** has seven naturally flowing pools, including the newest opened from an adjoining (old Yucca) bathhouse in 2002. At 10 ft by 20 ft, the pool is the largest in the hot-springs district. The standard price for the hot baths is $4.25 per person for a half-hour soak. Massage, Reiki, and reflexology therapists are on call for varying fees. Package prices are available, such as $35 for a 30-minute soak and a 30-minute massage. Owner Steve Kortemeier also has made available on the property a two-bedroom condominium, with kitchen, refrigerator, microwave, cable TV, in-room VCR, and a barbecue (standard rate of $95 nightly). ✉ *300 Austin Ave.,* ☎ *505/894–2228. AE, D, DC, MC, V.*

At the well-maintained **Geronimo Springs Museum** you can visit an authentic miner's log cabin that was transported from the nearby Gila National Forest or view the giant skull of a mammoth. Pottery on display includes examples of Mimbres, Tularosa, Alma, and Hohokam. The farm and ranch section has tools used by early settlers. ✉ *211 Main St.,* ☎ *505/894–6600.* 🎟 *$2.* ⊙ *Mon.–Sat. 9–5.*

## Dining and Lodging

$$–$$$$  ✕ **Los Arcos Restaurant and Bar.** Steaks and seafood are the draws at this slump block adobe-style establishment with a southwestern decor, complete with cactus garden. Homemade soups, desserts, and freshly baked bread add to the aromas and the ambience. ✉ *1400 N. Date St.,* ☎ *505/894–6200. AE, D, MC, V. No lunch.*

$–$$  ✕ **Town Talk Cafe.** Locals really do drop into this diner-style eatery in the heart of Truth or Consequences to catch up on the latest gossip. The breakfasts and other fare are standard but generous. ✉ *426 Broadway,* ☎ *505/894–3119. No credit cards.*

$$–$$$  ✕🏠 **Sierra Grande Lodge & Spa.** Far and away the classiest dining and
★  lodging option in Truth or Consequences, the area's newest inn (opened August 1, 2001) is affiliated with New York City's Raoul's restaurant. Remodeled from a two-story hot springs lodge originally built in 1937, the structure has Southwest flourishes giving it a pueblo appearance. Rooms have hardwood floors and cowboy themes. You can soak in an outdoor, kiva-style hot tub swirling with steamy water from natural, underground hot springs. Check out the backlit, colorful stained-

glass Elephant Butte mural (created in 1917) displayed in the restaurant. Chef Raum Fama has impressive credits, including a former association with the five-star Phoenician resort in Scottsdale, Arizona. With special arrangements, you can watch him at work in the "show kitchen" while you are seated at the chef's table. Dine on warm New Mexico goat cheese, lamb shank, or grilled filet mignon in red wine sauce. Restaurant reservations are advised on weekends. ⊠ *501 McAdoo St., 87901,* ☏ *505/894–6976,* FAX *505/894–6999,* WEB *www.sierragrandelodge.com. 16 rooms, 1 suite. Restaurant, some in-room hot tubs, cable TV, in-room VCRs, outdoor hot tub; no smoking. AE, D, MC, V. CP*

$ ⊡ **Best Western Hot Springs Inn.** Large rooms and modern furnishings make this lodge a restful haven. The oversize pool comes in handy on hot summer days. A steak house is next door. This establishment enthusiastically provides all manner of complimentary amenities, from shaving cream to sewing kits. ⊠ *2270 N. Date St., 87901, off I–25's Exit 79,* ☏ *505/894–6665. 40 rooms, 1 suite. In-room data ports, kitchens, microwaves, refrigerators, cable TV, pool, some pets allowed. AE, D, DC, MC, V.*

$ ⊡ **Charles Motel & Bath House.** This laid-back facility attracts healers and artists who explore spiritual and physical health through sometimes unorthodox methods. The therapies practiced here include massage, reflexology, Reiki, and Ayurvedic science. Costs depend on the treatment and its length, but $5 should buy you a good long soak in one of the nine indoor soaking tubs that take advantage of natural hot springs. In recent years, the motel added two new outdoor Jacuzzis atop the roof where $8 will buy you an hour-long soak. The single-story motel and its rooms are well maintained, if dated looking. The downtown Truth or Consequences location is convenient to small restaurants and shops. ⊠ *601 Broadway, 87901,* ☏ *505/894–7154. 20 rooms. Some kitchenettes, some microwaves, some refrigerators, cable TV, outdoor hot tub, spa, gift shop, meeting room, some pets allowed (fee). AE, D, MC, V.*

## Shopping

Paintings, sculptures, baskets, and postcards can be found at the **Main Street Gallery** (⊠ 306 Main St., ☏ 505/894–0615), an artists' cooperative open Wednesday–Saturday 1–5.

# Elephant Butte

❽ *5 mi east of Truth or Consequences on Hwy. 51.*

★ More than a million people each year visit **Elephant Butte Lake State Park,** whose 36,500-acre lake is New Mexico's largest. Bass, catfish, pike, and crappie fishing takes place year-round; trout are stocked in the Rio Grande below the dam in colder months. Elephant Butte is a world-class competition lake for bass fishing. Boaters come here in droves, and when the wind picks up so do the windsurfers. Special events include an April balloon festival and July drag-boat racing. The lake, which is also known as Elephant Butte Reservoir, was created by **Elephant Butte Dam,** a concrete structure 306 ft high and 1,674 ft long that was completed in 1916. The dam holds back water from the Rio Grande for irrigation purposes. The lake and Rio Grande below the dam attract many species of waterfowl, along with raptors and songbirds.

The state park straddles Elephant Butte Lake and the Rio Grande east of I–25 for about 50 mi (from south of Fort Craig to just north of Truth or Consequences). To take a **scenic drive** from Truth or Consequences, head east on Hwy. 51, turn north at Hwy. 179 for about 2 mi, head southeast on Hwy. 195, and take a loop drive of about 5 mi to Elephant Butte Dam. At the end of the dam turn north for overlooks of the lake water and a view of the rocky elephant-shape island formation that inspired the name of the reservoir (look for a head, with ears and a long trunk). To visit the **Dam Site Recreation Area** turn west on Hwy. 177, where you'll find a terraced picnic area with striking views and tall trees providing shade. A private concessionaire operates a restaurant, lounge, marina, and cabins. ⊠ *3 mi north of Truth or Consequences,* ☎ *505/744–5421,* WEB *www.emnrd.state.nm.us.* ⊡ *$4 per vehicle.*

## Dining and Lodging

**$–$$**   ✕ **Hodges Corner Restaurant.** Owners Ray and Linda Hodges believe in hearty food and lots of it—heapin' helpin's of thick barbecued pork ribs, cube steaks, and deep-fried fish. The atmosphere is ultracasual at this great stop for anglers who want to relax and chow down after a day of boating and fishing at Elephant Butte Lake. ⊠ *915 Hwy. 195, Elephant Butte,* ☎ *505/744–5626. D, MC, V.*

**$$**   ✕⊞ **Quality Inn.** Formerly known as the Inn at the Butte, this establishment sits atop a mesa offering serene views of Elephant Butte Lake. Rooms have either two queen-size beds or one king-size bed, and all have irons, hair dryers, and coffeemakers. Executive suites have a desk and speaker phone. The restaurant serves hamburgers and sandwiches. ⊠ *Hwy. 195 (Box E, Elephant Butte 87935),* ☎ *505/744–5431,* FAX *505/744–5044. 44 rooms, 4 suites. Restaurant, some microwaves, some refrigerators, cable TV, 2 tennis courts, pool, hiking, lounge, meeting rooms, some pets allowed (fee). AE, D, DC, MC, V. CP.*

**$–$$$**   ⊡ **Dam Site Resort.** Located in an official historic district, the Elephant Butte Dam site offers cabins with one to four bedrooms. All of the cabins have lake views, and some have kitchenettes (but no utensils). The combination bar-restaurant serves steaks, seafood, and sandwiches. On weekends between about Easter and Labor Day, dance bands play blues or rock on the outdoor patio, which also has a bar. A bed-and-breakfast opened in 2002 in a historic building that was administrative headquarters during the construction of the original dam. Decorated with everything from antiques from India to country-style furnishings, the rooms overlook the marina. ⊠ *77B Engle Star Rte., 87901, 5 mi east of the 3rd St. light in Truth or Consequences,* ☎ *505/894–2073,* FAX *505/894–0776. 16 cabins. Restaurant, some kitchenettes, lake, dock, windsurfing, boating, jet skiing, marina, waterskiing, fishing, lounge, playground, some pets allowed; no room phones, no room TVs. AE, D, DC, MC, V. CP.*

## Camping

⚠ **Dam Site Recreation Area.** At night, campfires flicker along the beaches of the many sandy coves of Elephant Butte Lake. The modern, primitive, and partially developed campsites are popular with anglers. ⊠ *3 mi north of Truth or Consequences,* ☎ *505/744–5421,* WEB *www.emnrd.state.nm.us. Flush toilets, pit toilets, partial hook-ups (electric and water), dump station, drinking water, showers, fire grates, fire pits, grills, picnic tables, restaurant, electricity, public telephone, ranger station, playground, swimming (lake). 127 developed sites, many primitive or partially developed tent sites.* ⊡ *$8–$14*

## Outdoor Activities and Sports

The **Dam Site Recreation Area Marina** (⊠ *77B Engle Star Rte., 5 mi east of the 3rd St. traffic light in Truth or Consequences,* ☎ *505/894–2041*) rents runabouts, ski boats, and pontoon boats. The vessels cost between $20 and $45 hourly ($110 and $220 daily). A $250 deposit is required for use of any boat.

*En Route*  As you head north on I–25 toward Socorro you can take a break at two attractions. At **Fort Craig National Historic Site,** signs describe the various buildings and solitary life at the outpost, where only a couple of masonry walls and numerous foundations remain. Historic markers are very informative, and a well-maintained gravel trail winds among the ruins. After the New Mexico Territory became part of the United States, the adobe Fort Craig was established to prevent raids by the Apache and Navajo peoples and to secure the trade routes within the region. The growth of Socorro and what is now Truth or Consequences can be traced to the protection the fort provided between 1854 and the mid-1880s, when it was decommissioned. Battles west of the Mississippi River during the American Civil War were relatively rare, but in 1862 the Confederate army crossed the Rio Grande and headed to Valverde, which is north of Fort Craig, with the goal of cutting off the fort from the Union military headquarters in Santa Fe. The Confederate forces first were sent into retreat but later won a few battles and made the Union forces withdraw. The Rebels later occupied Santa Fe for a few months. The roads to Fort Craig, which is about 40 mi south and east of Socorro, can become hard to pass during rainy weather. ⊠ *Off I–25's San Marcial exit 124 (follow signs from exit for about 10 mi),* ☎ *505/835–0412.* ▣ *Free.* ⊙ *Daily dawn–dusk.*

★ Snow geese, cranes, and eagles can be spotted from viewing platforms and directly through your car window at the popular **Bosque del Apache National Wildlife Refuge.** Besides serving as a rest stop for migrating birds, the Bosque del Apache also shelters mule deer, turkeys, quail, and other wildlife. Photo opportunities abound on the 15-mi auto loop tour; you can also hike through arid shrub land or bike through the refuge or take a van tour. In winter months, the refuge echoes with the haunting cries of whooping cranes flocking for the evening. Snow geese are so thick on lakes at times that shores are white with feathers washed ashore. ⊠ *1001 Hwy. 1, off I–25's San Marcial Exit 124 for northbound traffic and Exit 139 for southbound traffic, San Antonio,* ☎ *505/835–1828.* ▣ *$3 per vehicle.* ⊙ *Refuge daily dawn–dusk; visitor center weekdays 7:30–4, weekends 8:30–4:30.*

## Socorro

❾ *72 mi north of Truth or Consequences; 77 mi southwest of Albuquerque, south on I–25 and west on U.S. 60.*

The town of Socorro, population about 7,000, traces its roots back to the earliest Spanish expeditions into New Mexico, when explorer Juan de Oñate established (in 1598) a permanent settlement along the Rio Grande. Native Americans provided corn to the expedition, inspiring Oñate to give the community a name that means succor, or help. The first Spanish settlement was virtually erased during the Pueblo Revolt of 1680 and did not reestablish itself until 1816.

The business of Socorro is conducted in historic buildings that surround its square, which has a park with a gazebo and a plaque commemorating the arrival of Juan de Oñate. The town's claim to fame is the highly regarded New Mexico Institute of Mining and Technology (New Mexico Tech), founded in 1893. The institution's original specialties were chemistry and metallurgy, but along with scientific research now there are programs in medicine, engineering, and business.

More than 2,500 minerals and fossils are on display at the **New Mexico Bureau of Geology and Mineral Resources Mineral Museum,** among them samples from the area's ore-rich mining districts of Magdalena, Hansonburg, Santa Rita, and Tyrone. Many rocks here, from glittering pyrite to the deep-blue azurite, have exotic colors like those of trop-ical fish. Special tours can be arranged. ✉ *New Mexico Institute of Mining and Technology, 801 Leroy Pl. (from I–25's Exit 150, follow signs to institute)*, ☎ *505/835–5140.* ✆ *Free.* ☉ *Weekdays 8–5, week-ends 10–3. Sometimes closed weekends during academic holidays.*

Only a monument remains at **Trinity Site,** where the world's first atomic bomb exploded, on July 16, 1945. The resulting crater has been filled in, but the test site and monument are open for public viewing two days of the year. The McDonald ranch house, where the first plutonium core for the bomb was assembled, can be toured on those days. ✉ *5 mi south of U.S. 380. Turn east at the San Antonio exit off I–25, 10 mi south of Socorro. Drive 12 mi east on U.S. 380 and turn south onto a paved road, Hwy. 525, for 5 mi until the route dead-ends at Stallion Gate. Visitors (everyone must present photo identification) will be met at the gate off U.S. 380 and allowed to drive 17 mi east to the site,* ☎ *505/ 678–1134.* ✆ *Free.* ☉ *First Sat. of Apr. and Oct., gate opens 8–2.*

### Dining and Lodging

**$$–$$$$**  ✕ **Val Verde Steak House.** The curiosities inside this restaurant in the Val Verde Hotel, which opened in 1919, include an old oak-and-brass cooler and a series of mural landscapes, painted in 1923 by a patron who was working off his bar tab. The fare includes seafood such as shrimp and lobster, steak, and southwestern dishes. ✉ *203 Man-zanares St.,* ☎ *505/835–3380. AE, D, DC, MC, V.*

**$**  ✕ **Martha's Black Dog Coffeehouse.** Martha has an extensive offering of vegetarian items, but she does have dishes and deli sandwiches for carnivores, too. Meals are served three times daily, but closing hours vary. Call in ahead of time if it's past 6 PM. Locals make themselves at home here over coffee and homemade desserts. Art exhibits decorate the walls. ✉ *110 Manzanares,* ☎ *505/838–0311. AE, D, MC, V.*

**$$**  🛏 **Holiday Inn Express.** A favorite of groups and small conventions that otherwise might have limited options in such a remote area, this haven offers condensed versions of some of the luxuries of larger re-sorts. Its general manager was awarded one of the hotel chain's top awards for service and efficiency. You can expect the chain's usual qual-ity and contemporary, modern flourishes in standard rooms. ✉ *1100 California NE, 87801,* ☎ *505/838–0556,* 🖷 *505/838–0598. 120 rooms. In-room data ports, microwaves, refrigerators, cable TV, pool, gym, hot tub, laundry facilities, meeting rooms, some pets allowed (fee). AE, D, DC, MC, V. CP.*

**$**  🛏 **Super 8.** Pastel southwestern colors and prints of adobe architec-ture and pottery decorate this establishment's rooms, most of which have microwaves and refrigerators. K-Bob's, a franchise restaurant spe-cializing in steaks, is next door. ✉ *1121 Frontage Rd. (I–25's Exit 150), 87801,* ☎ *505/835–4626; 800/800–8000 central reservations;* 🖷 *505/ 835–3988. 88 rooms. Cable TV, pool, hot tub. AE, D, MC, V. CP.*

# HEADING WEST ON U.S. 60

Maybe you're a traveler who prefers to stay off the beaten path, to ven-ture to places you've never even heard of. If you're in the mood to take the slow road and encounter an authentic western America decades removed from today's franchise operations, head west on old Hwy. 60 out of Socorro and keep going—as far as the Arizona border if you'd like. The speed limit is 55, there's not a fast-food restaurant within 200 mi, and the scenery hasn't changed for 50 years.

This long, lonely highway opened in 1917 as the first numbered auto route to cross the United States. Called the Ocean to Ocean Highway,

U.S. 60 ran from Norfolk, Virginia, to Los Angeles. Earlier in the 20th century it was a "hoof highway," the route of cattle drives from Springerville, Arizona, to Magdalena, New Mexico. Walk into any café along this dusty roadside and you're still likely to be greeted by a blue-eyed cowboy in spurs on his way to brand a herd.

People really ranch here, much the way they have for more than 100 years. (Prior to the era of homesteaders and ranchers, the Apaches ruled.) Livestock production and timber are still the leading industries. Hwy. 60 takes you through the heart of Catron County, New Mexico's largest county by area. Notoriously politically incorrect and proud of it, this is a place where Confederate flags fly and animal trophies are proudly displayed.

After you've headed as far west as Quemado you can make an interesting loop by continuing north on Hwy. 36 to Hwy. 117, which skirts the east side of El Malpais National Monument (☞ Chapter 3), eventually hooking up with I–40 east of Grant. To get to Albuquerque take I–40 east.

## Magdalena

**❿** *27 mi west of Socorro on U.S. 60.*

Magdalena, population 300, enjoyed its heyday about a hundred years ago as a raucous town of miners and cowboys. It was once the biggest livestock shipping point west of Chicago. The Atchison, Topeka & Santa Fe Railway built a spur line from Socorro in 1885 to transport timber, wool, cattle, and ore. Lead, zinc, silver, copper, and gold all were mined in the area, but now there are more ghosts than miners.

The town took its name from Mary Magdalene, protector of miners, whose face is supposedly visible on the east slope of Magdalena Peak, a spot held sacred by the Indians of the area. To get a feel for the place, walk down to the Atchison, Topeka & Santa Fe Railway depot, now the town hall and library. Across the street is the Charles Ilfeld Warehouse, where the company's motto, "wholesalers of everything," is a reminder of that great trade empire of the late 19th century.

The biggest event of the year in Magdalena is the **Magdalena Old-Timers Reunion** (☎ 505/854–2719), held in early July. The festival, which draws about 5,000 and has the biggest parade in New Mexico after the State Fair's, began quietly 30 years ago. With the end of cattle drives and the shutdown of the rail spur in the early 1970s, cowboys began returning at the same time each year to greet each other and reminisce. Over the past three decades, the reunion has grown into an event-packed weekend including both kids' and adult rodeos, western swing dances on Friday and Saturday nights, a fiddling contest, a barbecue dinner, and an authentic chuck-wagon cook-off. The parade takes place Saturday morning, and the crowned reunion queen must be at least 60 years old. Most events are held at the Magdalena Fairgrounds, and admission is free. The deserted **Old Kelly Mine** (✉ Kelly Rd. off U.S. 60, ☎ no phone), 4 mi south of town, is reputed to be haunted, and during the Old Timers Reunion a 7K race finishes here (it begins in the village).

### Dining and Lodging

**$–$$** ✕ **Magdalena Cafe.** Burgers, hot sandwiches, and homemade pie and Mexican pineapple cake are served on red-and-white checkered tablecloths here. Thursday's dinner is quite the event around these parts, with a big $15.95 steak dinner and a $6.95 all-you-can-eat salad bar.

⊠ *U.S. Hwy. 60, across from Trail's End Supermarket,* ☎ *505/854–2696. No credit cards. No dinner Fri.–Wed.*

$ 🖭 **Western Bed & Breakfast Motel & RV Park.** To inspire dreams of riding the range, rooms of beveled pine are set off with western paintings and Indian artifacts, and some are Victorian-like with flowered upholstery and matching art. Quilts handmade in Magdalena decorate the walls. ⊠ *U.S. Hwy. 60, town center, 87835,* ☎ *505/854–2417,* FAX *505/854–3217. 6 rooms. AE, D, DC, MC, V. BP.*

## Shopping

Lebanese immigrant George Salome built **Salome Store** (⊠ U.S. Hwy. 60, at Oak St., ☎ 505/854–2341) in 1910, and his family still runs it. This general store with creaky wooden floors and a pressed-tin ceiling supplies locals with everything from boots and hats to groceries and feed. You'll also find saddles, dishes, giant jars of pickles on the counter, and sunbonnets hanging from elk antlers.

*En Route*   With its 27 glistening-white 80-ft radio-telescope antennas arranged in patterns, **Very Large Array** is a startling sight when spotted along the Plains of San Augustin. The complex's dish-shape ears, each weighing 230 tons, are tuned in to the cosmos. The array is part of a series of facilities that compose the National Radio Astronomy Observatory. The antennas, which provided an impressive backdrop for the movie *Contact,* based on the Carl Sagan book, form the largest, most advanced radio telescope in the world. The telescope chronicles the birth and death of stars and galaxies from 10 to 12 billion light-years away. Hundreds of scientists from around the world travel to this windy, remote spot to research black holes, colliding galaxies, and exploding stars, as well as to chart the movements of planets. Visitors are permitted to stroll right up to the array on a self-guided walking tour that begins at the unstaffed visitor center. The staff emphasize that their work does *not* involve a search for life on other planets. ⊠ *Off U.S. 60, 23 mi west of Magdalena,* ☎ *505/835–0424 Socorro County Chamber of Commerce.* 🖾 *Free.* ☉ *Daily 8:30–dusk.*

# Datil

*36 mi west of Magdalena on U.S. 60.*

More a crossroads than a town, Datil is named for the datelike fruit that once grew wild here.

## Dining and Lodging

$ ✕🖭 **Eagle Guest Ranch.** At the Datil intersection sits the one reason to stop, and it's a pretty good one. Since the Eagle opened in the 1920s, it has had various incarnations: roadside store, café, lounge, and dance hall. The dark-wood walls of the restaurant are saturated with tall tales, recollections of hard winters and dry summers, and the talk and laughter of big families and old friends who continue to share generous platters of food (mainly beef dishes, though there's a salad bar). The recipes for the pies served here are more than a half century old. On Friday only, Mexican food is served. The salsa could substitute for rocket fuel, and you'd better have an asbestos tongue if you order the red chile. Beer in a frosty Kerr canning jar will come to your mouth's aid. The guest rooms are low-end affairs, but if you're in need of accommodations in a place this remote, you have to think like an Old West traveler: "When you're at the Last Chance Hotel, you don't look for luxury." ⊠ *U.S. 60 at Hwy. 12 (Box 68, 87821),* ☎ *505/772–5612. Cable TV. 8 rooms. AE, D, DC, MC, V. Restaurant closed Sun.*

## Camping

⚠ **Datil Well Campground.** The well for which this campground is named was once an important stop on cattle drives. Along the ridges west of the campground there's a 3-mi trail through piñon-juniper and ponderosa-pine woodlands, with overlooks of the San Augustin Plains and surrounding mountains. ✉ *At intersection of U.S. Hwy. 60 and Hwy. 12, go left on Hwy. 12 (south) 5 mi,* ☎ *505/835–0412. Pit toilets, drinking water, fire pits, grills, picnic tables. 22 sites.* 🛏 *$5. No credit cards.*

# Pie Town

*21 mi west of Datil on U.S. 60.*

Do they still serve pie in Pie Town? The quest to find the answer is worth heading out on U.S. 60. During the 1930s and '40s, it was said, the best pie in New Mexico was served at a little café in Pie Town, a homesteading community west of the Continental Divide. Cowboys on cattle drives and tourists heading to California spread stories of the legendary pies. Thanks to the Pie-O-Neer Cafe, the tradition of great pie in this part of the world is alive and well.

Pie Town's reputation can be traced to 1922, when World War I veteran Clyde Norman came from Texas and filed a mining claim on the Hound Pup Lode. Gold mining didn't go as well as he'd hoped, but he began selling kerosene and gasoline, as well as doughnuts he'd brought from Magdalena in his Model T. Eventually, he learned to bake pies with dried apples, which were an immediate success. Spanish American War veteran Harmon L. Craig, who made a great sourdough, arrived in 1923 or '24, and the two went into partnership. The post office granted the place the name Pie Town in 1927.

Craig bought Norman out in 1932. He ran the mercantile end while his wife, Theodora Baugh, and her two daughters took over the pie baking. Nowadays, aficionados can dig in at the annual Pie Festival, held on the second weekend in September, with pie-eating and pie-baking contests, horny-toad races, and hot-air balloon flights.

## Dining

$ ✕ **Pie-O-Neer Cafe.** "Life goes on and days go by. That's why you should stop for pie." Such is the motto of one of New Mexico's most legendary roadside stops. Kathy Knapp serves three squares during the summer, but pie is her stock in trade. She always keeps these varieties on hand: apple, cherry, peach, coconut cream, lemon meringue, and banana cream. Her best sellers are the apple and the oatmeal-pecan. The butterscotch–chocolate chip and peanut butter pies are also big favorites, as is the apple-raisin-walnut. Everything here, from the cinnamon rolls to the chile-cheese fries, with your choice of green chile stew or Texas chili, is made from scratch. On some Sunday afternoons, local talent drops by for guitar strumming. The café closes at 7 PM in summer, and fall and winter hours are limited to 10–4. (Plans were in the works in 2002 to extend hours, however.) ✉ *U.S. 60,* ☎ *505/772–2900. AE, D, MC, V.*

# Quemado

**⑪** *22 mi west of Pie Town on U.S. 60.*

Quemado (pronounced kay-*ma*-dough) means "burnt" in Spanish, and the town is supposedly named for a legendary Apache chief who burned his hand in a campfire. The bustling village, which contains several motels and cafés, is busiest in fall, when it is a favorite base for hunters. **Quemado Lake,** about 20 mi south of town on Hwys. 32 and

103, is a man-made fishing and hiking area where it's not unusual to spot herds of elk.

**LIGHTNING FIELD –** The sculptor Walter De Maria created *Lightning Field*, a work of land art composed of 400 stainless-steel poles of varying heights (the average is 20 ft) arranged in a rectangular grid over 1 mi by ½ mi of flat, isolated terrain. Groups of up to six people are permitted to stay overnight between May 1 and October 31—the only way you can experience the artwork—at a rustic on-site 1930s cabin (the fee ranges from $85 to $135 per person, although those who can afford it are asked to pay up to $300 per person to help cover actual expenses of providing visitor meals and transportation). Dia Center for the Arts administers *Lightning Field,* shuttling visitors from Quemado to the sculpture, which is on private land to the northeast. High thunderstorm season is usually from July to mid-September; book way ahead for visits during this time. If you're lucky, you'll see flashes you'll never forget (though lightning isn't required to appreciate the artwork). ⊠ *Box 2993, Corrales 87048,* ☎ *505/898–3335 Corrales office and reservations; 505/773–4560 Quemado shuttle;* FAX *505/898–3336;* WEB *www. diacenter.org. Reservations essential. Closed Nov.–Apr.*

## Dining and Lodging

**$–$$**   ✕ **Snuffy's Steak House.** On the road to Quemado Lake, this true western bar serves steaks, burgers, and Mexican food. The enchiladas aren't bad, but this is a place to soak up local color. There's an antique bar, and the walls are plastered with pictures of homesteaders and folks with their fish and wild-game trophies. Snuffy's is open for breakfast on Saturday and Sunday and for early dinner (until 8) on Friday and Saturday. ⊠ *Hwy. 103,* ☎ *505/773–4672. MC, V. No dinner Sun.– Thurs.*

**$**   ✕🛏 **Largo Motel.** With plain, comfortable rooms, the Largo is as good a motel as you're going to find to wash off the trail dust and find a night's rest. The Largo has the best café in town, a busy little spot known for homemade corn tortillas and biscuits, gravy, and chicken-fried steak, as well as red and green chile. The Navajo tacos are famous. They serve "a real full plate," too. Above the spacious booths are mounted trophies (the owner is a hunting guide). ⊠ *U.S. Hwy. 60 on west side of town, 87829,* ☎ *505/773–4686. 6 rooms. MC, V.*

## Camping

△ **Quemado Lake Campgrounds.** Six campgrounds surround Quemado Lake, providing convenient access to hiking trails or lake fishing for planted rainbow trout. ⊠ *20 mi south of Pie Town on Hwys. 32 and 103,* ☎ *505/773–4678. Pit toilets, partial hook-ups (electric and water), dump station, drinking water, fire grates, fire pits, grills, picnic tables. Unlimited primitive sites, 60 developed sites, 16 sites with partial hook-ups.* ⬛ *RV sites $15, tent sites $10. No credit cards.*

# SOUTHWESTERN NEW MEXICO A TO Z

### AIR TRAVEL

El Paso International Airport is the main gateway to southern New Mexico. The major airlines with scheduled service to the airport are America West, American, Continental, Delta, Frontier, Southwest, and Azteca Airlines (specializing in flights to and from Mexico). Albuquerque International Sunport is 210 mi north of Las Cruces. *See* Air Travel *in* Smart Travel Tips A to Z for national airline phone numbers.

➤ AIRLINE: **Azteca Airlines** (800/445–9820).

➤ AIRPORTS: **Albuquerque International Sunport** (✉ 2200 Sunport Blvd. SE, Albuquerque, ☎ 505/842–4366). **El Paso International Airport** (✉ 6701 Convair Dr., El Paso, TX, ☎ 915/772–4271).

## BUS TRAVEL

Texas, New Mexico & Oklahoma Coaches, which is affiliated with Greyhound Lines, provides bus service throughout southwestern New Mexico (though not Silver City). Silver Stage Lines provides shuttle service to Las Cruces and Silver City from El Paso International Airport. Las Cruces Shuttle Service makes regular runs daily between El Paso International Airport and Las Cruces, Deming, and Silver City. Roadrunner City Bus operates public buses in Las Cruces.

➤ BUS COMPANIES: **Las Cruces Shuttle Service** (☎ 505/525–1784, WEB lascrucesshuttle.com). **Roadrunner City Bus** (☎ 505/525–2500). **Silver Stage Lines** (☎ 800/522–0162). **Texas, New Mexico & Oklahoma Coaches** (☎ 505/524–8518 in Las Cruces; 800/231–2222 for all other destinations).

## CAR RENTAL

You can rent a car from one of the national agencies at either Albuquerque International Airport or El Paso International Airport. Auto dealerships in some communities rent cars. Hertz has an office at the Las Cruces Hilton. *See* Car Rental *in* Smart Travel Tips A to Z for national rental agency phone numbers.

## CAR TRAVEL

Two major interstates travel through southwestern New Mexico, I–10 from west to east and I–25 from north to south. U.S. 70 connects Las Cruces to Alamogordo and the southeast. From Albuquerque, the drive is about two hours to Truth or Consequences, three hours to Las Cruces. Silver City can be accessed from minor highways leading off I–10 and I–25. From Las Cruces, I–10 leads south to El Paso.

The quality of the region's roadways varies widely, particularly in remote rural areas. Drive with caution on the narrow highways, which particularly in mountainous areas have no shoulders. On minor roadways, even if paved, be alert for curves, dips, and steep drop-offs.

## EMERGENCIES

In an emergency, dial 911.

Some Walgreens pharmacies in El Paso, Texas, and in Las Cruces stay open late or are open 24 hours. Wal-Mart and large supermarket chains such as Albertson's also have pharmacies.

➤ HOSPITALS: **Memorial Medical Center** (✉ 2450 S. Telshor Blvd., Las Cruces, ☎ 505/522–8641).

## PASSPORTS AND VISAS

On a day trip into Mexico, citizens of the United States and Canada need only carry a government-issue photo ID as documentation, but it's always a good idea also to have a valid passport or certified copy of a birth certificate. All other citizens must have a valid passport to enter.

### ENTERING MEXICO

Mexico has one of the strictest policies about children entering the country. Though it's not always checked for, all children, including infants, must have proof of citizenship for travel to Mexico. All children up to age 18 traveling with a single parent must also have a notarized letter from the other parent stating that the child has his or her permission to leave the home country. If the other parent is deceased or the child has only one legal parent, a notarized statement saying so must be provided as proof.

If you're visiting for less than 72 hours and are not traveling past a border town like Ciudad Juárez and into the country's interior, you don't have to pay Mexico's $20 visitor fee (tourist card). You do not have to buy Mexican auto insurance if you're only traveling to Mexico for the day. Be sure the insurance you do have covers you if you drive your vehicle across the border. If you're caught transporting a gun into Mexico, you can be jailed indefinitely.

➤ CONTACT: **Mexican Embassy** (☎ 202/728–1600, WEB www.embassyofmexico.org; http://travel.state.gov/mexico.html for travel information sheets).

## TOURS

El Paso–Juárez Trolley Co. has daily guided tours into Juárez, Mexico, for a $12.50 fee. Call for schedules and rates for special tours to the old Spanish missions of El Paso, Texas. Around and About Tours specializes in El Paso, Texas; Ciudad Juárez, Mexico; and tours of several days or a week into southern New Mexico. Volunteers from El Paso Mission Trail Association lead groups of at least 10 people on visits to the old Spanish missions of the El Paso area. A donation of at least $2.50 per person is requested.

➤ TOUR OPERATORS: **Around and About Tours** (✉ 6716 Mesa Grande Ave., El Paso, TX, ☎ 915/833–2650). **El Paso–Juárez Trolley Co.** (✉ 1 Civic Center Plaza, El Paso, TX, ☎ 915/544–0062). **El Paso Mission Trail Association** (✉ 1 Civic Center Plaza, El Paso, TX, ☎ 800/351–6024).

## TRAIN TRAVEL

Amtrak serves El Paso and Deming, New Mexico, on the *Sunset Limited,* which operates between Los Angeles, New Orleans, and Florida.
➤ CONTACT: **Amtrak** (✉ Union Station, 700 San Francisco St., El Paso, TX, ☎ 800/872–7245, WEB www.amtrak.com).

## VISITOR INFORMATION

➤ CONTACTS: **El Paso Convention & Tourism Department** (✉ 1 Civic Center Plaza, 79901, ☎ 915/534–0696 or 800/351–6024, WEB www.elpasocvb.com). **Las Cruces Convention & Visitors Bureau** (✉ 211 Water St., 88001, ☎ 505/541–2444 or 800/343–7827, WEB www.lascrucescvb.org). **Mesilla Visitor's Center** (✉ 2340 Avenida de Mesilla, 88046, ☎ 505/647–9698, WEB www.oldmesilla.org). **Silver City Murray Ryan Visitor's Center** (✉ 201 N. Hudson St., 88061, ☎ 800/548–9378 or 800/290–8330, WEB www.silvercity.org). **Truth or Consequences/Sierra County Chamber of Commerce** (✉ 201 S. Foch St., 87901, ☎ 505/894–3536, WEB www.truthorconsequencesnm.net).

# 9 BACKGROUND AND ESSENTIALS

Chile Time

Glossary

Menu Guide

Books and Movies

# CHILE TIME

Chile, an ancient, locally grown mainstay, is the defining ingredient of New Mexican cuisine. Combined with corn tortillas, beans, tomatoes, and potatoes, chile binds together the New Mexico that for centuries sustained indigenous people, the Spanish, and subsequent arrivals. A dedicated chile lover will travel any distance, down any highway in pursuit of a great chile sauce. From Chope's south of Las Cruces to M&J's Sanitary Tortilla Factory in Albuquerque and JoAnn's Ranch-o-Casados in Española (to name a few classic hot spots), the pursuit of the most flavorful—but not necessarily the hottest—chile remains a personal quest akin to proving one's honor.

When Christopher Columbus set out across the ocean in 1492, he was looking for a sea route to the lucrative spice trade of Asia. Instead, he stumbled onto the New World, where he tasted chile. He took some back to Spain, and from there chile spread around the world on trade routes, transforming the cuisines of Spain, Portugal, Italy, Hungary, North Africa, India, Nepal, Tibet, and China. In addition to its distinction as one of the world's favorite spices, chile is one of the oldest: it's believed to have originated 10,000 years ago in the Amazon region of South America in the area of Brazil and Bolivia.

How chile first arrived in New Mexico is the subject of debate. Some believe the Spanish introduced it to the Pueblo Indians on their travels north from Mexico. Others hold that chile was grown in New Mexico centuries prior to the arrival of the Spanish, having been introduced through trade with the peoples of Mexico and South America. It is interesting to note that chile is not used in the traditional ceremonies among the Pueblo Indians as is corn, but red and green chile dishes are served at all feasts and ceremonies.

The source of the chile's heat is the chemical capsaicin, found in the pepper's heart and membrane. The seeds themselves are not hot, but they absorb capsaicin from their contact with the heart and membrane. (Though "chile" is a Spanish spelling of *chili,* the Aztec, or Nahuatl, word for pepper, "capsicum," comes from the Latin *capsicon,* meaning chest or box.) In addition to providing a culinary delight to chile lovers, capsaicin has a long tradition as a healing substance and pain reliever. Medicinal uses of chile extend from prehistory into modern medicine. Chile may protect against blood clots and prevent heart attacks, and it is known to hinder cholesterol absorption. Chile is low in fat and high in vitamins A and C and beta-carotene. It also speeds up metabolism and helps digestion by intensifying stomach-acid production and sometimes working as a laxative. New Mexican old-timers chop up chile and place it on arthritic limbs; more recently topical creams made from capsaicin have become available. Chile-based products also bring relief from chronic pain caused by cluster headaches, shingles, and herpes—even amputation and other surgery.

Chile derives much of its reputation as a painkiller and bringer of well-being from the chemical effect the burning capsaicin has on the brain. When you eat or touch chile, the skin sends a pain signal to the brain, releasing endorphins, the hormones of pleasure. So, the same chemical reaction that produces "chile addiction" also blunts pain.

The green variety of chile, generically called "Hatch" (for the New Mexico town that produces the bulk of the state's crop), is the commercially developed type known as New Mexico 6-10 and the Big Jim. When it comes to red chile, the best is said to be grown from the old stock cultivated in Chimayó and other high mountain villages of the north—Española, Dixon, Velarde, and Peñasco.

By far the state's most important vegetable crop, New Mexico chile is grown on 30,000 acres, mostly in Luna and Doña Ana counties. Sixty percent of the nation's chile crop comes from the Land of Enchantment. Since 1980 chile consumption has doubled in the United States, much of it going into salsa, which in the 1990s surpassed ketchup to become the country's most popular condiment.

From mid-August through the fall, the New Mexican air is scented with the warm, enticing fragrance of chiles roasting out-of-doors in large, wire, propane-fired cages. Around State Fair time in September, people head for their favorite roadside stand to buy a sack of fresh-roasted green chiles. Once stored in the freezer, the chile is used all winter long, in stews, enchiladas, salsas, and burritos.

As the season progresses into October, it's time to buy a red chile ristra, a string of chiles, to hang full, heavy and sweet, near the front door, a sign of warmth and welcome. It's said the ristra brings good luck—and it certainly is convenient to have the makings of soul-warming red-chile salsa right at hand.

–Sharon Niederman

# GLOSSARY

Perhaps more than any other region in the United States, New Mexico has its own distinctive cuisine and architectural style, both heavily influenced by Native American, Spanish-colonial, Mexican, and American frontier traditions. The brief glossary that follows explains terms frequently used in this book. As befits a land occupied—in several senses of the word in some cases—by so many diverse peoples, the use of accents on place and other names is a tricky matter. For some people, among them many Hispanic residents, accents are a matter of identification and pride—Rio Grande, for instance, represents more clearly the linguistic origins of the current name of the river that runs so grandly through the state. On the other hand, though including the accent for Picurís Pueblo or Jémez Pueblo might be linguistically accurate, it's also a reminder of the Spanish conquest of Pueblo Native Americans. ("I couldn't care less whether you use accents or not—I don't," said a woman at the governor's office of Jemez Pueblo when asked whether having an accent above the first "e" in the pueblo's name would be more accurate.)

In general in this book we've applied accents when they're part of an official place or other name. Signs for and official documents of Española, for instance, tend to have a tilde above the "n" in the city's name. On the other hand, though the names of Capulin Volcano and the city of Raton are sometimes written Capulín Volcano and Ratón, we have not employed the accents because New Mexican residents rarely do. A generally workable solution, this strategy does lead to some apparent inconsistencies (Picurís Pueblo; Jemez Pueblo), an illustration of the conflicting cultural sentiments still at play within New Mexico.

## Art and Architecture

**Adobe:** A brick of sun-dried earth and clay, usually stabilized with straw; a structure made of adobe.

**Banco:** A small bench, or banquette, often upholstered with handwoven textiles, that gracefully emerges from adobe walls.

**Bulto:** Folk-art figures of a santo (saint), usually carved from wood.

**Camposanto:** A graveyard.

**Capilla:** A chapel.

**Casita:** Literally "small house," this term is generally used to describe a separate guest house.

**Cerquita:** A spiked, wrought-iron, rectangular fence, often marking grave sites.

**Corbel:** An ornately carved, decorative wooden bracket set between posts and beams.

**Coyote fence:** A type of wooden fence that surrounds many New Mexico homes; it comprises branches, usually from cedar or aspen trees, arranged vertically and wired tightly together.

**Equipal:** Pigskin-and-cedar furniture from Jalisco, Mexico, these chairs have rounded backs and bases rather than legs.

**Farolito:** Small votive candles set in paper-bag lanterns, farolitas are popular at Christmastime. The term is used in northern New Mexico only. People in Albuquerque and points south call the lanterns *luminarias,* which in the north is the term for the bonfires of Christmas Eve.

**Heishi:** Shell jewelry.

**Hornos:** Outdoor domed ovens.

**Kiva:** A ceremonial room, rounded and built at least partially underground, used by Native Americans of the Southwest. Entrance is gained from the roof.

**Kiva fireplace:** A corner fireplace whose round form resembles that of a kiva.

**Latilla:** Small pole, often made of aspen, used as a lath in a ceiling.

**Nicho:** A built-in shelf cut into an adobe or stucco wall.

**Placita:** A small plaza.

**Portal:** A porch or large covered area adjacent to a house.

**Pueblo Revival (also informally called Pueblo-style):** Most homes in this style, modeled after the traditional dwellings of the

Southwest Pueblo Indians, are cube or rectangle shaped. Other characteristics are flat roofs, thick adobe or stucco walls, small windows, rounded corners, and viga beams.

**Retablo:** Holy image painted on wood or tin.

**Santero:** Maker of religious images.

**Territorial style:** This modified Pueblo style evolved in the late 19th century when New Mexico was still a U.S. territory. The Territorial home incorporates a broad central hallway and entryway and adds wooden elements, such as window frames, in neoclassical style; some structures have pitched (often corrugated or flat metal) rather than flat roofs, and brick copings.

**Terrones adobes:** Adobe cut from the ground rather than formed from mud.

**Viga:** Horizontal roof beam made of logs, usually protruding from the side of the house.

## Flora and Fauna

**Cholla:** A term for various species of spiny cactus, which grow irregular branches with clustered berries.

**Collared peccary:** Known also as javelina hogs, these piglike animals are aggressive and highly protective of their young. They're commonly found in the mountains of southwestern New Mexico.

**Creosote:** Rare desert rain enhances the strong, medicine-like fragrance of this somewhat scraggly plant common to arid regions. Nicknamed greasewood for its oily resins, creosote produces evergreen leaves and small yellow or green flowers.

**Desert horned lizard:** Called horned or horny toads by locals, this species has a flattened body and rows of tiny spikes that resemble formidable armor.

**Desert tarantula:** It's a rare but startling sight to see thousands of large, dark tarantulas skittering across New Mexico highways after a heavy rain. With a leg span of up to 4 inches, this cousin of tropical spiders can look terrifying. It rarely bites, and its venom usually produces only a mild swelling on human skin.

**El lobo:** The Spanish term for the Mexican gray wolf once common in New Mexico but no longer found in the wild. Efforts are being made to reintroduce this genetically unique species to its original home range.

**Jackrabbit:** Tall, rangy, and graceful, this long-eared rabbit can sprint and hop at astonishing speeds.

**Juniper:** A shrub or tree, common to arid regions, with a waxy covering that retains moisture.

**Kangaroo rat:** This nocturnal rodent is a master of water conservation, as well as leaping, which helps it evade predators. Its kidneys expel very little water, and its body can convert a meal of dry seeds to moisture.

**Lechuguilla:** This fleshy desert plant has daggerlike leaves and tall stalks of yellow flowers.

**Mesquite:** Thorny branches and bean pods distinguish this common range plant, technically a small tree, which grows in thickets.

**Mexican freetail bat:** These bats are harmless to humans, except for the rare rabid individual. The half million bats living in Carlsbad Caverns during summer months can consume 3 tons of insects in one night.

**Mountain lion:** Solitary and stealthy, the mountain lion long has been a legend of the Old West. Habitats are disappearing, making remaining wildernesses of New Mexico a refuge for the creature.

**Mule deer:** The long ears of this timid deer explain the name. The animal thrives in virtually every corner of New Mexico, from forests to sand dunes.

**Ocotillo:** This common desert plant grows in clusters of thorny branches capped by red, tubular blossoms.

**Piñon pine:** These robust pines found in mountains and foothills throughout the Southwest survive drought through taproots that plunge as deep as 40 ft into the soil. The resinous wood produces fragrant scents from Santa Fe fireplaces, while tasty piñon nuts garnish foods.

**Prickly pear cactus:** The fleshy, rounded pads of this common cactus inspired its nickname "elephant ears."

**Pronghorn:** Look alongside roadways for a flash of white from the rear of this delicate creature, incorrectly called an antelope. Pronghorns roam in bands and prefer open rangeland.

**Quail:** Highly tolerant of dry weather, this sociable bird generally is found in a covey, which tries to sneak out of danger by running through the cover of brush. The birds take wing in short bursts of flight.

**Raptor:** A bird of prey, such as a hawk or owl.

**Roadrunner:** The crested head and speckled feathers of this desert dweller can be seen making mad dashes across or alongside New Mexico highways. The fearless fowl eats lizards and snakes. Its curiosity is well known to state residents, who sometimes find themselves face-to-face with a roadrunner peering through a window.

**Sagebrush:** This greenish-gray shrub carpets much of northern New Mexico, blooms with small yellow flowers, and smells slightly like the herb sage (to which it is not related). It's often collected, dried, and bundled into incense sticks or potpourri.

**Soaptree yucca:** White flowers adorn the broomsticklike protrusions of this plant, New Mexico's state flower.

**Tamarisk:** Imported from overseas, the tamarisk (or salt cedar) is a small evergreen found choking waterways throughout the Southwest. The nonnative plant is a major nuisance, sucking up precious moisture and providing very little benefit as animal habitat.

**Texas madrone:** The reddish, smooth bark of this unusual evergreen gives it the nickname "lady's legs." The tree dresses up with urn-shape white-and-pink flowers and red fruit. A relic of the last ice age, this variety is found only in isolated regions of west Texas and southeastern New Mexico. Look for it at Guadalupe Mountains National Park.

**Vinegaroon:** You'll know it when you see it. This dark, whip-tail scorpion appears fearsome at up to 3 inches long. It waves wicked-looking pincers and sprays an acid that reeks of vinegar. Yet, it's harmless to humans—unlike some of its more venomous cousins.

**Western diamondback:** This rattlesnake is usually found coiled under shady bushes or lounging in cool cave entrances. Watch your step.

# MENU GUIDE

**Aguacate:** Spanish for avocado, the key ingredient of guacamole.

**Albóndigas:** Meatballs, usually cooked with rice in a meat broth.

**Bolsa del pobre:** A seafood and vegetable dish; a specialty from Colima.

**Burrito:** A warm flour tortilla wrapped around meat, beans, and vegetables and smothered in chile and cheese; many New Mexicans also love breakfast burritos (filled with any combination of the above, along with eggs).

**Carne adovada:** Red chile–marinated pork.

**Chalupa:** A corn tortilla deep-fried in the shape of a bowl, filled with pinto beans (sometimes meat), and topped with cheese, guacamole, sour cream, lettuce, tomatoes, and salsa.

**Chilaquiles:** Often served at breakfast, this casserole-like dish consists of small pieces of fried tortillas baked with red or green chiles, bits of chicken or cheese, and sometimes eggs.

**Chile relleno:** A large green chile pepper peeled, stuffed with cheese or a special mixture of spicy ingredients, dipped in batter, and fried.

**Chiles:** New Mexico's infamous hot peppers, which come in an endless variety of sizes and in various degrees of hotness, from the thumb-size jalapeño to the smaller and often hotter serrano. They can be canned or fresh, dried or cut up into salsa. Most traditional New Mexican dishes are served either with green, red, or both types of chiles (ask for "Christmas" when indicating to your server that you'd like both red and green). Famous regional uses for green chile include green chile stew (usually made with shredded pork), green chile cheeseburgers, and green chile–and–cheese tamales.

**Chili:** A stewlike dish with Texas origins that typically contains beans, beef, and red chile.

**Chimichanga:** The same as a burrito only deep-fried and topped with a dab of sour cream or salsa. (The chimichanga was invented in Tucson, Arizona.)

**Chipotle:** A dried smoked jalapeño with a smoky, almost sweet, chocolaty flavor.

**Chorizo:** Well-spiced Spanish sausage, made with pork and red chiles.

**Enchilada:** A rolled or flat corn tortilla filled with meat, chicken, seafood, or cheese, an enchilada is covered with chile and baked. The ultimate enchilada is made with blue Indian corn tortillas. New Mexicans order them flat, sometimes topped with a fried egg.

**Fajitas:** A Tex-Mex dish of grilled beef, chicken, fish, or roasted vegetables and served with peppers, onions, and pico de gallo, served with tortillas; traditionally known as arracheras.

**Flauta:** A tortilla filled with cheese or meat and rolled into a flutelike shape ("flauta" means flute) and lightly fried.

**Frijoles refritos:** Refried beans, often seasoned with lard or cheese.

**Guacamole:** Mashed avocado, mixed with tomatoes, garlic, onions, lemon juice, and chiles, used as a dip, a side dish, a topping, or an additional ingredient.

**Hatch:** A small southern New Mexico town in the Mesilla Valley, known for its outstanding production and quality of both green and red chile. The "Hatch" name often is found on canned chile food products.

**Huevos rancheros:** New Mexico's answer to eggs Benedict—eggs doused with chile and sometimes melted cheese, served on top of a corn tortilla (they're good accompanied by chorizo).

**Pan de cazón:** Grilled shark with black beans and red onions on a tortilla; a specialty from Campeche.

**Posole:** Resembling popcorn soup, this is a sublime marriage of lime, hominy, pork, chile, garlic, and spices.

**Quesadilla:** A folded flour tortilla filled with cheese and meat or vegetables and warmed or lightly fried so the cheese melts.

**Queso:** Cheese; an ingredient in many Mexican and southwestern recipes (cheddar or jack is used most commonly in New Mexican dishes).

**Ristra:** String of dried red chile peppers, often used as decoration.

**Salsa:** Finely chopped concoction of green and red chile peppers, mixed with onion, garlic, and other spices.

**Sopaipilla:** Puffy deep-fried bread that's similar to Navajo fry bread (found in Arizona and western New Mexico); it's served either as a dessert with honey drizzled over it or savory as a meal stuffed with pinto beans or meat.

**Taco:** A corn or flour tortilla served either soft, or baked or fried and served in a hard shell; it's then stuffed with vegetables or spicy meat and garnished with shredded lettuce, chopped tomatoes, onions, and grated cheese.

**Tacos al carbón:** Shredded pork cooked in a mole sauce and folded into corn tortillas.

**Tamale:** Ground corn made into a dough, often filled with finely ground pork and red chiles; it's steamed in a corn husk.

**Tortilla:** A thin pancake made of corn or wheat flour, a tortilla is used as bread, as an edible "spoon," and as a container for other foods. Locals place butter in the center of a hot tortilla, roll it up, and eat it as a scroll.

**Trucha en terra-cotta:** Fresh trout wrapped in corn husks and baked in clay.

**Verde:** Spanish for "green," as in chile verde (a green chile sauce).

# BOOKS AND MOVIES

## General Interest

Classic books on New Mexico include *Death Comes for the Archbishop*, by Willa Cather, a novel based on the life of Archbishop Jean Baptiste Lamy, who built, among other churches, the St. Francis Cathedral in Santa Fe. Other significant works about the state include *Great River*, by Paul Horgan; *The Wind Leaves No Shadow*, by Ruth Laughlin; *Miracle Hill*, by Barney Mitchell; *Navajos Have Five Fingers*, by T. D. Allen; *Santa Fe*, by Oliver La Farge; *New Mexico*, by Jack Schaefer; and *Moon over Adobe*, by Dorothy Pillsbury. In a compelling personal style, *Enchantment and Exploitation* and *River of Traps*, both by William de Buys, chronicle the unique culture and concerns of the state.

Norman Zollinger's *Riders to Cibola* chronicles the conquistadors' search for the legendary Seven Cities of Gold. In 1974 Albuquerque author Tony Hillerman received an Edgar Allan Poe Award from the Mystery Writers of America for his book *Dance Hall of the Dead*. He has since written a series of mystery novels revolving around the character of a Navajo police officer. Hillerman also edited *The Spell of New Mexico*, an anthology of New Mexican writers. *A Sense of Place, a Sense of Time*, by pioneering landscape architect and environmentalist John Brinckerhoff Jackson, explores New Mexico's landscape, past and present. Several strands of New Mexico's history merge in Peggy Pond Church's *The House at Otowi Bridge*, the story of Edith Warner, an Anglo woman who lived near San Ildefonso Pueblo in the period before, during, and after the atomic bomb was developed in the neighboring town of Los Alamos. John Nichols has written many books about New Mexico, including the first two volumes of a memoir about his life in Taos: *If Mountains Die* and *The Last Beautiful Days of Autumn*.

Las Cruces author Linda G. Harris and photographer Pamela Porter offer an unusual look at New Mexico's past in *Houses in Time*. Harris's explanations of architectural styles intermingle with historical perspective. *The Wood Carvers of Cordova, New Mexico*, by Charles L. Briggs, is a prizewinning study of the making and selling of religious images in a northern New Mexico village. *Eliot Porter's Southwest* is the famed photographer's poetic view of the region, much of it focused around his Tesuque home. In *An Illustrated History of New Mexico*, Thomas E. Chavez, director of the Palace of the Governors in Santa Fe, uses quotes to provide context for his visual chronicle of New Mexican history.

The 1999 espionage controversy that raised eyebrows concerning security at Los Alamos lab is recounted in *A Convenient Spy: Wen Ho Lee and the Politics of Nuclear Espionage*, by Dan Stober and Ian Hoffman. *The Secret Mesa: Inside Los Alamos National Laboratory*, by Jo Ann Shroyer, gives a detailed look into this secret facility in the mountains northwest of Santa Fe. You can learn about the most fascinating archaeological site in the state in *People of Chaco: A Canyon and Its Culture*, by Kendrick Frazier.

## Native American Lore and Pueblo Life

*The Man Who Killed the Deer*, by Frank Waters, is a classic of Pueblo life. *Masked Gods*, by the same author, has a following that reaches cult proportions. J. J. Brody's illustrated book *Anasazi and Pueblo Painting* is an indispensable volume for art historians and students of southwestern culture. *Mornings in Mexico*, by D. H. Lawrence, contains a number of essays pertaining to Taos and the Pueblo ritual dances. *Pueblo Style and Regional Architecture*, edited by Nicholas C. Markovich, Wolfgang F. E. Preiser, and Fred G. Strum, covers the evolution of architecture in the Southwest, with particular emphasis on New Mexico.

## New Mexican Personalities

*Billy the Kid: A Short and Violent Life*, by historian Robert M. Utley, is considered the definitive work on the notorious outlaw. Utley also penned *High Noon in Lincoln*, another account involving the Kid. In *Edge of Taos Desert: An Escape to Reality*, New York socialite turned Taos art patron Mabel Dodge Luhan eloquently describes the transformative power Taos and the Pueblo Indians had on her life, beginning with her Taos arrival in 1917. A good biography is Lois Palken Rudnick's *Mabel Dodge Luhan: New Woman, New Worlds. The Life of D. H. Lawrence,* by Keith Sagar is a fine biography of the world-renowned author so strongly associated with (and buried in) New Mexico. Taos is also Georgia O'Keeffe country, and there is a wealth of books about the artist. Among the best is *Georgia O'Keeffe: Arts and Letters,* published by the New York Graphic Society in conjunction with a retrospective of her work at the National Gallery of Art, in Washington, D.C. Also worthy of note is the reissue of the coffee-table book *Georgia O'Keeffe,* with text by the artist herself. *Portrait of an Artist: A Biography of Georgia O'Keeffe,* by Laurie Lisle, and *O'Keeffe: The Life of and American Legend,* by Jeffrey Hogrefe, span the artist's life and career. *Georgia O'Keeffe: Some Memories of Drawings,* edited by Doris Bry, is a collection of the artist's major 1915–63 drawings, with comments on each.

## Albuquerque, Santa Fe, and Taos

*Albuquerque—A Narrative History,* by Marc Simmons, is a fascinating look at the city's birth and development. *Lautrec,* by Norman Zollinger, is an entertaining mystery set in Albuquerque. *The Wingspread Collectors Guide to Santa Fe and Taos* and *The Wingspread Collectors Guide to Albuquerque and Corrales* provide high-quality reproductions and useful information about art galleries, art, and crafts of the region; they also include listings of museums, hotels, restaurants, and historic sites. *A Short History of Santa Fe,* by Susan Hazen-Hammond, chronicles Santa Fe's history with text and photos. *Taos: A Pictorial History,* by John Sherman, contains numerous black-and-white historical photographs of the major characters, events, and structures that formed the backbone of Taos.

## Southern New Mexico

Roswell author Carole Larson gives a fascinating and comprehensive account of the sometimes violent settling of southeastern New Mexico in *Forgotten Frontier.* El Paso, Texas, author Leon Metz, a nationally recognized historian, has written many accounts of southern New Mexico, including mentions in the novel *Riders Along the Rio Grande: A Collection of Outlaws, Prostitutes and Vigilantes.* Historic photographs and colorful narratives are found in *Las Cruces: An Illustrated History,* by Linda G. Harris. Ferenc Morton Szasz tells a compelling story of the explosion of the world's first atomic bomb at the remote Trinity Site in *The Day the Sun Rose Twice. Tularosa,* by C. L. Sonnichsen, is a dramatic account of the Alamogordo area's old frontier.

## Movies

Northern New Mexico has provided memorable scenic backdrops for several feature films, particularly westerns. *Silverado* (1985) and *Wyatt Earp* (1994) were photographed in the Santa Fe vicinity. For television, two miniseries based on popular Larry McMurtry novels with Old West settings, *Lonesome Dove* (1989) and *Buffalo Girls* (1995), were shot near Santa Fe. *Lonesome Dove* was actually shot at Galisteo's movie ranch, Cook Ranch; most of the set there was blown up by accident during the filming of *The Wild Wild West* (1999). *The Milagro Beanfield War* (1988), directed by Robert Redford and based on the novel by Taos author John Nichols, was filmed in Truchas, on the High Road to Taos. Most agree the novel is far better than the film. Billy Bob Thornton's film adaptation (2000) of the novel *All The Pretty Horses* was shot in Las Vegas (New Mexico) and Santa Fe.

The Rio Grande Gorge Bridge in Taos and parts of Gallup appear in director Oliver Stone's *Natural Born Killers* (1994). Southern New Mexico provides settings for *Young Guns* (1988), *Gas, Food, Lodging* (1992), *White Sands* (1992), *Traffic* (2000), and *Mad Love* (1995). Other movies photographed around New Mexico include *Outrageous Fortune* (1987), with Bette Midler and Shelley Long, and *City Slickers* (1991), starring Billy Crystal.

Cinema classics shot in New Mexico include *Butch Cassidy and the Sundance Kid* (1969), which was filmed in Taos and Chama; *The Cowboys* (1972), the John Wayne movie shot in Chama, Galisteo, and Santa Fe's San Cristobal ranch; Clint Eastwood's *Every Which Way But Loose* (1978), which shows parts of Santa Fe and Albuquerque; and the countercultural anthem *Easy Rider* (1969), which inspired its star, Dennis Hopper, to buy Mabel Dodge Luhan's former home in Taos. Parts of John Ford's *The Grapes of Wrath* (1940), an adaption of the famous Steinbeck novel, were shot along the old Route 66 in Santa Rosa. The stunning Cumbres & Toltec Scenic Railroad in Chama thrilled viewers of *Indiana Jones and the Last Crusade* (1989).

The National Radio Astronomy Very Large Array of antennae in western New Mexico provided dramatic backdrops in the science fiction movies *Armageddon* (1998), *Contact* (1997), and *Independence Day* (1996). Los Alamos was featured in the Meryl Streep thriller *Silkwood* (1983). The alien-sighting history of New Mexico made the state a good setting for "star man" David Bowie in *The Man Who Fell to Earth* (1976), in which an Artesia church

service and White Sands National Monument are featured. You won't see White Sands in *Star Wars*, but recordings of missiles launched at White Sands Missile Range were used by the sound effects team. Carlsbad Caverns was the underground wonderland seen in the movies *King Solomon's Mines* (1950) and *Journey to the Center of the Earth* (1959).

For a view of New Mexico's sometimes checkered past, look for the documentary *The Silence of Cricket Coogler* (2000), which tells a sordid tale of mobsters, corrupt police and politicians, and a slain party girl in Las Cruces. The movie details events of the late 1940s and early 1950s, when a renegade grand jury hired its own lawyers, staged raids on illegal gambling halls, and revealed crimes that touched the highest levels of state government.

# INDEX

## Icons and Symbols

★ Our special recommendations

✕ Restaurant

🏠 Lodging establishment

✕🏠 Lodging establishment whose restaurant warrants a special trip

⚠ Campground

🐤 Good for kids (rubber duck)

☞ Sends you to another section of the guide for more information

✉ Address

☎ Telephone number

🕐 Opening and closing times

🎟 Admission prices

Numbers in white and black circles ③ ❸ that appear on the maps, in the margins, and within the tours correspond to one another.